FORMAL SEMANTICS OF
NATURAL LANGUAGE

FORMAL SEMANTICS OF NATURAL LANGUAGE

Papers from a colloquium sponsored by the
King's College Research Centre, Cambridge

EDITED BY
EDWARD L. KEENAN

Senior Research Fellow, King's College, Cambridge
(now Associate Professor, Department of Linguistics, UCLA)

CAMBRIDGE UNIVERSITY PRESS
CAMBRIDGE
LONDON . NEW YORK . MELBOURNE

Published by the Syndics of the Cambridge University Press
The Pitt Building, Trumpington Street, Cambridge CB2 1RP
Bentley House, 200 Euston Road, London NW1 2DB
32 East 57th Street, New York, N.Y. 10022, USA
296 Beaconsfield Parade, Middle Park, Melbourne 3206, Australia

First published 1975

Printed in Great Britain at the Alden Press, Oxford

Library of Congress Cataloguing in Publication Data

Cambridge Colloquium on Formal Semantics of Natural Language, 1973.
Formal semantics of natural language.
1. Semantics—Congresses. 2. Language and languages—Congresses. I. Keenan,
Edward L. II. Cambridge. University. King's College. Research Centre. III. Title.
P325.C27 1973   412   74–25657
ISBN 0 521 20697 9

CONTENTS

v

NOTES ON THE CONTRIBUTORS

DAVID LEWIS is Professor of Philosophy at Princeton University. He is the author of *Convention* (1969), of *Counterfactuals* (1973), and of articles on metaphysics, semantics, and philosophy of science.

BARBARA HALL PARTEE is Professor of Linguistics and Philosophy at the University of Massachusetts at Amherst. She is co-author with Robert P. Stockwell and Paul Schachter of *The Major Syntactic Structures of English* (1973) and editor of *Montague Grammar* (1975). Her main research interests are syntactic and semantic theory, structure of English, and Montague grammar.

R. D. HULL is currently researching at the University of Cambridge for a Ph.D. thesis entitled 'A Logical Analysis of Questions and Answers'. He is the joint author, with Edward Keenan, of 'The logical presupposition of questions and answers', in *Präsuppositionen in der Philosophie und der Linguistik* (1973).

NEIL W. TENNANT is Lecturer in Logic at the University of Edinburgh. His Ph.D. research was on the semantics of knowledge and belief.

J. E. J. ALTHAM is Assistant Lecturer in Philosophy at the University of Cambridge. He is the author of *The Logic of Plurality* (1971). His main research interests are in philosophical logic and in ethics.

JOHN LYONS is Professor of General Linguistics at the University of Edinburgh. He was the first editor of the *Journal of Linguistics* (1965–9); and his publications include *Structural Semantics* (1963), *Introduction to Theoretical Linguistics* (1968), *Chomsky* (1970), and, as editor, *New Horizons in Linguistics* (1970).

PIETER SEUREN is Reader in the Philosophy of Language at Nijmegen University, Holland. He is the author of *Operators and Nucleus: A Contribution to the Theory of Grammar* (1969), and the editor of *Generative*

Semantik: Semantische Syntax (1973), *Semantic Syntax* (1974). His research interests are in syntax and semantics, theory of reference, prelexical syntax.

ÖSTEN DAHL is Docent in General Linguistics at the University of Göteborg. He is the author of *Topic and Comment: A Study in Russian and General Transformational Grammar* (1969), and has written articles for *Language, Scando-Slavica*, and *Synthese* as well as textbooks in linguistics. His research interests are in semantics, theory of grammar, logic and language.

COLIN BIGGS is a Research Student in Linguistics at the University of Cambridge. His principal research interests are in linguistic theory and philosophy of language.

J. A. W. KAMP has held teaching posts at the University of California Los Angeles, Cornell University, the University of Amersterdam and the University of London. His research and publications have been primarily concerned with tense logic, modal logic, intensional logic, and the formal semantics and pragmatics of natural languages.

FRANTZ VON KUTSCHERA is Professor of Philosophy at the University of Regensburg. He is the author of *Die Antinomien der Logik* (1964), *Elementare Logik* (1967), *Einführung in die moderne Logik* (1971) with A. Breitkopf, *Wissenschaftstheorie-Grundzüge der allgemeinen Methodologie der empirischen Wissenschaften* (1972), and *Einführung in die Logik der Normen, Werte und Entscheidungen* (1973). His principal research interests are in philosophical logic, philosophy of language, philosophy of science, epistemology.

RENATE BARTSCH is Professor of the Philosophy of Language at the University of Amsterdam. Her publications include *Adverbialsemantik* (1972), and, together with Theo Vennemann, *Semantic Structures: A study in the Relation between Semantics and Syntax.*

CARL H. HEIDRICH is at present leading a research group on formal linguistics at the University of Bonn. His publications include 'Eine Einbettung von generativen Chomsky-Grammatiken in den Prädikatenkalkül', in *Forschungsberichte des IKP* (1974), *Vorlesungen über Montague-Grammatiken und Linguistische Logik* (forthcoming), and, as editor, *Formale Betrachtungen in Sprachtheorien* (1975). His principal research interests are in logic, model theory and semantics of natural languages, algebraic linguistics.

ARNIM VON STECHOW is Professor of Linguistics at the University of Konstanz (Germany). His publications include *Einführung in Theorie und Anwendung der generative Syntax* (1973–4) with A. Kratzer and E. Pause and 'ε-λ-kontextfreie Sprachen. Ein Beitrag zu einer natürlichen formalen Semantik', *Linguistische Berichte*, 34.

NICHOLAS JARDINE is Lecturer in History and Philosophy of Science and Senior Research Fellow, King's College, Cambridge. His publications include *Mathematical Taxonomy* (1971) and papers on the mathematical theory of classification and its applications. His main research interests are in philosophy of language, the role of natural kinds in scientific theories and renaissance concepts of method in mathematics and natural philosophy.

TIMOTHY C. POTTS is Lecturer in Philosophy at the University of Leeds. His publications include 'Fregean categorial grammar', in *Logic, Language and Probability* (1973), 'Modal logic and auxiliary verbs', in *Semantics and Communication* (1974), and 'Montague's semiotic: a syllabus of errors', in *Proceedings of the Logic Conferences at the University of York, 1973 and 1974*. His research interests are in formal linguistics, medieval philosophy, philosophy of mind, speculative theology, aesthetics.

GEORGE LAKOFF is Professor of Linguistics at the University of California at Berkeley. He is one of the founders of the Generative Semantics movement in American Linguistics. His principal research has been devoted to showing why semantics, pragmatics and psychological processing need to be integrated into a theory of syntax, and how that might be done. He is the author of *Irregularity in Syntax* and numerous articles, especially, 'On generative semantics', 'Linguistics and natural logic', 'Conversational postulates' (with David Gordon), ' "Hedges": a study in meaning criteria and the logic of fuzzy concepts', and 'Introducing cognitive grammar' (with Henry Thompson).

STEPHEN ISARD is at present with the Laboratory of Experimental Psychology at the University of Sussex. His publications include 'Free recall of self-embedded sentences' with G. A. Miller, 'Computability over arbitrary fields' with G. T. Herman, and 'Utterances as programs' with D. J. M. Davies.

PETR SGALL is a Professor at Charles University, Prague. His publications on general linguistics and generative grammar include *Vývoj flexe v indoevropských jazycích (The Development of Inflection in IE Languages)* (1958), *Die Infinitive im Rigveda* (1958), *Generativní popis jazyka a česká deklinace (Generative Description of Language and the Czech Declension)* (1967), and, as the main author, *A Functional Approach to Syntax* (1969), *Topic, Focus and Generative Semantics* (1973), and *Functional Generative Grammar in Prague* (1974).

THEO VENNEMANN is Professor of Linguistics at the University of California, Los Angeles and Professor-elect at the University of Munich. His publications include 'Explanation in syntax', in *Syntax and Semantics* (1973), 'An explanation of drift', in *Word Order and Word Order Change, Schuchardt, the Neogrammarians, and the Transformational Theory of Phonological Change* (1972) with Terence H. Wilbur, and *Semantic Structures: A Study in the Relation between Semantics and Syntax*. His research interests are in the theory of grammar and of grammar change.

YORICK WILKS has worked at Cambridge, Stanford, and now in Switzerland, on the analysis of the structure of natural language within the Artificial Intelligence paradigm. He has written numerous articles and is the author of *Grammar, Meaning and the Machine Analysis of Language* (1972).

JOSEPH EMONDS is an Assistant Professor at the University of California, Los Angeles. His publications include 'The place of linguistics in American Society', in *Papers from the 7th Meeting of the Chicago Linguistic Society*, and 'A reformulation of Grimm's Law', in *Contributions to Generative Phonology*. His principle research interest is in the development of the extended standard theory of generative syntax, and the results of most of this work will be collected in his forthcoming book, *Transformational Approach to English Syntax: Root, Structure-Preserving, and Local Transformations*.

CATHERINE FUCHS is at present a Lecturer in Formal Linguistics at the University of Paris, and is engaged on research on the formal semantics of natural language at the Centre National de la Recherche Scientifique. She is the author of *Considérations théoriques à propos du traitement formel du language* (1970), *Théorie de l'énonciation et problèmes de prédication* (1972), *Ordinateurs, programmation et langues naturelles* (1974), *Analyse du discours et linguistique* (1975), and *Initiation aux linguistiques contemporaines*.

JACQUES ROUAULT is Professor at the Social Sciences University of Grenoble, Institute for Computer Sciences, and Head of the Laboratory of Computational Linguistics and Applications. His publications include 'Etude formelle de l'opposition Situation/Propriété et des phénomènes de Voix et de Thématisation', International Conference on Computational Linguistics, Pisa (1973), 'Sémantique et traitement automatique des langues', Journées d'Etude sur la Parole, Orsay (1974), 'Les modèles logiques existants sont surtout un obstacle à la formalisation des théories linguistiques', Colloque Logique et Linguistique, Metz, and 'Vers une linguistique expérimentale des textes' (1975). His research interests are in the formalization of linguistic theories, computational linguistics.

MAURICE GROSS is Professor of Linguistics at the University of Paris and Director of the Laboratoire d'Automatique Documentaire et Linguistique. His major publications include *Notions sur les grammaires formelles* (1966) with A. Lentin, *Grammaire transformationnelle du français* (1968), *Mathematical Models in Linguistics* (1972) and *Méthodes en syntaxe* (1974). His research interest are in the problems in the foundation of syntax, formalization of syntactic rules and of generative transformational grammars.

EDWARD L. KEENAN is Associate Professor in the Department of Linguistics at the University of California, Los Angeles. His publications include 'Two kinds of presupposition in natural language', in *Studies in Semantics* (1970), 'Quantifier structures in English', *Foundations of Language* (1971), 'The logical presuppositions of questions and answers', in *Präsuppositionen in der Philosophie und der Linguistik*, 'Linguistics and logic', in *Linguistik und Nachbarwissenschaften* (forthcoming), articles in *Linguistic Inquiry* and papers presented to the Chicago Linguistic Society. He is an Associate Editor of *Linguistic Inquiry* and on the Advisory Board of Scriptor Verlag, Linguistics Series.

JOHN R. ROSS is Professor of Linguistics at the Massachusetts Institute of Technology. His Ph.D. thesis was entitled 'Constraints on Variables in Syntax'. His research interests are in universal grammar and the relationship of syntax and semantics.

ACKNOWLEDGEMENTS

I should like to express my thanks to King's College, Cambridge for having supported the colloquium from which these papers issue and to the Department of Linguistics, Cambridge University, for its help with the physical organization of the colloquium. In addition special thanks are due to Jacqueline Mapes and Angela Zvesper for their help in running the colloquium and preparing the manuscripts for publication. And finally, I would like to thank Colin Biggs, Bernard Comrie, Andrew Crompton, John Hawkins, and Nigel Vincent for their help in editing the manuscripts.

E.L.K.

INTRODUCTION

The papers in this volume are those given at the Cambridge Colloquium on Formal Semantics of Natural Language, April 1973. The purpose of that colloquium was twofold: to stimulate work in natural language semantics and to bring together linguists, philosophers, and logicians working in different countries and, often, from different points of view. Both purposes were, it seems to us, achieved, though of course it was not feasible to represent all countries and all points of view at a single conference.

The questions treated in the colloquium papers represent the following current areas of interest: problems of quantification and reference in natural language, the application of formal logic to natural language semantics, the formal semantics of non-declarative sentences, the relation between natural language semantics and that of programming languages, formal pragmatics and the relation between sentences and their contexts of use, discourse meaning, and the relation between surface syntax and logical meaning.

The papers have been loosely grouped under the six rubrics given in the table of contents. These rubrics were not given to the authors in advance and are intended only as a rough guide to the reader. E.L.K.

I QUANTIFICATION IN NATURAL LANGUAGE

Adverbs of quantification

DAVID LEWIS

Cast of characters

The adverbs I wish to consider fall into six groups of near-synonyms, as follows.

(1) Always, invariably, universally, without exception
(2) Sometimes, occasionally, [once]
(3) Never
(4) Usually, mostly, generally, almost always, with few exceptions, [ordinarily], [normally]
(5) Often, frequently, commonly
(6) Seldom, infrequently, rarely, almost never

Bracketed items differ semantically from their list-mates in ways I shall not consider here; omit them if you prefer.

First guess: quantifiers over times?

It may seem plausible, especially if we stop with the first word on each list, that these adverbs function as quantifiers over times. That is to say that *always*, for instance, is a modifier that combines with a sentence Φ to make a sentence *Always* Φ that is true iff the modified sentence Φ is true at all times. Likewise, we might guess that *Sometimes* Φ, *Never* Φ, *Usually* Φ, *Often* Φ, and *Seldom* Φ are true, respectively, iff Φ is true at some times, none, most, many, or few. But it is easy to find various reasons why this first guess is too simple.

First, we may note that the times quantified over need not be moments of time. They can be suitable stretches of time instead. For instance,

(7) The fog usually lifts before noon here

means that the sentence modified by *usually* is true on most days, not at most moments. Indeed, what is it for that sentence to be true at a moment?

3

Second, we may note that the range of quantification is often restricted. For instance,

(8) Caesar seldom awoke before dawn

is not made true by the mere fact that few of all times (past, present, or future) are times when Caesar was even alive, wherefore fewer still are times when he awoke before dawn. Rather it means that few of all the times when Caesar awoke are times before dawn; or perhaps that on few of all the days of his life did he awake before dawn.

Third, we may note that the entities we are quantifying over, unlike times,[1] may be distinct although simultaneous. For instance,

(9) Riders on the Thirteenth Avenue line seldom find seats

may be true even though for 22 hours out of every 24 – all but the two peak hours when 86% of the daily riders show up – there are plenty of seats for all.

Second guess: quantifiers over events?

It may seem at this point that our adverbs are quantifiers, suitably restricted, over events; and that times enter the picture only because events occur at times. Thus (7) could mean that most of the daily fog-liftings occurred before noon; (8) could mean that few of Caesar's awakenings occurred before dawn; and (9) could mean that most riders on the Thirteenth Avenue line are seatless. So far, so good; but further difficulties work both against our first guess and against this alternative.

Sometimes it seems that we quantify not over single events but over enduring states of affairs. For instance,

(10) A man who owns a donkey always beats it now and then

means that every continuing relationship between a man and his donkey is punctuated by beatings; but these continuing relationships, unlike the beatings, are not events in any commonplace sense. Note also that if *always* were a quantifier over times, the sentence would be inconsistent: it would say that the donkey-beatings are incessant and that they only happen now and then. (This sentence poses other problems that we shall consider later.)

---

[1] Unlike genuine moments or stretches of time, that is. But we may truly say that Miles the war hero has been wounded 100 times if he has suffered 100 woundings, even if he has been wounded at only 99 distinct moments (or stretches) of time because two of his woundings were simultaneous.

We come last to a sweeping objection to both of our first two guesses: the adverbs of quantification may be used in speaking of abstract entities that have no location in time and do not participate in events. For instance,

(11) A quadratic equation never has more than two solutions

(12) A quadratic equation usually has two different solutions

mean, respectively, that no quadratic equation has more than two solutions and that most – more precisely, all but a set of measure zero under the natural measure on the set of triples of coefficients – have two different solutions. These sentences have nothing at all to do with times or events.

Or do they? This imagery comes to mind: someone is contemplating quadratic equations, one after another, drawing at random from all the quadratic equations there are. Each one takes one unit of time. In no unit of time does he contemplate a quadratic equation with more than two solutions. In most units of time he contemplates quadratic equations with two different solutions.

For all I know, such imagery may sustain the usage illustrated by (11) and (12), but it offers no hope of a serious analysis. There can be no such contemplator. To be more realistic, call a quadratic equation *simple* iff each of its coefficients could be specified somehow in less than 10,000 pages; then we may be quite sure that the only quadratic equations that are ever contemplated are simple ones. Yet

(13) Quadratic equations are always simple

is false, and in fact they are almost never simple.

Third guess: quantifiers over cases

What we can say, safely and with full generality, is that our adverbs of quantification are quantifiers over cases. What holds always, sometimes, never, usually, often, or seldom is what holds in, respectively, all, some, no, most, many, or few cases.

But we have gained safety by saying next to nothing. What is a case? It seems that sometimes we have a case corresponding to each moment or stretch of time, or to each in some restricted class. But sometimes we have a case for each event of some sort; or for each continuing relationship between a man and his donkey; or for each quadratic equation; or – as in the case of this very sentence – for each sentence that contains one of our adverbs of quantification.

Unselective quantifiers

It will help if we attend to our adverbs of quantification as they can appear in a special dialect: the dialect of mathematicians, linguists, philosophers, and lawyers, in which variables are used routinely to overcome the limitations of more colloquial means of pronominalization. Taking m, n, p as variables over natural numbers, and x, y, z as variables over persons, consider:

(14) Always, p divides the product of m and n only if some factor of p divides m and the quotient of p by that factor divides n

(15) Sometimes, p divides the product of m and n although p divides neither m nor n

(16) Sometimes it happens that x sells stolen goods to y, who sells them to z, who sells them back to x

(17) Usually, x reminds me of y if and only if y reminds me of x

Here it seems that if we are quantifying over cases, then we must have a case corresponding to each admissible assignment of values to the variables that occur free in the modified sentence. Thus (14) is true iff every assignment of natural numbers as values of m, n, and p makes the open sentence after *always* true – in other words, iff all triples of natural numbers satisfy that open sentence. Likewise (15) is true iff some triple of numbers satisfies the open sentence after *sometimes*; (16) is true iff some triple of persons satisfies the open sentence after *sometimes*; and (17) is true iff most pairs of persons satisfy the open sentence after *usually*.

The ordinary logicians' quantifiers are selective: $\forall x$ or $\exists x$ binds the variable x and stops there. Any other variables y, z,...that may occur free in its scope are left free, waiting to be bound by other quantifiers. We have the truth conditions:

(18) $\forall x \Phi$ is true, under any admissible assignment f of values to all variables free in Φ except x, iff for every admissible value of x, Φ is true under the assignment of that value to x together with the assignment f of values to the other variables free in Φ;

(16) $\exists x \Phi$ is true, under any admissible assignment f of values to all variables free in Φ except x, iff for some admissible value of x, Φ is true under the assignment of that value to x together with the assignment f of values to the other variables free in Φ;

and likewise for the quantifiers that select other variables.

It is an entirely routine matter to introduce *unselective quantifiers* ∀ and ∃ that bind all the variables in their scope indiscriminately. Without selectivity, the truth conditions are much simpler; with no variables left free, we need not relativize the truth of the quantified sentence to an assignment of values to the remaining free variables.

(20) ∀Φ is true iff Φ is true under every admissible assignment of values to all variables free in Φ;

(21) ∃Φ is true iff Φ is true under some admissible assignment of values to all variables free in Φ

These unselective quantifiers have not deserved the attention of logicians, partly because they are unproblematic and partly because strings of ordinary, selective quantifiers can do all that they can do, and more besides. They have only the advantage of brevity. Still, brevity *is* an advantage, and it should be no surprise if unselective quantifiers are used in natural language to gain that advantage. That is what I claim; the unselective ∀ and ∃ can show up as the adverbs *always*, and *sometimes*.[1] Likewise *never*, *usually*, *often*, and *seldom* can serve as the unselective analogs of the selective quantifiers *for no x*, *for most x*, *for many x*, and *for few x*.[2]

To summarize, what we have in the variable-using dialect is roughly as follows. Our adverbs are quantifiers over cases; a case may be regarded as the 'tuple of its participants; and these participants are values of the variables that occur free in the open sentence modified by the adverb. In other words, we are taking the cases to be the admissible assignments of values to these variables.

But matters are not quite that simple. In the first place, we may wish to quantify past our adverbs, as in

(22) There is a number *q* such that, without exception, the product of *m* and *n* divides *q* only if *m* and *n* both divide *q*

---

[1] It is pleasing to find that Russell often explained the now-standard selective quantifiers by using an unselective adverb of quantification to modify an open sentence. For instance in *Principia* I, *9, we find the first introduction of quantifiers in the formal development: 'We shall denote "Φ*x always*" by the notation (*x*).Φ*x*...We shall denote "Φ*x sometimes*" by the notation (∃*x*).Φ*x*.'

[2] It is customary to work with assignments of values to all variables in the language; the part of the assignment that assigns values to unemployed variables is idle but harmless. But for us this otherwise convenient practice would be more bother than it is worth. In dealing with *usually*, *often*, and *seldom* we must consider the fraction of value-assignments that satisfy the modified sentence. Given infinitely many variables, these fractions will be ∞/∞ (unless they are 0 or 1). We would need to factor out differences involving only the idle parts of assignments.

So our adverbs of quantification are not entirely unselective: they can bind indefinitely many free variables in the modified sentence, but some variables – the ones used to quantify past the adverbs – remain unbound. In (22), *m* and *n* are bound by *without exception*; but *q* is immune, and survives to be bound by *there is a number q such that*, a selective quantifier of larger scope.

In the second place, we cannot ignore time altogether in (16)–(17) as we can in the abstract cases (11)–(15); (16)–(17) are not confined to the present moment, but are general over time as well as over 'tuples of persons. So we must treat the modified sentence as if it contained a free time-variable: the truth of the sentence depends on a time-coordinate just as it depends on the values of the person-variables, and we must take the cases to include this time coordinate as well as a 'tuple of persons. (Indeed, we could go so far as to posit an explicit time-variable in underlying structure, in order to subsume time-dependence under dependence on values of variables.) Our first guess about the adverbs is revived as a special case: if the modified sentence has no free variables, the cases quantified over will include nothing but the time coordinate. As noted before, the appropriate time-coordinates (accompanied by 'tuples or not, as the case may be) could either be moments of time or certain stretches of time, for instance days.

Sometimes we might prefer to treat the modified sentence as if it contained an event-variable (or even posit such a variable in underlying structure) and include an event-coordinate in the cases. The event-coordinate could replace the time-coordinate, since an event determines the time of its occurrence. If so, then our second guess also is revived as a special case: if there are no free variables, the cases might simply be events.

In the third place, not just any 'tuple of values of the free variables, plus perhaps a time- or event-coordinate, will be admissible as one of the cases quantified over. Various restrictions may be in force, either permanently or temporarily. Some standing restrictions involve the choice of variables: it is the custom in mathematics that λ is a variable that can take only limit ordinals as values (at least in a suitable context). I set up semi-permanent restrictions of this kind a few paragraphs ago by writing

(23) Taking *m*, *n*, *p* as variables over natural numbers, and *x*, *y*, and *z* as variables over persons...

Other standing restrictions require the participants in a case to be suitably related. If a case is a 'tuple of persons plus a time-coordinate, we may take it generally that the persons must be alive at the time to make the case admissible. Or if a case is a 'tuple of persons plus an event-coordinate, it may be that the persons must take part in the event to make the case admissible. It may also be required that the participants in the 'tuple are all different, so that no two variables receive the same value. (I am not sure whether these restrictions are always in force, but I believe that they often are.)

Restriction by if-clauses

There are various ways to restrict the admissible cases temporarily – perhaps only for the duration of a single sentence, or perhaps through several sentences connected by anaphoric chains. If-clauses seem to be the most versatile device for imposing temporary restrictions. Consider:

(24) Always, if x is a man, if y is a donkey, and if x owns y, x beats y now and then

A case is here a triple: a value for x, a value for y, and a time-coordinate (longish stretches seem called for, perhaps years). The admissible cases are those that satisfy the three if-clauses. That is, they are triples of a man, a donkey, and a time such that the man owns the donkey at the time. (Our proposed standing restrictions are redundant. If the man owns the donkey at the time, then both are alive at the time; if the participants are a man and a donkey, they are different.) Then (24) is true iff the modified sentence

(25) x beats y now and then

is true in all admissible cases. Likewise for

(26) Sometimes
(27) Usually } if x is a man, if y is a donkey, and if x owns y, x beats
(28) Often } y now and then

(29) Never } if x is a man, if y is a donkey, and if x owns y, does x
(30) Seldom } beat y now and then

The admissible cases are the triples that satisfy the if-clauses, and the sentence is true iff the modified sentence (25) – slightly transformed in the negative cases (29)–(30) – is true in some, most, many, none, or few of the admissible cases.

It may happen that every free variable of the modified sentence is restricted by an if-clause of its own, as in

(31) Usually, if x is a man, if y is a donkey, and if z is a dog, y weighs less than x but more than z

But in general, it is best to think of the if-clauses as restricting whole cases, not particular participants therein. We may have any number of if-clauses – including zero, as in (14)–(17). A free variable of the modified sentence may appear in more than one if-clause. More than one variable may appear in the same if-clause. Or it may be that no variable appears in an if-clause; such if-clauses restrict the admissible cases by restricting their time-coordinates (or perhaps their event-coordinates), as in

(32) Often if it is raining my roof leaks

(in which the time-coordinate is all there is to the case) or

(33) Ordinarily if it is raining, if x is driving and sees y walking, and if y is x's friend, x offers y a ride

It makes no difference if we compress several if-clauses into one by means of conjunction or relative clauses. The three if-clauses in (24) or in (26)–(30) could be replaced by any of:

(34) if x is a man, y is a donkey, and x owns y...

(35) if x is a man and y is a donkey owned by x...

(36) if x is a man who owns y, and y is a donkey...

(37) if x and y are a man and his donkey...

Such compression is always possible, so we would not have gone far wrong to confine our attention, for simplicity, to the case of restriction by a single if-clause.

We have a three-part construction: the adverb of quantification, the if-clauses (zero or more of them), and the modified sentence. Schematically, for the case of a single if-clause:

$$(38) \quad \left\{ \begin{array}{c} \text{Always} \\ \text{Sometimes} \\ . \\ . \\ . \end{array} \right\} + \text{if } \Psi + \Phi$$

But could we get the same effect by first combining Ψ and Φ into a conditional sentence, and then taking this conditional sentence to be the sentence modified by the adverb? On this suggestion (38) is to be regrouped as

(39)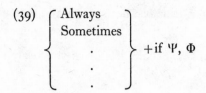

Sentence (39) is true iff the conditional *If* Ψ, Φ is true in all, some, none, most, many, or few of the admissible cases – that is, of the cases that satisfy any permanent restrictions, disregarding the temporary restrictions imposed by the if-clause. But is there any way to interpret the conditional *If* Ψ, Φ that makes (39) equivalent to (38) for all six groups of our adverbs? No; if the adverb is *always* we get the proper equivalence by interpreting it as the truth-functional conditional Ψ ⊃ Φ, whereas if the adverb is *sometimes* or *never*, that does not work, and we must instead interpret it as the conjunction Φ & Ψ. In the remaining cases, there is no natural interpretation that works. I conclude that the *if* of our restrictive if-clauses should not be regarded as a sentential connective. It has no meaning apart from the adverb it restricts. The *if* in *always if. . .,. . ., sometimes if. . .,. . .,* and the rest is on a par with the non-connective *and* in *between. . .and. . .,* with the non-connective *or* in *whether. . .or. . .,* or with the non-connective *if* in *the probability that. . .if. . .* It serves merely to mark an argument-place in a polyadic construction.[1]

Stylistic variation

Sentences made with the adverbs of quantification need not have the form we have considered so far: adverb + if-clauses + modified sentence. We will find it convenient, however, to take that form – somewhat arbitrarily – as canonical, and to regard other forms as if they were derived from that canonical form. Then we are done with semantics: the interpretation of a sentence in canonical form carries over to its derivatives.

The constituents of the sentence may be rearranged:

(40) If *x* and *y* are a man and a donkey and if *x* owns *y*, *x* usually beats *y* now and then

[1] What is the price of forcing the restriction-marking *if* to be a sentential connective after all? Exorbitant: it can be done if (1) we use a third truth value, (2) we adopt a far-fetched interpretation of the connective *if*, and (3) we impose an additional permanent restriction on the admissible cases. Let *If* Ψ, Φ have the same truth value as Φ if Ψ is true, and let it be third-valued if Ψ is false or third-valued. Let a case be admissible only if it makes the modified sentence either true or false, rather than third-valued. Then (39) is equivalent to (38) for all our adverbs, as desired, at least if we assume that Ψ and Φ themselves are not third-valued in any case. A treatment along similar lines of if-clauses used to restrict ordinary, selective quantifiers may be found in Belnap (1970).

(41) If x and y are a man and a donkey, usually x beats y now and then if x owns y

(42) If x and y are a man and a donkey, usually if x owns y, x beats y now and then

(43) Usually x beats y now and then, if x and y are a man and a donkey and x owns y

All of (40)–(43), though clumsy, are intelligible and well-formed.

Our canonical restrictive if-clauses may, in suitable contexts, be replaced by when-clauses:

(44) When m and n are positive integers, the power m^n can always be computed by successive multiplications

Indeed, a when-clause may sound right when the corresponding if-clause would be questionable, as in a close relative of (8):

(45) Seldom was it before dawn $\left\{ \begin{matrix} \text{when} \\ \text{? if} \end{matrix} \right\}$ Caesar awoke

Or we may have a where-clause or a participle construction, especially if the restrictive clause does not come at the beginning of the sentence:

(46) The power m^n, where m and n are positive integers, can always be computed by successive multiplications

(47) The power m^n (m and n being positive integers) can always be computed by successive multiplications

Always if – or is it *always when?* – may be contracted to *whenever*, a complex unselective quantifier that combines two sentences:

(48) Whenever m and n are positive integers, the power m^n can be computed by successive multiplications

(49) Whenever x is a man, y is a donkey, and x owns y, x beats y now and then

(50) Whenever it rains it pours

Always may simply be omitted:

(51) (Always) When it rains, it pours

(52) (Always) If x is a man, y is a donkey, and x owns y, x beats y now and then

(53) When *m* and *n* are positive integers, the power m^n can (always) be computed by successive multiplications

Thus we reconstruct the so-called 'generality interpretation' of free variables: the variables are bound by the omitted *always*.

Our stylistic variations have so far been rather superficial. We turn next to a much more radical transformation of sentence structure – a transformation that can bring us back from the variable-using dialect to everyday language.

Displaced restrictive terms

Suppose that one of our canonical sentences has a restrictive if-clause of the form

(54) if α is τ ...,

where α is a variable and τ is an indefinite singular term formed from a common noun (perhaps plus modifiers) by prefixing the indefinite article or *some*.

Examples:

(55) if *x* is a donkey...
(56) if *x* is an old, grey donkey...
(57) if *x* is a donkey owned by *y*...
(58) if *x* is some donkey that *y* owns...
(59) if *x* is something of *y*'s...
(60) if *x* is someone foolish...

(Call τ, when so used, a *restrictive term*.) Then we can delete the if-clause and place the restrictive term τ in apposition to an occurrence of the variable α elsewhere in the sentence. This occurrence of α may be in the modified sentence, or in another if-clause of the form (54), or in an if-clause of some other form. Often, but not always, the first occurrence of α outside the deleted if-clause is favoured. If τ is short, it may go before α; if long, it may be split and go partly before and partly after; and sometimes it may follow α parenthetically. The process of displacing restrictive terms may – but need not – be repeated until no if-clauses of the form (54) are left. For instance:

(61) Sometimes, if *x* is some man, if *y* is a donkey, and if *x* owns *y*, *x* beats *y* now and then

$\Rightarrow$

Sometimes if y is a donkey, and if some man x owns y, x beats y now and then

$\Rightarrow$

Sometimes, if some man x owns a donkey y, x beats y now and then

(62) Often, if x is someone who owns y, and if y is a donkey, x beats y now and then

$\Rightarrow$

Often, if x is someone who owns y, a donkey, x beats y now and then

$\Rightarrow$

Often, someone x who owns y, a donkey, beats y now and then

Instead of just going into apposition with an occurrence of the variable α, the restrictive term τ may replace an occurrence of α altogether. Then all other occurrences of α must be replaced as well, either by pronouns of the appropriate case and gender or by terms *that v* or *the v*, where v is the principal noun in the term τ. For instance,

(63) Always, if y is a donkey and if x is a man who owns y, x beats y now and then

$\Rightarrow$

Always, if x is a man who owns a donkey, x beats it now and then

$\Rightarrow$

Always, a man who owns a donkey beats it now and then

Now it is a small matter to move *always* and thereby derive the sentence (10) that we considered earlier. Sure enough, the canonical sentence with which the derivation (63) began has the proper meaning for (10). It is in this way that we return from the variable-using dialect to an abundance of everyday sentences.

I conclude with some further examples.

(64) Always, if x is someone foolish, if y is some good idea, and if x has y, nobody gives x credit for y

$\Rightarrow$

Always, if y is some good idea, and if someone foolish has y, nobody gives him credit for y

$\Rightarrow$

Always, if someone foolish has some good idea, nobody gives him credit for that idea

(65) Often, if y is a donkey, if x is a man who owns y, and if y kicks x, x beats y

⇒

Often, if y is a donkey, and if y kicks a man who owns y, he beats y

⇒

Often, if a donkey kicks a man who owns it, he beats it

(66) Often, if y is a donkey, if x is a man who owns y, and if y kicks x, x beats y

⇒

Often, if x is a man who owns a donkey, and if it kicks x, x beats it

⇒

Often, if it kicks him, a man who owns a donkey beats it

(67) Usually, if x is a man who owns y and if y is a donkey that kicks x, x beats y

⇒

Usually, if x is a man who owns a donkey that kicks x, x beats it

⇒

Usually, a man who owns a donkey that kicks him beats it

(68) Usually, if x is a man who owns y and if y is a donkey that kicks x, x beats y

⇒

Usually, if y is a donkey that kicks him, a man who owns y beats y

⇒

Usually, a man who owns it beats a donkey that kicks him

REFERENCES

Belnap, N. (1970). 'Conditional assertion and restricted quantification', *Noûs*, **4**, 1–12.

Russell, B. and Whitehead, A. N. (1912). *Principia Mathematica*, 1. London: Cambridge University Press.

Deletion and variable binding

BARBARA HALL PARTEE

Introduction

It is generally agreed that pronominalization and deletion under identity
are closely related phenomena; Postal (1970) and Jackendoff (1972) have
made particularly striking cases for the existence of close formal similarities
among pronominalization, reflexivization, and coreferential complement
subject deletion. Their claims are quite similar in spite of the differences
between the generative and interpretive semantics frameworks, and both
are concerned with complement subject deletion not only when it is
controlled by the next higher verb, i.e. ordinary Equi-NP Deletion, but
also when its 'controller' is several clauses away, i.e. what Grinder (1970)
analysed as 'Super-Equi NP Deletion'. What I want to explore in this
paper is the relation between pronominalization and deletion in the 'Super-
Equi NP Deletion' cases, as illustrated by (1) and (2).[1]

(1) John$_i$ thought it was foolish to shave himself$_i$

(2) John$_i$ thought it was foolish for him$_i$ to shave himself$_i$

I am going to argue that (1) and (2) are not simply optional surface variants,
but that their similarity rather results from an accidental convergence of
quite disparate processes. If my argument is correct, then on a generative
semantics approach (1) and (2) should have distinct underlying representations and on an interpretive approach their semantic interpretations
should be arrived at by distinct interpretive principles, even though for this
particular pair of examples there may be semantic rules which would show
the two sentences to be logically equivalent.

A preliminary observation is that in an environment where reflexivization is possible, an ordinary pronoun can never be understood as coreferential with the same antecedent.

[1] In the first few examples I use 'referential index' subscripts in the manner of Postal
and Grinder to indicate anaphoric relations between pronouns and their antecedents. Since
the analysis I will propose will not make use of referential indices as a theoretical device,
their use here should just be taken as a shorthand way of indicating what reading of a
sentence I am talking about. In later examples I omit indices, and trust that it will be clear
from the discussion which readings are relevant.

(3) The man$_i$ injured himself$_i$

(4) * The man$_i$ injured him$_i$

Similarly, where ordinary Equi-NP Deletion is possible, pronominalization is not an equivalent alternative.

(5) John was eager to start

(6) * John$_i$ was eager for him$_i$ to start

Thus whatever formal similarities can be captured among the three rules, generatively or interpretively, it has to be stated that reflexivization and Equi-NP Deletion must apply if they can, and pronominalization can only apply where neither of the other rules is applicable. Grinder (1970) tried to show that his rule of Super-Equi NP Deletion was collapsible with ordinary Equi-NP Deletion; but if it is, it then seems surprising that it should be optional, as the well-formedness of (2) suggests it must be. Kimball (1971) argues against Grinder's rule of Super-Equi, and proposes an alternative analysis of (1) based on a rule of Dative Deletion (which I will discuss in section 2), but still treats (1) and (2) as optional variants. What I will try to show is that the Super-Equi phenomenon, when properly analysed, is defined on variables (in the logical sense) and is always obligatory, and that the pronoun in (2) arises by a special process, 'pronominalization of laziness', and cannot be interpreted as a variable.

One exclusion must be noted at the outset. Whereas Grinder, Postal, and Jackendoff all apparently assume that complement subject deletion can be treated uniformly for infinitives and gerunds, I am dealing only with infinitives. The generalizations that I suggest for infinitives do not all carry over to gerunds, so if there is a way to treat them uniformly, this won't be it. Evidence for non-uniformity comes from pairs such as the following:

(7) (a) Smoking is harmful
    (b) It's harmful to smoke

(8) (a) Dropping bombs is dangerous
    (b) It's dangerous to drop bombs

On the one hand, all the sentences above seem to have a generic 'one' as the interpretation of the missing gerund or infinitive subject; but there is a difference between the gerunds and the infinitives with respect to the connection between who is doing the activity and who it is harmful or dangerous for. In the (b) sentences, with infinitives, the only interpretation is that the activity is harmful or dangerous for the one doing it; our analysis will follow Kimball's (1971) in positing a Dative with predicates like *harmful* or *dangerous* as central to the control problem with infinitives. But the (a) sentences, with gerunds, allow an interpretation where the activity is harmful or dangerous to some other unspecified party, e.g. the environment, or people who happen to be in the way of the smoke or the bombs. It should be noted that the counterexamples Grinder (1971) gives to Kimball's (1971) reanalyses of Super-Equi NP Deletion as Dative Deletion all involve gerunds. It may be that there is a generalization to the effect that gerund subject deletion can take place whenever infinitive subject deletion can though not vice versa. But nothing further will be said about gerunds here.

Returning to the main problem, I will now give some examples to support my claim that (1) and (2) are not as closely related as has been assumed.

(9) Only John believes that it would be inadvisable to vote for himself

(10) Only John believes that it would be inadvisable for him to vote for himself

Sentences (9) and (10) differ structurally in the same way as (1) and (2), but (9) and (10) are not synonymous. Sentence (10) can be paraphrased by (10′); what John and the others disagree about is the advisability of John's voting for himself, and no one else's voting is at issue.

(10′) Only John believes that it would be inadvisable for John to vote for himself

Sentence (9), on the other hand, cannot be so paraphrased; in this case, what is at issue is each person's opinion about his own voting, not each person's opinion about John's voting.

Sentences (11) and (12) show a similar distinction.

(11) Everyone considered it inadvisable to perjure himself

(12)(*) Everyone considered it inadvisable for him to perjure himself

Sentence (12) is well-formed if the *him* refers to someone outside the sentence altogether, but it cannot be interpreted with the *him* anaphorically bound to *everyone*. The difference between (11) and (12) is not surprising in the light of the data from ordinary Equi-NP Deletion, since (11) and (12) match the difference between (5) and (6). Yet it seems inconsistent with the equal acceptability and apparent synonymy of (1) and (2). The rest of this paper will be an attempt to resolve this conflict, making crucial use of a distinction between processes that involve identity of logical variables and processes that involve linguistic identity.

1. Pronouns as variables and pronouns of laziness

In Partee (1970) I discussed the question of whether it was possible to treat all instances of pronominalization in English uniformly, and suggested that it was not. Here I want to reinforce that claim, since I intend to exploit it in accounting for the problem sentences cited above. What I say is neutral, I believe, between a generative and an interpretive approach, but since it is virtually impossible to discuss the details of an analysis in terms that remain neutral, I will talk in generative terms; I believe the conversion to an equivalent interpretive analysis is straightforward. My approach to these matters is heavily influenced by the Montague framework, but I am not bringing that in explicitly here because of the additional technical apparatus it would demand.

It has been commonplace among logicians and more recently widespread among linguists to view pronouns in English as playing the role that variables play in logic. Such a view gives the only sensible account of the pronouns in sentences like (13).

(13) No prudent man will drive when he is drunk

The *he* in (13) is clearly not a substitute for the expression *no prudent man*; neither can it be said to refer to the entity denoted by *no prudent man*. Rather, the sentence must be analysed as being related on some level to the open sentence (13'), with the expression *no prudent man* introduced so that it binds both occurrences of the variable (the exact mechanism for this is irrelevant here).

(13') x will drive when x is drunk

Geach (1968) coined the term 'pronoun of laziness' to describe a different use of pronouns, one which can be equated with the earliest transformational account of pronominalization, namely the substitution of a pronoun to avoid repetition of an identical linguistic expression. A good example of a pronoun which can only be interpreted in this way was given by Karttunen (1969):

(14) The man who gave his paycheck to his wife was wiser than the man who gave it to his mistress

The *it* in (14) must be understood as *his paycheck*, and cannot be interpreted as a bound variable, at least not on the only natural reading for the sentence.

If examples such as these support the need for two separate pronominalization processes, there remains the problem of defining their domains, for it seems that many examples could be analysed either way with semantically equivalent results. For example, sentence (15) below could be analysed as related to (15′), with *John* binding both variables, or as derived from (15″), with *he* substituted for the second *John*.

(15)   John expected that he would win

(15′) x expected that x would win

(15″)   John expected that John would win

Parsons (1972) suggests that the pronoun of laziness analysis is possible whenever the antecedent is a proper name or a definite description, and not otherwise. This correlates with the fact that sentences like (13) with other sorts of quantifier phrases never allow such an interpretation. He also suggests that whenever a pronoun can be coherently represented as a bound variable, then that interpretation is to be taken as one of its possible analyses. The conclusion that sentences like (15) are indeed structurally ambiguous in spite of being semantically unambiguous is likely to be resisted by some linguists, but I know of no *a priori* arguments against it, and simplicity of the total system, if in fact that is a result, would argue for it.

Furthermore, for the case of (15), unexpected support for a real ambiguity turns up in the behaviour of *only*-phrases. It seems that *only*-phrases must be classed as permitting pronouns of laziness, but in a special way: if what follows the *only* is a proper noun or definite description, then subsequent occurrences of the same proper noun or definite description (minus the *only*) can be substituted for by a pronoun. On the other hand, *only*-phrases also act like quantifier phrases, with *only John* behaving like 'no one other than John'. If we substitute *only John* for *John* in (15), the resulting sentence is semantically ambiguous in a way that exactly parallels the syntactic ambiguity postulated for (15).

(16)   Only John expected that he would win

One source involves the open sentence (16′), quantified by *only John*:[1]

(16′) x expected that x would win

---

[1] See Bennett (1972) for an extension of Montague's (1970) fragment in which *only*-phrases are analysed syntactically and semantically as quantifier phrases.

The other source must be (16″), with the pronoun-of-laziness rule substituting *he* for *John*.

(16″) Only John expected that John would win

It might be protested that this is a hasty conclusion based on a superficial analysis of *only*-phrases, and that both interpretations could be treated as bound variables under a more sophisticated analysis that gives multiple-sentence sources for sentences with *only*-phrases, such as that proposed in Lakoff (1970). Since it would be too large a digression to go into that fully here, let me just mention one bit of evidence that supports my analysis, namely that the same restriction to proper names and definite descriptions holds for simple pronouns of laziness and for pronouns of laziness with *only*-phrases, so that, for instance, sentence (17) can have only the bound variable interpretation.

(17) Only one man expected that he would win

An analysis that treated both readings of (16) as bound variable interpretations would then have to explain why one of the bound variable analyses was blocked in cases like (17).

We have established so far, then, that ordinary pronouns can arise by two processes: as bound variables and as pronouns of laziness. Sentences where the antecedent of a pronoun is a proper noun or a definite description are structurally ambiguous, although the two structures often lead to equivalent interpretations. Now we should look at reflexive pronouns and at deletions, to see whether analogs of both processes apply there as well.

For reflexives, there are examples with quantifiers, like (18), which require the bound variable interpretation, and examples with proper nouns or definite descriptions, like (19), which could be analysed either way (with no difference in the resulting interpretation).

(18) Every man underrated himself

(19) The man in the brown hat shot himself in the foot

Such examples give evidence that reflexives must sometimes be analysed as variables, but are neutral on the question of whether there is a reflexive-of-laziness analysis as well. There are as far as I can determine no analogs to Karttunen's sentence (14) which would require a laziness interpretation. The one piece of differential evidence I know of comes from the classic example (20):

(20) Only Lucifer pities himself

If there were a reflexive-of-laziness process, then (20) should be ambiguous in the same way as (16), and one of its readings should be equivalent to (21).

(21) Only Lucifer pities Lucifer

But (20) is not ambiguous; it has only a bound variable reading, and cannot be interpreted as (21). And I know of no examples where a reflexive pronoun cannot be interpreted as a bound variable. (I would like to hold open the possibility that heavily stressed reflexive pronouns may perhaps be pronouns of laziness, but I will ignore that issue here and keep such examples out of the argument.)

Thus the only evidence that I can find that bears on the problem points to reflexivization as a process restricted to variables. In what follows I will argue that the same holds for complement subject deletion. Before going on, however, let us look back at the problematical examples we are concerned with and see if we can begin to formulate a hypothesis about what is going on. The examples are repeated below.

(1) John thought it was foolish to shave himself

(2) John thought it was foolish for him to shave himself

(9) Only John believes that it would be inadvisable to vote for himself

(10) Only John believes that it would be inadvisable for him to vote for himself

(11) Everyone considered it inadvisable to perjure himself

(12)(*) Everyone considered it inadvisable for him to perjure himself

Consider the *for him* in (2), (10), and (12), and the question of whether that *him* is a bound variable or a pronoun of laziness. I think analyses such as Grinder's and Postal's have implicitly assumed that it was a bound variable, although the question does not come up explicitly in their formulations. But Grinder at least used only proper names in his examples, and hence did not notice the problems posed by (9)–(12). It seems that we can approach a resolution of the problems by analysing the *him* in all these examples as a pronoun of laziness, especially if we can go on to argue that a bound variable in the same position is obligatorily deleted. Then the synonymy of (1) and (2) is just like the synonymy of the two analyses of (15), the non-synonymy of (9) and (10) is exactly parallel to the non-synonymy of the two analyses of (16); and the impossibility of (12) is accounted for by the restriction of pronouns of laziness to antecedents which are proper nouns or definite descriptions. So all we have left to do is to show why we cannot have a bound variable *him* in those positions. This will require some consideration of infinitives and *for*-phrases.

2. Deletion and variables in infinitive constructions

In this section I will try to show that, at least in the processes that relate to infinitives, whenever deletion is 'controlled' by noun phrase identity of some sort, the identity conditions are always between free variables and the deletion is obligatory. For ordinary Equi-NP Deletion, the case is quite easy to make and the conclusion is consistent with previous analyses in both generative and interpretive frameworks. For the phenomenon that Grinder has analysed as Super-Equi NP Deletion, I will argue in support of an analysis largely based on Kimball's rule of Dative Deletion, with some modifications related to the general claim above.

Consider first ordinary Equi-NP Deletion. The claim that the rule is obligatory when its structural description is met has never to my know-ledge been disputed, so I will not add arguments for it here. (The fact that some verbs, e.g. *try*, impose the further condition that the structural description of the rule *must* be met, is an independent matter, as is the problem of finding the most general way to specify which NP in the matrix sentence acts as the controller.) The claim that NP identity for Equi is identity of free variables can be verified from examples such as the follow-ing:

(22) No one tried to leave

(23) Only John expected to lose

(24) Only John expected that he would lose.

Example (22) is the sort that was originally adduced to show that Equi-NP Deletion must be regarded not as involving identity in linguistic form, but rather identity of the sort that logical variables represent.[1] If there were in addition a deletion-of-laziness phenomenon, then example (23) should be ambiguous in the way that example (24) is, but it is not. Hence I believe

---

[1] In recent extensions of Montague (1970), I have offered an analysis of *try* as taking a verb phrase complement rather than a sentential complement, so that Equi-NP Deletion is not involved (Partee (1972)). I believe such an analysis to be appropriate for those verbs which require (in the usual treatment) the structural description of Equi-NP Deletion to be met, but since I do not believe the difference between the analyses affects the present discussion I am keeping the standard analysis here.

it is clear (and uncontroversial) that ordinary Equi-NP Deletion is an obligatory operation on variables.[1]

In approaching the Super-Equi problem, one of the first things to worry about is the role of *for*-phrases. Kimball (1971) pointed out the frequent ambiguity of *for*-phrases as between Datives on adjectives and as part of an embedded complement. The two roles show up most clearly in examples where both can occur.

(25) It's unpleasant for me for you to leave such a mess

(26) It's good for the economy for everyone to have a job

(27) It's important for everyone for everyone to be happy

When only one *for*-phrase shows up, it is not always clear which role it is playing. Some adjectives, including *good* and *important*, appear to take Datives optionally; that is, the language seems to allow a distinction between asserting that something is good or important for someone and asserting that it is good or important in some absolute sense.[2] With such adjectives, a sentence with just one *for*-phrase is ambiguous.

(28) It's good for John to stay here
(28′) It's good [for John to stay here]
(28″) It's good for John [to stay here]

In the reading (28′), *good* is being used without a Dative.[3] In (28″) the Dative has triggered deletion of the embedded *for*-phrase. Now Kimball argues, and we want to support him, that deletion of an embedded *for*-phrase on identity with a Dative in the next higher clause works just like ordinary Equi-NP Deletion. Like some verbs, some adjectives require that the structural description of Equi be met: e.g. *foolish* requires that the

---

[1] I believe this claim is also consistent with Jackendoff's treatment of complement subject interpretation, once his 'table of co-reference' is refined to show what co-reference means between a pronoun and a quantifier phrase.

[2] Of course it can be argued that whatever is good must be good for someone, or perhaps for everyone, and similarly for *important*, etc.; but it seems to me that such arguments are real ones that the language permits us to debate, and that it would be entirely inappropriate for a linguist to decide *qua* linguist that no moral judgements were absolute. Linguists who argued that *good* always has an underlying Dative would end up having to take stands on philosophical issues in formulating the deletion rules that would permit *good* to end up with no Dative on the surface: e.g. a 'utilitarian linguist' might argue for 'for the greatest number'-deletion.

[3] Those who remain unconvinced by n. 2 above may posit some sort of free (i.e. uncontrolled) Dative deletion rule operating in (28′). Kimball suggests *for someone*-deletion, which seems semantically implausible in such a case. I know of no purely syntactic arguments on either side, and there may even be a further ambiguity in (28′) between an underlying structure with no Dative and an underlying structure with some freely deletable Dative.

embedded complement subject be identical to the Dative on *foolish*, disallowing (29).

(29) * It was foolish for John for Mary to leave

But if the Equi-NP Deletion rule as governed by adjectives with Datives is to be the same as the usual Equi-NP Deletion rule (where the controller is the subject or object of the matrix verb, or subject of an adjective like *eager*), we are faced with the problem that (30) and (31) are well-formed.

(30) It's good for John for John to stay here

(31) It's good for John for him to stay here

Ordinary Equi, as noted earlier, is obligatory and does not permit pronominalization as an equivalent option.

But note that (30) and (31) do not seem to be fully synonymous with (28) (on the reading (28″), which is the only relevant one since (30) and (31) clearly have a Dative). I would like to propose that (30) and (31) are related to an open sentence with two distinct free variables, i.e. (32), whereas (28″) is related to an open sentence with a single free variable, i.e. (33).

(32) It's good for x for y to stay here

(33) It's good for x for x to stay here

Then if Equi-NP Deletion is defined on variables and obligatory when the variables are identical, the data would be accounted for. But we have to make (32) and (33) plausible, and we have to try to explain why a similar option is not available with the standard cases of Equi, i.e. why (34) is not possible like (31) with an interpretation analogous to (32).

(34) * John is eager for him to stay here

The claim that (30) is an instance of (32) and not of (33) is supported by the fact that only those noun phrases which permit pronominalization-of-laziness can occur in the pattern of (31).

(35) * It's good for every student for him to have to meet deadlines

In non-extraposed form with either forward or backward pronominalization, (35) seems even worse, while (31) is still fine.

(31′) For John to stay here is good for him

(35′) * For every student to have to meet deadlines is good for him

(31″) For him to stay here is good for John

(35″) * For him to have to meet deadlines is good for every student

The explanation for this under the present hypothesis is that a pronoun can be anaphorically related to a quantifier phrase only on a bound variable interpretation, so (35) would have to come from (33), and (33) undergoes obligatory Equi-NP deletion; hence the only possible realization for the structure underlying (35) is (36).

(36) It's good for every student [to have to meet deadlines]

Further support for the distinction between (32) and (33) can be obtained from contrasts like the following:

(37) It may be good for Mike for him to be home all day, but it's bad for Mary

(38) It may be good for Mike to be home all day, but it's bad for Mary

The underlying variable structure of these might be represented schematically as follows:

(37′) It may be good for x for y to VP, but it's bad for z for y to VP

(38′) It may be good for x for x to VP, but it's bad for z for z to VP

Such pairs are not crucial evidence for this hypothesis as against alternatives, since the distinction could be accounted for simply by a cyclic ordering of rules even if *him* in (37) was treated as a bound variable.

Thus the data supports, if not exclusively, the hypothesis that Equi-NP Deletion is an obligatory operation on variables. Sentence (30), repeated below, is accounted for as arising via quantification over separate variables by the same NP, just as (39) below is, but sentence (30), unlike (39), permits the second occurrence of the NP to be replaced by a pronoun of laziness to form (31) (compare the ill-formedness of (40)). Sentence (31), then, does not show that Equi is sometimes optional.

(30) It's good for John for John to stay here

(39) It's good for everyone for everyone to have a job

(31) It's good for John for him to stay here

(40) * It's good for everyone for him to have a job

But now the converse problem, mentioned above in connection with example (34), still remains. Our analysis would seem to predict that an underlying structure like (41) below could have *John* substituted independently for each variable to give (42) and then pronominalization of laziness should yield (34).

(41) x is eager for y to stay here

(42) *?John is eager for John to stay here

At worst, we have just traded one set of cases where Equi is unpredictably optional for another set where substitution of the same NP for different variables is unpredictably forbidden. But note that it is only certain NPs for which the prohibition holds. In particular, it is only the NPs on which pronominalization of laziness can operate that cannot appear in sentences like (42). Thus (43) is perfectly well-formed.

(43) Everyone is eager for everyone to stay here

And a distinction which was left implicit earlier comes into play here. It was noted earlier that definite descriptions as well as proper nouns could be replaced by pronouns of laziness. But in contexts where a definite description is ambiguously referential or not, it is only on the referential reading that a pronoun of laziness can be used.

(44) Only the owner of the chicken farm thought that he should raise turkeys

Sentence (44) is ambiguous: the bound variable reading for the pronoun, which we are not interested in here, is the reading appropriate to the situation where everyone is contemplating raising turkeys; the reading that must be a pronoun of laziness is the one on which the chicken farmer is considering going into the turkey business against the advice of his friends. That reading should have as its source sentence (45) below.

(45) Only the owner of the chicken farm thought that the owner of the chicken farm should raise turkeys

Sentence (45) should in turn be ambiguous: the description *the owner of the chicken farm* should have both a referential and a non-referential reading, with the referential reading as the source for the pronoun of laziness in (44). (The non-referential reading does not permit any kind of pronominalization.) With a different subject for the higher clause, the usual ambiguity is clear enough, as in (46), but (45) itself strongly resists the referential reading.

(46) Smith thought that the owner of the chicken farm should raise turkeys

It seems likely that the reason (45) resists the referential reading is that pronominalization of laziness can apply to it to turn it into (44), and there is at least a stylistic preference to perform pronominalization whenever possible, especially when pronominalization can reduce ambiguity (though in this particular example, a new ambiguity is introduced when the original ambiguity is eliminated).

The facts just mentioned indicate, incidentally, that pronominalization of laziness does not depend merely on linguistic form, as the earlier discussion of it suggested, for if it did, (44) should share the non-referential reading of (45), which it clearly does not. It would be too strong to claim that pronouns of laziness were always referential, for (44) could in turn be embedded in some opaque context that would allow a non-referential reading for *the owner of the chicken farm*. The additional requirement needed may be that the scope of the NP being pronominalized and the scope of the antecedent must be identical; but that is only a tentative hypothesis and the question will have to remain open here.[1]

The question which is still at issue at this point, and to which this further discussion of pronouns of laziness is relevant, is why sentences like (34), repeated below, are not well-formed on any reading, when we seem to be led to predict a well-formed pronoun of laziness reading.

(34) *John is eager for him to stay here

Although I do not have a conclusive answer to this question, I would like to offer the beginnings of a hypothesis about it. One semantic difference between *good*, which does allow the same definite NP to substitute for distinct variables, and *eager*, which does not, is that *eager* denotes a subjective attitude of the subject of *eager* to the action or state denoted by the infinitive. *Good*, on the other hand, does not necessarily represent the attitude of the individual referred to by the Dative. Note that *feel good to*, unlike *be good for*, does express a subjective attitude of its Dative, and the corresponding restrictions hold.

(47) It felt good to John to touch Mary

(48) * It felt good to John for John to touch Mary

[1] One problem in refining the domain of pronominalization of laziness is that it is not clear how Karttunen's example, (14) above, can be treated if reference or identity of scope is reintroduced as a factor.

(49) * It felt good to John for him to touch Mary

In order for sentences like (34) and (48)–(49) to be generated, on the hypothesis that Equi is obligatory for identical variables, it would have to be possible to substitute *John* independently for each variable in structures like (50) and (51).

(50) x is eager for y to *VP*

(51) It felt good to x for y to *VP*

My tentative semantic explanation for the impossibility of doing so is that with subjective attitudes such as these, if *John* is the x, he cannot hold such an attitude about his own involvement in some action or state without recognizing that it is himself who is involved. Of course this is plausible only on a referential reading of the NP substituted for y; if we use a repeated definite description, a non-referential reading will be possible, but not a referential one, and accordingly not a pronoun.

(52) The stupidest official was eager for the stupidest official to be fired

(53) * The stupidest official was eager for him to be fired

To say that the holders of such attitudes necessarily know when it is themselves the attitudes concern (in the referential cases), is, I would suggest, an appropriate account for why a single free variable must be involved in such cases, and why, consequently, deletion is obligatory when the variable occurs in a position where Equi is applicable.[1]

If this hypothesis is correct, it may not be necessary to add any restrictions to the syntax to account for it, since the ill-formedness would be on the conceptual level. That is, (34) and (48) could be regarded as syntactically well-formed expressions of a conceptually anomalous proposition. If there is any point in marking the restrictions in the syntax, the appropriate verbs and adjectives could be marked with a syntactic feature that would be predictable from their semantic classification. But the syntactic restriction governed by these lexical items would be the rather complex one of prohibiting insertion of identical referential NPs for different free variables.

Let me quickly point out that much more work remains to be done before this tentative hypothesis even reaches a testable formulation. The semantic notions which are claimed to underlie the phenomena have not been made

---

[1] I believe these matters are related to the notion of 'quasi-indicator' developed by Castañeda (1966, 1967, 1968), but I have not explored the connections yet.

precise, and the influence of syntactic factors has not been fully explored. But at worst, if the hypothesis breaks down, there are some unexplained restrictions on the substitution of identical NPs for distinct variables, and the data involved have not been accounted for in any other account of Equi either.

This concludes the argument that deletion of a *for*-phrase controlled by a Dative in the next higher sentence is a case of ordinary Equi-NP Deletion and, like the other cases of Equi, is an obligatory operation defined on variables. Before turning to Super-Equi proper, we must briefly consider the possibilities of uncontrolled deletion of *for*-phrases.

If an adjective ends up with a bare infinitive, with no controller for deletion in the sentence, there are several possibilities for the underlying structure.

(54) It's against the law to park by a fire hydrant

If *against the law* takes no Dative, which seems plausible though not certain, then we must either posit infinitive phrases without accompanying *for*-phrases, or else allow certain *for*-phrases, e.g. *for one*, to be freely deletable.[1] Some evidence, though I think not crucial, for the latter comes from sentences like the following (assuming there is no controlling Dative in the underlying structure, which has not been conclusively established).

(55) It's a sin to covet one's neighbour's ox

(56) It's a crime against humanity to keep one's wealth to oneself

In other cases, an adjective which clearly does take a Dative ends up with no *for*-phrase.

(57) It's easy to learn to ski

(58) It's foolish to leave too many lights on

(59) It's dangerous to play with matches

In such cases, since identity between the understood Dative and the subject of the infinitive clearly holds, the best hypothesis seems to be that the under-

---

[1] In sentences with *would* in the main clause, *for me* and *for you* seem to be deletable as well, though they are not otherwise.

(a) It's a sin to kill oneself
(b) *It's a sin to kill myself
(c) It would be a sin to kill myself

The *would* suggests an underlying *if*-clause, but since I do not understand what is going on here, I will simply avoid examples with *would* in them.

lying structure has identical free variables, as in (60), to which Equi applies, and the Dative subsequently undergoes Free Dative Deletion (see Kimball (1971)).

(60) It's easy for x for x to learn to ski

Free Dative Deletion appears to be possible with *I*, *you*, and *one*; whether there are other possibilities, e.g. *someone*, I leave open.[1]

(61) It was stupid to leave your hat in the rain

(62) It's unpleasant to stay by myself in the house all day

(63) It's startling to find oneself viewed as part of the older generation

(64) * It's hard to get himself out of bed in the morning

It is difficult, and fortunately inessential to the present argument, to determine just how many ways ambiguous a given construction with a bare infinitive and no controller present is. The only essential point to be made is that there is such a thing as Free Dative Deletion, and probably also free deletion of *for one* in *for-to* constructions, when there is no Dative or other controller.

Among the sentences that Grinder (1970) cites as evidence for Super-Equi NP Deletion are some which could be equally well analysed as Free Dative Deletion such as (65) (Grinder's (1a)).

(65) Harry thought that it would be difficult to leave

Such a sentence does not provide evidence for Super-Equi unless it can be shown that it has a reading which could not be accounted for by Free Dative Deletion. Grinder clearly thinks it does, but his only direct evidence is the purported synonymy of (65) and (66), which is disputable.

(66) Harry thought that it would be difficult for him to leave

The strongest evidence for a deletion rule which operates over unbounded distance comes from sentences which show third-person reflexivization and related processes in infinitives, since such cases cannot arise by Free Dative Deletion (see (64)). Thus the critical examples are those like (67)–(69) (Grinder's (6a–c)).

---

[1] I'm inclined to doubt the possibility of *for someone*-deletion, partly because the pronoun for *someone*, either *he* or *they* depending on dialect, never shows up in the bare infinitives.

(67) Barbara explained why it was so natural to enjoy herself while singing the Gita

(68) Michael predicted that it would be trivial to design his own computer

(69) Kathleen claims that it is enjoyable to hold her breath for days at a time

In all of Grinder's examples of this type with infinitives (though not in all of those with gerundives) the adjective in the clause immediately above the infinitive is of the type that takes a Dative. Hence the deletion of the complement *for*-phrase can be analysed as controlled by the Dative, and the deletion that has the 'Super' properties Grinder describes is deletion of the Dative, as Kimball argued. All of Grinder's arguments about the notion of 'possible controller' and 'Deletion Path' apply to Dative Deletion; and recognizing the rule as Dative Deletion still leaves open the problem of specifying just what the possible controllers are (see Jackendoff (1972) for some semantically-based hypotheses). The only issue I want to take with the Grinder-Kimball Dative Deletion rule concerns its optionality. This is the point to which examples (9) and (10), repeated below, are relevant.

(9) Only John believes that it would be inadvisable to vote for himself

(10) Only John believes that it would be inadvisable for him to vote for himself

Similar examples which show Dative Deletion operating across a longer path are given below.

(70) Only John considers it likely to be unpleasant to shoot himself

(71) Only John considers it likely to be unpleasant for him to shoot himself

The sentences with and without the pronouns are not synonymous; only those without the pronoun permit the bound variable interpretation illustrated schematically in (72).

(72) [only John] $\hat{x}$ (x believes that it would be inadvisable for x for x to vote for x)

Furthermore, as pointed out earlier, a pronoun cannot occur when the controller is a quantifier phrase such as *everyone*. Thus it seems clear that when a pronoun does occur in such positions it is a pronoun of laziness and not a bound variable, so that Dative Deletion, like Equi-NP Deletion, is an obligatory rule defined on variables. The structures of (9) and (10) can be explained as follows:

(a) Sentence (9), where no pronoun shows up, has the structure illustrated in (72). On the first cycle, reflexivization occurs; on the second, the *for x* of the complement is obligatorily deleted by Equi-NP Deletion, controlled by the Dative *for x*. On the top cycle, Dative Deletion obligatorily deletes the Dative *for x* and the topmost *x* is filled by the NP *only John*.

(b) Sentence (10), with the pronoun of laziness, is ambiguous, since the *for him* can be either (i) a Dative or (ii) part of the *for-to* complement. Structure (i) is schematically illustrated in (73).

(73) [only John] $\hat{x}$ ([John] $\hat{y}$ (*x* believes that it would be inadvisable for *y* for *y* to vote for *y*))

Reflexivization and Equi occur as before, but Dative Deletion does not, since the variables are different. When *only John* and *John* are filled in, pronominalization of laziness can apply. Structure (ii) for sentence (10) is illustrated in (74); whether this is a real possibility depends on whether *inadvisable* requires a Dative or not, on which I have no strong opinions.

(74) [only John] $\hat{x}$ ([John] $\hat{y}$ (*x* believes that it would be inadvisable [for *y* to vote for *y*]))

Reflexivization occurs on the first cycle, but Equi cannot apply since there is no Dative, and nothing further happens until the NPs are filled in and pronominalization of laziness applies.

Thus even the Dative Deletion facts, where it originally seemed that deletion and pronominalization were in free variation, support the claim that deletion of an NP under identity conditions is always an obligatory operation on variables. It would be tempting to leap to the conclusion that all transformational operations which require NP identity are defined on variables and obligatory, but pronouns of laziness constitute one clear exception, and the Super-Equi data with gerunds need further investigation before the generalization can even be made firm for all deletion rules.[1]

[1] I am grateful to Emmon Bach for helpful discussion in the early stages of this paper; he is of course not responsible for any of its shortcomings.

REFERENCES

Bennett, Michael (1972). 'Accommodating the plural in Montague's fragment of English'. In Rodman (1972).

Castañeda, Hector-Neri (1966). '"He": a study in the logic of self-consciousness', *Ratio*, **8**, 130–57.

—— (1967). 'Indicators and quasi-indicators', *Am. Phil. Qtrly*, **4**, 85–100.

—— (1968). 'On the logic of attributions of self-knowledge to others', *J. Phil.*, **65**, 439–56.

Geach, Peter T. (1968). *Reference and Generality*. Ithaca: Cornell University Press.

Grinder, John (1970). 'Super Equi-NP Deletion'. In *Papers from the Sixth Regional Meeting of the Chicago Linguistic Society*, pp. 297–317. Chicago: Chicago Linguistic Society.

—— (1971). 'A reply to "Super Equi-NP Deletion as Dative Deletion"'. In *Papers from the Seventh Regional Meeting of the Chicago Linguistic Society*, pp. 101–11. Chicago: Chicago Linguistic Society.

Jackendoff, Ray S. (1972). *Semantic Interpretation in Generative Grammar*. Cambridge, Mass.: MIT Press.

Karttunen, Lauri (1969). 'Pronouns and variables'. In *Papers from the Fifth Regional Meeting of the Chicago Linguistic Society*, pp. 108–16. Chicago: Chicago Linguistic Society.

Kimball, John P. (1971). 'Super Equi-NP Deletion as Dative Deletion'. In *Papers from the Seventh Regional Meeting of the Chicago Linguistic Society*, pp. 142–8. Chicago: Chicago Linguistic Society.

Lakoff, George (1970). 'Repartee, or a reply to "Negation, conjunction, and quantifiers"', *Foundations of Language*, **6**, 389–422.

Montague, Richard (1970). 'The proper treatment of quantification in ordinary English.' Mimeographed, UCLA. (To appear in Hintikka, J. et al., eds., *Approaches to Natural Language*, Dordrecht: D. Reidel).

Parsons, Terence D. (1972). 'An outline of a semantics for English.' Dittograph draft, Univ. of Mass.

Partee, Barbara H. (1970). 'Opacity, coreference, and pronouns', *Synthese*, **21**, 359–85.

—— (1972). 'Some transformational extensions of Montague grammar.' In Rodman (1972).

Postal, Paul M. (1970). 'On coreferential complement subject deletion', *Linguistic Inquiry*, **1**, 439–500.

Rodman, Robert, ed. (1972). *Papers in Montague Grammar*. Occasional Papers in Linguistics No. 2, UCLA.

A semantics for superficial and embedded questions in natural language

R. D. HULL

We shall propose in this paper a formal semantics for elementary embedded questions, such as *John knows which student Mary invited*, *John can't remember who left early*, etc. The semantics for these sentences will be stated in terms of that for the corresponding 'direct' questions, e.g. *Which student did Mary invite?*, *Who left early?*, etc. So I shall first review the semantics of elementary direct questions, as proposed in Keenan and Hull (1973), and then generalize the analysis to cover the case of embedded questions:

1. Direct questions

1.1. *The intuition*

We consider a question such as (1):

(1) Which student did Mary invite?

to be basically a request for the identification of the student who Mary invited. An *answer* to the question is, linguistically, a noun phrase that refers to that individual. It might be an alternative description such as *the student who won first prize*, or perhaps just an elementary referring expression such as *John*, or even *him*. If the noun phrase does refer to the student in question, then it is a *true answer* to the question; otherwise, it is not.

In our semantics, then, question-answer pairs determine truth values. Questions themselves are, semantically, the sort of thing that makes a proposition from an answer phrase, but they do not themselves carry truth values. The basis of our semantics of questions lies in the definition of truth and falsehood for question-answer pairs – that is, in the definition of the question-answer relation.

1.2. *A more formal statement of the question-answer relation*

For the purposes of exposition, we will only consider singular questions of the form:

(2) (WH,NP_x,S) – (read 'Which NP
is such that S?'),

where NP is a *common noun phrase*, like *student*, *student who failed his exam* or *student who failed his exam who got drunk*.

Our syntax allows, by recursive definition, for an infinite number of possible common noun phrases. They are built up on a common noun, like *student*, by tagging on any number of relative clauses, progressively limiting the extension of the common noun phrase. The common noun phrase, NP_x, in (2), carries an index, x, which is a variable (pronoun) and which occurs as a free variable in S. Such a question requests the identification of the unique member of the extension of NP_x for which the sentence S is true. We call the extension of NP_x the *question set* of the question.

We let an *answer* A to the question (WH,NP_x,S) be any expression which refers (in a model) such as a proper noun, free pronoun, or a common noun phrase with a definite determiner like *The*. For each question-answer pair, we call the one-element set referred to by the answer the *answer set* of the question-answer pair. The question-answer pair is defined to be *true* just in case the answer set is contained in the question set of the question, and is identical with the unique member of the question set satisfying S. Thus the *truth* conditions for the question-answer pair $((WH,NP_x,S),A)$ are equivalent to those for A to identify the NP such that S. For example, (3):

(3) Which student left early?, Fred

is true just in case Fred is the student who left early.

The question-answer pair is *false* just in case the answer set is in the question set, but is distinct from the unique member of the question set satisfying S. Otherwise, the question-answer pair is given a third truth value here called *zero*. So, for instance, the question-answer pair (3) would get zero truth value if Fred wasn't a student – even if Fred did leave early.

In this way we can distinguish two ways in which an answer to a question can be untrue – one we term false, the other zero-valued. So, for instance, the answer (4b) to question (4a) is false just in case Fred is one of the men who left early, but he *did* apologize. *Fred* is a zero-valued answer to (4a) in the case where Fred did not leave early at all. This agrees with natural intuitions that there is a significant difference in the status of the answer in these two situations.

(4) a. Which man who left early didn't apologize?
     b. Fred.

Another point in favour of this analysis is that it makes a clear distinction between the questions (5a) and (5b):

(5) a. Which student came early and left late?
 b. Which student who came early left late?

Both questions have the same true answers – namely, those singular definite noun phrases that refer to the unique student who both came early and left late. However, the questions have different question sets; the question set of (5a) is the set of all students, whereas that of (5b) is the set of just those students who came early. Hence, if Fred is a student who neither came early nor left late, then *Fred* is a false answer to (5a), but takes zero value as an answer to (5b). This agrees with natural intuition about these two questions.

1.3. *Presuppositions of questions and answers*

As stated earlier, the question-answer pair behaves very much like a proposition, taking truth values, and having the same sort of meaning relations as do declarative sentences. Thus we may carry over the definitions of logical implication and presupposition from the analysis of declaratives in Keenan (1972), giving:

Definition 1: A question-answer pair (Q,A) *logically implies* a sentence S just in case, in every model in which (Q,A) is true, S is true.
Definition 2: A question-answer pair (Q,A) *logically presupposes* a sentence S just in case, in every model in which S is not true, (Q,A) takes the zero truth value.

These definitions account for:

Fact 1: The answer (6b) to the question (6a) asserts sentence (6c) and presupposes (6d):

(6) a. Which professor knows that Fred doesn't attend lectures?
 b. The professor who lives near Fred
 c. The professor who lives near Fred knows that Fred doesn't attend lectures
 d. Fred doesn't attend lectures

We then define the *logical presuppositions* of a question alone to be those sentences which are true in any model in which the question has a true answer. We are saying, then, that a question roughly presupposes that it has a true answer, and all the consequences of this. Thus we account for

Fact 2: The following (a)-questions presuppose the corresponding (b)-sentences:

(7) a. Which girl was surprised that Fred won?
   b. Fred won.
(8) a. Which barber shaves the King of France?
   b. There is exactly one King of France.

1.2. *Informativeness*

The analysis so far not only gives the satisfactory results described already, but also treats (9b) as an answer to (9a), an answer which can never be false:

(9) a. Which student did Mary invite to the party?
   b. The student who Mary invited to the party

Clearly this answer can never be false because, as long as there is a unique student such that Mary invited him to the party, (9b) refers to that student. (9b) is normally considered a very obstructive way to answer the question. Similarly, (10b) is considered an obstructive way to answer (10a):

(10) a. Which man washed the dishes?
    b. The man who didn't wash the dishes

We suggest that the unhelpfulness of (9) and (10) is attributable to the fact that in one case the answer can never be false, in the other it can never be true. In such cases the answers are conveying no information to the questioner, since he already knows all that they imply. This gives rise to our notion of an *informative answer* to a question: An answer A to a question Q is defined to be *logically informative* just in case there is some state of affairs in which it is true, and another state of affairs in which it is false as the answer to Q. Thus examples (9) and (10) would be *uninformative* by our definition.

Another example of uninformativeness arises with the question (11):

(11) Which student who left early left early?

Consider any answer A to the question; notice that A is a true answer just in case there is exactly one student such that he left early, and A refers to that student. However, A can never be false, for if it were then it would have to refer to a member of the set of students who left early and did not leave early – a set with no members. Since A can never be false, it is, by definition, a logically uninformative answer to (11); since A was arbitrary, (11) has the peculiar distinction of having *no* informative answers. This helps to explain why (11) is not a very natural type of question.

That concludes a summary of the analysis of this particular kind of superficial question. We now look at the way this analysis can be incorporated in an account of some types of embedded question:

2. Embedded questions

Leroy Baker (1968) has produced a useful analysis of the predicates which take 'indirect' or *embedded questions*. We will concentrate our attention in this exposition on just those embedded questions that are predicated by the verb *know*. Most of the predicates Baker classes with *know* can be treated similarly.[1]

2.1. *The intuition*

We consider a sentence such as (12):

(12) John knows (WH, NP_x, S)

to be stating that John can identify the NP such that S. That is, John knows a true informative answer to the question embedded in (12). We can express this knowledge by saying that for some true informative answer A to the question, (13) is true:

(13) John knows that $(A = (The, NP_x S))$

Notice the range of possible ways in which A could answer the question: If John is at a party and sees a student leaving the party early, the only way in which he may be able to identify that student is by pointing at him, or by some other direct identification, but even so the sentence (14) would be considered true. This direct identification corresponds to the answers like *him* dealt with in the question-answer analysis:[2]

---

[1] Thus, this analysis does not claim to account for predicates like *wonder, is a function of, depend, matter*, which also take embedded questions.

[2] This analysis is not entirely adequate, because it could be the case that there is no public way in which John's private visual impression of the student who left early can be expressed. If we were to allow our language to incorporate the notion of private names, perhaps in the style of Kaplan's *vivid names* (see Kaplan (1969)), then a full account could be given. Then each perceptual impression of one person on another would be codable in the language as such a private name, and such an impression would count as a possible, although inexpressible, answer to WH-questions.

(14) John knows which student left the party early

The answer need not be direct, though. Consider (15a): It is easy to conceive of a situation in which the sentence (15b) is true although John does not know the identity of the individual student who in fact *is* the smallest:

(15) a. John knows which student will be victimized.
　　 b. John knows that the student who is the smallest will be victimized.

Moreover, in such a situation it would be generally considered that (15a) is true. Hence, our analysis of embedded questions should account for the fact that (15b) implies (15a) and that such an indirect identification as *The student who is the smallest* is sufficient to make the embedded question true. Notice, however, that (16) (on the opaque reading) does *not* imply (15a):

(16) John knows that the student who will be victimized will be victimized

Anyone who knows that a unique student will be victimized and can make a simple deduction would know that the student who will be victimized will be victimized, but this is not the knowledge that is necessary for him to know which student will be victimized. So we see the necessity for the answer A identifying $(The, NP_x S)$ to be informative: *The student who is the smallest* is an informative answer to *Which student will be victimized?*, whereas *The student who will be victimized* is uninformative.

The following example illustrates the way in which the true informative answer A must be an *arbitrary* answer: The sentence (17a) is true in a given state of affairs if there is a true informative answer A to the question (17b) such that (17c) is true, in that state of affairs:

(17) a. John knows which competitor will win the contest
　　 b. Which competitor will win the contest?
　　 c. John knows that A is the competitor who will win the contest

The true informative answer A to the question (17b) can range from a direct identification of a particular competitor, by pointing for instance to a noun phrase such as *The competitor who writes the best slogan in less than ten words beginning 'I do linguistics because...'* And it is clear that John could know either answer was true without knowing that the other one was, both constituting sufficient conditions for John to know which competitor will win the contest.

We are now in a position to give a more formal statement of the truth and falsehood conditions for these embedded questions:

2.2. *More formal statement of the embedded question analysis*

Let Q be an abbreviation for the question (WH, NP_x, S). We define the sentence (18a), where z is a free variable, to be *true* just in case there is a true informative answer A to Q such that (18b) is true. (By '$A = (The, NP_xS)$' we mean that 'A' refers to the same individual in the world as does 'The, NP_xS'):

(18) a. z knows (WH, NP_x, S)
    b. z knows that $(A = (The, NP_xS))$

The sentence (18a) is defined to be *false* just in case for some true informative answer A to Q, (18b) is false, and for no such A is (18b) true. Otherwise (18a) takes the zero truth value.

2.3. *The grounding problem*

There is a problem that these definitions do not tackle: Notice that, in our definitions above, the answer A in (18b) is completely *arbitrary*, so it too could be a noun phrase containing an embedded question. So, to establish the truth of A as an answer to the original question, it would be necessary to evaluate the truth of this second embedded question. Equally well, this second embedded question may have answers involving embedded questions, and so on. So our allowing an arbitrary answer A in the formal analysis has produced a circular definition which can involve a derivation through an infinite number of embedded questions, never getting back to an answer grounded in reality.

Perhaps an example will illustrate this problem: According to our definitions (19a) can be true merely because John knows that (19c) is a true answer to (19b):

(19) a. John knows which student will pass the exam
    b. Which student will pass the exam?
    c. The student who knows which student will pass the exam

Now we *do* want to accept (19c) as a possible answer to the question (19b) because it *is* possible to conceive of a situation where there is an alternative means of identifying the student who knows which student passed the exam, and in this situation John's knowledge that (19c) answers (19b) would be sufficient for (19a) *John knows which student will pass the exam* to be true.[1] However, our analysis at present considers all arbitrary answers to (19b) *Which student will pass the exam?* in order to ascertain whether (19c) refers; so, in particular, the truth of (19c) as an answer to (19b) would have to be considered. That is, in order to ascertain whether (19c) is a true answer to (19b) we have to know whether (19c) is a true answer to (19b) before we start.

We solve this problem by introducing the idea of the *degree of directness* of an answer to a question. If the question and answer involve no embedded questions, then the answer has degree of directness zero, and the definitions for the question-answer relation go through as in the first part of this paper. However, if either the question or the answer contain an embedded question, then we have to consider the possible answers to this embedded question, and this in turn may mean we have to consider answers to other embedded questions. The degree of directness of the original answer is the number of such embedded questions we have to consider. Thus, by insisting that every answer to a question has a *finite* degree of directness, we limit the analysis to derivations involving finite chains of question-answer pairs. So that, to ascertain whether a particular question-answer pair is true we have to answer a finite number of other questions.

To illustrate this solution, consider the question-answer pair (20a):

(20) a. Which king rules France?, The king who knew which border post was unguarded.
     b. Which border post was unguarded?

The answer in (20a) cannot be an answer of degree zero because it contains an embedded question. However, if there was a true answer of degree zero, such as a name, to the question (20b), and if the king who rules France knew that this name referred to the border post that was unguarded, then (20a) would be a true answer with degree of directness one.

However, returning to our problem case (19), (19c) *The student who knows which student will pass the exam* cannot be a true answer of finite degree to the question (19b) *Which student will pass the exam?* solely on the grounds that the student referred to by (19c) knows that the student who knows which student will pass the exam will pass the exam, because this would involve answering the question (19b) an infinite number of times. And so this case is rejected by the analysis.

---

[1] For example, it could be that a student has managed to get access to the exam papers, and consequently is rightly confident that he is the one who will pass the exam.

A fuller account of the formalism of this analysis is given in the Appendix.

3. Summary

We have shown how natural language questions and answers can be given a logical representation in the same way as declarative sentences. We then presented an analysis of indirect questions, treating them both syntactically and semantically as questions embedded in complex declarative sentences. The results of this analysis show good agreement with intuitive understanding of the natural language constructions we are seeking to represent.

APPENDIX

1. The formal analysis

The interpreting function f_i for a state of the world (model) i is defined as in Keenan (1972) for the simple declarative sentences of the logical language $\mathscr{L}$.

Throughout the following, α may be a discourse name, a free variable, a proper name, or a noun phrase quantified by *The*.

By '$\alpha = (The, NP_x S)$', we mean that α identifies $(The, NP_x S)$.[1]

For question-answer pairs, we define:

$((WH, NP_x S), \alpha)$ is *true* in interpretation i just in case:

(i) $f_i \alpha \epsilon f_i NP_x$ AND
(ii) $\alpha = (The, NP_x S)$ is true in i.

It is *false* in i just in case:

(i) $f_i \alpha \epsilon f_i NP_x$ BUT,
(ii) $\alpha = (The, NP_x S)$ is false in i.

It is *zero-valued* in i just in case:

EITHER (i) $f_i \alpha \notin f_i NP_x$
   OR (ii) $\alpha = (The, NP_x S)$ is zero-valued in i.

For any question-answer pair (Q, A), A is an *informative answer* to Q just in case there is an interpretation i in which (Q, A) is true, and an interpretation j in which (Q, A) is false.

We have defined the truth values for question-answer pairs; we now introduce a new function F_i which, instead of mapping strings of $\mathscr{L}$ onto functions of the universe of discourse and truth values, like the interpreting function f_i, has a domain consisting of ordered pairs of $\mathscr{L}$-strings and markers, which are natural

---

[1] More formally, $(The, NP_x S, z)$ $(\alpha = z)$ if α is a discourse name or free variable, and $(\alpha, y)(The, NP_x S, z)(y = z)$, otherwise.

numbers indicating depth of derivation. For all $\mathscr{L}$-strings except those containing embedded questions, F_i operates just like the interpreting function with the derivation marker not there.

For example, for a common noun N, and for any natural number m, $F_i(N,m) = f_i(N)$, and the definition of truth in a model for a sentence quantified by *some* becomes:

$F_i((some,NP_x,S),m) = t$ iff there is a discourse name n such that
$\qquad\qquad F_i(n,m) \in F_i(NP_x,m)$, and $F_i(S_n^x,m) = t$.
$\qquad = z$ iff EITHER for all discourse names n such that
$\qquad\qquad F_i(n,m) \in F_i(NP_x,m)$, $F_i(S_n,m) = z$, OR where NP_x
$\qquad\qquad$ has the form $NP_y^* S^*$, $F_i((some,NP_y^*,S^*),m) = z$.
$\qquad = f$ otherwise.

For embedded questions, which we represent in the form: $know(z,(WH, NP_x,S))$,[1] we define, abbreviating '(WH,NP_x,S)' to 'Q', in the simplest cases:

$F_i(know(y,Q),0) = z$ in all situations (where z is the third truth value).
$F_i(know(y,Q),1) = t$ iff there is an informative answer α to Q such that
$\qquad\qquad F_i((Q,\alpha),0)=t$, and $F_i(know(y,\mathrm{Fact}(\alpha = (The,NP_xS))),0)$
$\qquad\qquad = t$.
$\qquad = f$ iff there is an informative answer α to Q such that
$\qquad\qquad F_i((Q,\alpha),0)=t$, and $F_i(know(y,\mathrm{Fact}(\alpha=(The,NP_xS))),0)$
$\qquad\qquad = f$, and for no such α is this last expression equal to t.
$\qquad = z$ otherwise.

That is, 'y knows Q' is true (to degree one) if there is a true informative answer α to Q to degree zero such that y knows that α identifies 'The,NP_xS'. This corresponds to the simplest cases of indirect questions as given in (15).

The more general definition, for all natural numbers m, is given by:

$F_i(know(y,Q),m) = t$ iff for some natural number $p<m$, there is an α such that
$\qquad\qquad F_i((Q,\alpha),p) = t$, and α is an informative answer to Q to
$\qquad\qquad$ degree p, and
$\qquad\qquad F_i(know(y,\mathrm{Fact}(\alpha = (The,NP_xS))),p) = t$.
$\qquad = f$ iff for some natural number $p<m$, there is an α such
$\qquad\qquad$ that $F_i((Q,\alpha),p) = t$, and α is an informative answer to
$\qquad\qquad Q$ to degree p, and $F_i(know(y,\mathrm{Fact}(\alpha = (The,NP_xS))),p)$
$\qquad\qquad = f$; and for no such p and α is this last expression
$\qquad\qquad$ equal to t.
$\qquad = z$ otherwise.

From the example (20), suppose the border post which was unguarded has name *Hastings*; then *Hastings* is a true informative answer of degree zero to (20b), and if there is a king who knew that *Hastings* identified the border post that was unguarded, then *The king who knew which border post was unguarded* refers, to degree one, and hence is a true answer to *Which king rules France?* to degree one

---

[1] *know* here is to be considered an arbitrary predicate from the class consisting of *know*, *remember*, etc. (see p. 39n.).

if this king *does* in fact rule France. If John knows that this is a true answer, then *John knows which king rules France* is true to degree two.

We define A to be an *informative answer to Q to degree m* just in case there is an interpretation i in which $F_i((Q,A),m) = t$, and an interpretation j in which $F_j((Q,A),m) = f$.

We define the interpretating function f_i for $\mathscr{L}$-sentences in terms of F_i:

$f_i(S) = t$ iff there is a natural number m' such that, for all $m > m'$, $F_i(S,m) = t$.
$\quad\,\, = f$ iff there is a natural number m' such that, for all $m > m'$, $F_i(S,m) = f$.
$\quad\,\, = z$ otherwise.

This makes the derivation of the truth of a sentence with embedded questions have a finite number m' of steps. In particular, if S is a question-answer pair (Q,A), then A is a true answer to Q with degree of directness m' just in case m' is the least natural number such that, for all $m > m'$, $F_i((Q,A),m) = t$.

REFERENCES

Baker, C. L. (1968). 'Indirect questions in English.' PhD thesis, University of Illinois.

Kaplan, D. (1969). 'Quantifying in'. In Donald Davidson and Jaakko Hintikka, eds., *Words and Objections: Essays on the Work of W. V. Quine* (1969). Dordrecht: Reidel Publishing Co.

Keenan, E. L. (1972). 'On semantically based grammar', *Linguistic Inquiry* **3**, 413–61.

Keenan, E. L. and Hull, R. D. (1973). 'The logical presuppositions of questions and answers'. In D. Franck and J. Petöfi, eds., *Präsuppositionen in der Linguistik und der Philosophie* (1973). Frankfurt: Athenäum.

Sortal quantification

J. E. J. ALTHAM AND NEIL W. TENNANT

This paper falls into two parts, the first by Altham, the second by Tennant. The second part contains the formal work; it sets forth a syntactic system for representing sortally quantified sentences of English, and provides semantics for the sentences so represented. Illustrations of the usefulness of the ideas presented are drawn from among the trickier kinds of sentences that have appeared in the literature. The first part gives some indication of the background to some of the ideas in the second part. It also shows the range of expressions that have some claim to treatment by the methods that follow.

Part 1

The standard logical quantifiers of classical predicate logic, $(\exists x)$, and $(\forall x)$ – the existential and universal quantifiers respectively – are familiar, as is also the idea that their workings in the system which is their home may serve as a source of syntactical and semantic insights into a class of English sentences containing such words as *some*, *none*, *every*, and *any*. The best known example of the use of this idea is perhaps the use of the logician's notion of the *scope* of a quantifier to explain why it is that in some contexts *any* may be replaced by *every* without change of truth value, whereas in other contexts the substitution must be made with *some*.

The English words *every*, *any*, and *none* can be qualified by certain adverbs, so that we may say, for instance, *nearly every*, *scarcely any*, and *almost none*. It seems an attractive idea to suppose that the effect of such adverbial modification is to form expressions representable by some further logical quantifiers. Once we are seized of this idea, the possible scope for quantificational representation quickly comes to seem quite broad. For instance, the sentence *Almost every man owns a car* is logically equivalent to *Few men do not own a car*, which in turn is equivalent to *Not many men do not own a car*. So *few*, and *many* seem ripe for quantificational representation. Moreover, since *He always comes to see me on Sundays* is equivalent to *He comes to see me every Sunday*, it looks promising to bring *always* into the group with the other terms for which a quantificational approach seems promising. Where *always* is properly given a temporal reading, it means something like *at all times*, and can be represented by universal quantification over times. There is indeed a pretty close correspondence between two sets of words as follows:

always ever often seldom sometimes never
every   any many few   some   none

The terms in the upper line interrelate in the same way as do those on the lower. For instance, just as *I have few books* is equivalent to *I do not have many books*, so *I seldom go to London* is equivalent to *I do not often go to London*.

In addition, the logician's eye discerns quantifiers in certain adjectives. Bertrand Russell pointed out long ago the invalidity of the syllogism:

> Men are numerous
> Socrates is a man
> Ergo, Socrates is numerous.

The first premiss is equivalent to *There are many men*. Analogous transcriptions can be made where other adjectives are concerned. For example *Storms are rare in this part of the world*, for which we might read *There are not many storms in this part of the world*, or *Storms do not often happen in this part of the world*.

Yet further quantifiers are discernible in natural language, unless the logician's eye deceives him. As well as *few, many*, and *nearly all*, we have *very few, very many*, and *very nearly all*, and yet more result from reiterated prefixing of *very*.

In their representations in a formal syntax, all the foregoing expressions come out as what Mr Tennant calls $(1,1)$-*quantifiers* – quantifiers which bind one variable in one formula. A formal syntax, together with appropriate semantics, which gave an appropriate treatment to all these would already be a significant generalization of classical quantificational methods on the pattern of ordinary logic. The further generalization to $(1,k,)$-quantifiers, binding one variable in an ordered k-triple of formulas, gives a further increase in power. Thus consider the sentence *There are exactly as many Apostles as there are days of Christmas*. The occurrence of *there are* puts one in mind of quantifiers, and the fact that *there are* occurs twice matches nicely in intuition with the idea that we have here a $(1,2)$-quantifier. It has been usual for logicians to represent sentences like this one in the language of set-theory, as asserting a one-one relation between the class of Apostles and the class of days of Christmas. The device of the $(1,2)$-quantifier avoids recourse to such higher-order logic in giving the syntax of such sentences.

It seems quite significant, in connection with these $(1,2)$-quantifiers, that we can build up additional ones in much the same way as we can $(1,1)$-quantifiers. For instance, from *more than* we can go to *many more than*, and *very many more than*. We have such expressions as *nearly as many as* and *almost as few as*, and so on.

We pass on now to matters of semantics. The simplest form of sentence involving what we call a plural quantification is one of the form *There are many Ps*. One thing that is clear about the truth conditions of this is that it is false if there is only one P. Next, it seems clear that in general how many Ps there need to be for there to be many Ps depends on the size of the envisaged domain of discourse. For instance, in *There are many Communists in this constituency*, the domain of discourse would probably be the electorate of the constituency in question. This domain is smaller than the one envisaged in *There are many Communists in Italy*, and consequently the number of Communists there have to be for there to be many Communists in this constituency is smaller than the number there have to be for there to be many Communists in Italy.

This very strongly suggests the use of a numerical method in providing appropriate semantics. This was done in Altham (1971) by selecting, for each application of the logic presented therein, a number n which is the least number of things there have to be with a certain property for there to be many things with that property. For the purposes of the logic it was unnecessary to specify exactly what number should be chosen, nor indeed can this realistically be done. The important points are that n is constrained to be >1, it varies with the domain of discourse, and its value relative to the numbers associated with other quantifiers should be correct. Thus the quantifier *a few* is given semantics in a way similar to those for *many*, in terms of the least number of things that must have some property if there are to be a few things with that property. This number again varies with the domain of discourse. If such numbers are termed threshold-numbers, then the essential condition is that the threshold-number associated with *a few* should be smaller than that associated with *many*.

This method can be used also in the case of the quantifiers compounded with *very*. Thus the threshold-number associated with *very many* will be $n+m$, with m positive, if n is the threshold-number for *many*. On the other hand, if k is the threshold for *a few*, the threshold for *a very few* will be $k-l$. Repetitions of *very* can be coped with similarly. The multiplicity of threshold-numbers is reduced, however, by the possibility of defining some quantifiers in terms of others. Thus *nearly all* is *not many not*.

In the cases considered so far, the range of quantification is not restricted by a phrase within the sentence itself, but is determined by the context. But very frequently the range of quantification is so restricted, and in this case quantifiers such as *many* are *sortal* quantifiers. A sentence *There are many things which are both P and Q* is one in which the quantifier is not sortal, and it is logically equivalent to *There are many things which are both Q and P*. In contrast *Many Ps are Q* involves a sortal quantifier, and is not equivalent to *Many Qs are Ps*. In *Many Ps are Qs*, the quantifier's range is restricted to the set of *Ps*. Thus the set of *Ps* here becomes the domain of discourse whose size determines an appropriate threshold-number. Consequently, since the set of *Ps* may not have even nearly the same cardinal number as the set of *Qs*, the threshold-number determined by one may be different from that determined by the other. The non-equivalence of the two sortally quantified sentences is a consequence of this fact. An example will make this clear. Compare the two sentences

(1) Many specialists in Old Norse are university officers
(2) Many university officers are specialists in Old Norse

It seems that (1) is true, and (2) is false. Because there are far more university officers than specialists in Old Norse, the threshold-number for *many university officers* is correspondingly larger than that for *many specialists in Old Norse*. Suppose n is the threshold-number for the latter, and it is true that there are n people who are both specialists in Old Norse and university officers. Then (1) is true. But the threshold number for *many university officers* is some number $m > n$, so that for (2) to be true it must be true that there are at least m people who are both specialists in Old Norse and university officers.

From these reflections we can arrive at the extra premiss which needs to be conjoined to *Many Ps are Qs* in order validly to infer *Many Qs are Ps*. This is that there are at least as many *Ps* as there are *Qs*. Thus, to take a plausible example, if many professional men own French motorcars, and there are at least as many professional men as owners of French motorcars, then it follows that many owners of French motorcars are professional men.

These points about relative sizes of threshold-numbers were seen in Altham (1971), but the treatment there in chapter 4 is unsatisfactory because incompletely formal. What is needed, and what Altham did not then have, is a way of representing a sentence such as *There are at least as many professional men as owners of French motorcars*. This defect is effectively remedied by the $(1,k)$-quantifiers explained by Tennant in the second part of this paper.

In the second part, a method of Hookway is reported which enables sortal quantifiers to be replaced everywhere by other, more complex, quantifiers that are not sortal. Here I indicate two informal possibilities of such reduction. First, it is clear that the sortal *Most Ps are Qs* is logically equivalent to *There are more things which are both P and Q than there are things which are P and not Q*, which involves a non-sortal $(1,2)$-quantifier. Similarly, we may think that many *Ps* are *Q* if not far from half the *Ps* are *Q*. In this case, we could give, as logically equivalent to (1),

(3) There are at least nearly as many specialists in Old Norse who are university officers as there are specialists in Old Norse who are not university officers.

(3) is not sortal. This transcription renders patent the lack of equivalence between (1) and (2), for (2) emerges as

(4) There are at least nearly as many university officers who are specialists in Old Norse as there are university officers who are not specialists in Old Norse.

Part 2

Between them, philosophers of language and linguists have identified certain expressions in natural language as *grammatical* quantifiers; that is, as expressions which combine with substantival general terms to produce new expressions which do not behave like naming phrases, either logically or grammatically. Some linguists have made a case for their incorporation as a category of operators in deep structure.

The logician has a wide array of *logical* quantifiers which may be offered as capturing their logical forces as they are ideally used in reasoning in natural language. A logical quantifier is here loosely understood as an expression in a logical system which binds variables in formulae, and which possesses an 'interpretation' given by the formal semantics for the system. In effect, this interpretation is a mapping f from ordered pairs of cardinals to the set $\{t,f\}$ of truth values; so that $Q_f x F x$ is true if and only if $f(\overline{\overline{A}}, \overline{\overline{D\text{-}A}}) = t$, where A is the set of members of the domain of discourse D of which F holds. Such quantifiers I shall call $(1,1)$-quantifiers because they bind one variable in one formula. They are due to Mostowski (1957). It is easy to define $(1,k)$-quantifiers binding one variable in an ordered k-tuple of formulae, thus:

$Qx(P_1x, \ldots, P_kx)$.

Such quantifiers are induced by mappings of ordered k-tuples of ordered pairs of cardinals to the truth values in the mathematically obvious way.

Which of these quantifiers may prove useful in the analysis of natural language? The following suggest themselves:

If $f_1(\langle a_1, b_1 \rangle, \langle a_2, b_2 \rangle) = t$ iff $a_1 = a_2 = 1$, then $\imath x(Px, Px \;\&\; Qx)$ can be given the reading *The P is Q.*

If $f_{\geqslant}(\langle a_1, b_1 \rangle, \langle a_2, b_2 \rangle) = t$ iff $a_1 \geqslant a_2$, then $\geqslant x(Px, Qx)$ can be given the reading *There are at least as many Ps as Qs*; similarly for *as many as* and *more than.*

If $f_0(\langle a_1, b_1 \rangle, \langle a_2, b_2 \rangle, \langle a_3, b_3 \rangle) = t$ iff $a_1 = a_2 = a_3 = 1$, then $Ox(Px, Qx, Px \;\&\; Qx)$ can be given the reading *Only the P is Q.*

If $f_{\alpha}(\langle a_1, b_1 \rangle, \langle a_2, b_2 \rangle, \langle a_3, b_3 \rangle) = t$ iff $a_1 = 1$, $a_2 = a_3 = 0$, then $\alpha x(Px, Px \;\&\; Qx, -Px \;\&\; -Qx)$ can be given the reading *All but the P are Q.*

If $f_{Mo}(\langle a, b \rangle) = t$ iff $a \geqslant b$, then *Mo x Px* can be given the reading *Most things are P*; if $f_M(\langle a, b \rangle) = t$ iff $a \geqslant n$ (where n depends on $\overline{\overline{D}}$) then *MxPx* can be given the reading *Many things are P*; and if $f_N(\langle a, b \rangle) = t$ iff $b < n$ then *NxPx* can be given the reading *Nearly all things are P*; these are Altham's *plurality* quantifiers (1971).

When Quine's policy of eliminating singular terms is followed, *John is bald* becomes $\imath x(Jx, Jx \;\&\; Bx)$, just as *The King of France is bald* becomes $\imath x(KFx, KFx \;\&\; Bx)$. The burden of the difference between proper names and descriptive phrases will then be shifted to the definition of *interpretation of non-logical constants in a model* by incorporating a *conventional constraint* on models to the effect that names, as predicates, are lexically identified as *naming* predicates and must, under any interpretation of the non-logical constants in any model, have no more than one member each in their extensions. Another conventional constraint on models is to the effect that E, the existence predicate, always has as extension the whole domain.

The range of quantification in natural language is usually restricted by a phrase after the quantifier, as noted by Harman (1970). Moreover, certain quantifiers in natural language are *irreducibly sortal* in the sense that a sentence containing a restricted quantification is not logically equivalent to a sentence containing an unrestricted quantification using the same quantifier. For example, *all* is not irreducibly sortal, because *All Ps are Qs* is equivalent to $\forall x(Px \supset Qx)$; but *many* is irreducibly sortal, because no such paraphrase is available for *Many Ps are Qs*. Since natural language contains such irreducibly sortal quantifiers, and since the hope prevails that logic may come to be a theory not only of truth conditions of sentences, but also of their deep structures, logical syntax and semantics should be developed accordingly.

Syntax

1. Definition of well-formed formula:
   (i) If P is an n-place predicate letter then $Px_{i_1},\ldots,x_{i_n}$ is a wff with exactly $x_{i_1},..,x_{i_n}$ as free variables;
   (ii) If X is a wff, then so is $-X$, with the same variables free;
   (iii) If X and Y are wffs then so are $X \& Y$, $X \vee Y$, $X \supset Y$, and $X \equiv Y$, with exactly the distinct free variables of X and Y free;
   (iv) If X and Y are wffs with x free, and if Q is a $(1,1)$-quantifier symbol, then $Q[X]^\wedge x\ Y$ is a wff with exactly the distinct free variables of X and Y, save x, free;
   (v) If X, Y and Z are wffs with x free, then $\imath[X]^\wedge x(Y, Y \& Z)$ is a wff with exactly the distinct free variables of X, Y and Z, save x, free;
   (vi) Similarly for whatever other $(1,k)$-quantifiers are adopted.

2. X is a *constituent* of X, $-X$, $X \& Y$, $X \vee Y$, $X \supset Y$, $X \equiv Y$, $Q[X]^\wedge x\ Y$, $Q[Y]^\wedge x\ X$, $\imath[X]^\wedge x\ (Y, Y \& Z)$, $\imath[Y]^\wedge x(X, X \& Z)$, etc.; $X \& Z$ is a constituent of $\imath[Y]^\wedge x(X, X \& Z)$, etc.; and the constituent relation is transitive.

3. X is a *sortalizer* of $Q[X]^\wedge x\ Y$, $\imath[X]^\wedge x(Y, Y \& Z)$, etc.

4. x is *bound* in X if and only if x is not free in X but is free in some constituent of X.

5. x *dangles* in X if and only if x is free in X but is bound in some constituent of X.

6. X is a *proper* wff if and only if no variable dangles in X.

7. *Abbreviations*
   (i) $\imath[X]^\wedge x(Y, Y \& Z) =_{df} \imath[X]^\wedge x\langle Y, Z \rangle$;
   (ii) $Q[Ex]^\wedge x\ X =_{df} QxX$; (where E is the existence predicate)
   (iii) $\imath[Ex]^\wedge \langle Y, Z \rangle =_{df} \imath x \langle Y, Z \rangle$; etc.

Strictly speaking, improper wffs are interpretable as open wffs; attention is drawn to them as deviants because they exemplify the results of misguided attempts to write down the logical forms of sentences containing 'pronouns of laziness', to borrow a phrase from Geach (1972a, 1972b).

Semantics

Tarski-style rules of satisfaction are easy to give for this logic. Suppose we have, for each quantifier symbol Q, the inducing function f_Q which is its interpretation. The satisfaction rules for the connectives and for atomic wffs are as usual; while for sortal quantification there is the following difference: the infinite sequence s of objects from domain D satisfies $Q[X]^\wedge x_i\ Y$ if and only if f_Q ($\langle$number of sequences (X,i)-differing from s which satisfy Y, number of sequences (X,i)-differing from s which do not satisfy $Y\rangle$) $= t$; and similarly for (I,k)-quantifiers for $k > I$; where s' (X,i)-*differs from* s if and only if for every $j \neq i\ s'_j = s_j$ and s' satisfies X. It follows that if X has no free variables, then it is satisfied by all sequences or by none, in which cases it is *true* or *false* respectively, with respect to the given interpretation of non-logical constants in the model at hand.

With this sortal logic we can provide many English sentences with more congruous logical forms than they would receive in the classical predicate logic. There are also English sentences which now can be coped with but which could not be accommodated at all in the old system. Geach provides a fund of examples, some of which we shall now consider.

(1) Almost every man who borrows a book from a friend eventually returns it to him

If one tries to write out the wff representing the logical form of (1) by turning the relative clause *who borrows a book from a friend* into a conjunct of a sortalizer, and then treating *it* and *him* as occurrences of the variables ranging over *book* and *friend* respectively, the result is

(2) $AE\ [Mx\ \&\ \exists[Bk\ y]^\wedge y \exists[Fzx]^\wedge z\ Bxyz]^\wedge x\ ERxyz.$

y and z dangle in (2). On the most likely reading

(3) Almost every man who borrows a book from a friend eventually returns each book thus borrowed to the friend from whom he borrowed it

the correct logical form is

(4) $AE\ [Mx\ \&\ \exists\ [Bk\ y]^\wedge y\ \exists\ [Fzx]^\wedge z\ Bxyz]^\wedge x$
$\forall[Bk\ w\ \&\ \exists[Fux]^\wedge u\ Bxwu]^\wedge w\ IV\ \langle Fxv\ \&\ Bxwv, ERxwv).$

Another example of Geach is

(5) The only man who ever stole a book from Snead made a lot of money by selling it

Analysing this along the lines of *The only P who is Q is R*, which has logical form $ʔ[Qx]^x \langle Px, Rx \rangle$, we get

(6) $ʔ[\exists[By]^y \, ʔz \, \langle Sz, \text{Stole } xyz \rangle]^x \langle Mx, ʔw \langle Bw \ \& \ ʔv \langle Sv, \text{Stole } xwv \rangle, MLMBSxw \rangle \rangle$.

Inspection will reveal that, according to our semantics, (6) has the same truth conditions as Geach's paraphrase

(7) As regards some book, the man of whom it holds good that this was the book he stole from Snead and that nobody else ever stole a book from Snead made a lot of money by selling it.

Pronouns of laziness compound the difficulties with Geach's examples in (1972c). Here he is concerned to discover why (A) is valid while (B), so similar to (A) in surface form, is not:

A. 1. Anything that counts as the personal property of a tribesman is suitable to offer to a guest by way of hospitality
  2. One thing that counts as the personal property of a tribesman is that tribesman's wife
  3. So, she is suitable to offer to a guest by way of hospitality
B. 4. Any woman whom every tribesman admires is beautiful by European standards
  5. One woman whom every tribesman admires is that tribesman's wife
  6. So, she is beautiful by European standards

If *woman whom every tribesman admires* were a genuine complex term (in Geach's sense) then (B5) would have the overall form *One P is the Q*. In our notation this is $ʔx\langle Qx, Px \rangle$. This naive reading of the logical form of (B5) would yield

(8) $ʔx\langle Wf \, xy, Wm \, x \ \& \ \forall[Ty]^y \, Ad \, yx \rangle$

in which *y* dangles. The complex term *woman whom every tribesman admires* does not function as a genuine logical unit, to use another phrase of Geach. In our terminology we would say that it should not be rendered as a constituent in the wff which correctly represents the logical form of (B5). Re-written as wffs of our sortal logic, the clearly valid (A) and invalid (B) are as follows:

A. 1. $\forall[\exists[Ty]^y \, PPxy]^x \, Sx$
  2. $\forall[Ty]^y \, ʔx \langle Wf \, xy, PPxy \rangle$
  3. $\forall[Ty]^y \, ʔx \langle Wf \, xy, Sx \rangle$

B. 4. $\forall[Wm\ x\ \&\ \forall[Ty]^\wedge y\ Ad\ yx]^\wedge x\ BESx$
  5. $\forall[Ty]^\wedge y\ \imath\ [Wm\ x]^\wedge x\ \langle Wf\ xy,\ Ad\ yx\rangle$
  6. $\forall[Ty]^\wedge y\ \imath x\ \langle Wf\ xy,\ BESx\rangle$

Note that if *a tribesman* were replaced in (A1) by *every tribesman* then (A) would be invalid in the same way as (B). This seems to be the real source of the difference between (A) and (B), and it is reflected in the different quantificational structures of (A1) and (B4) immediately above.

One example of quantificational structure which can be exhibited by a wff of our sortal logic, but not by one of classical logic, is that underlying the following (where italicization indicates emphasis):

(9) Nearly all the delegates had read mostly *soft-covered* books.

This involves quantifying into a sortalizer:

(10) $N[Dx]^\wedge x\ M[By\ \&\ Rxy]^\wedge y\ Sy.$

A final bothersome example which can be taken care of is the Bach–Peters sentence

(11) The pilot who shot at it hit the MIG that chased him.

The wff in our sortal logic which represents its logical form is

(12) $\imath x\langle Px\ \&\ \imath y\ \langle My\ \&\ Cxy,\ Sxy\rangle,\ \imath z\langle Mz\ \&\ Cxz,\ Hxz\rangle\rangle.$

From this can be extracted the phrase-marker (13) for deep structure

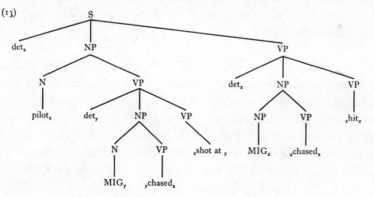

which I have not yet come across in the literature on the problem. Someone may be interested in finding the transformations taking (13) to (11). Note that a direct reading of (11) is

(14) The pilot who shot at the MIG that chased him, hit the MIG that chased him

in which the only pronominalization – *him* – is straightforwardly explained in terms of occurrences of the variable x in (11). *It* can then be introduced anaphorically, to get

(15) The pilot who shot at the MIG that chased him, hit it

which should be easily transformable into (11).

The same process of pronominalization seems to underlie

(16) Most boys who were fooling them kissed many girls who loved them.

This has logical form

(17) $Mo [Bx \& M[Gy \& Lyx]^{\wedge}y \, Fxy]^{\wedge}x \, M[Gz \& Lzx]^{\wedge}z \, Kxz \& Fxz$

The direct reading of (17) is

(18) Most boys who were fooling many girls who loved them kissed many girls who loved them

in which *them* comes from occurrences of the variable x in (17); anaphoric pronominalization then accounts for

(19) Most boys who were fooling many girls who loved them, kissed them

which should then be easily transformable to (16).

I hope these few examples have indicated that a logic of sortal quantification can contribute to an understanding of the grammar of complex terms and pronominalization.

Before we conclude, however, that sortality is a primitive phenomenon in the quantificational structure of sentences of a certain complexity, and that the syntactical device of sortalizers along with the corresponding modifications of the rules of satisfaction is the only way to cope with it, we should consider the implications of the following result obtained by investigating a suggestion of Chris Hookway (private communication): For every wff $Q_f[X]^{\wedge}x(Y_1 \ldots, Y_n)$ with Q_f a $(1,n)$-quantifier induced by f, there is an equivalent wff $Q_{f'}x(X, X\&Y_1, X\&Y_1, \ldots, X\&Y_n, X\&-Y_n)$ with $Q_{f'}$ a $(1, 2n+1)$-quantifier induced by f', with f and f' interdefinable thus:

$$f(\langle a_1, b_1 \rangle, \ldots, \langle a_n, b_n \rangle) = t \, (a_i + b_i \text{ constant})$$
$$\text{iff}$$

for all $c_0, c_1, \ldots c_{2n}$ such that $a_1 + b_1 + c_0 = a_1 + c_1 =$
$= b_1 + c_2 = \ldots = a_n + c_{2n-1} = b_n + c_{2n},$

$$f'(\langle a_1 + b_1, c_0 \rangle, \langle a_1, c_1 \rangle, \langle b_1, c_2 \rangle, \ldots, \langle a_n, c_{2n-1} \rangle, \langle b_n, c_{2n} \rangle) = t;$$

and for all $a_0, \ldots, a_{2n}, b_0, \ldots b_{2n}$ such that $a_i + b_i$ is constant and $a_1, \ldots, a_{2n} \leqslant a_0$,

$$f'(\langle a_1, b_2 \rangle, \langle a_1, b_1 \rangle, \ldots, \langle a_{2n}, b_{2n} \rangle) = t$$

$$\text{iff}$$

$$f(\langle a_1, a_2 \rangle, \langle a_3, a_4 \rangle, \ldots, \langle a_{2n-1}, a_{2n} \rangle) = t.$$

Thus every restricted (I, n)-quantification can be treated as an unrestricted $(I, 2n+I)$-quantification. If we opt always for the latter, we need not have sortalizers bracketed off in the syntax, but need only ensure that the sortalizing wff appears alone in the first position, and then as a conjunct in the appropriate fashion in each of the following $2n$ positions.

This underlines the indeterminacy of the syntactical representation of logical form; a syntactical structure represents *the* logical form of a sentence only modulo the formal semantics. We may feel that it is more 'natural' to bracket off the sortalizer as in the system developed above, and to introduce the notion of sequences (X, i)-*differing* from one another, but in Hookway's view this is to indulge a mere prejudice – we should not be concerned at all with mirroring even the most striking features of surface form in the wff representing logical form. All that matters is that the wff be so interpreted by the formal semantics that it capture the truth conditions of the sentence.

Moreover, which wff, or which abbreviation of it is chosen as a deep structure is immaterial since such notational variants can easily be transformed into one another. What *is* important is that there is a variable-binding configuration which is invariant with respect to the method of its representation by syntactical complexes; and it is this configuration which both logic and grammar must lay bare.

APPENDIX

Lewis' (this volume) adverbial quantifiers would appear to be easily representable as (n, I)-quantifiers in my sense:

$$Q[\Phi] x_{i1}, \ldots, x_{i_n} \Psi$$

Extra clauses in the recursive definition of wff are easily formulable, as are the corresponding clauses in the recursive definition of satisfaction:

s satisfies $Q[\Phi] \wedge x_{i1}, \ldots, x_{i_n} \Psi$ iff $f_Q(\langle a, b \rangle) = t$

where $a = \text{card} \{s' | s' (\Phi, i_1, \ldots i_n)\text{-differs from } s \text{ and } s' \text{ satisfies } \Psi\}$ and $b = \text{card} \{s' | s' (\Phi, i_1, \ldots, i_n)\text{-differs from } s \text{ and } s' \text{ does not satisfy } \Psi\}$, where $s' (\Phi, i_1, \ldots, i_n)\text{-differs from } s$ iff for all $j \neq i_1, \ldots, i_n s_{j'} = s_j$ and $s' \text{ satisfies } \Phi$.

$Q[\Phi] \wedge x_{i_1}, \ldots, x_{i_n}$ has the reading 'Q^*-ly, if Φ $then$ Ψ' where e.g. if Q is *most* then Q^*-ly is *usually*.

REFERENCES

Altham, J. E. J. (1971). *The Logic of Plurality*. London: Methuen.

Geach, P. T. (1927a). 'Referring expressions.' (1972b). 'Referring expressions again.' (1972c). 'Complex terms.' In *Logic Matters* (1972). Oxford: Blackwell.

Harman, G. (1970). 'Deep structure as logical form', *Synthese*, **21**, 275–97.

Lewis, D. 'Adverbs of quantification.' In this volume.

Mostowski, A. (1957). 'On a generalization of quantifiers', *Fundamenta mathematicae*, **44**, 12–36.

II REFERENCE AND CROSS REFERENCE

Deixis as the source of reference

JOHN LYONS

In this paper I shall be concerned with what Quine (1960:108) describes as the first two phases in the ontogenesis of reference.[1] Like Quine, I shall venture no psychological details as to the actual order in which 'the child of our culture' masters the 'provincial apparatus of articles, copulas, and plurals' as he 'scrambles up an intellectual chimney, supporting himself against each side by pressure against the others' (1960:102, 80, 93). What I have to say about the child's acquisition of the grammar of referring expressions is not incompatible, as far as I am aware, with any of the data that has been collected and discussed in the psycholinguistic literature: but I am not claiming that all children 'of our culture', and still less children of all cultures, must go through the same stages in the acquisition of their native language and that these stages must succeed one another in a fixed order. My purpose, rather, is to show how the grammatical structure and interpretation of referring expressions (other than proper names) can be accounted for in principle on the basis of a prior understanding of the deictic function of demonstrative pronouns and adverbs in what might be loosely described as concrete or practical situations. I will argue that the definite article and the personal pronouns, in English and other languages, are (in a sense of 'weak' to be explained below) weak demonstratives (see Sommerstein (1972); Thorne (1973)), and that their anaphoric use is derived from deixis. I will also argue, as part of this thesis, that the presuppositions of existence and uniqueness which logicians commonly associate with the use of the definite article derive from general conditions governing singular definite reference – more especially deictic reference – and do not distinguish the definite article in English from the demonstratives *this* and *that*, but that they are grammaticalized as separable components in the underlying structure of demonstrative and definite noun phrases in English.

[1] What I have to say in this paper derives, in large part, from discussions with my colleagues, Renira Huxley, Martin Atkinson, and Patrick Griffiths working on the SSRC-sponsored Language Acquisition Project in Edinburgh. My ideas on deixis and localism have also been much influenced by the work of other colleagues in Edinburgh, notably John Anderson and James Peter Thorne. Needless to say, we have somewhat different views on these questions; and none of my colleagues would agree, I think, with all the points made in this article.

In this paper I will construct a language-system which is simple, but rich enough, I believe, to characterize the grammatical and semantic structure of children's early sentences in many languages and also to serve as a basis for the development, differently in different languages, of the more complex sentences of adults. I will call this simple language-system Quasi-English.

There are three grammatically distinct classes of singular definite referring expressions in English: proper names, pronouns, and definite noun phrases. In many languages, however, common nouns may also be used without a determiner as singular definite referring expressions; and they frequently occur with this function in the earliest utterances of English-speaking children. We will therefore build this feature into the grammar of Quasi-English; but we will assume that the semantic distinction between names and common nouns, in certain cases at least, is already established. Our main problem is to show how phrases like *this man*, *that man*, and *the man* can be derived within the grammar, in a syntactically and semantically revealing way, from underlying structures which contain neither a demonstrative adjective nor a definite article. In doing so, we shall make use of two transformational processes, adjectivalization and apposition, both of which, I am inclined to believe, are universal.

We will operate with just four terminal syntactic categories: names (Nm), common nouns (N), verbs (V), and deictics (D). For reasons of convenience and familiarity, we will also make use of the standard auxiliary symbols NP and VP, and present the rules of the base in terms of phrase structure grammar. The rules of the base component of Quasi-English at a very early stage are as follows:

PS rules: (1) S → NP NP
          (2) S → NP VP
          (3) NP → {Nm, N, D}
          (4) VP → {N, V, D}
Lexicon: (i) Nm: {*John, Daddy,...*}
          (ii) N: {*dog, house, table,...*}
          (iii) V: {*big, bark, swim,...*}
          (iv) D: {*there*}

As they stand, these rules will generate a set of binary syntagms, which we may think of as kernel sentences, in Harris's (1957) rather than Chomsky's (1957) sense of this term: each of these sentences, when uttered, will be associated with a particular intonational and stress contour which will, in part, serve to determine the interpretation of the utterance as an exclamation, statement, question, wish, etc. If we wanted the system to generate all the sentential constructions that a child is capable of producing at the age at which the mean length of his utterances (measured in terms of the number of forms in each utterance) is about 1.5 (see Bowerman (1973)), we should need to introduce two-place verbs and we might also have to allow for the deletion of either the subject or the verb, and even the object. One further deficiency in the system, considered as a grammar for the generation of the sentences underlying the utterances of children at an early stage of their linguistic development, is its failure to account for locative and possessive structures, which appear to be well established in children's speech soon after they pass the holophrastic stage. I will say something about these structures later.

Before we introduce the transformational rules and extend the system in a particular direction, some comments on the rules and categories of the base-component of Quasi-English are in order. Rules (1) and (2) distinguish two subtypes of kernel sentences: equative and predicative. I assume, without evidence, that this distinction is grammaticalized in all languages, though differently in different languages: by case, by the use of one copula rather than another, by the use of determiners, etc. In English, the distinction is grammaticalized, partly in terms of the permutability of noun phrases in equative sentences and their non-permutability in predicative sentences and partly in terms of the restrictions governing the internal structure of predicative nominals (i.e. nouns and noun phrases derived by rules corresponding to VP→N in the grammar of Quasi-English).[1] Whether or not the distinction between equative and predicative sentences is justifiable on purely syntactic grounds in all languages, the semantic distinction between equative and predicative statements is surely fundamental. Russell's sentence *Scott is the author of Waverley* is not only ambiguous (out of context) as an utterance; it is also syntactically ambiguous as a sentence of English. *The Morning Star is the Evening Star*, on the other hand, is not a syntactically ambiguous sentence of English: nor is any utterance of this sentence, I assume, ambiguous with respect to the semantic distinction drawn between equative and predicative statements.

I have introduced into the grammar of Quasi-English the principle that the subject precedes the predicate. It has been argued recently that the traditional grammatical distinction of subject and predicate is purely a matter of surface structure (Fillmore (1968); Anderson (1971)); and there is some force in this argument. It should not be forgotten, however, that

---

[1] I also assume that equative-structures underlie such so-called cleft sentences as *The one who did this is John* (see Halliday (1967:223)).

the grammatical distinction was traditionally associated, on the one hand, with the logical distinction of particular and universal terms in the proposition expressed by a sentence and, on the other, with the semiotic distinction of topic and comment in utterance (Lyons (1968a: 343)). In twentieth-century linguistic theory, it has also been associated with the semantic distinction between the actor, or agent, and the action; and subdivisions within topic and comment have also been recognized (Halliday (1970)). Granted that some or all of these distinctions need to be drawn in the grammatical and semantic analysis of any fully developed adult language, it is perhaps reasonable to assume that they tend to coincide in child language. It has, in fact, been suggested in the literature that the topic-comment construction is 'attributable to the innate capabilities of the child' and that the grammatical distinction of subject and predicate develops out of this in languages like English (Gruber (1967: 39)). The topic-comment distinction correlates highly of course with the logical distinction of particular and universal terms, as it does with the semantic distinction (where it is independently determinable) of actor and action. The principle that the topic precedes the comment is one that is widespread in languages. In traditional discussions of the subject-predicate distinction, this was commonly explained in terms of the naturalness of first mentioning, or identifying, what you are going to talk about and then saying what you have to say about it (Sandmann (1954)). I do not wish to make too much of the subject-predicate distinction. But it can hardly be dismissed as a superficial feature of the grammatical structure of certain languages.

Little need be said about the recognition of names, common nouns, and verbs as distinct categories in a very early stage of language-acquisition. Most logicians in modern times have, I suppose, grouped common nouns with predicates, and have distinguished them from names and pronouns; more recently, some linguists have taken a similar view (e.g. Bach (1968)). But there are very few languages, if any, in which grammarians have found it difficult to distinguish nouns and verbs in terms of their syntactic distribution; and the distinction seems to be well established in the child-language data that I have seen. It will be observed that in Quasi-English nouns may be used as either referring or predicative expressions; but that names may be employed only as referring expressions and verbs as predicative expressions. We will not discuss here the distinctions between noun subtypes (e.g. mass/count, concrete/abstract).

Quasi-English has a single deictic particle which is neutral with respect to any distinctions of gender or proximity. Its function is to draw attention to some feature of the situation or some entity in the situation, and it will be normally accompanied by some paralinguistic movement of the head or hands indicating the direction to which the addressee should turn in order to identify the feature or entity in question. We may think of the deictic as meaning something like '*Look!*' or '*There!*'.[1] The child's utterances, whether they contain a recognizably deictic form or not, will often be purely expressive, rather than communicative in the full sense: they will be indicative of his own interest in some feature of the environment. It is also important to realize that, even at a stage when we feel entitled to say that the child is drawing the attention of an addressee to some feature or entity, it will not always be clear that part of his utterance identifies a referent and part of it says something about the referent. Utterances such as *Book there* or *There book* might be intended and understood to mean '*I want that book*', '*Give me that book*', '*There's the book!*', '*Look, a book!*', '*That's a book*', and so on.[2] We are not concerned here with the way in which the child's developing control of a language enables him to differentiate and make explicit various semiotic functions. From now on, we will concentrate primarily upon those binary syntagms analysable grammatically as being of [D + VP] or [NP + D] structure and interpretable, as utterances, as being composed of a referring expression (the topic) and a predicative expression (the comment); and we will say nothing about any selection restrictions that hold between particular subjects and particular predicates.

Quasi-English does not distinguish the pronominal and the adverbial function of the deictic. Any theory of deixis must surely take account of the fact (much discussed in philosophical treatments of ostensive definition) that the gesture of pointing of itself will never be able to make clear whether it is some entity, some property of an entity, or some location that the addressee's attention is being directed to. Identification by pointing, if I may use the term 'pointing' in a very general sense, is deixis at its purest; and it is only when deixis operates within at least a rudimentary language-system that ostensive definition, as such, becomes feasible. The single deictic particle of Quasi-English is intended to be the linguistic counterpart of pointing; more precisely, as we shall see later, of non-directional

---

[1] The etymology of such forms as *voici* and *voilà* in French is revealing in this connection.

[2] Utterances like *There's a book* in English cannot be interpreted satisfactorily in terms of reference and predication. The function of the whole utterance is perhaps best described as quasi-referential (or quasi-predicative). It draws attention to an object (and by doing so it frequently introduces it as the topic about which a comment will then be made in subsequent utterances). But drawing attention to the object in such cases cannot be sharply distinguished from saying something about it. Quasi-reference is perhaps ontogenetically more basic than either reference or predication.

pointing. There is perhaps no language with a single deictic particle which operates exactly in this way, being neutral with respect to pronominal and adverbial (or prolocative) function, on the one hand, and with respect to distinctions of spatial proximity, gender, etc., on the other. We will presently introduce some of these distinctions, although it is not clear that any particular one of them must be grammaticalized in all languages.

However that may be, we will now move on to extend the grammar (and lexicon) of Quasi-English by introducing into the language a syntactic (and lexical) distinction between a deictic pronoun (D_1) and a deictic adverb (D_2). As far as language acquisition is concerned, this distinction may be thought of as partly reflecting and partly supporting the child's recognition of the difference between referring to an entity and referring to a place. It is my assumption that, even if the adult language did not draw a distinction between deictic pronouns and adverbs, by virtue of the universal and extralinguistic principle that deictics with pronominal function (like proper names) cannot be used as predicative expressions, a deictic which derives from VP in the grammar would necessarily be interpreted as having an adverbial function. When I say that the distinction between pronouns and adverbs, once it is acquired, not only reflects, but also supports, the child's recognition of the difference between referring to an entity and referring to a place, I have in mind the fact that, on the basis of the grammatical distinction, he will come in time to see a parallel difference of meaning between such sentences as *Thát's the park* and *Thère's the park*, on the one hand, and *Thát's John* and *Thère's John*, on the other.[1]

There are various ways in which we can extend the grammar and lexicon of Quasi-English to incorporate the distinction between deictic pronouns and adverbials. Let us do so here by simply replacing rule (4) with

(4′) $VP \rightarrow \{N, V, D_2\}$;

by adding

(5) $D \rightarrow \{D_1, D_2\}$;

and by substituting for (iv) the following two rules in the lexicon:

(iv′) $D_1 \rightarrow \{that\}$
(v) $D_2 \rightarrow \{there\}$.

These rules allow a deictic adverb to occur as the subject of a predicative

---

[1] For a discussion of the meaning of such sentences and a formalization of some of the conditions of appropriate utterance associated with them, see Atkinson and Griffiths (1973).

sentence and as either the topic or comment in an equative sentence. Briefly, there are two reasons for this decision. First of all, by deriving both D_1 and D_2 from D in these positions, and D_2 directly from VP in predicate position, we make explicit what was earlier said to be a universal principle governing the interpretation and distribution of deictics. Secondly, there are positive reasons for wanting to derive D_2 from NP. Sentences like *It's cold there* create problems for any theory of predication which operates solely with entities and properties (or classes); and as has often been pointed out, we can make statements about places, just as we can make statements about things. Russian, for example, would translate *It is cold there* as *Tam xolodno* (literally '*There* (*is*) *cold*'); and I see no reason why the semantically equivalent English sentence should not be derived from an underlying structure in which *there* is the subject and *cold* the predicate. This analysis is broadly equivalent to that which has been proposed, in terms of case-grammar, by Fillmore (1968) and Anderson (1971).

The semantic justification for generating sentential structures with a deictic adverbial subject and a nominal predicate is perhaps more dubious. English allows us to say either *This place is cold* or *It is cold here*. But it forces us to say *This* (*place*) *is a city* rather than *It is a city here*.[1] In principle, however, there seems to be no reason why a language should not permit reference to a place or region by means of a deictic adverbial in order to predicate of that place or region that it belongs to a certain class. There would of course be selection restrictions holding between the adverbial subject and the predicative noun. But there are similar selection restrictions holding between a nominal or pronominal subject and a predicative noun. We will not, therefore, exclude the possibility of a deictic adverb occurring as the subject of either a verbal or a nominal predicate.[2]

Let us now turn our attention to what are traditionally regarded as noun phrases composed of a demonstrative adjective and a noun: e.g. *that dog*. The most obvious way of generating such phrases, and one which would formalize the traditional conception of their structure, is by means of an adjectivalization transformation, identical with that which derives

---

[1] Place-denoting nouns (whether common or proper) are not as fully assimilated to entity-denoting nouns in all languages as they are in the Indo-European languages. In Chinese, for example, place-nouns are distinguished from entity-nouns in that they can occur as locative adjuncts or complements without a postposed locative morpheme.

[2] Quasi-English also generates such equative structures as $D_2\ D_2$, which can be thought of as establishing an identity between two places. This is syntactically parallel to the identity established between two entities by $D_1\ D_1$ (*That's it*, in English) or D_1 Nm (*That's John*). In English, of course, we say *This* (*place*) *is London* rather than *Here is London*. But a locative phrase can be in equative apposition with a deictic adverb in such sentences as *It is cold here in London*. It is arguable, therefore, that even in English we should admit such underlying equative structures as $D_2 +$ Locative.

attributive adjectives from predicative adjectives (in such phrases as *good dog*) and attributive nouns from predicative nouns (in such phrases as *girl student*). Up to a point this is semantically satisfactory. For there does seem to be a semantic similarity between the following pairs: < *The dog is good, the good dog* >; < *The student is a girl, the girl student* >; < *The book is on the table, the book on the table* >; < *The dog is (over) there, the dog over there = that dog* > (see Thorne (1972)). Notice, however, that this parallelism also suggests that the demonstrative adjective in English encapsulates in some way both the definite article (which we have not yet accounted for) and the adjectivalized adverb: *that dog* is interpretable, under one interpretation at least, as *the dog (over) there*. Moreover, there are both syntactic and semantic problems attaching to the derivation of demonstrative adjectives in English from predicative deictic adverbs. Transformations of this kind should produce semantically endocentric complex predicative expressions (*good dog, girl student, book on table*). It is arguable that *that dog* is, in certain instances at least, semantically endocentric (when it is used in explicit or implicit contrast with *this dog*), but it cannot be employed as a predicative expression. Furthermore, when it is used as a referring expression, it cannot be regarded as being syntactically endocentric and having *dog* as its head, since in adult English (in contrast with Latin, Russian, Chinese, Malay, Turkish, etc.) singular countable nouns cannot be used as referring expressions without having some kind of determiner or quantifier adjoined and preposed to them. Quasi-English, as we have so far presented it, is more like Turkish, Latin, and Russian in this respect; but even in these languages, it should be noted, demonstrative noun phrases cannot be used as predicative expressions.

What then are the alternatives? There would seem to be two. We could take *that* as a pronominal head deriving *dog* by means of an adjectivalizing transformation from a predicative nominal. This would be syntactically satisfactory, since it would make phrases like *that dog* endocentric with respect to *that* (i.e., it would account for the fact that demonstrative noun phrases have the same distribution as demonstrative pronouns); it would also account for the more general fact that, not only in English, but also in Turkish, Latin, Russian, etc., demonstrative noun phrases are excluded from predicate position in predicative sentences. Analysed in this way, *that dog* would mean '*that entity which is a dog*' ('*which is a dog*' being construed restrictively). However it requires but little reflection to see that this interpretation, though perhaps not absolutely excluded, is very unusual.

The second alternative is to take *dog* as being in apposition with *that* in such phrases as *that dog*; and this is undoubtedly more attractive. There are many languages in which nouns or noun phrases seem to operate as optional appositional adjuncts of obligatory personal or demonstrative pronouns (Keenan (1972:446–50)). But there are two kinds of apposition relevant to the present problem, and each of them is naturally handled in current versions of generative grammar by means of non-restrictive clause formation (Motsch (1965)). Consider *That man, John Smith, is very rich;* and *That man, an oil magnate, is very rich.* The appositional phrase *John Smith* is most appropriately derived from the comment position of an underlying equative structure [*That man* [*that man be John Smith*] *be very rich*].[1] Now *that dog* in English is in fact interpretable as a referring expression, it seems to me, in either of the two ways suggested by these two types of apposition: (i) '*that entity – the dog*'; (ii) '*that entity – a dog*'. The first interpretation, however, is perhaps the more normal, both *that* and *dog* having reference and being co-referential: the individual in question is identified simultaneously, as it were, by deixis and description. Since demonstrative pronouns, common nouns, and proper names all occur as referring expressions at a very early stage in the utterances of English-speaking children, if we are forced into adopting a single ontogenetic source for demonstrative noun phrases, it is perhaps preferable to opt for the grammaticalization of an equative appositional link between the demonstrative pronoun and the associated noun.

But do we need to opt for one of the appositional processes to the exclusion of the other, or indeed for apposition to the exclusion of adjectivalization, even in a synchronic grammar of adult English? The predicative appositional link is what seems to be required for the semantic interpretation of such utterances as *That fool won't do it* and in general for the analysis of demonstrative noun phrases with what Donnellan (1966) calls an attributive function. And we have already seen that there are some reasons for deriving at least one component of the demonstrative adjectives from predicative deictic adverbs. Since adjectivalization and both kinds of apposition are required anyway in English, my proposal is that we incorporate all three ways of deriving demonstrative noun phrases within the grammar.

A further question now arises: can any two, or all three, of the three transformations operate in the derivation of the same demonstrative noun phrase? And if so, how are they ordered? To discuss this question in detail would take up too much space; and a decision one way or the other would

---

[1] In principle, it could also be derived from the subject position of a predicative syntagm, [*That man* [*John Smith be very rich*] *be very rich*]; and perhaps also from the topic position of an equative syntagm, [*That man* [*John Smith be that man*] *be very rich*]. I will simply discount these alternatives.

seem to be irrelevant to the further points I wish to make in this paper. Let me simply say that the two types of apposition appear to be mutually exclusive on semantic grounds, but that either could be combined, in principle, with adjectivalization. Now it is a language-particular fact about English that countable nouns cannot be used as singular definite referring expressions without a demonstrative or other determiner; and that the demonstrative always precedes the noun with which it is associated, as it also precedes any adjectival modifiers of that noun. These facts are most naturally accounted for if we incorporate in the grammar of English (though not necessarily of all languages) the principle that adjectivalization presupposes apposition, but that apposition may take place without adjectivalization, in the derivation of demonstrative noun phrases. Every such noun phrase, e.g. *that dog*, will be four-ways ambiguous in terms of its grammatical structure: (i) '*that entity* $(D_1) - a\ dog$ (N)'; (ii) '*that entity* $(D_1) - the\ dog$'; (iii) '*that entity* $(D_1) - a\ dog$ (N) *which is there* (D_2)'; (iv) '*that entity* $(D_1) - the\ dog$ (N) *which is there* (D_2)'. These structures can be distinguished symbolically (without introducing the definite article as an underlying category) as follows: (i) (D_1-N); (ii) $(D_1=N)$; (iii) $(D_1-(D_2N))$; (iv) $(D_1=(D_2N))$. In these formulae, '$=$' symbolizes equative apposition and '$-$' symbolizes predicative apposition; these are different types of paratactic constructions, each of which resists classification in terms of a simple dichotomy of endocentricity and exocentricity (see Nida (1966:17)). '(D_2N)' symbolizes an endocentric construction composed of an adjectivalized deictic adverbial and a noun. It should be clear that the grammar of Quasi-English also generates a number of other constructions in which D_2 is in predicative apposition with either D_1, N, (D_1-N), or $(D_1=N)$. All of these are in fact interpretable; and we shall return to a subclass of them later.[1]

Let us now concentrate on the equative-appositional interpretations (which I have assumed to be more normal). The derivation of *that dog* by means of both equative apposition and adjectivalization might proceed as

---

[1] A phrase like *on the table there* (in, say, *Put it on the table there*) is ambiguous with respect to the distinction between adjectivalization and predicate apposition; and this distinction is also neutralized in *on that table* and (in an appropriate context) *on the table*. More obviously distinct, semantically and syntactically, from either of these is a third interpretation of the phrase under which *there* is in equative apposition with the whole locative phrase *on the table* (see p. 67 n.2). In this case, however, it is perhaps more usual for the deictic adverb to precede the locative phrase (just as it is more usual for a deictic pronoun to precede an appositional noun phrase). But *Put it there on the table* is itself structurally ambiguous. It can also mean, roughly, '*Put it on this part (of the surface) of the table*'. The grammatical rules presented here cannot account for this construction, which, I suspect, should be included among so-called inalienable possessives; and these I take to be a subclass of part-whole locatives.

follows: [*that* [*that* = *dog* [*dog there*]]] ⇒ [*that* [*dog there*]] ⇒ [*that* [*there dog*]] ⇒ [*that-there dog*] ⇒ [*that dog*]. The hyphenization of *that-there* at the penultimate stage is intended to represent informally a process of amalgamation which has the effect of uniting the two underlying forms in a single surface form.[1] However this process of amalgamation is formalized, its effect would be to incorporate both a pronominal and an adjectival component in the resultant form *that;* and this, as we have seen, is what is required under the interpretation of phrases like *that dog* when they are in contrast, explicit or implicit, with *this dog*.[2] Let us assume, however, that in Quasi-English amalgamation does not take place, so that *that dog* is derived without adjectivalization of a predicative deictic adverb (and contrasts semantically with such phrases as *this dog*, once we introduce the distinction of deictic proximity), whereas *that there dog* is derived as a grammatical phrase, syntactically equivalent to *that good dog*.

How does Quasi-English compare with Standard English (apart from its lack of the amalgamation process)? So far it does not distinguish syntactically or semantically between the definite article, the demonstratives, and the so-called third-person pronouns. It is well known that these three (or four) categories are related diachronically. Postal (1967) has argued, correctly I believe, that they are also synchronically relatable in the grammar of English; and he has suggested that they should all be derived, synchronically, from underlying structures containing the definite article. Sommerstein (1972) and Thorne (1973), on the other hand, have taken the view that the third-person pronouns and the definite article are to be regarded as being basically demonstratives. This latter hypothesis is to be preferred on several grounds. First of all, there are many languages that have demonstratives, but lack a definite article or formally distinct third-person pronouns. Secondly, in all the Indo-European languages which distinguish between either the article and the demonstratives or the third-person pronouns and the demonstratives, the demonstratives are diachronically prior. Finally, and most importantly, the function and distribution of the article and the third-person pronouns, and the grammaticalization of definiteness as it is in fact grammaticalized in English, are explicable

---

[1] There is no natural way of formalizing this process of amalgamation, as far as I can see, in Chomskyan transformational grammar. The best we can do is to substitute *that* for the string *that* + *there* (rather than simply to delete *there*) and this creates labelling problems for the derived phrase marker.

[2] In certain dialects of English *that there dog* is a perfectly grammatical phrase; and it is stressed in a way that suggests that *there* is enclitic. This does not seem to be the case for the Standard English *that dog there*, which, as the alternative correlated stress patterns would suggest, is interpretable as either '*that entity – the dog which is there*' or '*that entity – the dog – it is there*'. We have not dealt with the second interpretation (but see p. 70 n.1).

by means of the hypothesis that they derive synchronically (and perhaps also ontogenetically) from demonstratives. Since the main lines of the argument in favour of this hypothesis are to be found in Sommerstein (1972) and Thorne (1973), I can be relatively brief at this point.[1]

The English third-person pronouns (*he/she/it*) are distinguished for gender, but not for the deictic distinction of proximity; the demonstratives (*this/that; here/there*) are distinguished for proximity, but not for gender; the definite article is distinguished for neither gender nor proximity, and (unlike the demonstrative and third-person pronouns) cannot be used as a referring expression. In English it is not possible to refer to an individual deictically (other than by using a proper name) without incorporating within the referring expression some information about the location of the referent or about one or more of its properties. The phrase *this man*, used deictically, informs the addressee that the referent is in or near the place where the speaker is and that it is a male, adult, human being; *he* informs the addressee that it is male, but says nothing about its location in relation to the speaker; *this* gives the information that it is located near the speaker, but implies or presupposes nothing about any of the properties of the referent, except (in predicative utterances) that it is non-personal. This last proviso is required, because the use of the demonstrative and personal pronouns in English is governed by the further, and more specific, principle, that *that* and *this* cannot be used as referring expressions, in predicative utterances, to refer to persons (and animals): *That is good* cannot mean '*That person is good.*'[2]

Now, it is important to realize that in the deictic distinction of proximity, as it operates in English, *this* and *here* are semantically marked in relation

[1] There are certain differences between Sommerstein's (1972) and Thorne's (1973) proposals. Briefly (and to put it in my own terms), Sommerstein treats the definite article as a demonstrative pronoun and Thorne derives it by the adjectivalization of *there*. I believe that each of these proposals is correct, as far as it goes, but incomplete.

[2] 'Person' must here be understood to include a variety of personified individuals, not only supernatural beings and domestic pets, but also, under certain circumstances, ships, cars, and other artefacts. The grammar, or the rules of semantic interpretation, must also allow for the de-personification of babies unfamiliar to the speaker. The details are more complex. One general principle seems to be that reference to an individual by name constitutes (or is evidence of) personification in English and precludes deictic or anaphoric reference to the same individual, by the same speaker, in a predicative utterance by means of a neuter pronoun: e.g. *The baby is a year old now and it/he/she is beginning to talk* vs. **Little Lesley is a year old now and it is beginning to talk.* In practice, one can of course know the name of a child or animal without knowing its sex; and this creates problems for the choice of *he* or *she*, which cannot be avoided, if the name is used, by simply employing *it*. There would seem to be further restrictions on the use of the demonstrative and personal pronouns with reference to infants (and animals?). *It* in *It's very good* (but not *that* or *this* in *That/this is very good*) can be used to refer to a baby, but not, I think, in such sentences as *It's very beautiful*.

to *that* and *there*: the opposition is proximal vs. non-proximal, not proximal vs. distal (or distal vs. non-distal). It is only when there is an explicit or implicit contrast with the proximal term in the opposition that the non-proximal demonstratives imply or presuppose remoteness from the speaker. As *bitch* is to *dog* with respect to the lexicalized opposition of sex, so *this/here* is to *that/there* with respect to the opposition of deictic proximity. To say that *dog* has two meanings because it is the unmarked term in this lexical opposition would be to misunderstand the nature of semantic marking as it operates in the grammatical and lexical structure of languages. Similarly for *that* and *there*; and it is, incidentally, the failure to appreciate the significance of this point that vitiates Allan's (1971, 1972) arguments against my proposals relating to existential sentences (Lyons (1967, 1968b)).[1] Let us, however, purely for convenience of exposition distinguish weak and strong forms of the non-proximal demonstratives (as Allan does) by means of subscripts – $that_1$ and $there_1$ being weak, and $that_2$ and $there_2$ being strong. The use of the strong forms of the demonstratives will always imply a contrast with the marked terms *this* and *here;* but the use of the weak forms of the unmarked demonstratives correlates, to some degree, with the distribution of strong and weak stress (see Sommerstein (1972); Thorne (1973)); the correlation, however, is quite complex, since strong stress serves a number of different semantic functions in English.

Let us now build into the grammar of Quasi-English this deictic distinction of proximity. We will do this initially by simply amending rules (iv') and (v) of the lexicon

---

[1] Allan (1971) argues (against what he calls the Fillmore-Lyons hypothesis) that $there_1$ cannot be a thematic copy of the locative phrase in existential sentences because it differs syntactically and semantically from the locative proform $there_2$ and because there is another way of thematizing the locative phrase: *viz.* by applying the independently motivated *have*-transformation. I cannot answer for Fillmore, but I at least never suggested that the preposed $there_1$ was an element which 'copied' all the features of the predicative locative phrase under thematization. It was an important part of my hypothesis that the predication of existence involved the extraction from the locative phrase of only the deictically neutral locative component and the copying (if copying is indeed the appropriate transformational mechanism) of this in the preposed $there_1$. I still believe that this gives a more satisfactory explanation of the meaning and function of $there_1$ in existential sentences than any alternative that I am aware of. Allan's own positive proposals fail to account for the formal identity of $there_1$ and $there_2$; and they depend upon the to me unacceptable notion of incorporating the existential operator in the deep structures of natural language (see below, p. 81, n. 1). As for the alternative means of thematization with the *have*-transformation, it should be obvious that what is 'thematized' in this case is the nominal part of the locative phrase: i.e. neither the whole phrase nor the locative element as such. *There is a book on the table* makes a predication about a book, whereas *The table has a book on it* makes a predication about the table. This distinction is unaffected by the fact that English also treats place-denoting nouns, syntactically, like entity-denoting nouns in a variety of constructions (see p. 67, nn. 1 and 2).

(iv″) $D_1 \rightarrow \{that_1, that_2, this\}$
(v′) $D_2 \rightarrow \{there_1, there_2, here\}$

The grammar will now generate such kernel sentences as $That_1$ big, $That_2$ big, This big, Dog $there_1$, Dog $there_2$, Dog here. It will also generate by means of apposition $That_1$ dog big, $That_2$ dog big, This dog big; and by means of both apposition and adjectivalization $That_1$ $there_1$ dog big, $That_1$ $there_2$ dog big,..., $That_2$ $there_1$ dog big,..., This here dog big, as well as $That_1$ good dog big, etc.[1] The amalgamation rule (if we introduce it into the grammar at this point) will operate according to the principle that a marked or strong demonstrative absorbs a weak form. (This is obviously more neatly formalizable in componential terms; and I will presently reanalyse the deictics in a componential framework.) Thus: this $there_1 \Rightarrow this$; $that_1$ $here \Rightarrow this$; $that_1$ $there_1 \Rightarrow that_1$; $that_1$ $there_2 \Rightarrow that_2$; $that_2$ $there_1 \Rightarrow that_2$.

All that is required in order to generate a definite article in Quasi-English is a rule (whose historical counterpart in the development of English was presumably a purely phonological rule based on stress):

$that_1 \Rightarrow the$.

We now have such phrases in Quasi-English as the dog, the big dog, this dog, that dog, etc. We also have such sentences as The big (i.e. 'He/she/it is big'). The next step is to incorporate in the grammar of Quasi-English rules which will exclude such structures. But before we do so, it is worth noting that, if English had such sentences as these, it would have a demonstrative pronoun (as Classical Greek had in certain environments: Sommerstein (1972)) which was neutral with respect to distinctions of proximity with respect to the location of the speaker: and this pronoun would be the linguistic equivalent, when used to refer to an entity in the situation, of non-directional pointing. It would be an entity-referring expression without sense.

There are various ways in which we can go about incorporating in Quasi-English gender distinctions in the demonstratives comparable with the distinctions found in the set $\{he, she, it/that\}$ in English. What we want to say, it seems to me, is that the speaker of English, when he wants to refer to a person by means of a demonstrative pronoun (in the utterance of

---

[1] Some of these sentences are, of course, contradictory – $That_2$ here dog big, This $there_2$ dog big, etc.; and some are redundant – This here dog big, $That_2$ $there_2$ dog big, etc. We can obviously exclude either or both of these classes, if we wish to, by means of semantic rules. How we exclude these sentences (or their underlying structures), and indeed whether we exclude them or not, is irrelevant to the argument.

a predicative sentence), is forced by the structure of English (as he is not so forced by the structure of certain other languages: e.g. Turkish) to give the addressee the information that the referent is a person and the further information that the referent is male or female; and that he cannot give any information (linguistically) about the deictic location of a personal referent (within a phrasal referring expression)[1] without introducing into the referring expression an appositional noun (or the nominal dummy *one*); but that, when he refers to a non-personal entity, he can locate it deictically, by using the marked or the strong demonstrative, or choose not to locate it deictically, by using the weak demonstrative. We also want to relate *this* to *here* and *that* to *there* rather more satisfactorily than we have done so far. Without entering upon a wholesale reinterpretation of the syntactic categories in terms of features (see Chomsky (1970)), we can perhaps formalize these facts about English well enough for the present purpose by making a more restricted use of complex symbols, as follows:

Base rules:

(1) $S \rightarrow NP\ NP$

(2) $S \rightarrow NP\ VP$

(3) $NP \rightarrow \{Nm, N, D\}$

(4) $VP \rightarrow \{N, V, D_2\}$

(5) $D_2 \rightarrow [+D, -entity]$

(6) $D \rightarrow [+D, \pm entity]$

(7) $[+entity] \rightarrow [\pm person]$

(8) $[+person] \rightarrow [\pm female]$

(9) $\left. \begin{array}{c} [-person] \\ \\ [-entity] \end{array} \right\} \rightarrow [\pm proximate]$

(10) $[-proximate] \rightarrow [\pm distal]$

Lexicon:

(i) Nm: $\{John, Daddy, \ldots\}$

(ii) N : $\{dog, house, table, \ldots\}$

(iii) V : $\{big, bark, swim, \ldots\}$

(iv) $\begin{bmatrix} +D \\ -entity \\ +proximate \end{bmatrix}$: *here*

(v) $\begin{bmatrix} +D \\ -entity \\ -proximate \\ +distal \end{bmatrix}$: *there$_2$*

---

[1] By a 'phrasal referring expression' I mean an expression which does not include an embedded clause (in terms of the traditional distinction between phrases and clauses).

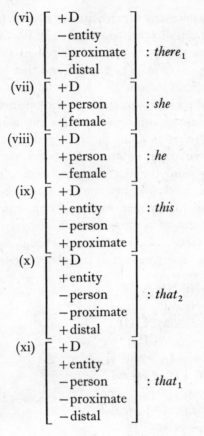

$$\text{(vi)} \begin{bmatrix} +D \\ -\text{entity} \\ -\text{proximate} \\ -\text{distal} \end{bmatrix} : \textit{there}_1$$

$$\text{(vii)} \begin{bmatrix} +D \\ +\text{person} \\ +\text{female} \end{bmatrix} : \textit{she}$$

$$\text{(viii)} \begin{bmatrix} +D \\ +\text{person} \\ -\text{female} \end{bmatrix} : \textit{he}$$

$$\text{(ix)} \begin{bmatrix} +D \\ +\text{entity} \\ -\text{person} \\ +\text{proximate} \end{bmatrix} : \textit{this}$$

$$\text{(x)} \begin{bmatrix} +D \\ +\text{entity} \\ -\text{person} \\ -\text{proximate} \\ +\text{distal} \end{bmatrix} : \textit{that}_2$$

$$\text{(xi)} \begin{bmatrix} +D \\ +\text{entity} \\ -\text{person} \\ -\text{proximate} \\ -\text{distal} \end{bmatrix} : \textit{that}_1$$

This grammar is not entirely satisfactory: apart from anything else, the usual problems with binary features in relation to Boolean conditions have led me to introduce [±distal] into the deictic system. Using [−entity] rather than [+locative] might also be regarded as unsatisfactory. As part of the grammar of adult English, it has certain other inadequacies which we need not go into here.

One point, however, should be mentioned. There is an obvious redundancy in the grammar of Quasi-English as it stands. The demonstrative noun phrases, *this dog*, *that dog*, and *the dog*, are all structurally ambiguous, not only with respect to the nature of the link between the demonstrative and the noun (and this seems to me semantically justifiable), but also with respect to the internal structure of *this*, *that*, and *the*. For example, *this* in *this dog* is either a purely pronominal deictic (with the feature [+proximate]) or an amalgam of a pronominal and an adjectivalized deictic (i.e. *that*₁ *here*, *this there*₁, *this here = this*). But *this* and *that* in what we have taken to be their purely pronominal function are also generated within the system from *that₁ here* and *that₁ there* (*here* and *there* being taken restrictively or non-restrictively according to whether the transformational rule is one of adjectivalization or predicative apposition: (D_2D_1) vs. (D_1-D_2)). I have assumed, perhaps wrongly, that the child might learn and use the demonstratives in their purely pronominal usage before he has mastered the syntactic relation between *this* and *here* and between *that* and *there*. However, it is perhaps plausible to suppose that there will come a time when the child internalizes the relevant transformational relationships and restructures his grammar accordingly. Whatever the psychological validity of this hypothesis, descriptive economy in writing the grammar of English would be served by the elimination of the redundancy referred to, since no distinction of meaning seems to be associated with the alternative derivations. All we need to do by way of restructuring the grammar is to delete [− person] from the disjunction of features on the left-hand side of rule (9).

Given the componential analysis embodied in the above set of grammatical rules and the associated lexicon, we can not only reformulate our amalgamation rule (prior to lexicalization) in terms of strings of deictic complex symbols, but we can also prohibit the application of either the adjectivalizing or appositional transformation to instances of D_1 (i.e. [+ entity] deictics) that contain the feature [+ person].[1] The substitution of *the* for *that₁* will operate as before, except that it will need to be made conditional upon the association with *that₁* within the same NP of a transformationally derived predicative or equative N. A further rule may then be added, to rewrite *that₁* as *it*, on condition that it has no appositional adjunct within the same NP.[2]

We need not go further with construction of Quasi-English. It now reflects, though perhaps not in the most satisfactory way, what I take to be the central grammatical distinctions of English in so far as they apply to the structure, function, and semantic interpretation of singular definite referring expressions. I would remind the reader, at this point, that I am not assuming that a 'child of our culture' learning English will necessarily proceed, as we have done, in the construction of the grammar of the language, first distinguishing between a pronominal and an adverbial

---

[1] This will have the effect of excluding as ungrammatical such strings as *he good man, *she girl, etc. There are other ways of excluding such strings.

[2] In English *that₁* and *it* are partly in complementary distribution and partly in free variation in particular syntactic environments. However, it is my assumption that the form of the non-proximate, non-distal, non-personal demonstrative pronoun that is used to refer to entities in the situation is always *it*.

deictic, then mastering the deictic distinction of proximity, and finally distinguishing the personal pronouns *he* and *she* from the demonstratives *this* and *that*. What I have tried to show is that it is possible to see the language-specific features of English developing, ontogenetically, from a possibly universal base.

Philosophers have devoted a lot of attention to the question of uniquely referring expressions; and they have emphasized the logical similarity, from this point of view, between proper names and definite descriptions. Many of them have claimed that the use of the definite article implies or presupposes that there is one and only one entity that satisfies the description contained in the noun phrase. There is, however, no reason to associate any implication or presupposition with the definite article as such. When the speaker refers to a specific individual, by whatever means, he tacitly accepts the convention that he will provide any information (not given in the context) that is necessary for the addressee to identify the individual in question (see Thorne (1973:564)). Uniqueness of reference is always, in principle, context-dependent in this sense; and it applies just as much to the use of the personal pronouns and the demonstratives (and indeed to the use of proper names) as it does to the use of the definite article. It is therefore no argument against our analysis of the definite article as a demonstrative pronoun ($that_1$) or an amalgam of a demonstrative pronoun and a demonstrative adverb ($that_1$ *there* $\Rightarrow that_1 \Rightarrow the$), that it is functionally different from the marked and the strong forms of the demonstratives ($that_2$ and *this*) with respect to its presupposition of uniqueness. The pronominal component in the definite article, $that_1$, has exactly the same function as has the same component in the other forms of the demonstrative adjectives: that of informing the addressee that a specific individual (or group of individuals) is being referred to which satisfies the description. The difference is that $that_2$ and *this* encode as part of the description offered to the addressee information about the deictic location of the referent. In context, *this dog* and *the dog* will both be construed as uniquely-referring expressions; but the former will be descriptively more informative (by virtue of the grammaticalization of [+proximate] in the adjectivalized deictic adverb amalgamated with the pronoun).

Philosophers in their discussions of the logical structure of definite descriptions have also made much of their presupposition or implication of existence; and this is particularly interesting from the point of view of the analysis of the demonstrative adjectives and the definite article that has been proposed here. As we have seen, the demonstratives $that_2$ and *this* (when they are used deictically) serve to inform the addressee that some specific individual (or group of individuals) is being referred to and also to locate the referent in relation to the here-and-now of utterance. If something has a spatio-temporal location, it must exist; and it is arguable that any notion of 'existence' that we can operate with is based upon our intuitive understanding of physical existence as spatio-temporal location. I have suggested elsewhere that existential sentences, in English and many languages, are derivable from structures in which the underlying subject is, typically, an indefinite noun phrase and the underlying predicate a locative (Lyons (1967, 1968b)). I now want to relate this suggestion, very briefly, to the proposals made in this paper about the ontogenesis of referring expressions in English.

We begin by introducing the notion of deictic existence: location in a physical space, whose coordinates are established by the utterance of sentences of a given language-system. The deictic coordinates vary somewhat from one language to another; but the zero-point, presumably, will always be the moment and place of utterance. The English demonstratives *this/here* and *that/there*, when they are used as deictic referring expressions (or within deictic referring expressions), can be interpreted as instructing, or inviting, the addressee to direct his attention to a particular region of the deictic space in order to find the referent. *There is a boy here* (which I take to be derived from the underlying predicate structure *Boy (be) here*) means, roughly, '*A boy is (to be found) in the place where I (as I am now speaking) am (to be found)*'. In terms of the analysis of demonstrative noun phrases proposed above *this boy* derives from *that$_1$ here boy* (*here* being taken either restrictively or non-restrictively, and *boy* being associated with *that$_1$* in one of several ways): it therefore presupposes or implies that the referent is located in the deictic space. So too does *that man* (derived from *that$_1$ there$_2$ man*). But what about *the man*? This is derived either from *that$_1$ man* or *that$_1$ there$_1$ man*. That it should have a double derivation is perhaps inelegant. Let us, however, not stop to consider the possibility of either eliminating this apparent redundancy or motivating it by reasons other than those of formal simplicity in the grammar. Let us ask, instead, what interpretation we can assign to the weak deictic adverbial *there$_1$* in the underlying string *that$_1$ there$_1$*.

Despite what certain philosophers have said about the non-predicability of existence, it seems to me that existential sentences, with either a definite or an indefinite noun phrase as subject, are meaningful. Normally, in everyday discourse, we are not concerned to assert or deny the existence of entities in any absolute sense of 'existence'. It is much more common to say that such-and-such an individual is (or is not) in a particular place (*John Smith is in London, John Smith is here*, etc.) or that an individual (or class of individuals) satisfying a certain description is (or is not) in a particular place (*There is a girl in my soup, There are some unicorns here*). Granted that *John Smith is here* and *There are some unicorns here* are derivable from underlying structures in which the proximal deictic adverbial occurs as the predicate and that we interpret these sentences in terms of the notion of deictic existence, it is my proposal that what might be called absolute existential sentences such as *John Smith exists* and *There are unicorns* (or *Unicorns exist*) are derived syntactically from the same underlying structures, except that it is *there$_1$* which occurs as the predicate. Just as the meaning of the weak demonstrative pronoun *that$_1$* is derived by abstraction from the gesture of pointing, so the weak demonstrative *there$_1$* is derived by abstraction from the notion of location in the deictic context. If the underlying structure of *the man* is taken to be *that$_1$ there$_1$ man* (derivable in various ways as we can see), this can be said to separate and segmentalize the components of context-dependent uniqueness of reference (*that$_1$*) and existential presupposition or implication (*there$_1$*).

Furthermore, the structural ambiguity of *that$_1$ there$_1$ man* – $(D_1 = (D_2N))$, $(D_1-(D_2N))$, $(D_1=(N-D_2))$, $(D_1-(N-D_2))$ – may account, in part at least, for the enduring controversy as to whether existence is presupposed, implied or asserted in definite noun phrases. If adjectivalization (restrictive relative clause formation in current versions of transformational grammar) is associated with presupposition and apposition (i.e. non-restrictive relative clause formation), not necessarily with assertion, but with an independent illocutionary act (Thorne, 1973), the distinction between (D_2N) and $(N-D_2)$ can be held to represent the difference between the presupposition and the assertion of existence. It is not difficult, I believe, to contextualize the phrase *the man* (as well as *that man* and *this man*) in such a way that the other structural ambiguities are seen to be relevant.

Another point should be made about existential sentences. The standard predicate calculus analysis of sentences with what appears to be a singular definite referring expression as subject, runs into trouble because it makes them assert (or, still worse, deny) what is either asserted or presupposed by the referring expression. *God exists* (and its contrary) is analysable satisfactorily enough (under one interpretation) as $(\exists x)$ (*x be omnipotent* & *x be eternal* & ...). But this analysis will clearly not do for utterances which refer, by name, to individuals (unless one pushes the descriptive-backing theory of proper names to its extreme: see Searle (1969:162)); and I would argue that *God* should be interpretable in *God exists* as a proper name. In the grammar of Quasi-English, we can generate sentences like *God (be) there₂* and *God (be) here* (cf. *John Smith is there, John Smith is here*) which are surely meaningful with *there₂* and *here* taken as deictic predicative expressions. We can also generate *God (be) there₁*. It is my contention that our understanding of *God exists*, under one interpretation, is based upon our abstraction from the notion of deictic existence of more or less of the spatio-temporal implications of the weak form of the deictic adverb. Whether we are willing or able to carry out this psychological process of abstraction, and how far we go with it, depends of course upon our metaphysical or theological preconceptions or decisions. But that is another question entirely. The point is that the linguistic analysis of absolute existence in terms of an abstraction from deixis enables us, should we so wish, to assign an analysis to existential sentences with a singular definite referring expression as subject which is free from the at times counter-intuitive analysis imposed upon them by the use of the existential quantifier.[1]

It should also be stressed that what we may now call the existential adverb *there₁* (i.e. the weak form of the [−proximal] deictic adverb) can be interpreted within the same underlying structure in two or more different ways. One way is to take it as anaphoric, rather than as absolutely existential. For example, *That man does not exist* can be interpreted as meaning (discounting all but one of the analyses of *that man*) '*The entity (that₁) – a man which is there₁ – is not there₁*'. If *there₁* in the noun phrase is construed as anaphoric (i.e. as locating the referent in the universe of discourse) and the second predicative *there₁* as being absolutely existential, the sentence does not necessarily deny what it presupposes, any more than does the sentence *That man is not there* (which contains two occurrences of *there₂* in its underlying structure).

Finally, consider the relationship between anaphora and deixis. It is my assumption that the anaphoric use of pronouns and adverbs is secondary to their basic function as deictics (Lyons (1968a:275ff.)). Anaphora involves the transference of what are basically deictic, and more specifically spatial, notions to the temporal dimension of the context of utterance and the reinterpretation of deictic existence in terms of what might be called

---

[1] To introduce the existential quantifier into the underlying structures of natural languages without giving it an interpretation in terms of some intuitive notion of existential predication is, to my mind, to put the cart before the horse; and I would suggest that the most satisfactory interpretation of existential quantification is in terms of a basically locative predicate, as proposed here. $(\exists x)(x = a)$, which Hintikka (1969) has put forward as an analysis of '*a* exists' (in connection with Quine's famous dictum, that to be is to be the value of a variable), is interpretable intuitively as 'an x is *there₁* which is identical with *a*'.

textual existence. The referent of course does not exist in the text. But it is located in the universe of discourse (which derives its temporal structure from the text) by means of an antecedent expression which either introduces or identifies a referent. Subsequent reference to this referent by means of an anaphoric expression identifies the referent in terms of the textual location of the antecedent. If there is no other referent in the universe of discourse which satisfies the description incorporated in the predicative noun *man*, it will be sufficient to use *the man* (i.e. *that*₁-(*there*₁ *man*)) in order to re-identify the person in question. He is the one such referent that has textual existence: i.e. he is there, in the weak sense of *there*. It is in this sense that I interpret Thorne's (1973:564) analysis of the anaphoric meaning of *there*. There are of course complexities attaching to the analysis of the function and distribution of anaphoric distinctions in English and other languages. It suffices for my present purpose that anaphora should be seen as, in principle, derivable from deixis.

It is also my assumption – and this will surely not be challenged – that reference to entities outside the situation of utterance, indefinite and opaque reference, reference to hypothetical entities (treated as hypothetical in the utterance), and various other kinds of reference that have puzzled philosophers and linguists are at least ontogenetically secondary. The fact that the referring expressions used in such cases are comparable in terms of their grammatical structure with deictically referring expressions suggests that their use and function is derivative, and depends upon the prior existence of the mechanisms for deictic reference by means of language. It is because I make this assumption that I hold the view that deixis is, in general, the source of reference. Although I have said nothing in this paper about locative expressions other than deictic adverbs, it should be clear that my proposals can be construed as offering support for at least a modified version of the localist hypothesis (Anderson (1971)).

REFERENCES

Allan, Keith (1971). 'A note on the source of "there" in existential sentences', *Foundations of Language*, **7**, 1–18.
—— (1972). 'In reply to "There₁, there₂"', *Journal of Linguistics*, **8**, 119–24.
Anderson, John M. (1971). *The Grammar of Case: Towards a Localistic Theory*. Cambridge Studies in Linguistics, **4**. London and New York: Cambridge University Press.
Atkinson, M. and Griffiths, P. (1973). 'Here's here's, there's, here and there'. In *Edinburgh Working Papers in Linguistics*, **3**.
Bach, Emmon (1968). 'Nouns and noun phrases'. In Bach and Harms (1968).

Bach, Emmon and Harms, R. T., eds. (1968). *Universals in Linguistic Theory.* New York: Holt, Rinehart & Winston.

Bowerman, Melissa M. (1973). *Early Syntactic Development.* Cambridge Studies in Linguistics, **11**. London and New York: Cambridge University Press.

Chomsky, N. (1957). *Syntactic Structures.* Janua Linguarum, Series Minor, **4**. The Hague and Paris: Mouton.

—— (1970). 'Remarks on nominalization'. In R. Jacobs and P. Rosenbaum, eds., *Readings in English Transformational Grammar.* Boston: Ginn.

Donnellan, Keith (1966). 'Reference and definite descriptions', *Philosophical Review*, **75**, 281–304. (Reprinted in D. D. Steinberg and L. A. Jakobovits, eds., *Semantics.* London and New York: Cambridge University Press, 1971.)

Fillmore, C. J. (1968). 'The case for case'. In Bach and Harms (1968).

Gruber, J. S. (1967). 'Topicalization in child language', *Foundations of Language*, **3**, 37–65.

Halliday, M. A. K. (1967). 'Notes on transitivity and theme in English: Part 2', *Journal of Linguistics*, **3**, 199–244.

—— (1970). 'Language structure and language function'. In J. Lyons, ed., *New Horizons in Linguistics.* Harmondsworth: Penguin.

Harris, Z. S. (1957). 'Co-occurrence and transformation in linguistic structure', *Language*, **33**, 283–340.

Hintikka, Jaako (1969). *Models for Modalities: Selected Essays.* Dordrecht-Holland: Reidel.

Keenan, E. L. (1972). 'On semantically based grammar', *Linguistic Inquiry*, **4**, 413–61.

Lyons, J. (1967). 'A note on possessive, existential and locative sentences', *Foundations of Language*, **3**, 390–6.

—— (1968a). *Introduction to Theoretical Linguistics.* London and New York: Cambridge University Press.

—— (1968b). 'Existence, location, possession and transitivity'. In B. Rootselaar and J. F. Staal, eds., *Logic, Methodology and Philosophy of Science, III.* Amsterdam: North Holland.

Motsch, W. (1965). 'Untersuchungen zur Apposition im Deutschen', *Studia Grammatica*, **5**, 87–132.

Nida, E. A. (1966). *A Synopsis of English Syntax.* The Hague: Mouton.

Postal, P. M. (1967). 'On so-called "pronouns" in English', *Georgetown University Monograph Series on Languages and Linguistics*, **19**, 177–206.

Quine, W. V. (1960). *Word and Object.* Cambridge, Mass.: M.I.T. Press.

Sandmann, M. (1954). *Subject and Predicate.* Edinburgh University Publications, Language and Literature, **5**. Edinburgh: Edinburgh University Press.

Searle, J. R. (1969). *Speech Acts.* London and New York: Cambridge University Press.

Sommerstein, Alan (1972). 'On the so-called definite article', *Linguistic Inquiry*, **3**, 197–209.

Thorne, J. P. (1972). 'On the notion "definite" ', *Foundations of Language*, **8**, 562–8.

—— (1973). 'On non-restrictive relative clauses', *Linguistic Inquiry*, **3**, 552–6.

Referential constraints on lexical items

PIETER SEUREN

The following represents a very provisional report on work going on. The author is fully aware of the fact that there are many uncertainties, unclarities and errors in the text as presented here. Yet it seems that the observations which are made are of a certain interest, and that the ideas put forward deserve some consideration in so far as they indicate a general direction in which an explanatory solution to the problem under consideration might be found.

It is a very widespread phenomenon, in many if not all languages, that verbs are semantically decomposable into a fairly general transitive verb and a generic object. An example from English is *brew*, which is made up of *make* and *beer*, or *advise*, which is *'give advice'*. Assuming this observation to be correct, we must posit a rule in the grammatical semantics of English, which incorporates the object into a lexical verb. Let us speak of *Object-Incorporation*. Sometimes, as in the case of *brew*, the incorporation is optional, since we also have *brew beer*. Further details could be worked out, such as the fact that an adjective qualifying the object ends up as an adverb: *advise someone well*, but these are not our concern here.[1]

What does concern us here is the fact that the object which is the object of Object-Incorporation is always a generic NP (or a sortal NP, if you like), but never a referring expression. It is not possible to have a lexical item decomposable into, for example, *'make the beer'*, where *the beer* is used to refer to some beer which either actually exists or has just been mentioned (although it may not exist).

Likewise, we detect an ambiguity in, for example:

(1) This is a joke about a horse

where either a specific horse is mentioned, which this is said to be a joke about, or the kind of joke specified that this is said to be. Only the latter meaning, not the former, corresponds to:

[1] The alternation between dative and accusative in *give advice to somebody* and *advise somebody* follows from Object-Incorporation if the indirect object is taken to derive from a bare NP preceding the object-NP. Further arguments, especially in connection with Predicate Raising, are given in Seuren (1972).

84

(2) This is a horse-joke

Elements cannot be incorporated into a compound noun when they have what we may reasonably call a referring function. Only sortal expressions allow this to happen to them. Many similar observations can be made. The following sentences are synonymous only in the non-referring sense of (3a):

(3) a. I like to work in a garden
    b. I like gardening

It is in keeping with these observations (especially (2)) that referring expressions cannot occur in compound words other than in head position. An expression such as *that coathanger* has *hanger* as the head of the compound noun, and the deictic *that* relates to that and not to *coat*. It is unthinkable that any such expression could be analysed as '*hanger of that coat*'.

If rules are to be formulated at all to relate semantic representations to surface structure, they will have to bring together elements from various positions in semantic trees under one category node, since semantically composite lexical items and compound-words occur under one category node in surface structure. Various observations made by McCawley and others suggest that there is not a direct and immediate transition from semantic trees to lexicalized phrase-markers, but, rather, that the various elements making up the contents of a lexical item are first brought together under a category node, as a sub-tree, and then replaced by a lexical item or a morphologically compound word. Following a well-known terminology, we might call such sub-trees *islands*.[1] We will, in this paper, formulate two constraints on the entering of such lexical islands. Both constraints will be formulated in terms involving the notion of 'referring expression'.

The constraints are not, however, limited to the entering into lexical islands by referring expressions. Other elements are also sometimes prohibited from entering a lexical island, but the prohibition seems to depend on external referring expressions. Take, for example, the following two sentences:

(4) a. Alcoholics are getting younger
    b. Alcoholics are rejuvenating

The (a)-sentence is ambiguous in a way the (b)-sentence is not. It either refers to one set of people, alcoholics, and says these are getting younger,

---

[1] It is perhaps worth speculating that such islands form the domain of morphological rules, where, for example, command relations hold not with respect to S-nodes but with respect to any category-node dominating the domain.

instead of getting older as would be expected. This reading it shares with (4b). But it can also mean, quite naturally, that, given two sufficiently distant moments in the not too remote past, those who were alcoholics at the earlier moment tended to be older than those who were alcoholics at the later moment, and that the present is one of these moments. Let us distinguish the two readings by saying that the former involves single reference, but the latter multiple reference with regard to whoever is or was an alcoholic. The lexical verb *rejuvenate* does not allow for multiple reference.

The same is true for *have forgotten* vis-à-vis *no longer remember*.[1] In (5), the (a)-sentence allows for multiple reference in the object, but the (b)-sentence does not. (a) and (b) are synonymous only on the single reference reading:

(5) a. I no longer remember the names of my students
    b. I have forgotten the names of my students

De Rijk (1968) provides abundant evidence that there is a significant area of overlap in the ways expressions *no longer remember* and *have forgotten* are used, where the two are synonymous. A simple case is:

(6) a. I no longer remember John's address
    b. I have forgotten John's address

Both expressions require that the subject did, at some time in the past, know or remember the object. Failing this, neither expression can be used truthfully. De Rijk quotes Shakespeare to support this point (*The Taming of the Shrew*, Act V, sc. 1, 49):

Vincentio: Come hither, you rogue. What, have you forgot me?
Biondello: Forgot you! No, Sir: I could not forget you, for I never saw
           you before in all my life.

Both expressions are factive: the object-*S* is taken to be true by the speaker:

(7) a. Kissinger, conveniently, no longer remembered that he had
       agreed to a deadline.
    b. Kissinger had conveniently forgotten that he had agreed to a
       deadline.

Hence the implicit contradiction in sentences such as:

(8) a. I no longer remember that today is my birthday.
    b. I have forgotten that today is my birthday.

[1] This observation is due to R. P. G. de Rijk. It prompted him to write 'A note on prelexical predicate raising' (1968).

De Rijk presents this observation not as an argument against semantic decomposition of lexical items, but as a problem which has to be solved if such a procedure is to be at all viable. George Lakoff (1971:272) proposes that lexical decomposition does not imply complete synonymy between the analysans and the lexical item, but only an inclusion of meaning: 'McCawley's conjecture...only requires that the meaning of *cease to know* be *contained* in the meaning of *forget*, which it is.' According to him a lexical item may mean more than its analysans. In this case, he maintains, *forget*, includes '*cease to know*', but it means '*cease to know due to a change in the mental state of the subject*'. This answer to the problem raised by de Rijk is, however, too facile. For one thing, it does not rule out the multiple reference reading for *forget* (*have forgotten*). I may cease to know the names of my students (although I used to be able to retain their names in the old days) due to a change in my mental state: my memory is no longer what it used to be. Moreover, the rider '*due to a change in the mental state of the subject*' appears ad hoc in the light of a host of parallel observations, for which this rider would provide no solution. Thus we have, apart from (4):

(9) a. I am no longer satisfied with my teachers
   b. I have become dissatisfied with my teachers
(10) a. I no longer have my watch with me
   b. I have lost my watch

We must, instead, try to formulate the general principle accounting for the observations made, in so far as they are related by some general principle. It has proved to be a fruitful and promising method to set up possible semantic analyses for the sentences involved, or at least to specify certain minimal properties which their semantic analyses may reasonably be thought to have, and then to state what constraints can be detected holding between semantic representations and surface structure, especially in connection with lexical items.

Let us assume the following two semantic analyses for the two readings of (5a):

(11) a. it used to be the case that:
       I knew x [x were the names of my then students]
     and:
       now:
         not:
           I know y [y are the names of my now students]
   b. it used to be the case that:

> I knew x [x are/were the names of my now/sometime students]

and:

> now:
>
> not:
>
> I know x.

The details are not important. What counts is the minimal claim that there are two propositions with verb *know* and the subject *I* in both (a) and (b), and that these two readings are distinguished principally by the occurrence of a separate referring expression 'y[y are the names of my now students]' in the second proposition of one, but not the other reading.

Both (a) and (b) can be taken to reduce to:

(12) I used to know the names of my students and now I do not know them

or a suitably abstract form corresponding to this. (Notice that the pronoun *them* in (12) is ambiguous between single and multiple reference.) A further reduction could lead to (5a).[1]

For (5b), which contains the lexical verb *have forgotten*, let us assume the formation of a lexical island of something like the form '*used to know and then (now) not know*', through application of a particular form of Conjunction Reduction. We would expect both (11a) and (11b) to reduce to a structure corresponding to:

(13) I [used to know and now not know] the names of my students

after which the lexical item *have forgotten* could be substituted for the island. It appears, however, that reduction to (13) is possible only for (11b), not for (11a). This is borne out by the observation made in (5), and also by the fact that:

(14) I used to know but don't know any longer the names of my students

does not allow for a multiple reference reading. It is reasonable to assume that *used to know but don't know any longer* forms one single constituent in (14), labelled 'V', and, thus, an island. Apparently, the formation of such an island is blocked for (11a), but not for (11b). Since the critical difference between the two is the occurrence of a separate referring expression in (a), one is led to infer that it is that expression, occurring in that position, which is responsible for the blocking.

---

[1] Disregarding the difference between *know* and *remember*, which seems irrelevant in this context.

This inference is confirmed by an analysis of (4). The NP *alcoholics* occurring in both sentences of (4) is of a category which is still poorly understood. It is not even certain whether or not such NPs should be deemed to contain a quantifier. If they do, the logical properties of the quantification are unclear. If they do not, the mode of reference remains problematic. I shall assume that such NPs do not contain quantification but rather a variety of the definite article. Not only does this assumption make the present analysis more regular; it is also in keeping with the fact that ordinary, canonical forms of quantification applied to *alcoholics* in (4a) do not lead to multiple reference ambiguity:

(15) a. All alcoholics are getting younger
b. Some alcoholics are getting younger

The definite article, on the other hand, does lead to multiple reference:

(16) The alcoholics of most countries are getting younger

In order to analyse (4) we must have some theory of the comparative. Whether or not the comparative-analysis adopted here (and mainly taken from Seuren (1973)) is correct is largely immaterial to the present argument, as long as it is agreed that two propositions are involved in the comparative, the second of which is usually shortened. Let us now consider the following semantic analyses for the two readings of (4a):

(17) a. for all moments i, j (i and j are recent; i precedes j):
    there is an extent e such that:
      at j:
        x [x be alcoholics] be young to e
    and:
      at i:
        not:
          y [y be alcoholics] be young to e
b. for all moments i, j (i and j are recent; i precedes j):
    there is an extent e such that:
      at j:
        x [x be alcoholics] be young to e
    and:
      at i:
        not:
          x be young to e

Let there be a lexical island *be young to some extent e at j and at i not* (with *i* and *j* defined as in (17)), for which the verb *rejuvenate* can be substituted, then the formation of such an island and the subsequent insertion of *rejuvenate* must be blocked for (17a), which contains a separate referring expression in the second proposition of the *and*-conjunction. The parallel with (11a) is obvious.

Can we now formulate a principle, or constraint, which could account for all observations made so far? It seems the following might be a viable starting point:

A. If a referring expression R commands a node A in the semantic representation of a sentence, then any lexical island absorbing A must still be commanded by a constituent R' whose head is derived from R or from any expression making the same reference.

In (11a) and (17a) the referring expressions under the variable y command the predicates *know* and *be young*, respectively. For (11a) a lexical island of anything like the form *used to know and now not know* would entail the loss, through deletion, of the second referring expression relating to names of students, i.e. the expression under the variable y. Such a lexical island can therefore not be formed for (11a). A similar argument applies to (17a). There is no obstacle to such an island, however, when the sentence is derived from (11b). The island will then be commanded by the referring expression under x, which makes the same reference as the deleted x. The same, again, applies to (17b).

Constraint A prevents the incorporation of a referring expression such as *the beer* into a lexical verb which would then stand for '*make the beer*', since the referring expression would no longer command the verb *make*, as it did in the semantic representation. Likewise, if *a garden* in (3a) is a referring expression it commands *work* (or its semantic forbear) in semantic structure. This prevents it from being incorporated into a lexical verb *gardening*, since it would then no longer command the lexical island of which *work* has become a part. If, as seems reasonable, we extend this explanation to cover compound nouns such as *horse-joke* in (2), we must stipulate that the ordinary command-relation, as mentioned in constraint A, which is defined with respect to S-nodes, breaks down inside compounds. It might be suggested that the ordinary notion of S-command ceases to apply inside lexical islands generally (see p. 85, n. 1), and that a notion of C-command takes over (where C is any category-node dominating the lexical island). Further support would have to be derived from the study of morphological processes, however, for such a proposal to be made in seriousness.

There is another category of cases where the difference between referring and non-referring expressions seems to be crucial for the formation of lexical islands. As is well-known, McCawley proposes, in various papers, to derive the verb *kill* from an underlying structure containing at least the elements '*cause to become dead*'. This analysis has been both confirmed and disconfirmed. It was confirmed by Morgan (1969) who observed that a sentence such as:

(18) I almost killed John

has a threefold ambiguity. It can mean that the speaker almost brought himself to killing John, or the speaker did something which would have killed John if he had been less lucky, or that the speaker reduced John to such a state that he almost died.[1] The three readings correspond to different semantic trees, where *almost* modifies *cause*, *become*, or *dead*, respectively:

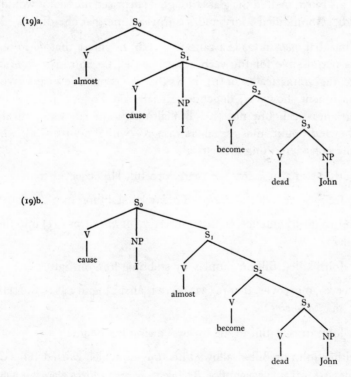

---

[1] It is worth noting that (18) translates differently into French according to the reading it has. The first reading corresponds to something like *J'aurais tué Jean*; the second is adequately rendered as *J'ai failli tuer Jean*, whereas in the third reading the sentence translates as *J'ai presque tué Jean*.

(19)c.

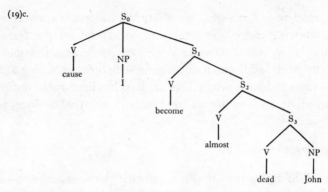

McCawley's analysis was disconfirmed, however, by Fodor (1970) in an article entitled 'Three reasons for not deriving "kill" from "cause to die"'. Fodor's first reason is perhaps less compelling than the other two. He gives the following two sentences:

(10) a. Floyd melted the glass though it surprised me that it would do so
     b. *John killed Mary and it surprised me that she did so

Assuming that *melt* in (a) is a causative verb, he infers that *do-so* replacement is permissible for the verb under 'cause', i.e. intransitive *melt*, and that the ungrammaticality of (b) shows that *kill* cannot be a causative verb. This argument, however, depends crucially on Fodor's judgement that (a) is grammatical, but not (b). But although the ungrammaticality of (b) is beyond doubt, most speakers disagree with Fodor on (a), which is generally considered ungrammatical.

His other two arguments are more forceful. He observes that:

(21) John caused Bill to die on Sunday by stabbing him on Saturday.

is a good English sentence, but that insertion of *kill* turns (21) into the very dissimilar:

(22) John killed Bill on Sunday by stabbing him on Saturday.[1]

He observes, moreover, that in (23) there is an ambiguity as to the semantic subject of *swallowing*:

(23) John caused Bill to die by swallowing his tongue.

Here either John or Bill swallowed his tongue, which caused Bill's death.[2]

---

[1] Fodor gives (22) as ungrammatical. This does not seem correct, since it is a perfectly good way of expressing the contradictory proposition which it does express.

[2] There is a further ambiguity according to whether *his* is or is not reflexive. Pragmatic difficulties arising in connection with two of the four possible readings can be left out of account here.

But if *kill* is inserted here, only *John* can be the semantic object of *swallowing*:

(24) John killed Bill by swallowing his tongue.

These observations are no doubt correct. And they put a serious difficulty in the way of McCawley's analysis of *kill*.

Let us, in accordance with general assumptions adhered to in this paper, consider temporal adverbials such as *on Sunday* and *by*-phrases as in (21)–(24) to be operators in semantic structure. A partial analysis of (21) will then be:

(25)

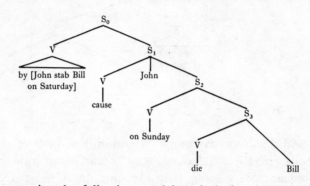

Likewise, we can give the following partial analysis for the two readings of (23):

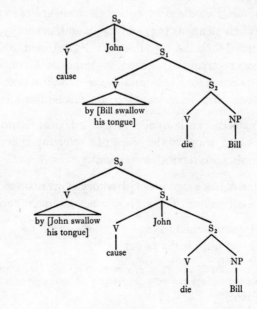

We agree in principle with Fodor when he argues that the subject of the by-phrase is deleted when it is co-referential with the subject of the S immediately underneath it. We thus see that *John* is deleted in (25) and (26b), and Bill in (26a).

We now notice that *kill* can be used only in (26b), not in (25) or (26a). We notice furthermore, that, according to the same principles of analysis, (22) is analysed as follows:[1]

(27)

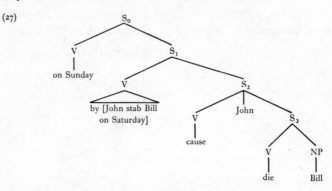

It would thus seem as though *kill* can only be inserted when its component elements ('*cause*', '*become*', '*dead*') occur, in semantic representation, in subsequent *S*s, without alien elements intervening. This restriction cannot be correct, however, since (19) shows that *almost* does occur as an alien element in between the component parts of *kill* without preventing the insertion of *kill*. I would suggest that the answer lies in the referring function of the alien elements (25) and (26a), and, generally, in all cases where such elements block the insertion of a lexical item. *Almost*, on the other hand, is not a referring expression: its semantic function is purely logical. In order to account for the seemingly contradictory observations made, the following constraint on lexical insertion can be formulated:

B. No material can be made part of a lexical island when, thereby, it moves into or out of the scope of a referring operator (or an operator containing a referring expression).

Constraint *B* has a certain explanatory power, since it accounts for the following observations. The verb *miss* occurs in the sense of '*not hit*':

(28) a. I missed the target
     b. I did not hit the target

---

[1] Since, as was noted in p. 92 n. 1, sentence (22) is in some ways contradictory, the analysis presented in (27) can only be partial and incomplete: it does not show up the inherent contradiction.

Yet, although we have (29a), insertion of *miss* results in the ungrammatical (29b).

(29) a. I did not hit anything
b. *I missed anything
c. I missed everything

The correct semantic counterpart of (29a) is (29c).

The verb *refuse* occurs in the sense of '*not accept*' and '*not give*'. These two senses can be seen to be closely related: both are reducible to '*not allow to have*'. When the subjects are equal the result is '*not accept*', otherwise *refuse* corresponds to '*not give*'.[1] Here again, we see that *anything* must be replaced by *everything* when the lexical verb *refuse* is used:

(30) a. He did not accept anything
b. *He refused anything
c. He refused everything

Analysing (29a) according to the principles adopted and investigated here, we find:

(31)

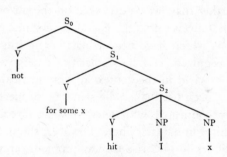

The element '*for some x*' is considered a referring operator. Constraint *B* now prevents the formation of a lexical island of which both *not* and *hit* would form part, since material would have to be moved across the scope boundaries of the referring operator. The verb *miss* cannot be inserted here, but it can be inserted when we have a logically equivalent[2] semantic phrase-marker:

[1] *Give* is analysable as '*cause to have*'. '*Cause not to have*' is logically equivalent to '*not allow to have*', and gives a more precise analysis for the one sense of *refuse* than '*not give*'.
[2] The equivalence is not complete: (32) presupposes the existence of certain things to be hit, whereas (31) does not, or not necessarily. In fact, (29a) is ambiguous from this point of view, and only in the presupposition-loaded sense is it equivalent to (29c). See Seuren (forthcoming) for an elaboration of this presuppositional difference.

(32)

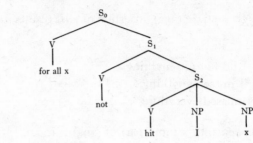

The same applies, of course, to (30).[1]

A final word remains to be said about the notion 'referring expression' which plays a crucial role in the formulation of the two constraints on lexicalization formulated above. This notion has been used here in a twofold opposition. On the one hand it is set against generic or sortal expressions (as *milk* in *Drinking milk is something I like*). On the other hand it is opposed to the notion of purely logical, or truth-functional, expressions, such as *almost, probably, not*, etc. It is clear that more is needed to make the concept of referring expression precise and satisfactory. It is equally clear, however, that an attempt at clarifying that notion would take us very far afield, further than seems desirable for the purposes of this paper.

It is felt, however, that there is some semantic property common to those expressions which have been labelled 'referring expressions' here. Once this is recognized, certain regularities emerge which appear to have an explanatory yield in the context of grammatical semantics. The term *referring* has been used since the semantic property in question seems very intimately connected with what has been recognized as 'reference' in philosophical literature. There, however, the notion is also far from clear and continues to give rise to new problems and new attempts at solving them. (The literature is so abundant that any reference would be arbitrary.) One way in which the ideas presented in this paper might be helpful consists in using the two lexical constraints as tests for problematic cases. When it is felt that the results enhance our insight and reveal further regularities, we have some reason for encouragement.

As an example we might consider the case of proper names. It has often been said that proper names have no 'meaning' but only 'reference' (no 'connotation' but only 'denotation'). This purely referential definition of proper names has also, however, been denied quite frequently. If proper

---

[1] It should be clear that the constraints formulated above are of a transderivational, or global nature, in Lakoff's sense. Semantic structure keeps plaguing later derivational stages, in this case lexical island formation.

names are indeed purely referential, then our constraints could predict that they can *never be incorporated into* a lexical island. We observe, however, that they can:

(33) a. Fred is a Nixon-admirer
     b. Charlie is a Stalinist
     c. Albert has been through a process of complete Spiro-Agnewification

We are now faced with a dilemma: are our constraints incorrect, or is the theory at fault according to which proper names have no other semantic function than reference? A closer scrutiny of the semantic subtleties of the sentences in (33) may well help us to decide here. We might ask if the names *Nixon, Stalin* and *Spiro Agnew* in (33a, b, and c), respectively, actually refer to the well-known public figures who bear or bore those names. Or do they fulfil the function of sortal specification? It is known, of course, that proper names are sometimes used as sortals:

(34) Frank is a second Nixon

We notice, furthermore, that when the name *Nixon* is unambiguously used to refer to that person, its incorporation into a lexical island strikes us as highly unnatural:

(35) a. Two weeks ago John was Nixon's guest
     b. *Two weeks ago John was a Nixon-guest

It does seem appropriate to say that in (33a) it is specified what kind of admiration Fred has, more or less as in:

(36) To admire a man like Nixon is a crime of opinion

Nor should it pass unobserved that (33c) does not mean that Albert is now identical with Spiro Agnew: this sentence does not entail an identity crisis.

Whatever the answers to questions such as these are, the proposals put forward in this paper provide us with more powerful tools to develop and test hypotheses and to refine our semantic notions than was hitherto the case.

REFERENCES

De Rijk, R. P. G. (1968). 'A note on prelexical predicate raising', unpublished. To appear in Seuren, ed. (forthcoming).

Fodor, J. A. (1970). 'Three reasons for not deriving "kill" from "cause to die" ', *Linguistic Inquiry*, **1**:4, 429–38.

Kiefer, F. and Ruwet, N., eds. (1973). *Generative Grammar in Europe*. Foundations of Language Supplementary Series. Dordrecht: Reidel.

Lakoff, G. (1971). 'On generative semantics'. In Steinberg and Jakobovits (1971), 232–96.

Morgan, J. L. (1969). 'On arguing about semantics,' *Papers in Linguistics*, **1**:1, 49–70.

Seuren, P. A. M. (1972). 'Predicate Raising and Dative in French and sundry languages.' Unpublished.

—— (1973). 'The comparative'. In Kiefer and Ruwet, eds. (1973), 528–64.

—— (forthcoming). 'Negative's travels'. In Seuren, ed. (forthcoming).

—— ed. (forthcoming). *Semantic Syntax*. Oxford: Oxford University Press.

Steinberg, D. D. and Jakobovits, L. A. eds. (1971). *Semantics. An Interdisciplinary Reader in Philosophy, Linguistics and Psychology*. Cambridge: Cambridge University Press.

On generics

ÖSTEN DAHL

In this paper,[1] I am going to discuss two closely related phenomena, namely generic tense and generic noun phrases. By 'generic tense' I am referring to cases such as the following:

(1) Beavers build dams
(2) I write with my left hand
(3) John smokes cigars
(4) Dogs bark
(5) The sun rises in the east
(6) Oil floats on water
(7) John does not speak German
(8) A gentleman does not offend a lady

Examples of generic noun phrases are the italicized constituents in the following sentences:

(9) *Beavers* build dams
(10) *A beaver* builds dams
(11) *The beaver* builds dams

I shall mainly be concerned with the types exemplified by (9) and (10), i.e. indefinite generic noun phrases.

I am going to claim in this paper that the common semantic property of all generic expressions is that they are used to express law-like, or nomic, statements. The first thing to be done is to make this concept clear. A suitable way of doing so to a linguistic audience may be by using the following example, taken from Chomsky and Halle (1968). Suppose only inhabitants of Tasmania survive a future war, they say. 'It might then be a property of all then existing languages that pitch is not used to differentiate lexical items.' Still, we would not want a linguistic theory to include this among the universals of language, since the property that pitch is not used

[1] I have benefited from discussions with Jens Allwood and Thore Pettersson, who read an earlier draft of this paper and drew my attention to several weak points in the argumentation. Some of the ideas presented in the paper are the results of discussions with Lars-Gunnar Andersson, whose work on generic pronouns was presented in Andersson (1972).

99

as a distinctive feature would not be an *essential* property of human languages, i.e. it would not be a necessary consequence of the innate endowments of the speakers. We must thus differentiate between two types of statements about all languages which we can refer to as accidental generalizations and nomic or law-like statements.[1] In an accidental generalization, we talk only about a set of actual cases, whereas nomic statements concern also possible, non-actual cases.

A way to formalize the difference between accidental and nomic generalizations is offered by modal logic. By now, everyone should be familiar with the concept of a possible world (or a possible state of affairs). However, the concept of an 'alternativeness relation between possible worlds' is perhaps in need of some clarification. As most people should know, modal logic interprets 'necessary' and 'possible' as 'true in all possible worlds' and 'true in some possible worlds' respectively. In most cases talking about 'all possible worlds' does not help us very much; we want to restrict the domain in some way. For this purpose, the notion of an alternativeness relation is introduced. Rather than saying that a proposition p is true in all possible worlds we say that p is true in all worlds which have a certain relation to the actual world. For example, we might want to consider all possible worlds in which Einstein's theory of relativity is true. Consider now the following statement, uttered by a future Tasmanian linguist:

(12) No human language uses pitch as a lexical feature

This can be interpreted both as an accidental generalization and a nomic statement. Consider the set of possible worlds in which humans have the same genetic endowments as in our world. In the nomic interpretation, (12) is a statement about this very set: in any world in this set, any human language will be such that it does not use pitch as a distinctive feature. In the 'accidental' interpretation, on the other hand, we are only talking about the actual world (or rather, our Tasmanian linguist is talking about his actual world). Generally, nomic statements involve the consideration of alternative worlds or states of affairs.

---

[1] Some important treatments of the problems connected with nomic statements are Goodman (1947), Reichenbach (1947), von Wright (1963), Popper (1972), Stalnaker and Thomason (1970). Kimball (1969), of which I have regrettably seen only chapter 4, uses the concept of 'nomicity' to explain what we here refer to as 'generic tense', but he does not discuss the possibilities for a formal treatment within model logic, nor does he (as far as I know) relate generic noun phrases to nomicity in any systematic way.

The term 'nomic' should not be confused with the homophonous term 'gnomic', which is used in traditional grammars of Classical Greek to refer to the use of the aorist in 'proverbial' expressions. The relations between generic and gnomic tense remain somewhat mysterious, but clearly they cannot be equated.

Depending on the character of the alternativeness relation, we may get rather different types of nomic statements. One important distinction is between *descriptive* nomic statements, i.e. those which express physical, biological, etc., laws, and *normative* ones, i.e. those which express social (moral) norms, customs, regulations and so on.[1] A descriptive nomic statement tells us what holds in e.g. the 'physically possible worlds', a normative nomic statement tells us what holds e.g. in 'the morally perfect worlds'. Since our own world is clearly a physically possible world, but not so obviously a morally perfect one, an important consequence follows: the norms expressed in normative nomics may be broken, whereas the laws of descriptive nomics may not.

The most important consequence of the different properties of accidental and nomic generalizations is that the latter can be used for making predictions. Thus, the following argument is valid only if the first sentence is understood as expressing a nomic generalization.[2]

(13) My friends vote for the Socialists. Hence, when you have become my friend, you'll vote for the Socialists.

In (13), we have made a prediction about the future. We can also make inferences of another type from nomic statements, which one could perhaps call predictions in a wide sense, namely inferences to counterfactual statements. Thus, the following is a valid argument, if the first sentence is understood nomically:

(14) My friends vote for the Socialists. Hence, if you had been my friend, you would have voted for the Socialists.

It is clear from the semantic analysis of nomic statements that we gave why it is possible to make such inferences from them, although it is not possible to make them from accidental generalizations. Counterfactual statements concern non-actual states of affairs – what could have been the case. Nomic statements, but not accidental generalizations, tell us something about such states of affairs.

There is an important relation between the concepts 'nomic statement' and 'dispositional property'. A classical example of a dispositional property

---

[1] I am painfully aware of the risks for misinterpreting the term 'normative nomic statement' so as to imply that the statement is issued as an exhortation to obey the norm. 'Normative', in this context, should only be interpreted in the sense 'involving a norm'.

[2] Strictly speaking, this is not quite true. There is a hidden condition here: that the nomic statement will 'rest in force' for a sufficient period of time. In most cases of everyday reasoning, one can take for granted that this condition is fulfilled, but there is no logical necessity for it.

is 'soluble in water'. Such a property shows itself only under certain conditions: to test whether something is soluble in water, we must put it in
water. Still, we want to be able to call a thing soluble in water, even if it has
never been in contact with this liquid and will perhaps never be. Thus, the
conditions for something having this property rest upon its behaviour in
certain states of affairs, which may never be actualized. In other words,
saying that something has a dispositional property is tantamount to making
a nomic statement.

The treatment of nomic or law-like statements is complicated by two
things, which may be somewhat difficult to distinguish from each other.
The first is that when in formulations of nomic statements, there is often an
implicit restriction on the cases in which the law or rule applies, with the
import 'under normal conditions' or the like. For example, if we say

(15) Dogs have four legs

this is certainly a nomic, non-accidental generalization about dogs, although it is a fact that some dogs do not have four legs, due to some innate
or acquired defect. What is meant is obviously that under normal conditions, all dogs have four legs. There is clearly a danger of circularity here:
it is possible in most cases to interpret 'under normal conditions' so as to
make the statement empty, e.g. if we include into the defining qualities of
a normal dog that it have four legs. Nevertheless, some such 'normalcy'
condition is probably hidden in most nomic statements without causing any
trouble for the reasoning.

The second problem is that laws may also be of a 'probabilistic' or
'statistical' type. An example of this would be the following statement:

(16) Every second Englishman prefers whisky to gin

This is not a generalization in the sense that it attributes some property to
all members of a certain class, but still it can be interpreted in two ways –
'nomically' and 'accidentally'. In the accidental interpretation, we are
talking about the proportions of whisky and gin drinkers among a set of
actual individuals, in the nomic, we are talking about the probability for
any Englishman – actual or potential – to prefer whisky to gin. As before,
only the nomic interpretation allows us to make predictions about new
cases.

In everyday discourse, we do not very often talk about exact probabilities, but statements of the following type are quite frequent:

(17) Englishmen tend to like whisky

We can refer to approximate 'laws' of this sort as 'tendencies'. Notice the difference between a statement which formulates a 'tendency' and a statement with a hidden 'normalcy' condition. The existence of a tendency does not imply that the cases which do not comply with the tendency are in any way abnormal. We have not said in (17) that any 'normal' Englishman likes whisky. On the other hand, the presence of a normalcy condition does not imply that the law becomes probabilistic rather than deterministic. If the normalcy condition is fulfilled, all cases will follow the law. Thus, it would be strange to say

(18) Dogs tend to have four legs

in view of the fact that any normal dog has exactly four legs.

Let us now consider the application of what we have said to generic tense. My suggestion is that when we use generic tense, we state that a law or a principle of some sort 'is in force' at a certain time. In other words, we make a nomic statement. Notice that since the validity of a law or norm may very well be restricted in time, there is nothing in this account of generic tense that implies that it is in some way 'timeless' or 'valid for all time', as is occasionally suggested. This is also the way it should be, in my opinion. There is nothing in the sentences (1–8) themselves that necessitates that they have always been valid and will always be valid, on the contrary, several of them are naturally interpreted as concerning temporally restricted laws or norms. Notice that there is not only a generic present, but also generic pasts and generic futures:

(19) When I was a boy, I wrote with my left hand, but now I write with my right hand, although I will probably write with my left hand again when I grow older.

Thus, what a generic sentence such as (2) basically states is that the principle that I write with my left hand is valid now. As we have seen, there are many types of laws, norms, and principles, and the sentences that describe them are as varied. We have already talked about two main types of nomic statements: descriptive and normative. This distinction is useful also in analysing generic tense. Sometimes it gives rise to different possibilities for the interpretation of a single sentence. Consider, for instance, (7). This sentence may be interpreted as saying that John does not have the ability to speak German, but also as saying that although he knows German, he does not speak it, as a matter of principle. In the first case, we refer to what is possible given John's innate and acquired capacities and abilities, in the second, what is allowed by the principles of behaviour he has set up for himself. We see the difference if we consider what would happen if we suddenly heard John speak German: the first interpretation would then clearly be refuted, but not so obviously the second, since people sometimes break their principles of behaviour. Although this case may seem relatively clear, not all cases are. It is often a rather arbitrary decision whether to look upon a certain sentence as expressing a descriptive or a normative statement, due to the fact that if there is a prescriptive norm, there is mostly also an objective regularity in behaviour.

Generic sentences differ not only with regard to the nature of the alternativeness relation involved in them, there are also differences of another sort.

Lawler (1972) makes a distinction between universal and existential generics (i.e. cases of generic tense). As examples of these two types, he gives the following two sentences, respectively:

(20) Delmer walks to school
(21) Nephi's dog chases cars

of which the following would, according to him, be 'reasonable paraphrases':

(20′) On all occasions when Delmer goes to school, he walks
(21′) There have existed occasions of Nephi's dog chasing cars.

In other words, 'universal generics' would be in essence, 'universal quantification' over occasions, events, time or the like, whereas 'existential generics' would correspond to statements containing an existential quantifier.

The distinction made by Lawler is no doubt relevant, although, as we shall see, one needs to refine it in various ways. Let us look more closely at his claims. First, if we are quantifying over something in (20) and (21), what are we quantifying over? Lawler seems to prefer to assume that the domain of quantification is 'occasions' or 'events'. In a number of cases, such as:

(22) The Vice-President succeeds the President, and the Speaker of the House succeeds the Vice-President

he notes that we should rather be talking of 'possible events'. What Lawler does not notice is that all generics are, in a way, about possible events. Thus, we understand (20) not only as meaning that in any observed event of Delmer's going to school he has been walking but also as meaning that he will walk to school tomorrow, if tomorrow is a school day, and that he would have walked to school today, if he had been free today. Similarly, (21) is not synonymous to (21′) (this would imply that the generic present tense is equivalent to the present perfect) but rather that Nephi's dog is – at this moment – disposed to chasing cars, i.e. that if he sees a car in a few minutes, it is not excluded that he will chase it. (We would hardly judge (21) as true if Nephi's dog had lost his legs, or been administered a personality-changing anti-car-chasing drug. (21′), on the other hand, would still be true under these conditions.)[1]

Therefore, I would suggest the following reinterpretation of Lawler's universal–existential distinction: A generic statement means that a certain law or principle is valid at a certain time, i.e. it characterizes a certain set of worlds defined by some alternativeness relation. In the 'universal' cases, we say that something holds for all the worlds in the set in question, in the 'existential' cases, we say that something holds for some of the worlds. For instance, in (21) we say that in any alternative state of affairs where Delmer goes to school, he walks. In other words, the universal cases correspond to the necessity operator in modal logic, and the existential cases to the possibility operator.

There is, however, a rather subtle distinction which makes the universal–existential dichotomy insufficient. Consider the sentence

(23) Does John eat artichokes?

In what situation would we answer (23) by 'yes' or 'no'? There are clear cases of both: suppose, for example, that John is known to eat artichokes for breakfast every day, or on the other hand, that he is the chairman of the National Anti-Artichoke League. But suppose now that we are in the following situation: We are having John to dinner, and we know that John

---

[1] In addition, there are a number of unclarities in Lawler's discussion of the universal–existential distinction. He seems to mix up at least two problems: (a) whether the interpretation of the sentence involves a set of 'occasions' which is quantified over with universal quantification, (b) whether any of the constituents in the sentence is 'focused'. Thus, he paraphrases the universal reading of *Garth drinks coffee* as *Garth drinks nothing but coffee*, although a paraphrase analogous to (20′) would be rather *On all occasions, Garth drinks coffee*, which does not exclude that he drinks tea at the same time. Similarly, Lawler quotes (i) with the possible paraphrases (ii) and (iii).

  (i) DeVar eats vegetables
  (ii) DeVar is a vegetarian (i.e. does not eat anything but vegetables)
  (iii) DeVar will eat vegetables if you give them to him

According to him, (ii) is a universal and (iii) an existential reading. However, it is perfectly possible to interpret (iii) as universal in the first of the two senses mentioned above, namely as synonymous with

  (iv) On all occasions when DeVar is offered vegetables, he eats them

where nothing at all is said about his eating only vegetables.

has never seen an artichoke in his life, but, since he is eager to try everything new, he will certainly accept if he is offered one. We are now considering whether it is advisable to buy artichokes for our dinner or not. I think we experience a certain hesitation here, and that there are actually two possibilities hidden in (23), paraphrasable as follows:

(24) a. Does John have a habit of eating artichokes?
b. Do John's principles of behaviour allow him to eat artichokes?

In our situation, the answer to (a) would be 'no' but the answer to (b) 'yes'. (24b) fits with the proposed analysis of existential generics:

(25) Is there an alternative world compatible with John's principles of behaviour where he eats artichokes?

but for (24a) we need something else. A 'habit', as we usually understand it, is something more than just the absence of a negative principle. For a person to have a habit, for example of smoking, the behaviour in question should be exercised at times, and preferably regularly. In fact, to the extent that a habit is a behaviour-guiding principle, it is a principle which requires a certain behaviour rather than just allows it. Let us try to make clear what this would mean in a possible-world analysis. If a certain behaviour is required by some principle, it means that the behaviour is performed in all worlds which are compatible with the principle. However, the problem is messed up by the intrusion of the time dimension. In the earlier cases, we have been able to talk about 'alternative worlds' and 'alternative states of affairs' indiscriminately, thus interpreting 'alternative world' implicitly as 'the alternative to the world as it is at a given time'. In the case of habits, however, this is not sufficient, since having e.g. a habit of smoking does not mean that one smokes in all alternative states of affairs, i.e. at all times in all alternative courses of events. Rather, what one says is that in any alternative course of events – i.e. any succession of world-states – one smokes at some times. A possible way of expressing this would be to say that if I have a habit at time t, all the world-states which are alternatives to the world at t are followed by some world-state where I smoke. There is a further problem that I do not quite see how to solve within a formal analysis: the requirement that the behaviour be performed regularly, i.e. sufficiently often. Clearly, there is no fixed interval that can be chosen: a habit of going to Mallorca does not need to be exercised as often as a habit of smoking cigarettes. Perhaps, every type of activity is associated with a rough interval at which it must be performed for there to be a habit.

If what we have said about habits is correct, Lawler's existential cases fall into two classes, one of which is more similar to the universal cases. In fact, it could be regarded as an in-between category: although we talk about what happens in all worlds, we talk about what happens at some – not all – times in these worlds.

In the beginning of this paper, I gave only an 'ostensive' definition of generic tense by quoting a number of clear cases. A possible objection to my approach would be that even if the semantics I have provided is correct at least for some of the more natural interpretations of them, I have not demonstrated that 'generic tense', if we use this term the way I do, is a category which has any interesting grammatical properties. One way of giving an answer to this is to show that there are languages where 'generic tense' is marked morphologically. At first glance, English might seem to be such a language, since in many cases, the choice of a simple rather than a progressive tense necessitates a generic reading:

(26) I smoke
(27) I am smoking

However, the generic–non-generic distinction is clearly not the main distinction underlying the opposition between simple and progressive tenses. (28), for example, may be both generic and non-generic.

(28) I smoked

We have to look for other languages. Turkish seems to be a suitable candidate. In this language, there is an opposition between so-called 'aorist' and 'non-aorist' tenses. Since I cannot claim first-hand knowledge of Turkish, I shall have to rely on the formulations in Lewis (1967). Lewis (1967:117) describes the difference in meaning between the aorist present forms *yaparim* 'I do' and the corresponding ordinary present *yapıyorum* in the following way: 'Fundamentally, *yaparım* means "I am a doer" and according to the context it may represent : "I habitually do"; "by and large I am the sort of person who does"; "I am ready, willing and able to do"; "I shall do". *yapıyorum* means: "I have undertaken, and am now engaged in, the job of doing"; "I am doing now"; "I am doing in the future", i.e. "I have the job in hand".' Hopi is another language we can mention. The 'nomic' category in Hopi according to Whorf (1956:114) 'does not declare any particular situation, but offers the statement as a general truth, e.g. English: "She writes poetry, he smokes only cigars, rain comes from the clouds, certain dinosaurs laid eggs in the sand" '.

We shall now proceed to the second major topic of this paper, viz. generic noun phrases. It has been frequently pointed out that there is a clear connection between generic tense and generic noun phrases. Thus, the possibilities of interpreting an indefinite noun phrase as generic or non-generic often depend on the generic or non-generic character of the verb of the sentence. Consider, for example:

(29) A dog is barking
(30) A dog barks

There is hardly any doubt that the natural interpretation of *a dog* is non-generic in (29) and generic in (30). The restriction is clearly semantic. In a language such as Swedish, where there is no difference in the verb in sentences of this type, the translation of (29–30) still has two natural interpretations rather than four:

(31) En hund skäller

An adequate semantic analysis should, then, account for this connection.

My claim about indefinite generic noun phrases is that they always involve a quantification over possible objects rather than over actual ones. Consider the following 'minimal pair':

(32) a. A member of this club does not drink whisky
     b. The members of this club do not drink whisky

The intuitive semantic difference between (a) and (b) is to me the following: In (a), we state that there is an obligation for members of the club not to drink whisky, or at least that it is expected of them that they will not drink whisky. In (b), this is not necessarily the case: it is quite compatible with this statement that it just happens that the persons who are members of the club do not like whisky. This difference should come out clearly when we compare the following arguments:

(33) A member of this club does not drink whisky: hence, since you will now be accepted as a member, you will have to stop drinking.
(34) The members of this club do not drink whisky: hence, since you will now be accepted as a member, you will have to stop drinking.

I claim that (33) is a valid argument, but (34) need not be. Here's another example of a 'minimal pair' to make the point clearer:

(35) Superpowers do not take account of the views of smaller countries; China is now becoming a superpower; hence, China will not take account of the views of smaller countries.
(36) The superpowers do not take account of the views of smaller

countries; China is now becoming a superpower; hence, China will not take account of the views of smaller countries.

Talking about superpowers, we can either say that any possible superpower will have a certain property (i.e. that it is an essential property of superpowers) or that the entities that happen to be superpowers have this (accidental) property. It seems to me that whereas definite noun phrases allow both possibilities indefinite generic NPs can only be interpreted in accordance with the first. To support this claim further, I provide the following examples:

(37) Superpowers are referred to by abbreviations the first letter of which is U

(38) The superpowers are referred to by abbreviations the first letter of which is U

Provided that the superpowers are the USSR and the USA, (38) is a true statement (at least on one reading), whereas (37) seems rather nonsensical in view of the absurdity of the idea that having an abbreviation in U is an essential property of superpowers.

We must now specify the rules for interpreting generic noun phrases, and relate them to the interpretation of generic tense. We have said that generic indefinite noun phrases range over possible objects. It has been proposed to add the quantifiers of normal predicate calculus quantifiers that have another range: 'for all possible x...' and 'for some possible x...' (cf. Lambert and van Fraassen (1970)). It is not clear to me what this proposal actually implies: at least if you consider that a possible object may exist in several different possible worlds, an expression such as 'for all possible objects x, x has the property p' does not seem to be well defined since x might have p in one world and lack it in another. We might interpret the expression as meaning 'in all worlds w, any object x in w has the property p'. However, in this case the introduction of the two types of quantifiers seems unnecessary, if we have already introduced modal operators. We shall stick to this later solution: that of interpreting generic noun phrases as equivalent to a universal quantification within the scope of a modal operator. There are still problems, however. Consider the following sentences:

(39) Fido barks

(40) A dog barks

If we interpret (39) as a statement about Fido's habits along the lines we suggested above, we might paraphrase it as follows:

(41) In all alternative worlds, Fido barks sometimes

But (40) is a bit more complicated. The following are possible alternatives:

(42) In all alternative worlds, all dogs bark sometimes
(43) In all alternative worlds, all dogs are such that in all alternative worlds, they bark sometimes

(43) would correspond to an expression in modal logic containing two modal operators, for example:

(44) $\Box \forall x \Box F x$

whereas (42) would just contain one:

(45) $\Box \forall x F x$

In some systems of modal logic, (44) and (45) would be equivalent. It is not clear that there is any difference between the two alternatives in natural language, either, and if there is a difference, the choice between the two is not obvious. There are a few things which might speak in favour of choosing (43) rather than (42), in spite of its being more complicated. First, (43) seems more parallel to (41), in the sense that the same thing is here said of all possible dogs as is said of Fido in (41). Second, two modal operators will be necessary to formalize existential generics, if there are any. Cf.

(46) Educated Swedes speak English

This cannot be paraphrased as

(47) In some alternative worlds, all educated Swedes speak English

but must rather be

(48) In all alternative worlds, all educated Swedes are such that in some alternative worlds, they speak English

Another possible argument in favour of something like (43) is the following. In some cases, we have two generic noun phrases in one sentence, e.g.

(49) Dogs treat cats harshly

Theoretically, we could interpret this sentence in two ways: as ascribing to dogs the essential property of treating cats harshly, or as ascribing to cats the essential property of being treated harshly by dogs. In actual practice, however, we would tend to choose the first alternative as more natural. In other words, we would interpret the set of worlds referred to in (49) as defined by the inherent character of dogs rather than by the inherent character of cats. We might then want to give this a reflection in the formalization by giving the noun phrase *dogs* another status than the noun phrase *cats*. This might be done by placing the former outside the scope of the innermost modal operator, if there are two or more in the formula. However, I would prefer to regard what I have said in the last few paragraphs as rather loose speculation. Too much in the semantics of generic expressions is still unclear.

REFERENCES

Andersson, L.-G. (1972). 'Man – ett pronomen,' *Gothenburg Papers in Theoretical Linguistics*, **15**.

Chomsky, N. and Halle, M. (1968). *The Sound Pattern of English*. New York: Harper & Row.

Goodman, N. (1947). 'The problem of counterfactual conditionals', *Journal of Philosophy*, **44**, 113–28.

Kimball, J. P. (1969). 'Selections on tense and mood and conditional sentences.' Unpublished M.I.T. thesis.

Lambert, K., ed. (1970). *Philosophical Problems in Logic. Some Recent Developments*. Dordrecht: Reidel.

Lambert, K. and van Fraassen, B. C. (1970). 'Meaning relations, possible objects, and possible worlds.' In Lambert (1970).

Lawler, J. M. (1972). 'Generic to a fault.' In *Papers from the Eighth Regional Meeting Chicago Linguistic Society*. Chicago: Chicago Linguistic Society.

Lewis, G. L. (1967). *Turkish Grammar*. Oxford: The Clarendon Press.

Popper, K. (1972). *The Logic of Scientific Discovery*. 6th revised impression. London: Hutchinson.

Reichenbach, Hans (1947). *Elements of Symbolic Logic*. New York: The Macmillan Co.

Stalnaker, R. and Thomason, R. (1970). 'A semantic analysis of conditional logic', *Theoria*, **36**, 23–42.

Whorf, B. L. (1956). *Language, Thought, and Reality*. Selected writings of B. L. Whorf, ed. by J. B. Carroll. Cambridge, New York and London: The Technology Press, Wiley, and Chapman & Hall.

Wright, G. H. von (1963). *Norm and Action*. London: Routledge and Kegan Paul.

Quantifiers, definite descriptions, and reference[1]

COLIN BIGGS

When the Messenger in *Through the Looking Glass* told the King that nobody walked faster than he did, Alice was puzzled that the King accused the Messenger of being a liar: on the grounds that if nobody walked faster than he did, then nobody would have got there first. Clearly NPs like *nobody* (if indeed they are NPs) do not refer in any straightforward way. I shall, to give a label, call such surface structure NPs as *nobody, all men, every stupid academic* 'quantified NPs': they correspond to what Geach (following W. E. Johnston) calls 'applicatival phrases' (being phrases formed from a general term plus an applicative). But if quantified NPs do not refer in any straightforward way, do they refer at all? Moreover, in general what requirements does the presence of such NPs impose on the semantics of host sentences?

Clearly anything like an adequate answer to such questions would take us over much ground. I shall here confine myself to examining a small subset of the possible concatenations involving quantified NPs. In so doing I hope to shed some light on the behaviour of definite descriptions in certain roles.

One possibility for concatenation with quantified NPs has been much discussed in the literature of linguistics: that involving the co-habitation within a sentence of two quantified NPs having superficially the same structure, and being composed of the same morphological units. In such cases, it is not uncommon for a writer to claim that the two tokens are, in fact, tokens of the same type. Consider, for example, sentences like (1):

(1) All optimists expect all optimists to be President

The same phenomena is exhibited in the behaviour of definite descriptions, as in (2):

(2) The shortest linguist in the world expects the shortest linguist in the world to be discriminated against

Some speakers have a 'bizarreness reaction' to sentences such as (1) and

[1] The following is an essentially unrevised version of the paper I presented at the colloquium; indeed, the main change is the title. Again I am indebted to Terence Moore for his encouragement and comment.

(2), finding them at best awkward or cumbersome in their use of what is (superficially) the same phrase twice. We can, perhaps, remove those qualms by asking speakers of such uncharitable dialects to substitute pronouns for the first token in each sentence, with the specification that those pronouns have the same reference as the phrases for which they are substituted if the latter have a reference, and that where there is a failure of reference they (the pronouns and the NPs for which they go proxy) have the same denotation.[1] Thus we get (3) and (4) (subject to the above specifications):

(3) They expect all optimists to be President
(4) He expects the shortest linguist in the world to be discriminated against

We have just made mention of the notion of pronouns going proxy for full, or bloated, NPs. It is just such a notion that has, on occasion, prompted consideration of such sentences as (1) and (5):

(5) Everyone hates everyone

If pronouns are co-referential with their antecedents, as linguists and philosophers have often supposed, and if they do in fact go proxy for their antecedents (behaving as what Geach calls 'pronouns of laziness'),[2] then how do we account for the fact that (5) and (6) are not paraphrases?

(6) Everyone hates himself

And, allowing that some pronouns are so lazy as to disappear, as in

(7) All optimists expect to be President

how do we account for the fact that (1) and (7) are not paraphrases? Confronted with such data, most people seem to have abandoned, at least for such cases, the notion that pronouns go proxy. It is not my wish, in this paper, to defend that notion, but rather to show that the evidence from sentences such as those we have just considered does not support, in the way they envisage, their abandoning of that notion. In seeing why this is the case, we shall understand the semantics of such sentences somewhat better.

---

[1] I am here using the terms 'reference' and 'denotation' in much the sense that, say, Donnellan (1966) uses them.
[2] See Barbara Partee's contribution to the present volume.

I shall argue (A) *that no string containing two co-referential tokens*[1] *of a quantified NP is a plausible underlying structure for a sentence such as* (7) and (B) *that no such string is a possible surface structure sentence.* Hence, rather than its being *surprising* that the sentence pairs *All optimists expect all optimists to be President* and *All optimists expect to be President* differ in meaning, it is to be *expected* that they differ in meaning – for the thesis that they ought to be paraphrases was based on a view of co-reference co-occurrence restrictions explicitly denied by (A) and (B). Those who reject pronouns of laziness will not find (A) surprising.

To see in some detail why I make the second claim (B) we can usefully consider a different proposal which has been much discussed in the literature; namely, the higher-verbs proposal. In this time of rapidly changing ideas and theories, some may think the higher-verbs proposal must have been an idea of Dionysius Thrax – although it is, of course, only a few years old. I consider it here both for its relevance to claim (B) and also because it would seem that George Lakoff (1971:238b), whilst rejecting the higher-verbs proposal as such (in that he rejects the VP node), offers as semantic representations schemata which, in essentials, repeat much of what is wrong with the higher-verbs proposal.

In a paper from the Harvard Computational Laboratory entitled 'English quantifiers' Guy Carden (1968) actually gives as motivation for an analysis of quantifiers as higher verbs the fact that sentence pairs such as those we have been considering are not paraphrases but he assumes (what we are questioning via claim (B)) that the two NPs in surface sentences such as *All optimists expect all optimists to be President* are co-referential, and satisfy the requirements for Equi-NP Deletion. To distinguish such a sentence from *All optimists expect to be President* (where we have just one token), he is led to postulate deep structures for such sentence pairs involving higher Ss, with quantifiers appearing as verbs of those Ss: the deep structure for the sentence containing one token has one higher verb (as in diagram (1)); the deep structure for the sentence containing two tokens is correspondingly more complex, having two higher verbs (as part of S_0 and as part of what we might characterize as the matrix S of the complement structure). The derivation of the surface structures is crucially dependent upon an intriguing process called Q-magic which lowers a quantifier into the next S down the tree where it is adjoined as left daughter of the NP. It is the mark of a true magician that he never lets his audience

---

[1] There are, of course, serious difficulties in specifying what it is for two items to be co-referential, and in specifying what the relation is between the linguist's notion of 'co-reference' and the philosopher's notion of 'reference'. For an attempt in this area see Postal (1970); also Biggs (1973).

(1)

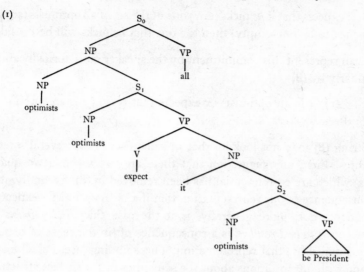

know how the trick was performed. Carden respects that tradition. All we do know is that the derived structure in our example is as follows:

(2)

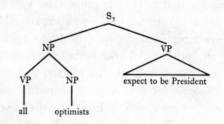

(One of the puzzling features of this derived structure concerns the status of the category configuration in which a VP is immediately dominated by a NP which is in turn immediately dominated by an S.[1])

Such an account offers us no insight into the semantic distinction between the sentence pairs under consideration. Indeed, in that it marks the two tokens *all optimists* as co-referential, it does not even produce the correct surface structure. Let me suggest another analysis for such sentences. Intuitively, the utterer of a sentence such as *All optimists expect all optimists to be President* is, in sincerely uttering the sentence, characteristically making a promise to his audience of the form:

Consider the set of all optimists and if you (the audience) pick any one of them (supposing the set to be non-empty) you will find that the one you

---

[1] One is reminded, in this respect, of Strawson's general caution concerning trees – see, for example, Strawson (1971), chapter 7.

pick expects that if *he* picks (any) one of the set of all optimists (supposing the set to be non-empty) then the one that *he* picks will be President.

We can represent this commitment by the speaker more formally and more familiarly by (8):

(8) $(\forall x)$ (x is an optimist $\rightarrow x$ expects that $((\forall y)$ (y is an optimist $\rightarrow y$ be President))

String (8) may not look all that unusual, but it has several interesting features. First, any suggestion that there are two tokens (two quantified NPs) which are co-referential has been removed in (8). Secondly, it is not a consequence of our representation that if x is an optimist x expects to be President; nor, more generally, is it the case that *All optimists expect (themselves) to be President* is a consequence of (in the sense of being logically entailed by) that representation. These findings are, I shall maintain, in line with our intuitions about the semantics of the surface structure (1). Consider, for example, the claim that if x is an optimist it is not a consequence of our representation that x expects to be President. Clearly if x does not realize that he is an optimist (and I take it to be plausible that this could be the case) then he may well expect all optimists to be President without expecting himself to be President – even though he is a member of the set of all optimists.[1] I take it that the natural sentence (1) is vague in that it is not committed on this matter, and that it is desirable that the representation reflect this lack of commitment. Hence our sample representation is very much in line with the observation that the sentence pairs are not paraphrases; for the representation shows that if the two-token sentence is true it does not follow that the one-token sentence is true, and it is not difficult to see that the other half of the equivalence fails to hold either, for a representation of (7) will be of the form:

(9) $(\forall x)$ (x is an optimist $\rightarrow x$ expects to be President)

Notice that string (9) is in line with the prediction of claim (A).

The representation I have offered in (8)[2] suggests, then, that the two

---

[1] For a discussion of this and related phenomena see Castañeda (1966) and references therein.

[2] I am not entirely sure how to interpret George Lakoff's schemata (1971:238b), but I suspect that they are at least compatible with (8) and (9). Where he errs, it seems to me, is in thinking that *the* important feature of his schemata is that which they share with Carden's higher-verbs proposal and his own prior higher-verbs proposal: the positioning of quantifiers in underlying representations in a higher clause than the quantified. Such a preoccupation causes no serious problems, as it happens, for such quantifiers as *all*, but if we look (as he does) at other quantifiers, such as *many* and *few*, then his representations fall wide of the mark. For, as Altham (1971) has carefully argued, quantification involving

tokens in such sentences as (1) are not co-referential. It will be instructive, for reasons which will be made clear later, to test our intuitions about such 'two-token' sentences by considering a further example. First we must distinguish two types of reading for sentences containing *all* as a quantifier. Consider (10) and (11):

(10) All linguists are clever
(11) All linguists know about transformational grammar

The statement expressed by (10) is, of course, contingently true or false, but what is important is that the statement is TIMELESS – that is, the reader or hearer does not understand the statement as concerned with *all linguists* at a particular time. Clearly, however, it is an empirical fact that the statement expressed by (11) *is* understood by the reader or hearer to be a statement about *all linguists* today, to be a TIMELY statement.

We can now consider an example to illustrate our representation; using, say, a TIMELY statement.

The important thing about quantified NPs in Ss with a TIMELY reading is that they refer to or denote a (possibly large but) finite set. Let us suppose, for present purposes, that the set of linguists referred to or denoted by *all linguists* in (11) is a two-membered set: {Noam, Chomsky}. If we now consider (12):

(12) All linguists expect all linguists to know about transformational grammar

we can see that this too is a TIMELY statement. Moreover, the reference of the first token and the denotation of the second token are variable. That is to say, all linguists (i.e. – contingently – Noam and Chomsky) expect *all linguists* (whoever they may be) to know about transformational grammar. Should Noam and Chomsky abandon linguistics in favour, say, of political science, and be replaced by some newly-fledged linguists, then (13) may well be false but (14) true:

(13) Noam and Chomsky expect to know all about transformational grammar

many, for example, is, logically, *double* quantification (one of the quantifiers being existential, the other universal). (See especially (7)–(9).) Altham's analysis requires a caveat, however, since although it provides an intuitively appealing representation for sentences such as *Many optimists like few pessimists* (these being sentences comparable to those Lakoff considers), where the existence of what Altham calls a *manifold* (a set containing many members) is asserted, the analysis as it stands would predict, wrongly, that in uttering *John expects that many optimists will come* I commit myself to the existence of a manifold. Clearly there is a class of verbs, of which *expect* is a member, whose behaviour in sentences containing quantified NPs requires special study.

(14) Noam and Chomsky expect all linguists to know all about transformational grammar.

Clearly then the two tokens in sentences of the sort we have been considering are, as our representation indicated, not co-referential.

We noted earlier in the paper that definite descriptions also permit the
co-habitation within a sentence of superficially similar tokens, as in (2)

(2) The shortest linguist in the world expects the shortest linguist in the
world to be discriminated against

Let us now see briefly how we might analyse such sentences, for in so
doing we shall see similarities to our previous sentences. First notice that
(2) is ambiguous. Suppose that I know the shortest linguist in the world
expects the shortest linguist in the world to be discriminated against but
I also know that he does not realize that he *is* the shortest linguist in the
world; then I can report this fact not by uttering (15)

(15) The shortest linguist in the world expects (himself) to be discriminated against

but rather by uttering (2). This reading for (2) will not concern us here
(although it is an interesting one).[1] The reading with which we are concerned can be represented as follows:

He (the shortest linguist in the world) expects that $(\forall x)$ (x is the shortest
linguist in the world $\rightarrow x$ is discriminated against).

Here, then, despite the fact that at any given moment in time there is one
and only one shortest linguist in the world, the NP *the shortest linguist in the
world* is acting as a variable.[2] The closest that we come in English to a paraphrase of this reading is probably (16):

(16) The shortest linguist in the world expects that if and when there is
a shortest linguist in the world then he is discriminated against

---

[1] See above, p. 116 n. 1. In my PhD thesis, Cambridge (in preparation) I also consider
this reading.

[2] This analysis of definite descriptions in certain roles should not be confused with a
stipulation of Frege's in the *Grundgesetze* (1893:49–50) that where it is not the case that
one and only one object falls under a concept such as

ξ is the unique King of France

then – here I use the more familiar Peano–Russell notation – $\ulcorner(\imath x)\,\phi\urcorner$ is to be rendered as
$\ulcorner\hat{x}\,\phi\urcorner$. See Quine (1951:146–52) for a brief discussion of Frege's stipulation.

This representation too reveals that the two tokens (as in the case of quantified NPs) are not co-referential. Again, notice that given (2) on this second reading, it does not follow that

(17) The shortest linguist in the world expects that he will be discriminated against

Of course, it will come as no surprise to some to see definite descriptions in certain roles being represented as variables – for they would analyse all NPs as variables. But *then* it is no longer clear how we would adequately distinguish the two readings for (2) – where, we would argue, only the latter involves a definite description as a variable. The evidence presented here would suggest, I think, that an approach which regards all NPs as variables would destroy important semantic distinctions in such sentences as we have been lately considering.

I have tried to indicate in this paper the considerable semantic complexity of certain sentence types – specifically those involving the co-habitation within a sentence of two tokens of, allegedly, the same type. It has been my aim to indicate that – even at the level of surface structures – they are, in fact, tokens of quite different types. Understanding this, we can reformulate some of our notions about reference. There is nothing magical, of course, about the number *two*: we can readily construct sentences involving three or more tokens. The semantics for such sentences will be correspondingly more complex, but are construable on essentially similar lines.

REFERENCES

Altham, J. E. J. (1971). *The Logic of Plurality*. London: Methuen.
Biggs, C. (1973). 'Problems and non-problems about reference'. Presented at the Annual Meeting, Linguistics Association of Great Britain.
Carden, G. (1968). 'English quantifiers'. Report NSF-20 from Harvard Computational Laboratory, Cambridge, Mass.
Casteñeda, H-N. (1966). 'He: a study in the logic of self-consciousness', *Ratio*, **8**, 130–57.
Donnellan, K. (1966). 'Reference and definite descriptions', *Philosophical Review*, **75**, 281–304; reprinted in Steinberg and Jakobovits.
Frege, Gottlob. (1893). *Grundgesetze der Arithmetik*, vol. I, translated and edited by M. Furth (1964) as *The Basic Laws of Arithmetic*. Berkeley: University of California Press.
Lakoff, G. (1971). 'On generative semantics'. In Steinberg and Jakobovits.
Postal, P. (1970). 'On coreferential complement subject deletion', *Linguistic Inquiry*, **1**, 439–500.

Quine, W. V. (1951). *Mathematical Logic*. Revised edition, Cambridge: Harvard University Press.

Steinberg, D. and Jakobovits, L., eds. (1971). *Semantics*. Cambridge: Cambridge University Press.

Strawson, P. F. (1971). *Logico-Linguistic Papers*. London: Methuen.

III INTENSIONAL LOGIC AND SYNTACTIC THEORY

Two theories about adjectives[1]

J. A. W. KAMP

1.

I will discuss two theories about adjectives. The first theory dates from the late 1960s. It is stated in Montague (1970) and Parsons (1968). According to this theory the meaning of an adjective is a function which maps the meanings of noun phrases onto other such meanings; e.g. the meaning of *clever* is a function which maps the meaning of *man* into that of *clever man*, that of *poodle* onto that of *clever poodle*, etc. Predicative uses of adjectives are explained as elliptic attributive uses. Thus *This dog is clever* is analysed as *This dog is a clever dog* – or as *This dog is a clever animal*, or perhaps as *This dog is a clever being*. Which noun phrase ought to be supplied in this reduction of predicative to attributive use is in general not completely determined by the sentence itself, and to the extent that it is not, the sentence must be regarded as ambiguous.

The main virtue of this doctrine is that it enables us to treat, within a precise semantical theory for a natural language – as e.g. that of Montague – adjectives in such a way that certain sentences which are, or might well be, false are not branded by the semantics as logically true. Examples of such sentences are:

(1) Every alleged thief is a thief
(2) Every small elephant is small
(3) If every flea is an animal, then every big flea is a big animal

Each of these sentences would come out logically true in Montague's model theory if it were to treat adjectives as ordinary predicates, so that the logical form of (1), for example, would be $(\forall x)(A(x) \wedge T(x) \rightarrow T(x))$.

[1] Since I presented the outline of this paper at the Cambridge conference I – and, I hope, this paper – have profited from discussions with and comments by Michael Bennett, Richard Grandy, Hidé Ishiguro, David Lewis, Richmond Thomason and, in particular, George Lakoff. I was equally fortunate to hear Sally Genet's paper on comparatives at the summer meeting of the Linguistic Society of America in Ann Arbor, which proposed an approach similar to that taken here. Only after the present paper had already been given its final form did I become acquainted with Kit Fine's article 'Vagueness, truth and logic' which expresses on the topic of vagueness, which is the central theme of the second part of my paper, views very similar to those which can be found here. I know that I would have been able to offer a better contribution to this volume if I had known about Fine's work earlier.

Moreover, the theory allows us to express in very simple mathematical terms some important semantical features which some, though not all, adjectives possess. In order to give precise formulations of such features, it is necessary to make some assumptions about the comprehensive semantical theory in which this particular doctrine about adjectives is to be embedded. These assumptions can all be found in Montague (1970). I regard them as basically sound, but would like to point out to those who have strong qualms about possible world semantics that the distinctions drawn by the definitions below do not depend on these assumptions as such.

The assumptions are the following:

(a) Each possible interpretation (for the language in question) is based upon (i) a certain non-empty set W of possible worlds (or possible situations, or possible contexts) and (ii) a set U of individuals.

(b) A property relative to such an interpretation is a function which assigns to each $w \in W$ a subset of U (intuitively the collection of those individuals which satisfy the property in that particular world (or context) w).

(c) The meaning of a noun phrase in such an interpretation is always a property.

Thus the meanings of adjectives in an interpretation of this kind will be functions from properties to properties.

We may call an adjective *predicative in* a given interpretation if its meaning F in that interpretation satisfies the following condition:

(4) there is a property Q such that for each property P and each $w \in W$,
$$F(P)(w) = P(w) \cap Q(w).$$

Once we have singled out a given class $\mathscr{K}$ of admissible interpretations, we can also introduce the notion of being *predicative* simpliciter: an adjective is *predicative* (with respect to the given class $\mathscr{K}$) if and only if it is predicative in each interpretation (belonging to $\mathscr{K}$).

Predicative adjectives behave essentially as if they were independent predicates. If for example *four-legged* is treated as predicative then any sentence *If every N_1 is an N_2 then every four-legged N_1 is a four-legged N_2*, where N_1 and N_2 are arbitrary noun phrases, will be true in each admissible interpretation in all the worlds of that interpretation.

Predicative adjectives are, roughly speaking, those whose extensions are not affected by the nouns with which they are combined. Typical examples are technical and scientific adjectives, such as *endocrine, differentiable, superconductive*, etc.

We may call an adjective *privative in* a given interpretation if its meaning F in that interpretation satisfies the condition

(5) for each property P and each $w \in W$ $F(P)(w) \cap P(w) = \phi$

Again, an adjective will be called *privative* if (5) holds on all admissible interpretations.

A privative adjective A is one which, when combined with a noun phrase N produces a complex noun phrase AN that is satisfied only by things which do not satisfy N. If A is a privative adjective then each sentence *No AN is an N* will be a logical truth. Adjectives that behave in this way in most contexts are e.g. *false* and *fake*. I doubt that there is any English adjective which is privative (in the precise sense here defined) in all of its possible uses.

An adjective is *affirmative in* a given interpretation if its meaning satisfies

(6) for each P and w,
  $F(P)(w) \subseteq P(w)$

It is *affirmative* if (6) holds in all admissible interpretations.

Clearly all predicative adjectives are affirmative. But there are many more. In fact the vast majority of adjectives are affirmative. Typical examples of affirmative adjectives which are not predicative are *big*, *round*, *pink*, *bright*, *sharp*, *sweet*, *heavy*, *clever*.

Finally, an adjective is *extensional in* a given interpretation if

(7) there is a function F' from sets of individuals to sets of individuals such that for every P and w $(F(P))(w) = F'(P(w))$

and *extensional* if (7) holds in all admissible interpretations.

Thus a predicative adjective is in essence an operation on extensions of properties: if two properties have the same extension in w then the properties obtained by applying the adjective to them also have the same extension in w.

Clearly all predicative adjectives are extensional. Non-extensional adjectives are for example *affectionate* and *skilful*. Even if (in a given world) all and only cobblers are darts players, it may well be that not all and only the skilful cobblers are skilful darts players;[1] and even if all men were fathers the set of affectionate fathers would not necessarily coincide with the set of affectionate men.[2]

---

[1] This example was given at the conference by Professor Lewis.
[2] This example was given to me by Dr Hidé Ishiguro of University College, London.

It is an interesting question whether there are any adjectives which are extensional but not predicative. It has been suggested[1] that in particular such adjectives as *small, tall, heavy*, and *hot* belong to this category. Indeed these adjectives are evidently not predicative, whereas their extensionality follows from a certain proposal according to which they derive from their comparatives in the following way. Let A be an adjective of this kind, and let $\mathscr{R}$ be the binary relation represented by the phrase *is more A than*. The function $\mathscr{A}$ from properties to properties which is associated with A is then characterized by

(8) for any property P and world w $\mathscr{A}(P)(w) = \{u \in P(w):$ for most $u' \in P(w) \langle u, u' \rangle \in \mathscr{R}(w)\}$

It will soon be evident why I have not much sympathy for analyses of positives in terms of comparatives generally. At this point, however, I only want to express some reservations which concern (8) in particular. That (8) cannot be right is brought out by the fact that it logically excludes the possibility that, for any property P, most Ps are small Ps and only a few are large Ps. Thus what we usually call a small car in England would according to (8) not be a small car; for we call most English cars small. (One might perhaps reply that this only shows that by *small car* we mean *car of a small model*. But that does not quite do. After all, it is the *individual* cars we call small.) In this case the conflict between usage and the consequences of (8) arises from the fact that cars are naturally divided into categories; and it is to these, if anything, that (8) applies.

There is yet another reason why (8) might fail for *small*. We might have a clear concept of what is the normal size of objects satisfying a certain property, even if objects of that size which have the property do not or only rarely occur. It is conceivable to me that we would then call almost all members of a species S small members of S if there was strong biological evidence that only accidental and abnormal circumstances C prevent the majority from growing into a height which most members of the species would reach under conditions we would regard as normal. Yet we might still be unwilling to call them small members of S-under-the-circumstances-C; for as objects falling under that second description they should be expected to have the size they do have. If, moreover, S and S-under-C had precisely the same extensions the case would tend to show that *small* is not purely extensional. But that it is so difficult to come up with a concrete and convincing example of this sort is perhaps an indica-

---

[1] Cf. Bartsch and Vennemann (1972), part II.

tion that for all practical purposes *small*, and similar adjectives, are indeed extensional.

2.

This theory of adjectives is of course not new. The observation that *John is a good violinist* cannot be analysed as *John is good and a violinist* is probably too old to be traced back with precision to its origin.[1] What is perhaps new in the doctrine as I have stated it here is the emphasis on the fact that what has for a long time been observed to be a feature of certain adjectives is a common feature of them all. *All* of them are functions from noun phrases to noun phrases. Some adjectives (expressed in (4)), however, possess a certain invariance property that makes them behave as predicates, which when combined with a noun phrase give a complex equivalent in meaning to the conjunction of the predicate represented by the adjective and that represented by the noun phrase.

Even if this theory does accomplish the rather simple-minded tasks for which it was designed, one may feel dissatisfied with it for a variety of reasons. Here I will mention only one (although I believe there are other grounds for dissatisfaction as well): The theory is incapable of providing an adequate treatment for the comparative and superlative. For reasons of convenience I will concentrate on the comparative and leave the superlative aside; but the theory which will emerge from our considerations will handle the superlative as well.

From a naïve point of view the comparative is an operation which forms out of an adjective a binary predicate. I believe that this naïve point of view is correct: that when we learn a language such as English we learn the meanings of individual adjectives and, moreover, the semantic function which this comparative-forming operation performs *in general*, so that we have no difficulty in understanding, on first hearing, the meaning of the comparative of an adjective of which we had thus far only encountered the positive. If this is so then the meaning of an adjective must be such that the comparative can be understood as a semantic transformation of that meaning into the right binary relation.

It is quite obvious that if adjectives were ordinary predicates no such transformation could exist. How could we possibly define the relation *x is bigger than y* in terms of nothing more than the extension of the alleged predicate *big*?

---

[1] A clear exposition of a view about the adjective *good* which is essentially what is here proposed for adjectives in general can be found in Geach (1956). Notice, however, that not only does *good*, as Geach makes clear, fail to be a predicate; it is not even extensional (cf. *skilful* above).

Could functions from properties to properties serve as the basis for such a transformation? This is a more problematic question. One might for example characterize the transformation as follows:

For any adjective A with meaning $\mathscr{A}$ in a given interpretation we have for any $u_1, u_2 \in U$ and $w \in W$

(9) u_1 is more A than u_2 in w iff

(a) for every property P such that u_1 and u_2 both belong to $P(w)$ if u_2 belongs to $\mathscr{A}(P)(w)$ then so does u_1

(b) there is a property P such that $u_1, u_2 \in P(w)$, $u_1 \in \mathscr{A}(P)(w)$, and $u_2 \notin \mathscr{A}(P)(w)$.

This definition is in the right direction. But I doubt that it will do. In particular, I doubt whether (b) is a necessary condition. Take *tall*, for example. According to (9) u_1 is taller than u_2 only if there is a property P that applies to both of them and such that u_1 is a tall P while u_2 is not. But suppose that u_1 is taller than u_2 by a tiny bit. Can we then find a P which satisfies this condition? The question is not easy to answer. Let us suppose for the sake of argument that *tall* can be correctly defined by (8) as *taller than most*. Then the question depends on whether we can find a property P such that u_1 is taller than most Ps while u_2 is not. But this can only be the case if there are enough things in the extension of P which have heights intermediate between those of u_1 and u_2. And perhaps there are no such things at all. Now, in our discussion of extensional adjectives we found that (8) is probably not adequate in any case. So there may be after all a property P which satisfies the condition. In this manner we might succeed in saving (9) by imploring the assistance of some bizarre property whenever we need one. But I find this solution ad hoc and unsatisfactory. What underlies the possibility of making comparative claims is that adjectives can apply to things in various degrees. It is my strong conviction that when we learn the meaning of an adjective we learn, as part of it, to distinguish with greater or lesser precision to what degree, or extent, the adjective applies to the various entities to which it applies at all. Once we have learned this we are able to understand the comparative of the adjective without additional explanation, provided we understand the function of the comparative in general.

In order to give my view on the primacy of positive over comparative an adequate foundation I will develop a semantical framework in which the idea of a predicate being true of an entity to a certain degree can be made coherent and precise. This specific problem is closely related to such general features of natural languages as vagueness and contextual disambiguation; indeed I hope that the theory which I will outline will provide an adequate framework for the treatment of these problems as well.

Before stating what at this point I believe to be the most promising framework for our purpose, I first want to make some remarks on a theory of formal logic which has been often proposed just for the solution of the problems with which I want to deal, viz. multi-valued, or many-valued logic.

Most systems of multi-valued logic available in the literature are systems of propositional calculus. In view of our purpose, our interest should lie with multi-valued predicate logic. But for reasons of exposition I will consider the simpler propositional logics.

Multi-valued logics differ from ordinary two-valued logic in the first place by their model theories. Indeed many such systems are syntactically indistinguishable from standard formulations of ordinary propositional calculus; and I will consider for the time being only such systems of multi-valued logic, all of which have the same syntax, based upon an infinite set $q_1, q_2, q_3, \ldots$ of propositional variables. Starting with these we can recursively construct complex formulae, i.e. $\neg(\phi)$, $\wedge(\phi, \psi)$, $\vee(\phi, \psi)$, $\rightarrow(\phi, \psi)$, $\leftrightarrow(\phi, \psi)$ from already constructed formulae ϕ and ψ. (I will write $(\phi \wedge \psi)$ for $\wedge(\phi, \psi)$, etc.) Let us call this language of propositional logic L_o.

A multi-valued semantics for L_o will provide for this language a model theory based upon some set TV (of 'truth values') the cardinality of which is ≥ 2. Two-valued propositional calculus emerges as a case where TV contains exactly two elements. A *model* for L_o according to such a model theory based upon TV is a function which assigns to each variable q_i an element of TV. Such a function uniquely determines the (truth) values of the complex formulae of L in virtue of another component which specifies for each t_i in TV what the value is of $\neg \phi$ given that t_i is the value of ϕ; for each t_i, t_j in TV what the value is of $(\phi \wedge \psi)$ given that ϕ has t_i and ψ has t_j; and similarly for the other connectives.

The definition of logical truth requires a third component of the theory which singles out a proper non-empty subset TV_t of TV, the set of 'designated' truth values. A formula will be regarded as *logically true* if in each model it has a value belonging to TV_t. *Logical consequence* can be defined in an analogous manner.

Thus we come to the following formal definition:

A *multi-valued model theory* (in short m.m.t.) *for* L_o is a triple $\langle TV, TV_t, F \rangle$ where (i) TV is a set of cardinality ≥ 2;
(ii) TV_t is a proper, non-empty subset of TV;

(iii) F is a function which maps each n-place connective of L_0 onto a n-place function from TV into itself.

A *model for L_0 relative to the m.m.t.* $\langle TV, TV_t, F \rangle$ is a function from $\{q_1, q_2, q_3, \ldots\}$ into TV.

Let $\mathscr{M} = \langle TV, TV_t, F \rangle$. The truth value of a formula ϕ of L_0 in a model M relative to $\mathscr{M}$, $[\phi]_{,\mathscr{M}}$ is defined by the clauses:

(i) $[q_i]_M = M(q_i)$;

(ii) $C(\phi_1, \ldots, \phi_n) [^{\mathscr{M}}_M] = F(C) ([\phi_1]^{\mathscr{M}}_M, \ldots, [\phi_n]^{\mathscr{M}}_M)$ for any n-place connective C of L_0.

ϕ is *logically true in $\mathscr{M}$* iff $[\phi]^{\mathscr{M}}_M \in TV_t$ for all models M relative to $\mathscr{M}$.

Clearly the classical semantics for propositional calculus is the model theory $\langle \{0,1\}, \{1\}, F_c \rangle$ where $F_c(\neg), F_c(\wedge), \ldots \ldots, F_c(\leftrightarrow)$ are the functions defined by the usual two-valued truth tables for these connectives.

It is natural to require of a model theory for L_0 based upon a truth value set of cardinality $\geqslant 2$ that it has the feature:

(10) there are two particular elements of TV – let us call them 0 and 1 – such that

(i) $1 \in TV_t$;

(ii) $0 \notin TV_t$;

and (iii) for each connective C, the restriction of $F(C)$ to $\{0,1\}$ is the usual two-valued truth table for C (i.e. there are among the truth values two, which we might think of as 'absolute falsehood' and 'absolute truth', with respect to which the connectives behave in the ordinary classical manner).

It appears that those model theories for L_0 which have been seriously proposed in the literature do indeed satisfy (10).[1] The vast majority of these theories assume, moreover, a linear ordering of the members of TV with respect to which 0 is the smallest and 1 the largest element. The formal properties of the theory, as well as its philosophical relevance, then depend on the characterization of the functions $F(C)$. Clearly there are, whenever the cardinality of TV is greater than 2, various such functions which do not violate (i). The question is which of these 'correctly capture' the function of the connectives *not, and, or,*...given a particular interpretation of what the truth values in TV really represent. Let us consider the case where $TV = \left\{ 0, \dfrac{1}{n-1}, \dfrac{2}{n-1}, \ldots, \dfrac{n-2}{n-1}, 1 \right\}$ and where these numbers represent 'degrees of truth' – the higher the number the higher the degree.

[1] For references see Rescher (1969).

What function F would adequately reflect our intuitions about the semantic behaviour of these connectives in this case? I think there are no such functions. The reason is that the connectives *not, and, or,*...are not functions of degrees of truth. This becomes evident almost immediately when one reflects upon the definition of $F(\neg)$. The natural suggestion here is that $F(\neg)\left(\dfrac{k}{n-1}\right) = 1 - \dfrac{k}{n-1}$, i.e. that the negation of a proposition is true exactly to the degree that that proposition itself fails to be true. And this indeed is a definition of $F(\neg)$ which is commonly accepted.

Now let us assume that n is odd so that one of the truth values is $\frac{1}{2}$. What value would $F(\wedge)$ assign to the pair of arguments $(\frac{1}{2},\frac{1}{2})$? It is plausible that the value should be $\leqslant \frac{1}{2}$. For how could a conjunction be true to a higher degree than one of its conjuncts? But which value $\leqslant \frac{1}{2}$? $\frac{1}{2}$ seems out because if $[\phi]_M^{\mathcal{M}} = \frac{1}{2}$ then, if we accept our definition of $F(\neg)$, $[\neg\phi]_M^{\mathcal{M}} = \frac{1}{2}$. So we would have $[\phi \wedge \neg\phi]_M^{\mathcal{M}} = \frac{1}{2}$, which seems absurd. For how could a logical contradiction be true to *any* degree? However, if we stipulate that $(F(\wedge))(\frac{1}{2},\frac{1}{2}) = 0$, we are stuck with the even less desirable consequence that if $[\phi]_M^{\mathcal{M}} = \frac{1}{2}$, $[\phi \wedge \phi]_M^{\mathcal{M}} = 0$. And if we choose any number between 0 and $\frac{1}{2}$, we get the wrong values for both $\phi \wedge \neg\phi$ and $\phi \wedge \phi$.[1]

This argument indicates why we cannot represent the connectives accurately within the narrow framework of multi-valued semantics based upon linearly ordered truth-value sets. The reason can be expressed thus: the truth value of a complex formula – say $\phi \wedge \psi$ – should depend not just on the truth values of the components – i.e. ϕ and ψ – but also on certain aspects of these formulae which contribute to their truth values but cannot be unambiguously recaptured from them.

The possibility of treating the connectives truth-functionally in two-valued model theory (while not in model theories based on larger linearly ordered sets of truth values) is a reflection of the fact that two-element sets are the only linearly ordered truth-value sets which can be regarded as Boolean algebras in the following sense:

If we define the Boolean operations $\cap$, $\cup$, $-$ in the usual manner in terms of the ordering relation $\leqslant$ of a linearly ordered set TV (i.e. if we put $C \cap C' = df$ the largest C'' under $\leqslant$ such that $C'' \leqslant C$ and $C'' \leqslant C'$; $C \cup C' = df$ the smallest C'' such that $C \leqslant C''$ and $C' \leqslant C''$; and $\bar{C}$ as the largest C' such that $C \cap C' = \phi$), then, if TV consists of two elements, 0 and 1, we obtain the two-element Boolean algebra $\langle \{0,1\}, \cap, \cup, - \rangle$. But as soon as TV

---

[1] This argument is certainly not new. It can be found e.g. in Rescher (1969). Yet it seems to have failed to discourage people from trying to use multi-valued logic in contexts where the argument shows it to be inadequate.

contains more than two elements the resulting algebra is not a Boolean algebra. In particular the equation $C \cup \bar{C} = 1$ will no longer be satisfied by all elements C.

3.

This last observation suggests in which direction a solution to our difficulty might be found: we should choose as truth-value sets not linear orderings, but rather sets which, like the two-valued system, display the structure of the propositional calculus, viz. Boolean algebras. We may then, if we want to, further 'reduce' these Boolean algebras to linearly ordered systems; in this reduction different Boolean values may be assigned the same element of the linear ordering. But this will no longer affect our semantic characterization of the connectives, as these will now be defined in the Boolean truth-value space and thus not directly on the linearly ordered, 'ultimate' truth values themselves. It may now happen that even if ϕ and ψ have the same ultimate value, $\phi \cap \chi$ has a different ultimate value from that of $\psi \cap \chi$ (viz. in certain cases where the Boolean values of ϕ and ψ which reduce to the same ultimate value are nevertheless distinct).

This idea is by now quite familiar to logicians. Yet it is surprising that its use for the specific problems with which we are here concerned occurred as late as it did; for there is a branch of mathematics, viz. probability theory, in which it has been accepted as the standard solution to what is in many ways the same problem as the one we are facing here. I am referring to the theory of probability in the definitive mathematical form that Kolmogorov (1970) gave it in the 1930s. In this theory one associates with a proposition in first instance a certain set. With this set is associated in turn a real number in the closed interval [0:1]. This number gives the probability of the proposition. Now while the set associated with the conjunction of two propositions is a simple function of the sets associated with the conjuncts, viz. their intersection, there is no way of telling in general the probability of the conjunction on the basis of just the probabilities of the conjuncts; and this is as it should be, for when p and q each have probability $\frac{1}{2}$, the probability of $p \wedge q$ could, intuitively, be anything between 0 and $\frac{1}{2}$.

Perhaps the main philosophical problem which this approach raises is that of giving a plausible interpretation of the sets with which propositions are associated. I will consider here only one doctrine, according to which the elements of the sets are regarded as possible worlds, or possible situations. Thus the probability of a proposition is measured in terms of the set of those possible worlds in which it is true. Seen in this light, probability theory is closely connected with the possible-world semantics for modal and other types of non-extensional logic. Both theories associate with a given sentence in any particular interpretation a set (of possible worlds, points of reference, contexts, etc.).

Of course, probability theory and intensional logic are concerned with different sorts of problems. In intensional logic we are primarily concerned with the analysis, in terms of the set of all possible 'worlds' (as well as, perhaps, various structural properties of this set), of the semantical function of certain non-truth functional operators, such as *it is necessarily the case that*. In probability theory one does not consider such intensional operators, but concentrates on the probability function which associates real numbers with the sets, and investigates how the probabilities of certain complex expressions depend on the probabilities of their components – often under certain assumptions about these components, such as independence or disjointness.

There is another theory of formal semantics which fits within the general frame which we are now discussing, viz. the theory of partial interpretations and supervaluations. This theory is, in its simplest form, a generalization of ordinary two-valued model theory, which allows for the possibility that in a given interpretation for a certain formal language (say, of ordinary first order logic with description operator) some sentences of the language are neither true nor false. Yet, in order to avoid the – from a certain standpoint undesirable – consequence that whenever p is without truth value, so are, among others, $p \wedge \neg p$ and $p \vee \neg p$, one considers the collection of all interpretations which extend the given interpretation by filling out its truth gaps in a consistent manner. If a formula comes out true in each of these completions it will be regarded as true in the interpretation even if it is not assigned a truth value directly by the (incomplete) recursive definition of truth. Similarly it will be counted as false in the interpretation if it is false in each of its completions.

One may view this process again as one of assigning, in a given interpretation, sets to sentences: to each sentence is assigned the set of all completions in which it is true. Sentences already true in the given interpretation, and also such sentences as $p \vee \neg p$ where p itself is not assigned a truth value directly, will be assigned the set of all completions, those already false as well as sentences such as $p \wedge \neg p$ will be assigned the empty set; only sentences which neither have a truth value in virtue of the recursive truth definition nor have the form of a logical identity or contradiction may be assigned intermediate sets.

The theory, which was first introduced by Van Fraassen (1969) suggests in what way the framework under discussion might be used in an analysis of vagueness. Vagueness is one of the various reasons why certain sentences may be without truth value. Thus if we regard the world, or any specific speech situation in it, as providing an interpretation for English, what it provides is at best a *partial* interpretation.[1] For such a partial interpretation we may consider the various completions in which all instances of vagueness are resolved in one way or another. The quantity of such completions in which a certain sentence is true ought then to be in some sense a measure for the degree to which the sentence is true in the original interpretation. Such considerations would of course apply not only to adjectives but to other parts of speech as well, in particular to those grammatical categories which, like adjectives, are usually treated as 1-place predicates in simple-minded predicate-logic-symbolizations of English sentences, viz. common nouns and intransitive verbs. (I will later try to say something about systematic differences between the semantic behaviour of adjectives and that of these other two categories.)

These considerations naturally lead to a modification of the model theory for formal or natural languages which I will exemplify for a rather simple case, viz. first order predicate logic. The example will make it clear enough how one could adapt in a similar fashion more complicated model theories – such as those for intensional logics or for fragments of natural languages.

Let us consider the language L for predicate logic, the logical symbols of which are $\neg$, $\wedge$, $\exists$, and the variables v_1 v_2, v_3,..., and the non-logical symbols of which are the n-place predicate letters Q_i^n ($n = 1,2,3,...$; $i = 1,2,3,...$).

A *classical model for* L is a pair $\langle U,F \rangle$ where (i) U is a non-empty set and (ii) F assigns to each Q_i^n an n-place relation on U.

The *satisfaction value of* a formula ϕ of L *in* $M = \langle U,F \rangle$ *by* an assignment a of elements of U to the variables (in symbols $[\phi]_{M,a}$) is defined by the usual recursion:

(i) $[Q_i^n (v_{i_1}...v_{i_n})]_{M,a} = 1$ iff $\langle a(v_{i_1}),...,a(v_{i_n}) \rangle \in F(Q_i^n)$

(ii) $[\neg\phi]_{M,a} = 1$ iff $[\phi]_{M,a} = 0$

(iii) $[\phi \wedge \psi]_{M,a} = 1$ iff $[\phi]_{M,a} = 1$ and $[\psi]_{M,a} = 1$

(iv) $[(\exists v_i)\phi]_{M,a} = 1$ if for some $u \in U$ $[\phi]_{M,[a]_{v_i}^u} = 1$

---

[1] Of course there are other factors whose effect is that a situation of speech will in general determine only a partial interpretation; for example, many predicates are not applicable to individuals of certain kinds – and yet not every statement which attributes a predicate to such a semantically improper object should be regarded as illformed. Such other sources of interpretational incompleteness, however, will here not concern us.

A sentence ϕ of L is *true in M* if $[\phi]_{M,a} = 1$ for some a.

For any model M, Tr_M will be the set of sentences of L which are true in M and Fa_M, the set of sentences of L false in M.

A *partial model* for L is a pair $\langle U,F \rangle$ where (i) U is a non-empty set and (ii) F assigns to each letter Q_i^n an ordered pair $\langle F^+(Q_i^n),F^-(Q_i^n) \rangle$ of disjoint n-place-relations on U.

N.B. I will assume throughout that M is a model and is of the form $\langle U,F \rangle$.

The *satisfaction value* of a formula ϕ in M by an assignment a is now defined by:

(i) (a) $[Q_i^n(v_{j_1},\ldots,v_{j_n})]_{M,a} = 1$ if $\langle a(v_{j_1}),\ldots,a(v_{j_n}) \rangle \in F^+(Q_i^n)$

   (b) $[Q_i^n(v_{j_1},\ldots,v_{j_n})]_{M,a} = 0$ if $\langle a(v_{j_1}),\ldots,a(v_{j_n}) \rangle \in F^-(Q_i^n)$

(ii) (a) $[\neg\phi]_{M,a} = 1$ if $[\phi]_{M,a} = 0$

   (b) $[\neg\phi]_{M,a} = 0$ if $[\phi]_{M,a} = 1$

(iii) (a) $[\phi \wedge \psi]_{M,a} = 1$ if $[\phi]_{M,a} = 1$ and $[\psi]_{M,a} = 1$

   (b) $[\phi \wedge \psi]_{M,a} = 0$ if $[\phi]_{M,a} = 0$ or $[\psi]_{M,a} = 0$

(iv) (a) $[(\exists v_i)\phi]_{M,a} = 1$ if for some $u \in U$ $[\phi]_{M,[a]_{v_i}^u} = 1$

   (b) $[(\exists v_i)\phi]_{M,a} = 0$ if for all $u \in U$ $[\phi]_{M,[a]_{v_i}^u} = 0$

Again a sentence ϕ is said to be *true in M* if $[\phi]_{M,a} = 1$ for some a; and ϕ is *false in M* if for some a $[\phi]_{M,a} = 0$

Again Tr_M is the set of true, and Fa_M the set of false sentences of L in M. But now it is clearly possible that certain sentences are neither true nor false in M, so that $Tr_M \cup Fa_M$ does not coincide with the set of all sentences of L.

The partial model $M = \langle U,F \rangle$ is said to be *at least as vague as* the partial model $M' = \langle U,F' \rangle$ (in symbols: $M \subseteq M'$) if for each Q_i^n:

$$F^+(Q_i^n) \subseteq F'^+(Q_i^n) \text{ and } F^-(Q_i^n) \subseteq F'^-(Q_i^n)$$

(Thus $Tr_M \cup Fa_M \subseteq Tr_{M'} \cup Fa_{M'}$.)

To each classical model $\langle U,F \rangle$ for L corresponds a unique partial model, viz. the model $\langle U,F' \rangle$ where for each Q_i^n, $F'^+(Q_i^n) = F(Q_i^n)$ and $F'^-(Q_i^n) = U^n - F(Q_i^n)$. Classical models, as well as the partial models corresponding to them, will be referred to as *complete* models.

A classical model M is called a *completion* of a partial model M' if M' is at least as vague as (the partial model corresponding to) M.

4.

In the theory of supervaluation one considers partial models in conjunction with *all* their completions. What I want to do here is formally almost the same – but with one crucial exception. Rather than all completions of a given partial model, we consider only a certain subset of them. In addition we consider a probability function over a field of subsets of this set of completions,[1] which contains, in particular, for each formula and assignment of elements to its free variables the set of all completions in which the former satisfies that assignment. (This condition warrants that each sentence has a measure.) The complex consisting of the partial model, the set of completions, the field over that set and the probability function over that field I will call a *vague model*. Formally

A *vague model for L* is a quadruple $\langle M, \mathscr{S}, \mathscr{F}, p \rangle$ where
   (i) M is a partial model for L;
   (ii) $\mathscr{S}$ is a set of classical models for L which are completions of M;
   (iii) $\mathscr{F}$ is a field of subsets over $\mathscr{S}$
   (iv) for each $\phi \in L$ and assignment a in the universe of M, $\{M' \in \mathscr{S}: [\phi]_{M',a} = 1\} \in \mathscr{F}$; and
   (v) p is a probability measure on $\mathscr{F}$.[2]

Let $\mathscr{M} = \langle \langle U, F \rangle, \mathscr{S}, \mathscr{F}, p \rangle$ be a vague model for L. For any formula ϕ of L and assignment a of elements of U to the variables the *degree of satisfaction of ϕ by a in $\mathscr{M}$*, $[\phi]_{\mathscr{M},a}$, is defined as $p(\{M' \in \mathscr{S}: [\phi]_{M',a} = 1\})$. Thus, in particular, if $\phi \in Tr_M$ then $[\phi]_{\mathscr{M}} = 1$ and if $\phi \in Fa_M$ then $[\phi]_{\mathscr{M}} = 0$.

The idea behind the notion of a vague model is this. At the present stage of its development – indeed, at any stage – language is vague. The kind of vagueness which interests us here is connected with predicates. The vagueness of a predicate may be resolved by fiat – i.e. by deciding which of the objects which as yet are neither definitely inside nor definitely outside

[1] A *field of subsets* of a given set X (or: a *field over X*) is a set of subsets of X, such that (i) $X \in \mathscr{F}$; (ii) $\Phi \in \mathscr{F}$; (iii) if $Y, Y' \in \mathscr{F}$ then $Y \cap Y'$, $X - Y \in \mathscr{F}$.

A *probability function over* a field $\mathscr{F}$ over X is a function p whose domain is $\mathscr{F}$, whose range is included in the real interval $[0,1]$, and which has the properties: (i) $p(X) = 1$; (ii) if $Y \in \mathscr{F}$, then $p(X - Y) = 1 - p(Y)$; and (iii) if $\mathscr{G}$ is a countable subset of $\mathscr{F}$ such that (a) whenever $Y, Y' \in \mathscr{G}$ and $Y \not\equiv Y'$ then $Y \cap Y' = \Phi$; and (b) $\cup \mathscr{G} \in \mathscr{F}$; then $p(\cup \mathscr{G}) = \sum_{Y \in \mathscr{G}} p(Y)$.

[2] From the mathematical point of view this notion is unproblematic only if the universe U is finite. In that case we do not really need to require that p satisfy the condition (iii) of n. 1, but only the weaker condition obtained by replacing the word *countable* in (iii) by *finite*. (iii) is necessary when U is denumerable; in that case, however, as well as when U is uncountable, it may happen that no intuitively correct models exist. The only way in which I can see how to cope with these cases involves non-standard analyses. I do not want to go into this here.

its extension are to be in and which are to be out. However, it may be that not every such decision is acceptable. For there may already be semantical principles which, though they do not determine of any one of a certain group of objects whether it belongs to the extension or not, nevertheless demand that if a certain member of the group is put into the extension, a certain other member must be put into the extension as well. Take for example the adjective *intelligent.* Our present criteria tell us of certain people that they definitely are intelligent, of certain others that they definitely are not, but there will be a large third category of people about whom they do not tell us either way. Now suppose that we make our standard more specific, e.g., by stipulating that to have an I.Q. over a certain minimum is a necessary and sufficient criterion for being intelligent. Further, suppose that of two persons u_1 and u_2 of the third category u_1 has a higher I.Q. than u_2. Then, whatever we decide this minimum to be, our decision will put u_1 into the extension if it puts u_2 into it. Finally, let us assume for the sake of argument that any way of making the concept of intelligence precise that is compatible with what we already understand that concept to be is equivalent to the adoption of a certain minimum I.Q. Then there will be no completions in the partial model that reflect the present state of affairs and in which u_2 is put into the extension of the predicate but u_1 is not.

Formally, if Q_1^l represents the adjective *intelligent* and the model $\langle M, \mathscr{S}, \mathscr{F}, p \rangle$ reflects the situation just described, and M, in particular, that which obtains before any of the possible precise definitions has been adopted, then u_1 and u_2 are both members of $U - (F^+(Q_1^l) \cup F^-(Q_1^l))$ and there is no model $M' \in \mathscr{S}$ such that $u_2 \in F(Q_1)$ and $u_1 \notin F(Q_1)$.

My original motivation in setting up this framework was to give a uniform characterization of the operation which transforms adjectives into their comparatives. Let us see if this is now possible.

The relation *x is more A than y* (where A is any adjective) can be defined in terms of the relation *x is at least as A as y* by

(11) *x is more A than y* if and only if *x is at least as A as y* and it is not the case that *y is at least as A as x*

Therefore a semantic characterization of this second relation will automatically give us one for the first as well. As there are minor but undeniable advantages in discussing the relation *at least as...as* I will concentrate on that concept.

Let us assume that some of the one-place predicates of L represent adjectives, in particular Q_j^l. We add to L the operator symbol $\geqslant$. $\geqslant$ forms out of one one-place predicate Q_i^l a two-place relation $\geqslant(Q_i^l)$. $\geqslant(Q_i^l)(x,y)$ should be read as x *is at least as* Q_i^l *as* y. (What relation $\geqslant(Q_i^l)$ might represent when Q_i^l is not an adjective is of no concern to us now.) Let L' be the language resulting from the addition of $\geqslant$ to L. Let $\mathcal{M} = \langle M, \mathcal{S}, \mathcal{F}, p \rangle$ be a vague model for L. In order to expand $\mathcal{M}$ to a model for L' we must determine the positive and negative extensions of the relation $\geqslant(Q_i^l)$ in M as well as its extensions in all the members of $\mathcal{S}$. To begin we will consider just the positive extension in M. Two possible definitions come to mind. According to the first an element u_1 of U stands (definitely) in the relation to u_2 if for every member M' of $\mathcal{S}$ in which u_2 belongs to the extension of Q_i^l u_1 belongs to that extension as well. So we get, representing the positive extension of $\geqslant(Q_i^l)$ in M as $F^+(\geqslant(Q_i^l))$,

(12) for all $u_1, u_2 \in U$, $\langle u_1, u_2 \rangle \in F^+(\geqslant(Q_i^l))$ iff $[Q_i^l(v_1)]_{\mathcal{M},a_2} \subseteq [Q_i^l(v_1)]_{\mathcal{M},a_1}$ (where a_1 and a_2 are any assignments with $a_1(v_1) = u_1$ and $a_2(v_1) = u_2$, respectively)

According to the second definition u_1 stands in the relation to u_2 if the measure of the set of completions in which u_1 belongs to the extension of Q_i^l is at least as large as that of the set of completions in which u_2 belongs to the extension. So we obtain

(13) for all $u_1, u_2 \in U$, $\langle u_1, u_2 \rangle \in F^+(\geqslant(Q_i^l))$ iff $p([Q_i^l(v_1)]_{\mathcal{M},a_2}) \leqslant p([Q_i^l(v_1)]_{\mathcal{M},a_1})$ where a_1 and a_2 are as above

Before we consider the relative merits of these definitions let us first remove a flaw which they share. Neither (12) nor (13) allows for the possibility that the comparative relation holds between two objects for each of which it is beyond doubt that it satisfies the positive. For if both u_1 and u_2 belong to $F^+(Q_i^l)$ then $[Q_i^l(v_1)]_{M,a_1} = [Q_i^l(v_1)]_{M,a_2} = 1$ and so both (12) and (13) would exclude $\langle u_1, u_2 \rangle$ from $F^+(\geqslant(Q_i^l))$.

It seems that the only way in which we could meet this difficulty without departing too much from our present format is this: Instead of a vague model, consisting of a partial model M, a field $\mathcal{F}$ over a set $\mathcal{S}$ of completions of M and a probability function p over that field, we need to consider models $\mathcal{M}$, in which the set $\mathcal{S}$ comprises besides completions of M also complete models which in certain ways conflict with M. Such models will represent (hypothetical) situations in which the standards for a predicate are set so high that certain objects which already have that predicate in M now fail to have it – or else in which the standards are set so low that objects belonging to the negative extension of the predicate in M now fall in its positive extension. This leads us to the following modification of the notion of a vague model:

A *graded model for L* is a quadruple $\langle M, \mathcal{S}, \mathcal{F}, p \rangle$, where

(i) M is a partial model for L

(ii) $\mathcal{S}$ is a set of classical models for L with universe U

(iii) $\mathcal{F}$ is a field over $\mathcal{S}$

(iv) For each formula ϕ of L and each assignment a to elements of the universe of M, $\{M' \in \mathcal{S} : [\phi]_{M',a} = 1\} \in \mathcal{F}$

(v) $\{M' \in \mathcal{S} : M' \text{ is a completion of } M\} \in \mathcal{F}$; and

(vi) p is a probability function over $\mathcal{F}$.

We may then define the degree of truth of a sentence of L just as before except that we now consider the conditional probability of a certain set of completions of M on the set of all completions of M in $\mathcal{S}$. On the other hand the characterization (13) of the comparative of Q_i^1 is now no longer vulnerable to the objection which led us to the introduction of graded models.

Let us consider an example. Suppose that Q_1^1 represents the adjective *heavy*; that all other predicates represent properties of, and relations between, material objects, and (for simplicity) that Q_1^1 is the only vague predicate. Let U be the set of material objects and let $\mathcal{M} = \langle M, \mathcal{S}, \mathcal{F}, p \rangle$ be a graded representation (restricted to material objects) of the actual world. What should in this case $\mathcal{S}$ and p be? As regards $\mathcal{S}$ a simple answer seems possible in this special case: For each particular real number r there will be a member M of $\mathcal{S}$ in which the extension of Q_1^1 consists of those objects whose weight (in grams) exceeds r.

It is not possible to say precisely what the function p should be. But this much seems beyond doubt: there should be a strictly monotonic function f from the set of all positive real numbers into the interval $[0,1]$ so that for any object u with weight r, $p([Q_1^1(v_1)]_{\mathcal{M},a} = f(r)$ (for some a with $a(v_1) = u$). Thus, the greater u's weight, the larger the class of members of $\mathcal{S}$ in which Q_1^1 is true of u, and the greater the measure (or 'intermediate truth value') of the formula $Q_1^1(v)$ under a_1.

5.

We should now compare (12) and (13). According to (12) u_1 is at least as heavy as u_2 just in case the set of models in which u_1 *is heavy* is true includes the class of those which render u_2 *is heavy* true; and this will be the case if and only if u_1 has greater or equal weight. Indeed, within the context of the present example, (12) is precisely the proposal that can be found in Lewis (1970), where it is attributed to David Kaplan.

According to (13) u_1 will be at least as heavy as u_2, provided u_2 *is heavy* is true in a set of models with measure greater than or equal to that of the set of models in which u_2 *is heavy* is true. Again this will be true if and only if u_1 has greater or equal weight. Thus for this special case the two definitions are equivalent.

But this need not always be so. Suppose for example that Smith, though less quick-witted than Jones, is much better at solving mathematical problems. Is Smith cleverer than Jones? This is perhaps not clear, for we usually regard quick-wittedness and problem-solving facility as indications of cleverness, without a canon for weighing these criteria against each other when they suggest different answers. When faced with the need to decide the issue, various options may be open to us. We might decide that really only problem-solving counts, so that after all, Smith is cleverer than Jones; or we might decide on a particular method for weighing the two criteria – so that Smith's vast superiority at solving problems will warrant that in spite of Jones's slight edge in quick-wittedness Smith is cleverer than Jones; or we might decide that only quick-wittedness counts; and this time Jones will come out as the cleverer of the two.

It is not clear how the probability function of a graded model $\mathcal{M}$ representing this situation should be defined. Yet, if we assume that the third decision is less plausible than either the first or the second, then we should expect members of $\mathcal{S}$ which are compatible with that decision to have no more weight than those which are compatible with other decisions. Further, relatively few models of the first sort will be such that Jones belongs to the extension of *clever* and Smith not; for Jones is not that much quicker in conversation. But, because of the disparity in problem-solving ability, many models compatible with the first decision, as well as a good many that are compatible with the second, will have Smith in the extension of *clever* but not Jones. Given all this, we would expect the measure of the set of members of $\mathcal{S}$ in which Smith belongs to the extension to be greater than that of those members where Jones belongs to the extension. So by (13) and (11) we would have to conclude that Smith is cleverer than Jones.

But do we want to say this? I think not. Before any decision has been made it is true neither that Smith is cleverer than Jones nor that Jones is cleverer than Smith. This intuitive judgement is in agreement with (12), according to which Jones and Smith are incomparable in respect of cleverness. Indeed, it is (12) which, in my opinion, captures the comparative correctly – at least to the extent that it gives a necessary and sufficient condition for *definite* membership in the positive extension of $\geq(Q_l^i)$. That (13) cannot be right becomes even more evident when we realize that it implies that for any objects u_1 and u_2 and adjective A, either u_1 is at least as A as u_2 or u_2 is at least as A as u_1; and this should fail to be true in general whenever we have two, largely independent, criteria for applicability of the adjective, but no clear procedure for weighing them.

We saw that for *heavy* (12) and (13) are equivalent (provided p has been correctly specified). The same is true for a number of other adjectives which, like *heavy*, may be called 'one-dimensional'. With each such adjective is associated a unique measurable aspect. The (numerical) value of that aspect for a given object determines whether or not the adjective applies. For *heavy* the aspect is weight. Other examples are *tall* (associated with height) and *hot* (associated with temperature).

But such adjectives are rare. Even *large* is not one of them. For what precisely makes an object large? Its height? or its volume? or its surface? or a combination of some of these? Here we encounter the same phenomenon that has already been revealed by our discussion of *clever*. There is no fixed procedure for integrating the various criteria. Often it is the context of use which indicates how the criteria should be integrated or, alternatively, which of them should be taken as uniquely relevant.

This is one of the various ways in which contexts disambiguate. Formally, contextual disambiguation can be represented as a function from contexts to models less vague than the ground model. While incorporating this idea into the framework already adopted, I will at the same time eliminate a feature of vague and graded models which is unrealistic in any case but would be particularly out of place in the context-dependent models defined below: Thus far I have assumed that all the members of $\mathscr{S}$ are complete models. But this is unnatural if we want to think of these models as the results of semantical decisions that could actually be made. For most decisions will fail to render the relevant predicates completely sharp. They will only make them sharper. (Indeed, we may with Wittgenstein, doubt that we could ever make any concept completely sharp.) It therefore appears more natural to posit that the members of $\mathscr{S}$ are partial models. It is possible, moreover, that one of these contextually determined models is less vague than another, viz. when, intuitively speaking, the semantic decision reflected by the second goes in the same direction, but not as far as, that reflected by the first. Thus $\mathscr{S}$ will be partially ordered by the relation *as vague as*.

I just suggested that a context picks from this set a particular model – which functions, so to speak, as the ground model of the graded model which represents the speech situation determined by that context. The various sharpenings acceptable from the viewpoint of that context would then be represented by those members of $\mathscr{S}$ which are at most as vague as the new ground model. But I am not convinced that this is absolutely correct. For it could conceivably be the case that two different contexts specify for a given predicate two different criteria from the set of those which are prima facie plausible and which, though they happen to determine the same new ground model, will not permit exactly the same further sharpenings. So the context should select a certain subset of $\mathscr{S}$ of contextually admissible further sharpenings. In addition, the context must select a subset of admissible modifications. This set we could not even hope to reconstruct from the new ground model alone.

Thus far the probability function p was defined over a class of complete models. This would now seem to be impossible as we no longer require that $\mathscr{S}$ consists of – or even that it contains any – complete models. Yet the intuition behind the function p – which I tried to convey in the example concerning *heavy* – makes it appear unnatural to define p as a function over sets of *partial* models, especially as these sets may now be expected to contain models one of which is vaguer than the other; it is, so to speak, the number of possible *ultimate* results of repeated sharpening that p should measure, and not, the number of intermediate steps that one may take on the way to these ultimate complete models.

A solution to this dilemma can be found if we assume that all individual cases of vagueness can be resolved, though not all at once; and this assumption does appear to be unexceptionable. Thus we will impose on the set $\mathscr{S}$ the following condition:

(14) if $\langle U, F_1 \rangle \in \mathscr{S}$ and $\langle u_1, \ldots, u_n \rangle \in U^n - (F_1{}^+(Q_i^n) \cup F_1{}^-(Q_i^n))$, then there is a member $\langle U, F_2 \rangle$ in which Q_i^n is less vague than $\langle U, F_1 \rangle$ and such that $\langle u_1, \ldots, u_n \rangle \in F_2{}^+(Q_i^n) \cup F_2{}^-(Q_i^n)$.

Under this assumption we may construct complete models as the unions of maximal chains in $\mathscr{S}$: Let $\mathscr{S}$ be a set of partial models for L which all have the same universe U. Then $\mathscr{S}$ is a *chain under the relation 'vaguer than'* if for any two of its members $\langle U, F_1 \rangle$, $\langle U, F_2 \rangle$ either

(i) for each predicate Q_j^n of L, $F_1{}^+(Q_j^n) \subseteq F_2{}^+(Q_j^n)$ and $F_1{}^-(Q_j^n) \subseteq F_2{}^-(Q_j^n)$ or

(ii) for each predicate Q_j^n of L, $F_2{}^+(Q_j^n) \subseteq F_1{}^+(Q_j^n)$ and $F_2{}^-(Q_j^n) \subseteq F_1{}^-(Q_j^n)$.

A subset $\mathcal{S}'$ of a set $\mathcal{S}$ of models with universe U, is a *maximal chain in $\mathcal{S}$* if (i) $\mathcal{S}'$ is a chain (under the relation *vaguer than*) and (ii) for any $M' \in \mathcal{S} - \mathcal{S}'$, $\mathcal{S}' \cup \{M'\}$ is not a chain. The *union of* a chain $\mathcal{S}$ of models with universe U is the model $\langle U, F_\infty \rangle$ where for each $Q_j^n F_\infty{}^+(Q_j^n) =$

$$\underset{\langle U,F \rangle \in \mathcal{S}}{\cup} F^+(Q_j^n) \text{ and } F_\infty(Q_j^n) = \underset{\langle U,F \rangle \in \mathcal{S}}{\cup} F(Q_j^n)$$

If U is countable then (14) entails that

(15) The union of each maximal chain of $\mathcal{S}$ is complete

However, (15) does not follow automatically from (14) when U is uncountable. Since it is property (15) in which we are primarily interested in connection with the function p, I will make it, rather than (14), one of the defining conditions of graded context-dependent models.

A *graded context-dependent model for L* is a quintuple $\langle M, \mathcal{S}, \mathcal{C}, \mathcal{F}, p \rangle$ where

(i) M is a partial model;

(ii) $\mathcal{S}$ is a set of partial models with the same universe as M;

(iii) The union of each maximal chain of $\mathcal{S}$ is complete;

(iv) $\mathcal{C}$ is a function the range of which consists of pairs $\langle M', \mathcal{S}' \rangle$ where (a) $M' \in \mathcal{S}$; (b) $\mathcal{S}' \subseteq \mathcal{S}$ and (c) the union of each maximal chain of $\mathcal{S}'$ is complete;

(v) $\mathcal{F}$ is a field over the set $\overline{\mathcal{S}}$ of unions of maximal chains of $\mathcal{S}$;

(vi) (a) for each formula ϕ and assignment a the set of members M' of $\mathcal{S}$ such that $[\phi]_{M',a} = 1$ belongs to $\overline{\mathcal{S}}$; (b) $\{M' \in \overline{\mathcal{S}}: M \subseteq M'\} \in \mathcal{F}$; (c) for each $\langle M', \mathcal{S}' \rangle$ in the range of $\mathcal{C}$ if $\overline{\mathcal{S}}'$ is the set of unions of maximal chains of $\mathcal{S}'$ then $\{M'' \in \overline{\mathcal{S}}': M' \subseteq M''\} \in \mathcal{F}$;

(vii) p is a probability function over $\mathcal{F}$.

We will refer to context-dependent graded models by means of the abbreviation cgm. Henceforth $\mathcal{M}$ will always be a cgm and will always be equal to $\langle M, \mathcal{S}, \mathcal{C}, \mathcal{F}, p \rangle$; M will be called the *ground model* of $\mathcal{M}$; similarly if $\mathcal{C}(c) = \langle M'_c, \mathcal{S}'_c \rangle$ then M'_c is called the *ground model* (in $\mathcal{M}$) *with respect to c*.

Again we denote the set of members of $\overline{\mathcal{S}}$ in which ϕ is true under a as $[\phi]_{\mathcal{M},a}$, where $\overline{\mathcal{S}}$ is again the set of unions of maximal chains of $\mathcal{S}$.

Similarly, if $\mathscr{C}(c) = \langle M_c, \mathscr{S}_c \rangle$, $[\phi]_{\mathcal{M},c,a}$ is the set of members of $\overline{\mathscr{S}}_c$ in which ϕ is true under a.

The domain of $\mathscr{C}$ should be thought of as the set of contexts. Contexts may be more or less specific; correspondingly Dom $\mathscr{C}$ may contain elements c and c' such that $M_c \leqslant M_{c'}$ and $\mathscr{S}_c \subseteq \mathscr{S}_{c'}$; in this case c will be at least as specific as c'. Thus the members of Dom $\mathscr{C}$ are partially ordered by the relation $\leqslant$, defined by: $c \leqslant c'$ iff $M_c \subseteq M_{c'}$ and $\mathscr{S}_c \subseteq \mathscr{S}_{c'}$. One may wonder if for every member M' of $\mathscr{S}$ there should be a c such that M' is the ground model with respect to c. This would mean that for any possible sharpening of a predicate there is a context which indicates that the predicate should be understood in precisely *that* sharper way. I have no argument to show that this assumption is false; yet I see no gain from it; thus I prefer not to make it.

In a cgm it is possible that while the relation $\geqslant (Q^I)$ does not hold in the ground model it does hold in the ground models of certain contexts. Thus assume Q_I^I represents the adjective *clever*; further assume that c_1 represents a context in which *clever* must be understood as '*good at solving problems*'; that c_2 represents a context in which *clever* must be understood as '*quick-witted*'; and that c_3 represents a context on which both quick-wittedness and the ability to solve problems are to be regarded as constitutive of cleverness. Then we may expect that if $a_1(v_1) = $ Smith and $a_2(v_1) = $ Jones,

(a) $[Q_I^I(v_1)]_{\mathcal{M},c_1,a_2} \subseteq [Q_I^I(v_1)]_{\mathcal{M},c_1,a_1}$; and

(b) $[Q_I^I(v_1)]_{\mathcal{M},c_2,a_1} \subseteq [Q_I^I(v_2)]_{\mathcal{M},c_2,a_2}$

while nothing definite can be said about the relation between $[Q_1(v_1)]_{\mathcal{M},c_3,a}$ and $[Q_I^I(v_1)]_{\mathcal{M},c_3,a_2}$ until more is known about whether, and in what way, c_3 determines how the two criteria for *clever* are to be weighed. In order that (a) and (b) formally guarantee that in c_1 Smith is cleverer than Jones, while in c_2 Jones is cleverer than Smith, we must specify, parallel to (13)

(16) if $\mathscr{C}(c) = \langle \langle U, F_c \rangle, \mathscr{S}_c \rangle$ and $u_1, u_2 \in U$ then $\langle u_1, u_2 \rangle \in F_c^+(\geqslant (Q_i^I))$ if and only if $[Q_i^I(v_1)]_{\mathcal{M},c,a_2} \subseteq [Q_i^I(v_1)]_{\mathcal{M},c,a_1}$.

Since not every member of $\mathscr{S}$ is necessarily the ground model with respect to some context, (16) may not define the positive extension of $\geqslant (Q_i^I)$ for some of these models. This is of little practical importance. If we insist on defining the extensions in these models as well, we may stipulate that for any such model $\langle U, F \rangle$, $\langle u_1, u_2 \rangle \in F_1^+(\geqslant Q_i^I))$ if and only if for some $c, \mathscr{C}(c) = \langle M_c, \mathscr{S}_c \rangle$, $\langle U, F_1 \rangle \in \mathscr{S}_c$, $M_c \subseteq \langle U, F_1 \rangle$ and $\langle u_1, u_2 \rangle \in F_c^+(\geqslant (Q_i^I))$.

What is the negative extension of $\geqslant(Q_i^l)$? It should consist in the first place of those pairs $\langle u_1, u_2 \rangle$ of which it is definitely true that u_2 is more Q_i^l than u_1, i.e. in view of (12), those pairs for which

(17) $[Q_i^l(v_1)]_{\mathcal{M},a_1} \subsetneq [Q_i^l(v_1)]_{\mathcal{M},a_2}$.

One might question this condition on the ground that it makes u_2 *is more Q_i^l than u_1* definitely true also when the difference between u_1 and u_2 is only marginal. But I do not believe that the objection is well-founded. However marginal the difference, if it is a difference in an aspect which is irrevocably bound to the predicate, so that no context can break this tie, then the relation definitely obtains irrespective of whether it is difficult, or even physically impossible, to observe this.

This leaves us with those pairs $\langle u_1, u_2 \rangle$ such that neither $[Q_i^l(v_1)]_{\mathcal{M},a_1} \subseteq [Q_i^l(v_1)]_{\mathcal{M},a_2}$ nor $[Q_i^l(v_1)]_{\mathcal{M},a_2} \subseteq [Q_i^l(v_1)]_{\mathcal{M},a_1}$. Which of these should go into $F^-(\geqslant(Q_i^l))$? I think none. As long as there are some acceptable ways of sharpening Q_i^l which render u_1 at least as Q_i^l as u_2, the falsehood of u_1 *is at least as Q_i^l as u_2* cannot be definite.

I introduced the probability function to show how the notion of 'degrees of truth' can be made coherent. But so far the function has served to no good purpose. In particular it has proved useless for the characterization of the comparative: once more it turned out to be necessary to define the operation on the sets themselves rather than on the numerical values to which p reduces them.

However, there are expressions the analysis of which does seem to require the function p. Consider *rather*. *Rather* forms adjectives out of adjectives, e.g. *rather tall* out of *tall*, *rather clever* out of *clever*, etc. When is a person rather clever? Before I can discuss the really important aspects of this question, I should first settle a minor point. *x is rather clever* sometimes seems to deny that x is clever, while on other occasions it appears to be entailed by the fact that x is clever – just as e.g. *most x are F* sometimes seems to entail *not all x are F*, while on other occasions it seems to be entailed by *all x are F*. I think that both cases, as well as a great many similar ones, ask for an explanation involving Grice's theory of implicature: *most x are F* is a consequence of *all x are F*; but when uttered by a speaker whom the hearer assumes to know whether all x are F, it will convey that not all x are F – for if all x were F, why would not the speaker have said so? Similarly, *rather clever* is weaker than *clever*. But one would use the longer phrase only if one had doubts that the shorter applies.

Thus *x is rather clever* is weaker than *x is clever*. *x* is rather clever if a certain lowering of the standards for cleverness would make *x* clever, i.e. if the proportion of members of $\mathscr{S}$ in which *x* belongs to the extension of *clever* is large enough. Indeed the closer *x* is to being truly clever, the smaller is the modification of the standards that is required, and thus the larger will be the class of those models where *x* is in the extension.

It should be noted that just as *x* may pass the test of cleverness for different reasons, so he may also pass that of being rather clever in a variety of ways. Thus it is possible that *x*, *y* and *z* are all rather clever (though not unambiguously clever); *x*, because he is remarkably quick-witted, while hopeless at mathematical problems; *y*, because he is good at such problems, though slow in conversation; and *z*, because he has both capacities to a moderate degree. For any two of *x*, *y*, *z*, there will be certain modifications of standards which will warrant membership in the extension of *clever* for one but not for the other. Thus it will be true of the set of members of $\mathscr{S}$ in which, say, *x* is in the extension of clever and the set of those members of $\mathscr{S}$ where the extension contains, say, *y*, that neither will include the other. Yet they both guarantee membership in the extension of *rather clever*, essentially because they are both large enough. It is this intuition concerning the largeness of sets which *p* tries to capture.

Thus if *clever* is again represented by Q_1^l, then we may put:

u_1 is rather clever if and only if $[Q_1^l(v_1)]_{\mathcal{M},a_1} \geqslant p_0$ (where p_0 is some number in $(0,1)$.

Obviously p_0 should be less than $p(\{M' \in \mathscr{S}: M \subseteq M'\})$; but not much more can be said about it. For of course p_0 is not fixed. If that were so, *rather clever* would be a sharp predicate, which evidently it is not.

The vagueness of *rather* could be represented in the following way. We associate with each $c \in \mathrm{Dom}\ \mathscr{C}$ a pair of real numbers r_c^-, r_c^+ between 0 and 1 such that whenever $c \leqslant c'$, then $r_c^- \leqslant r_{c'}^- < r_{c'}^+ \leqslant r_c^+$. The positive and negative extensions of *rather* Q_1^l in the ground model M_c w . r . t . c are then defined as the sets

$$\{u \in U: [Q_i^l(v_1)]_{\mathcal{M},c,a} > r_c^+ \cdot p(\{M' \in \mathscr{S}_c: M_c \subseteq M'\})\}$$
$$\{u \in U: [Q_i^l(v_1)]_{\mathcal{M},c,a} < r_c^- \cdot p(\{M' \in \mathscr{S}_c: M_c \subseteq M'\})\},$$

respectively; finally the intermediate value of *u is rather* Q_i^l in the ground model is given by $p(\{M' \in \mathscr{S}: u$ belongs to the positive extension of *rather* Q_i^l in $M'\})$.

There are a number of words which, like *rather*, form adjectives out of adjectives and which can be analysed along similar lines. Another prominent example is *very*. The extension of *very* Q_i^l is again a function of $[Q_i^l(v_1)]_{\mathcal{M},a}$. The limit which $[Q_i^l(v_1)]_{\mathcal{M},a}$ must exceed in order that $a(v_1)$ belong to the extension of *very* Q_i^l must be larger, and not smaller, than $p(\{M' \in \mathscr{S}; M \subseteq M'\})$.

6.

For traditional logic adjectives, nouns and intransitive verbs are all of a kind – viz. one-place predicates. My second theory of adjectives tries to vindicate this view against the one expressed earlier which puts adjectives into a different category than verbs and nouns. Yet it is an undeniable fact about ordinary English that while the comparative is in general a natural operation on adjectives, similar operations on nouns are of relatively little importance, and on verbs they are virtually non-existent. This suggests a difference between adjectives on the one hand and verbs and nouns on the other hand. I will leave verbs out of consideration in the following discussion, as they present problems quite different from those with which this paper is concerned. But I will try to say something about the difference between adjectives and nouns. Why is it that comparisons involving nouns are in general so much more dubious than those which involve adjectives? *This is more a table than that* sounds awkward and is perhaps never unequivocally true, except in the cases in which it is evident that this is a table and that is not (but then we can say precisely this, and thus do not need the first phrase). Yet it appears that nouns too are vague, some of them just as vague as certain adjectives. Why does not their vagueness allow for equally meaningful comparatives? To discover the reasons, it is advantageous to reconsider 'one-dimensional' adjectives.

For any such adjective Q_i^l it will be the case that, for arbitrary a_1, a_2,

(18) either $[Q_i^l(v_1)]_{\mathcal{M},a_1} \subseteq [Q_i^l(v_1)]_{\mathcal{M},a_2}$ or
$[Q_i^l(v_1)]_{\mathcal{M},a_2} \subseteq [Q_i^l(v_1)]_{\mathcal{M},a_1}$;

and this ensures that u_1 *is more* Q_i^l *than* u_2 always has a definite truth value.

We have already seen that most adjectives do not satisfy (18) unambiguously. u_1 *is cleverer than* u_2 could remain without truth value in the ground model. Yet there should still be a fair proportion of pairs $\langle u_1, u_2 \rangle$ where u_1 and u_2 both lie in the extension gap of *clever*, but for which (18) holds (with $a_1(v_1) = u_1$ and $a_2(v_1) = u_2$). And, for the same reason, there are many contexts c in which (18) holds (with $[Q_i^l(v_1)]_{\mathcal{M},c,a_1}$ for $[Q_i^l(v_1)]_{\mathcal{M},a_1^1}$, etc.), so that in c each comparative sentence involving Q_i^l is either definitely true or definitely false. On the other hand, if Q_i^l is a noun then (18) will in general be satisfied for very few pairs of objects which both fall in the extension gap of Q_i^l.

A very rough explanation for this formal distinction is the following: In order for an object to satisfy a noun it must in general satisfy all, or a large portion, of a cluster of criteria. None of these we can promote to the sole criterion without distorting the noun's meaning beyond recognition. We cannot, therefore, compare the degrees to which two different objects satisfy the noun in terms of their degrees of satisfaction of just one of its many criteria; and in order to compare them by comparing their ratings with respect to a variety of these criteria we need a method for integrating these various ratings. And such a method is in general not part of the meaning of the noun.

There is another aspect to the difference between nouns and adjectives which is related to the one discussed above, but perhaps even more important in connection with the former's resistance to comparatives. Nouns, though potentially just as vague as adjectives, tend in actual practice to behave much more like sharp predicates. Take *cat*. In principle there could be all sorts of borderline cases for this predicate – but in actual fact there are very few at best. The same is true, be it in slightly varying degrees, of *table*, *rock* or *word*. Thus nouns often have very small, or no, extension gaps in the actual world – even if it is easy to think of possible worlds in which these gaps would be enormous. This gives an additional explanation of why comparatives involving nouns should be of relatively little use. For they are particularly important in those cases where neither of the two objects compared belongs unambiguously to the positive or to the negative extension of the predicate in question. And these cases will seldom arise when the predicate is a noun.

It is an interesting question how nouns 'manage' to be as sharp as they are. The explanation must be more or less along the following lines: Even if each of the several criteria for the noun may apply to actual objects in varying degrees, these criteria tend to be, with respect to the actual world, *parallel*: an object which fails to satisfy a few of them to a reasonable degree will generally fail to score well with regard to almost all of them. Consequently, it will either be recognized as definitely inside the extension of the noun, or else as definitely out. The nature of this parallelism is very much that of a physical law – it is a feature of our world, and thus in essence empirical. This is one of the ways in which the actual **structure of** the world shapes the conceptual frame with which we operate, and one of the reasons why it is difficult to separate the empirical from the purely conceptual.

Where the simple comparative of a predicate is non-sensical, addition of certain special expressions can restore its meaningfulness. Examples of such expressions are: *in a sense, as far as function is concerned, with regard to shape*.[1]

Let us consider this last phrase. How should we analyse

(19) with regard to shape u_1 is more a table than u_2?

First we should determine the logical type of the expression *with regard to shape*. This is really a problem which does not belong in this paper. I will therefore give an answer which is convenient in connection with the issues which concern us here and does not distort them. I will treat *is more... than...with regard to shape* as an atomic, i.e. not further analysable, expression which stands for a new comparative operation – one which again forms binary relations out of predicates. This new comparative differs from the one considered thus far in the following way: The phrase *with regard to shape* places us so to speak in a context where shape is singled out as the only criterion for whatever the property is in respect of which the comparison is made. Let us suppose that there are such contexts – contexts in which those predicates to which shape is at all relevant are evaluated with respect to shape alone. Then (19) should be true in the ground model if and only if u_1 *is more a table than* u_2 is true in each of these contexts.

I should like to make a brief comment at this point on the nature of contexts and the role which in my opinion they ought to play in semantic analysis of the sort of which I have tried to give instances in this paper. We could give an alternative, but evidently equivalent, account of (19) by stipulating that the phrase *with regard to shape transforms* the context in which (19) is used *into* one where shape is the only relevant issue. For our account of (19) it does not make much difference which line of explanation we choose. However, I believe that the solution to certain other semantical problems can be found only if we investigate not only the effect of the various aspects of context on the meanings of expressions used in those contexts, but also the mechanisms which *create*, or *modify*, contextual aspects. A proper understanding of these mechanisms seems essential to the

---

[1] An extensive discussion of such expressions can be found in Lakoff (1972). Lakoff calls such expressions 'hedges', a term I will adopt here too.

analysis of more extended pieces of discourse – such as told, or written stories.[1] Given that such understanding must eventually be reached in any case, an account of (19) along the lines of the second proposal may well ultimately be the more desirable. It seems, however, too early to pass judgement on this matter.

At any rate it is important to realize that contexts are made up of verbal and nonverbal elements alike. The same contextual aspect may on one occasion be manifest through the setting in which the utterance is made, while on another occasion its presence is signalled by a particular verbal expression. Exclusive preoccupation with shape, for example, can be evident to both speaker and audience either because they have been discussing shape and nothing but shape all along (think of a session about shape during a conference on industrial design); or because the previous sentence was *But let us now concentrate exclusively on shape*; or because the sentence itself contains the qualifying phrase *with regard to shape*. The three cases differ as regards the degree of permanence with which the feature in question is part of the context. In the first case, preoccupation with shape will last throughout the session; and a special verbal effort would be necessary to remove it; in the last the modification will be in force only during the evaluation of the particular phrase to which *with regard to shape* is attached; the second case is somewhere between the two. Indeed, without further information it is not possible to say whether the modification is valid just for the present sentence, for everything this particular speaker is going to say right now, or for the remainder of the entire discussion.

Another expression of the sort we have just been discussing is *in a sense*.[2] What is it to be clever in a sense? That depends on what are the various possible senses of the word *clever*. It will help to consider such related sentences as *Smith is clever in the sense that he is good at solving problems* or *Jones is clever in the sense of being quick-witted*. The expressions following *clever* in these two sentences have, again, the effect of transforming the context, viz. into one where *clever* is given a more specific sense. The truth value of the sentence should therefore be the same as it is in any of these contexts. The contexts in question are the same as those created by antecedent specifications like *Let us understand by 'clever': 'good at solving problems'*. Each such specification will single out a set of contexts in which *clever* is understood correspondingly. *x is clever in a sense* is then true if

---

[1] Cf. Isard (1973). Others whom I know to have developed similar ideas are Thomas Ballmer of the Technische Universität, Berlin, and David Lumsden of University College, London.
[2] Cf. Lewis (1970:65).

there is such a set of contexts such that *x is clever* is true in each of its members.

But which are the acceptable specifications of a given noun or adjective? This is a question to which no definite answer can be given; for the notion of an acceptable specification of a given concept is itself subject to just that sort of vagueness with which this paper is concerned. Clearly not every logically possible definition is acceptable; for if this were so, then all statements of the form

(20) *x* is a...in a sense

would be true. But what is an acceptable specification can if necessary be stretched very far indeed. That is why it is so hard to establish that a particular sentence of the form (20) is false.

I want to conclude this discussion of hedges with a few remarks on the expression *to the extent that*. Let us consider Lakoff's example:

(21) To the extent that Austin is a linguist he is a good one

Once more I will leave questions concerning the ultimate logical form of the expression aside. It will be adequate for our present interests if we regard *to the extent that* as a two-place sentential operator which forms out of two formulas ϕ and ψ the compound formula

(22) to the extent that ϕ, ψ.

The semantical analysis of this connective brings into focus a problem connected with contextual disambiguation which I have so far failed to mention: to what extent does the sharpening of one predicate affect other predicates? Clearly the decisions concerning two different words cannot in all cases be independent. Sharpening of the noun *leg* will yield sharpening of the adjective *four-legged* as well. Yet there are many pairs of adjectives such that a sharpening or modification of one does not carry with it any perceptible semantic change in the other. This is true in particular of *linguist* and *good*. This is important for the following account of (21).

The truth conditions of (22) are essentially these: (22) is true (in its actual context of use *c*) if ψ is true in all contexts in which ϕ is true and which are as similar to *c* as is possible, given that they make ϕ true. In the case of (21) these contexts will be contexts in which we have modified the semantics for *linguist* in such a way that Austin is now definitely inside its extension, and have left the semantics otherwise as much the same as the modification of *linguist* permits. In particular *good* would, it seems to me, not be affected seriously by the modification. The truth of the main clause of (21) in such a context is to be understood in the usual manner.

It is interesting to compare (21) with the slightly more complicated

(23) To the extent that Austin and Russell are linguists, Austin is at least as good a linguist as Russell

This sentence will be true in c if in every maximally similar context c' in which *linguist* has been modified in such a way that both Austin and Russell are in its extension, it is true that Austin is at least as good a linguist as Russell. When is it true in c' that Austin is at least as good a linguist as Russell? This will be the case if the pair ⟨Austin, Russell⟩ belongs to the positive extension of ⩾(good linguist) with respect to c', i.e. if the set of members of $\mathscr{S}_{c'}$ in which *Austin is a good linguist* is true includes the set of those members in which *Russell is a good linguist* is true. It is important that this account will give us the intuitively correct truth conditions for (23) only if the members of $\mathscr{S}_{c'}$, involve modifications of *good* but not of *linguist*.

It is clear from this brief discussion that a formal elaboration of such analyses within the framework provided by cgm's requires a great deal more structure on the set of contexts than I have given.

7.

I have claimed that vagueness is often reduced by context. This doctrine is void, however, unless it is accompanied by a concrete analysis of those contextual factors which contribute to such reduction of vagueness and of how they succeed in doing so. To provide such an analysis is a difficult task, the completion of which will perhaps forever elude us. Yet I feel I ought to say something on this topic, more, in fact, than I actually have to offer. But let me mention at least one contextual aspect which plays a central role in almost all cases where adjectives occur in attributive position. That aspect is the noun to which the adjective is attached. In a great many cases the noun alone determines, largely or wholly, how the adjective should, in the given context, be understood. Indeed, if we assume that the noun is the *only* factor, we are back with the first theory according to which adjective meanings are functions from noun-phrase meanings to noun-phrase meanings.

But of course the noun is not always the only determining factor. *Smith is a remarkable violinist* may be true when said in comment on his after-

dinner performance with the hostess at the piano, and false when ex-
claimed at the end of Smith's recital in the Festival Hall – even if on the
second occasion Smith played a bit better than on the first.

It would be desirable to give a general account of how the meaning of the
noun determines that of the adjective that combines with it. Here I will
mention just one aspect of this problem. One of the main purposes of the use
of an adjective in attributive position is to contribute to the delineation of the
class of objects that the complex noun-phrase of which it is part is designed
to pick out – or, alternatively, to help determine the particular individual
which is the intended referent of the description in which the adjective
occurs. In order that the adjective can be of any use at all for these purposes, it should, in the presence of the noun in question, have an extension
which, so to speak, cuts the extension of the noun in half – i.e. if we assume
for the sake of this argument that both noun and adjective (in the presence
of the noun) are sharp, and that $\bar{A}$ is the extension of the adjective, and $\bar{N}$
that of the noun, then both $\bar{N}-\bar{A}$ and $\bar{N}\cap\bar{A}$ should be substantial proportions of $\bar{N}$. Thus in order to be able to use the adjective profitably in combination with an unlimited number of nouns, we should let the noun
determine the criteria and/or standards for the adjective in its presence in
such a way that the above condition is in general fulfilled. (The proposal
(8), p. 126, obviously meets this requirement.)

The distinctions between nouns and adjectives adumbrated in the
previous section are of course far from absolute. *Four-legged*, for example,
has virtually no extension gap – which is hardly surprising given the
manner in which it is derived from the noun '*leg*'. And indeed it yields
comparatives as infelicitous as those derived from most nouns. *This is more
four-legged than that* would on most occasions sound positively non-
sensical. *Blue*, though apparently not derived from a noun, also gives rise
to rather strained comparatives. *This is bluer than that* is sometimes a
meaningful statement, but would fail to be more often than not. So it seems
that *heavy* and *four-legged* are really very far apart and that they will
ultimately require analyses that are fundamentally different.

This brings us to a likely objection against the theory I have outlined.
Does it not blur fundamental distinctions between different kinds of
adjectives? Yes, undoubtedly it does. Still, I feel that what it reveals about
adjectives in general is important. But this conviction should not bar the
way to accounts that deal in detail with small provinces of the wide realm
of all those concepts to which it claims to apply. It should be pointed out in
this connection that the second theory itself can hardly be regarded as
comprehending all adjectives. Is *alleged* a predicate, even in the most

diluted sense? It seems not. Of course we can still maintain that in each particular context of use it behaves as a predicate, in so far as the accompanying (or tacitly understood) noun phrase determines to which objects in that context the adjective applies. But this is just a restatement of the first theory in slightly different terms. The original intuition which led to the second theory seems to be inapplicable to *alleged*. The same can be said to be true, to an almost equal degree, of adjectives such as *fake*, *skilful*, or *good*. Where precisely we should draw the boundaries of the class of adjectives to which the second theory applies I do not know. For example, does *skilful* belong to this class? Surely we must always ask 'skilful what?' before we can answer the question whether a certain thing or person is indeed *skilful*; this suggests that the theory is not applicable to the word *skilful*. Yet there appears to be some plausibility in the view that *having a good deal of skill* does function as a predicate – be it a highly ambiguous one as there are so many different skills. Here the question whether we face an expression that stands for a function from properties to properties or rather an ambiguous predicate which is disambiguated by accompanying expressions for properties has perhaps no definite answer. Both views appear to be equally plausible accounts of the same phenomenon. So it may be impossible to determine in a non-arbitrary manner how far the domain of our theory extends. But then it probably does not matter whether we can or not. This will certainly be unimportant once we have a complementary theory which deals specifically with such adjectives as *alleged*, *fake*, *skilful* and *good*. It is bad to be left with a semantic phenomenon that is explained by no theory; but it does no harm to have two distinct theories which give equally adequate, albeit different, accounts of those phenomena that fall within the province of both.

8.

To conclude, let me mention some of the questions which I should have liked to discuss and which I believe can be treated within the framework I have set up.

In the first place there are intransitive verbs. I have avoided them throughout, even though they too appear to be one-place predicates and to display a good deal of vagueness. In particular I have failed to give any account of what semantically differentiates verbs from adjectives, or, for that matter, from nouns. My excuse for this is that the proper understanding of these differences involves the consideration of tense, of the time spans during which a predicate is true of an object, and of similar issues which seem to require for their formal elaboration a framework which incorporates a good deal of tense logic.

Secondly, I have given only the scantest attention to hedges. I think that my framework is basically suitable for their analysis, although more structure on the set of contexts will be needed than I have provided.

Thirdly, I have considered only the simplest kind of comparatives. Examples of comparatives which are considerably more difficult to treat, are

Jones is more intelligent than he is kind
This building is higher than that is long
Smith is much cleverer than Jones and
Smith is more cleverer than Jones than Jones is than Bill

(accepting this as English).

The last two sentences in particular, present problems of a rather different kind than those I have tackled in this article. Their analysis requires more mathematical structure than has been built into the models here considered. The difference between the formal framework needed there and the one I have presented is essentially that between metric and arbitrary topological spaces. These and other problems I hope to consider in some other paper.

REFERENCES

Bartsch, R. and Vennemann, T. (1972). *Semantic Structures*. Frankfurt: Athenäum.

Geach, P. (1956). 'Good and evil', *Analysis*, **17**. Also in P. R. Fort, ed. (1967). *Theories of Ethics*. Oxford: Oxford University Press.

Isard, S. (1973). 'Changing the context.' This volume.

Kolmogorov, L. (1970). *Foundations of the Theory of Measurement*. New York: Chelsea.

Lakoff, G. (1972). 'Hedges: a study in meaning criteria and the logic of fuzzy concepts', *Chicago Linguistic Society*, **8**.

Lewis, D. K. (1970). 'General semantics', *Synthèse*, **22**. Also in G. Harman and D. Davidson, eds. (1971). *Semantics of Natural Language*. Dordrecht: Reidel.

Montague, R. (1970). 'English as a formal language.' In *Linguaggi nella Societá e nella Technica*. Milan: Editione di Communitá.

—— (1974). *Formal Philosophy*, ed. with an introduction by R. H. Thomason. New Haven: Yale University Press.

Parsons, T. (1968). 'A semantics for English.' Unpublished.

Rescher, N. (1969). *Many-Valued Logic*. New York.

Van Fraassen, B. (1969). 'Presuppositions, supervaluations and free logic.' In K. Lambert, ed., *The Logical Way of Doing Things*. New Haven: Yale University Press.

Partial interpretations

FRANZ VON KUTSCHERA

1. Statement of the problem

Natural languages contain many expressions which are grammatically
well-formed but meaningless; they are assembled from meaningful words
or morphemes[1] in accordance with the syntactic rules of the language but
no meaning is conferred upon them by the semantic rules of the language.
When we call expressions or utterances 'meaningless' here without further
qualification, that will just be for the sake of brevity. We want to indicate by
that term that the expressions or utterances are semantically anomalous in
such a way that they will generally evoke responses like '*What do you
mean?*' or '*What are you talking about?*' There is no implication that they
are on a par with totally meaningless expressions as *Krz is thwing*.

Let us take six typical examples of such well-formed but meaningless
expressions:

(1) *Incompletely defined functors*: Many predicates are not defined for all
syntactically permissible arguments. Thus the verb *to run* is defined
for animals with locomotive appendages, for humans, machines,
fluids and for noses, not however for plants, minerals or numbers.
And the German verb *lachen* is defined only for humans and the sun.
The sentence *Der Mond lacht*, though constructed grammatically
just as *Die Sonne lacht*, has, in distinction to the latter, no meaning.

(2) *Non-existing objects*: Sentences about objects which do not exist or
no longer exist form a significant sub-category of example (1). The
sentences *Odysseus is (now) shaving himself* and *Eisenhower is (now)
sick* are meaningless but not the sentences *Professor Snell is dreaming
of Odysseus* or *Nixon remembers Eisenhower*. Thus many predicates
are defined for non-existent objects while others are not. Since the
question of whether a human being is alive or dead is purely empirical, syntax cannot refer to this distinction.

(3) *Invalid presuppositions*: A presupposition of a statement or utterance
A is a state of affairs which is not itself asserted in *A*, but which

---

[1] Meaningless expressions do not rate as words of the lexicon upon which the syntax is
based.

must be the case if both *A* and the (colloquial) negation of *A* are to be meaningful. Thus the sentence *John gave up smoking* presupposes that John previously smoked. *Jack knows that there is a university in Regensburg* presupposes that Regensburg does indeed have a university. The utterance *As a doctor I realize how dangerous this symptom is* presupposes that the speaker is a physician. These presuppositions are not part of the content of the sentences but rather preconditions to them being meaningful at all. Such presuppositions, being again matters of empirical fact, cannot be accounted for syntactically.

Invalid presuppositions also appear in the following special cases:

(4) *Definite descriptions with unfulfilled normality conditions*: Description terms as *Russell's book* or *George VI's son* have no meaning because the describing predicate fails to apply to exactly one object as the *normality condition* of descriptions requires. Whether this condition holds or not is again an empirical question, not a syntactic one.

(5) *Empty generalizations*: In ordinary discourse the sentence *All of John's children have red hair* is meaningless if John does not have any children. In general a sentence of the form *All A's are B* is only meaningful if there are *A*s. Such a sentence thus presupposes that sentence *As exist*. This should not in every case be understood to mean that there must exist 'real objects' which are *A*s – sentences like *All the Greek Gods were assimilated into the Roman Pantheon* indicate to the contrary that they can also be 'possible objects'. These presuppositions of descriptions and generalizations were first noticed by P. F. Strawson.

(6) *Quantifying into intensional contexts*: W. V. Quine (1953) has repeatedly emphasized that it is senseless to quantify into intensional contexts, as in the sentences *There is a number x such that x is necessarily greater than 7* or *There is a person x such that Philip is unaware that x denounced Catiline*. A quantification of this sort is only meaningful under the *normality condition* that the use of the predicate depends solely upon the extension and not upon the intension of the argument indicated by the variable as is the case in deontic contexts like *There is a person x who is obliged to examine the students* (see Kutschera (1973), section 1.6).

In this paper we propose to discuss how the problem of grammatically well-formed but meaningless expressions can be handled within the general framework of intensional semantics developed by R. Montague.[1] This semantic system refers primarily to an artificial language L of the logic of types and will be treated exclusively as such in the following. Rules for the interpretation of a natural language S can be derived from this system only when an analysing relation between the expressions of L and those of S is defined.

Let us first take a general look at possible courses toward solving our problem. We shall disregard solutions which syntactically exclude meaningless expressions as being not well-formed. One could in this manner, for instance with respect to (1), introduce a many-sorted language with several object domains and several varieties of constants and variables of the same category so that every single-place predicate would be defined for exactly one object domain. The examples given under (1), however, already indicate that this is a hopeless undertaking since the predicates of a natural language are not all defined on sets that can be delineated by such simple classifications as 'animal', 'human', 'abstract object', etc. Such an attempt becomes even more dubious in case (2) and collapses completely in cases (3)–(6). The problem permits only semantic solutions if unpleasant interference between syntax and semantics is to be avoided.[2]

Semantic solutions offer themselves in the following ways:

(a) *Completing the semantic interpretation*: We might stipulate, for instance, that a basic predicate takes on the value *false* for an argument for which it is not defined – *17 runs* and *The moon laughs* are then false sentences, just as *Odysseus is shaving* and *Eisenhower is sick*. Furthermore the interpretation of description terms is extended, for instance in the sense of Frege, in such a way that they have a meaning even when the normality condition is not met. Generalizations are interpreted in such a way that they are true when their presuppositions are not fulfilled.[3] And in the cases mentioned under (3), finally, one can resort to the device of including the presuppositions into the assertions. Thus the sentence *John gave up smoking* would be interpreted as meaning *John used to smoke but doesn't any more*. Supplementing the semantic interpretation in this way has been the customary procedure in logic since Frege.

(b) *Incomplete 2-valued interpretations*: One uses a 2-valued semantics but permits interpretations which do not assign a meaning to every syntactically well-formed term. Functors can then be interpreted as partial

---

[1] Reference will be mainly to Montague (1970).

[2] Syntax and semantics interfere with one another, for instance, if forming a description term is permitted only when the normality condition is provable.

[3] For a complete interpretation of generalizations in intensional contexts, see **2.3.1**(c).

functions so that a sentence $F(a)$ remains meaningless when the reference of a does not belong to the domain over which F is defined. Expressions involving presuppositions are only interpreted if these are valid. This is the solution proposed by D. Scott (1970).

(c) *3-valued interpretations*: Along with the truth values of sentences *true* and *false* one introduces a third value *meaningless*, and assigns meaningless proper names an object *meaninglessness* as reference and thus constructs a 3-valued semantics. A 3-valued semantics has been offered for predicate logic for instance by Woodruff (1970), but he only considers such meaningless expressions as arise from the use of meaningless proper names. For this reason we shall discuss a more general 3-valued semantics below.

(d) *Sets of 2-valued interpretations*: Proceeding from the idea that meaningless expressions arise when only limited information is available about the interpretation of a language, one represents such limited semantic information by the set T of 2-valued interpretations M which are eligible relative to that information. T then assigns to an expression A the value α, if for all $M \in T$, $M(A) = \alpha$. If there is no such α, then T is not defined for A. This procedure leads therefore to considering a term meaningless if the semantic information is compatible with different interpretations for this term. If, for instance, a predicate $F(x)$ is only defined over a proper subset U' of the object domain U, then all possible continuations of this partial function on U are considered as possible interpretations of F. If the constant a designates an object from $U - U'$, these interpretations provide different values for $F(a)$ so that $F(a)$ is characterized as meaningless with respect to the set of these interpretations. And if the normality condition for descriptions does not hold, then every assignment of an object to this term would be a possible interpretation of the term so that it again is meaningless relative to the set of these interpretations.

Such an approach has been developed especially by B. van Fraassen (1969). It refers, however, only to the language of elementary predicate logic in an extensional interpretation.

Completing semantic interpretations in accordance with proposal (a) leads to several inadequacies in the semantic analysis of natural language sentences. First of all one has to determine which predicates are to be basic predicates. For instance should *sick* be taken as a basic predicate and *healthy* as *not sick* or vice versa. Both cannot be taken as basic because otherwise the sentence *Eisenhower is neither sick nor healthy* would be correct, in contradiction to the analytic sentence *Anyone who is not healthy is sick*. Such conventions are, however, very artificial for natural languages and they always end up by making sentences false which ordinarily are considered true: If *work* and *to be lazy* are basic predicates, then the sentence *Anyone who never works is lazy* is false by virtue of the new semantic conventions, since numbers do not work. Most importantly, however, the distinction between the assertion of a sentence and its presupposition gets lost and its meaning is thereby distorted. If one interprets the sentence *John gave up smoking* to mean *John used to smoke and doesn't any more* then the negation of this sentence maintains *John didn't use to smoke or John still smokes* and in contradistinction to *John didn't give up smoking* is true even if John never smoked.

The proposal (a) therefore offers no satisfactory solution to our problem, so we can limit ourselves henceforth to a discussion of proposals (b), (c) and (d), i.e. those concerning partial interpretations which do not assign every term a meaning. Our primary objective will be to work out and compare these proposals within the framework of Montague's semantics. It will turn out that (b) and (c) have essentially the same effect while proposal (d) does not lead to satisfactory results.

We will start off in the next section by defining the ordinary, complete, 2-valued interpretations in the sense of Montague, in order to elucidate where the partial interpretations differ from them.[1]

2. Fundamentals of intensional semantics

2.1. The syntax of L

The language L upon which intensional semantics is based is constructed in the following way:
We determine first the *categories* of L-expressions.

2.1.1.

(a) σ, v are categories.
(b) If τ, ρ are categories, then $\tau(\rho)$ is also a category.
(c) If τ is a category, then $\iota(\tau)$ is also a category.

σ is the category of sentences, v the category of proper names, $\tau(\rho)$ is the category of functors which produce expressions of category τ from arguments of category ρ, $\iota(\tau)$ is the category of intensions of expressions of the category τ.

[1] These definitions are taken from Kutschera (1975) where they are intuitively explained.

The *alphabet* of L consists of the symbols λ, $\equiv$, μ, δ, (,) and infinitely many constants and variables of every category. The category of an expression will often be noted by use of an upper index.

The symbol * is not a part of L. $A[*]$ is a finite series of basic L-symbols together with this symbol, and $A[a]$ is the expression resulting from replacement in $A[*]$ of all occurrences of * by a.

The well-formed expressions or *terms* of L are determined by

2.1.2.

(a) Constants of the category τ of L are terms of the category τ of L.

(b) If F is a term of the category $\tau(\rho)$ ($\tau \neq \iota$) and a is a term of the category ρ of L, then $F(a)$ is a term of the category τ of L.

(c) If $A[a]$ is a term of the category τ, a is a constant of the category ρ and x is a variable of the category ρ of L which does not occur in $A[a]$, then $\lambda x(A[x])$ is a term of the category $\tau(\rho)$ of L.

(d) If a and b are terms of the same category of L, then $a \equiv b$ is a term of the category σ of L.

(e) If A is a term of the category τ of L, then $\mu(A)$ is a term of the category $\iota(\tau)$ of L.

(f) If A is a term of the category $\iota(\tau)$ of L, then $\delta(A)$ is a term of the category τ of L.

Where brackets are not necessary to delineate clearly the range of an operator λ, μ or δ, they will be left out in the following.

L_1 shall be that sublanguage of L in which the operators μ and δ do not appear and only constants and variables of those categories which can be constructed solely in accordance with rules (a) and (b) of 2.1.1.

2.2. *Extensions*

For clarity's sake the semantics of L will be constructed in several stages, in the first of which the expressions of L are assigned only extensions. For this purpose we will restrict ourselves to the sublanguage L_1.

2.2.1. Let $E_{\tau,U}$ be the *set of possible extensions* of the terms of L_1 of the category τ relative to the object domain U.

(a) $E_{v,U} = U$

(b) $E_{\sigma,U} = \{w,f\}$

(c) $E_{\tau(\rho),U} = E_{\tau,U}{}^{E_{\rho,U}}$

w represents the truth value *true* and f the truth value *false*. A^B is the set of functions with domain B and a range included in A.

2.2.2. An *extensional interpretation* of L_1 over the (non-empty) object domain U is a 1-place function M with the following properties:

(a) $M(a) \in E_{\tau,U}$ for all constants a of the category τ.

(b) $M(F(a)) = M(F)(M(a))$ for all terms in accordance with 2.1.2(b).

(c) $M(\lambda x A[x])$ is that function f from $E_{\tau(\rho),U}$ for which $f(M'(b)) = M'(A[b])$ holds for all M' with $M' \underset{b}{=} M$. The term $\lambda x A[x]$ is formed in accordance with 2.1.2(c) and the constant b of the same category as x shall not occur in $\lambda x A[x]$.

(d) $M(a \equiv b) = w$ iff $M(a) = M(b)$ for all terms in accordance with 2.1.2(d).

In (c) $M' \underset{b}{=} M$ means that the two interpretations M and M' differ at most in the values they assign the constant b.

2.2.3. We define following Montague:

(a) $\wedge x^\tau A := \lambda x^\tau A \equiv \lambda x^\tau (x^\tau \equiv x^\tau)$

(b) $\neg A := A \equiv \wedge x^\sigma (x^\sigma)$.

(c) $A \wedge B := \wedge x^{\sigma(\sigma)} (B \equiv (x^{\sigma(\sigma)}(A) \equiv x^{\sigma(\sigma)}(B)))$

(d) $A \vee B := \neg(\neg A \wedge \neg B)$

(e) $A \supset B := \neg A \vee B$

(f) $\vee x^\tau A := \neg \wedge x^\tau \neg A$.

2.2.4. It is often useful to introduce *names for non-existing objects* like *Odysseus*. Taking U as the set of 'possible objects' and a subset U' of U as the set of 'real objects', then where E is a constant of category $\sigma(v)$ and a is a constant of category v we postulate

(e) $M(E(a)) = w$ iff $M(a) \in U'$.

If we then define

(g) $\wedge . x^v A[x^v] := \wedge x^v (E(x^v) \supset A[x^v])$

(h) $\vee . x^v A[x^v] := \neg \wedge . x^v \neg A[x^v]$

the following principles hold

$A[a] \wedge E(a) \supset \vee . x A[x]$

$\wedge . x A[x] \wedge E(a) \supset A[a]$.

This means that quantification with $\bigwedge$. and $\bigvee$. takes into account only existing objects.

2.2.5. Descriptions can be introduced in L_1 in such a way that $\iota x A[x]$ is a term of L_1 of category τ if $A[b]$ is a term of category σ, b a constant and x a variable of category τ of L_1; x should not occur in $A[b]$. It can then be postulated in extension of 2.2.2:

(f)　$M(x A[x]) = \alpha$

if there is exactly one M' such that $M' \underset{a}{=} M$ and $M'(A[a]) = w$ and if for this M' $M'(a) = \alpha$ (a being a constant of the same category as x and one which does not occur in $\iota x A[x]$; otherwise we let $M(\iota x A[x]) = M(a_0)$ where a_0 is a fixed constant of the category τ.

If the description operator is only to refer to existing objects, it can be defined by

(i)　$\iota . x^v A[x^v] := \iota x^v (A[x^v] \bigwedge E(x^v))$.

2.3. Intensions

Considering now the assignment of intensions to the expressions of L let us shift over from L_1 to L. L can be characterized as a modal language of the logic of types. According to Carnap the intension of an expression should be taken as that function which determines its extension for every possible world. $i \in I$ are to be indices for these possible worlds.

The extension of a functional expression such as *it is necessary that p* is often dependent not only on the extension but also on the intension of the argument p. Thus the arguments of the functor *it is necessary that*... are assigned the category $\iota(\sigma)$ for propositions (intensions of sentences) instead of the category σ for sentences. Since however the intension of p can be expressed by $\mu(p)$, it is possible to maintain, as Frege did, that the extensions of functional expressions always depend on the extensions of their arguments if one writes *it is necessary $(\mu(p))$* instead of *it is necessary that p*.

Supplementing the conventions 2.2.1 by

(d)　$E_{\iota(\tau), U} = E_{\tau, U}{}^I$

we define:

2.3.1. An *intensional interpretation* of L over the (non-empty) universe domain I with the (non-empty) object domain U is a 2-place function $M_i(A)$ such that the following holds for all $i \in I$:

(a) $M_i(a) \in E_{\tau, U}$ for all constants a of the category τ.

(b) $M_i(F(a)) = M_i(F)(M_i(a))$ for all terms according to 2.1.2(b).

(c) $M_i(\lambda x A[x])$ is that function f from $E_{\tau(\rho), U}$, for which: $f(M_i'(b)) = M_i'(A[b])$ holds for all M' with $M' \underset{b}{=} M$, and $M_j'(b) = M_j(b)$ for all $j \neq i$ from I. The term $\lambda x A[x]$ is constructed in accordance with 2.1.2(c) and the constant b of the same category as x shall not occur in $\lambda x A[x]$.

(d) $M_i(a \equiv b) = w$ iff $M(a) = M(b)$ for all terms according to 2.1.2(d).

(e) $M_i(\mu(A)) = \lambda^* i M_i(A)$.

(f) $M_i(\delta(A)) = M_i(A)(i)$.

λ^* is to be a symbol of the metalanguage for functional abstraction. $M' \underset{b}{=} M$ now means that the intensional interpretations M and M' differ at the most with regard to the values $M_i(b)$ and $M_i'(b)$ for any number of $i \in I$.

$M_i(A)$ is the *extension* of the term A in world i, $\lambda^* i M_i(A)$ its *intension*.

If the variable x in $\lambda x\, A[x]$ does not occur within the scope of an operator μ, then one can also define: $M_i(\lambda x A[x])$ is that function f from $E_{\tau[\rho], U}$ for which $f(M_i'(b)) = M_i'(A[b])$ holds for all M' with $M' \underset{b}{=} M$; for then for all M' and M'' with $M' \underset{b}{=} M$, $M'' \underset{b}{=} M$ and $M_i'(b) = M_i''(b)$ we have $M_i'(A[b]) = M_i''(A[b])$. This does not hold however when $\lambda x A[x]$ is the expression $\lambda x^v G^{\sigma(,((\sigma))}(\mu(F^{\sigma(v)}(x^v)))$ for which $\mu(F(a))$ can depend on the intension of a, i.e. on the values of $M_j(a)$ with $j \neq i$. In this case the expression $\lambda x\, G(\mu(F(x)))$, which is to be interpreted as a function from $E_{\sigma(v), U}$, has no reasonable meaning. The construction of the terms $\lambda x A[x]$, however, cannot be restricted to those cases in which x does not occur in the scope of an operator μ since there are also interpretations of G and F for which the truth value of $G(\mu(F(a)))$ does not depend on the intension but only upon the extension of a. Such contexts are, for instance, deontic contexts like $O(\mu(F(a)))$ (i.e. $F(a)$ is obligatory). In such contexts we cannot do without terms such as $\lambda x A[x]$, $\wedge x A[x]$, or $\vee x A[x]$. It is therefore necessary to permit syntactically the construction of all the terms $\lambda x A[x]$ and they must then be interpreted in such a way that they have the usual meaning if the normality condition obtains, i.e. if $M_i(A[a])$ does not depend upon the $M_j(a)$ with $j \neq i$. And that is what condition (c) does.

In L we can define, besides the operators under 2.2.3, modal operators as

(j) $\Box A := \mu(A) \equiv \mu(\wedge x^v(x^v \equiv x^v))$
(k) $\Diamond A := \neg \Box \neg A.$

If for every i a set U_i of objects existing in i is given with $U_i \subset U$, then operators for quantifying over existing objects can be introduced in analogy to 2.2.4 with the help of the existence predicate E for which $M_i(E(a)) = w$ now holds iff $M_i(a) \in U_i$. Since statements about the quantity of objects existing in a world are to be formulated with such quantifiers, no sentence of the form *It is necessary that there are exactly k objects* is analytically true unless all the U_i have the same cardinality.

2.4. Pragmatic relations

We shall disregard here the meaning dependencies which derive from the linguistic context in which an expression occurs (Kutschera (1975)), and take account only of the fact that the meaning of an utterance may depend on its non-linguistic, situational context, e.g. by making use of indexical expressions. If the semantically relevant pragmatic parameters are summarized in an index $j \in \mathcal{J}$ – the *point of reference* of an utterance – then we can define:

2.4.1. A pragmatic interpretation of L over the universe with domain I and the (non-empty) index set $\mathcal{J}$ is a 3-place function $M_{i,j}$ such that for all $j \in \mathcal{J}$, $M_{i,j}$ is an intensional interpretation of L over I in the sense of 2.3.1.

We call $M_{i,j}(A)$ the *extension* of statement A at the point of reference j with regard to i, $\lambda^* i \, M_{i,j}$ its *intension*, $\lambda^* j M_{i,j}(A)$ the *extension* of A with regard to i and $\lambda^* ij M_{i,j}(A)$ the *intension* of A.

3. Partial 2-valued interpretations

3.1. Extensions

After these preparatory steps we can now take up method (b) of section 1 and specify in greater detail what is meant by an incomplete 2-valued interpretation of the language L. We begin again by assigning extensions to the expressions of L_1.

Every complete 2-valued interpretation of M over U in the sense of 2.2.2 assigns a possible extension from $E_{\tau(\rho), U}$ to a functional constant F of the category $\tau(\rho)$. These functions are defined for all arguments from

$E_{\rho,U}$. If $M(a){\in}E_{\rho,U}$ has been defined, then $M(F(a))$ is also defined. Thus in handling case (1) from section 1 of incompletely defined functors by the use of incomplete 2-valued interpretations, partial functions must be permitted as possible extensions of functors. The set of possible extensions must therefore be defined in the following way:

3.1.1.

$$E^+_{\nu,U} = E_{\nu,U}$$
$$E^+_{\sigma,U} = E_{\sigma,U}$$
$$E^+_{\tau(\rho),U} = E^+_{\tau,U}{}^{(E^+_\rho,U)}.$$

$A^{(B)}$ is to be the set of partial functions from B into A, i.e. functions with a domain included in B and a range included in A.[1]

If $E_{\tau,U}$ in 2.2.2 is everywhere replaced by $E^+_{\tau U}$, if no demand is made in (a) that $M(a)$ be defined for all constants a of the categories ν and σ, and if the conditions (b)–(d) are taken to hold only in the case where the values of M in the recursive conditions are defined, then we get the definition of the concept of a *partial extensional interpretation* of L. $M' \underset{b}{=} M$ in condition (c) is now to indicate that $M'(b)$ or $M(b)$ can also be undefined. Therefore we attach to (c) the supplementary condition that $M'(b)$ should be defined. The conditions $f(M'(b)) = M'(A[b])$ in (c) is meant to include that $f(M'(b))$ be undefined iff $M'(A[b])$ is undefined.

3.1.2. If definition (a) from 2.2.3 is taken over, then $M(\Lambda xA[x]) = w$ holds in case $M(\lambda xA[x])$ is a complete function taking on the value w for every argument. Otherwise $M(\Lambda xA[x]) = f$ holds since $M(\lambda xA[x])$ is always defined. Consequently according to definition (f) from 2.2.3 $\mathsf{V}xA[x]$ is true in every case where $M(\lambda xA[x])$ is a partial function, no matter whether this function takes on the value w for a particular argument or not. Thus definition (a) is not suitable. In order to arrive at quantifiers Λx and $\mathsf{V}x$ referring only to the objects for which $A[x]$ is defined we introduce an operator $\sim$ such that $a \sim b$ is a term of L_1 if a and b are terms of the same category $\tau(\rho)$, and postulate:

$M(a \sim b) = w$ iff $M(a)$ and $M(b)$, restricted to the common domain of definition, are identical – in case this domain is not empty.

---

[1] If $M(F^{\tau(\rho)})$ is the totally undefined function from $E^+_{\tau(\rho),U}$, then $F^{\tau(\rho)}$ remains undefined. Since we also wish to admit the case where M is undefined for some *constants* – thou h it is of no special interest n the present context – we can also include totally undefined func- tions into the set $E^+_{\tau(\rho),U}$.

With

(a') $\wedge x^{\tau}A[x^{\tau}] := \lambda x^{\tau}A[x^{\tau}] \sim \lambda x^{\tau}(x^{\tau} \equiv x^{\tau})$

and (f) we can then introduce suitable quantifiers and keep the rest of the definitions in 2.2.3.

Definition (a'), however, does not solve the problem of colloquial generalizations of the form *All As are B* mentioned in section 1. In common usage such a sentence is only about the *A*s – i.e. it has a truth value iff there are *A*s and *B* is defined for all *A*s. For representing such sentences restricted generalizations can be introduced, for instance by stipulating

$M(\underset{A[x]}{\wedge} xB[x]) = w$ iff for all M' with $M' \underset{b}{=} M$ and

$M'(A[b]) = w$ $M'(B[b]) = w$ holds – provided that there is such an M' and that for all such M', $M'(B[b])$ is defined.

Names of non-existing objects can be handled as in 2.2.4. However, instead of defining descriptions as in 2.2.5 as well for the case where the normality condition is not met, using partial interpretations we can restrict the definition to the normal case, i.e. the case in 2.2.5(i).

3.2 Intensions

If in extension of 3.1.1.we postulate

$$E^{+}_{\iota(\tau),U} = E_{\tau,U}{}^{(I)},$$

we can define *partial intensional interpretations* in the same correspondence to 2.3.1 as we defined extensional interpretations in correspondence to 2.2.2. Having, however, emphasized in sections 1 and 2.3 that quantification into intensional contexts is only meaningful under the normality condition, 2.3.1(c) must be replaced by:

(c') $M_i(\lambda xA[x])$ is that function f from $E^{+}_{\tau(\rho),U}$ for which $f(M'_i(b)) = M'_i(A[b])$ holds for all M' with $M' \underset{b}{=} M$ and $M'_i(b)$ defined – provided that for all M', M'' with $M' \underset{b}{=} M$, $M'' \underset{b}{=} M$ and $M'_i(b) = M''_i(b)$ (for which both these values are defined) $M'_i(A[b]) = M''_i(A[b])$. Otherwise $M(\lambda xA[x])$ shall be the totally undefined function from $E^{+}_{\tau(\rho),U}$. $\lambda xA[x]$ shall be a term according to 2.1.2(c) in which the constant b of the same category as x does not occur.

With regard to *partial pragmatic interpretations* we also permit that $M_{i,j}(A)$ be not defined for all $j \in \mathcal{J}$.

The introduction of intensions and pragmatic relations provides a suitable framework for treating presuppositions.

3.2.1. A sentence B of L is a *presupposition* of A relative to interpretation M iff for all $i \in I$ and $j \in \mathcal{J}$ $M_{i,j}(A)$ is only defined if $M_{i,j}(B) = w$. If $M_{i,j}(B)$ is not dependent on j, then we call B a *purely intensional presupposition*, and if $M_{i,j}(B)$ is not dependent upon i, we call B a *purely pragmatic presupposition*.

According to this definition a sentence has an intension (as partial function) in a world i even if it has no extension in i because of a non-fulfilled presupposition. A description whose normality condition is not met is thus not completely without meaning, it just does not denote anything.

It is obvious that *material* implications cannot be used for the definition of presuppositions, if B is called a presupposition of A iff A and non-A both imply B. Otherwise every factually correct sentence B would be a presupposition to every other sentence A. Just as obvious, however, is the fact, that this implication cannot be understood in the sense of an entailment with reference to a set of interpretations (such that every interpretation which would make A true or false would make B true) because the question of whether B is a presupposition of A depends on the interpretation of A and B as long as we are considering the general case under point (3) in section 1 and not only the special cases in (4) and (5). For this reason the proposal of van Fraassen (1969) for handling presuppositions is not generally applicable. Only by reference to possible worlds and intensions can a general dependency of the assignment of an extension to A upon the truth value of B be determined with respect to one and the same interpretation M.

4. 3-valued interpretations

We turn now to the proposal to account for meaningless but grammatically well-formed expressions within the framework of a 3-valued logic. Since there is a multiplicity of 3-valued logics, we must first consider the principles such a logic should be based upon.

We wish to interpret the third value of sentences along with w and f – we will call it o^σ – as 'meaningless' in the sense of 'left indeterminate in truth value by the semantic conventions'. We adopt an extensive interpretation of the value o^σ according to which a sentence is characterized as meaningless if one of its components is meaningless. The orientation is towards partial 2-valued interpretations which also assign no truth value to a sentence if they are not defined for its components. The object is generally to establish a close correspondence between 2- and 3-valued interpretations so that for every 3-valued interpretation N there is a 2-valued interpretation M which assigns all sentences A with $N(A) \neq o^\sigma$ the same truth value as N, and vice versa: i.e. for every 2-valued interpretation M there is a 3-valued interpretation N which assigns every sentence A for which $M(A)$ is defined the same truth value as M. On the basis of this correspondence the theorems of 3-valued ogic will be exactly those of 2-valued logic. In natural languages we use in fact 2-valued logic, excepting, however, the metatheoretical principle of bivalence which requires that every sentence be true or false.[1]

A 3-valued logic can now be constructed on these lines corresponding either to the semantics of section 2 or to the semantics of section 3. We will only carry out the latter project here since the use of partial functions is unavoidable, as for instance in the treatment of presuppositions of indirect sentences. The truth value of a sentence of the form $F(\mu(A))$ – e.g. *John said that Jack gave up smoking* – depends on the partial function $\lambda{*}i\, M_i(A)$ and is not invariant with regard to a change in its domain of definition. And in general the reference to the frequent occurrence of only partially defined concepts which we made in section 1 already suggests strongly the use of partial functions as possible extensions.

4.1. Extensions

We will define first extensional 3-valued interpretations for the language L_1 and assign every category τ a single object 'meaninglessness' o^τ. o^σ will be assigned to a meaningless sentence, o^v to a meaningless proper name. The objects $o^{\tau(\rho)}$ will be introduced below.

The set of possible extensions of the category τ for the object domain is determined in analogy to 2.2.1 in the following way:

4.1.1.

$$E^*_{v,U} = U \cup \{o^v\}$$
$$E^*_{\sigma,U} = \{w, f, o^\sigma\}$$

---

[1] For the distinction between accepting the object language principle of *tertium non datur* and accepting the metalinguistic principle of bivalence see van Fraassen (1969).

$E^*_{\tau(\rho),U}$ is the set of functions f from $E^*_{\tau,U}{}^{E^*_\rho,U}$ which take the value o^τ for the argument o^ρ.

$o^{\tau(\rho)}$ shall be that function from $E^*_{\tau(\rho),U}$ which takes the value o^τ for all arguments.

4.1.2. An *extensional 3-valued interpretation* of L_1 over the (non-empty) object domain U is a 1-place function N with the following properties:

(a) $N(a) \in E^*_{\tau,U}$ for all constants a of L_1 of the category τ.

(b) $N(F(a)) = N(F)(N(a))$ for all terms in accordance with 2.1.2(b).

(c) $N(\lambda x A[x])$ is that function f from $E^*_{\tau(\rho),U}$ with $f(N'(b)) = N'(A[b])$ for all $N' \underset{b}{=} N$ and $N'(b) \neq o^\rho$. $\lambda x A[x]$ is a term according to 2.1.2(c) and the constant b of the same category as x shall not occur in $\lambda x A[x]$.

(d) $N(a^\tau \equiv b^\tau) = w$ for $N(a^\tau) \neq o^\tau$ and $N(a^\tau) = N(b^\tau)$; $N(a^\tau \equiv b^\tau) = f$ for $N(a^\tau) \neq o^\tau \neq N(b^\tau)$ and $N(a^\tau) \neq N(b^\tau)$; and otherwise $N(a^\tau \equiv b^\tau) = o^\sigma$ – for all terms according to 2.1.2(d).

The intuitive ideas for the construction of a 3-valued logic as formulated above can then be made precise in the following way:

4.1.3. An extensional 3-valued interpretation N and an extensional partial interpretation M (in the sense of 3.1) shall be called *correlated* if

(a) M and N are based on the same object domain;

(b) for all constants a^τ with $\tau = \nu,\sigma$ $M(a^\tau)$ is defined iff $N(a^\tau) \neq o^\tau$; if $M(a^\tau)$ is defined, then $M(a^\tau) = N(a^\tau)$;

(c) for all constants $a^{\tau(\rho)}$, $M(a^{\tau(\rho)})$ is the totally undefined function from $E^+_{\tau(\rho),U}$ iff $N(a^{\tau(\rho)}) = o^{\tau(\rho)}$; otherwise $M(a^{\tau(\rho)}) = N(a^{\tau(\rho)})/D(N(a^{\tau(\rho)}))$.

$D(N(a))$ is the set of arguments $\neq o^\rho$, not assigned the value o^τ by $N(a)$, while f/E is the function f restricted to E.

This correlation is a one-to-one correspondence between all 3-valued and all partial interpretations.

4.1.4. If N and M are correlated then everything which applies to the constants of L_1 according to 4.1.3 applies also to all terms of L_1.

This statement can be proved by induction on the degree of the terms, i.e. on the number of occurrences of logical operators in them, where brackets which express function-argument positioning according to 2.1.2(b) are also counted as operators.

We define:

4.1.5. A partial interpretation M *satisfies* a sentence A weakly if $M(A) = w$ or if $M(A)$ is undefined. A 3-valued interpretation N *satisfies A weakly* if $N(A) \neq f$.[1] A shall be called *weakly valid* if all partial interpretations satisfy A weakly. Furthermore A shall be called *weakly 3-valid* if all 3-valued interpretations satisfy A weakly.

From 4.1.4 we then obtain the theorem:

4.1.6. The weakly 3-valid sentences of L_1 are exactly the weakly valid sentences of L_1.

If the 3-valued semantics had been constructed corresponding to the semantics of section 2 instead of section 3, we would have obtained in place of 4.2.6 the theorem: The weakly 3-valid sentences are exactly the logically true sentences, i.e. the sentences satisfied by all complete 2-valued interpretations.

For the definitions of 2.2.3 corresponding remarks apply as were made in 3.1.2. We postulate

$$N(a^\tau \sim b^\tau) = w, \text{ if } N(a^\tau) \neq o^\tau \neq N(b^\tau) \text{ and } N(a^\tau)/D(N(a^\tau)) \cap D(N(b^\tau))$$
$$= N(b^\tau)/D(N(a^\tau)) \cap D(N(b^\tau)); N(a^\tau \sim b^\tau) = o^\sigma, \text{ if } N(a^\tau) = o^\tau \text{ or } N(b^\tau) = o^\tau; \text{ and otherwise } N(a^\tau \sim b^\tau) = f.$$

Names of non-existing objects and description terms can be treated in direct analogy to 3.1.

4.2. Intensions

The definition of 3-valued intensional interpretations also follows directly from 2.3 and 3.2. We let

$$E^*_{\iota(\tau),U} = E_{\tau,U}{}^I.$$

$o^*_{\iota(\tau)}$ is to be that function from $E^{*(\tau)}_{\iota}{}_{,U}$ which assigns every $i \in I$ the value o^τ.

In correspondence to 3.2 condition (c) of 2.3.1 in the definition of intensional 3-valued interpretation takes the form:

(c'') $N_i(\lambda x A[x])$ is that function f from $E^*_{\tau(\rho),U}$ for which $f(N'(b)) = N'(A[b])$ holds for all N' with $N' \underset{b}{=} N$ and $N'(b) \neq o^\rho$ – in case $N'_i(A[b]) = N''_i(A[b])$ holds for all N', N'' with $N' \underset{b}{=} N, N'' \underset{b}{=} N,$

---

[1] The concept 'satisfies weakly' was introduced by Woodruff (1970).

and $N_i'(b) = N_i''(b) \neq o^\rho$. Otherwise $N_i(\lambda x A[x]) = o^{\tau(\rho)}$. We choose b as in 2.3.1.

The definitions and theorems 4.1.3 to 4.1.6 carry over to intensional 3-valued interpretations, and introducing pragmatic interpretations in 3-valued semantics requires no additional considerations either.

Summing up we can say: The 3-valued semantics we have sketched above derives in a simple and straightforward way from the semantics of partial 2-valued interpretations of section 3 by assigning undefined expressions the object 'meaninglessness'. 3-valued logics can, of course, also be constructed in quite different ways, but these are barred to us here since our intention has been to interpret the value 'meaninglessness' as 'indeterminate in value by a 2-valued semantic interpretation' and to let 3-valued logic coincide with the 2-valued logic of natural languages.

5. Sets of interpretations

In building up our 3-valued semantics we understood the characterization of terms as 'meaningless' in an extensional sense in which a sentence $A \lor B$, for instance, is meaningless if A or B is meaningless. In a narrower sense we could also call a sentence 'meaningless' if it could be assigned the value '*true*' as well as '*false*' by additional semantic stipulations. In this sense a sentence $A \lor B$ is not meaningless if B is true even if A is meaningless. And a sentence of the form $A \lor \neg A$ is never meaningless.

If meaningless expressions are to be understood in this way, (non-empty) sets T of 2-valued interpretations M suggest themselves as an adequate tool of semantic analysis. If a is a term of L, it is interpreted by a set T in such a way that

(a) $T(a) = \alpha$ in case $M(a) = \alpha$ holds for all $M \in T$, and
(b) $T(a)$ remains undefined, if there is no such α.

Intuitively this procedure can be described thus: if only limited information about a (2-valued) interpretation of L is available, take the set T of all interpretations M compatible with this information, and assign a term a a meaning α if and only if this meaning can be derived from the given information, i.e. if and only if all $M \in T$ assign a the value α.

The sentences true for all such sets T are obviously exactly the logically true sentences, i.e. the sentences true under all interpretations. Thus we get in a trivial way a result corresponding to 4.1.6.

We are, however, not concerned here with all the interpretations of L

that can be defined by arbitrary sets T. We have addressed ourselves rather to the problem, that an interpretation can be fixed for all constants of L and can still be indeterminate for some terms of L. We are therefore interested primarily in those sets T for which $T(a)$ is defined for all (or at least most) constants a, and must ask, therefore, if partial 2-valued interpretations can be represented by sets of complete 2-valued interpretations, i.e. if working with sets of interpretations we can get the same results as working with partial interpretations.

Let us confine our attention to the assignment of extensions. If we take sets of complete interpretations in the sense of 2.2.2 we can account for the fact, that a term $a^{\tau(\rho)}$ denotes a partial function f from $E_{\rho,U}$ into $E_{\tau,U}$ – we can set $T(a^{\tau(\rho)}) = f$, if $E \subset E_{\rho,U}$ is the most comprehensive set, such that $M(a^{\tau(\rho)})/E = f$ holds for all $M \in T$ – but those partial functions cannot appear as arguments of other functions since we are using $E_{\tau,U}$ instead of $E_{\tau,U}^{+}$ as sets of possible extensions. We have seen, however, that the use of partial functions as arguments is indispensable for an adequate treatment of meaningless terms. We cannot, therefore, represent partial interpretations by sets of complete interpretations; so the use of such sets leads to unsatisfactory results.

There remains then only the recourse of using some sort of completed partial interpretations. Their definition is to be derived from that of a partial interpretation M with the additional stipulation that if $M(a^{\tau})$ is undefined, $M'(a^{\tau})$ is to be an arbitrary object from $E_{\tau,U}^{+}$ for the completed interpretation M'. If T_M is the set of all completions of M, then T_M is defined exactly for those terms a, for which M is defined, and for them we have $M(a) = T_M(a)$.

But even if partial interpretations can be represented by sets of interpretations by this procedure, it is still quite unacceptable since the notion of a completed partial interpretation is intuitively wholly unreasonable. If M' is such an interpretation, $M'(F^{\tau(\rho)})$ a partial function, and $M'(a^{\rho})$ an object not belonging to the domain of this function, $M'(F^{\tau(\rho)}(a^{\rho}))$ is still supposed to be defined. Such a stipulation can, of course, not yield an intuitively acceptable concept of interpretation.

Partial interpretations cannot therefore be represented in a reasonable way by sets of interpretations.

The definition of an interpretation by a set of interpretations furthermore is not recursive: $T(A \supset B)$ does not depend directly on the values $T(A)$ and $T(B)$ and can be defined even if both $T(A)$ and $T(B)$ are undefined. This is not in accordance with the general semantic principle that the meaning of a sentence derives from the meaning of its constituents.

And finally we want to quantify with the operator μ over interpretations M_i in intensional semantics. If every M_i is a complete interpretation, we cannot account for the presuppositions of A by $\mu(A)$ and cannot use partial functions $\lambda^* i M_i(A)$ as arguments of functors. If, on the other hand, we were to work with sets T_i of interpretations and quantify with μ over such sets, we would use values of interpretations as well as sets of interpretations in the recursive definition in a rather obscure fashion.

For these reasons the attempt to represent incomplete interpretations by sets of interpretations seems to be unsuccessful, or at least to become so complicated and artificial as to be without interest.

For a simple and adequate treatment of well-formed but meaningless terms there remain then only the 2-valued semantics of partial interpretations and 3-valued semantics. Both come to the same thing on the definitions in section 4. Since, however, in our 3-valued interpretations the value 'meaningless' is understood in the sense of 'indeterminate under 2-valued semantic conventions', the notion of partial interpretation is to be regarded as the more fundamental one.

REFERENCES

Fraassen, B. C. van (1969). 'Presuppositions, supervaluations, and free logic'. In K. Lambert, ed., *The Logical Way of Doing Things*, pp. 67-91. New Haven Yale University Press.

Kutschera, F. v. (1973a). *Einführung in die Logik der Werte, Normen und Entscheidungen*. Freiburg.

—— (1975). 'Grundzüge der logischen Grammatik'. To appear in S. J. Schmidt, ed. *Pragmatic* II. Munich.

Lambert, K. (ed.) (1970). *Philosophical Problems in Logic*. Dordrecht: Reidel.

Montague, R. (1970). 'Universal grammar', *Theoria*, **36,** 373-98.

Quine, W. V. (1953). 'Reference and modality'. In W. V. Quine, *From a Logical Point of View*, pp. 139-59. Cambridge, Mass.

Scott, D. (1970). 'Advice on modal logic'. In Lambert (1970), pp. 143-73.

Woodruff, P. W. (1970). 'Logic and truth value gaps'. In Lambert (1970), pp. 121-42.

Subcategorization of adnominal and adverbial modifiers

RENATE BARTSCH

1.

The topic of this paper[1] is the role of adnominal and adverbial modifiers in sentence semantics. Before going into details I will sketch the framework in which this special problem will be treated. The framework is that of Natural Generative (NG) Grammar (Bartsch and Vennemann (1972)). A natural generative grammar comprises the following rules:

1.1. *From the point of view of linguistic production*

(a) Formation rules of a properly extended predicate logic (PEPL), i.e. a predicate logic extended by predicates over sentence intensions and by several sorts of individual variables and constants (multi-sortal logic).

(b) Formation rules of a categorial grammar of a natural language.

(c) Constituent building rules. They map forms built according to PEPL (a), the semantic representations, onto forms built in accordance with categorial syntax (b). If the formation rules of PEPL are understood as the generative component of the grammar, then the constituent building rules are conversion rules with semantic representations as input and categorial forms as output. The rules of categorial syntax then have to be understood as restrictions on the forms of the output of constituent building rules and thus as restrictions on the constituent building rules themselves.

(d) Lexicalization rules.

(e) Morphological rules.

(f) Serialization rules.

(g) Intonation rules.

The semantic representations as well as the forms of categorial syntax are not linearly ordered but only hierarchically ordered. Serialization rules

[1] I am grateful to Theo Vennemann (UCLA) for clarifying discussions of this paper and for valuable suggestions concerning both content and presentation.

apply to the forms of categorial syntax after lexicalization rules and morphological rules have applied. The serialization rules of English serialize, e.g. (*because of the rain(fast(run)))* as [[[*run*]*fast*]*because of the rain*], and the serialization rules of German serialize the same categorial structure (*wegen des Regens(schnell(laufen)))* as [*wegen des Regens*[*schnell*[*laufen*]]]. The serialization rules serialize in cases of natural serialization from left to right or from right to left depending on language type (Vennemann (1972a); Bartsch and Vennemann (1972)).

1.2. From the point of view of linguistic analysis and interpretation

The surface syntactic structure of a sentence in a natural language is connected with its interpretation by two formal languages, the language specified by categorial syntax and the language generated by the syntax of PEPL. The categorial structure of a complex expression is inferred from the knowledge that certain lexical expressions can be used in certain syntactic relations and from their position in the expression, from morphological information and intonation. Forms of categorial syntax are to a certain degree interpretable, namely to the extent that subcategorial differences are not involved.[1] Thus, e.g., in (*blond'* (*boy'*)) and in (*alleged'* (*murderer'*)) the adnominal adjective can be interpreted – following Montague (1970) – as a function that maps the intensions of common nouns on

---

[1] If b is an expression of natural language then b' denotes its disambiguated meaning. The expression b' is an expression in the vocabulary of intensional logic in Montague's system and it is an expression of categorial grammar in NG grammar. Each lexical item b contains some syntactic information, e.g., *beautiful'* can be used at least as an adnominal modifier, as an adverbial modifier, and as a predicative adjective. If C is a category in which b' can be used, then b' in the category C can be assigned an extension. The intension $^\wedge b'_c$ of b'_c is a function which, when applied to a universe of individuals, a possible world i, and a point of time j yields the extension of b'_c relative to that universe, that possible world and that point of time. Whether a predicate operator, and in particular an adnominal or adverbial operator, is to be interpreted as a function on the extension or the intension of the operand depends on subcategorial information. E.g., *red'* and *big'* are extensional operators (i.e. interpretable as functions on extensions of predicates) and *alleged'* and *fake'* are intensional operators (i.e. interpretable as functions on intensions of predicates). This difference is not expressed in the forms of categorial syntax or intensional logic but rather in subcategorial distinctions. In a Montague grammar all predicate operators are functions on intensions. Thus all expressions of one categorial form receive a single interpretation. Since verbs and common nouns are translated into expressions of a single type in intensional logic *beautiful girl'* and *dance beautifully'* receive the same kind of interpretation, namely *beautiful'* ($^\wedge girl'$) and *beautiful'*($^\wedge dance'$) of the same type, even though *beautiful'* is a very different kind of function in both cases: *beautiful girl'*(x)$\not\Leftrightarrow$*beautiful'*(x), but *dance beautifully'*(x) $\not\Leftrightarrow$*beautiful'*(x). In NG grammar *beautiful* is analysed as one semantic content used in *two* different functions indicated by the subcategories A_1 and Av_1. In this example not only the subcategorial but also the categorial difference is relevant to the interpretation. But this categorial distinction is also eliminated in intensional logic.

the extensions of the compound common nouns, viz. the extensions of *blond boy'* and *alleged murderer'*, respectively. But this interpretation does not specify the meaning difference between *blond* and *alleged* as adnominal operators. It is a subcategorial difference that makes *blond'* to be a standard operator and interpretable as a function over extensions of predicates, and *alleged'* a non-standard operator which is interpreted as a function over intensions of predicates.[1] Consequently NG-theory provides for rules that explicate the kind of functions performed by adnominal and adverbial modifiers by assigning them different logical forms. These rules translate the categorial forms into forms of PEPL, using the subcategorial information obtained from the syntactic and lexical structure of the analysed sentence. These conversion rules are the inverse rules of the constituent building rules mentioned in section 1. On the level of PEPL, there are no operators on predicates, in particular no adnominal or adverbial modifiers.

This position differs from Montague's in the following respects: In Montague (1970), there is a single interpretation common to all categorial forms with adverbial and adnominal modifiers, namely $\alpha'(^\wedge\beta')$ with α' as the translation of the verb or noun modifier α and with β' as the translation of the verb or noun β into a single type of intensional logic. If this is done, differences like 'standard–non-standard', 'predicative–non-predicative' are eliminated, and restrictions on the order of application of adnominals and adverbials of different subcategories, as well as their restricted occurrence with verb negation, are unmotivated on the level of categorial forms and the corresponding forms of intensional logic. The categorial distinction between adformula phrases (adsententials or sentence adverbials) and adverbial phrases is not sufficient to catch all subcategorial differences that have to be taken into account to guarantee syntactic well-formedness of sentences with adverbial constructions. E.g.,

(1) a. Surprisingly John ran because of the rain
    b. *Because of the rain surprisingly John ran
(2) a. Because of the rain John ran fast
    b. John ran fast because of the rain
    c. *John ran because of the rain fast

In $\alpha'(^\wedge\beta')$ it is not explicated what kind of function α' is. Since there is no subcategorial information about α', the precise nature of the function α' can only be inferred from the lexical content of α. But this is insufficient because morphology, word order, and intonation are often necessary to

---

[1] There are also standard intensional operators, e.g. *regrettably, surprisingly.*

determine the subcategory in which α is used, i.e. what kind of function α' is. E.g.,

(3) a. Strangely John sings 'America the beautiful'.
  b. John strangely sings 'America the beautiful'.
  c. John sings 'America the beautiful' strangely.

In (3a) we have an adsentential:

$(strange'_{As_2} (John\ sings\ 'America\ the\ beautiful''_S)_S)$.

In (3b) we have an adverbial:

$(strange'_{Av_4} (sing\ 'America\ the\ beautiful''_V)_V)$.

In (3c) we have an adverbial:

$(strange'_{Av_1} (sing\ 'America\ the\ beautiful''_V)_V)$.

The interpretations of these categorial forms depend on the subcategorial index, i.e. the subscript attached to the main category symbol. α' in As_2 is interpreted as a function on senses (intensions) of sentences, α' in Av_4 is interpreted as a function on intensions of predicates, and α' in Av_1 is interpreted as a functions on extensions of predicates. Thus the interpretation of the categorial form (3a) is: The sentence is true iff *John sings 'America the beautiful''* is true in all worlds compatible with all states of affairs whose being the case is strange. The interpretation of the complex verb in (3b) is that *strange'* in Av_4 is a function which maps the sense of the verb *sing 'America the beautiful''* on the extension of this verb in all worlds compatible with all states of affairs whose being the case is strange. Obviously, (3a) and (3b) are logically equivalent under these interpretations. The interpretation of the complex verb in (3c) is that *strange'* in Av_1 is a function that maps the extension of *sing 'America the beautiful''* (in the real world) on the extension of *sing 'America the beautiful' strangely'*. This function is an intersection function (or at least a subsection function). The interpretation of (3c) is not equivalent with that of (3b) or (3a).[1]

Since the information from morphology, position, and intonation is lost on the level of $\alpha'(^\wedge\beta')$ forms of intensional logic, it is obvious that a translation into intensional logic as proposed by Montague is insufficient. I can think of two ways to remedy this situation. We either carry subcategorial information into intensional logic, as was proposed in Bartsch and Vennemann (1972: § 1.4). Or we interpret categorial forms, including

---

[1] There may be speakers who get a second reading of (b) equivalent to that of (c). But this only shows that the position of *strangely* in front of the verb admits the interpretation of *strange* in two different subcategories.

subcategorial information, directly via PEPL, without an intermediate level of intensional logic of a kind where all categorial forms Adnominal + Noun or Adverbial + Verb receive a single representation in which the subcategorial differences are disregarded. This is the procedure of Bartsch (1972), Bartsch and Vennemann (1972), and of the present paper.

2.

After this survey of syntax and semantics in NG grammar from the points of view of production and analysis, I will discuss adnominal and adverbial modifiers in detail. This discussion amounts to the explication of a portion of the connection between categorial syntax and PEPL.

In the course of the successive application of constituent building rules (or their inverses) we receive forms as inputs and outputs of these rules that are partially formed according to the syntax of PEPL and partially according to the syntax of categorial grammar (hybrid forms). These rules are therefore formulated in a language which is the union of both syntaxes plus a few rules providing for the well-formedness of the hybrid forms. In this union of two languages the constituent building rules and their inverse rules can be formulated as equivalence relationships between formulas. They can be understood as meaning rules for whole classes of categorial expressions, namely meaning rules for expressions containing certain subcategories. The following is an example of such a rule:

$$\square\ (\forall a')(\forall b')(\forall c')(((a'_{A_1}(b'_N)_N)(c'_T)_S) \leftrightarrow ((a'_P(c'_T)_S) \wedge (b'_P(c'_T)_S)_S))$$

For this we write the shorter:

$$((a'_{A_1}(b'_N)_N)(c'_T)_S)\ \approx\ ((a'_P(c'_T)_S) \wedge (b'_P(c'_T)_S)_S).$$

'$\approx$' represents the metalinguistic notion of being necessarily equivalent.[1] An example for the above formula is:

This is a red house. $\approx$ *This is red, and this is a house.*

One of the rules taking care of the well-formedness of hybrid forms is used with the above example: All nouns, verbs and predicative adjectives are represented as predicates (P) in PEPL.

In section 1 the inverses of constituent building rules were presented as conversion rules converting categorial forms into PEPL forms. These conversion rules are equivalence relationships in a language which is the

---

[1] The subscripts indicate the subcategory (A_1; adnominal modifier of subcategory 1, N: common noun, T: term, P: predicate, S: sentence). Thus, e.g., the notation b_N indicates that b is used in the category of common nouns.

union of both syntaxes. However, they can also be understood as a kind of meaning rule for subcategories. If the relation between categorial syntax and extended predicate logic is understood in this way, the categorial forms can be regarded as forms introduced into the syntax of PEPL by definitions, typically abbreviatory definitions. This position concerning the structure of a grammar was proposed by Vennemann at a colloquium held in Berlin, winter semester 1972/3. While in the former view forms of two formal languages are connected by rules formulated in a third language, the idea of this position is that the syntactic constructions of a specific language are introduced into the universal syntax of PEPL as language-specific structures, where these are formed according to certain universal principles discussed in Bartsch and Vennemann (1972), and in Vennemann (1972a,b). These language-specific structures are categorial forms, the *raison d'être* of which is precisely that they conform to these principles. Thus, expressions consisting of an adnominal or adverbial operator and a noun or verb are defined by 'definitions in use' analogously to the definition of, e.g., the iota-operator for definite descriptions, a device for the formation of complex terms. Understanding the constituent building rules and their inverses as definitions in use, we can then write, with the above example,

$$((a'_{A_1}(b'_N)_N)(c'_T)_S) \Leftrightarrow_{\text{def}} ((a'_P(c'_T)_S) \wedge (b'_P(c'_T)_S)_S).$$

If this view is adopted the rules of categorial syntax are formation rules that do not belong to the generative component of the language.[1] They are rather restrictions on the outputs of constituent building rules like, as regards the above example, (CR1).

(CR1) $a'_P(c'_T) \wedge b'_P(c'_T) \rightsquigarrow (a'_{A_1}(b'_N)_N)(c'_T).$

Thus they are restrictions on the possibilities for abbreviatory definitions. We should notice, however, that not only the categorial form $((a'_{A_1}(b'_N)_N)$ can be realized in natural language but also the PEPL form $a'_P(c'_T) \wedge$

---

[1] Reasons for not assuming that categorial syntax belongs to the generative components are given in Bartsch and Vennemann (1972:§1.2) and Vennemann (1972a). A further argument for not treating categorial syntax as the generative component derives from the fact that this component would generate many constructions with adverbials which are not well-formed. To prevent this the categorial rule 'If a is an adverb and b is a verb then $a(b)$ is a verb' has to be replaced by a set of very complicated rules which restrict the possible combinations of adverbials in such a way that all constructions are syntactically well-formed and interpretable. If, on the other hand, PEPL is the generative component, the co-occurrence and order-of-application problem is taken care of by the formation rules of PEPL and does not arise on the categorial level. Only well-formed forms of PEPL are converted into categorial forms by rules conforming to certain principles which reflect the hierarchies in the application of predicates on the PEPL level in adverbial operator-operand hierarchies on the categorial level.

$b'_P(c'_T)$.[1] However, speakers hardly ever say things like *this is a house and this is red* instead of *this is a red house*. Sentences of the form $(a'(b'_P)_P)(c'_T)$ are preferred to sentences of the form $a'_P(c'_T) \wedge b'_P(c'_T)$ because of their greater compactness and the resulting perceptual advantages (Vennemann (1972a,b)).

Since the formation rules of PEPL and their semantics, as well as the rules of categorial syntax, can be assumed to be known – even though there exists considerable differences in the rule systems presented by individual authors – I can in the following concentrate on the constituent building rules and their inverses which connect categorial forms and forms for PEPL.

3.

Among the adnominal modifiers I will treat the subcategories exemplified by the following expressions: *red house, big mouse, alleged murderer of Smith*.

The meaning *red'* of *red* is used in the subcategory A_1; *big'* is used in A_2; *alleged'* is used in A_3. *House', mouse', murderer of Smith'* are used in N.

Among the adverbial modifiers I will treat the subcategories exemplified by the following expressions: *dance beautifully, run fast, write carefully, exceed in length, run because of the rain, allegedly murdered Smith, regrettably murdered Smith*.

Beautifully' is used in the subcategory Av_{11}; *fast'* in Av_{12}; *carefully'* in Av_{13}; *in length'* in Av_2; *because of the rain'* in As_1 and Av_3; *allegedly'* in Avr_{41} and As_{21}; and *regrettably'* in Avr_{42} and As_{22}. *Dance', run', write', murdered Smith'* are used in V_1, and *exceed'* is used in V_2.

3.1. Adnominal modifiers

(1) *red house*

(CR1) $((a'_{A_1}(b'_N)_N)(c'_T)_S) \rightsquigarrow ((a'_P(c'_T)_S) \wedge (b'_P(c_T)_S)_S)$

From (CR1) we obtain:

$(red'_{A_1}(house'_N)_N)(c_T) \rightsquigarrow red'_P(c_T) \wedge house'_P(c_T)$

The categorial form *red'* (*house'*) can be interpreted directly: *red'* in the

---

[1] A very general constituent building rule has to apply in order to obtain $c'_T(\delta_1)(a'_P) \wedge c'_T(\delta_1)(b'_P)$ as a categorial form in accordance with the categorial syntax of Bartsch and Vennemann (1972), where terms appear with case marking applied to n-place predicates, in particular n-place verbs and n-place adjectives (prepositions), yielding $n-1$-place predicates. (0-place predicates are the limiting case, namely, sentences.) Then by lexicalization a'_P is replaced by a predicative adjective and b'_P is replaced by a common noun. A morphological rule then has to apply and we obtain $c_T(\delta_1)(a_{AP}(be_{V_{AUX}})_V) \wedge c_T(\delta_1)(b_N(be_{V_{AUX}})_V)$. By morphological rules $c_T(\delta_1)$ becomes the nominative form of c.

category A_1 is interpretable as a function that maps the extension of *house'* on the extension of *red house'*. That this is insufficient becomes apparent from the following example where the adnominal is also a function on the extension of predicates, but a different kind of function.

(2) *big mouse*

Rule (CR') below is a special case of a constituent building rule which applies to all kinds of constructions with relative adjectives and comparison. (CR'') is a special case of a constituent building rule which serves to construct $n-1$-place predicates from n-place predicates by applying terms in the appropriate case marking to n-place predicates.

$$(\text{CR}') \quad >((f_D^M(c_T)_T), N_{Y,D}) \rightsquigarrow (d'_{Av2}(\rangle_{P2})_{P2})(c'_T, N_{Y,D})$$
$$(\text{CR}'') \quad a'_{P2}(c'_T, b'_T) \rightsquigarrow ((b'_T(\delta_2)_{KT})(a'_{P2})_{P1})(c'_T)$$

KT is the category of terms with a case marking. δ_2 is a case. In (CR2) below it is apparent that relative adjectives are intersection functions.

$$(\text{CR2}) \quad ((d'_{A_2}(b'_N)_N)(c'_T) \rightsquigarrow (((N_{b',D}(\delta_2)_{KT})(d'_{Av_2}(>_P{}^2)_P{}^2)_P)(c'_T) \wedge b'_P$$
$$(c'_T)))$$

By these rules we obtain:

$$(big'_{A_2}(mouse'_N)_N)(c'_T) \rightsquigarrow >(f_{Big'}(c'_T), N_{mouse', \; Big'}) \wedge mouse'_P(c'_T)$$

Note that *Big'* is lexicalized as *size*.[1]

(3) *alleged murderer*

$$(\text{CR3}) \quad (a'_{A_3}(b'_N)_N)(c'_T) \rightsquigarrow a'_{P_I}(^\wedge(b'_P(c'_T)_S)_{T_S})$$

P_I designates the subcategory of intensional sentence predicates and T_S indicates the subcategory of sentential terms, i.e. terms that are arguments for intensional sentence predicates. By (CR3) we obtain:

$$(alleged'_{A_3}(murderer'_N)_N)(c'_T) \rightsquigarrow (alleged'_{P_I}(^\wedge(murderer'_P(c'_T)_S)_{T_S})_S)$$

If categorial syntax is directly interpreted by intensional logic, *alleged'* (*murderer'*) is interpreted as *alleged'* applied to the intension of *murderer'*, i.e. $^\wedge murderer'$. In this way to the compound noun *alleged murderer'* there is assigned as an extension the extension of *murderer'* in all possible worlds compatible with what is alleged.

---

[1] $N_{Mice, \; Size}$ is the norm or average of the sizes of mice. In the treatment of relative adjectives and comparison in Bartsch and Vennemann (1972) *d-er than* $N_{Y,D}$ is analysed as $(N_{Y,D}(\delta_2)\,(d'(>)))$, where d' is a predicate limiting adverbial (in the example also lexicalizable as *in size* in *exceed in size*). δ_2 is a case marker for the term $N_{Y,D}$.

3.2. *Adverbial modifiers*

I can be brief about rules for adverbials because this topic is discussed at great length in Bartsch (1972) and also to some extent in Bartsch and Vennemann (1972: § 5).

(1) *dance beautifully*

In (CR5) $B(x,r)$ means *x is involved in r*. *x* is a variable over thing-individuals, and *r* is a variable over processes, including action processes.

(CR5) $(a'_{Av_1}(b'_V)_V)(x_T) \rightsquigarrow a'_P(\imath r)(B_P(x_T, r_T) \wedge b'\text{-PROCESS}_P(r_T)_S)_T)$

By (CR5) we obtain:

$(beautiful'_{Av_{11}}(dance'_V)_V)(x_T) \rightsquigarrow$
$beautiful'_{A_1}((\imath r)(B_P(x_T, r_T) \wedge dance'\text{-PROCESS}_P(r_T)_S)_T)$

(2) *run fast*

By (CR5') we obtain:

$(fast'_{Av_{12}}(run'_V)_V)(x_T) \rightsquigarrow$
$fast'_{A_2}((\imath r)(B_P(x_T, r_T) \wedge run'\text{-PROCESS}_P(r_T)_S)_T)$

(3) *write carefully*

Here (CR5) applies as before. There is furthermore a selectional restriction for *careful'*, namely that *r* is an action process.

(4) *exceed in length*

Predicate limiting adverbials like *in length* are treated in Bartsch (1972, Appendix) and Bartsch and Vennemann (1972: § 5).

(CR6) $(a'_{Av_2}(b'_{Pn})_{Pn})(x_{1T}, \ldots, x_{nT}) \rightsquigarrow b'_{Pn}((a'_F(x_{1T})_T), \ldots, (a'_F(x_{nT})_T))$

F is the category T/T i.e. *a'* in that category maps a term on a term, namely *x* on *length of x*. In the notation of (CR') a'_F was represented by f_A^M, e.g., f_{Length}^M. By (CR6) we obtain:

$(in\ length'_{Av_2}(exceed'_{V2})_{V2})(x_T, y_T) \rightsquigarrow >((f_{Length}^M(x_T)_T), (f_{Length}^M(y_T)_T)).$

The right-hand side can be realized by *the length of x exceeds the length of y*.

(5) *run because of the rain*

(CR7) $(a'_{Av_3}(b'_V)_V)(c_T) \rightsquigarrow a'_P((\imath v)[b'_P(c_T)_S]^*(v_T)_T)$

The right-hand side can be realized as *That c runs is because of the rain*, for the present example. By (CR7) we receive:

$$(because\ of\ the\ rain'_{Av_3}(run'_V)_V)(x_T)$$
$$because\ of\ the\ rain'_P((\imath v)[run'_P(x_T)_S]^*(v_T)_T)$$

A further analysis of the internal structure of the adverbs of the sub-category Av_3 is given in Bartsch (1972). Depending on topicalization, the phrases used in the category Av_3 can also be used in the category of adsententials, As_1. In this case a constituent building rule would apply by which the categorial structure $(a'_{As_1}(b'_S)_S)$ is built. This structure is realized as *Because of the rain x runs*, for the present example. In Bartsch (1972) the structure with the adsentential was an intermediate step in the derivation of the structure with the adverbial. Vennemann (personal communication) has suggested deriving both constructions by two different constituent building rules directly from the predication over the event (on the right-hand side of the rule (CR7)), where the application of these rules depends on topicalization.

(6) *allegedly murdered Smith*

$$(CR8)\ (a'_{Av_{41}}(b'_V)_V)(c_T) \rightsquigarrow a'_{P_I}(^\wedge(b'_P(c'_T)_S)_{T_s})$$

By (CR8) we obtain:

$$(alleged'_{Av_{41}}(murdered\ Smith'_V)_V)(x_T) \rightsquigarrow$$
$$alleged'_{P_I}(^\wedge(murdered\ Smith'_P(x_T)_S)_{T_s})$$

The right-hand side can be realized as *It is alleged that x murdered Smith*, and the left-hand side as *x allegedly murdered Smith*. The corresponding construction with the adsentential results from the application of (CR9), by which we obtain:

$$(alleged'_{As_{21}}(murdered\ Smith'_P(x_T)_S)_S)$$

$$(CR9)\ a'_{As_{21}}(b'_P(c'_T)_S) \rightsquigarrow a'_{P_I}(^\wedge(b'_P(c'_T)_S)_{T_s})$$

The complex predicate obtained by (CR8) can also be directly interpreted in intensional logic: to $(allegedly'(^\wedge murdered\ Smith'))$ is assigned the extension of *murdered Smith'* in all worlds compatible with what is alleged. Thus *Paul allegedly murdered Smith* is true iff Paul is a member of this extension. In this way *allegedly* is taken as an intensional operator over predicates. In *Allegedly Paul murdered Smith*, *allegedly* is a 'pragmatic' operator on a sentence such that *Allegedly Paul murdered Smith* is true iff

Paul murdered Smith is true in all worlds compatible with what is alleged. In *That Paul murdered Smith is alleged, alleged* is an intensional sentence predicate such that this sentence is true iff *that Paul murdered Smith* is a member of the set of those states of affairs that are alleged. Thus all three sentences are necessarily equivalent under the point of view of truth conditions.

(7) *regrettably murdered Smith*

The analysis is similar to that of (6), except that *regret* is a factive verb. *I regret that Paul murdered Smith* presupposes that Paul murdered Smith. The assertion is merely that I regret that fact. In *Regrettably Paul murdered Smith* as well as in *Paul regrettably murdered Smith* it is asserted that Paul murdered Smith and it is furthermore expressed that that is regrettable. Though *that Paul murdered Smith* is presupposed for the assertion *it is regrettable*, it is not presupposed for the sentences with adverbials or adsententials. Thus in those sentences something is asserted which at the same time becomes a presupposition for the speaker because otherwise the predicate *regrettable* could not apply. However, it is not a presupposition for the hearer because he may challenge the information that Paul murdered Smith by answering *No, that is not the case* to *Paul regrettably murdered Smith*. The sentence *That Paul murdered Smith is regrettable* is semantically represented by

$(regrettable'_{P_l}(^\wedge Paul\ murdered\ Smith'_S)_{T_S})_S)$ with the following condition of use: ⟨Paul murdered Smith⟩.

Here ⟨ ⟩ indicates that the proposition included belongs in the presupposition pool of the discourse. The opposition factivity versus nonfactivity is relevant to the conditions of application for factive verbs but not to the logical form of the sentence itself.[1] Because of the difference in presuppositions, factive verbs can be used in phrases like *I regret the fact that*...or *the fact that*...*is regrettable*. For the adverbials of Av_{42} and the adsententials of As_{22} the constituent building rules (CR8²) and (CR9²) are posited:

(CR8²) $(a'_{Av_{42}}(b'_V)_V)(c'_T) \rightsquigarrow b'_P(c'_T) \wedge a'_{P_l}(^\wedge(b'_P(c'_T)_S)_{T_S})$.
(CR9²) $a'_{As_{22}}(b'_P(c'_T)_S) \rightsquigarrow b'_P(c'_T) \wedge a'_{P_l}(^\wedge(b'_P(c'_T)_S)_{T_S})$.

[1] This proposal for the treatment of factivity was made by Vennemann (1972a); for an opposing view, see Kiparsky and Kiparsky (1971), and Keenan (1972).

4. Summary and conclusion

In Montague (1970), adnominal and adverbial modifier constructions are interpreted via their translation into intensional logic. They all have a single interpretation, viz., as functions on the intensions of predicates:

$$\alpha_A \beta_N \text{ ———} \rightarrow \alpha'(^\wedge\beta')$$
$$\beta_V \alpha_{Av} \text{ ———} \rightarrow \alpha'(^\wedge\beta').$$

Important differences between these constructions are eliminated, with the consequence that inferences such as *red ball'*$(x) \Rightarrow$ *red'*(x), *red ball'*$(x) \Rightarrow$ *ball'*(x) cannot be drawn on the level of intensional logic. Therefore, a further transformation of $\alpha'(^\wedge\beta')$ is necessary depending on subcategorial information contained in the operator α'. But at this point only lexical semantic information of α is available – which is insufficient for determining subcategories. Contrary to this proposal the categorial syntax of NG grammar has operator-operand relationships such as $\alpha'_{A_i}(\beta'_N)$, α'_{Av_i}-(β'_V), and $\alpha'_{As_i}(\beta'_S)$. Bidirectional conversion rules convert these categorial forms, together with the subcategorial information referred to by the index i, into forms of a properly extended predicate logic (PEPL), and conversely. Furthermore, this approach is preferable to that of Montague because it explains why adsententials, adverbials, and adnominals are restricted in their order of application to sentences, verbs, or nouns, and why they behave differently with regard to verb negation (see Bartsch (1972)).

There are two more fundamental advantages to the NG approach. First – as I have indicated here – Montague's approach requires that all co-occurrence and order-of-application restrictions for syntactic forms be incorporated into categorial syntax, something which gives rise to immense complications. This can be understood as an argument against all approaches which regard categorial syntax as the generative component of a grammar. By contrast, this problem is in NG grammar transferred to PEPL, where it is easily handled by its formation rules which are sensitive to selectional restrictions between predicates and individuals of various kinds. Second – and this goes beyond the present discussion – Montague's approach does not provide a single level of representation where word order regularities can be formulated in a uniform way and, in addition, in such a way that universals of word order and word order change are considered (Vennemann (1972a), Bartsch and Vennemann (1972. § 6.2)).

REFERENCES

Bartsch, Renate. (1972). *Adverbialsemantik*. Frankfurt a.M.; Athenäum.

Bartsch, Renate and Vennemann, Theo. (1972). *Semantic Structures. A Study in the Relation between Semantics and Syntax*. Frankfurt a.M.: Athenäum.

Keenan, Edward, (1972). 'On semantically based grammar', *Linguistic Inquiry*, 3, 413–61.

Kiparsky, Paul and Kiparsky, Carol. (1971). 'Fact'. In D. Steinberg and L. Jacobovits, eds. (1971). *Semantics – An Interdisciplinary Reader in Philosophy, Linguistics, Anthropology, and Psychology*. Cambridge: Cambridge University Press.

Montague, Richard. (1970). 'The proper treatment of quantification in ordinary English.' Department of Philosophy, University of California. Los Angeles. MS.

Vennemann, Theo. (1972a). 'Explanation in syntax.' To appear in John Kimball, ed. (1973). *Syntax and Semantics II*. San Francisco: Seminar Press.

—— (1972b). 'Warum gibt es Syntax? Syntaktische Konstruktionsprinzipien in logischer und psychologischer Sicht.' To appear in *Zeitschrift für Germanistische Linguistik*, No. 2 (1973).

Should generative semantics be related to intensional logic? Remarks on lexical factorization and semantic structure

CARL H. HEIDRICH[1]

I.

As far as I know there has been no attempt to relate generative semantics (GS) to intensional logic (IL) in a complete and systematic manner. Indeed at first sight one may well doubt that a relation can be established at all. So the first question we shall be concerned with here is with which parts of the theory of GS one should try to establish such a relation. And the second will be with which methods should be used.

If both theories could be formulated as formal, or mathematical theories, then we could try to construct mappings between them. As Montague (1970b) has shown, intensional languages and intensional logic can be formulated as mathematical theories. But I know of no formalization of GS.

Another systematic way to attack this problem is *reduction*, which means roughly, the *embedding* of one theory into another. This can be done for parts of theories as well and it is that approach I shall take here. To this extent then, no complete solution to the embedding problem will be given.

It is well known that Montague's theory contains both syntax and semantics (i.e. a model theory). Concerning the syntax of GS, Partee (1972), to give one example, has formulated transformations in a Montague-type syntax. This does not mean that the syntax or the surface structure of both theories are comparable. The incomparability has to do with the role of semantic structure in GS, which has been characterized in the following way:

> ...'generative semantics', which states that the rules of grammar are just the rules relating logical forms to surface forms of sentences (Lakoff (1972: 194)).

or

> ...the semantic representation of a sentence is a representation of its inherent logical form...(Lakoff (1971: 277)).

[1] I thank E. L. Keenan very much for having corrected my English.

188

or

> I will in fact argue that symbolic logic, . . ., provides an appropriate system for semantic representation within the framework of transformational grammar (McCawley (1971: 219)).

Now Montague's theory of translation as formulated in Montague (1970a,b) fulfills exactly the conditions given in the first quotation.

Concerning the second, it is not clear to me what 'is' really means; a complete identification could not be meant. And to this extent the third quotation is helpful because it says, that 'logic provides an appropriate system *for* semantic representation'. Again, this is true for Montague's theory, of which the logic represents in a special way an enlarged Tarskian semantics which is set-theoretical in structure.

Here, now, is the crucial point in respect to the reduction process. GS, as far as I see, has not yet clearly defined any elements or entities which constitute the semantic structure to be represented by logical structure. One may quote McCawley (1972: p. 2):

> . . .a semantic structure is a labeled tree. . .the terminal elements of the trees are:. . .some kind of semantic units, namely 'indices' and the kinds of things that logicians call 'predicates' and 'operators'. . .

But this quotation is not very elucidating if compared with a possible world semantics. Consequently the problem I shall discuss here is a first attempt at a reduction of the predicates of GS to predicates in intensional structures.

It is very easy to establish this reduction for predicates, in the sense of GS, like *cause, come, die, perceive, look, see, persuade*, etc., if they are simple, but problems arise if predicates are complex or factored, if various types of deep complement embeddings are necessary at all. In this case GS uses transformational rules like 'Predicate Raising', 'Subject Raising', '(Super)-Equi-NP Deletion', 'Psych-Movement', to derive structure in such a way that lexical insertion can take place. It will be seen that the complexity of factorization determines the type of logic that represents semantical structure.

Some preliminary and general remarks are in order. It is somewhat accidental that we begin our analysis with factorization processes. But they have been discussed by authors of different schools. Joshi (1972) has noted several examples from the literature, and discusses, himself, a class of about 60 verbs of seeing. He uses 29 predicates and constructs representations for 10 verbs of seeing, representations for the others being then derivable.

This can be considered as an attempt to study interdefinability of factored elements. Fillmore (1971) may be mentioned in this connection too. Joshi uses the same types of rules as mentioned above but the formal objects in his discussions are not trees but rather operators and operands. The variety of syntactical elements is then reduced to only two types.

This is not far from recent developments in GS. What I have in mind can be generally called *normalization*, of syntactic categories, class concepts, functors and arguments, for instance. The *contentives* of E. Bach are the outcome of normalization. They have been adopted with modifications by Lakoff, Ross, McCawley, Postal and others as predicates and arguments, or predicates and indices, and the apparent connection with the categories of logic has been stated explicitly by McCawley. The widely adopted predicate-argument-argument...or V-S-O representation is a natural consequence. So it seems appropriate to treat the different approaches together because Montague as well uses some factorization, as in e.g. the case of *seek*.

There is still, however, an important difference between the objects used in GS and in Joshi's representation. It is known that GS interprets conjunctions for example as predicates. Joshi interprets some nominals, preposition-nominal complexes or adjectives as operators. It is interesting to see that even in these cases the two approaches are comparable for certain types of factors. Finally there is a very difficult problem regarding the syntactic role of transformation rules as mentioned above. If they are applied successively or iteratively and if they take underlying structures directly into surface structure, then one must deal with complex phrases like infinitive constructions, gerunds or complex adjuncts. In terms of Montague's theory of translation we might try to construct directly their relation to a logic, given a syntactic theory. But I shall not attempt this here, due to the technicality of the task. Moreover we would need justification for the correctness of the syntactic rules. This justification cannot itself be purely syntactic or formal. I want to refer here again to Joshi (1972) where explicit methodological considerations can be found. Of course justification of various types, as for example the description of the structure of the transformational cycle, can be found in the GS literature.

The idea of looking for a reduction as proposed above came from Joshi (1972), where the problem of merging predicates is explicitly formulated.

> The choice of a suitable representation and the corresponding formulation of suitable predicate collapsing rules is still very much of an open problem (Joshi (1972: 83)).

2.

I shall introduce first some notation and some functional concepts. With these concepts the various types of normalization can be expressed. This means that we can map a normalization, for instance that of GS, onto our concepts. I shall use only one type of normalization of GS and the one of Joshi.

I define:

Type 1 symbols: a_1, a_2, a_3,...together with (the words) *John*, *Fred*, *tree house*, etc.

Type 2 symbols:

(i) P_1, P_2, P_3,...together with *cause*, *try*, *seek*, *see*, etc.
(ii) if $\mathscr{P}$, $\mathscr{Q}$, and $\mathscr{R}$ are type 2 symbols then so are $\mathscr{P}/\mathscr{Q}/$, $\mathscr{P}/\mathscr{Q}\mathscr{R}/$, $/\mathscr{P}\mathscr{Q}/$, $/\mathscr{P}\mathscr{Q}\mathscr{R}/$.

Type 2 symbols may be called predicators or operators. They are n-placed for $n > 0$. For $n = 0$ we have:

Type 3 symbols: F_1, F_2, F_3,...together with $\mathscr{P}(\ell_1, \ell_2 \ldots \ell_n)$ where $\mathscr{P}$ is an n-place predicator and for $1 \leqslant j \leqslant n$ ℓ_j is either a type 1 symbol or a type 3 symbol.

The a_i, P_i, and F_i are normally taken as variables, but in special cases may be taken as constants. If only finitely many are used I write a, b, c, P, Q, R.

I shall introduce three primitive types of functions ρ, μ, σ which are defined for elements of type 1–3 symbols as arguments. Identities will be allowed: $\mathscr{A} = \mathscr{B}$ for $\mathscr{A}, \mathscr{B}$ from the same set of type symbols.

The functions are as follows, where i, j mark place numbers.

(1) $\rho^i(\mathscr{P}(\ldots, \mathscr{A}_i, \ldots), \mathscr{B}) = \mathscr{P}(\ldots, \mathscr{B}_i, \ldots)$
   $\mathscr{P}$ a predicator, $\mathscr{A}$ a type 1 or type 3 symbol, $\mathscr{B}$ a type 3 symbol.
(2) $\mu^i(\mathscr{P}_1(\ldots, \mathscr{A}_i, \ldots), \mathscr{P}_2(\mathscr{B})) = \mathscr{P}_1/\mathscr{P}_2/(\ldots, \mathscr{B}_i, \ldots)$
   $\mathscr{P}_1, \mathscr{P}_2$ predicators, $\mathscr{A}$ type 1 or 3 symbol, $\mathscr{B}$ a type 1 or 3 symbol or a sequence of such symbols.
(3) (i) $\sigma^{ij}(\mathscr{P}(x_1, \ldots, \langle a \rangle_i, \ldots, \langle \ell \rangle_j, \ldots, x_n)) = \mathscr{P}(x_1, \ldots, \langle \ell \rangle_{j-1}, \ldots, x_{n-1})$
    (ii) $\sigma^{ji}(\mathscr{P}(x_1, \ldots, \langle a \rangle_i, \ldots, \langle \ell \rangle_j, \ldots, x_n)) = \mathscr{P}(x_1, \ldots, \langle a \rangle_i, \ldots, x_{n-1})$

$\mathscr{P}$ a predicator, $\langle a \rangle$, $\langle \ell \rangle$ n, m-place (argument) sequences of type 1 symbols respectively and such that $n \leqslant m$ and $\langle a \rangle$ a subsequence of $\langle \ell \rangle$ in the case of (i), $m \leqslant n$ and $\langle \ell \rangle$ a subsequence of $\langle a \rangle$ in the case of (ii).

The restriction in the last condition to type 1 sequences is possible only in simple cases. Some variants of (2) are used:

(4) $\mu^{ij}(\mathscr{P}_1(\ldots, \mathscr{A}_i, \ldots, \mathscr{B}_j, \ldots), (\mathscr{P}_2(\mathscr{C}), \mathscr{P}_3(\mathscr{D}))) = \mathscr{P}_1 / \mathscr{P}_2 \mathscr{P}_3 / (\ldots, \mathscr{C}_i, \ldots,$
    $\mathscr{D}_j, \ldots)$

(5) $\hat{\mu}^i(\mathscr{P}_1(\ldots, \mathscr{A}_i, \ldots), \mathscr{P}_2(\mathscr{B})) = /\mathscr{P}_1\mathscr{P}_2/(\ldots, \mathscr{B}_i, \ldots)$

For (4,5) conditions as above.

(6) $\bar{\mu}(\mathscr{P}_1(\mathscr{A}_1, \mathscr{A}_2), \mathscr{P}_2(\mathscr{B}_1, \mathscr{B}_2)) = /\mathscr{P}_1\mathscr{P}_2/(\mathscr{B}_1\mathscr{B}_2)$
    With $\mathscr{A}_1$, $\mathscr{B}_1$ being both of the same type either 1 or 3.

(7) $\tilde{\mu}(\mathscr{P}(\mathscr{P}_1(\langle a \rangle), \mathscr{P}_2(\langle \ell \rangle)), \mathscr{P}_2(\langle \ell \rangle)) = /\mathscr{P}_1\mathscr{P}\mathscr{P}_2/(\langle a \rangle, \langle \ell \rangle)$
    where $\mathscr{P}, \mathscr{P}_1, \mathscr{P}_2$ are predicators and the argument sequences $\langle a \rangle$, $\langle \ell \rangle$ are either identical or $\langle a \rangle$ is a subsequence of $\langle \ell \rangle$.

Finally I define the function π. Let $\mathscr{A}$ be a type 3 symbol which is a n-tuple predicator and $\mathscr{B}$ any type 3 symbol. I shall express the fact that $\mathscr{B}$ is one of the arguments of $\mathscr{A}$ by $\alpha(\mathscr{B}, \mathscr{A})$.

(8) $\pi(\mathscr{A}) = \mathscr{A}' :\leftrightarrow (\exists \mathscr{B})(\alpha(\mathscr{B}, \mathscr{A}) \& \phi(\mathscr{A}, \mathscr{B}) = \mathscr{A}')$
    $\pi(\mathscr{A}) = \mathscr{A}' :\leftrightarrow (\exists \mathscr{B}, \mathscr{C})(\alpha(\mathscr{B}, \mathscr{A}) \& \alpha(\mathscr{C}, \mathscr{A}) \& \mu^{ij}(\mathscr{A}, (\mathscr{B}, \mathscr{C})) = \mathscr{A}')$
    where ϕ stands for one of the μ-functions not identical with μ^{ij}, $\mathscr{A}$, $\mathscr{B}$, $\mathscr{C}$ stand for allowed arguments and $\mathscr{A}'$ for the defined value of ϕ, μ^{ij}.

In case of (2), $\mathscr{P}_2$ is a *right adjunct* to $\mathscr{P}_1$. Left adjuncts can be defined in an obvious way but I shall not use them. (5, 6) will be called *couples* and (7) is a *conjunct*.

It is easy to establish a formal system for the concepts just introduced. Obviously the next step is to exemplify some of the normalizations within these concepts. This will be done by constructing a mapping onto the new concepts.

The first example is the factorization of *kill* given by McCawley. For simplicity I shall leave out indices and the *do* predicator. To show two nontrivial applications of the function μ I shall assume that *not-alive* is one predicator. In this first example (9′) I shall establish the mapping, called v, completely in all stages. It is assumed that it is defined for a set $\mathscr{T}$ of semantic trees as domain and with the set $\mathscr{S}$ of identities of type 3 symbols as its range. In what follows mappings are realized by writing arrows between domain and range and by writing '$\mapsto$' between elements of domain and range to indicate the effect of a mapping. So

(9) $v: \mathscr{T} \longrightarrow \mathscr{P}\mathscr{S}$

$t \mapsto \mathscr{S}'$, for

$t \in \mathscr{T}$, $\mathscr{S}' \in \mathscr{P}\mathscr{S}$, $\mathscr{P}$ 'power set of'.

(9')

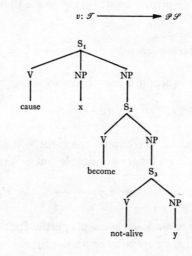

$\{F_1 = P_1(a, F_2), F_2 = P_2(F_3), F_3 = P_3(b)$ and $P_1 =$ cause, $P_2 =$ become, $P_3 =$ not-alive$\}$

To have a short form for representations I shall write the domain element in a linear form without labelled bracketings. These can be re-established in an obvious manner having one tree representation at the beginning. The domain element will have the form:

$S_1 = cause\ (x,\ become\ (not\text{-}alive(y)))$

and the range element is

$F_1 = P_1\ (a, P_2(P_3(b)))$

using replacement of such identities having only variables. Using the other identities we get a form which is identical with the S_1 representation. We first apply π to the rightmost predicator P_3 of F_1:

$$\pi(P_2(P_3(b))) = P_2/P_3/(b) \leftrightarrow (\exists P_3(b))(\mu^1(P_2^1(P_3(b)),\ P_3(b)) = P_2/P_3/(b))$$

The α condition can be left out because of the identities noted in the range element of $\mathscr{S}$. It can be seen that the effect of π is what Predicate Raising does. μ is a merging function producing a right adjunct and a new predicator to which we apply ρ:

$$\rho(P_1(a,P_2(P_3(b))),\ P_2/P_3/(b)) = P_1(a,P_2/P_3/(b))$$

We could not provide for this embedding without ρ because we will not get an identity of the form $F_2 = P_2/P_3/(b)$ from the original tree by the mapping υ. So what $\rho o \pi$, the application of ρ after π, does would usually be done by tree-pruning principles. It is easy to see that $\rho o \pi$ preserves υ for it contains

$$S'_1 = cause\ (x,\ become\ not\text{-}alive(y)) \longmapsto F'_1 = P_1(a,P_2/P_3/(b))$$

Applying the same procedure once again we have

$$\pi(P_1(a,P_2/P_3/(b)) = P_1/P_2/P_3//(a,b)$$

(I leave it to the reader to compute the right side of the formulae in (8).)
To this result ρ is no longer applicable but υ is still preserved:

$$S'' = cause\ become\ not\text{-}alive\ (x,y) \longmapsto F''_1 = P_1/P_2/P_3//(a,b)$$

The next step is to work out some properties for our functions. The first question is whether they are total or partial functions. This will depend on the ultimate (semantic) units allowed in factorizations.

For the class of verbs of seeing as discussed in Joshi (1972) the functions turn out to be partial. One can partially reduce the problem to cases of two or three predicators. According to Joshi one can raise the question as to whether there are μ functions such that

(10) $\mu_1(by\ sight(perceive(a,P)),\ perceive(a,P))$
(11) $\mu_2(possible(perceive(a,P)),\ perceive(a,P))$

and μ_1, μ_2 are independent functions in the sense that disjoint classes of lexical realizations are possible. He observed, which seems very interesting, that letting *by sight* operate on the first argument of μ_2 and *possible* on the first argument of μ_1 lexical gaps may be found. On the other hand if *by sight* operates in a more complicated embedding on two arguments then having applied μ_1, μ^{ij} for $P_2 = P_3$ and a new function of *factoring out* the couple $/P_1P_2/$ no gaps will occur, but verbs in a non-visual sense will occur. This is a very complicated problem about which I have not much information.

From the facts expressed by $\alpha(\mathcal{B},\mathcal{A})$ in (8) it follows that only adjacent predicates may occur as second arguments in μ functions. With the same example as in (9) I am able to point at an analogous problem in this case if π is applied to the leftmost predicator first. It is clear that υ is again preserved.

(12) Let F_1 be as in (9). Then we have first
$$\pi(P_1(a,P_2(P_3(b)))) = P_1/P_2/(a,P_3(b))$$
and secondly
$$\pi(P_1/P_2/(a,P_3(b))) = P_1/P_2//P_3/(a,b).$$

In both cases we do not need the ρ function so that tree pruning is completely covered by π. The reason is that the values of π can be directly identified with new Fs. This is the first result. The second is that from the formal point of view of functional applicability we cannot decide whether or not

(13) *cause/become/not-alive//(a,b)* $\neq$ *cause/become//not-alive/(a,b)*

i.e. we have to decide whether μ is associative or not.

I can find no motivation in GS for opting for one or the other case. All that can be said seems to be that the structure for *kill*-insertion is the one resulting from (9). Of course this question has to do with occurrences of ambiguity; as Partee (1972: pp. 11f.) has pointed out in the case of certain infinitive constructions.

A calculus for predicate collapsing functions without such a decision can contain only *rules* that lead exactly to forms as in (9) for classes of 3-tuples of predicators. But then we still must decide if iterations are allowed, as in

(14) *cause*(Fred, *cause*(Bill, *become*(*not-alive*(John))))
    i.e. Fred causes Bill to kill John

In some cases even identities cannot be excluded. In the case of the following example due to Joshi

(15) John perceives by sight that something is a cat
    we may identify it with
(16) By sight John perceives it to be a cat

Using the action predicator *do* as Ross suggests, we may even identify (15) with

(17) John perceives a cat and he does it by sight

Quite another form of identity occurs if, following Joshi, one takes not only verbs in the classical sense as predicates but also operators as *by sight* to express the act of seeing. I shall use the predicator *by act* for a factorization of 'kill' which may be

(18) *by act(effect(a, become(not-alive(b))))*.

This factorization is nearly identical to the result of an analysis to be found in McCawley (1972) where he uses the *do* predicator instead of *by act*.

Factorizations of lexical items may have an intrinsic order with regard to their embedded predicators. Traditionally speaking most of them are infinitive or gerund constructions in which clear forms of coordination and subordination appear. But this is far from being standard even ignoring ambiguities as such. Transitivity of π application may have to do with independence from subordination to the left and to the right.

In what follows I present some examples which may give evidence for coordination or subordination. The discussion is limited by the fact that we have no functions representing Subject raising and Psych-movement. The case of *try-find* as an infinitive construction will be handled by applying μ^2:

(19) $\mu^2(try(a, find(a,b)), find(a,b)) = try/find/(a,(a,b))$

Applying σ we get

(20) $\sigma^{12}(try/find/(a,(a,b))) = try/find/((a,b))$,

i.e. σ turns out to copy Equi-NP Deletion. On the other hand for *seem*, taken intransitively as in (21),

(21) John seems to write

I would propose

(22) $\hat{\mu}^1(seem(write(\text{John})), write(\text{John})) = /seem\ write/(\text{John})$

In this case *seem* takes a proposition in the sense of McCawley (1971: p. 229) as complement.

A nominative +infinitive construction as in

(23) I expect to see John

could be represented as

(23') *expect(I, see(I, John))*

Applying $\bar{\mu}$ we have

(24) $\bar{\mu}(expect(\text{I}, see(\text{I, John})), see(\text{I, John})) = /expect\ see/(\text{I, John})$

No Equi-NP Deletion is necessary. $\bar{\mu}$ includes a part of the subject raising function so that it can be taken as a natural extension of μ. But I do not have enough evidence to conclude that both of (25) should be handled in a way similar to (23).

(25) a. Bombs cease to fall
    b. Bombs cease falling

Some evidence comes from cases like

(26) I enjoy hearing John talk

which may be represented as

(27) $enjoy(\text{I}, hear(\text{I}, talk(\text{John})))$.

After application of $\bar{\mu}$ we have

(28) $/enjoy\ hear/(\text{I}, talk(\text{John}))$

which, after μ application, becomes

(29) $/enjoy\ hear//talk/(\text{I, John})$

The introduction of μ^{ij} is necessary to manage such examples as (Joshi (1972: p. 52))

(30) I looked towards the sky in order to see the plane

A similar case occurs in Dowty (1972: p. 63):

(31) $cause\ (do(\text{John}, F_1), become(not\text{-}alive(\text{Harry})))$.

Applications of $\tilde{\mu}$ yield, e.g.

(32) You come and have tea

i.e.

(33) $and(come(a), have(a,b))$

Applying $\tilde{\mu}$ and σ we get

(34) $/come\ and\ have/((a,b))$
(35) You try and come

For this we get, by the same procedure,

(36) $and(try(\text{you}), come(\text{you}))$

(37) $/try\ and\ come/((\text{you}))$.

The last examples show directly that the $\bar{\mu}$ function is not commutative, i.e. (32) and (35) are not paraphrases of

(38) Have tea and come

(39) You come and try

This section has shown clearly that predicate collapsing rules produce very complicated predicator structures which may not have formal properties such as associativity and commutativity.

3.

It follows from section 2 that with the help of a set $\mathscr{S}$ we can handle many of the normalizations occurring in the literature. To construct a reduction for GS with respect to intensional logic (IL) it is sufficient to map a set $\mathscr{S}$ into a possible world semantics for IL. By this I mean that the predicators which are type 3 symbols will be mapped into the set of predicates of a possible world semantics. The set $\mathscr{S}$ contains for this reason the identities allowed and all of the type 3 symbols. This task is not difficult to perform as far as the formalism is concerned in order for the predicates of GS to be interpreted consistently. The philosophic and linguistic importance of this reduction is not only a question of taste: either an effective semantics is available or it is not.

Before I construct a mapping I have to point out some restrictions in connection with the functions μ^i, μ^{ij}, $\hat{\mu}^i$, $\bar{\mu}$, $\tilde{\mu}$. μ clearly gives the usual embeddings. Predicate structures of the types produced by μ^i are available in IL. In most of Montague's published papers IL is a second order logic characterized by the fact that predicate variables are embedded only into predicate constants whereas predicate variables take only individual variables and individual constants as arguments. Because I shall leave out the syntactic part one should bear this restriction in mind in what follows.

The embeddings related to applications of the other functions are not realized in IL as far as I could show. In case of *seem* for instance Montague usually takes phrases like *John seems to John*... In Montague (1970a) there appear cases which are nearly similar to (5) and (6) in that he uses such forms as *try to* as units the category of IV//IV, i.e. they are IV modifying phrases. In comparison with the result of this section I want to say that I am trying to find other types of predicate mergings than those treated here. With respect to higher levels and types of embeddings second order logic has to be extended.

To simplify the reduction we let the subset of type 2 symbols contain *seek, find, try* as predicators of GS. I shall use (19) and (20).

A possible world semantics may be introduced roughly as follows: let I and U be two sets, the possible worlds and the possible individuals respectively. For each $i \in I$ let U_i be a subset of U, the set of individuals existing in or relative to the world i. Let $U^n = U \times \ldots \times U$ be the n-fold cartesian product of U, the elements of which are represented as n-tuples $\langle u_1, \ldots, u_n \rangle$. Functions P_L from I to subsets of U^n may be defined as mappings:

(40) $P_L: I \longrightarrow \mathscr{P} U^n$

$\quad\quad i \mapsto \{ \langle u_1, \ldots, u_n \rangle \}$

where $\mathscr{P}$ here indicates 'power set of'. The range of P_L is called the 'extension' of P_L. From the point of view of extensional logic the subsets of U^n constitute set-theoretical or extensional relations used in interpretations of predicate and function signs of extensional languages.

The functions P_L are the *predicates of individuals* in intensional semantics. According to Montague we may say for a n-place predicate P_L and a possible world i that the predicate holds for the set $\{ \langle u_1, \ldots, u_n \rangle \}$ as values of $P_L(i)$ relative to the world i.

To apply and to illustrate this new concept of a predicate means to give I a certain structure. Nothing has been said of the forms of elements $i \in I$ which are normally called 'indices' or 'points of reference'.

Let us take an action, for instance John's seeking of Pegasus. From an ontological point of view this action has what I shall call several *aspects* – namely, the 'action', 'persons', and possibly 'zoological objects'. To be able to refer to these aspects, which may turn out to be questionable ontological entities, one may introduce a type of name-like sign usually written '⟨Action⟩', '⟨Zool.obj.⟩', '⟨Person⟩', etc. From the philosophical point of view it is necessary to believe that such aspects exist in some sense. '⟨Action⟩', etc., will be taken as indices. It must be said that an index like '⟨Person⟩' is not to be seen as an ultimate unit but it may be taken as one provided it functions suitably for aspects of actions as it does in the example. So let ⟨Person⟩, ⟨Zool.obj.⟩ $\in I$. Having sets at hand we may be able to define aspects for instance '⟨Action⟩'. To this end we form $I' = I \times I = \{ \langle \langle \text{Person} \rangle, \langle \text{Person} \rangle \rangle, \langle \langle \text{Person} \rangle, \langle \text{Zool.obj.} \rangle \rangle, \langle \langle \text{Zool.obj.} \rangle,$

$\langle$Person$\rangle\rangle$, $\langle\langle$Zool.obj.$\rangle$, $\langle$Zool.obj.$\rangle\rangle\}$. Then we take $R \subseteq I \times I$ such that $R = \{\langle\langle$Person$\rangle$, $\langle$Zool.obj.$\rangle\rangle\}$ and define

(41) $\langle$Action$\rangle := \langle\langle$Person$\rangle$, $\langle$Zool.obj.$\rangle\rangle$

The R relation may be called an 'intensional relation' between relevant aspects. Further an intensional predicate P_L like $seek_L$ may then be defined as

(42) $seek_L$: $I' \longrightarrow \mathscr{P}U^2$

$\qquad \langle$Action$\rangle \mapsto \{\langle u_1, u_2 \rangle\}$

Let U contain just two elements, say u_1, u_2 such that u_1 is a person to which we may refer by using a name 'John', and u_2 being a mythical object about which John can find information in handbooks of iconography and which is to that extent extensionally determined. The possible world is completely fixed by containing a person, possibly living at the present moment, and a mythical zoological object.

The reduction of the predicate $seek \in \mathscr{S}$ to $seek_L$ can now be completed. Let $seek$ (a,b) be contained in $\mathscr{S}$ and also $find(a,b)$, $try(a,F)$ and let the set $\mathscr{Q}_L$ contain $seek_L$ together with $find_L$ and try_L to be introduced later. Let χ be the following mapping

(43) χ: $\mathscr{S} \longrightarrow \mathscr{Q}_L$

$\qquad P \longmapsto P_L$ for every P, and such that for each sequence of arguments $(\mathscr{A}_1, \ldots, \mathscr{A}_n)$ of the allowed type in $\mathscr{S}$ there exists $i \in I$ such that $(+)\chi(P(\mathscr{A}_1, \ldots, \mathscr{A}_n)) = P_L(i)$

From the condition $(+)$ it follows that we always have $(\mathscr{A}_1, \ldots, \mathscr{A}_n) = i$, i.e. the argument sequences of predicators are not mapped to sequences of U elements. Next I define try_L and $find_L$:

(44) a. $find_L$: $R \longrightarrow \mathscr{P}U^2$

$\qquad \langle\langle$Person$\rangle$, $\langle$Zool.obj$\rangle\rangle \longmapsto \{\langle u_1, u_2 \rangle\}$

b. try_L: $I \times R \longrightarrow \mathscr{P}(U \times \mathscr{P}U^2)$

$\qquad \langle\langle$Person$\rangle$, $\langle$Action$\rangle\rangle \longmapsto \{\langle u_1, A \rangle\}$,

for a set of pairs A.

One point is apparent here in respect to $find_L$: the character of the intensional relations is such that the same type of relation may be used for different extensional relations.

A consequence of this reduction is that we can show what predicate raising is in semantical terms – namely, that which corresponds to $try/find/$. Let $try_L/find_L/$ indicate the corresponding function in $\mathscr{Q}_L$. This is to be the function ψ_i, which is the restriction of a function ψ to indices i, on $(I \times R) \times R$ with values in $I \times R$ such that

(45) $\psi_i(\langle\langle\text{Person}\rangle,\langle\text{Action}\rangle\rangle,\langle\langle\text{Person}\rangle,\langle\text{Zool.obj.}\rangle\rangle)$
        $= \langle\langle\text{Person}\rangle,\langle\langle\text{Person}\rangle,\langle\text{Zool.obj.}\rangle\rangle\rangle$

i.e. predicate raising is the result of merging the index of (44a) into the index of (44b) by using the identity (41). The following diagram illustrates the situation

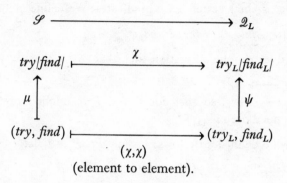

(element to element).

So ψ is to be

(45′) $\psi: \mathcal{Q}_L \times \mathcal{Q}_L \longrightarrow \mathcal{Q}_L$
        $((44\text{a}), (44\text{b})) \longmapsto$
        $(\langle\langle\text{Person}\rangle,\langle\langle\text{Person}\rangle,\langle\text{Zool.obj.}\rangle\rangle\rangle) \longmapsto \{\langle u_1,\langle u_1,u_2\rangle\rangle\})$

It is a bit trickier to establish the equivalence of *try* $(a, find(a,b))$ and *seek*(a,b) in intensional logic. To do this we have to map the index of *seek*$_L$ onto that of *try*$_L$/*find*$_L$/. Let ϕ be this mapping. Then we have to have

$$\phi(\langle\langle\text{Person}\rangle,\langle\langle\text{Person}\rangle,\langle\text{Zool.obj.}\rangle\rangle\rangle) = \langle\langle\text{Person}\rangle,\langle\text{Zool.obj.}\rangle\rangle$$

The effect of ϕ is that one of the indices '$\langle\text{Person}\rangle$' is to be filtered out. The question is, which one. I shall show that it is the second one in the above argument. If we map '$\langle\langle\text{Person}\rangle, \langle\text{Zool.obj.}\rangle\rangle$' onto '$\langle\text{Zool.obj.}\rangle$' then the relational aspects of a 2-place relation is reduced to a 1-place by filtering out one component. So we obtain

(46) $\omega: I \times I \longrightarrow I$
        $(i,j) \longmapsto j$

A natural interpretation of this function in accordance with Montague is that if (i,j) is the index of an action relative to i and j then j is the index of an action too. Equivalently, using predicates to be definable on $I \times I$ and on I: if P_L is a predicate on (i,j), and P'_L is a predicate on j then i is filtered out in P_L. In analogy to Montague's terminology I shall write for a predicate P_L on (i,j) on which ω has operated $\hat{\imath} P_L[j]$. ω applied to $find_L$ gives

$$(47)\ \hat{\imath}\, find_L \colon I \longrightarrow \mathscr{P}U$$
$$\langle \text{Zool.obj.} \rangle \longmapsto \{\langle u_2 \rangle\}.$$

This may be expressed as the predicate of *finding Pegasus* or as *to find Pegasus*. Let $\hat{\mathcal{Q}}_L$ be a set of those predicates. We define ϕ' to produce

$$(48)\ \phi'\,(try_L/find_L/) = try_L/\hat{\imath}\, find_L/$$

To this end let $\gamma(\omega)$ be a function such that

$$\gamma(\omega) \colon \mathcal{Q}_L \longrightarrow \hat{\mathcal{Q}}_L$$
$$P_L \longmapsto \hat{P}_L,\ \text{so that for } i,\ j \in I,\ \omega \text{ applied to } (i,j), P_L(i,j) \text{ is}$$
mapped onto $\hat{\imath}P_L[j]$.

ϕ' can now be defined as follows: for any $P_{1L}, P_{2L} \in \mathcal{Q}_L$ let

$$(48')\ \phi'(P_{1L}/P_{2L}/) := \psi(P_{1L}, \gamma(\omega)(P_{2L})) = P_{1L}/\hat{P}_{2L}/$$

Now we are home, because we define ϕ so as to map

$try_L/\hat{\imath}\, find_L/$ onto $seek_L$, i.e.

$$(49)\ \phi(\phi'(try_L/find_L/) = seek_L$$

As the last result taking (20) into account we have that ϕ' of (48) copies exactly Equi-NP Deletion showing also what the infinitive construction in

(50) John tries to find Pegasus

is to be.

Because I have treated here only the semantical parts of the two theories, GS and IL, it is obviously impossible to interpret ϕ as lexical insertion. ϕ can at best be interpreted as some sort of equivalence between two predicates. The question of equivalences of predicates has been discussed by Lakoff (1972) if interpreted as meaning postulates and by Montague (1969, 1970a) in connection with definitions in intensional logic and as translations of intensional locutions into intensional logic.

4.

To summarize the discussion consider the diagrams (51) and (52):

(51)

$$\mathbf{GS} = (\mathscr{T}, (\text{Tree pruning, Predicate Raising, Equi-NP Deletion}))$$

$v \downarrow$

$$\mathbf{A}' = (\mathscr{S}, (\rho^i, \mu^i, \sigma^{ij})) \text{ of type } (2,2,1)$$

$\varepsilon \downarrow$

$$\mathbf{A} = (\mathscr{S}, (\mu^i, \sigma^{ij})) \text{ of type } (2,1)$$

$\chi \downarrow$

$$\mathbf{P}_L = (\mathscr{Q}_L \cup \hat{\mathscr{Q}}_L, (, \psi, \varphi')) \text{ of type } (2,1).$$

By using examples I have shown how to map **GS**, taken as an algebra-like structure, onto **A'**. **A'** is an algebra over $\mathscr{S}$ with ρ^i, μ^i, σ^{ij} as its operations, leaving for simplicity the other μ-functions out of this summary. This result of section 2 is used in section 3 but for a simpler algebra **A** without ρ^i, because of the special example used. **A** is then mapped onto an IL, i.e. onto an algebra that contains the predicates of IL, such that the operations of **A**, that correspond by ε and v to transformations in **GS**, are mapped onto operations of **P**$_L$. The effect of the mapping χ from **A** onto **P**$_L$ and the resulting correspondence of the operations of the different structures is as in (52). In the general case the mappings will not be onto but into the structures. To have a short notation let T indicate *try*, F indicate *find*.

(52)

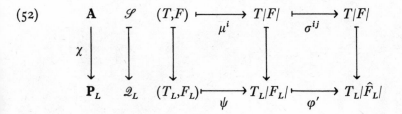

REFERENCES

Dowty, D. R. (1972). 'On the syntax and semantics of the atomic predicate CAUSE', *Chicago Linguistics Society*, **8**, 62–74.

Fillmore, C. J. (1971). 'Verbs of judging'. In C. J. Fillmore and D. T. Langendoen, eds., *Studies in Linguistic Semantics*, pp. 273–88. New York: Holt.

Joshi, A. K. (1972). 'Factorization of verbs. An analysis of verbs of seeing'. Unpublished manuscript (partly to be published in C. H. Heidrich, ed., *Semantics and Communication*. Amsterdam: North-Holland Publ. Co.).

Lakoff, G. (1971). 'On generative semantics'. In D. J. Steinberg and L. A. Jacobovits, eds., *Semantics*, pp. 232–96. Cambridge: Cambridge University Press.

—— (1972). 'Linguistics and natural logic', *Synthese*, **22,** nos. 1/2, 151–271. Also in D. Davidson and G. Harman, eds. (1972), *Semantics of Natural Language*. Dordrecht: Reidel.

McCawley, J. D. (1971). 'Where do noun phrases come from?' In D. J. Steinberg and L. A. Jacobovits, eds., *Semantics*, pp. 217–31. Cambridge: Cambridge University Press.

—— (1972). 'Syntactic and logical arguments for semantic structures'. Unpublished manuscript. Also in publications of the Indiana University Linguistics Club.

Montague, R. (1969). 'On the nature of certain philosophical entities'. In *The Monist*, **53,** 159–94.

—— (1970a). 'The proper treatment of quantification in ordinary English'. In K. J. J. Hintikka, J. M. E. Moravcsik, P. Suppes, eds. (1973), *Approaches to Natural Language*. Dordrecht: Reidel.

—— (1970b). 'Universal grammar', *Theoria*, **36,** 373–98.

Partee, B. (1972). 'Some transformational extensions of Montague grammar'. In R. Rodman, ed., *Papers in Montague Grammar*, Occasional Papers in Linguistics No. 2, UCLA., pp. 1–24.

Transformational semantics

ARNIM VON STECHOW

1. Purpose

In this paper I want to present the general framework of a semantic theory which can describe partial meaning relations between sentences of natural languages; relations such as *partial synonymy, partial consequence, partial incompatibility*. I will call such a theory henceforth *semantics* and sometimes also *grammar*. Three features are important for the kind of semantics proposed here: first, the theory *only* makes use of transformational rules (henceforth: T-rules) which are stated within a formalism that is a modified and generalized version of the formulation of Ginsburg and Partee (1968) and Brockhaus (1972).[1] Second, logical systems developed within the framework of predicate logic can be embedded into this theory without difficulties. The system can be connected with a model theory. And third, the theory lends itself to later justification from speech act theory.

I mention these points explicitly because I think that a semantics of natural language should be conceived in such a way as to make use of the results of three important contemporary linguistic schools: *transformational grammar* as worked out by Harris, Chomsky and others; *formal logic* in the widest sense including model theory, and *speech act theory* (Austin, Searle and others).[2]

Nevertheless, a semantic theory cannot simply be a chaotic mixture of these or other different approaches, but the goals of such a theory should be determined independently in a clear way.

In this paper I discuss the goals of a semantic theory, and then propose a criterion of adequacy. I do not claim to define new goals (for instance, on the whole I could accept the task which D. Lewis (1972) attributes to semantics), but probably I will place the emphasis a little differently from other authors. In any case, this approach may be regarded as a technical and, I claim, feasible, variant of other contemporary approaches.

A semantics for a subset of German which meets the conditions stated below is published in Kratzer, Pause and Stechow (1973). In addition to

[1] The formalism used here has been worked out by E. Pause (1973).
[2] Bar-Hillel pleads for a synthesis of these three directions of scientific inquiry in Staal (1969).

E. Pause and A. Kratzer, I owe much to discussions with U. Egli and K. Brockhaus.[1]

2. The data of semantics: partial meaning relations

I will now try to clarify what things my semantic theory talks about. I choose here as objects of semantics partial meaning relations between sets of sentences in natural languages.[2] (The role of the adjective 'partial' will be explained later.)

To be more explicit, consider the following sentences:

(1) Franz-Josef schlägt den Bruder von Willy
(2) Herbert ist der Bruder von Willy
(3) Franz-Josef schlägt Herbert
(4) Franz arbeitet
(5) Karl arbeitet
(6) Maria schläft
(7) Maria schläft nicht
(8) Maria schläft und Franz und Karl arbeiten
(9) Maria ist größer als Karl
(10) Mary is bigger than Charles
(11) Hast du Karl um einen Gefallen gebeten?
(12) Est-ce que tu as demandé un service à Charles?

Among others, the following partial meaning relations hold.[3]

(a) In German the relation of *partial consequence* (*P-consequence*, *P-entailment*) holds between {(1), (2)} and {(3)}.

(b) In German {(4), (5), (6)} and {(8)} are *P-synonymous* (or the two sets *have a certain meaning in common*, they are *partially logically equivalent*).

(c) In German the relation of *P-contradiction* holds between {(6)} and {(7)}. Equivalently we say that (6) *P-contradicts* (7), i.e. we identify unit sets with their elements.

---

[1] I use some definitions developed by K. Brockhaus without special reference. I wish to thank S. Plötz for helping me with some formulations in English.

[2] Needless to say the objects of a semantic theory could be defined in quite a different way. One could, for instance, make a theory of utterance meaning or investigate the meanings of speech acts. I would not object to calling such theories semantic theories as well.

[3] I use *meaning, sense* and *intension* synonymously in this paper. For declarative sentences these concepts coincide with the concept of *intension* of Lewis (1972). Lewis however distinguishes between *meaning* and *intension*. I do not deny the value of such a distinction but for the purpose of this paper it is not necessary. So, in this context, one could speak also of *partial sense relations* or *partial intensional relations*.

(d) The German sentence (9) is *P-synonymous* with the English sentence
(10).

(e) Between the German sentence (11) and the French sentence (12)
the relation of *P-synonymy* holds.

Partial meaning relations are intuitively given for the speaker of one or
more languages. This certainly does not mean that the speaker is able to
express statements like (a) to (e). These statements belong to the observation language, i.e. they are the data of the semantic theory.[1] I do not say
how an observer can get such data nor do I claim that this will be an easy
task for him.

It should be noted that partial meaning relations are not restricted to
sentences of one language only, as (d) and (e) show. Furthermore, they are
not limited to declarative sentences as can be seen by (e), where partial
synonymy between interrogative sentences is asserted.[2] Perhaps there are,
in addition, partial meaning relations like the relation of *question-answer*
between different types of sentences.

For partial meaning relations holding between sets of declarative sentences an explication in terms of truth conditions can be given in a well-
known way as follows.

When a declarative sentence s is uttered in a context C the result of the
utterance act may be a true or a false *assertion*.[3] In the first case we will say
that s is true in C in a particular one of its meanings, whereas in the second
case we say that s is false in C in a particular one of its meanings. Now we
may define:

Definition 1

(i) a sentence s of a language L_i *P-entails* a sentence t of a language L_j
iff there is no context C such that s is true in C in a particular one of
its meanings and t is false in C in a particular one of its meanings.

[1] I refer to data as statements in the observation language following Wunderlich (1973)
and ultimately Carnap. I think this is reasonable because in this way it is not concealed that
data are always the results of an intellectual activity which is tacitly presupposed for the
purposes of a certain theory but which may be itself the object of a theory serving other
purposes. Thus, I consider here sentences of natural languages as observable objects. For
other purposes the concept of sentence may be regarded as a theoretical one. See, for
instance, Kasher (1972).

[2] Statements like (e) are the basis for an adequacy criterion for sentence translation in
different natural languages.

[3] Or sometimes no assertion at all. But I will deliberately neglect this possibility. I use
the word *context* in a very general way to include all situational factors, for instance, the
indices of Lewis (1972).

Thus, the P, i.e. 'partially', refers to two fixed meanings of s and t respectively.

Similarly,

(ii) a sentence s of L_i is *P-synonymous* with sentence t of L_j iff

    (a) there is no context C such that s is true in a particular one of its meanings and t is false in a particular one of its meanings and

    (b) there is no context C such that t is true in the last mentioned meaning and s is false in the first mentioned meaning.

The relation of P-synonymy coincides, if I am right, with the paraphrase relations as proposed in Hiż (1964).

It should be noted that partial meaning relations have other properties than the usual 'corresponding' logical relation as *consequence, logical equivalence*, and so on. For instance, the relation of P-consequence is reflexive and the relation of P-synonymy is reflexive and symmetric, whereas the relation of consequence is reflexive and transitive, and the relation of logical equivalence is reflexive, symmetric and transitive, i.e. an equivalence relation. Yet, the partial meaning relations will be described with the aid of logical relations in our grammar. These are the reasons why we qualify the relations studied here as partial relations.

It should be evident how other partial meaning relations for declarative sentences can be explained in terms of truth conditions and how these relations can be extended to sets of sentences.[1]

Thus, the general form of the data our theory is to describe is the following.

(iii) The set of sentences $\mathcal{M}$ of the language $\mathcal{L}_j$ stands in the partial sense relation r_i to the set of sentences $\mathcal{M}'$ of the language $\mathcal{L}_k$. This we abbreviate as:

$$r_i(\mathcal{M}, \mathcal{L}_j, \mathcal{M}', \mathcal{L}_k).$$

3. Generative and interpretative semantics

In this section I introduce some theoretical concepts which are necessary for understanding the criterion of semantic adequacy of a grammar as given in the next paragraph.

---

[1] There are exactly 16 partial meaning relations for declarative sentences which can be false and true only. Important relations which have not yet been mentioned are: *converse P-consequence, P-contrariness, P-subcontrariness*.

Let V be a finite vocabulary and V^* the set of all finite strings over V. Then every L, with $L \subset V^*$ is a *formal language* (over V). The elements of L are called *syntactic strings*. If to every syntactic string of a formal language L one or several elements of a set B of 'formal meanings' or *semantemes* are assigned, then L is a *semantically interpreted language* (SIL). That is to say, a SIL is a relation $R \subset V^* \times B$, and to a syntactic string $x \in L$ a semanteme is assigned iff $(x, \alpha) \in R$. If, furthermore, for some SIL, say R, a finite number of 2-place *semantic relations* $\rho_1, \ldots \rho_n \subset 2^B \times 2^B$ are given, then R is a *SIL with relations*. (2^B is the power set of B.)

Semantic relations like CONS, SYNO, NEGA, . . . will be the theoretical counterparts of P-consequence, P-synonymy, P-contradictoriness, . . . and so on respectively.

We make the following terminological conventions for SILs.

Definition 2: A *generative semantics* is a SIL $R \subset V^* \times B$ where

(i) the set of semantemes B is generated by a formal system;
(ii) R is defined by means of transformational rules such that $(x, \alpha) \in R$ iff x can be derived from α in a finite number of steps by means of the transformational rules.

Definition 3: An *interpretative semantics* is a SIL $R \subset V^* \times B$ such that

(i) L is generated by a recognition syntax;
(ii) R is defined in such a way that $(x, \alpha) \in R$ if and only if α can be determined for x in a finite number of steps.

According to the concepts introduced above there are interpretative and generative semantics with or without (semantic) relations. In an interpretative semantics for a given syntactic string x all the semantemes α such that $(x, \alpha) \in R$ can be found in an effective way. In a generative semantics for a semanteme α all syntactic strings such that $(x, \alpha) \in R$ can be determined effectively.

A few words concerning these notions might be necessary. First, I do not claim that in the literature these concepts are always used as they are here. It is possible that so-called generative semantic theories are not generative semantics in our terminology because it is not always clear whether for a given semanteme all of its syntactic strings can be obtained in a finite number of steps. This might not be the case if filter transformations are used.

On the other hand, grammars as suggested in Chomsky's *Aspects* can be regarded, perhaps, as interpretative semantics in the above sense: certain remarks of Chomsky's suggest that L (that is, the terminal strings of the surface structures) is defined by a transformational grammar which is supposed to be a recognition grammar.[1] Therefore, for each $x \in L$ all of its deep structures can be obtained effectively. Now, take as semantemes interpreted deep structures where the interpretation is made with projection rules. If the projection rules are computable functions, then to each syntactic string, all of its semantemes can be found in a mechanical way.

The third thing which should be noticed is that the concepts Definition 2 and Definition 3 are technical ones which are not to be interpreted in psycholinguistic terms. (At least, such an interpretation is not intended.) Also, the 'direction' from formal meanings to syntactic strings in a generative semantics and the reverse one in an interpretative semantics reflects formal properties of semantic theories which may be useful for some purposes, for instance for mechanical translation. But formal meanings or semantemes must not be interpreted as meanings qua observable, psychological objects, as is done in Bartsch and Vennemann (1972).[2] Semantemes are not interpreted at all in my theory. They are constructs which serve to describe partial meaning relations. I will try to use for the semantic theory a transformational grammar which is both a generative and an interpretative semantics.[3]

4. Semantic adequacy of a grammar

In this section I will give a criterion of semantic adequacy for grammars. I will not give a precise description of the kind of transformational grammar I use, but the formalism is quite similar to the one developed by Ginsburg and Partee (1968). There are however some modifications, among which the following should be noted. First, apart from singularly T-rules, T-rules with more than one argument structure are allowed ('generalized' T-rules). And second, the applicability of the T-rules to structures is not dependent on a 2-dimensional tree representation.[4]

[1] This point is not clear. It depends upon how the grammars sketched in *Aspects* are formalized. Chomsky's restrictions for T-rules are too weak to get recognition grammars. See Kimball (1967) and Pause (1973).

[2] See e.g. Bartsch and Vennemann (1972; 3ff.). I do not say that a theory which takes meanings as observable objects is not possible. I simply am not speaking about these objects. It would not be an objection to my approach that I do not speak about what really happens in a speaker when he is speaking or listening. If I am right, a criticism of Chomsky's work done by Bartsch and Vennemann is based upon an analogous mistake. See Bartsch and Vennemann (1972: 8 ff.).

[3] See also Chomsky (1971: 187ff.), where he opposes a superficial antagonism between a 'syntactically based' and a 'semantically based' grammar i.e. an interpretative and a generative semantics in my terminology.

[4] No use is made of the notion of 'concatenation of graphs'.

The formalism is introduced in a rigorous way in Kratzer, et al. (1973). The T-grammar G we use consists essentially of an infinite set B of base structures or semantemes generated by a context-free base grammar and two kinds of T-rules, 'semantic' T-rules, and 'syntactic' T-rules. The *semantic T-rules* are grouped together into sets *Cons, Nega,*...which are used for defining semantic relations like CONS, NEGA,... $\subset 2^B \times 2^B$. The *syntactic T-rules* correlate base structures with surface structures. The terminal strings of the latter are interpreted as sentences of natural languages. With the sets of syntactic rules *English, German, French* and so on, SILS like ENGLISH, GERMAN, FRENCH $\subset V^* \times B$ are *definable*, where V is the terminal vocabulary of our grammar G. In other words, syntactic strings occurring in the domain of ENGLISH, GERMAN and so on are interpretable as English and German sentences respectively if G is adequate. All syntactic T-rules are singular T-rules.

I will now give a preliminary idea of the adequacy criterion for G. Consider the German sentences (6) and (7) between which the relation of P-contradictoriness holds. If G is adequate, then there are base structures α, β such that the relations in the following diagram hold. The arrows

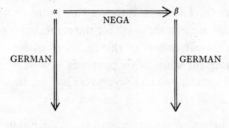

(6) P-contradicts (7)

symbolize that $(\alpha, \beta) \in$ NEGA, that $((6), \alpha)$ and $((7), \beta)$ both belong to GERMAN. Thus, the intuitive relation of P-contradictoriness corresponds to the formal relation NEGA. I will now give some details of how the relations in question are definable in a T-grammar G. After that I will formulate the adequacy criterion. First a set *Tautolog* of 'tautological' structures is introduced: *Tautolog* is the set of structures derivable in G which have the form S(MOD(taut)α). Structures or trees are finite sets of nodes with labelling functions. The nodes are finite sequences of natural numbers fulfilling certain conditions.[1] I use obvious linear or 2-dimensional representations for structures. Greek letters are variables over structures. The following structure β belongs to *Tautolog*.

$\beta = $ S(MOD)(taut)PROP(seq γ γ)

[1] A definition of a tree is given, for instance, in Lewis (1972: 183ff.).

where

$$\gamma = \text{PROP(VERB}_1(\text{TEMP(praes)VERB('arbeit'))NP}_1(\text{NAM(NOM-('karl')))).}$$

One realization of β in English is *If Charles works then he works*. The subtree β can be represented in a 2-dimensional notation equivalently as β_1, β_2 or β_3 (see following diagram). T-rules make no essential use of an

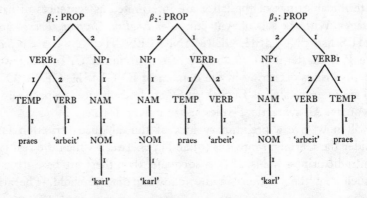

ordered tree notation. I insist a little on this point in order to meet the objections that trees are not adequate for the representation of semantemes because a certain 'linear order' of the nodes must be established which might be inadequate for some other purposes.[1] Now, by giving the definitions of the semantic relations CONS and SYNO we show in an exemplary way how the semantic relations are defined in G:

Definition 4: The set of semantemes $\{\alpha_1, \ldots, \alpha_n\}$ stands in the relation CONS to $\{\alpha\}$ iff there is a sequence of structures $(\beta_1, \ldots, \beta_k)$ such that $\beta_k = \alpha$ and each $\beta_i (1 \leq i \leq k)$ is either an element of $\{\alpha_1, \ldots, \alpha_n\}$ or an element of *Tautolog* or the result of an application of a T-rule of *Cons* on structures preceding in the sequence.

Definition 5: Similarly, $(\alpha, \beta) \in \text{SYNO}$ iff $(\alpha, \beta) \in \text{CONS}$ and $(\beta, \alpha) \in \text{CONS}$. It is clear that in predicate logic the relation of derivability corresponds to Definition 4. It should be evident how these relations can be extended

---

[1] Such an argument is found in Bartsch and Vennemann (1972. 17ff.). The notation used by Bartsch and Vennemann is somewhat more general than my notation, since they have ordered and unordered trees which are connected by 'serialization rules', whereas I only use unordered trees. The 'serialization' in the formalism used here only takes place when the notion of 'terminal string of a tree' is defined. This has the consequence that for some languages semantemes are translatable in a less complicated way into surface structures than in other languages. If one does not want this, some technical changes of the formalism, for instance the serialization rules of Bartsch and Vennemann are necessary. The semantic transformations are not affected by these changes.

to pairs (Δ, Γ) of sets of semantemes such that Γ is not necessarily a unit set. The relations of 'syntactic derivability' in G, that is, SILs, are defined as usual. For instance:

Definition 6: Between the syntactic string $x \in V^*$ and the base structure α the relation ENGLISH holds iff there is a (surface) structure β such that:

(i) the terminal string of β is x, and
(ii) there is a sequence of (intermediate) structures $(\beta_1 \ldots, \beta_k)$ such that $\alpha = \beta_1$, $\beta = \beta_k$ and β_i is the result of an application of a T-rule of *English* to β_i ($1 \leq i \leq k$).

Now we are able to give a more definitive adequacy criterion for a semantic representation of natural language. For this purpose we establish a fixed correspondence between natural languages like English, German, French, ...and the SILs ENGLISH, GERMAN FRENCH,...respectively. Furthermore, a fixed correspondence between the partial meaning relations P-consequence, P-synonymy, P-negation,...and the semantic relations CONS, SYNO, NEGA,..., respectively is established.

Definition 7 (Adequacy of G): G is *semantically adequate* iff statements (i) and (ii) both hold:

(i) if (A) then (B),
(ii) if (B) then (A), where,

(A): $\mathcal{M} = \{s_1, \ldots, s_m\}$ and $\mathcal{M}' = \{t_1, \ldots, t_n\}$ are finite sets of sentences such that $r_i(\mathcal{M}, \mathcal{L}_j, \mathcal{M}', \mathcal{L}_k)$ holds.
(B) There are sets of base structures $\Gamma = \{a_1, \ldots, \alpha_m\}$ and $\Delta = \{\beta_1, \ldots, \beta_n\}$ such that (B.1) and (B.2) hold.
(B. 1) Between Γ and Δ the semantic relation ρ_i holds, where ρ_i corresponds to the partial meaning relation r_i.
(B. 2) $(s_p, \alpha_p) \in R_j$ and $(t_q, \beta_q) \in R_k$ where R_j and R_k are the SILs which correspond to $\mathcal{L}_j$ and $\mathcal{L}_k$ respectively for $p = 1$, ..., m and $q = 1, \ldots, n$

Condition (i) states the *completeness*, condition (ii) the *soundness* of G.

The content of this definition should become clear by considering again diagram 1. Note that we use the same notation both for syntactic strings and for sentences. Therefore, no correspondence rules between sentences and syntactic strings are necessary. Yet, the notion of sentence, as it is introduced here, belongs to the observation language and the notion of syntactic string, to the theoretical language. If, for instance, syntactic strings were represented in a phonological notation and sentences in a traditional orthography, then correspondence rules for the correlation of the two concepts would be necessary.

5. Defining semantic relations using model theory

In the preceding section I have proposed to define semantic relations, i.e. subsets of $2^B \times 2^B$, by means of T-rules, and thus in a constructive way.

It is known that with the methods of model theory semantic relations are definable which are not definable with the aid of rules within formal systems (i.e. semantic T-rules in our grammar).[1] Such relations can be defined by means of suitable (model theoretical) interpretations in essentially the same way as proposed in Lewis (1972). The only difference is that Lewis uses a categorical syntax as base grammar whereas I use a (reduced) context-free syntax. Now, to each context-free rule of the base grammar

$$P_i = A \to B_1 \ldots B_k$$

a (compound) intension $\zeta_i(\zeta_{P_1}, \ldots, \zeta_k)$ is assigned. That is, to each non-terminal node of a tree which is 'expanded' by the syntactic rule P_i into k nodes to which the intensions $\zeta_1, \ldots, \zeta_k$ have already been assigned the intension $\zeta_{Pi}(\zeta_{i1}, \ldots, \zeta_k)$ is assigned. Thus, to the rule P_i correspond interpreted subtrees shown in the diagram below.[2] Now, by means of model

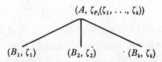

theoretical concepts the semantic relations CONS*, SYNO*,... $\subseteq 2^B \times 2^B$ are definable which are not identical with the relations, CONS, SYNO,..., introduced above. Such a theory would be more general in certain respects but it would be a non-constructive theory.[3] I believe that partial meaning relations can always be described in an approximately adequate manner with the aid of a constructive theory. So, I see no practical need to accept

---

[1] For instance, the relation of consequence in higher predicate logic. See also Keenan (1970) where semantic relations are defined that probably cannot be generated by means of a formal system.

[2] The idea to interpret trees in this way is found also in Montague (1970). See also Brockhaus and Stechow (1971).

[3] *Constructive* is used here in the sense that semantic relations must be generated by means of a formal system.

a non-constructive theory. Yet, in order to meet objections, the following possibility exists: one can define the above relations CONS*, SYNO* and so on within the same grammar as outlined in this paragraph. Then an alternative adequacy criterion using these relations can be given. So, there might be partial meaning relations that hold but are not covered completely by the grammar using the first, 'constructive' adequacy criterion. However, with respect to them, the grammar is still complete according to the 'model theoretic' adequacy criterion. Thus, the advantage of the two approaches can be combined within one grammar.

6. Concluding remarks

Let me now say a few words about the relations between semantics and speech act theory (pragmatics). Although my opinion on this matter is not quite definite yet, it seems to me that, in any case it is to be the role of speech act theory to help justify the semantic data

$$(13) \quad r_i\left(\mathcal{M},\mathcal{L}_j,\mathcal{M}',\mathcal{L}_k\right).$$

I have no clear idea how this can be done. The relation of consequence could perhaps be defined in pragmatical terms, along the following lines:

Definition 8: *s P-entails t* iff there is no context where the speaker is *allowed to assert s* in a particular one of its meanings and to *deny t* in a particular one of its meanings.

In other words, in each situation, where the speaker asserts *s* in a particular one of its meanings he is *obliged* (by social convention) to assert *t* in a particular one of its meanings. See Brockhaus and Stechow (1971). I will not insist on this point. Let me only remark that statements of the form (13) are evidently open to such justification.

REFERENCES

Bartsch, R. and Vennemann, T. (1972). *Semantic Structures*. Frankfurt: Athenäum.

Brockhaus, K. (1970). 'Bemerkungen zur generativen Syntax mit Transformationsregeln', *Linguistische Berichte*, **8**, 1–9.

—— (1972). 'Aussagesätze, Behauptungen, Sinnrelationen.' In *Arbeitspapier* No. 4. Universität Bern, Institut für Sprachwissenschaft.

Brockhaus, K. and Stechow, A. v. (1971). 'On formal semantics: a new approach', *Linguistische Berichte*, **11**, 7–36.

—— (1973). 'Mathematische Verfahren in der Linguistik'. In Dietrich Sinemus, ed., *Grundriß der Literatur – und Sprachwissenschaft*, Vol. II: *Sprachwissenschaft*. Deutscher Taschenbuch Verlag.

Chomsky, N. (1971). 'Deep structure, surface structure, and semantic interpretation'. In D. D. Steinberg and L. A. Jacobovits, eds., *Semantics*. Cambridge: Cambridge University Press.

Egli, U. (1972). 'Zur integrierten Grammatiktheorie', *Linguistische Berichte*, **21**, 1–14.

Ginsburg, S. and Partee, B. (1968). *A Mathematical Model of Transformational Grammars*. SDC, TM Series, Scientific Report No. 21.

Hiż, H. (1964). 'The role of paraphrase in grammar'. In *Monograph Series on Languages & Linguistics*, No. 17, Report of the 15th Annual R.T.M. on Linguistics and Language Studies, ed. C. I. J. M. Stuart.

Kasher, A. (1972). 'Sentences and utterances reconsidered', *Foundations of Language*, **8**, 313–45.

Keenan, E. L. (1970). 'A logical base for a transformational grammar of English'. *Transformations and Discourse Analysis Papers*, No. 85. Philadelphia: University of Pennsylvania.

Kimball, J. (1967). 'Predicates definable over transformational derivations by intersection with regular languages', *Information and Control*, **11**, 177–95.

Kratzer, A., Pause, E. and Stechow, A. v. (1973). *Einführung in Theorie und Anwendung der generativen Syntax*. Frankfurt: Athenäum.

Lakoff, G. (1971). *Linguistik und natürliche Logik*, Werner Abraham, ed. German translation, U. Fries and H. Mitterman. Frankfurt: Athenäum.

Lewis, D. (1972). 'General Semantics'. In D. Davidson and G. Harman, eds., *Semantics of Natural Language*, pp. 169–219. Dordrecht: Reidel.

Montague, R. (1970). 'English as a formal language'. In *Linguaggi nella Società e nella Tecnica*. Milano: Edizioni di Communità.

Montague, R. and Schnelle, H. (1972). *Universal Grammatik*. Braunschweig: Vieweg.

Pause, E. (1973). *Transformationssyntaxen; Generative Kraft-Entscheidbarkeit – Analyse*. To appear Frankfurt: Athenäum.

Staal, J. F., ed. (1969). 'Formal logic and natural languages' (A symposium), *Foundations of Language*, **5**, 256–84.

Wunderlich, D. (1973). 'Grundlagen der Linguistik'. Unpublished manuscript. In preparation.

IV QUESTIONING MODEL THEORETIC SEMANTICS

Model theoretic semantics and natural language

NICHOLAS JARDINE

My aim in this paper[1] is to describe the ways in which model theoretic semantics is used in the study of formal languages, and thence to evaluate it as a tool for the study of natural language. I shall argue that model theoretic semantics is primarily valuable as a theory of consequence; and that, whilst as a tool for the study of natural language it enjoys certain philosophical advantages over other theories of consequence, the fashionable claim that it can provide a theory of truth and meaning for natural language is misguided.

From its conception in the 1930s model theory has led a double life. It has been at once an uncontroversial tool of formal logic and a controversial tool of philosophical and linguistic analysis (recently it has acquired a third and perhaps less transient life as an object with certain algebraic and topological properties of interest to pure mathematicians, see, e.g., Rasiowa and Sikorski (1963)).

To prepare the ground we categorize roughly the uses of model theory:

In the study of formal languages

1. A theory of truth value assignment and consequence;
2. A construction for proving metalogical theorems about independently defined formal systems;
3. A heuristic for the development and teaching of formal systems.

In the study of natural language

4. A theory of consequence;
5. An explication of certain connections between extension, truth value assignment and consequence;
6. A framework for the discussion of questions of ontology;
7. A theory of truth and meaning.

[1] I should like to thank Dr T. J. Smiley, Dr E. Keenan, and Dr P. N. Pettit for helpful criticism.

4–7 have long been of interest to philosophers. Their importance for linguists has been greatly enhanced in the past decade by the work of Mostowski (1952), Kripke (1963a,b), van Fraassen (1969), Montague (1970) and others. These authors have developed model theoretic semantics for systems of many valued, sortal, free, tense and modal logic which (at least in some grand synthesis) are widely believed to be sufficiently power-ful to capture substantial fragments of natural language (I shall have more to say later about this notion of capture).

1–7, above, form a natural sequence, understanding of each being facilitated by a grasp of its predecessors, so I have adopted this as my order of presentation. The discussion of the uses of model theory in the study of formal languages is mainly expository, and attempts only a slight debunk-ing by showing that model theory is not, as is often supposed, indispensable for these purposes. Special emphasis is placed on the role of model theory as a theory of consequence and its relation to other recently developed approaches to the study of consequence. The discussion of the uses of model theory in the study of natural language is critical.

A couple of terminological points and a warning: The phrase *formal language* is used for a set of well-formed formulae determined by syntactic formation rules, and the phrase *formal system* is used for a formal language on which additional structure is defined. Natural language is often abbre-viated to NL, model theoretic semantics to MTS, and truth value seman-tics to TVS. The exposition in sections 1 and 2 presupposes familiarity with at least the notation of model theory. The reader will find all that is needed in digestible form in Hunter (1971).

The lengthy and technical preliminary to an assessment of the claim that MTS can provide theories of truth and meaning for fragments of natural language would be otiose were there some short and sweet argument which established or refuted the claim. Informal arguments purporting to do one or the other have appeared in the literature from time to time, and two of them deserve mention.

A direct argument against the claim occurs to many students when they first encounter Tarski's adequacy criterion for a definition of truth. It rests on the ignoble suspicion that there can be little profit in saying the same thing twice – once in the object language and once in a metalanguage. When linguists or philosophers use model theory in the study of some fragment of NL the metalanguage in which the truth conditions of sentences are expressed is itself a fragment of NL. So how can this approach help one to understand the fragment of NL when to understand the truth conditions he must already understand a fragment of NL which contains either the very fragment of NL studied or some translation of it? The trouble with this charge of circularity is its vagueness. Precisely which uses of model theory is it supposed to vitiate and how exactly does it do so?

A direct argument for the claim is to be found in Davidson's (1967) influential paper 'Truth and meaning'. He offers an analytic argument which purports to show that a definition of truth which satisfies Tarski's adequacy criterion satisfies a highly plausible adequacy criterion for a theory of meaning. In the first appendix I examine this argument and show that it fails.

1. Model theory, consequence, and related properties of formal systems

We first indicate, informally, what is meant when it is said, misleadingly, that classical semantics provides a definition of truth in a language.

A model is specified as a set, the domain of the model, and an extension for each non-logical constant of the object language. In the standard semantics for the first order predicate calculus the extension of an individual constant in a model is an element of the domain, and the extension of an n-place predicate is an n-ary relation on the domain. The fundamental definition shows how the extension of an atomic formula is determined by the extensions of the constants appearing in it, and how the extension of a non-atomic formula is determined by the extensions of the atomic formulae from which it is built up. The extension of an open formula is the set of assignments of elements of the domain to variables which satisfy it. And the extension of a sentence is its truth value, truth being conventionally identified with the set of all assignments to variables, and falsity with the empty set.

Suppose that L is the set of sentences of a language. Then for each member a of L the fundamental definition gives rise to a condition of the form:

'a is true iff . . .'

The sentence which replaces the three dots in this schema is not a member of L. It is a sentence which states that a model for L has a property corresponding to the truth of a. Thus, the fundamental definition does not yield a definition of truth for a, but only a necessary and sufficient condition for the truth of a in terms of each model for L.

Tarski's (1936) first full account of the semantical theory of truth has often been misunderstood by philosophers who have perhaps been misled by his remark that the definition of truth makes no use of other semantical notions. In fact his construction of the truth predicate for the Huntington calculus makes use of the notion of satisfaction and hence implicitly of the notion of extension. In later papers (see, e.g. Tarski and Vaught (1957)) model theory is used to clarify the notion of satisfaction, and the theory of truth is explicitly presented as an explication of truth in terms of extension in a model.

It should be noted that, even if a single model for L is given, there is in general no effective procedure for determining truth values of sentences in L. For example, Church proved that there is no recursive algorithm for calculating the truth values of sentences of elementary number theory. The fundamental definition gives an effective procedure determining a truth condition for each sentence in terms of a property of the model; but there can be no algorithm which decides whether or not the model has the property.

Usually, of course, more than one model is available, so that the fundamental definition only constrains the truth values of sentences of L. It is through these constraints that the internal properties of the system can be defined. Thus, let M be a model for the language whose set of sentences is L. We may define a map ϕ_M from L to $\{0,1\}$ by:

$\phi_M(a) = 1$ if a is true in M;
$\phi_M(a) = 0$ if a is false in M.

If a class $\mathbf{M}$ of models is specified, the corresponding set $\Phi_\mathbf{M}$ of maps from L to $\{0,1\}$ defined by:

$$\Phi_\mathbf{M} = \{\phi_M : M \in \mathbf{M}\},$$

summarizes the constraints on truth value imposed by the fundamental definition and the specification of $\mathbf{M}$.

The basic internal property of L which may be defined semantically is the consequence operation. Loosely, sentence a is a consequence of a set A of sentences if a is true whenever all members of A are true. More formally, given a class of models $\mathbf{M}$, we may define a map $con_\mathbf{M}$, from $\mathscr{P}(L)$ to $\mathscr{P}(L)$, by:

$$con_\mathbf{M}(A) = \cap\{\phi^{-1}[1] : \phi \in \Phi_\mathbf{M} \text{ and } A \subset \phi^{-1}[1]\}.$$

Let us compare the semantic definition of consequence with the more direct proof theoretic definition. A set of axioms is specified, and finitely many rules of inference are laid down. A sequence of sentences is a proof if every member of the sequence is either an axiom, or a premiss, or follows from its predecessors by one of the rules of inference. A sentence is a consequence of a set A of sentences if it is the last element of some proof whose premisses are taken from A. The map *con* so defined, carrying a set of sentences A to the set of all its provable consequences, has the following properties:

(1) $A \subset con(A)$;
(2) if $A \subset B$, then $con(A) \subset con(B)$;
(3) $con(con(A)) = con(A)$;
(4) if $a \in con(A)$, then there is a finite subset F of A such that $a \in con(F)$.

The first three of these properties define a closure operation, and the map con_M, derived from a class **M** of models, also satisfies them. The fourth property, which arises from the finitistic nature of the definition of proof, is not a general property of semantically defined consequence.

The fact that the map *con*, whether defined semantically or proof-theoretically, is a closure operation on the set of sentences suggests another useful property of formal systems. To any closure operation there corresponds a closure system. Thus, if *con* is a map from $\mathscr{P}(L)$ to $\mathscr{P}(L)$ satisfying (1), (2) and (3), above, and if a set **T** of subsets of L is defined by:

$$\mathbf{T} = \{T \subset L : con(T) = T\},$$

then

$$con(A) = \cap\{T \in \mathbf{T} : A \subset T\}.$$

Moreover, the intersection of any collection of members of **T** is a member of **T**. If *con* is the map which carries a subset of L to the set of all its consequences, then the members of the corresponding **T** are precisely the sets of sentences which are theorems of theories in L. For the theory whose axioms are the members of a set $A \subset L$ has as its theorems the set $con(A)$, and since $con(con(A)) = con(A)$, $con(A) \in \mathbf{T}$. And if $T \in \mathbf{T}$, since $con(T) = T$, the theory whose axioms form the set T has exactly T as its set of theorems.

We call a set T of sentences such that $con(T) = T$ a *theory set*. Let us see how the theory sets in a language relate to its semantics. We have a class of models **M**, a set of truth value assignments Φ_M defined *via* the fundamental semantic definition, and a semantic consequence map con_M. Let us call the sets T, such that $con_M(T) = T$, the **M**-*theory sets*, and denote the set of such sets $\mathbf{T}_M$. For each model M in **M** the set $\phi_M{}^{-1}[1]$ of sentences true in M has the following properties:

(1) $\phi_M^{-1}[1] \in \mathbf{T}_M$;

(2) for each $a \in L$, either $a \in \phi_M^{-1}[1]$ or $\sim a \in \phi_M^{-1}[1]$;

(3) there is no $a \in L$ such that $a \in \phi_M^{-1}[1]$ and $\sim a \in \phi_M^{-1}[1]$.

Thus $\phi_M^{-1}[1]$ is not only a theory set, but is also complete, by (2) above, and consistent, by (3) above.

Now it follows directly from the definition of con_M that every **M**-theory set is the intersection of sets $\phi_M^{-1}[1]$, where M ranges over some subclass of the class **M** of models. Since no set satisfying (2) above is contained in any larger set satisfying (3), it follows that every complete consistent **M**-theory set is equal to $\phi_M^{-1}[1]$ for some model M. So given a set $\mathbf{T_M}$ of theory sets, derived *via* Φ_M and con_M from a class of models, we can recover the set Φ_M of truth value assignments. They are just those maps from L to $\{0,1\}$ which, for some complete consistent **M**-theory set T, map each sentence in T to 1 and each sentence not in T to 0.

In summary we have shown how three internal properties of a formal system are defined given a fundamental semantic definition and specification of a class of models. First, we can say which maps from the set of sentences to $\{0,1\}$ are admissible assignments of truth value; that is, we define Φ_M. Secondly, we can say which sentences are consequences of which sets of sentences; that is, we define con_M. Thirdly, we can say which sets of sentences constitute the theorems of theories; that is, we define $\mathbf{T_M}$. And we have shown that if one of Φ_M, con_M, $\mathbf{T_M}$ is given the other two are determined.

Of course, the class of models is not itself determined by these internal properties. Let us consider the relation of isomorphism between models. Informally two models are isomorphic if they have the same structure and differ only in content. Formally, let M and M', with domains D and D', be models for a language L. Let f be a $1:1$ map from D onto D'. Then f induces maps from the cartesian power D^n onto D'^n for each integer n. So, for each integer n, f induces a map from n-ary relations on D to n-ary relations on D', and from n-ary functions on D to n-ary functions on D'. The map f is said to be an isomorphism of models if the extension of each non-logical constant of L in M' is the image of its extension in M under the appropriate induced map. Two models are isomorphic if there is an isomorphism of models between them.

It follows from the definition that if M and M' are isomorphic models, $\phi_M = \phi_{M'}$, and that if **M** and **M'** are classes of models such that for each $M \in \mathbf{M}$ there is an $M' \in \mathbf{M'}$ isomorphic to M, and vice versa, then $\Phi_M = \Phi_{M'}$. So given an assignment of truth values it is not possible to recover the class of models from which it was derived, and *a fortiori* not possible to specify the extension of any non-logical constant. We shall hark back to this point in the final section.

So far we have considered extensional semantic systems like the standard model theory for the predicate calculus. But, with some slight modifications, our account extends to more complicated semantic systems such as Kripke's (1963a,b) semantics for modal logics, Kaplan's (1964) semantics for intensional languages, Montague's (1970) semantics for pragmatic languages, and the systems outlined by Lewis (1970) and Scott (1970). In these systems there is specified for each model a set **I** whose elements are variously called points of reference, indices, or possible worlds. An index is supposed to specify the time, place, speaker and other information needed to determine the logical relations between sentences which involve tense, modality, and indexical reference.

In such systems the fundamental semantic definition yields truth conditions of the form:

'a is true at i iff ...',

for each sentence a of the object language, for each index i. It is therefore possible to have a more complicated recursion in the algorithm which generates truth conditions for sentences than is allowed in the simple extensional case. To specify a model the extension of each non-logical constant at each index is specified. The map which carries each index to the extension of a particular constant at that index is called the *intension* of the constant (this device was introduced by Carnap (1947) and Church (1951)). The fundamental semantic definition derives the intensions of atomic formulae from the intensions of the constants which occur in them, and derives the intensions of non-atomic formulae from the intensions of the atomic formulae from which they are built up. The intension of a sentence is a specification of its truth value at each index.

The motive behind such systems is so to generalize the classical extensional semantics as to capture the ways in which the assignment of truth value to a sentence uttered at a given time and place, by a given speaker (etc.) is constrained by the assignment of truth values to other sentences under various conditions of utterance. This is what gives this kind of semantics its intuitive appeal for the treatment of tense, modality and indexical reference.

In such systems the fundamental definition does not lead to a single assignment of truth values to sentences of L for each model M. Instead, for each model M an assignment of truth values is determined for each member of the index set $\mathbf{I}_M$, associated with M, so that we obtain not a single map, but a set of maps:

$$\{\phi_{M,i}: i \in \mathbf{I}_M\}$$

from L to $\{0,1\}$.

If $\mathbf{M}$ is a class of models we may define $\varPhi_\mathbf{M}$ by:

$$\varPhi_\mathbf{M} = \cup\{\{\phi_{M,i}: i \in \mathbf{I}_M\}: M \in \mathbf{M}\}.$$

From this set of maps from L to $\{0,1\}$ the consequence operation on L and the theory sets in L can be derived.

So we see how both extensional and Kripke-style intensional semantic systems generate a set of maps from sentences of the object language to $\{0,1\}$ which can be identified as the admissible truth value assignments. And these maps can be used to define the consequence operation on the language and the theory sets in the language.

2. Metalogical and heuristic uses of formal semantics

Many of the standard proofs of symbolic logic use model-theoretic apparatus. For example, to prove that a set of proper axioms for a first order theory is proof-theoretically consistent, in the sense that it is impossible to derive a contradiction from them, it suffices to prove that the set is semantically consistent, in the sense that there is a model for the theory in which all the axioms are true.

Such proofs depend on the fact that the first order predicate calculus is semantically complete. That is, the consequence operation $con_\mathbf{M}$, defined as in the previous section in terms of the class $\mathbf{M}$ of models for the calculus, is the same as the consequence operation defined proof-theoretically in terms of axioms and rules of inference. So an assertion about proof-theoretic consequence can be proved by proving the corresponding assertion about semantic consequence.

For many such proofs we can dispense with model-theoretic apparatus altogether, by specifying directly a set of truth value assignments which is complete in the sense that the consequence operation derived from it corresponds to the proof-theoretic consequence operation. One application of this approach is due to Leblanc (1968) who used it to investigate a reading of quantification somewhat different to the usual reading.

On the standard reading of quantification, it is possible for an existentially quantified sentence to be true when no sentence derived from it by substitution of constants for free variables in the open formula is true.

Intuitively this reading feels right because the object, or objects, which instantiate the existential sentence may not be named. On the substitutional reading of quantification an existentially quantified sentence is true if and only if some substitution of names for free variables of the open formula yields a true sentence. The set Ψ of truth value assignments appropriate for this reading of quantification may be defined as follows for a first order predicate calculus with infinitely many individual constant symbols.

Let L be the set of *sentences* of a first order predicate calculus with infinitely many individual constant symbols. We define Ψ as the set of maps ψ from L to $\{0,1\}$ such that:

(1) $\psi(a \to b) = 0$ iff $\psi(a) = 1$ and $\psi(b) = 0$;

(2) $\psi(\sim a) = 0$ iff $\psi(a) = 1$;

(3) $\psi((\exists\alpha)a) = 0$ iff $\psi(a(t/\alpha)) = 0$ for all constant terms t.

We define a map con_Ψ from $\mathscr{P}(L)$ to $\mathscr{P}(L)$ by:

$$con_\Psi(A) = \cap\{\psi^{-1}[1]: \psi \in \Psi \text{ and } A \subset \psi^{-1}[1]\}.$$

The relation between the consequence operation derived from this set Ψ of truth value assignments, and the consequence operation derived from the usual set Φ is as follows:

(1) $con_\Phi(A) \subset con_\Psi(A)$ for all subsets A of L;

(2) if infinitely many of the constant terms of L do not occur in the members of A, and hence *a fortiori* if A is finite, $con_\Phi(A) = con_\Psi(A)$.

These remarks follow from Beth's (1959) considerations of the class of those models for the predicate calculus in which every element of the domain is the extension of some individual constant of the language. Leblanc and Meyer (1970) have extended this approach to languages of higher order. (2), above, is an important result because it shows that the two readings of quantification yield the same valid proofs.

It should be noted (contrary to what is widely assumed in the literature) that there is no necessary connection between the reading of quantification and the mode of specification of truth value assignments. Truth value assignments appropriate for the substitutional reading of quantification can be specified model-theoretically, following Beth (1959); and a set Φ of truth value assignments appropriate for the standard reading is specified directly in appendix 2.

One historical reason why model theoretic constructions have been preferred to direct constructions like the Φ given in appendix 2 is a preference, arising from the famous Hilbert programme, for the use of finitistic constructive methods in metalogical proofs. Many of the standard model theoretic constructions used for consistency and completeness proofs satisfy this stringent requirement, whereas, for example, the topological proof of the completeness of Φ, mentioned in appendix 2, does not. In fact model theoretic constructions have no monopoly of finitistic approaches (see, e.g., Hintikka (1955)). And many logicians have taken the proof by Gödel that any finitistic axiomatization of arithmetic is either inconsistent or incomplete as showing the futility of the Hilbert programme.

The heuristic value of model theoretic semantics is unquestionable. There can be no doubt that the intuitions behind many developments in symbolic logic have been of a semantical type, and that construction of semantical apparatus may, for some logicians, be a psychologically necessary bridge between those intuitions and a full internal description of a formal object language. And what is useful in the development of formal systems may remain useful in helping others to understand them. Thus Kripke's (1963a) semantics for propositional modal logics serves not merely as a construction for deriving new modal logics and proving consistency and other metalogical theorems. The demonstration that various propositional modal logics arise from different restrictions on accessibility relations between possible worlds makes the logics much easier to understand.

But which considerations a logician chooses to train his intuitions and to instruct others is largely a matter of taste and fashion. There are no *a priori* grounds for preferring model theoretic apparatus to constructions which dispense with model theory, such as the direct construction of admissible truth value assignments. Indeed, such direct constructions have recently become quite popular. Hintikka (1969) has used admissible truth value assignments as a heuristic in discussions of modality and propositional attitudes; Leblanc (1968) has suggested that direct construction of admissible truth value assignments may be easier to teach to students with a mathematical background than the standard extensional semantics of the first order predicate calculus; and Curry (1963: chapter 8) has used theory sets in the exposition of modal logics. As a theory of truth value assignment and consequence, model theoretic semantics owes much of its prestige to having been first in the field.

3. Model theory and natural language

It is increasingly fashionable for linguists to claim that substantial fragments of NL can be captured by formal languages. This is an interesting contingent claim. As a minimal adequacy criterion for such capture we may require that *effective* translation rules be specified which take into account contextual information to transform sentences of NL into well-formed formulae of the formal language, and do so in such a way that the entailments which hold amongst the natural language sentences are preserved by a consequence operation defined on the formal language (like 'grammaticality' the notion of 'entailment amongst NL sentences' is by no means clearcut, and for practical purposes would be construed by linguists so as to allow a generous measure of arbitrary decision for doubtful cases). By this minimal criterion no substantial fragment of natural language has yet been captured, although the recent work of Winograd (1972) provides the first real grounds for optimism.

The illusion that much has been achieved in this field may arise from the relative ease with which NL sentences can often be generated from sentences of a formal language. But whilst this *may* be a valuable first step towards the construction of rules which 'go the other way', in itself it merely corroborates the uncontroversial claim that NL can capture fragments of many formal languages.

To see the gulf which lies between translation from a formal language into NL and its converse, consider definite pronouns. To generate pleasingly colloquial NL representatives for sentences of a predicate calculus it is fairly easy to write programmes which eliminate or reduce repetition of names and definite descriptions by introducing definite pronouns, and which do so without introducing unacceptable ambiguities. But 'going the other way' it is exceedingly difficult to write a programme which disambiguates the reference of definite pronouns using contextual information to find the admissible substitutions of names and definite descriptions.

In what follows I shall consider the hypothetical case where a fragment of NL is captured by a formal language. In this hypothetical case it follows from the definition of capture that if MTS provides the theory of consequence for the formal system (and the work of Kripke (1963a,b) and others has shown that this is not too restrictive a clause), then it provides a theory of consequence for the fragment of NL. So the claim that MTS can provide a theory of consequence for fragments of NL, the fourth of the uses of MTS listed in the introduction, is no more controversial than the contingent claim that fragments of NL can be captured by formal languages for which MTS provides a theory of consequence.

However, apart from the fact that it may be easier to work with, there is no reason to prefer MTS to TVS (or even proof-theory) if all we want is a theory of consequence. The question we must ask is – when a fragment of NL is captured by a formal language does MTS give us insights into the structure of NL which other approaches to the theory of consequence do not?

As a preliminary let us define *NL-extension*. The NL-extension of a referring expression is the object it designates; the NL-extension of a predicative expression is the set of objects to which it 'applies' (i.e. of each of which it could be predicated by a true sentence).

Now consider the two readings of quantification and the two kinds of semantics discussed in section 2. We showed that the two readings of quantification, the standard and the substitutional, yield the same consequence operation on finite sets of sentences. So from the point of view of provability there is nothing to choose between them. And we showed that, contrary to what is generally supposed, for each reading of quantification an appropriate set of truth value assignments can be set up *either* using MTS *or* using TVS. So we have four adequate approaches to the theory of consequence (apart from proof-theory).

There are two reasons, one good and one debatable, for one who studies NL to prefer the pair ⟨MTS; standard reading⟩ to other pairs.

1. If ⟨MTS; standard reading⟩ is adopted and NL-extension is identified with extension in a model an explication of certain relations between extension, truth value assignment and consequence is obtained. This explication, which is outlined in the first section, is rightly accounted as a paradigm of philosophical analysis. It is obvious that TVS can yield no such explication, and to adopt ⟨MTS; substitutional reading⟩ and identify NL-extension with extension in a model is to commit oneself to an absurd denial of the existence of unnamed objects.

2. If ⟨MTS; standard reading⟩ is adopted and NL-extension is identified with extension in a model, Quine's celebrated 'to be is to be the value of a bound variable' can be used to find out what kinds of objects we are committed to by NL assertions. Quine (1969) has argued that to adopt the substitutional reading is to turn one's back on questions of ontology. This matter is discussed in appendix 3.

The first of these bonuses got by adopting ⟨MTS; standard reading⟩ and identifying NL-extension with extension in a model should be welcomed with a modicum of caution. The MTS for a formalized fragment of NL does not, as is sometimes assumed, in any way determine the NL-extensions of terms. To make this clear let us recapitulate the remarks in section 1 about isomorphism of models. If more than one assignment of truth values to sentences is available (as is usually the case for a fragment of NL!), more than one isomorphism class of models is available. Even if a complete assignment of truth values were given the class of models would be determined, at best, only up to isomorphism. In any isomorphism class there are models which differ on *all* non-empty extensions. For example, in any isomorphism class there is one model at least whose domain consists of odd integers and one whose domain consists of even integers. It follows that it is not possible within a language to specify the extension of any term or even to specify what kinds of objects its expressions have as extensions. (We take the arguments given by Quine (1969) as an attempt to generalize this result to show that under no circumstances can language users ascertain that each applies some expression to the same objects or to the same kinds of objects as do the others.) Were extensions determined by the internal structure of a language it might be possible to interpret MTS as a theory of truth and meaning for NL without making further assumptions about NL. But matters stand otherwise.

We are now in a position to tackle the last and most controversial question. By equating NL-extension with extension in a model we have obtained an elegant account of the connections between extension, truth value assignment and consequence, and a licence to practise the dubious science of ontology. What more must we assume to establish MTS as a theory of truth and meaning? Before proceeding to the business of destruction we outline briefly, and with no attempt at rigour, some of the reasons why MTS appears so attractive as a theory of truth and meaning.

First we note that the Fregean approach to the theory of meaning into which MTS fits so neatly deals with the descriptive contents of sentences, and largely ignores the sort of study of meaning which concerns itself with the conditions for performance and recognition of the various kinds of speech acts – assertions, commands, warnings, etc.

Amongst the principles of the Fregean approach are: (1) 'To understand the meaning of a sentence is to understand what it is for the sentence to be true'; and (2) 'To understand the meanings of the logically simple constituent expressions of a sentence together with its syntax is to understand the meaning of the sentence'. If MTS is taken as a theory of truth, then we may translate (1) into 'To understand the meaning of a sentence is to understand its semantic truth condition'. The reader of section 1 will remember that the semantic truth condition of a sentence specifies certain (set-theoretic) relations between the extensions of its logically simple constituents. For example, assuming 'is an apple' and 'is green' to be logically simple expressions, the semantic truth condition for 'All apples are green' is 'Ext(is an apple) is included in Ext(is green)'. So, on our interpretation of

(1), to understand the meaning of a sentence is to understand something about the extensions of certain logically simple expressions. It is worth asking why semantic truth conditions are chosen as accounts of what it is for sentences to be true rather than some other sort of truth conditions. Why should we not choose, for example, the truth conditions given by TVS which specify for each sentence an assignment of truth values to atomic sentences of the language?

To answer this question it is necessary to consider the connection between the meanings of logically simple expressions of a language and their extensions. Suppose that we accept the principle that to understand the sense of a logically simple expression is to understand how in principle to recognize whether an object is (in the case of a referring expression), or is a member of (in the case of a predicative expression) its extension. We may then argue as follows. Suppose that someone understands the syntax of a sentence and the meanings of its logically simple constituents. The logical syntax of the sentence determines the form of its semantic truth condition, and the principle mentioned above ensures that someone who understands the meanings of the logically simple constituents of the sentence knows in principle what it is for the truth condition to be satisfied. Such a person may plausibly be said to understand the semantic truth condition of the sentence. So the answer to our question is that by choosing to interpret 'what it is for a sentence to be true' in (1), above, as 'the semantic truth condition of a sentence' we obtain a nice explication of (2).

The part of this account which I shall question is the initial assumption that the semantic truth condition for a formalization of a sentence of NL can be interpreted as 'what it is for the sentence to be true'. The semantic truth condition of a sentence is expressed in a metalanguage as an assertion about the extensions of the logically simple expressions of the language. If we are to interpret such an assertion as what it is for the corresponding sentence to be true, we are bound to accept the following principles.

C1. Were someone to ascertain what the truth condition specifies about the extensions of logically simple expressions he would have sufficient grounds for saying that the sentence was true.

C2. The truth condition specifies uniquely all that someone would have to ascertain *about the extensions of the logically simple expressions of the language* in order to ascertain the truth of the sentence.

These are relatively weak epistemological conditions. It should be noted

that their adoption is consistent with a rejection of any form of verifica-
tionism. Thus C1 does not entail the palpably absurd conclusion that
semantic truth conditions are effective recipes for verifying or falsifying
sentences. Further, C2 does not entail the equally absurd conclusion that
ascertainment of what the semantic truth condition specifies is the only
way in which a sentence could be verified. It merely says that if you are
going to try and verify a sentence by ascertaining things about the extensions
of logically primitive expressions, then the semantic truth condition tells
you *all* that you would have to ascertain.

We now show that C2 entails a most implausible assumption about
natural language. Let us define an expression of NL as *primitive* if there is
no object for which under all circumstances it would be necessary to know
the truth value of a sentence for which a truth condition was provided in
order to recognize whether or not that object is (in the case of a referring
expression), or is a member of (in the case of a predicative expression) its
extension. C2 cannot be true unless all the logically simple expressions of a
language are primitive. For, consider a truth condition which mentions a
logically simple expression which is not primitive. The truth condition can
no longer be interpreted as specifying uniquely what one would have to
ascertain about the extensions of logically simple expressions of the
language in order to ascertain the truth of the sentence, for in order to
ascertain the truth of the sentence *in this way* it would be necessary to
ascertain also whatever it was about the extensions of logically simple expressions that the truth conditions for one or more other sentences specified.

It follows that MTS can be interpreted as a theory of truth and meaning
for NL only if it is assumed that every expression of NL is either a primitive expression or one which can be replaced by some explicit construction
out of primitive expressions. This is one of the basic assumptions of logical
positivism, or rather, to be more precise, it is an assumption needed to
make sense of logical positivism. It would be out of place here to go into
the standard objections to this assumption, but it is perhaps worth indicating the nature of the dilemma it poses for the would-be interpreter of
MTS as a theory of truth and meaning for NL.

A sentence challenges the primitive status of an expression of NL if
under all conceivable circumstances a person's decision whether or not
some object is to be assigned to its extension would be affected by his
assignment of truth value to the sentence. If forced to concede that such a
challenge is successful the semantic enthusiast must choose, on pain of
having to abandon altogether his claim that MTS provides a theory of
truth and meaning for NL, one of several unpalatable alternatives. He may

banish the challenging sentence from the language. He may replace the challenged expression by some construction out of other allegedly primitive expressions, and banish the sentence which he uses to express the construction from the language. Or he may banish the challenged expression itself from the language. In practice the first two courses are often made to look quite impressive by relegating the banished sentences to the metalanguage in which truth conditions are expressed and calling them 'meaning postulates'. But the important point is that on pain of incoherence MTS cannot be interpreted as providing an analysis of the meanings of such sentences. Of course, the dilemma does not directly yield anything like a refutation of the interpretation of MTS as a theory of truth and meaning for NL. For a refutation we should need a demonstration that there would be no end to the process of impoverishment and reconstruction of NL which the semantic enthusiast could be forced to undertake; or, alternatively, a demonstration that were NL so reconstructed as to render all logically simple expressions primitive it could no longer be used for the purposes for which NL is in fact used.

Faced with the necessity of admitting that MTS cannot provide a complete analysis of truth and meaning for NL, and with the spectre of a demonstration that it may provide no such analysis, the semantic enthusiast may, as a last resort, claim that MTS is to be interpreted only as an approximate or idealized theory of truth and meaning for NL. This line of defence may turn out to be justified. It may ultimately happen that some modification or extension of MTS can be interpreted as a theory of truth and meaning in such a way as to preserve something like the present account of the relations between the syntax and meaning of a sentence and the meanings of its constituents, whilst dispensing with the untenable assumption. I suspect, however, that the defence will not be vindicated. It is usual for a profitable idealization in natural science to be so designed that the scientist can see, at least in outline, how to extend or modify the theory so as to dispense with some or all of the simplifying assumptions. But although recent extensions of MTS, such as that outlined at the end of section 1, have vastly increased the range of formal languages to which it can be applied, no one has, as far as I know, proposed a modification or even a sketch of a modification of MTS which could be interpreted as a theory of truth and meaning for NL without the untenable assumption.

Conclusion

If the arguments given above are correct, the interpretation of MTS as a theory of truth and meaning for NL, an interpretation persuasively urged by Davidson (1967), Montague (1970) and Lewis (1970), is misguided. To the linguist interested in the use of formal languages as sources of underlying structures for NL sentences MTS is perhaps the most useful of several alternative approaches to the theory of consequence. For the philosopher it provides a beautiful explication of certain connections between extension, truth value assignment and consequence, and a framework for the discussion of ontological questions. But its interpretation as a theory of truth and meaning for NL, whilst it yields a coherent account of the dependence of the meaning of a sentence on the meanings of its constituents together with its syntax, does so at the cost of an untenable assumption about NL.

I think that the specific flaw which I have indicated in the interpretation of MTS as a theory of truth and meaning for NL is merely symptomatic of the general inadequacy of any approach which divorces the analysis of the descriptive contents of sentences from the study of the rules which govern the performance and recognition of the various kinds of speech acts. But to argue for a connection between the specific flaw and the general inadequacy, let alone to indicate what a theory of meaning not subject to either would look like, would take me far beyond the confines of this already overlong paper.

APPENDIX 1

Davidson's analytic argument

Davidson (1967) first considers and effectively shows up the vacuity, as theories, of accounts which reify meanings. And he points out that syntactic theories which discriminate the well-formed or meaningful sentences of a language from the ill-formed or meaningless are not theories of meaning. He then considers sentences of the form:

'*s* means that *p*',

where '*s*' is to be replaced by a structural description of a sentence and '*p*' by a sentence. He suggests as an adequacy criterion for a theory of meaning that it should provide for each sentence *s* a matching sentence '*p*', which 'gives the meaning' of *s*.

The analytic argument by which Davidson infers that a theory which specifies for each sentence a truth condition satisfying Tarski's adequacy criterion is an adequate theory of meaning goes as follows (Davidson (1967:310)):

> The theory will have done its work if it provides, for every sentence *s* in the language under study, a matching sentence (to replace '*p*') that, in some way

yet to be made clear, 'gives the meaning' of *s*. One obvious candidate for the matching sentence is just *s* itself, if the object language is contained in the metalanguage; otherwise a translation of *s* in the metalanguage. As a final bold step, let us try treating the position occupied by '*p*' extensionally: to implement this, sweep away the obscure 'means that', provide the sentence that replaces '*p*' with a proper sentential connective, and supply the description that replaces '*s*' with its own predicate. The plausible result is

(*T*) *s* is *T* if and only if *p*.

What we require of a theory of meaning for a language *L* is that without appeal to any (further) semantical notions it place enough restrictions on the predicate 'is *T*' to entail all sentences got from scheme *T* when '*s*' is replaced by a structural description of a sentence of *L* and '*p*' by that sentence.

Any two predicates satisfying this condition have the same extension, so if the metalanguage is rich enough, nothing stands in the way of putting what I am calling a theory of meaning into the form of an explicit definition of a predicate 'is *T*'. But whether explicitly defined or recursively characterized, it is clear that the sentences to which the predicate 'is *T*' applies will be just the true sentences of *L*, for the condition we have placed on satisfactory theories of meaning is in essence Tarski's Convention *T* that tests the adequacy of a formal semantical definition of truth.

In fact to secure equivalence of the schemata '*s* means that *p*' and '*s* is *T* iff *p*', where 'is *T*' is a predicate which applies to just the true sentences, we need a further assumption not mentioned by Davidson. It is necessary to preclude the case where, for some structural description '*s*', '*s* means that *p*' is true whatever sentence replaces '*p*'.

With this additional premiss the argument can be made explicit as follows. We denote the schema '*s* means that *p*' by *. On the assumption that the position occupied by '*p*' in * is extensional the following four cases only can arise for any particular substitution for '*s*':

(1) * is true whatever sentence is substituted for '*p*';
(2) * is false whatever sentence is substituted for '*p*';
(3) * has the same truth value as whatever sentence is substituted for '*p*';
(4) * has the opposite truth value to whatever sentence is substituted for '*p*'.

(1) is ruled out by the extra premiss given above. (2) is ruled out by Davidson's assumption that * is true when the sentence replacing '*p*' is that specified by the structural description replacing '*s*'. Let us define 'is *T*' as a predicate of sentences such that *s* is *T* if case (3) holds. Then, since (1) and (2) are excluded, *s* is not *T* only if case (4) holds. It follows directly that * is equivalent to '*s* is *T* iff *p*' for all substitutions of structural descriptions for '*s*' and sentences for '*p*'. It must now be shown that a truth predicate which satisfies Tarski's adequacy criterion satisfies also the defining condition for the predicate 'is *T*', given above. This follows directly from Davidson's assumption that * is true whenever '*p*' is replaced by the sentence specified by the description which replaces '*s*'.

Of the three premisses used in this argument, the only counterintuitive one is the treatment of the role of '*p*' in '*s* means that *p*' as extensional. Nowhere is it independently justified. The discussion which precedes the analytic argument does indeed cast doubt on the reification of meanings, and the proposed adequacy criterion for a theory of meaning is attractive. But acknowledgement of the intensionality of the role of '*p*' in sentences of the form '*s* means that *p*' does not force a reification of meanings; so even a cast-iron refutation of all approaches which reify meanings would not justify the alternative treatment of the role of '*p*' as extensional. But in the absence of independent justification Davidson's interpretation of the analytic argument collapses. For the identification of the semantical theory of truth as a theory of meaning is achieved only by covertly introducing the semantical notion of truth in the extensionality premiss. Indeed the argument lends itself to the converse of Davidson's interpretation. For it establishes that a plausible way of identifying the semantical theory of truth as a theory of meaning entails the extensionality of the role of '*p*' in sentences of the form '*s* means that *p*'. And this looks more like the conclusion of a *reductio ad absurdum* than a premiss.

APPENDIX 2

Truth value semantics for standard quantification, by C. J. Jardine

First, we define a set Θ of maps from the set of well-formed formulae to $\{0,1\}$. Let $L+$ be the set of well-formed formulae, and L the set of sentences. If a in $L+$ is a formula whose first element is an existential quantifier, the scope of which is the whole of the rest of the formula, then we denote by a/V the set of all formulae derivable from a by first making a substitution of variables for the bound variables (preserving distinctions between variables), and then deleting the initial quantifier. We define Θ as the set of maps θ from L to $\{0,1\}$ such that

(1) $\theta(\sim a) = 0$ iff $\theta(a) = 1$;
(2) $\theta(a \rightarrow b) = 0$ iff $\theta(a) = 1$ and $\theta(b) = 0$;
(3) if a is a formula for which a/V is defined, then
$\theta(a) = 0$ iff $\theta(x) = 0$ for all $x \in a/V$.

Let $\theta|_L$ be the restriction of the map θ to the set L. We may now define the required set of maps Φ from L to $\{0,1\}$ by:

$$\Phi = \{\theta|_L : \theta \in \Theta\}.$$

There are two ways of proving the set Φ to be complete. Either we may prove directly that the map con_Φ, defined by:

$$con_\Phi(A) = \cap \{\phi^{-1}[1] : \phi \in \Phi \text{ and } A \subset \phi^{-1}[1]\},$$

is the same as the proof-theoretic consequence operation. This proof uses topological methods to be found in Rasiowa and Sikorski (1963), and dispenses with model theoretic constructions altogether. Or we may prove as follows that Φ is equal to the semantically defined set Φ_M and use the standard semantic completeness theorem.

We have to show that for each $M \in \mathbf{M}$, $\phi_M \in \Phi$; and that for each $\phi \in \Phi$ there is an $M \in \mathbf{M}$ such that $\phi = \phi_M$.

Suppose $M \in \mathbf{M}$. Then by the Löwenheim–Skolem theorem there is an $M' \in \mathbf{M}$ with countable domain such that $\phi_{M'} = \phi_M$. Since M' has countable domain there will be assignments of elements of the domain to variables in L which assign each element to a variable. Consider such an assignment and define a map θ from L^+ to $\{0,1\}$ by

$\theta(a) = 1$ iff a is satisfied by the assignment in M'.

It is clear that θ obeys the conditions for membership of Θ. Since any sentence is satisfied by all assignments or by none, $\theta|_L = \phi_{M'}$. Hence $\phi_M \in \Phi$.

Suppose $\phi \in \Phi$. Then there is a $\theta \in \Theta$ such that $\phi = \theta|_L$. Consider the following model M for L. The domain of M is the set of variables of L. If P is an n-place predicate of L, the extension of P is the set of those n-tuples $\langle \alpha_1, \ldots, \alpha_n \rangle$ of variables such that $\theta(P(\alpha_1, \ldots, \alpha_n)) = 1$. Now consider the assignment of variables to elements of the domain of L which assigns each variable to itself. The recursive definition of satisfaction together with the conditions on membership of Θ give us that $\theta(a) = 1$ iff a is satisfied by this assignment, and hence that $\phi = \phi_M$. $\square$

Extension of the definition of Θ from the pure first order predicate calculus to the first order predicate calculus with individual constants and functions is easy but notationally complex.

APPENDIX 3

Quantification and ontology

We consider the case where a fragment of NL is formalized by a formal language with an existence predicate $\mathbf{E}$. The natural course in giving model theoretic truth conditions for sentences of the form '$\mathbf{E}(t)$' is to use

(1) $\mathbf{E}(t) \equiv (\exists x)(x = t)$

as a definition, x ranging over the domain of a model. In a truth value semantics, however, the natural course is to use

(2) $(\exists x)(A(x)) \equiv (\exists x)(\mathbf{E}(x) \text{ and } A(x))$

as a definition in giving truth conditions for sentences of the form '$(\exists x)(A(x))$', and to regard sentences of the form '$\mathbf{E}(t)$' as atomic. So in the model theoretic approach existence is defined in terms of existential quantification, and in the truth value semantic approach existential quantification is defined in terms of existence.

Let us now take as our criterion of ontological commitment the validity of sentences of the form '$\mathbf{E}(t)$,' and consider the four approaches to the theory of consequence outlined in section 2. If we adopt the standard reading of quantification and MTS the criterion translates into 'to be is to be the value of a bound variable' and can be justified by pointing out that we have identified NL extension with extension in a model and that x in (1) ranges over the domain of a model. If we adopt the standard reading and TVS the criterion can be justified only by pointing out that it yields the same results as would be got using MTS with the standard reading. If we adopt the substitutional reading of quantification and TVS the criterion can be justified only if it can be proved that for the particular formal language the two readings of quantification yield the same valid formulae. Finally, if we adopt the substitutional reading and MTS the criterion cannot be justified because we are committed to a denial of the existence of unnamed objects. So of these four approaches to the theory of consequence only the standard reading of quantification and its model theory yields an internally justified criterion of ontological commitment.

Of course, as several authors have recently pointed out, the application of the ontological commitment criterion to particular fragments of NL is a fishy business because of the dependence of the answers obtained on the rules used to translate NL assertions into a formal language to which the criterion can be applied.

REFERENCES

(A few of the items listed are works not specifically cited in the text from which I derived general guidance.)

Beth, E. W. (1959). *The Foundations of Mathematics*. Amsterdam: North Holland.

Carnap, R. (1947). *Meaning and Necessity*. Chicago: University of Chicago Press. (Enlarged edn., Chicago, 1956.)

Church, A. (1951). 'A formulation of the logic of sense and denotation'. In P. Henle, H. M. Kallen, and S. K. Langer, eds., *Structure, Method and Meaning*, pp. 3–24. New York: Liberal Arts Press.

Curry, H. B. (1963). *Foundations of Mathematical Logic*. New York: McGraw-Hill.

Davidson, D. (1967). 'Truth and meaning', *Synthese*, **17**, 304–23.

Dummett, M. E. (1958–9). 'Truth', *Proceedings of the Aristotelian Society*, **59**, 141–62.

Fraassen, B. C. van (1969). 'Presuppositions, supervaluations and free logic'. In Lambert, K., ed., *The Logical Way of Doing Things*, pp. 67–91. New Haven: Yale University Press.

Hesse, M. B. (1970). 'Is there an independent observation language?' In R. G. Colodny, ed., *The Nature and Function of Scientific Theories*. Pittsburgh: University of Pittsburgh Press.

Hintikka, J. (1955). 'Form and content in quantification theory', *Acta Philosophica Fennica*, **8**, 7–55.

—— (1969). *Models for Modalities*. Dordrecht: Reidel.

Hunter, G. (1971). *Metalogic: an Introduction to the Metatheory of Standard First-order Logic*. London: Macmillan.

Kaplan, D. (1964). 'Foundations of Intensional Logic'. Doctoral Dissertation, University of California, Los Angeles.

Kripke, S. A. (1963a). 'Semantical analysis of modal logic. I. Normal propositional calculi', *Zeitschrifte für mathematische Logik*, **9**, 67–96.

—— (1963b). 'Semantical considerations on modal logic', *Acta Philosophica Fennica*, **16**, 83–94.

Leblanc, H. (1968). 'A simplified account of validity and implication for quantificational logic', *The Journal of Symbolic Logic*, **33**, 231–5.

Leblanc, H. and Meyer, R. K. (1970). 'A truth-value semantics for the theory of types'. In K. Lambert, ed., *Philosophical Problems in Logic*, pp. 77–101. Dordrecht: Reidel.

Lewis, D. (1970). 'General semantics', *Synthese*, **22**, 18–67.

Montague, R. (1970). 'Pragmatics and intensional logic', *Synthese*, **22**, 68–94.

Mostowski, A. (1952). 'On a generalization of quantification', *Fundamenta Mathematicae*, **44**, 12–36.

Quine, W. V. O. (1960). *Word and Object*. Cambridge, Mass.: M.I.T. Press.

—— (1969). *Ontological Relativity and other Essays*, pp. 26–68. New York: Columbia University Press.

Rasiowa, H. and Sikorski, R. R. (1963). *The Mathematics of Metamathematics*. Warsaw: Polska Akad. Nauk.

Scott, D. (1970). 'Advice on modal logic'. In K. Lambert, ed., *Philosophical Problems in Logic*, pp. 143–73.

Searle, J. (1969). *Speech Acts: an Essay in the Philosophy of Language*. Cambridge: Cambridge University Press.

Tarski, A. (1936). 'Der Wahrheitsbegriff in den formalisierten Sprachen', *Studia Philosophica*, **1**, 261–405. Translation (by J. H. Woodger) in *Logic, Semantics, Metamathematics*, pp. 152–278. Oxford (1956).

Tarski, A. and Vaught, R. L. (1957). 'Arithmetic extensions of relational systems', *Compositio Mathematica*, **13**, 81–102.

Winograd, T. (1972). *Understanding Natural Language*. Edinburgh: Edinburgh University Press. And concurrently in *Cognitive Psychology*, **3**.

Model theory and linguistics

TIMOTHY C. POTTS

Model theory is a mathematical technique for investigating certain properties of formal systems: properties such as consistency, completeness, the finite model property and having a decision procedure. Instead of looking for proofs based directly upon the formal system being studied, the method is to relate it to other formal systems whose properties are already known, by defining a translation from the former to the latter. Where this can be carried through, the systems thus related to the one under investigation are termed 'models' of it and known properties of the models can then be extrapolated to the new system. If a natural language or a fragment of a natural language constitutes a formal system, then the technique can be applied to it also, for the same purposes. There is now a prevalent impression among linguists, however, that model theory can provide a theory of *meaning* for natural language. The thesis of this paper is that any such hope will certainly be disappointed and that the mistake has arisen from confusion among mathematicians about the correct description of their own procedure.

This confusion is illustrated by the following descriptions of model theory from a recent book on mathematical logic: 'Model theory is the study of the relations between languages and the world, or more precisely between formal languages and the interpretations of formal languages' (Crossley et al. (1972:20)). The idea which links these two descriptions is that interpretations of formal languages are not, as I have claimed, other formal languages, but *structures*, 'the world' being the structure which interprets a natural language. Thus, by applying model-theoretic techniques to natural languages, we shall elucidate their relationship to the world and thereby provide an account of the meanings of their expressions. For no theory of meaning will be adequate if it explains the use of language solely by reference to language itself; at some stage, it must break out of the confines of language and show how the latter 'hooks onto the world'. The suggestion that model theory has this power has been reinforced by an ill-chosen piece of terminology, according to which a model is said to provide a 'semantics' for a formal system; it is then natural to suppose that this must also be a theory of meaning.

Since model theory is concerned with formal systems, natural languages will not come within its scope unless they, too, can be regarded as formal systems. Consequently, this must be established first: can we agree with Montague when he said 'I reject the contention that an important theoretical difference exists between formal and natural languages' (1970:189)? Are they even two species of the same genus, as the term 'formal language' suggests?

In describing a language as natural, we mean that it has grown up in the course of the everyday life of a people. The implied contrast is with a *technical* language, devised by a minority for a special purpose. Thus the notation of mathematics might be described as a technical language, though in this case the distinction is not a sharp one; to the extent that mathematics is applied in everyday life, its notation is annexed by natural language. It might, perhaps, be better to speak of general-purpose and special-purpose rather than of natural and technical languages. This has the merit of underlining the necessity for taking the purposes of a language into account if we are to understand it.

'Formal' does not belong to this system of classification, as may be seen from the procedure by which a formal language is specified. The first step is to list the signs which it contains, grouping them into their various kinds or categories; the second is to define a formula of the language by saying how signs of the various categories may be combined. We can always try to carry out this procedure with any existing language, whether general- or special-purpose. It could also be used to create a new language, but then the signs would not qualify as a language until they had been given, in addition, a use; an existing language, by contrast, already has an established use. To claim that an existing language is a formal language is, therefore, ambiguous: we must distinguish between a stronger claim, to the effect that it *has* already been specified formally, and a weaker claim, to the effect that it *can* be specified formally.

The language of arithmetic is a formal language in the strong sense. Implicitly, the procedure has also been applied to natural languages since the dawn of grammar, which has traditionally distinguished parts of speech and described how expressions belonging to the various parts of speech may be combined into sentences, with the aim of excluding nonsensical expressions. But whatever the devotees of a particular school of grammar may urge, there is no general agreement among linguists that the task has yet been successfully accomplished. The criterion of success would be an effective procedure for deciding, of any expression, whether or not it is nonsense, i.e. our definition of a formula would capture all and only those expressions which have a sense in the language concerned. Montague's opinion must therefore be regarded as a profession of faith that such a definition can be given. Perhaps this faith is essential for a grammarian.

His view is, nevertheless, badly expressed, for there remains an exceedingly important theoretical difference between *many* formal languages (in the strong sense) and *any* natural language. Many formal languages, being special-purpose, lack the degree of multiplicity which a general-purpose language demands. This is not just a matter of vocabulary: it can also affect the range of categories and the possibilities of combination of expressions belonging to those categories. In particular, it is essential to a natural language that we should be able to use it not only to say what is the case, but also to ask questions, give commands, express wishes, intentions and emotions, and so on. Neither of the two most celebrated formal languages, that of arithmetic and predicate logic, has the requisite multiplicity for all of these employments. The question which we have to ask with regard to a given formal language is whether it *could* be used as a general-purpose language, even though, as a matter of fact, it is not so used; if the answer is 'No', then there is a major theoretical difference between it and any natural language.

The purpose of giving a formal specification of a natural language, as it emerges from traditional grammar, is to distinguish sense from nonsense. Model theory, however, presupposes that formal languages are specified with a view to constructing formal *systems*, in which formulae may be *derived* from other formulae. One way of achieving this is to lay down rules allowing us to pass from one or more types of formula to another type of formula. The alternative method, which is that employed in model theory, is to divide the signs of the language into two groups (which may cut across the categories), specifying a range of *values* which may be assigned to signs of the first group. For signs of the second group, procedures are laid down which allow us to compute the value of any formula given the values assigned to any signs of the first group which it may contain. Some, but not all values are then *designated* and a formula α is said to be *derivable* from a set of formulas Γ just in case α has a designated value whenever every member of Γ has a designated value. The proposition that α is derivable from Γ will then be a *truth* of the formal system, truth in this case being relative to the system in question.

It is in no way essential to a formal language that its formulae be accounted true or false; on the other hand, if an existing language is to be taken into the service of a formal system, there must be some analogue of derivability. To cite a special-purpose language, the rules of chess might be cast into a formal system in which derivability corresponded to a permissible move in the game. Both with special- and with general-purpose languages, however, derivability has traditionally been identified with logical consequence, the historical motivation for constructing formal systems having been to classify valid argument-patterns and to provide a foundation for mathematics. Since a valid argument cannot lead from true premises to a false conclusion, by making the values of formulae truth values and the designated value 'true', derivability is made to coincide with logical consequence. The price to be paid for this requirement, however, is that formulae are equivalent to propositions and so our formal language, instead of drawing the borderline between sense and nonsense, marks off expressions having a truth value from all others, whether the latter make sense or not.

This restriction might be defended on methodological grounds as a necessary preliminary. It does, indeed, confine us to a fragment of natural language by singling out deductive argument as its central use, but it could plausibly be maintained that a successful account of this aspect of language would constitute a bridgehead from which extensions could be constructed to cover other uses. Our formal language would have to be extended to allow for new types of formula whose values were not truth values; an example of what might be needed can be found in Kenny (1966). Furthermore, if model theory can tell us the circumstances in which a proposition is true, then it will have justified its title to be regarded as genuine semantics; for 'to understand a proposition means to know what is the case, if it is true' (Wittgenstein (1922:4.024)). It is here that the model-theoretician's appeal to structures becomes relevant.

We need to distinguish first between *being* a structure and *having* a structure. Something *is* a structure if it has distinguishable parts or *elements* which are inter-*related* in a determinate way. At the same time, two different things, each of which is a structure, can in certain circumstances be said to have the *same* structure, e.g. two houses built to the same design. It is nearly always possible for us to distinguish the elements of a given structure in more than one way; the inter-relationships of the elements will then alter, too. Thus the structures of sentences, as the disputes of grammarians and logicians illustrate, can be very variously described.

A model, in the everyday sense, is also a structure, e.g. the cardboard or balsa wood structure which an architect makes to sell a design for a building to a client who cannot read architectural drawings. But let us begin with the clearest case of all, a model of an actually existing building: the model will then be a model of the building in virtue of having a structure which is also a structure which the building has. This, in turn, requires that for each element in the model we are able to distinguish a corresponding element in the building such that the spatial relationships between the elements distinguished in the model are proportionate to those between the corresponding elements distinguished in the building.

In ordinary language, the term 'model' is reserved to three-dimensional structures. If this restriction were waived, we could also call the architect's drawings a model of the building, for it would again be possible to correlate elements in the drawings with elements in the building so as to yield corresponding inter-relationships. Due allowance would have to be made, of course, for the loss of one dimension in the drawings, a deficiency which is compensated by certain conventions. Both the drawings and the cardboard model would then qualify as models of the building, each of them having a structure which is also a structure of the building. But now suppose that we have only the drawings and the cardboard model: the building has not yet been constructed. How can we say that they are models of a building, when there is no building of which they are models? and how can we say that they are models of the *same* building? For we certainly do talk of models in these circumstances and, indeed, models (including drawings) are of *most* use to us in making new structures.

These considerations show that the expression *is a model of* is, in logician's parlance, 'intensional'. Accordingly, we cannot say that what makes something which is a structure a model is that there is something else which is also a structure and that both have a structure in common. Anything which *is* a structure is capable of being a model: it will become a model if it is used by someone with a certain intention, as a proxy for something different in kind yet having the same structure. The justification for saying that the architect's drawings and his cardboard structure are models of a building is, then, that he uses them to show his client and the contractor what the building is to be like; and we can say that both are models of the same building because a *direct* correlation is possible between their elements and between the inter-relationships of their elements.

We have extended the everyday notion of model to include two-dimensional drawings. Can we take this a step further and allow a verbal description to count as a model (a 'word-picture')? Theoretically, it would be possible for our architect to write out a description of his building, although, if the contractor had to work from it alone, the description would have to be inordinately lengthy. He could first specify the elements of the building (this is already, to some extent, what the quantity surveyor does) and then state their inter-relationships. We should notice, however, that the conventions of linguistic description differ very fundamentally from those of architectural draughtsmanship. In the latter, spatial relationships are still represented spatially and the *scale* of the drawing is one of its most vital features. In the linguistic description, by contrast, we should not find, e.g. that if one element was twice as far from a second element as a third, the name of the first was written twice as far from the name of the second as the name of the third. Instead, the different spatial relationships between the elements would be represented by the use of different linguistic expressions and be understood via their customary meanings.

The linguistic description which I have envisaged will employ a certain vocabulary. To simplify matters, suppose that this vocabulary consists of only two types of expression: names of elements and expressions for the relationships between elements. We could then specify this as a formal language containing two types of sign, element-names and relational expressions, a list of each being appended. A formula would be defined as a relational expression flanked by two element-names. The description of the building would then consist of the set of all true formulae of this language. Now suppose that the building is designed on some kind of modular pattern, so that the description can be simplified by describing each type of module once only and adding how many modules there are and how they are inter-related. It might then be possible to use our formal language in order to set up a formal system in which, by the application of suitably framed rules, the whole description could be derived from a fragment of it. We then treat the formulae in the fragment as axioms, i.e. as truths of the system by stipulation, so that other formulae derivable from the axioms will be truths of the system too.

It seems that we could now claim that our formal system is also a model of the building, for the axioms and theorems of the system together give a complete description of it. In the mathematician's terminology, the building is an 'interpretation' of the formal system and, by a curious inversion of everyday language, he also calls the building a 'model' of the formal system. From this point onwards, I shall use 'model' in the mathematical sense. If a putative model of a given formal system is a perceptible structure, we can determine whether the axioms of the system are true by observation of the structure. Whether the rules of derivation are sound and complete can also be checked in the same way: If every theorem says something true of the structure, then the rules are sound; if there is no formula of the system which says something true of the structure and yet is neither an axiom nor a theorem, then the rules are complete. By reference to the structure, we can thus determine whether any formula of our formal language is true or false; but it should be noted that while we could distinguish between tautological (or contradictory) and contingent statements about the structure in ordinary language, there would be no such distinction in the formal system, even supposing both types of proposition to be representable in its formulae.

In model theory, the structures which are correlated with formal systems are abstract structures and thus inaccessible to perception. This is supposed to make no essential difference, but, if we look closely at the correlation procedure, we discover that the analogy of a building and its linguistic description gives a totally misleading picture of what is really being done. I have developed that analogy, nevertheless, precisely because I believe that mathematicians and logicians are confused upon this point. Only the essentials of the correlation procedure will be described here; in particular, I shall not consider intensional models of the kind developed by Montague, upon which I have written elsewhere (Potts (1975)).

Since abstract structures are not perceptible, they must be introduced by description in some language; this is called the metalanguage, while the signs of the formal language with which the structure is to be correlated constitute the object-language. The structure is conceived as consisting, in the first instance, of a set of elements, which are named in the metalanguage and with each of which an element-name of the object-language is then correlated. The elements of the structure are also *ordered*, for otherwise it would be just a heap of elements. Following standard mathematical practice, the relations between the elements are then conceived as ordered subsets of the elements and the relational expressions in the object-language are treated as names of these sets. It then remains to give a truth-definition for formulae of the object-language, i.e. to specify how their truth values can be read off or computed by reference to the model structure.

Suppose, then, that aRb is a formula of the object-language, that the element-names a and b have been correlated respectively with the elements x and y in the structure and the relational expression R with the set of ordered pairs Z in the structure; aRb will then be true just in case $\langle x,y \rangle \in Z$. But we must now be able to determine whether the latter is true and, for this purpose, the metalanguage must be used. The latter could itself be a special-purpose language, e.g. the language of arithmetic. For instance, we might specify that

$$\langle x,y \rangle \in Z \text{ iff } x = y^2$$

But it may be a general-purpose language, e.g.

$\langle x,y \rangle \in Z$ iff x is to the right of y

The point is that, somehow, the meaning of '$\langle x,y \rangle \in Z$' must be explained; ostension is ruled out *ex hypothesi* because the structure is abstract, so it is essential to appeal instead to some language, whether technical or natural, which has an established use. This applies to model-theoretic truth definitions in general, as anyone can check for himself by turning up a few examples in the literature.

It should now be obvious that the abstract structure is a mere beetle in the box. The whole procedure is just a roundabout way of correlating expressions of the object-language with expressions of the metalanguage. We are not really studying the relations between a formal language and an abstract structure, but between two languages. Model theory is, rather, an exercise in *translation*. We have given meanings to the formulae of our object-language by specifying how they are to be translated into propositions of an established language with which it is assumed that we are already familiar; to this extent it is true that model theory is concerned with meaning. To go back to the architect, the correct analogy is with a translation procedure from, say, drawings to a cardboard model, which ensures that a cardboard model constructed from the drawings has a structure in common with the drawings. It is not necessary for the building to have been constructed for the architect to make a cardboard model from the drawings, for he already knows (implicitly) the procedure for translating the drawings directly into a cardboard model.

Thus it is just a confusion to suppose that model theory can say anything about the relation of language to the world; it can, at best, only elucidate one language by reference to another. This is all that is needed for its proper, mathematical application, for if the metalanguage is itself a formal language whose properties have already been studied, then the possibility of specifying a translation from the object to the metalanguage allows us to conclude that the object-language has corresponding properties. Talking of a structure in this connection is then quite harmless, though redundant. Similarly, saying that the relational expressions of a formal system denote ordered pairs of elements in the structure is of no consequence whatever, because the truth-definition tells us how to translate expressions of the form '$\langle x,y \rangle \in Z$' into the metalanguage. These expressions are mere intermediaries and anything would do, provided that the final correlation between object and metalanguage were suitably effected; so the question whether relational expressions have a meaning by denoting sets of ordered pairs need not concern us.

In applying model theory in linguistics, neither the object-language nor the supposed structures, but rather the metalanguage is of primary concern. Suppose, for the sake of argument, that a fragment of a natural language has been formally specified and is taken as our object-language. We then have two choices of metalanguage: either another formal language, used in known formal systems, or another (perhaps the same) language which is not, as yet, embodied in any formal system. The latter could be either special- or general-purpose.

If we take the first option, the result of carrying through a truth-definition will be to correlate our fragment of natural language with a formal system or systems whose properties are already known; we are then in a position to prove that our object-language, under this translation, has corresponding properties. We cannot, however, claim to have explained the meanings of the expressions of the object-language, for the latter already has an established use; we have not elucidated *that* use, but shown instead that it could be given a different use, namely the established use of the metalanguage, in virtue of which certain propositions are true in the latter and others false. This option, therefore, offers no contribution to semantics.

There is an additional problem if the chosen metalanguage is that of predicate logic. Predicate logic was originally devised in order to represent the logical structures of natural language propositions. For this purpose, it utilizes two quite different types of sign. First, its formulae contain schematic signs, e.g. predicate-letters, which represent any linguistic expression of a specified category; their intended meanings, accordingly, can only be explained by appeal to a general-purpose language which already has an established use. Second, its formulae also contain non-schematic signs, whose meanings are given by a truth-definition also in a general-purpose language and, in practice, the definition will utilize at least some of the expressions which are represented by the non-schematic signs.

This option will consequently reduce to the second, for by introducing predicate logic we are tacitly appealing to the metalanguage which stands behind it, namely natural language. Taking the second option, then, use of a special-purpose language as metalanguage will again provide no contribution to semantics, for it will only show that the original fragment of natural language *could* be used for that purpose, without explaining how it is actually used. If, on the other hand, the metalanguage is a different general-purpose language from the object-language, the truth-definition becomes a formal procedure for translating from one natural language into another. If both languages are the same, the whole of the object-language being contained in that part of the metalanguage being used for the truth-definition, the result will be a vicious circularity. Supposing, however, that the fragment of natural language chosen as object-language is not used at all in the truth-definition, the result will be a componential analysis of the expressions and is thus genuine semantics, but we do not need the elaborate apparatus of model theory in order to conduct componential analyses.

REFERENCES

Crossley, J. N., Ash, C. J., Brickhill, C. J., Stillwell, J. C. and Williams, N. H. (1972). *What is Mathematical Logic?* London: Oxford University Press.

Davidson, D. (1965). 'Theories of meaning and learnable languages'. In Bar-Hillel, ed., *Logic, Methodology and Philosophy of Science*, pp. 384–94. Amsterdam: North-Holland.

Kenny, A. (1966). 'Practical inference', *Analysis*, **26**, 65–75.

Montague, R. (1970). 'English as a formal language'. In *Linguaggi nella Società e nella Tecnica*, pp. 189–223. Milan: Edizione di Comunità.

Potts, T. C. (1975). 'Montague's semiotic: a syllabus of errors'. In M. Bell, *York Papers in Logic and Semantics*. Dordrecht: Reidel.

Wittgenstein, L. (1922). *Tractatus Logico-Philosophicus*. London: Routledge and Kegan Paul.

V PRAGMATICS AND SENTENCES IN CONTEXT

Pragmatics in natural logic[1]

GEORGE LAKOFF

I would like to discuss two aspects of pragmatics that in recent years have been treated very differently: indexicals and conversational implicatures. Montague and Scott proposed to handle indexicals by adding to points of reference (sometimes called 'indices') extra coordinates for speaker, hearer, time and place of utterance. This proposal places indexicals among those phenomena to be dealt with by formal logic, and such systems have in recent years been articulated by Lewis and Kamp, among others. Implicatures on the other hand, were taken by Grice to be by nature informal inferences of a fundamentally different kind than logical inferences, and hence not to be dealt with by the apparatus of formal logic. In other papers I have dropped hints to the effect that indexicals and implicatures should be treated somewhat differently than they are in the Montague–Scott and Grice proposals. I would like to elaborate a bit on those hints.

The basic suggestion is this:

(I) If the goals of what I have called natural logic are adopted, then it should in time be possible to handle indexicals without any extra coordinates for speaker, hearer, and time and place of utterance, and it should also be possible to handle implicatures without any kinds of extralogical inference.

The basic ingredients of the suggestion are as follows:

(A) The so-called performative analysis for imperatives, questions, statements, promises, etc.
(B) The limitation of points of reference to assignment coordinates for variables and atomic predicates.
(C) The commitment of natural logic to the formal semantic characterization of *all* natural language concepts, including those having

[1] Copyright © by George Lakoff, 1973. All rights reserved by the author. This work was partially supported by grants GS 35119 and GS 38476 from the National Science Foundation to the University of California. An earlier version of this paper was presented at the University of Texas Conference on Performatives, Implicature, and Presuppositions.

to do with social interaction, such as sincerity, politeness, formality, cooperation, etc.

(D) Global, transderivational, fuzzy correspondence grammars.

Let us start with what has been called the *performative analysis* – which is not a single proposal, but a family of various partial proposals made by grammarians like Sanctius, Lancelot, and Whitney, and more recently by Postal, Robin Lakoff, Ross, Sadock, J. McCawley, and myself, among others. The positions held by these people vary a great deal, and it is not my purpose to try to survey them here. What they have in common is that they would analyse imperative sentences like *Leave* as having logical structures containing a performative imperative predicate with arguments referring to speaker and hearer, essentially the same logical structure as that needed for the (surface) sentence *I order you to leave*, which contains a surface performative predicate (*order*) and surface arguments referring to speaker and hearer (*I* and *you*). In support of such an analysis, a large amount of syntactic evidence has been offered; it is my opinion that there is enough correct evidence of this sort to strongly support such a proposal for imperatives. Ross has, in addition, observed that syntactic evidence of the same sort in nearly the same amount is available to support a parallel performative analysis for declaratives. Thus, a declarative sentence like *There exist unicorns*, which contains a surface performative declarative predicate (*state*) and surface arguments referring to speaker and hearer (*I* and *you*). Whereas most of the evidence to date for these proposals has been syntactic in nature, I would like to provide some evidence in favour of them of a semantic-pragmatic nature.

Let us first consider two proposals for providing formal semantics for performative sentences, one made by David Lewis (1972) and one made by myself (1972a). Lewis adopts the Montague–Scott proposal for the use of *indices* (Montague's term) or *points of reference* (Scott's term) to account for indexicals in the framework of general intentional logic as outlined by Montague.

We may take indices as *n*-tuples (finite sequences) of the various items other than meaning that may enter into determining extensions. We call these various items *coordinates* of the index, and we shall assume that the coordinates are given some arbitrary fixed order.

First, we must have a *possible-world coordinate*. Contingent sentences depend for their truth value on facts about the world, and so are true at some possible worlds and false at others. A possible world corresponds to a possible totality of facts, determinate in all respects. Common nouns also have different extensions at different possible worlds; and so do some names, at least if we adopt the position (defended in Lewis, 1968a) that things are related to their counterparts in other worlds by ties of strong similarity rather than identity.

Second, we must have several *contextual coordinates* corresponding to familiar sorts of dependence on features of context. (The world coordinate itself might be regarded as a feature of context, since different possible utterances of a sentence are located in different possible worlds.) We must have a *time coordinate*, in view of tensed sentences and such sentences as 'Today is Tuesday'; a *place coordinate*, in view of such sentences as 'Here there are tigers'; a *speaker coordinate* in view of such sentences as 'I am Porky'; an *audience coordinate* in view of such sentences as 'You are Porky'; an *indicated-objects coordinate* in view of such sentences as 'That pig is Porky' or 'Those men are Communists'; and a *previous discourse coordinate* in view of such sentences as 'The afore-mentioned pig is Porky'.

Third, it is convenient to have an *assignment coordinate*: an infinite sequence of things, regarded as giving the values of any variables that may occur free in such expressions as 'x is tall' or 'son of y'. Each variable employed in the language will accordingly be a name having as its intension, for some number n, the *nth variable intension*: that function whose value, at any index i, is that thing which is the nth term of the assignment coordinate of i. That thing is the extension, or value, of the variable at i. (Note that because there is more than one possible thing, the variable intensions are distinct: nothing is both the n_1th and the n_2th variable intension for two different numbers n_1 and n_2.) The extensions of 'x is tall' of 'son of y' depend on the assignment and world coordinates of indices just as the extensions of 'I am tall' and 'son of mine' depend on the speaker and world coordinates. Yet the assignment coordinate cannot naturally be included among features of context. One might claim that variables do not appear in sentences of natural languages; but even if this is so, it may be useful to employ variables in a categorial base. In any case, I seek sufficient generality to accommodate languages that do employ variables.

. . .Thus an *index* is tentatively any octuple of which the first coordinate is a possible world, the second coordinate is a moment of time, the third coordinate is a place, the fourth coordinate is a person (or other creature capable of being a speaker), the fifth coordinate is a set of persons (or other creatures capable of being an audience), the sixth coordinate is a set (possibly empty) of concrete things capable of being pointed at, the seventh coordinate is a segment of discourse, and the eighth coordinate is an infinite sequence of things (Lewis (1972:175–6)).

Later, Lewis gives his account of the semantics of nondeclarative sentences, after rejecting a proposal by Stenius:

I prefer an alternative method of treating non-declaratives that requires no revision whatever in my system of categories, intensions, and meanings. Let us once again regard S as the category *sentence*, without discrimination of mood. But let us pay special attention to those sentential meanings that are represented by base structures of roughly the following form.

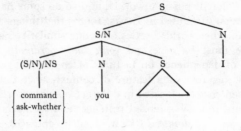

Such meanings can be represented by *performative sentences* such as these.

> I command you to be late.
> I ask you whether you are late.

(See Austin, 1962, for the standard account of performatives; but, as will be seen, I reject part of this account.) Such meanings might also be represented, after a more elaborate transformational derivation, by non-declaratives.

> Be late !
> Are you late?

I propose that these non-declaratives ought to be treated as paraphrases of the corresponding performatives, having the same base structure, meaning, intension, and truth-value at an index or on an occasion. And I propose that there is no difference in kind between the meanings of these performatives and non-declaratives and the meanings of the ordinary declarative sentences considered previously.

Lewis, however, refrains from going all the way with the performative analysis; in particular, he refuses to embrace a similar analysis for declaratives.

> If someone says 'I declare that the Earth is flat' (sincerely, not play-acting, etc.) I claim that he has spoken truly: he does indeed so declare. I claim this not only for the sake of my theory but as a point of common sense. Yet one might be tempted to say that he has spoken falsely, because the sentence embedded in his performative – the content of his declaration, the belief he avows – is false. Hence I do not propose to take ordinary declaratives as paraphrased performatives (as proposed in Ross, 1970) because that would get their truth conditions wrong (Lewis (1972:210)).

The analysis Lewis adopts for non-declarative performatives resembles, in its essential parts, the proposal I made (1972a,b) for all performatives, including declaratives:

> ...it is claimed that the logical forms of imperatives, questions, and statements should be represented as in (A).

(A)

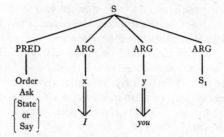

In (A), S_1 represents the propositional content of the command, question, or statement. Note that in statements it is the propositional content, not the entire sentence, that will be true or false. For example, if I say to you 'I state that I am innocent', and you reply 'That's false', you are denying that I am innocent, not that I made the statement. That is, in sentences where there is an overt performative verb of saying or stating or asserting, the propositional content, which is true or false, is not given by the sentence as a whole, but rather by the object of that performative verb. In 'I state that I am innocent', the direct object contains the embedded sentence 'I am innocent', which is the propositional content. Thus, even in statements, it should not be surprising that the illocutionary force of the statement is to be represented in logical form by the presence of a performative verb.

In the analysis sketched in (A), the subject and indirect object of the performative verbs are represented in logical form by the indexical expressions x and y. Rules of grammar will mark the subject of the performative verb as being first person and the indirect object as being second person. Thus, logical forms need not contain any indication of first person or second person, as distinct from third person. If there are other instances of the indexical expressions x and y in S_1, they will be marked as being first and second person respectively by the grammatical rule of person-agreement, which makes a NP agree in person with its antecedent. Thus all occurrences of first or second person pronouns will be either the subject or indirect object of a performative verb or will arise through the rule of person-agreement. The analysis given in (A) and the corresponding account of first and second person pronouns makes certain predictions. Since the structure given in (A) is exactly the same structure that one finds in the case of non-performative verbs of ordering, asking, and saying, it is predicted that rules of grammar involving ordinary verbs of these classes, which occur overtly in English sentences, may generalize to the cases of performative verbs, even when those verbs are not overtly present in the surface form of the sentence, as in simple orders, questions, and statements (G. Lakoff (1972a: 560–1)).

The analysis of (A) not only permits the statement of grammatical generalizations, but it also permits one to simplify formal semantics. Consider, for example, the notion of an 'index' as given by Scott (1969). Scott assumed that indices would include among their coordinates specifications of the speaker, addressee, place, and time of the utterance, so that truth conditions could be stated for sentences such as 'Bring what *you now* have to *me* over *here*'. Under an analysis such as (A), the speaker and addressee coordinates could be eliminated from Scott's indices. Moreover, if (A) were expanded, as it should be, to include indications of the place and time of the utterance, then the place and time coordinates could be eliminated from Scott's indices.[9] Truth conditions for such sentences could then be reduced to truth conditions for sentences with ordinary adverbs of place and time. Moreover, truth conditions for sentences such as 'I am innocent' and 'I state that I am innocent' could be generalized in terms of the notion 'propositional content', namely, S_1 in (A). Thus, (A) can be motivated from a logical as well as a grammatical point of view (G. Lakoff (1972a:569)).

I saw Lewis' paper after writing the above, but before receiving the proofs, and added footnote 9 at the last minute:

[9] This becomes clearer if one considers Lewis' treatment in *General Semantics* rather than Scott's. Lewis distinguishes between 'contextual coordinates' and an 'assignment coordinate'. The contextual coordinates are for such things as speaker, audience, time of utterance, and place of utterance. The assignment coordinate gives 'the values of any variables that may occur free in such expressions as "x is tall" or "son of y"'.

The assignment coordinate will have to assign a value corresponding to the the speaker for person variables, since the speaker would presumably be in the worlds in question. The same for the audience. If times are assigned to time variables by the assignment coordinate, presumably the time of the utterance will be included. And if places are assigned to place variables, one would assume that the place of the utterance would be given by the assignment coordinate. Given this, and the analysis given in (A), the contextual coordinates become superfluous, since the job that they would do in Lewis' system would be done automatically by the assignment coordinate together with the analysis in (A). Since (A) involves no new types of structure – the same predicates occur in nonperformative uses and have to be given anyway – we have a considerable gain. What we have done is to largely, if not entirely eliminate pragmatics, reducing it to garden variety semantics (G. Lakoff (1972a:655)).

The principal place where Lewis and I differ is on the analysis of declaratives. My feeling is that the reason he gives for rejecting the performative analysis for declaratives is a bad one. According to Lewis, if a speaker uttered (1)

(1) I state that the earth is flat

and someone replied

(2) a. That's true
    or
   b. That statement is true

then, Lewis claims, the speaker of (2a) or (2b) would not be committing himself to the earth's being flat but only the first speaker's having said so. Lewis is simply wrong – natural language does not work that way. The speaker of (2a) or (2b) *is* committing himself to the earth's being flat.

Lewis' proposal is reminiscent of the classic story (probably fabricated) of the Pittsburgh judge who was caught taking bribes. When called before a grand jury, the judge took the stand under oath and said 'I swear that I have never taken a bribe'. The district attorney then brought the judge to trial for perjury, and produced witnesses to the effect that a bribe had taken place. The judge's defence was that he had not committed perjury at all, since all he said was 'I swear that I have never taken a bribe' and he had indeed sworn that he had never taken a bribe. The case was thereupon dismissed by the trial judge, who happened to be an old friend of the defendant judge. On Lewis' account, justice was served in this case. On my account, it was not.

Part of the confusion in Lewis' discussion arises because the English surface adjective *true* has certain conditions for appropriate use for just about all English speakers, with the exception of those logicians and philosophers who have made that surface adjective into a technical term. When Austin said that a performative sentence was neither 'true' nor 'false', and that such terms could only be applied to statements, he was using 'true' and 'false' in their ordinary senses. A statement is something stated or at least statable, that is, that can be the direct object of a predicate of stating. It should be added that the normal English surface adjectives *true* and *false* are also limited by an additional condition on their appropriate use, namely, that any statement that they are predicated of must have previously been asserted or at least entertained. Consider sentences like:

(3) a. It is true that it is raining outside
    b. It is false that it is raining outside

One could not just go up to someone out of the blue and appropriately say such sentences. The question has to have previously come up as to whether it is raining. Though (4a and b) will be true and false together in all situations in which they are both appropriate, they are appropriate in very different classes of situations.

(4) a. It is raining outside
    b. It is true that it is raining outside

Since logicians rarely if ever consider conditions for appropriate use, and since performatives were never discussed in classical logic, the surface adjective *true* has come to be used as a technical term by many logicians. Within the tradition of formal semantics, *true* has been made into the relative term *true in a model* (*given a point of reference*), which is equated with the technical term *satisfied in a model* (*given a point of reference*). If I understand Lewis correctly, he is using the surface adjective *true* in this sense. Consider Lewis' claim (Lewis 1972: 210):

(5) 'I would wish to say that "I bet you sixpence it will rain tomorrow" is true on an occasion of an utterance if the utterer does bet his audience sixpence that it will rain on the following day; and, if the occasion is normal in certain respects, the utterer does so bet; therefore his utterance is true'

This statement does not make much sense if one takes the surface adjective *true* in its ordinary sense. Imagine the following discourses.

(6) a. I bet you sixpence it will rain tomorrow
    b. That's false, because you don't have a penny to your name. You didn't just make a bet
    b'. That's true – you did just bet me sixpence
(7) a. I hereby christen this battleship the *S.S. Borman*
    b. That's false, you have no authority to give a name to that ship!
    b'. That's true – you did just give that name to that ship
(8) a. I hereby pronounce you husband and wife
    b. That's false, you have no authority to marry those people!
    b'. That's true, he did just marry them

The (b) and (b') sentences are all inappropriate responses; Austin was right that the surface adjectives *false* and *true* cannot be appropriately predicated of performatives. For this reason, Lewis' statement in (5) may not match the intuitions of most speakers of English, including many ordinary language philosophers and linguists. However, it makes perfectly good sense if *true* in (5) is taken to mean *satisfied in a model* (*given a point of reference*). 'Truth conditions' in Lewis' sense are meant to be satisfaction conditions, not conditions under which one can appropriately use the surface adjective *true*.

This shows up pretty clearly in the proposal I made in 'Performative antinomies':

What we need to do is to extend the assignment of truth values for non-performative sentences to the assignment of felicity values for performative sentences. Just as we have valuations like $V_w[P] = 1$ for 'P is true in world w', where P is nonperformative, we will let $V_w[P] = 1$ stand for 'P is felicitous in world w', where P is performative (G. Lakoff (1972b:570)).

There I use the neutral '1' to indicate satisfaction, both in the case of performatives and nonperformatives. When I speak of felicity values, I do not mean to suggest, incidentally, that there is a new kind of value called a *felicity value*, but rather that there is only one kind of value, a satisfaction value, and that the surface adjectives *felicitous* and *true* are to be taken as indicating satisfaction in the case of performatives and nonperformatives respectively. This is also what I had in mind (1971:335–6) when I pointed out that the presuppositions of performative verbs in their nonperformative uses were identical to certain of the felicity conditions for those verbs in their performative uses.

An important point to bear in mind with respect to both Lewis' discussion and mine is that if so-called 'truth conditions' are satisfaction conditions in the model-theoretical sense, then in both Lewis' proposal and mine they are meant to apply to logical structures, *not to surface structures*. In both systems it is nonsense to think of a surface sentence being satisfied in a model at a point of reference, since satisfaction conditions are given only for logical structures, not for surface strings. Under the performative analysis for declaratives, all of the satisfaction conditions will come out to be correct, and the use of the surface adjective *true* in ordinary English will be accounted for (see appendix 1).

(9)

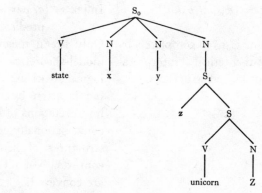

(10) a. I state to you that unicorns exist
    b. Unicorns exist

Both the sentences in (10a and b) will have (9) as their approximate logical structures. The satisfaction conditions for the statement to be made will be those for S_0. The satisfaction conditions for the content of the statement to be true will be those for S_1. The surface adjective *true* will be predicated of what is stated, i.e., the object of the verb of stating, namely, S_1. That is why someone who replies to (10a) by saying *That's true* or *That statement is true* will be committing himself to the truth of S_1 in (9).

Let us review the essential points of the two proposals:

(11) LEWIS' PROPOSAL

a. Satisfaction in a model is defined for all performatives except for the implicit declarative performative.

b. Performative predicates have the same satisfaction conditions as nonperformative predicates.

c. Logical structures contain pronouns *I, you, here, now,* etc.

d. Transformational grammars are assumed.

e. Logical structures are not universal (at least because they contain English pronouns *I, you,* etc.)

f. Index = $\{w,s,h,t,p,d,a\}$[1]

g. Meaning is given completely by model-theoretical interpretations of logical structures.

MY PROPOSAL

Satisfaction in a model is defined for all performatives including the implicit declarative performative.

Performative predicates have the same satisfaction conditions as nonperformative predicates.

Pronouns *I, you, here, now,* etc. are not in logical structure, but are 'introduced' by rules of grammar as replacements for variables.

Global transderivational correspondence grammars are assumed.

Logical structures are taken to be universal.

Index = $\{a,$ partial assignments to predicates$\}$

Only literal meaning is given by model-theoretical interpretations of logical structures. Conveyed meaning is given by model-theoretical interpretations of logical structures conversationally entailed by logical structures of sentences in given contexts. Not all literal meanings are conveyed.

It should be noted that the adoption of the performative analysis for implicit declaratives allows one to avoid having pronouns like *I, you, here,* and *now* in logical structure, and hence allows one to get rid of pragmatic

---

[1] w = world coordinate　　p = place coordinate
s = speaker coordinate　d = demonstrative coordinate
h = hearer coordinate　　a = assignment coordinate
t = time coordinate

coordinates for speaker, hearer, time and place of utterance. But what is more important, defining satisfaction in a model for *all* performatives as I propose allows one to define entailment for all performative cases in the same way as entailment is defined for all nonperformative cases, namely:

(12) $X \cup \{P\}$ entails Q (where P and Q are logical structures and X is a finite set of logical structures) if and only if Q is satisfied in all models at all points of reference at which X and P are satisfied.

If one can give for performatives the same account of satisfaction and entailment as one gives for nonperformatives, the following possibilities open up:

(13) a. One may not need separate theories for speech acts and for descriptions of speech acts. For example, the satisfaction conditions for the predicate *promise* in *I promise to marry you* and *I promised to marry you* can be the same.
b. It is conceivable that conversational implicatures may turn out to be logical entailments of performative utterances in certain contexts.
c. It should be possible to give a uniform characterization of performative antinomies.
d. Indirectly conveyed meanings for embedded sentences can be treated in exactly the same way as indirectly conveyed meanings for performatives.

Let me begin with indirectly conveyed meanings. Gordon and I (1971)[1] included the following in our proposal for what we called conversational postulates:

(14) *sincere(x, state(x,y,P)) ⊃ believe(x,P)* ['if x is sincere in stating P to y, then x believes P']

At the time, we assumed that this and the other postulates we proposed were to be added specially to handle what Heringer has called 'indirect illocutionary force', that is, indirectly conveyed meanings in the case of performatives. I now think that we were wrong to segregate them off in that way. I would now consider (14) to be a normal part of natural logic, that is, a meaning postulate relating the meanings of *sincere*, *state*, and *believe*. (14) is one of the things that you know if you know the meanings of *sincere*, *state*, and *believe*. Logicians have sometimes worried about giving satisfaction conditions for *believe*, but to my knowledge, none has ever

[1] See p. 264, n. 1.

tried to give them for *state* and *sincere*. But if one were to accept the goals of natural logic, one would have to provide satisfaction conditions for all natural language concepts, including these. In an adequate natural logic, (14) would have to be satisfied in all models at all points of reference.

(15) a. Spiro was sincere in stating that Tricky Dick had betrayed him
      b. Spiro believed that Tricky Dick had betrayed him

If (14) is taken to be a meaning postulate of natural logic, and if (12) is taken to define semantic entailment, then (15a) semantically entails (15b). Now consider (16).

(16) a. Sam was being sincere
     b. Sam stated that Tricky Dick had betrayed him
     c. Sam believed that Tricky Dick had betrayed him

Letting (16a) be X and (16b) be P in the definition of (12), then (16b), taken in a context where (16a) is assumed to be true, will semantically entail (16c), given (14) as a meaning postulate. Moreover, (17′) will be a contradiction, given (14) and (17) as meaning postulates and an assumption of rationality.

(17) $believe(a, believe(a,S)) \supset believe(a,S)$

Note that (17) will suffice here and that it is not necessary to assume its converse, which is probably false.[1]

(17′) Sam was sincere in stating that Tricky Dick had betrayed him but that he believed that Tricky Dick had not betrayed him

---

[1] I am also assuming that (i) is a meaning postulate

(i) $believe\ (x,P\ and\ Q) \supset believe\ (x,P)\ and\ believe\ (x,Q)$

Part of assuming rationality consists of assuming that the person involved does not have contradictory beliefs

(ii) $believe(x,P) \supset \neg believe(x,\neg P)$

Given (14), (17), (i) and (ii), (17′) will yield a contradiction.

(iii) a. $sincere(a, state(a,b,P\ and\ believe(a,\neg P)))$ $[= (17′)]$
      b. $believe(a,P\ and\ believe(a,\neg P))$ [from (14)]
      c. $believe(a,P)\ and\ believe(a,believe(a,\neg P))$
      d. $believe(a,believe(a,\neg P))$ [simplification,c]
      e. $believe(a,\neg P)$ [from (17)]
      f. $believe(a,P)$ [simplification,c]
      g. $\neg believe(a,\neg P)$ [from (ii)]
      h. $believe(a,\neg P)\ and\ \neg believe(a,\neg P)$ [e and g]

CONTRADICTION

Since (17′) yields a contradiction given an assumption of rationality, the only way to make (17′) noncontradictory would be to assume that Sam in (17′) held contradictory beliefs.

If (14) is true at all points of reference in all models, then (17') cannot be true in any model at any point of reference. For the same reason, (18a) will entail (18b) in a natural logic.

> (18) a. Sam stated that Tricky Dick had betrayed him but that he did not believe that Tricky Dick had betrayed him
> b. Sam was not being sincere

Given the performative analysis for declaratives, the definition of entailment in (12), and the independently motivated meaning postulates of (14), (17), and (i) and (ii) in p. 264, n. 1, Moore's paradox can be accounted for automatically.

> (19) a. Tricky Dick betrayed me, but I don't believe that Tricky Dick betrayed me
> b. The speaker is not being sincere (assuming that he does not hold contradictory beliefs)

(19a) can never be said sincerely and rationally, and that is accounted for given (12), (14), (17), and (i) and (ii) in p. 264, n. 1, together with the performative analysis for declaratives. Moreover, if we adopt the postulates in (20) that Gordon and I proposed, we can give similar accounts of the oddness of the sentences in (21).

> (20) a. *sincere*$(x, promise(x,y,P)) \supset intend(x,P)$
> b. *sincere*$(x, request(x,y,P)) \supset want(x,P)$
> c. *sincere*$(x, request(x,y, tell(y,x,P))) \supset want(x, tell(x,P))$
>
> (21) a. I promise to marry you, but I don't intend to
> b. Please close the window, but I don't want you to
> c. Who left, but don't tell me

None of these can ever be used sincerely and rationally.

What is interesting about such cases is that supposedly pragmatic paradoxes can be accounted for with just the apparatus of formal semantics, provided we adopt the performative analysis for all cases and the given meaning postulates, which are required independently for an adequate account of truth conditions in nonperformative cases.

There is another class of supposedly pragmatic paradoxes that can be handled by purely semantic means provided that we adopt a uniform performative analysis with definitions of satisfaction and entailment that hold for both performative and nonperformative predicates. These are what I have called the 'performative antinomies', cases like:

(22) a. Don't obey this order
    b. I promise not to keep this promise
    c. I advise you not to follow this advice
    etc.

An account of these was given in G. Lakoff (1972b), where the principles in (23) were proposed.

(23) a. An order is felicitous only if it is (logically) possible for it to be obeyed.
    b. A promise is felicitous only if it is (logically) possible for it to be kept.
    c. A piece of advice is felicitous only if it is (logically) possible for it to be followed.

It is assumed that an order is felicitous if and only if the logical structure representing it has a satisfaction value of 1.

Given (23) and the usual satisfaction condition for ' $\Diamond P$ ', namely (24), we can account for the performative antinomies of (22).

(24) $V_w[\Diamond P] = 1$ iff $(\exists w')$ $(Rww'$ & $V_{w'}[P] = 1)$
where w and w' are possible situations.

Take (22a). The order in (22a) can be obeyed if and only if it is not obeyed. If $P = $ *you do not obey this order*, then there will be no possible situation in which P is true, since in every possible situation in which P is true it is also false. Hence, there is no situation in which the value of ' $\Diamond P$ ' can equal 1. Consequently, (22) can never be a felicitous order.

What we have done in the case of (22a) is to account for what appears to be a pragmatic paradox by using only the devices of formal semantics, taken together with the performative analysis for imperatives and the principles of (23). Similar accounts can be given for (22b) and (22c).

Although declarative antinomies were not discussed in G. Lakoff (1972b), it turns out that they exist and can be handled in the same way. The declarative antinomy can be given by any of the following sentences:

(25) a. You do not believe this statement
    b. I state that you do not believe this statement
    c. You believe that this statement is false
    d. I state that you believe that this statement is false

Each of the sentences of (25) has the following property: It is true if and only if you believe it is false, and it is false if and only if you believe it is true. Hence you cannot have a correct belief about it.

Given the performative analysis for declaratives, we can account for all the declarative antinomies in exactly the same way as we accounted for the nondeclarative antinomies, provided we add the principle:

(23) d. A statement is felicitous only if it is (logically) possible for it to be believed.

As before there will be no possible situation in which ' $\Diamond believe(y,P)$' will be satisfied, since y can believe P if and only if y does not believe P. Thus, ' $\Diamond believe(y,P)'$ will always be false and so each of the statements in (25) will always be infelicitous.

Note, incidentally, that the principles of (23) are needed independently to account for natural logic entailments in nonperformative cases:

(26) a. Sam ordered Olga not to obey the order he was then giving
    b. Sam did not give a felicitous order
(27) a. Sam stated to Olga that she did not believe the statement he was then making
    b. Sam did not make a felicitous statement

The principles in (23) are needed to account for the inferences from the (a) to the (b) sentences above.

What we have shown so far is that, in the case of performative antinomies as in the case of the Moore paradoxes, the principles needed to account for natural language entailments in nonperformative cases will, given a uniform performative analysis, automatically give an account of what goes wrong in performative antinomies. This is no mean accomplishment. For what appeared to be paradoxes of a pragmatic nature can be accounted for by the use of independently needed formal semantic apparatus, given a uniform syntactic performative analysis for declaratives as well as for imperatives, promises, etc. Even if there were no purely syntactic evidence for a performative analysis, these results suggest that we would want to have one anyway – just so that the Moore paradoxes and performative antinomies could be accounted for by independently needed apparatus in formal semantics. It is especially interesting that purely syntactic evidence buttresses this result from the area of model-theoretical semantics. And it is striking that the same types of arguments obtain in both cases.

(28) THE FORM OF SYNTACTIC ARGUMENTS FOR PERFOR-
MATIVE ANALYSES

  (i) We need certain rules to account for given syntactic phenomena in nonperformative sentences.

  (ii) Given the performative analysis, the same rules will automatically account for the corresponding syntactic phenomena in
performative sentences for which additional and different rules
would be needed if we do not adopt a performative analysis.

(29) THE FORM OF SEMANTIC-PRAGMATIC ARGUMENTS
FOR THE PERFORMATIVE ANALYSIS

  (i) We need certain apparatus in natural logic to account for
certain semantic facts in nonperformative sentences. (The
apparatus includes definitions of satisfaction for certain classes
of predicates, meaning postulates, and a definition of entailment.)

  (ii) Given the performative analysis, the same apparatus will
automatically account for the corresponding 'pragmatic' facts
in the case of performative sentences; while additional and
different apparatus would be needed if we do not adopt a
performative analysis.

The convergence of the syntactic evidence for the performative analysis
with the semantic-pragmatic evidence seems to me to strongly confirm
the need for some version of the performative analysis (though not necessarily any of the particular ones proposed by Sanctius, Lancelot, Whitney,
Postal, R. Lakoff, Ross, or Sadock).

I suggested above that the performative analysis should enable us to
frame the theory of speech acts within formal semantics. Actually, the idea
for doing this is implicit in the approach to the theory of speech acts given
in chapter 3 of Searle (1969), where Searle gives truth conditions for third-
person descriptions of speech acts and lets them *be* the felicity conditions
for those acts. Similarly, in a natural logic, satisfaction conditions would
be given for each atomic predicate, including all of the performative
predicates; the satisfaction conditions are at once both truth conditions and
felicity conditions. The sincerity conditions given in (14) and (20) are
examples of meaning postulates that function as conditions on satisfaction.
Searle's *essential conditions* might take the form of meaning postulates like
that in (30).

(30) *Request(x,y,P) ⊃ attempt(x, cause(x,P))*

(30) expresses Searle's essential condition for requests, which is that a request counts as an attempt on the part of the speaker to get the hearer to do the action requested. The need for (30) as a meaning postulate independently of performative asentences can be seen in (31).

(31) a. Henry requested of Jill that she take her clothes off
      b. Henry attempted to get Jill to take her clothes off

It should follow from the meaning of *request* that if (31a) is true then (31b) is true. Thus the meaning postulate in (30) is needed to account for entailments in nonperformative sentences.

Searle's preparatory conditions are especially interesting, since at least some of them are presuppositional in nature. For example, consider the condition on orders that says that the speaker has authority over the hearer. An inspection of nonperformative sentences shows that this is a presupposition, not merely an entailment.

(32) a. Sam ordered Harry to get out of the bar
      b. Sam didn't order Harry to get out of the bar
      c. Sam may order Harry to get out of the bar

Each of the sentences in (32) entails that Sam has authority over Harry.

Given a uniform performative analysis, there are only two ingredients required for a theory of speech acts: (i) an account of satisfaction conditions for all performative predicates; and (ii) an account of culture-specific assumptions about social interaction, at least in so far as they pertain to conversational interaction. We have discussed (i) at length; it is needed independently to account for nonperformative uses of performative predicates and requires only the apparatus of formal semantics. What about (ii) – the culture-specific assumptions? What Searle had in mind for these were such assumptions as (33):

(33) In normal conversations, you assume that the person you are talking to is being sincere, unless you have a good reason for not assuming it.

Thus, in an example like (16) above, (16a) ('Sam was being sincere') would be taken to be part of the culture-specific assumptions of speaker and hearer in a normal conversation. There is some doubt in my mind as to whether (33) is really a *culture-specific* assumption, rather than a truth which follows from the meaning of the concepts 'normal' and 'conversation'. The latter seems to me more likely, in which case (33) would just be a theorem of natural logic. (33) just does not seem to me to be the sort of thing that would vary a great deal from culture to culture.

Be that as it may, there are real examples of culture-specific assumptions that have to be characterized in order to understand various aspects of speech acts in a given culture. But this does not mean that we need to go beyond the resources of formal semantics to provide an account of speech acts. In particular, we do not need any new notion of pragmatic or non-logical inference. Ordinary semantic entailment will suffice, just as it sufficed in the case of (16) above. Cultural assumptions play the same role in semantic entailment as any other assumptions.

This brings us to conversational implicature. I would like to suggest (modestly) that implicatures are not 'loose' or informal inferences. Given the performative analysis, implicatures should turn out to be a species of semantic entailment, providing one had an adequate natural logic and an adequate analysis of the relevant culture-specific principles of social interaction. Grice's theory of conversational implicature is based on the 'cooperative principle', the idea that certain 'maxims' are to be followed in conversational situations in which the participants are cooperating. Grice's maxims can be restated as principles like the following:

(34) a. If x is cooperating with y, then x will do only what is relevant to the enterprise at hand, unless his actions make no difference to the enterprise [MAXIM OF RELEVANCE]
   b. If x is cooperating with y, then x will not do less than is necessary to make the enterprise successful
   c. If x is cooperating with y, then x will not greatly exceed his needed contribution [MAXIMS OF QUANTITY]
   etc.

It seems to me that principles like those in (34) should follow from the meaning of *cooperate*, rather than being special culture-specific principles of social interaction. Since natural logic is committed to the study of all natural language concepts, including *cooperation*, principles like those in (34) should fall within the purview of formal semantics within natural logic, and no separate set of pragmatic principles should be necessary for hand-ling them. So far, unfortunately, neither linguists nor logicians have done any serious formal study of the logic of cooperation. Until such studies are done, we cannot say for sure whether implicatures can be handled using normal semantic entailment or whether a new, informal mode of inference needs to be characterized. What we can do now is (i) provide some evidence in favour of the proposal, (ii) show that apparent counter-examples are not real, and (iii) show that similar cases in the realm of indirectly conveyed meaning show promise of eventually being dealt with within formal semantics.

Some evidence in favour of the proposal comes from work on the presuppositions of complex sentences by Lakoff and Railton (1971) and by Karttunen (1973). They observed that in sentences, S, of the form *If A, then B*, where B presupposes C, S presupposes C with respect to context X, unless $X \cup A \Vdash C$. This principle is meant to handle cases like the following:

(35) a. If Jack has children, then all of Jack's children are bald
     b. If Nixon invites Angela Davis to the White House, then he will regret having invited a black militant to his residence

Assuming these sentences are of the form *If A, then B*, then in (35a), B presupposes that *Jack has children* ($=C$). Therefore $A = C$, and so $X \cup A \Vdash C$, for any X at all. In (35b), B presupposes that *Nixon will have invited a black militant to his residence* ($=C$). Therefore in any context X in which it is assumed that *Angela Davis is a black militant* and that *the White House is Nixon's residence*, the condition $X \cup A \Vdash C$ will be met, and so C will not be a presupposition of (35b) with respect to those contexts X.

If implicatures are really entailments in context, then we would expect the above principle, which is stated in terms of entailment in context to work in the case of implicatures. That is, suppose we have a sentence of the form *If A, then B*, where B presupposes C and where in a context X, A implicates C. If implicature is really entailment in context, we would expect the entire sentence *If A, then B* not to presuppose C with respect to X. This prediction is borne out, as the following example shows:

(36) If Sam askes Professor Snurd to write him a recommendation to graduate school, and Professor Snurd writes the recommendation, saying only that Sam has nice handwriting, then Sam will regret that Professor Snurd wrote him a bad recommendation

In (36), B presupposes that *Professor Snurd will have written Sam a bad recommendation* ($=C$). Consider every situation X in which it is assumed that if, in recommending someone for graduate school, a professor writes only that the student has a nice handwriting, then the professor is writing a bad recommendation. It will be the case that $X \cup A \Vdash C$. Thus, it is predicted that (36) as a whole does not presuppose C with respect to such contexts X, which is the case. But the inference from saying only that a student has nice handwriting to giving a bad recommendation is a classic case of a

Gricean implicature. (36) indicates that implicatures work like entailments in context with respect to the phenomenon of presupposition cancelling. Other implicatures seem to work the same way. Since implicatures *can* be treated as entailments in context, (36) gives us reason to believe that they *should* be treated as such, since then the presuppositional facts of (36) will be accounted for by the same principle that accounts for the presuppositional facts of (35).

In addition to providing evidence for our conjecture, we can show that apparent counter-examples are not real and that similar cases in the realm of indirectly conveyed meaning show promise of being dealt with within formal semantics. Probably the main objection to trying to treat implicatures via formal semantics is that implicatures are cancellable, while entailments are not. Consider the following examples.

(37) a. John has three children
     b. John has three children – and he may even have six
(38) a. John caused Harry to leave
     b. John caused Harry to leave – but Harry may not have left

On Grice's account (37a) invites the interference by means of conversational implicature that John has only three children, but does not entail it. The implicature can be cancelled, as in (37b). (37a) differs from (38a) in that (38a) has an entailment – Harry left – not an implicature. Any attempt to cancel the entailment, as in (38b) leads to a contradiction. Clearly there is a difference between (37a) and (38a), but this does not mean that the formal semantic mechanism of entailment cannot be used to handle both cases. Let me explain. The definition of entailment given above in (12) was context-dependent entailment; this is the usual model-theoretical notion. One special case of that is context-independent entailment, as defined in (39).

(39) CONTEXT-INDEPENDENT ENTAILMENT
     P entails Q if and only if Q is satisfied in all models at all points of reference at which P is satisfied.

(38a) is a case of context-independent entailment; (37a) is not. I would like to suggest, however, that (37a) is a case of context-dependent entailment. If so, then (37a) will entail that John has only three children in some contexts, but not in others. The function of the cancellation phrase in (37b) will then be to limit the contexts appropriate for the use of the sentence to those in which the entailment does not hold.

To provide support for this claim we need to show that cancellation of implicatures is context-dependent. That turns out to be fairly easy to do.

(40) a. We've got a job for a welfare recipient who has at least three children – and the more the better. Do you definitely know someone who fills the bill?

　　b. We've got a job for a junior executive with children, but no more than three. Do you definitely know someone who fills the bill?

(41) Exactly how many children does John have?

Consider the sentences of (37) as being replies to (40) and (41). If (37a) is a reply to (40a), the implicature is cancellable, as shown by the fact that (37b) is a relevant and appropriate response. However, if (37a) is taken as a reply to (40b) or (41), the implicature is not cancellable, as shown by the fact that (37b) is not an acceptable response in these cases. The reason is fairly clear. The implicature is based on principle (34b). (34b) will be part of X in '$X \cup \{P\}$ entails Q' in (12). Whether or not implicatures arise due to (34b) will depend on what else is assumed in context, namely, what else X contains that is relevant to the 'success of the conversational enterprise'. In this case, the relevant issue is whether it matters that John has more than three children. In (40a) it does not. In (40b) and (41), it does. My claim is that if examples like the above could be suitably formalized, the presence or absence of implicatures could be handled using context-dependent entailment, as defined in (12).

Although no significant work has yet been done on the problem of formalizing Gricean implicatures, there has been considerable investigation of other types of indirectly conveyed meanings, or in Heringer's terminology, 'indirect illocutionary force'. At present, these studies suggest that indirectly conveyed meanings might be handled using the apparatus of context-dependent semantic entailment, together with global and trans-derivational rules of grammar.

The basic idea is this: Grammars are taken as generating quadruples of the form (42).

(42) (S,L,C,CM), where S is a sentence (more strictly its phonetic representation), L is a model-theoretically interpreted logical structure (representing the literal meaning of the sentence), C is a consistent set of logical structures (the models in which they are satisfied represent the contexts in which the sentence has the literal meaning of L), and CM is a sequence of logical structures

(representing the conveyed meanings of the sentence relative to context C – the last member of the sequence is the 'ultimately conveyed meaning')

More specifically, pairs of the form (S,L) are characterized by derivations, that is, sequences of trees linking S and L. Each derivation D uniquely characterizes a pair (S,L). Thus one could alternatively say that a grammar generates triples of the form (D,C,CM), where D determines a pair (S,L). Derivations are not well- or ill-formed in and of themselves, but only with respect to contexts C and conveyed meanings CM. Derivations are characterized by local and global correspondence rules. Transderivational rules are constraints that specify which derivations are well-formed with respect to which contexts and which conveyed meanings.

The need for distinguishing literal from conveyed meaning is fairly obvious, as cases of sarcasm show. Take a sentence like (43).

(43) Harry is a real genius

Depending on context, (43) can be understood as being either literal or sarcastic. In contexts where it is to be taken sarcastically, the literal meaning is not conveyed at all – instead its polar opposite, namely, *Harry is an idiot*, is conveyed. Although in most normal cases that linguists and logicians and philosophers of language have talked about, the literal meaning of the sentence is conveyed and perhaps other meanings as well, in sarcasm, the literal meaning is not conveyed at all. Interestingly enough, there are linguistic rules that correlate with sarcasm. R. Lakoff has observed that American English (at least many dialects) has a rule of sarcastic nasalization, whereby the sentence as a whole or the portion one is being sarcastic about is nasalized. Thus, if (43) or the sarcastic portion of it – *real genius* – is nasalized, the sentence can only have a sarcastic reading. This nasalization rule therefore seems to have a transderivational condition on it limiting the conveyed meaning of the sentence to the polar opposite of the literal meaning.

The reason that conveyed meanings are given as a sequence is that sentences often convey more than one meaning at once – the literal meaning plus one or more others. Take the following cases.

(44) Can you pass the salt?

(45) I want a beer

(46) Why don't you ask Harriet for a date?

(47) Your mother would like it if you asked Harriet for a date

Each of these sentences has a literal reading, and in certain situations the literal meaning can be conveyed. For example, (44) is literally a question about the addressee's abilities, and can be used as such, say, by a doctor trying to determine how well his patient's injured arm was healing. Of course, (44) is more frequently used to convey a request. (45) is literally a statement about the speaker's desires, and might be used as such, say, by a starving captive in reply to his sadistic captor's question 'What do you want most?'. More typically, it would be used to convey a request. (46) and (47) have very different literal meanings, but could both be used as suggestions to the effect that the addressee ask Harriet for a date.

But where these sentences convey requests or suggestions, their literal meanings are also conveyed, and in fact the nonliteral meanings arise only by virtue of the literal meanings being conveyed. Thus, (44) in the right context can be both a question about one's abilities and by virtue of that, a request. Gordon and I proposed that the appropriate way to account for the relation between literal and conveyed meanings was by using context-dependent entailment together with the performative analysis. We suggested that there existed what we called 'conversational postulates' on which such relations were based, and that the literal meanings taken together with the postulates would, given the performative analysis and context-dependent entailment, entail the conveyed meanings. (48) is an example of one our our proposed postulates (slightly revised).

(48) *assume(x, not relevant(want(x,Q)))* & *say(x,y,want(x,Q))⊃request (x,y,Q)*
[If x assumes that it is not relevant that he wants Q and he says to y that he wants Q, then he is requesting that y do Q]

Thus, (48) would account for the fact that (45) is a request in exactly those contexts where the mere question of my *desire* for a beer was irrelevant. Given the performative analysis for (45) and context-dependent entailment, (48) will do the job.

It ought to be pointed out that there is independent motivation for (48) from nonperformative cases.

(49) a. Sam assumed that the pure question of his desires was irrelevant
b. Sam said to Mary that he wanted a beer
c. Sam requested that Mary get him a beer

(49a) and (49b) together entail (49c).

Gordon and I, in setting up postulates like (48) and calling them 'conversational postulates' were assuming that they were culture-specific principles of social interaction. I now have some doubt about that, and think that they may simply be meaning postulates or theorems of natural logic that happen to contain performative predicates.

In summary, let me state what I hope to have convinced you of:

(50) a. There is strong semantic-pragmatic evidence supporting a uniform performative analysis.
b. Given a uniform performative analysis, the treatment of indexicals in natural language does not require that additional coordinates for speaker, hearer, and time and place of utterance be added to points of reference.
c. No additional pragmatic theory is necessary for an account of speech acts and conversational implicatures, provided that one accepts the goals of natural logic and the need for global transderivational grammars.

APPENDIX 1

An important point to bear in mind with respect to both Lewis' discussion and mine is that if so-called 'truth conditions' are taken to be satisfaction conditions in the model-theoretical sense, then in both Lewis' system and mine they are meant to apply to logical structures, *not directly to surface structures*. In both systems it makes no sense to think of a surface sentence being directly satisfied in a model at a point of reference, since satisfaction conditions are given for logical structures and not for surface strings. Because of this, a certain confusion can arise when one does not distinguish between the normal English surface adjective *true* and the technical term *true in a model*, taken to mean *satisfied in a model*. One can speak in English of a surface sentence as being *true* or *false* in the non-technical senses of those terms. Superficially it might appear that the normal English surface adjective *true* could be predicated of a surface sentence, while the technical *true* meaning *satisfied in a model* cannot.

We can see more easily what is going on here if we consider such classic examples as the following (from Postal (1969), and Borkin (1971)).

(1) a. IBM went up six points
b. IBM stock went up six points
(2) a. Proust is impossible to read
b. Proust's works are impossible to read
(3) a. This page is illegible
b. The writing on this page is illegible
(4) a. This page is impossible to understand
b. What is expressed by the writing on this page is impossible to understand

In each case the (a) sentence is understood in the same way as the (b) sentence.

Proust in (2a) is understood as referring to *Proust's works*, while *Proust* in (5a) refers to the remains of Proust's body, while *Proust* in (5b) refers to the person himself.

(5) a. Proust is buried in France
   b. Proust wrote a lot

Similarly, *this page* in (3a) refers to the writing on the page and in (3b) refers to the content of what is written (or printed) on that page, while in (6) it refers to the physical page itself.

(6) This page weighs 1/50th of a gram

There are various ways in which one might try to deal with such sentences as (1a)–(4a). Postal has suggested that the (a) sentences in those cases be derived from the structures underlying the (b) sentences via a deletion rule (or rules), and the constraints on such sentences cited by Borkin and Lawler have given plausibility to such a suggestion. On the other hand, if one dislikes the deletion solution, one might propose instead a semantic solution whereby, for instance, the logical structure of (2a) would have the surface name *Proust* corresponding to the same logical structure element(s) as the surface name *Proust* in (5b), but would have different references in the two sentences. So far as I have been able to tell, such a suggestion would be difficult to implement adequately in terms of formal semantics for the following reason: Somehow the surface NP *Proust* in (2a) does not simply refer to Proust's works. In a sense, it also refers to Proust himself, and if it refers to Proust's works, it does so by means of its reference to the writer himself. This is exactly what happens under Postal's proposal. If the logical structure of (2a) is the same as that of (2b) and if *Proust* in (2a) is derived via a deletion rule from the structure underlying *Proust's work*, then in the logical structure of (2a) *Proust* refers to the man himself, and *Proust's works* refers to the man's works. Under Postal's proposal, the ordinary reference assignments used in formal semantics will suffice; while under the alternative proposal, we would have to control the reference of a description or a proper name in a different way. An obvious suggestion would be a 'pragmatic' solution, adding to points of reference a new coordinate for each proper name and each description in the language, i.e., an infinite number of new coordinates, and one would somehow have to mark each description and proper name in a logical structure to tell whether it was to have its ordinary reference or whether it was to refer to what was specified in its 'pragmatic' coordinate. Such a solution would not only have to have an additional infinite sequence of pragmatic coordinates, as well as having special markings in logical structure for ordinary vs. 'pragmatic' reference, but it would also have all the complications that would go along with Postal's proposal in addition. The reason is that there are empirical constraints on what a surface NP can ordinarily be understood as referring to. For example, *Proust* in (2a) cannot be understood as referring to the works that Proust did *not* write, nor as referring to Shakespeare's works, nor as referring to the works that my cousin Herbie believes that Proust wrote, nor as referring to this paper (which I have not given the title *Proust*). The principal unsolved problem with Postal's proposal is how to constrain his proposed deletion rule so as to get the right surface NPs from the right underlying NPs. Exactly the same problem would remain in the pragmatic proposal. It is for this reason that I prefer Postal's deletion proposal. It requires less apparatus. Both proposals require the same constraints, but Postal's proposal uses the ordinary formal semantic apparatus to account for reference, and does not require extra pragmatic coordinates, that is, extra indicators of nonordinary reference.

Let us now return to the surface adjective *true*. Note that (7a) is understood to mean the same as (7b).

(7) a. That sentence is true
   b. The proposition that the logical structure of that sentence expresses is true

That sentence in (7a) has the same reference as *the proposition that the logical structure of that sentence expresses* in (7b), while in (8) it refers to the sentence itself.

(8) That sentence contains five words

The problem is exactly that encountered in (1)–(4) above, and I would again suggest Postal's proposed solution: derive (7a) from the structure underlying (7b) by a deletion rule. Under this proposal, the English adjective *true* would not be predicated of surface sentences themselves, but only of propositions expressed by the logical structures of those sentences. And in both Lewis' proposal and mine, propositions are expressed not by surface sentences directly, but by the logical structures associated with those surface sentences. Thus, according to both our proposals, truth is predicated not of a surface sentence, but of the proposition expressed by the logical structure associated with the surface sentence.

In other words, in order to give satisfaction conditions for a given surface structure S, we must first pick out a logical structure S related to it by the grammar of the language. The question is: can one always find a unique logical structure S associated with any given surface structure S? It should be observed that the problem of determining satisfaction conditions for a surface S overlaps in part with the problem of assigning reference to surface structure nominals. Given a surface structure N, we must pick out a logical structure N associated with it, and then find out what that logical structure N refers to at a given point of reference. The question here is whether one can always find a unique logical structure N associated with an arbitrary surface structure N. Under Postal's beheading proposal, the answer to this question in general is no. For example, in (2a),

(2) a. Proust is impossible to read

the surface N *Proust* would have associated with it *two* logical structure Ns, one of which would refer to Proust and the other, to Proust's works. Thus the question 'What does the surface N *Proust* refer to in surface sentence (2a)?' makes no sense, since surface Ns can be said to refer only by virtue of there being an associated logical structure N that refers. If the question is rephrased, as it should be, to 'What does the logical structure N associated with the surface structure *N Proust* in (2a) refer to?', it becomes clear that the question makes no sense since the presupposition is false. It should also be noted that the fact that such a question does not have a sensible answer in no way creates a problem for the assignment of reference so far as the logical structure of (2a) is concerned.

The situation is the same with surface structure *S*s. Surface structure *S*s will not in general be associated with unique logical structure *S*s and therefore, it may make no sense to ask for the satisfaction conditions for a surface structure *S*. Consider (8a) for example.

(8) a. It is possible for anyone to win

In (8a), *for anyone to win* is a surface *S* (at least on one reading). Assuming for the sake of discussion that the logical structure of (8a) is (8b) [we have left out the declarative performative, since it is irrelevant for the moment], we might ask what are the satisfaction conditions for the surface structure *S for anyone to win*?

(8) b.

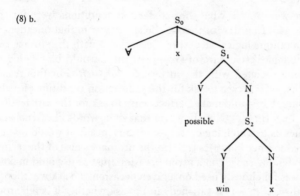

For this to be a sensible question, there would have to be a unique logical structure *S* in (8b) that *for anyone to win* in (8a) is associated with. But there is no such *S*. The reason is that there are certain necessary conditions given in (9) that must be met in order for an *S*-node in a surface structure tree to be 'associated with' an *S*-node in a logical structure tree in discussions about the 'truth' of a surface structure sentence or clause.

(9) Let S_s be a surface structure *S*-node and S_l be a logical structure *S*-node.
   a. The logical structure elements that correspond to the surface structure elements dominated by S_s are all dominated by S_l.
   b. The surface structure elements that correspond to the logical structure elements dominated by S_l are all dominated by S_s.

S_2 is not a candidate, since the logical structure element corresponding to *anyone* is not dominated by S_2. And S_0 is not a candidate since it dominates *possible*, which does not correspond to any element in the surface *S* 'for anyone to win'. Thus in general it does not make sense to ask for satisfaction conditions for a random surface structure *S*.

Suppose, for the sake of discussion, that the grammar of English pairs the logical structure (11) with the surface sentence (10).

(10) John left

(11)

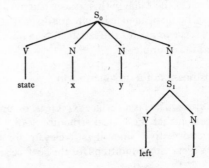

Suppose we were to ask what the satisfaction conditions were for the surface S *John left* (= 10). In order for there to be an answer to that question, there would have to be a unique logical structure S associated with the surface S of (10). But if (11) is the logical structure of (10), then there would be two logical structure Ss, not one, associated with the surface S, *John left*. For this reason, it would make no sense in this case to ask for the satisfaction conditions for the surface S, *John left*, though it would make perfect sense to ask for the satisfaction conditions of either S_0 or S_1 in (11). Note however that since words like 'true' and 'felicitous' can give clues as to which logical structure S is meant, it would make sense to ask whether the sentence in (10) is true (in the ordinary sense of the term, rather than in Lewis' extended sense) on a given occasion, just as it would make sense to ask whether it was felicitously used on a given occasion. To ask whether (10) is true is to ask whether S_1 in (11) is satisfied, and to ask whether it is felicitously asserted is to ask whether S_0 is satisfied.

As we have seen, it makes sense to talk about satisfaction in a model *directly* only for logical structure Ss; and it makes sense to talk about satisfaction in a model indirectly for a surface structure S only if there is a unique logical structure S which is associated by the grammar with that surface S and in terms of which satisfaction can be directly defined. We are in the same position with respect to entailment, which after all is defined in terms of satisfaction. Strictly speaking, entailment is a relation between logical structures, not surface sentences. We can define entailment indirectly for surface sentences just in case we can associate a unique logical structure S with each of the surface sentences. Consider the following examples.

(12) a. John and Bill left
     b. John left
(13) a. I state that John and Bill left
     b. I state that John left

Under the performative analysis for declaratives, the (a) and (b) sentences in (12) and (13) will be associated with the logical structures in (14a) and (14b)

(14) a.

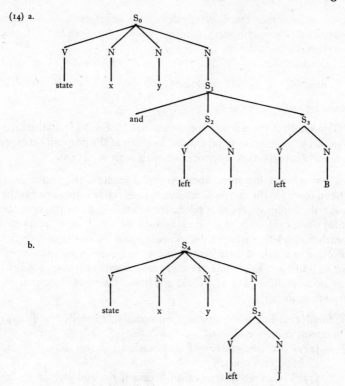

b.

respectively. With respect to (14) we can say the following about entailment.

(15) a. S_1 entails S_2
     b. S_0 does not entail S_4

Since entailment is a relation directly defined between logical structures and only indirectly between sentences depending on which logical structure Ss they are associated with, we can only talk about entailment relations in (12) and (13) if we know which logical structure Ss we are talking about. Consider for example the sentences in (13). If we can find a locution to make it clear that we are associating (13a) with S_1 and (13b) with S_2, then we can speak of an entailment relation of the appropriate sort holding.

(16) That (13a) is a true statement on occasion t entails that (13b) is a true statement on occasion t.

By using the locution about true statements, we make it clear that we are associating (13a) with S_1 and (13b) with S_2, since:

(17) a. (13a) is a true statement on occasion t if and only if S_1 in (14a) is satisfied on occasion t.
     b. (13b) is a true statement on occasion t if and only if S_2 in (14b) is satisfied on occasion t.

The point again is that when we speak of true statements, we are speaking of direct objects of statement predicates, not whole sentences or the logical structures corresponding to them.

Now consider (18).

(18) Sentence (13a) entails sentence (13b)

(18) would be understood as meaning (19).

(19) The truth of the proposition expressed by the logical structure S associated with sentence (13a) entails the truth of the proposition expressed by the logical structure S associated with sentence (13b).

Without any special locutions about true statements, the constraints of (19) would be in force for the entire surface sentences (rather than just for the surface S marking the direct object of a predicate of stating, as in the case above). By (9a), (13a) and (13b) could not be associated with S_1 and S_2 respectively, but rather with S_0 and S_4 respectively. Since S_0 and S_4 describe speech acts it is inappropriate to speak of their 'truth'; moreover, there is no entailment relation between S_0 and S_4. Thus, there are two reasons why (19) does not hold.

Let us now consider (12). If we use the 'true statement' locution, we get the same results as in (16).

(16') That (12a) is a true statement on occasion t entails that (12b) is a true statement on occasion t.

(17') a. (12a) is a true statement on occasion t if and only if S_1 in (14a) is satisfied on occasion t.

b. (12b) is a true statement on occasion t if and only if S_2 in (14b) is satisfied on occasion t.

But because (12) contains no overt performative verb, (12) displays a difference with respect to (13) when one looks at statements parallel to (18) such as (18').

(18') Sentence (12a) entails sentence (12b).

(18') is understood as (19').

(19') The truth of the proposition expressed by the logical structure S associated with sentence (12a) entails the truth of the proposition expressed by the logical structure S associated with sentence (12b).

(18') is unlike (18) in that principle (19) permits both S_0 and S_1 to be 'associated with' the surface S dominating sentence (12); and (19) also permits both S_4 and S_2 to be 'associated with' the surface S dominating sentence (12b). But since one can only speak of S_1 and S_2 as being 'true', while it is inappropriate to speak strictly of the 'truth' of S_0 and S_4, the surface nominals *sentence (12a)* and *sentence (12b)* in (18') wind up being associated with S_1 and S_2 respectively. Since there is an entailment relation between S_1 and S_2, (18') not only makes sense, but is true.

The point here is that the grammar of English may assign sentence (12a) the logical structure (14a), while the surface nominal *sentence (12a)* in the *sentence* (18') may be taken as referring to the content of only a subtree of (14a), namely

S_1. The reason why I have taken the trouble to discuss this matter at such length is that a failure to make such distinctions can lead one into making a fallacious argument against the performative analysis for declaratives. (20) contains the gist of such an argument.

(20)   (i)   (14a) is the logical structure of sentence (12a) and (14b) is the logical structure of sentence (12b).
     (ii)   Sentence (12a) entails sentence (12b).
    (iii)   But (14a) [= S_0] does not entail (14b) [= S_4].
   (iv)   Therefore, assuming that entailment is based on logical structure, (i) cannot be correct.

The argument is fallacious. In order to make the argument correct, we would have to assume in addition:

(21)   *Sentence (12a) entails sentence (12b)* is true if and only if the logical structure of sentence (12a) entails the logical structure of sentence (12b).

But this need not be a correct assumption, as we saw above. The truth of (20 ii) [= (18′)] depends upon what the surface nominals *sentence (12a)* and *sentence (12b)* refer to in that sentence. As we have seen, these surface nominals may be understood as referring to the proposition expressed by a subtree of the logical structure of the surface sentence. This is not particularly strange, considering the general complexities that we have seen to be involved in the assignment of reference to surface nominals, and the general constraints in (9) above.

APPENDIX 2

Given transformational grammar of the Aspects vintage, it made sense to ask 'Do transformations preserve meaning?' Within generative semantics, this question does not make sense, for various reasons. First and most obviously, there are no transformations. In their place there are correspondence rules which may have global and/or transderivational constraints associated with them. Secondly, the role of correspondence rules is to correctly relate surface structures and logical structures, given various constraints involving context, conveyed meanings, etc. The rules will have to account correctly for all aspects of meaning; but the term 'preserving meaning' will be itself meaningless in such a theory. Since there is more to meaning than just the model-theoretical interpretations of logical structures – in particular, those features of meaning associated with context and conveyed meanings – one would not expect all aspects of the meaning of a sentence to be given by the model-theoretical interpretation of the logical structure of the sentence. The rule of performative deletion, as discussed by R. Lakoff (1973), is a case in point. As Lakoff observes, overt performatives are used under different contextual conditions than nonovert performatives. Thus, sentences with overt performatives would differ in their contextual meaning from sentences with nonovert performatives. This would be accounted for in the grammar of English by placing transderivational conditions concerning context on the rule of performative deletion.

If one had a theory like the Aspects theory, with transformations and a notion of deep structure, and if one stated performative deletion in such a theory as a transformation, then performative deletion would, as expected, not be a meaning-preserving transformation in such a theory, since the contextual constraints on sentences in the derivation of which the rule has applied would differ from those in which the rule had not applied. But this issue does not arise in generative semantics, since the notion of 'preserving meaning' does not make sense in such a theory. In generative semantics, meanings are assigned to sentences by rules of grammar. One may ask whether they are assigned correctly or incorrectly, but not whether they are 'preserved'.

APPENDIX 3

Ross and Sadock, in their versions of the performative analysis, assume that the logical structure of every sentence has a performative predicate expressing the literal content of that speech act which is performed when the speaker utters the given sentence in an appropriate situation. I am not making such an assumption, but rather two weaker assumptions:

(I) Every sentence when used in a given situation to perform a speech act has associated with it in that situation a logical structure which contains a performative predicate which expresses the literal content of the speech act.

(II) Every sentence which contains in its surface structure a deictic (or 'indexical') element, i.e., an element which has meaning only with reference to a speech act, has in its logical structure a performative predicate which expresses the literal content of that speech act.

(I) and (II) leave open the possibility that there are sentences of natural languages which do not have any deictic elements and which can be considered in the abstract apart from any implicit or explicit speech act. Such sentences do seem to occur in English, though they constitute a very tiny proportion of sentences of the language. They include certain sentences about mathematics and the physical sciences, as well as definitions. Compare the following two groups of sentences.

(1) a. Two plus two equals four
b. Force equals mass times acceleration
c. Whales are mammals
(2) a. My uncle came here yesterday
b. Whales are becoming extinct
c. The earth has one satellite
d. That is a wombat

Though the sentences in (1) have surface structure present tense elements, those tense elements have no relation to the time that such sentences were uttered (written, etc.). They are true (or false) independent of who utters them, or when or where or under what circumstances they are uttered, and independently of whether they are uttered at all. Thus the tenses in (1) are not deictic elements. The tenses in (2) are, however, deictic elements. The truth of each sentence in (2) depends on when it is uttered. Moreover, the truth or falsity of (2a) depends on who utters it and where the utterance takes place. (2d) depends for a truth value on what the speaker refers to by *that*.

A tiny proportion of natural language sentences have no deictic elements in them at all, and if we ignore instances where such sentences, including those in (1), are considered in the abstract rather than being asserted by a speaker, then my proposals in (I) and (II) become identical with the Ross–Sadock proposal. The disparity between our positions, though miniscule so far as natural language phenomena on the whole are concerned, is important with respect to the history of the study of formal semantics. Formal semantics grew out of the study of formal logic, which in turn concerned itself primarily if not wholly with non-deictic sentences abstracted away from speech situations, since it was concerned with mathematics (and science in general). Mathematics can be formalized without taking speech acts into account. However, when formal semantics is extended from its traditional domain to natural languages as wholes, the study of nondeictic sentences abstracted from speech situations pales into insignificance. Not that such cases should not be accounted for; (I) and (II) are set up to account for them. According to (I) and (II), sentences like those in (1) would be associated with two logical structures; one for cases in which the sentence is uttered in the performance of a speech act – typically an assertion, and another in which the sentence is considered in the abstract, as logicians usually consider them. In the former (speech act) case, the logical structure of the sentence would contain a performative predicate expressing the literal content of the speech act; in the latter case, since the sentence can be totally abstracted from any speech act situation, there would be no performative predicate in logical structure.

The Ross–Sadock proposal requires that all logical structures contain performatives in the appropriate place; my proposal requires no such constraint. (I) and (II), rather than being constraints placed on grammars, would simply fall out automatically once the principles governing the occurrence of deictic elements were stated correctly. Each surface structure deictic element would correspond to some argument in logical structure that would be a clause-mate of some performative predicate. Thus, the presence of a deictic element would require the presence of a performative predicate in logical structure; correspondingly, if a sentence contained no deictic element, no performative predicate would be required – one might be there or not. If a performative predicate were there, then in order for the logical structure to be satisfied in a model, some speech act would have to occur. With no performative predicate, there would be no corresponding speech act, and we would get the consideration-in-the-abstract case.

REFERENCES

Borkin, A. (1971). 'Coreference and beheaded NP's'. Unpublished paper.

Gordon, D. and Lakoff, G. (1971). 'Conversational postulates'. *Chicago Linguistic Society*, **7**.

Grice, H. P. (1967). 'Logic and conversation'. Unpublished MS.

Karttunen, L. (1973). 'Presuppositions of compound sentences', *Linguistic Inquiry*, **4**, 2.

Lakoff, G. (1971). 'Presuppositions and relative well-formedness'. In Jacobovits and Steinberg, *Semantics*. Cambridge: Cambridge University Press.

—— (1972a). 'Linguistics and natural logic'. In G. Harman and D. Davidson, *Semantics for Natural Language*. Dordrecht: Reidel.

—— (1972b). 'Performative antinomies', *Foundations of Language*,

Lakoff, G. and Railton, P. (1971). 'Some types of presupposition and entailment in natural language'. Unpublished MS.

Lakoff, R. (1973). 'The logic of politeness: Or, minding your P's and Q's', *Chicago Linguistic Society*, 9.

Lewis, D. (1972). 'General semantics'. In G. Harman and D. Davidson, *Semantics for Natural Language*. Dordrecht: Reidel.

Postal, P. (1969). 'Anaphoric islands', *Chicago Linguistic Society*, 5.

Searle, J. (1969). *Speech Acts*. Cambridge: Cambridge University Press.

Changing the context

STEPHEN ISARD

Introduction

In recent years, the 'point of reference' has received considerable attention as a way of representing context in formal treatments of natural language. It encodes such information as who is speaking to whom, the time, what entities exist and what relations hold among them. It is an attempt to mirror the way in which the context forms a background against which a sentence can be true or false.

However, utterances do more than merely display themselves before a context and then vanish. They alter the context and become part of it. For instance, if I say

(1) I am a foreigner

I have not only said something with a truth value depending on the situation in which I speak, I have also created a new situation in which

(2) a. I just told you that I was a foreigner

will be true if I address it to the same audience, and

(2) b. He just told you that he was a foreigner

will be true if used by a third party. The usual sort of analysis in terms of reference points sets out truth conditions for (2a) and (2b) that make them true if appropriate entities stand in a 'telling' relation. But there is nothing in the analysis of (1) which expresses its power to put the entities into the relation. What I would like to propose is that we invest (1) with such power. That is, that we associate with sentences not just mappings from reference points to truth values but also operations which alter reference points, in order to represent the fact that not only are sentences interpreted in context, they contribute to context as well.

I shall attempt in this paper to point out some cases in which this approach yields a more satisfying explanation, and some examples of phenomena whose semantics seem to be involved much more with changes wrought by an utterance than with truth. As a general observation, I feel that a theory which allows a speaker to accomplish something by speaking makes a more promising start towards a larger theory of language use than one which just passes judgements on the propriety of what has been said.

Pronoun reference

One aspect of English in which context plays a crucial role is determining the referents of pronouns. Reference points are usually constructed so that the speaker and hearer can be 'looked up', and this provides referents for *I* and *you*. The treatment of *he*, *she* and *it* tends to be different (see, e.g., Montague (1970)) in that these words are taken to be multiply ambiguous, being surface representations of any of an infinite sequence of variables. Once a decision has somehow been made as to which variable is being represented in a sentence such as

(3) He was staring blankly out of the window

the value assigned to that variable becomes one of the factors in the reference point which determines whether the sentence is true. Of course, in the case where the variable is bound by a quantifier or other operator, as it would be in

(4) Anyone who believes that needs his head examined

neither the choice of variable nor its assignment is important, and the syntactic ambiguity, if it should really be called such, is not matched by any plethora of meanings.

Now, a more traditional account of (3) is that the pronoun *he* must have an antecedent somewhere in previous discourse and the reference of *he* is the same as that of the antecedent, as in the situation where (3) is preceded by

(5) I just looked in on the president

Partee (1972) and others have discussed difficulties that arise when this account is taken too literally, in particular when it is assumed that there is a single entity to which both antecedent and pronoun refer, but what must clearly be rescued from it is the idea that the interpretation of *he* can depend on what has gone before. One way of capturing this would be to have noun phrases like *the president* in (5) set the assignment of some variable, which the *he* in (3) could then represent. But this faces us with the pseudo-problem of making certain that the pronoun in the succeeding sentence represents the variable whose assignment has been set. It would not do to have the president waiting as the value of the first variable and then have (3) turn out to be about some underling who happened to be the value of the twenty-seventh. The brute force technique of making the president the value of all the variables will not work if we are to cope with exchanges like

(6) What did John say about Dick? He said that he looked like a drunken giraffe on ice skates

where two people are referred to by *he* in the same sentence.

The way in which to avoid this issue is to let *he*, *she* and *it* represent not variables, but more complex functions on the point of reference, which are able to take into account things like who has been recently mentioned, and in what role. The previous sentences must, of course, supply this information to the point of reference. Winograd (1972), although he does not discuss it in these terms, operates such a scheme for *it* with considerable success.

Notice that, since the antecedent of a pronoun may occur in the same sentence as the pronoun itself, as in

(7) The egg broke when I dropped it

the pronoun functions must have access to some information provided by the present sentence as well as previous ones.

Another small point, but worth remembering, is that a thing need not have been explicitly mentioned in order to be fair game for a pronoun. It only needs to be sufficiently prominent in the speaker and hearer's focus of attention. If a child reaches towards the lion's cage in order to pat the nice kitty, the zookeeper can say

(8) Be careful, he might bite you

without any previous reference to the lion. Therefore it is important to represent not just what has been mentioned, but what is being attended to. Atkinson and Griffiths (1973) have made suggestions about the representation of attention in a formalism of this general sort.

On the other hand, ordinary pronouns, as opposed to demonstratives, do seem to show a certain preference for mentioned items. Thus

(9) First square 19 and then cube it

is an instruction to perform both the squaring and cubing operations on the number 19, while

(10) First square 19 and then cube that

tells you to cube the square, which has not been explicitly mentioned, but has come to attention as the result of the first operation.

The situation changes if we actually mention the square, as in

(11) First take the square of 19 and then cube it

which I, at least, find ambiguous, since the *it* might refer to either 19 or its square.

Demonstratives

In the zoo scene just described, use of *he* without heavy stress was acceptable because the child was already paying attention to the lion. We can contrast this situation with one in which the keeper, standing before a group of cages, points in turn to the occupants of two of them and says

(12) *That* is dangerous, but *that* is not.

The function of the *that*s is not just to refer to something already attended to, but to indicate that the speaker is doing something, in this case something extra-linguistic, to distinguish a referent that his addressee may or may not have been attending to previously. If the keeper were to turn his back to the cages and put his hands in his pockets before uttering (12) his audience would be understandably confused.

Lewis (1970) considers the possibility of having an 'indicated object coordinate' in his points of reference, to provide referents for demonstratives. He sees a difficulty in the fact that the indicated object can change in the course of a sentence such as (12) and puts forward a solution involving sequences of indicated objects and a sequence of different words $that_1$, $that_2$, etc., with the nth word referring to the nth object.

I think it would be desirable to try to capture more directly the intuition that the indicated object changes. In fact, it seems worth noting that the indicated object *must* change in sentences like (12), where the second *that* receives stress.

We do not say

(13) That bit me so I kicked that

without stressing the second *that*, and in this case it must be something other than the biter that received the kick. If someone, a small child perhaps, *were* to utter (13) without stress on the second *that*, it would probably receive the interpretation that he had kicked whatever bit him, but I would consider this non-standard usage.

The moral, I think, is that the stress should be taken as a sign that the indicated object must be updated before we proceed any further. We must change the point of reference in mid-sentence. One can, in fact, concoct examples more natural than the child's use of (13) above in which unstressed *that* occurs and no updating takes place. Consider

(14) If you try to pat that lion, that lion will bite you
(15) I did that because I *felt* like doing that.

Notice that these are also cases in which *it* could replace *that*,

(16) If you try to pat that lion, it will bite you
(17) I did that because I *felt* like doing it

which is to be expected in view of the fact that indicated, but not newly indicated, objects are already in the focus of attention, and so are eligible for representation by ordinary pronouns. But in cases like (11) above where there are several objects being attended to, *it* might refer to any of them, while *that* shows a preference for the one on which attention has been focused most recently, as in (10).

Atkinson and Griffiths have treated, in their somewhat different framework, sentences like

(18) There goes a mouse!

whose interaction with the context in which it is spoken is rather complex. As in the cases above, the addressee must do some updating to clear away his initial question of *where?*. However, the extra twist here is that the speaker is using the mousehood of the object in question as part of his technique for drawing the addressee's attention to it. In some cases at least, the addressee cannot really be certain that he knows where 'there' is until he has found a mouse. Thus if there is a great stream of small rodents rushing past and the speaker sees a mouse among them, he can call the hearer's attention to it with (18), but he is less likely to use

(19) That's a mouse

because (19) involves, essentially, pointing it out first and predicating about it afterwards, and in the situation described, pointing out will be quite difficult.

In support of this analysis, or at least in support of the claim that (18) is certainly not the innocent existential assertion that it might at first glance appear to be, let me introduce two additional facts about it. First, it does not seem to have a negation. This is not to say that the addressee cannot object with

(20) That's no mouse

or

(21) There's no mouse there

but one might expect on purely syntactic grounds to be able to negate (18) with something like

(22) There doesn't go a mouse

and one cannot. I would claim that this is a symptom of the fact that (18), not being a simple assertion, does not have a corresponding denial, and the objections (20) and (21) do not so much say that (18) is false, as that the speaker, in trying to direct the audience's attention to a mouse, is attempting the impossible.

The other point is that (18) cannot be reported like an ordinary assertion. We do not say

(23) He said that (or told me that) there went a mouse

If the addressee found a mouse when he looked, he might say

(24) He pointed out a mouse to me

but otherwise he must resort to something like

(25) He tried to point out a mouse to me, but I didn't see one

Incomplete utterances

Longuet-Higgins (1972) has considered the problem of what information must be available for the successful interpretation of incomplete utterances like

(26) Will John?

He has constructed a computer program which maintains what amounts to an updatable point of reference, including such information as what people and events have been recently mentioned and whether in main or subordinate clauses. In a sequence of questions such as

(27) Did Charlie arrive after Al?

(28) Just after?

(29) Did Derek?

he is able to understand (29) as

(30) Did Derek arrive just after Al?

An interesting point that emerges in his work is that there are signals, notably change of tense, which indicate that certain information should be wiped out. In (27)–(29) above, the time clause *after Al* is understood as implicitly attached to (28) and (29). However, if we were to continue with

(31) Is Ed coming?

it would be improper to attach the clause, and it would continue to be wrong even if we switched back into the past tense with

(32) Did Bob?

Speech acts

Austin (1962) has taken the position that the speaker of a sentence such as

(33) I bet you 2½p that it will rain tomorrow

performs an act, the act of betting, and that his sentence has no truth value. Lewis (1970) argues that (33) should be assigned a truth value and that under normal circumstances this value will be 'true', because the speaker claims to be making a bet, and he *is* making a bet. He sees the situation as analogous to one in which I say 'I am tracing a line in the dust with my finger' while tracing a line in the dust with my finger. But Lewis is working within a framework where truth is defined with respect to points of reference, and the suggestion (Lewis (1970:59) that a sentence can be true because it is uttered would seem to require that its utterance must somehow be able to make points of reference where it is uttered into ones where it is true.

This is, of course, just what we are advocating here. That the formal consequence of Austin's act of betting should be to change the point of reference. The question of whether (33) itself should have a truth value then becomes much less important, because we have ensured that

(34) I have bet you 2½p that it will rain tomorrow

will be true immediately after an utterance of (33) under the sort of circumstances where Lewis wants to make (33) itself true.

The connection between sentence pairs such as (1), (2) and (33), (34) has led to proposals (see, e.g., Ross (1970)) that, for instance, (1) should be given a syntactic analysis making it look like *I assert to you that I am a foreigner*. I have no immediate quarrel with such an analysis as long as the semantic force of the *I assert to you* part is seen as operating upon the reference point, rather than determining the truth of the sentence.

However, I would not propose to account in this fashion for all of the ways in which one's speech can be reported. If I say

(35) That fool Cuthbert turned up at the party

it is then true that I have referred to Cuthbert as a fool, but I would be extremely wary of a syntactic analysis on the lines of *I refer to Cuthbert as a fool in the course of asserting to you that he turned up at the party (which, by the way, I also mention)*.

On the other hand, (35) must somehow record my allusion to Cuthbert in the point of reference. I think the appropriate course is to build some knowledge of how the language is used into the meaning of *refer to . . . as . . .* and have the point of reference store just a record of my sentence and its occasion of use. To say that I referred to Cuthbert as a fool is then to say that one of my sentences applied the description *fool* to Cuthbert, but not that the sentence announced that it was doing this. It just did it.

Proofs

So far we have discussed changes in the situation which the speaker can bring about with a minimum of help from his addressee. We have been taking for granted that the addressee understands what has been said and remembers it for a reasonable period of time. There has not been any assumption that the addressee necessarily believes what he is told, or otherwise acts upon it. In Davies and Isard (1972) we discussed some effects that speakers can try to achieve with more active cooperation of the addressee. In particular, changes in his beliefs and predispositions as well as in his focus of attention.

I would like here to touch on a sort of intermediate case, that in which the speaker is trying to convince his audience of something. This does need a certain amount of cooperation from the addressee, in that it often requires some effort to follow an argument. On the other hand, if he does follow it, he accepts its conclusion on his own, so to speak, and not just because the speaker has asked him to, as in the case of an ordinary assertion.

In a chain of reasoning, as opposed to just any series of true assertions, the speaker is trying, with each link of the chain, to put the hearer's system of beliefs into a state where it will automatically accept the next link that is presented. In a mathematical proof, for instance, it is not sufficient just for all the lines to be true. They have to be in the right order with the right size steps between them. *Therefore the result follows from Rolle's Theorem* might make a good ending for a proof of the Mean Value Theorem, but it certainly will not do for an opening line.

In many formal deductive systems, especially systems of natural deduction, proofs are not defined just as sequences of formulae, but as sequences of lines which contain formulae and some other symbols as well. In Quine (1959), for instance, one finds lines of the form

$$*(6) \quad (x)Gx \ (5)y$$

where 6 is the number of the line itself, 5 is the number of the line from which it is said to follow, and the other symbols indicate the application of certain rules of inference, and have a bearing on what can be legitimately inferred later on.

I would contend that certain words and expressions in English, like *hence, therefore, by the Third Sylow Theorem*, and *let y be such a number* play the same sort of role as these extra trappings in natural deductive systems. That is, they do not affect the truth, with respect to any model, of the assertion with which they are associated. Instead, they say something about the sequence of changes of belief that the speaker is trying to induce. To say that something follows by the Third Sylow Theorem is not just to say that it is true in all models where the Third Sylow Theorem holds. This would make every theorem follow by every other one. The claim is rather that the hearer of the proof can, by combining the Third Sylow Theorem in some manner with other of his beliefs, come to believe the new assertion as well.

Conclusion

I have tried to make a case for constructing a formalism to capture the way in which language interacts with the context in which it is used. I want to do this partly because I believe that there are aspects of English which cannot be understood otherwise, but mostly because I think it is an intrinsically interesting problem in its own right, and one through which the claim that the study of language will illuminate the workings of the mind can be borne out.

While it might appear that I am suggesting a journey into wild and uncharted territory, this is not really the case at all. High level computing languages present a paradigm case of languages which can alter the context with respect to which they are being interpreted. A glance through, e.g., Burstall et al. (1971), will reward the reader with many examples of expressions which alter their environment while computing their truth values, and many with no truth values at all. Furthermore, these languages even meet the criteria of learnability and scrutability set out by Davidson (1970) and they are learned by people and 'scruted' by machines every day.

Acknowledgements

I am indebted to Martin Atkinson, Kit Fine, Patrick Griffiths, Christopher Longuet-Higgins, John Lyons and Barry Richards both for stimulating discussions on these topics and for criticisms of an earlier draft manuscript.

I was supported by a research grant from the S.R.C. during the period when this paper was written.

REFERENCES

Atkinson, M. and Griffiths, P. D. (1973). 'Here's here's, there's, here and there'. In *Edinburgh Working Papers in Linguistics*, **3**.

Austin, J. L. (1962). *How to do Things with Words*. Cambridge, Mass.: Harvard University Press.

Burstall, R. M., Collins, J. S. and Popplestone, R. J. (1971). *Programming in POP-2*. Edinburgh: Edinburgh University Press.

Davidson, D. (1970). 'Semantics for natural languages'. In B. Visentini, ed., *Linguaggi nella Società e nella Tecnica*, pp. 177–88. Milan: Edizioni di Communità.

Davies, D. J. M. and Isard, S. (1972). 'Utterances as programs'. In D. Michie and B. Meltzer, eds., *Machine Intelligence*, **7**, 325–39. Edinburgh: Edinburgh University Press.

Lewis, D. (1970). 'General semantics', *Synthese*, **22**, 18–67.

Longuet-Higgins, H. C. (1972). 'The algorithmic description of natural language', *Proceedings of the Royal Society London B*, **182**, 255–76.

Montague, R. (1970). 'Universal grammar', *Theoria*, **36**, 373–98.

Partee, B. H. (1972). 'Opacity, coreference, and pronouns'. In G. Harman and D. Davidson, eds., *Semantics of Natural Languages*, pp. 415–41.

Quine, W. V. (1959). *Methods of Logic*. New York: Henry Holt.

Ross, J. R. (1970). 'On declarative sentences'. In R. Jacobs and P. Rosenbaum, eds., *Readings in Transformational Grammar*, pp. 222–77. Boston, Mass.: Blaisdell.

Winograd, T. (1972). *Understanding Natural Language*. Edinburgh: Edinburgh University Press.

Conditions of the use of sentences and a semantic representation of topic and focus

PETR SGALL

The main objective of this paper is to discuss the correspondence between the semantic structure of sentences and a structuring of the universe of discourse in a given time-point of the discourse.

Some possibilities of a classification of presuppositions, assertions and also allegations with respect to the distinction between a given world (state of affairs) and the points of reference (pragmatic context of an utterance token) are analysed in section 1. Chomsky's use of the term 'presupposition' is rejected as misleading, since the topic (i.e. the elements not belonging to the focus of the sentence) refers to items not only known, but activated in the given time-point of the utterance (section 2). Chomsky's range of permissible focus is shown to be determined by the hierarchy of communicative dynamism of the sentence (given by a systemic ordering of participants of verbs in the grammar and by contextual boundness); his choice of focus corresponds to the placement of the juncture between contextually bound and non-bound elements (section 3). If the scale of communicative dynamism of the participants of a verb is denoted, in semantic representation (SR), by a linear ordering of the participants, and the placement of boundness juncture is included, too, then – as demonstrated on crucial examples in section 4 – a semantically-based generative description can be formulated in which neither global constraints nor semantically relevant transformations are needed.

1.

For decades, structural linguists have pointed out the distinction between linguistic meaning and cognitive or ontological content (in other terms, between the form and the substance of the content, *Bedeutung* and *Bezeichnung*, etc.),[1] arguing that only the former is a proper object of linguistic study, while the latter is connected with rather complex conditions given by the situation referred to so that it cannot be fully accounted for by

[1] See Hjelmslev (1943), and, in a somewhat extreme formulation, Coseriu (1970).

linguistic means alone. Within algebraic linguistics, transformationalists (especially the adherents of generative semantics) study the level of content directly (cf. Rohrer (1971:81 and 88–99)) without exploring the above-mentioned dichotomy, whereas some others regard the semantic structure of the sentence to be a matter of meaning, not of content.[1]

In logic, the discussions concerning sentences and their uses, utterances and statements (initiated by Strawson (1972), Bar-Hillel (1954)), and illocutionary acts (Austin (1962), Searle (1970), and others), though bringing insights of basic importance, display what was called 'neglect of linguistics' by Bar-Hillel (1965:292).

Thus, the empirical findings of linguistics were not formulated with regard to the requirements of modern methodology, and the results of logical discussions were not systematically applied in linguistic investigations. Only in the past few years does this difficult situation begin to change; a true dialogue between linguistic and logical semantics has started with the writings of Montague (1970a,b), Dana Scott (1970) and others, and with reactions of linguists to these and other logical analyses. In resuming and commenting on some of them, Dahl (1972) arrives at results showing that at least one aspect of the dichotomy of content and meaning can already be discussed explicitly. By this we mean, first of all, his analysis of Montague's 'sense' and 'meaning'. As Dahl's analysis of the example of *the leader of the British Labour Party* shows, the meaning is constant for different uses of the phrase, while the sense varies not only with varying speech situations, but also with other points of reference (the time-point of the event, in this case). This variation of the sense – and, with it, of the ontological content – makes the sense rather inaccessible for direct linguistic analysis. The meaning of the sentence is determined (not always uniquely, but with a finite number of resulting values) by the structure of the sentence, whereas the number of senses of a sentence may be infinite. It is the relationship between meaning and sense, which most probably cannot be described recursively or computed, in the sense of computibility discussed by Bar-Hillel (1966:283–5).

This supports the view that an SR of a sentence should not be conceived of as denoting a sense of the sentence (or its ontological content, which includes reference to some individual phenomena of a certain possible

---

[1] In the functional generative description, as elaborated in the Prague group, this dichotomy was discussed and illustrated by Sgall and Hajičová (1970); in Panevová and Sgall (1973) it is shown that in some situations such sentences as *The animal we saw is/was a chipmunk* can be used with an identical content, though their meaning is not identical; in Weisheitelová and Sgall (1971: 176) such examples as *I know whether Tom is here* are characterized as rather odd with respect to their content but not to their meaning.

world and a certain pragmatic context). If transformationalists using a performative hypersentence in the sense of the Ross–Sadock hypothesis actually attempt to account directly for the content or for the sense (see Dahl (1972)), then the hypersentence in an SR would have to include elements referring unambiguously to an individual speaker, hearer, place and time point of an utterance of a sentence having this SR. This is, of course, not the case, and so in this respect the SR differs from the sense, and also from a statement (having a truth value), as well as from a formula of the (modified, complemented, etc.) predicate calculus.

There are at least two other aspects in which an SR should differ from a logical formula. The first of them concerns the fact that the statements entailed by an SR do not belong to a single level, i.e. the meaning of a sentence cannot be defined as the set of all statements entailed by the sentence. The distinction between presupposition and assertion (meaning proper) is well known, and it can be argued that the use of iota and lambda operators or similar means makes it possible to render this distinction in the form of logical formulae, too. But it should be noticed that beside meaning proper (the negation of which is entailed by the corresponding negative SR) and presuppositions (entailed by negative as well as by positive SRs) also a third type has been found, namely *allegation* (which is entailed by a positive SR, while neither it itself, nor its negation are entailed by the corresponding negative SR); see Hajičová (1971; in press)[1].

Let us illustrate our viewpoint with an example:[2]

(1) My husband caused a misunderstanding between two lawyers living in Washington, D.C.

(2) The speaker is a woman

(3) There live(d) at least two lawyers in Washington, D.C.

(4) There was a misunderstanding between two lawyers living in Washington, D.C.

(5) The speaker's husband caused a misunderstanding between two lawyers living in Washington, D.C.

[1] Keenan and Hull's (1973) Definition 2 would characterize every allegation as an assertion, so that (4), which is entailed by (1), but not by its negation (6), would be considered as an assertion of (1), see point (c) of their Definition; but then – with the common understanding of *assertion* or *meaning proper* – (4) would have to be false in any state of affairs in which (6) is true; see the discussion in Strawson (1952, esp. p. 213), and Fillmore (1969, pp. 120ff.).

[2] The surface sentences replace here certain SRs for the sake of simplicity only; some of the points where a difference between a sentence and one of its SRs (as well as a corresponding statement) is relevant will be discussed below, in a rudimentary form; a more comprehensive discussion can be found in Sgall, Hajičová, and Benešová (1973). It should be noted that we deal only with declarative sentences. Where necessary, the word bearing the intonation centre is written in capital letters.

(6) My husband didn't cause a misunderstanding between two lawyers
     living in Washington, D.C.

Under a certain reading (1) presupposes (2) and (3), and (5) can be said
to characterize the meaning proper of (1) – if surface paraphrases may be
used to illustrate roughly, without an explicit elaboration, some items
important for the present discussion. But (4) is an allegation of (1), since it
is entailed by it, but neither it nor its negation is entailed by (6).

If we are allowed to abbreviate *the fulfillment of x by the given world and
the given points of reference is a necessary condition for the given use (utterance
token) of y to be true (or meaningful)* by '*x is a semantic prerequisite of the
truth (or meaningfulness) of y*, then we can say:

(a) *meaning proper* is a semantic prerequisite of the truth of a use of a
     sentence, the corresponding negative SR being connected in the same
     way with a negation of the given meaning;
(b) a *presupposition* is a semantic prerequisite of the meaningfulness of
     an SR (as well as of its negative counterpart);
(c) an *allegation* is a semantic prerequisite of the meaningfulness of an
     SR in which the allegation is not negated (i.e. it is not inside the
     scope of a negation operator).

It would be possible to say that (2) is a pragmatic presupposition, and
(3) a logical one,[1] in the sense of Keenan (1971), and, furthermore, that an
SR should be so formulated as to determine the logical presuppositions,
while the pragmatic ones can be specified only with respect to individual
utterance tokens or occurrences of the sentence (under the given reading),
i.e., more exactly with respect to specific points of reference. Meaning
proper and allegation could be classified along similar lines. In this case the
hypersentence with *I, you, here* and *now* would be adequate. But let us
examine briefly Keenan's (1971) classification of presuppositions: He
distinguishes between logical and pragmatic presuppositions, the former
being defined 'solely in terms of abstract sentences and the world', and the
latter concerning the necessity that the context of an utterance be appropriate (where '*utterance*' means utterance token, and context includes the
speaker, addressee or audience, and the physical and 'cultural' environment
of the utterance). Let us add here some remarks on his reasoning.

First, Keenan's logical presuppositions concern not only an 'abstract
sentence', but also, in a sense, its utterance tokens: some of them can meet
the presuppositions, being either true (as (7) when referring to a couple

[1] But see below, as for the question of the time-point of (3).

named Fred and Sally who met in Chicago), or untrue (as (7) when referring to a couple bearing these names who met elsewhere), and others may
'make no sense at all', i.e. not meet the logical presuppositions of the
sentence (as (7) when referring to two people named Fred and Sally who
have not met at all).

(7) CHICAGO is where Fred met Sally

Second, it is not exact to say that *Fred met Sally* is a presupposition of
(7); what is presupposed is that he met her before the time point of uttering (7). Similarly, we were not exact in saying above that (3) is a presupposition of (1); rather, every statement having the form of (1) presupposes that
at a time point prior to the uttering of this statement at least two lawyers
lived in Washington, D.C. Only if (1) were replaced by such a sentence as
(1') and (3) by (3'), we could say that the chosen SR (in all its utterance
tokens used as statements) presupposed (3').

(1') My husband caused a misunderstanding concerning the prime
    numbers greater than 17
(3') There are prime numbers greater than 17

Thus we see that only in such specific cases (where the expression is not
indexical) can the presuppositions be defined 'solely in terms of abstract
sentences [more precisely, by their SRs] and the world'. In the general
case, the presupposition is a statement (with all points of reference being
specified), and it is determined not by an SR as such, but by a corresponding statement.

Third, it is necessary to account for presuppositions concerning the
pragmatic context; for instance, the sex of the speaker may be relevant in
English as well as in languages having specific forms of gender with verbs
or personal pronouns. The sentence (8) may be uttered (leaving jokes
aside) only by a male speaker, similarly as (9) requires a speaker having a
sister.

(8) My wife is fond of Chomsky's EST
(9) My sister came LATE to-night

If a traveller in a bus utters the sentence (10), having seen that the driver
is long-haired and not having realized in time that, in the given country,
this does not determine the sex of a person uniquely, he may commit an
error consisting in the use of a false presupposition of a similar kind (the
physical environment of the utterance is involved here, if we understand
the term correctly); this error is of the same nature (in the aspect of interest

to us here, i.e. the relationship between sentences, utterances, presuppositions, the given world and the environment of the utterance) as if (11) instead of (12), or (13) instead of (14) is used.

(10) Our driver must know her bus well if she dares to go through these narrow streets of the Old TOWN

(11) The blond lady in the third row has nice HAIR

(12) The blond gentleman in the third row has nice HAIR

(13) This time John's victory was caused by HARRY

(14) This time John's defeat was caused by HARRY

On the other hand, if the French sentence (15) is used (or if a German speaker uses *du* instead of *Sie*) in such a case where the addressee is neither an animal, a child, a person socially inferior to the speaker, nor personally intimate with him,[1] a sentence has been used which is not appropriate from a certain point of view that does not affect its truth conditions: the addressee may react indignantly or harshly, but he will understand.

(15) Tu es dégoûtant

Furthermore, one should take into consideration also cases in which the 'semantic prerequisites' concern the given world as well as the points of reference: if, in (1), we replace *Washington, D.C.* by *our town*, this NP is then connected (in Keenan's terms) with a logical and a pragmatic presupposition at the same time: the statement presupposes that there is a town with two lawyers in the given world, and also that the sentence is uttered by a speaker living in such a town.

We may conclude that a distinction is to be made between presuppositions and between conditions restricting the appropriate use of a certain sentence from a social point of view. The former, i.e. presuppositions, are determined and either met or non-met by a statement, i.e. by a particular utterance token of the given sentence.[2] The status of the latter conditions has much in common with stylistic criteria, and we do not pay attention to them in the sequel. Among Keenan's examples those taken from French

---

[1] It could be added that the use of *du* and *Sie*, etc., in some cases (e.g. between people who meet and communicate regularly) is given by a convention of usage.

[2] To say that a statement determines a presupposition P or that a statement presupposes P (by which our previous formulation is made more precise) means, of course, that every speaker who makes the statement presupposes P (the two variants of the case frame of the verb *presuppose* are parallel to the two variants of that of *mean, complete, open, break*, etc.); if Garner (1971:28) argues against claiming that a statement does the presupposing by objecting that with *the present king of France* 'there *is* no statement to do the presupposing', it should be noticed that the presupposition as a matter of fact is determined even here by the statement including this noun phrase: *There is no person that would claim to be the present king of France* (as uttered in different periods) shows that the NP itself is not neccessarily connected with the presupposition.

and Biloxi may belong to the latter type, the other being genuine presuppositions.

Other difficulties are connected with the well-known indeterminacy of proper names (in general they do not have a unique reference, see Bar-Hillel (1954)), as well as with the fact that such expressions as *in front of a house* may be understood with this or that sense of *in front of* (concerning either the relative position of the house and the speaker – i.e. the pragmatic context, or only the shape and position of the house; see Piťha (1972:248f; Dahl:1972). Even such sentences where proper names can be understood as unambiguous, as *Shakespeare was a great poet* or *Napoleon I was defeated at Waterloo* are connected with semantic prerequisites concerning the pragmatic context: before the birth of the cited hero they could not be used appropriately, with a truth value (in Bar-Hillel's terms they are indexical since they contain tensed verbs). Only tautologies (analogical to Carnap's L-true statements), true in all possible worlds, have the property of all their utterance tokens being true, independently of the pragmatic context or of the points of reference.

2.

Another (and deeper) distinction between the common shape of logical formulae and the semantic structure of the sentence is derived from the fact that the sentence developed as a form of a message, of an element of communication. When uttering a sentence, a speaker wants to make the hearer(s) change in some respect some points of the information stored in his (their) memory. The sentence is adapted to its functioning in communication in that it contains a distinction between those items of the universe of discourse shared by the speaker and hearer that should be identified easily by the hearer as points in which the change of information should be anchored, and those items that specify the change itself.[1] The former items correspond to the elements of the topic (or contextually bound segment)[2] of the sentence, the latter to those of the focus. Not every element of the universe of discourse can be referred to by (a part of) the topic of a sentence. A certain hierarchy (having, perhaps, the form of a partial ordering) of these elements must be assumed, and only elements above a certain level or 'threshold' in this hierarchy (i.e. items not only known to the speaker

---

[1] See Õim's (1973) formulations concerning the messages as 'instructions for the hearer to modify his knowledge of the word in definite points and in definite ways' (p. 363); also Keenan and Hull's (1973) notions of informativeness and of discourse presuppositions.
[2] Regarding this notion, see section 3 below.

and to the hearer, but having been activated or foregrounded by the preceding co-text or situation) can be referred to by the topic. We shall see in section 4 that this dichotomy must be taken into account if the semantics of sentences containing two different operators (e.g. a quantifier and negation) is to be accounted for.

To understand well the role these two types of units play in the course of the change of the structure of the universe of discourse during the process of communication, it is useful to notice that Chomsky's terminological identification of presupposition and that part of the sentence which does not belong to the focus obscures the matter. If the sentence could be divided into focus and presupposition, then two sentences differing only in the position of the boundary between these two parts would differ in that the presuppositions of one of them would be included in those of the other, i.e. the former could be used appropriately in all cases in which the latter could, but not vice versa. As the examples (16) and (17) show, this is not the case.[1]

(16) a. Charles went / to his aunt for MONEY
    b. Charles went for money / to his AUNT
    c. Charles went to his aunt / for MONEY

(17) a. Henry brought / Jane a BOOK
    b. Henry brought a book / to JANE
    c. Henry brought Jane / a BOOK

In (16b) the NP *money* is included in the topic, from which it follows that it is presupposed, while in (16a) it is in the focus, and, being indefinite (at least in one of the possible SRs), it is not presupposed; in (16c), the NP *his aunt* is included in the topic, while in the examples (a) and (b) it is in the focus; but being a definite NP, it is connected with a corresponding presupposition. This would lead to a result according to which (16b) could be used only in the cases in which (16a) and (16c) could. But this is not the case. The sentence (16b), and not (16a) can be used as an answer to such a question as *To whom did Charles go for money?* Furthermore, the conditions of use of (16a) and (16c) are not identical (as they should be, according to Chomsky's use of the term presupposition), since only the former can be used as an answer to *Where did Charles go?* if his aunt is not in the foreground of the stock of knowledge shared by the speaker and the hearer; on the other hand, such a question as *For what did Charles go to his aunt?* can be answered by (16c) but not by (16a).

---

[1] The sign '/' denotes the juncture between the topic and the focus (i.e. the quoted surface sentence stands for an SR meeting this condition).

The three sentences of the example (17) have similar properties, and here also the use of none of them is narrower than that of some other, since for each of them there are questions which can be answered only by this SR (and every question represents a certain type of situation).

This shows that presuppositions are not the only kind of conditions of use of a sentence. Among other types of conditions (not to speak about various other pragmatic aspects of the situation of the discourse) there are those covered by the vague formulation of 'what is spoken about', or, in other words, what part of the stock of knowledge shared by the speaker and the hearer(s) has already been activated in the given part of the discourse (by the preceding context or by the given situation), i.e. what is in the foreground of the shared knowledge.

This distinction can be illustrated more clearly by the fact that an element of the foreground of the shared knowledge can be referred to in two distinct ways in an utterance token: either it is only mentioned as an element known to the hearer, identifiable, recoverable (in Halliday's meaning of the term), its relationship to other item(s) being stated in the utterance; or else it is used as a part of the 'new information', it is brought into a relation to another known item, being chosen among other possible candidates that could bear this relation to that item. In the former case the given element is included in the topic, like *his aunt* in (16c) or *money* in (16b), in the latter case it is inside the focus. On the other hand, an element not belonging to the foreground of the stock of shared knowledge can be used only in the focus, when it is first mentioned in a coherent text.[1]

There are situations and contexts allowing a free choice between these two possibilities of a use of an NP. If, for instance, the hearer knows that the speaker stays at his aunt's and that he and his aunt both lend money to his brother Charles from time to time, and Charles was just mentioned as having gone to his aunt's house, then the speaker can choose one of the SRs of the example (16); if it is more or less clear that this time Charles has gone for money, he chooses (b); if it is fairly clear that Charles visited the aunt, he chooses (c); and if neither of the two can be supposed to be known to the hearer, then the speaker chooses (a).

A similar example is that of (18) followed by (19a) or (19b):

(18) Yesterday was the last day of the Davis cup match between Australia and the U.S.

(19) a. Australia WON the match
   b. The match was won by AUSTRALIA

---

[1] By such a use in the focus, this element enters, in the given time-point of the text, the foreground of the stock.

Here the motives for the choice of (19a) or (19b) as following (18) are given by the conditions of the formulation of the text itself rather than by the situation.[1]

In other cases the choice between the two quoted possibilities of a use of an NP is not free, e.g. (20) can be followed only by (21), where *some money* is inside the topic, and not by (22), where this NP is included in the focus:[2]

(20) John looked for some MONEY
(21) He GOT some (money)
(22) He got some MONEY

3.

Chomsky's (1968) notions of focus and of the range of permissible focus are closely related to some of the notions that have been studied in Europe under such headings as topic and comment, information focus, functional sentence perspective, etc.[3] If we understand Chomsky's notions well, then in the sentences (23) and (24) the range of permissible focus permits various choices of focus, most of which are denoted in our examples by the occurrences of the symbol '/', but also *found in the garden* and *studies at Oxford* may be chosen as foci. In (25) and (26) the choice of focus is determined uniquely, the focus includes here the locative NP only.

(23) Harry / found / Jane / in the GARDEN
(24) Harry / studies / chemistry / at OXFORD
(25) It was in the GARDEN where Harry found Jane
(26) It is at OXFORD where Harry studies chemistry

This can be checked by questions answered properly[4] by the given sentences: the questions (27) to (30) can be answered by (23), while e.g. (31) to (33) cannot, the proper answer to them being (34), in the given situation.

(27) Where did Harry find Jane?

---

[1] See also the examples given in Sgall (1974) and Kuno's (1972:275ff.) example (2–3).
[2] Unless *money* were in contrast to a following context such as...*but he lost a FRIEND*.
[3] For questions of topic/comment articulation (TCA) see e.g. Firbas (1964; 1971), Sgall (1967; 1972a); one of the characteristic features of the focus is what Kuno (1972) calls 'exhaustive listing'; see Keenan and Hull (1973:§3.3) about complete and incomplete answers.
[4] The relationship between questions and answers as considered here concerns sentences only, but in other respects it fulfils, if I am not mistaken, conditions parallel to those required by Keenan and Hull (1973).

(28) Whom did Harry find where?

(29) What did Harry do then?

(30) What about Harry and Jane?

(31) What happened in the garden?

(32) What did Harry do in the garden?

(33) Whom did Harry find in the garden?

(34) Harry found JANE in the garden

An empirical investigation of many sentences in Czech[1] (where the word order is connected more closely with TCA than in English, so that some properties of TCA are more accessible here, since the word order is more transparent than intonation) has led to the following results, which are, as far as the author is able to say, valid also for English:

1. Every element of a topic is contextually bound, i.e. it always refers to an item that is activated in the given time-point of the utterance of that sentence (or, in the sense of section 2, it is above a certain threshold of the hierarchy concerning the given universe of discourse at that moment).

2. For at least some of the participants of the same verb token (Tesnière's *actants* and *circonstants*, Fillmore's cases, etc.) a linear ordering can be defined,[2] called the systemic ordering and denoted by S, such that if, in an SR, none of these participants is contextually bound, for every pair of participants P_j, P_k it holds that if there is a permissible focus including P_k and not including P_j, then $S(P_j, P_k)$ holds.

3. The verb token governing the participants P_i may be contextually bound or non-bound; the main verb of the sentence is in the focus if it is non-bound, and outside the focus, if it is bound.

4. For every SR of a sentence there is a linear ordering C defined for all its elements (i.e. for the verb and for all of its participants), having the following properties:

4a. if $C(P_i, V)$ holds, then P_i is contextually bound and outside the focus (i.e. in the topic);

4b. if $C(V, P_i)$ holds, then P_i is non-bound and included in the focus;

4c. if P_j and P_k are included in the focus, then $C(P_j, P_k)$ holds iff also $S(P_j, P_k)$ holds.

The ordering C can be interpreted as the scale of communicative dynamism (cf. Firbas (1964; 1971), Sgall (1967; 1972a), if this scale is

---

[1] See Sgall (1973) for a more detailed discussion; only the structure of the sentence nucleus (verb and its participants) rather than that of the NP is studied here.

[2] It is not clear whether this ordering is language dependent or general, but at least the position of some of the main participants seems to be identical in such languages as English and Czech or Russian.

attributed not to the surface shape but to an SR of the sentence. If this ordering is denoted by the left-to-right order of the elements of the SR,[1] then the SR may have the following shape

$$\text{(x)}\ P_{a_1}, \ldots, P_{a_j}, V, P_{a_{j+1}} \ldots, P_{a_n}$$

Besides that, it is necessary to denote the bound or non-bound character of the verb. In the sequel, we use the superscript b in case the verb is bound.

4.

Let us suppose that the participants Agentive, Dative, Instrument, Objective, Origin have, under the systemic ordering S, this order. In an SR the participants that are contextually non-bound, i.e. included in the focus, are ordered in accordance with S and they follow the verb. If they are bound, they precede the verb and their mutual order is conditioned by other factors. Thus, the SR has the shape (x), where all the pairs (P_r, P_s) for $r > a_j$, $r + 1 = s \leq n$, are elements of S (this binary relation being regarded as a set of pairs). The rules of transductive components of the description (transformational or other) determine then certain changes in their linear ordering, as was illustrated by the two elementary rules formulated in Sgall (1972a, b). Using the present notation, we can state them briefly as follows:[2]

(i) If (P_r, P_s) is an element of C and (P_s, P_r) is an element of S, it is possible to exchange the positions of the two participants in the representation of the sentence.

(ii) If the condition of (i) holds and (i) has not been applied, replace V by its conversion form $V_{r,s}$, exchange the position of the two NPs and assign a derived case value to each of them (i.e. the preposition *by* instead of Agentive or Instrument, the preposition *to* instead of Dative, and zero instead of Objective or Origin).

We may say quite briefly and informally that, in English, if an Objective is contextually bound, while the Agentive of the given sentence is included in the focus (i.e., if the Objective is topicalized), there are at least two possibilities: either the order Objective – Verb – Agentive is retained in

---

[1] This order is not extrinsic, but has been stated on the basis of a comparative study of languages with 'fixed' and 'free' word order; even in the latter class of languages, word order in the general case is relevant for the semantic interpretation of sentences, contrary to what is claimed by Bartsch and Vennemann (1972:38).

[2] The position of the verb and other necessary adjustments of the rules are discussed elsewhere (see p. 299 n.2). As for the tentative ordering, some arguments suggested by Kirkwood support the placement of Origin before Objective.

surface structure and a passive form of the verb is used (cf. (35b) below), or the order is reversed to Agentive – Verb – Objective, but the Agentive may then bear the intonation centre. In other cases, where e.g. the Origin is topicalized, the situation is similar, only an 'inversion form' of the verb other than passive is used (the form with *into* replacing *out of* in our examples (38b) and (39b) below; it is shown in Sgall (1972b), on the basis of independent evidence, that these inversion forms are to be regarded as secondary forms of the corresponding 'deep structure verbs'). The verb stands, in the surface form of English sentences, in the second position, and can be followed by contextually bound elements, even if it is non-bound. A more detailed (and more exact) discussion of these and other questions (including the semantics of negation) is given in Sgall, Hajičová and Benešová (1973); here we would like to illustrate our point by some of the much discussed examples that require, within the usual transformational framework, either such strong devices as Lakoff's global constraints, or such obliteration of the framework as Chomsky's direct semantic interpretation of (phonetically interpreted) surface structures. The non-synonymous sentences differing only in the scope of focus (i.e. in the placement of the boundness juncture and, eventually, in the scale of communicative dynamism), have different SRs (or deep structures, in Chomsky's terminology), and the transduction rules do not make it possible to derive a sentence from the SR of its non-synonymous counterpart.

We give here, under every example, its SR, with many simplifications; the inner structure of NPs is not examined here; the participants of a verb are each included in a pair of parentheses (so that our notation is equivalent to a dependency tree, which is compatible with Fillmore's Case Theory as well as with the general properties of a TG, see Robinson (1970)), and the types of participants (cases) are denoted by subscripts; the superscript b is added iff the verb is contextually bound (in our examples the sentences are ambiguous on this point,[1] which is denoted by the inclusion of this superscript in parentheses). Notice that the participants standing to the left of the verb in the SR are contextually bound, while those standing to its right are not. The intonation centre of the sentences is denoted by capital letters.

(35) a. Many men read few BOOKS
((many men)$_{Ag}$ read$^{(b)}$ (few books)$_{Obj}$)

---

[1] The verb is unambiguously contextually bound, e.g., in cleft sentences. For the treatment of negation see Hajičová (in press); since a contextually bound verb can be either preceded or followed by the operator of negation, the SRs in example (37) below correspond only to some readings of the quoted sentences.

b. Few books are read by many MEN
   ((few books)$_{Obj}$ read $^{(b)}$(many men)$_{Ag}$)

(36) a. Each of us knows two LANGUAGES
   ((each of us)$_{Dat}$ know$^{(b)}$ (two languages)$_{Obj}$)

b. Two languages are known to each of US
   ((two languages)$_{Obj}$ know$^{(b)}$ (each of us)$_{Dat}$)

(37) a. Many arrows didn't hit the TARGET
   ((many arrows)$_{Inst}$not hit$^{(b)}$ (the target)$_{Obj}$)

b. The target wasn't hit by many ARROWS
   ((the target)$_{Obj}$ not hit$^{(b)}$ (many arrows)$_{Inst}$)

(38) a. Every oak developed out of an ACORN
   ((every oak)$_{Obj}$ developed$^{(b)}$ (an acorn)$_{Orig}$)

b. Every acorn developed into an OAK
   ((every acorn)$_{Orig}$ developed$^{(b)}$ (an oak)$_{Obj}$)

c. An OAK developed out of every acorn
   ((every acorn)$_{Orig}$ developed$^{(b)}$ (an oak)$_{Obj}$)

(39) a. I made every canoe out of a LOG
   ((I)$_{Ag}$ made$^{(b)}$ (every canoe)$_{Obj}$ (a log)$_{Orig}$)

b. I made every log into a CANOE
   ((I)$_{Ag}$ (every log)$_{Orig}$ made$^{(b)}$ (a canoe)$_{Obj}$)

c. I made a CANOE out of every log
   ((I)$_{Ag}$ (every log)$_{Orig}$ made$^{(b)}$ (a canoe)$_{Obj}$)

It can be seen that the sentences (b) and (c) have identical SRs, in each of our last two examples, while – as required by Fillmore (1970) – our rules do not allow for an analogous counterpart of the sentences (a); see the discussion in Sgall (1972b). In all cases, the distinction between topic (or Chomsky's presupposition) and focus is determined uniquely by our SRs (by the ordering of the verb and its participants and by the presence or absence of the superscript on the verb).

Our framework allows for a unified and relatively simple description of topic and focus both in languages with grammatically 'fixed' word order as well as in those with relatively 'free' word order, and no global constraints or semantically relevant transformations are needed.

REFERENCES

Austin, J. L. (1962). *How to Do Things with Words.* Oxford.

Bar-Hillel, Y. (1954). 'Indexical expressions', *Mind*, **63**, 359–79. Reprinted in and quoted from Bar-Hillel (1970), pp. 69–88.

—— (1965). 'Kybernetika a lingvistika' ('Cybernetics and Linguistics'). In *Kybernetika ve společenských vědách*, pp. 255–64. Prague. Translated in and quoted from Bar-Hillel (1970), pp. 289–301.

—— (1966). 'Do natural languages contain paradoxes?', *Studium generale*, **19**, 391–7. Reprinted in and quoted from Bar-Hillel (1970), pp. 273–85.

—— (1970). *Aspects of Language*. Jerusalem.

Bartsch, R. and Vennemann T. (1972). *Semantic Structures*. Frankfurt a. M.

Chomsky, N. (1968). 'Deep structure, surface structure and semantic interpretation'. Mimeo. Printed in and quoted from N. Chomsky, *Studies on Semantics in Generative Grammar* (1972), pp. 62–119. The Hague.

Coseriu, E. (1970). 'Semantik, innere Sprachform und Tiefenstruktur', *Folia linguistica*, **4**, 53–63.

Dahl, Ö. (1972). 'On points of reference', *Logical Grammar Reports*, No. 1. Göteborg.

Fillmore, C. J. (1969). 'Types of lexical information'. In F. Kiefer, ed., *Studies in Syntax and Semantics*, pp. 109–37. Dordrecht-Holland.

—— (1970). 'Subjects, speakers, and roles', *Synthese*, **21**, 251–74.

Firbas, J. (1964). 'On defining the theme in functional sentence analysis', *TLP*. **1**, 267–80. Prague.

—— (1971). 'On the concept of communicative dynamism in the theory of functional sentence perspective', *Sb. prací fil. fak. brněnské univ.*, A **19**, 135–44.

Garner, R. (1971). ' "Presupposition" in philosophy and linguistics'. In C. J. Fillmore and D. T. Langendoen, eds., *Studies in Linguistic Semantics*, pp. 22–42. New York.

Hajičová, E. (1971). 'Some remarks on presuppositions', presented at the conf. on comput. ling. in Debrecen, 1971, *Prague Bull. of Math. Ling.*, **17** (1972), 11–23.

—— (in press). 'Negation and topic vs. comment', *Philologica Pragensia*, **16** (1973), 81–93.

Hjelmslev, L. (1943). *Omkring sprogteoriens grundlaeggelse*. Copenhagen. Quoted from *Prolégomènes à une théorie du langage*. Paris, 1968.

Keenan, E. L. (1970). 'A logical base for a transformational grammar of English.' Doctoral dissertation. Mimeo.

—— (1971). 'Two kinds of presuppositions in natural language.' In C. J. Fillmore and D. T. Langendoen, eds., *Studies in Linguistic Semantics*, pp. 45–52. New York.

—— (1972). 'On semantically based grammar', *Linguistic Inquiry*, **3**, 413–61.

Keenan, E. L. and Hull, R. D. (1973). 'The logical presuppositions of questions and answers.' Mimeo. To appear in D. Franck and J. Petöfi, eds., *Präsuppositionen in der Linguistik und der Philosophie* (1973). Frankfurt: Athenäum.

Kuno, S. (1972). 'Functional sentence perspective', *Linguistic Inquiry*, **3**, 269–320.

Montague, R. (1970a). 'Universal grammar', *Theoria*, **36**, 3, 373–98.

—— (1970b). 'Pragmatics and intensional logic', *Synthese*, **22**, 68–94.

Õim, H. (1973). 'On the semantic treatment of predicative expressions.' In F. Kiefer and N. Ruwet, eds., *Generative Grammar in Europe*, pp. 360–86. Dordrecht.

Panevová, J. and Sgall, P. (1973). 'Čas a vid českého a ruského slovesa' ('Tense and aspect of the Czech and Russian verb'), *Slavia*, **42**, 16–24.

Piťha, P. (1972). 'Nekotoryje zamečanija k obrabotke morfologii obstojatel'stva mesta v generativnom opisanii česskogo jazyka s neskol'kimi urovnjami' ('Notes on morphemics of adverbial of place in a functional (multilevel) description of Czech)', *Prague Studies in Math. Ling.*, **3**, 241–57.

Robinson, J. J. (1970). 'Dependency structures and transformational rules,' *Language*, **46**, 259–89.

Rohrer, C. (1971). *Funktionelle Sprachwissenschaft und transformationelle Grammatik*. Munich.

Scott, D. (1970). 'Advice on modal logic'. In K. Lambert, ed., *Philosophical Problems in Logic*, pp. 143–73. Dordrecht–Holland.

Searle, J. R. (1970). *Speech Acts*. Cambridge.

Sgall, P. (1967). 'Functional sentence perspective in a generative description', *Prague Studies in Math. Ling.* **2**, 203–25.

—— (1972a). 'Topic, focus, and the ordering of elements of semantic representations', *Philologica Pragensia*, **15**, 1–14.

—— (1972b). 'Fillmore's mysteries and topic vs. comment', *Journal of Ling.*, **8**, 283–8.

—— (1973). 'Kontextové zapojení a otázková metoda' ('Contextual boundness and the question test'), *Slovo a slovesnost*, **34**, 202–11.

—— (1974). 'Zur Stellung der Thema-Rhema-Gliederung in der Sprachbeschreibung'. In F. Daneš, ed., *Papers on Functional Sentence Perspective*, Marianské Lázne.

Sgall, P. and Hajičovà, E. (1970). 'A "functional" generative description', *Prague Bull. of Math. Ling.*, **14**, 3–38. Printed in *Revue Roumaine de ling.*, **15** (1971), 9–37.

Sgall, P., Hajičová, E. and Benešová, E. (1973). *Topic, Focus, and Generative Semantics*. Kronberg

Stalnaker, R. C. (1970). 'Pragmatics', *Synthese*, **22**, 272–89.

Strawson, P. F. (1952). *Introduction to Logical Theory*. London. Quoted from the 5th ed. London, 1967.

Weisheitelová, J. and Sgall, P. (1971). 'K syntaxi některých typů českých zájmen' ('Some remarks on the syntax of some types of Czech pronouns'), *AUC – Slavica Pragensia*, **13**, 167–78. Prague.

Topics, sentence accent, ellipsis: a proposal for their formal treatment

THEO VENNEMANN

1. Introductory note

My goal in this paper is a very modest one. I cannot even begin to discuss the numerous empirical aspects of the phenomena listed in the title, nor can I give a survey of the literature on these subjects in a short paper of this sort. All I can reasonably attempt here is to suggest an explication of the three concepts *topic, sentence accentuation,* and *ellipsis,* which may at best be the concepts associated with these expressions by several linguists, and at worst, are only my own.[1] I will do this by making a proposal for the representation of the semantics of topicality, of sentence accentuation, and of ellipsis – as I understand these expressions – in natural generative (NG) grammar. This theory of grammar is characterized in Vennemann (1971 and 1973a) and in Bartsch and Vennemann (1972). My remarks here are an extension of ideas and notation in Bartsch (1972, especially chapter 4) and are drawn to a large extent from the third section of Vennemann (1973b).

In formulating my remarks, I shall try to abide by a methodological principle which was used as a procedural guideline in Bartsch and Vennemann (1972), e.g. chapter 6.1, where we give different semantic representations for constructions with negative adverbs than we do for sentences with negation verbs, and which I propose explicitly in Vennemann (1973b). This principle says that any two discourses that have different surface syntactic representations must have different semantic representations (where I use 'semantic' in a broad sense, where some perhaps would use another expression, e.g. 'pragmatic' or 'pragmato-semantic'). I intend to apply this principle even in cases where the discourses (or pieces of such) are synonymous; in fact, it is precisely for such cases that the principle is important.

My goal is, then, more specifically, to propose a system of semantic (or pragmato-semantic) notation in which discourse sentences with identical

---

[1] I am grateful to Renate Bartsch for several clarifying discussions of the proposals made in this paper.

truth conditions but different topic-comment structure, different sentence accent, or different degrees of verbal explicitness receive different semantic representations. I will deal here only with certain simple declarative sentences (in which, furthermore, I will disregard tense and aspect), but I believe it will become apparent that the system can be extended to other sentence types.

2. Presuppositions

I assume a model of semantic (or pragmato-semantic) representation in which presuppositions are not carried and characterized inside their matrix structures as, e.g., in Bartsch (1972), but in a special 'presupposition pool' which does not belong to individual sentences only but to entire discourses or, at least, stretches of discourses. The information contained in this pool is constituted from general knowledge, from the situative context of the discourse, and from the completed part of the discourse itself.

Each participant of a discourse is operating with his own presupposition pool. His pool grows as the discourse proceeds. Each utterance made by another participant adds information to the pool; in particular, each statement that is not challenged becomes presuppositional for the remainder of the discourse. His own utterances likewise add information to his presupposition pool, viz. at least the information that he has made them, which is very important information indeed; e.g., this information prevents him, in most cases, from saying the same things over again.

Each participant of a discourse proceeds as if there existed only one presupposition pool for all participants of the discourse, his own. In fact, his presupposition pool can be characterized as the set of all assumptions relevant to the discourse which he believes are shared by all the participants. At least this is so in a normal, honest discourse. A discourse can continue undisturbed as long as the assumption of the shared presupposition pool can be entertained. As soon as the participants notice that this assumption is wrong, the discourse – or a particular portion of the discourse – ends, and a discussion of the discrepant presuppositions begins, i.e., a new discourse – or a new portion of the discourse – begins, during which no participant entertains the discrepant presuppositions as presuppositions. The way this happens is well known; one only has to think of appropriate reactions to such discourse fragments as the following: '*What do you think of the rumour that the present king of England is bald?*' '*You should stop beating your wife.*' '*Why don't you admit that your theory is wrong?*' Note also the following actually recorded discourse. Policeman at the front door: '*Does Mrs Miller, the widow, live here?*' Lady: '*I am Mrs Miller, but I am not a widow.*' Policeman: '*You want to bet?*'

Presuppositions, then, have the status of axioms relative to a discourse. Just as the axioms of a calculus delimit the range of possible extensions of the calculus, the presuppositions of a discourse delimit the range of possible continuations of the discourse. When a presupposition is violated by a certain continuation of the discourse, the discourse collapses, exactly as a calculus collapses when a certain extension violates an axiom. Natural language discourse does not tolerate contradictions any more than axiomatic calculi.

Following Bartsch I mark presuppositions by enclosing them in angled brackets ⟨ ⟩. These brackets have the status of a pragmatic relational predicate which characterizes propositions as axiomatic relative to a discourse. Since I limit my remarks to declarative sentences, I will leave the assertive part of semantic representations unmarked in this paper.

To illustrate with an example of Fillmore's discussed in Vennemann (1973a) and in Bartsch and Vennemann (1972), I represent the statement *John is even taller than Bill* semantically as a bipartite structure consisting of the presupposition *Bill is tall*, $\langle f_T^M(x_2) > N_{T,Y} \rangle$, and the assertion *John is taller than Bill*, $f_T^M(x_1) > f_T^M(x_2)$, as in (1b).

(1) a. John is even taller than Bill
   b. $\langle f_T^M(x_2) > N_{T,Y} \rangle$
   $f_T^M(x_1) > f_T^M(x_2)$

Both parts of the representation may, of course, be conjoined for the purpose of drawing inferences. E.g., *John is tall* may be inferred from *John is even taller than Bill* because (2b) may be inferred from (1b) via (3), which is simply an application of the law of transitivity for the relation > *more than*.

(2) a. John is tall
   b. $f_T^M(x_1) > N_{T,Y}$
(3) $f_T^M(x_1) > f_T^M(x_2)$ & $\langle f_T^M(x_2) > N_{T,Y} \rangle \Rightarrow f_T^M(x_1) > N_{T,Y}$

3. Topics

I understand the expression 'discourse subject' as referring to some individual phenomenon, such as a physical object, a set of physical objects, a process, or an event, that is uniquely determined relative to a discourse. In a manner of speaking, a discourse is about its discourse subjects. The discourse subjects may be given by general knowledge, including knowledge shared just by the interlocuters, e.g. *the Queen, John, John's wife*; or by the situative context of the discourse, e.g. *your hat, today*; or by the preceding part of the text of the discourse, e.g. *a concert of the Berlin Philharmonics last year, a pink unicorn, several essays, some John*. If a participant in the discourse mentions a discourse subject given by general knowledge or by means of deixis within the situative context, he naturally presupposes the unique existence of the discourse subject in the real or some possible world and can, therefore, refer to it by means of an individual name, a definite description, or a deictic expression. If he introduces a discourse subject textually, he uses an indefinite description (which presupposes the existence in the real or some possible world of the kind of phenomenon described by the predicate(s) used in the indefinite description). From the first mentioning on, the unique existence of the discourse subject introduced textually is presupposed, and the discourse subject will in the continued discourse be referred to by an individual name, a definite description, or a text-deictic expression, i.e. a pronoun. Let us, from now on, use the expression 'discourse subject' in the sense of 'previously-mentioned discourse subject'. We can then say that a discourse participant mentioning a discourse subject presupposes the unique existence of the discourse subject in the real or some possible world. Let a be a discourse subject of a discourse. Let a be uniquely identified for the discourse by the predicate F (more generally, by an open sentence with one free variable, but that is a trivial generalization). The proper way of representing a semantically then is by means of a unique existential proposition in the presupposition pool, as in (4).

(4) $\langle (\exists x)(F(x) \,\&\, (\forall y)(F(y) \supset y = x)) \rangle$

I will indicate unique existence by writing the numeral one on top of the existential quantifier. More generally, I indicate the existence of exactly n objects of a given kind by writing the numeral n on top of the existential quantifier, a convention used by H. Arnold Schmidt in his lectures. Let f_P^M be a functor mapping a set on its power (its cardinal number, or number of elements in the set). I define:

(5) $(\overset{n}{\exists}x)H(x) =_{\mathrm{df}} f_P^M(\{x:H(x)\}) = n$
for natural numbers $n = 1, 2, \ldots$

With this definition, I can rewrite (4) as (6).

(6) $\langle (\overset{1}{\exists}x)F(x) \rangle$

I understand the expression 'topic' or 'topic of a discourse' as referring to a discourse subject on which the attention of the participants of the discourse is concentrated. Such concentration of attention is usually, though not always, brought about by an immediately preceding textual mentioning of the discourse subject. Let the discourse subject a of (4)–(6) become topic of its discourse. Let C be a predicate such that $C(x)$ means 'the attention of the interlocutors is concentrated on x'. Then a is characterized as a topic of its discourse by the presupposition (7).

(7) $\langle(\overset{1}{\exists}x)(F(x)\ \&\ C(x))\rangle$

As all phenomena whose unique existence is presupposed, topics can be referred to by means of individual names, deictic expressions, and definite descriptions. E.g., we can refer to the topic a of (7) by means of the definite description (8).

(8) $(\imath x)(F(x)\ \&\ C(x))$

Since the predicate C will occur whenever topics are involved, I introduce a further abbreviation, the use of C as an index on the existential and descriptive operators, as in (9).

(9) a. $(\overset{n}{\exists}_c x)H(x) = {}_{df}(\overset{n}{\exists}x)(H(x)\ \&\ C(x))$
   b. $(\imath_c x)H(x) = {}_{df}(\imath x)(H(x)\ \&\ C(x))$

With these definitions, the topicality of a can be expressed as in (10), and a itself can be referred to by the expression in (11).

(10) $\langle(\overset{1}{\exists}_c x)F(x)\rangle$
(11) $(\imath_c x)F(x)$

As I said before, topics share the property of being based on presuppositions with all other phenomena that can be referred to by means of definite descriptions (or deictic expressions or individual names). That definite descriptions are based on presuppositions can, of course, be tested easily with the usual negation and question tests. Note also that the statement *The present king of England is bald* in a discourse must be immediately rejected by all interlocutors who know that no such object exists; the discourse ends immediately because a discrepancy in the presupposition pools is noticed: The participant who states *The present king of England is bald* entertains the presupposition that there is exactly one object which is presently king of England; the interlocutors who know the world better entertain a presupposition which is incompatible with that of the speaker.

They must end the discourse (or the completed portion of the discourse) by saying something like '*The present king of England? There is no such thing*'. One can see why: not ending the discourse would be tantamount to accepting the speaker's presupposition as true, and it would mean that in the continuation of the discourse they would be operating with a contradictory set of axioms.

4. Topics and comments, themes and rhemes

I understand the expression 'comment' as referring to a statement involving topics (in the sense just discussed). E.g., in the following discourse, '*Where is John?*' – '*He is at home*', the answer is a comment on *John*, who is among the topics of the discourse. Within a comment, I call a topic a theme, and a non-topical predicate predicated of a topic, a rheme. (The expressions 'theme' and 'rheme' need not be reserved for comments, or statements in general, but can be applied to other utterance types.) Thus, in the discourse, *he* refers to the theme of the commental statement *He is at home*, and *is at home* is a verbalization of its rheme.

Let us now look at a particular statement more closely. Let us analyse the topic-comment relations, the theme-rheme structure, of the statement (12).

(12) Mary is singing strangely

We notice immediately that this written string is a representation not of one, but of several different commental statements (comments), at least of the three indicated by the following questions:

(12) a. How is Mary singing?
     b. What is Mary doing strangely?
     c. Who is singing strangely?

Question (12a) introduces, or refers to, two topics of the discourse, viz. Mary, and Mary's singing. *Mary* is an individual name. Individual name expressions can be used both as terms (or noun phrases), as in (12) and (12a), and as noun predicates, e.g. in German dialects *der Hans, die Maria* (*the John, the Mary*). As predicates, individual names have no intensions, and an extension whose power is one, i.e. an extension containing exactly one element. Other term expressions, e.g. definite and indefinite descriptions, may likewise be used as predicates. The need for this will become apparent later. I mark an expression commonly used as a term by a subscript P when it is used as a predicate. The topicality of *Mary* is represented in (13).

(13) $\langle(\overset{1}{\exists}_c x)\,\text{Mary}_P(x)\rangle$

Mary's singing refers to an action process in which Mary is involved and which is a singing process. Using Bartsch's notation: r as a variable over states and processes, $P(x,r)$ for *x is involved in r*, and $F\text{-}V(r)$ for *r is an F-ing process*, I represent the topicality of *Mary's singing* as in (14).

(14) $\langle(\overset{1}{\exists}_c r)(P(\text{Mary},r)\ \&\ \text{Sing-}V(r))\rangle$

Here *Mary* is used like $(\iota_c x)Mary_P(x)$. See (13). Now the semantic representation of (12), as an answer to (12a), is given in (15a).

(15) a. Presuppositions: (13), (14).
Strange$((\iota_c r)(P(\text{Mary},r)\ \&\ \text{Sing-}V(r)))$

Just looking at (15a), and at (13) and (14), tells us that *Mary* and *Mary's singing* are the themes, and *Strange* is the rheme of (12) as an answer to (12a).

I give the representation of (12) as an answer to (12b) and (12c) in (15b) and (15c), respectively.

(15) b. (13)
$\langle(\overset{1}{\exists}_c r)(P(\text{Mary},r)\ \&\ \text{Strange}(r))\rangle$
$\text{Sing-}V((\iota_c r)(P(\text{Mary},r)\ \&\ \text{Strange}(r)))$
c. $\langle(\overset{1}{\exists}_c x)(\overset{1}{\exists}_c r)(P(x,r)\ \&\ \text{Sing-}V(r)\ \&\ \text{Strange}(r))\rangle$
$\text{Mary}_P((\iota x)(\overset{1}{\exists}_c r)(P(x,r)\ \&\ \text{Sing-}V(r)\ \&\ \text{Strange}(r)))$

In (15c), though (13) is not presupposed, it is presupposed that the interlocutors know which individual the name predicate *Mary* refers to in the discourse, $\langle(\overset{1}{\exists}x)Mary_P(x)\rangle$. This is simply a condition on the use of individual names, and I will not repeat it below. If a personal name is used without such a presupposition being entertained, *some* or *one* has to be used: *Some Mary is singing strangely, One Mr Miller would like to talk to you*, etc. Note that the presupposition $\langle(\overset{1}{\exists}x)Mary_P(x)\rangle$, other than (13), does not make *Mary* topical. – I mention briefly that not only (12), but also the questions (12a–c) are ambiguous. E.g., one further meaning of (12c) can be paraphrased by *Who all is singing strangely?*. Such ambiguity is important because it may cause discrepancies in presupposition pools, but I cannot pursue it further in this paper.

Concluding this section, I return for a moment to the methodological principle mentioned in section 1. Since (12)–(12a) is represented semantically as in (15a), (12)–(12b) as in (15b), and (12)–(12c) as in (15c), how can we represent (16a–c)?

(16) a. Mary's singing is strange
  b. What Mary is doing strangely is singing
  c. The one who is singing strangely is Mary

I propose the following representations.

(17) a. $\langle(\overset{1}{\exists}_c r)(P(\text{Mary},r) \ \& \ \text{Sing-}V(r))\rangle$
  $\text{Strange}((\imath_c r)(P(\text{Mary},r) \ \& \ \text{Sing-}V(r)))$

  b. $\langle\overset{1}{\exists}_c r)(P(\text{Mary},r) \ \& \ \text{Strange}(r))\rangle$
  $\text{Sing-}V((\imath_c r)(P(\text{Mary},r) \ \& \ \text{Strange}(r)))$

  c. $\langle(\overset{1}{\exists}_c x)(\overset{1}{\exists}r)(P(x,r) \ \& \ \text{Sing-}V(r) \ \& \ \text{Strange}(r))\rangle$
  $\text{Mary}_P((\imath_c x)(\overset{1}{\exists}r)(P(x,r) \ \& \ \text{Sing-}V(r) \ \& \ \text{Strange}(r)))$

While I must admit that my intuitions about the theme-rheme structure of some of the sentences represented here are somewhat weak, so that some details may require correction, I am confident that the difference is in fact one of topicalization. This seems to me especially transparent not only in the three readings of (12), but also in the pair (12)–(12a) vs. (16a), which I repeat here, together with questions to which they may be answers.

(18) a. [How is Mary singing?]
  Mary is singing strangely
  $\langle(\overset{1}{\exists}_c x)\text{Mary}_P(x)\rangle$
  $\langle(\overset{1}{\exists}_c r)(P(\text{Mary},r) \ \& \ \text{Sing-}V(r))\rangle$
  $\text{Strange}((\imath_c r)(P(\text{Mary},r) \ \& \ \text{Sing-}V(r)))$

  b. [How is Mary's singing?]
  Mary's singing is strange
  $\langle(\overset{1}{\exists}_c r)(P(\text{Mary},r) \ \& \ \text{Sing-}V(r))\rangle$
  $\text{Strange}((\imath_c r)(P(\text{Mary},r) \ \& \ \text{Sing-}V(r)))$

In (18a), both *Mary* and the *singing* process in which she is involved are topical. In (18b), only the singing process is topical, and the mentioning of Mary only serves to identify the process. If my hypothesis that the difference between the commental statements (18a) and (18b) is one of topicalization is correct, then we must formulate syntactic rules in such a way that they are sensitive to differences of topicalization, differences that are as subtle as those in the proposed semantic representations of (18a–b).

In concluding this section, I want to draw attention to the correlation – in my representations – between topicalization and embedding. Topics, as themes, have a tendency to appear at a low level of embedding in surface syntactic structures, preferably as sentence subjects. In (18b) where there is only one theme, this tendency is easily implemented: the topic *Mary's singing* appears as sentence subject. In (18a) where there are two themes, *Mary* and her *singing*, the tendency is implemented by raising the name term *Mary* from its embedded position in the logical representation of the *singing* process and placing it, as a typical term expression, in sentence subject position, while the process itself is realized as a verb. The correlation between argument raising and topicalization is schematized graphically in (19).

(19)

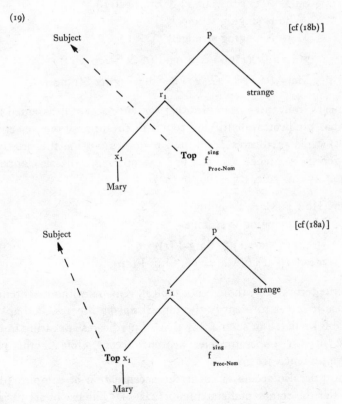

5. Topicalization and sentence accent

We saw earlier that statement (12) can have various theme–rheme structures depending on which topics it is a comment on. The difference in theme-rheme structure is correlated with a difference of sentence accentuation. See (20).

(20) a. [How is Mary singing?]
Mary is singing stríngely
$\langle(\overset{1}{\exists}_c x)\mathrm{Mary}_P(x)\rangle$
$\langle(\overset{1}{\exists}_c r)(P(\mathrm{Mary},r)\ \&\ \mathrm{Sing}\text{-}V(r))\rangle$
$\mathrm{Strange}((\imath_c r)(P(\mathrm{Mary},r)\ \&\ \mathrm{Sing}\text{-}V(r)))$

b. [What is Mary doing strangely?]
Mary is sínging strangely
$\langle(\overset{1}{\exists}_c x)(\mathrm{Mary}_P(x))\rangle$
$\langle(\overset{1}{\exists}_c r)(P(\mathrm{Mary},r)\ \&\ \mathrm{Strange}(r))\rangle$
$\mathrm{Sing}\text{-}V((\imath_c r)(P(\mathrm{Mary},r)\ \&\ \mathrm{Strange}(r)))$

c. [Who is singing strangely?]
Máry is singing strangely
$\langle(\overset{1}{\exists}_c x)(\overset{1}{\exists}_c r)(P(x,r)\ \&\ \mathrm{Sing}\text{-}V(r)\ \&\ \mathrm{Strange}(r))\rangle$
$\mathrm{Mary}_P((\imath_c x)(\overset{1}{\exists}_c r)(P(x,r)\ \&\ \mathrm{Sing}\text{-}V(r)\ \&\ \mathrm{Strange}(r)))$

It appears from these examples that sentence accent is assigned in such a way that predicates identifying topics in presuppositions reject sentence accent, while predicates predicated of topics outside the presupposition pool receive sentence accent. The examples in (16) also appear to be covered by this rule, e.g. (16a) in (21).

(21) [How is Mary's singing?]
Mary's singing is stránge
$\langle(\overset{1}{\exists}_c r)(P(\mathrm{Mary},r)\ \&\ \mathrm{Sing}\text{-}V(r))\rangle$
$\mathrm{Strange}((\imath_c r)(P(\mathrm{Mary},r)\ \&\ \mathrm{Sing}\text{-}V(r)))$

Here the term *Mary*, though not topical, remains without sentence accent because it serves to identify the topical *singing* process. Perhaps the rule can be formulated in such a way that all predicates appearing in the scope of the Iota-C ($\imath_c$) operator reject sentence accent, while all other predicates receive sentence accent.

The rule also seems to cover the accentuation of complex predicates. Consider the commental statements (22a–c). (The use of set variables and plural predicates follows Bartsch (1973)).

(22) a. [Which of the red objects does Mary want?]
Mary wants the red hóuse

$\langle(\overset{1}{\exists}_c x)\mathrm{Mary}_P(x)\rangle$

$\langle(\overset{1}{\exists}_c X)\mathrm{Red}_{\mathrm{Plural}}(X)\rangle$

$\langle(\overset{1}{\exists}_c x)(\mathrm{Want}(\mathrm{Mary},x) \ \& \ x\in(\imath_c X)\mathrm{Red}_{\mathrm{Plural}}(X))\rangle$

$\langle(\exists x)(x\in(\imath_c X)\mathrm{Red}_{\mathrm{Plural}}(X) \ \& \ \mathrm{House}(x))\rangle$
$\mathrm{House}((\imath_c x)(\mathrm{Want}(\mathrm{Mary},x) \ \& \ x\in(\imath_c X)\mathrm{Red}_{\mathrm{Plural}}(X)))$

b. [Which of the houses does Mary want?]
Mary wants the réd house

$\langle(\overset{1}{\exists}_c x)\mathrm{Mary}_P(x)\rangle$

$\langle(\overset{1}{\exists}_c X)\mathrm{House}_{\mathrm{Plural}}(X)\rangle$

$\langle(\overset{1}{\exists}_c x)(\mathrm{Want}(\mathrm{Mary},x) \ \& \ x\in(\imath_c X)\mathrm{House}_{\mathrm{Plural}}(X))\rangle$

$\langle(\exists x)(x\in(\imath_c X)\mathrm{House}_{\mathrm{Plural}}(X) \ \& \ \mathrm{Red}(x))\rangle$
$\mathrm{Red}((\imath_c)(\mathrm{Want}(\mathrm{Mary},x) \ \& \ x\in(\imath_c X)\mathrm{House}_{\mathrm{Plural}}(X)))$

c. [Which of the objects does Mary want?]
Mary wants the réd hóuse

$\langle(\overset{1}{\exists}_c x)\mathrm{Mary}_P(x)\rangle$

$\langle(\overset{1}{\exists}_c X)\rangle$, i.e. $\langle(\overset{1}{\exists} X)C(X)\rangle$

$\langle(\overset{1}{\exists}_c x)(\mathrm{Want}(\mathrm{Mary},x) \ \& \ x\in(\imath_c X))\rangle$

$\langle(\exists x)(x\in(\imath_c X) \ \& \ \mathrm{Red}(x) \ \& \ \mathrm{House}(x))\rangle$
$\mathrm{Red}((\imath_c x)(\mathrm{Want}(\mathrm{Mary},x) \ \& \ x\in(\imath_c X)))$
$\& \ \mathrm{House}((\imath_c x)(\mathrm{Want}\,(\mathrm{Mary},x) \ \& \ x\in(\imath_c X)))$

Of course, *the red house* can also be thematic in a commental statement, in which case it does not receive any sentence accent at all.

There seem to exist rules for the ways sentence accents influence each other in a kind of sandhi fashion, depending on the categorial realization of the accented predicates, their relative order, their position in the sentence, the syntactic type of the language, the semantic structure of the lexical items employed, and other factors. I ventured a hypothesis about the categorial aspect of this in Vennemann (1973b), but it is in all likelihood wrong; so I shall not repeat it here. I should mention, however, that I believe that this problem must be investigated on the basis of observations and generalizations such as those in Bolinger (1972).

6. Pronominalization and ellipsis

In the final section of this paper I will make a proposal for the formal representation of ellipsis at the pragmato-semantic level. The expression 'ellipsis' is used by some, e.g. von Kutschera (1971:27), for pronominalization or, as he says, the use of 'indicators' such as *I, he, here, now*; I assume that zero realization of semantic structure in certain contexts would be subsumed under this concept of ellipsis. Others – and I tend to sympathize with them – distinguish between pronominalization, or the use of 'indicators' in the somewhat broader sense just exemplified, on one hand, and contextual zero realization of semantic structure, or what some call deletion, on the other.

Under certain conditions, chief among them the condition that a pronominal expression, or 'indicator', establishes reference unambiguously, a topic is not usually thematized by means of an individual name or a definite description but by means of a pronoun, or 'indicator'. Consider the commental statement in (18b)–(21), repeated here as (23).

(23) [How is Mary's singing?]
Mary's singing is stránge
$\langle (\overset{1}{\exists}_c r)(P(\text{Mary},r) \,\&\, \text{Sing-}V(r)) \rangle$
$\text{Strange}((\imath_c r)(P(\text{Mary},r) \,\&\, \text{Sing-}V(r)))$

Now, (23) is a rather verbose statement. A more concise verbalization would be *It is strange*. While in (23) the predicates identifying the topic are fully lexicalized, in *It is strange* the topic is referred to by means of the pronoun *it* and only the commental predicate 'Strange' is fully lexicalized. Apparently one who uses the sentence *It is stránge* to make a statement goes about the construction of his sentence as follows: 'There is exactly one process in which Mary is involved and which is a singing process and which we are talking about; since the attention of my interlocutor(s) is directed to this individual phenomenon anyway, as indicated by the question [(23)], there is no point in repeating the entire verbiage; I'll just use a minimal verbalization for this phenomenon in order to establish reference and go straight on to the predication: *It is stránge*.' I express this additional abbreviatory step of minimalization of verbalization by means of introducing a referential constant in the presuppositional representation of a topic, as in (24) which should be compared to (23).

(24) [How is Mary's singing?]
It is stránge
$\langle (\overset{1}{\exists}_c r)(P(\text{Mary},r) \,\&\, \text{Sing-}V(r)) \rangle$
$r_1 =_{\text{df}} (\imath_c r)(P(\text{Mary},r) \,\&\, \text{Sing-}V(r))$
$\text{Strange}(r_1)$

I employ the same mode of representation where pronominal reference to several topics is involved, e.g. (25) which should be compared to (20a); 'r_1' is used in (25) in the category of predicates just as individual name terms were used earlier.

(25) [How is Mary singing?]
  She is doing it st")(rángely
  $\langle (\overset{1}{\exists}_c x) \text{Mary}_P(x) \rangle$
  $x_1 =_{df} (\imath_c x) \text{Mary}_P(x)$
  $\langle (\overset{1}{\exists}_c r)(P(x_1, r) \ \& \ \text{Sing-}V(r)) \rangle$
  $r_1 =_{df} (\imath_c r)(P(x_1, r) \ \& \ \text{Sing-}V(r))$
  $\text{Strange}((\imath_c r)(P(x_1, r) \ \& \ [r_1]_P(r)))$

Compare also (26) to (22b).

(26) [Which of the houses does Mary want?]
  She wants the réd one
  $\langle (\overset{1}{\exists}_c x) \text{Mary}_P(x) \rangle$
  $x_1 =_{df} (\imath_c x) \text{Mary}_P(x)$
  $\langle (\overset{1}{\exists}_c X) \text{House}_{\text{Plural}}(X) \rangle$
  $X_1 =_{df} (\imath_c X) \text{House}_{\text{Plural}}(X)$
  $\langle (\overset{1}{\exists}_c x)(\text{Want}(x_1, x) \ \& \ x \in X_1) \rangle$
  $\langle (\overset{1}{\exists} x)(x \in X_1 \ \& \ \text{Red}(x)) \rangle$
  $\text{Red}((\imath_c x)(\text{Want}(x_1, x) \ \& \ x \in X_1))$

If my proposal for the semantic representation of pronominalization is correct, we must construct syntactic rules in such a way that they are sensitive to the difference between an Iota definite description and a referential constant. The pronominal actualization of a referential constant is determined by the semantics of its definite description, e.g. plurality, and by properties of the lexical items that would be used in a full verbalization of the definite description, e.g. gender.

So far the methodological principle that different surface syntactic structures should have different pragmato-semantic representations has served us well: We have succeeded in formulating different semantic representations for surface syntactic structures that differ only in their theme-rheme composition and concomitant accentuations, or in full verbalization versus pronominalization. In doing this, we remained entirely within a logic that was extended by a pragmatic relational predicate characterizing propositions as presuppositional, i.e. axiomatic, relative to a discourse, and by a pragmatic relational predicate characterizing a discourse subject as being a focus of attention of the participants of a discourse, i.e. as a topic. (We also made use of the introduction of referential constants for certain definite descriptions.)

As we finally turn to ellipsis in the narrower sense, viz. that of zero lexicalization (or deletion), one may feel inclined to abandon the principle and speak of free choice, optional rules, or the like. Compare (27a, b, c).

(27) [How is Mary's singing?]
    a. Mary's singing is stránge
    b. It is stránge
    c. Stránge

We have managed to distinguish between (27a) and (27b); but what shall we do with (27c)? Here we seem to be entering the domain of stylistic and also social variation that seems to lie beyond the domain of properly extendable logic. On the other hand, one could argue that the same is true, to some extent, even of pronominalization, because the choice between full lexicalization and pronominalization of topics is also governed in part by stylistic and social parameters. Therefore, I will remain true to my principle and try to represent ellipsis at the level of semantic representation. I will do this by means of a syntactic predicate Z characterizing a thematic referential constant as subject to zero lexicalization if the syntactic rules of the language permit this.

(27c') [How is Mary's singing?]
    Stránge

$$\langle(\overset{1}{\exists}_c r)(P(\text{Mary},r) \ \& \ \text{Sing-}V(r))\rangle$$
$$r_1 = {}_{df}(\imath_c r)(P(\text{Mary},r) \ \& \ \text{Sing-}V(r))$$
$$Z(``r_1")$$
$$\text{Strange}(r_1)$$

This, I think, is all that can be done about the difference among commental statements such as (27a, b, c) at the level of pragmato-semantic representation. The empirical investigation of the stylistic and social parameters which control the application of the pragmatic and syntactic functions of referential constant introduction and zeroing goes beyond the domain of the theory of grammar, and certainly beyond the goals of this paper.[1]

---

[1] The above is the text of the paper which I submitted prior to the Colloquium. The following remarks are based on the discussion that followed the presentation of an abridged version of the paper at the Colloquium. Unfortunately I do not recollect all of the

REFERENCES

Bartsch, Renate (1972). *Adverbialsemantik: Die Konstitution logisch-semantischer Repräsentationen von Adverbialkonstruktionen* (Linguistische Forschungen, **6**). Frankfurt am Main: Athenäum-Verlag.

—— (1973). 'The semantics and syntax of number and numbers'. To appear in John Kimball, ed., *Syntax and Semantics II*. New York: Seminar Press.

Bartsch, Renate and Vennemann, Theo. (1972). *Semantic structures: A Study in the Relation between Semantics and Syntax* (Athenäum-Skripten Linguistik, **9**). Frankfurt am Main: Athenäum-Verlag.

Bolinger, Dwight. (1972). 'Accent is predictable (if you're a mind-reader)', *Language*, **48**, 633–44.

Kutschera, Franz, v. (1971). *Sprachphilosophie*. Munich: W. Fink.

Vennemann, Theo (1971). 'Natural generative phonology'. Paper read at the annual meeting of the Linguistic Society of America, St Louis, Mo., 1971.

—— (1973a). 'Explanation in syntax'. To appear in John Kimball, ed., *Syntax and Semantics II*. New York: Seminar Press.

—— (1973b). 'Warum gibt es Syntax? Syntaktische Konstruktionsprinzipien in logischer und psychologischer Sicht'. To appear in *Zeitschrift für Germanistische Linguistik*, **1**, No. 2.

valuable discussion now, three months after the Colloquium. What follows should therefore be understood as a *subjective* rendering of *some* of the interchanges concerning my paper that occurred at the Colloquium.

Mr Schnelle remarked that situations may occur in which it would be inappropriate to challenge the presuppositions of someone saying *The present king of France is bald* because of some specific social relation among the interlocutors of a specific social setting. This seems correct to me; it must be considered in a discussion of presupposition. On the other hand, it seems to me that there is something special about a discourse in which a statement such as *The present king of France is bald* goes by unquestioned as opposed to one in which it does not. From the point of view of linguistic communication, as contrasted with the totality of social interaction, the former discourse strikes me as pathological, the latter as normal; and even within a larger framework of social interaction the latter seems to represent an 'unmarked' type, while the former seems 'marked' and properly characterizable only by confrontation with the 'unmarked' type. That too must be considered in a discussion of presupposition.

It was remarked (I forget by who) that it is incorrect to say that 'natural language does not tolerate contradictions any more than axiomatic calculi' because contradictions in calculi do occur and may go unnoticed for a long time. This seems to me to be to some extent correct; what I should say is probably something like 'Natural language does not tolerate obvious contradictions any more than axiomatic calculi' and that a discourse collapses when a contradiction (such as a violated presupposition) is noticed by the interlocutors (in an honest discourse). That a contradiction is never accepted can be seen when someone says (with a sentence used earlier at this Colloquium), *Wittgenstein was a linguist and he was not a linguist*. Such a statement is never seriously interpreted as a contradiction, but a non-contradictory interpretation is constructed, e.g. 'Under one definition of "linguist" Wittgenstein was a linguist, but under another one he was not', or 'Wittgenstein fulfilled some of the conditions that qualify a person as a linguist, but not all'. The same is true, incidentally, of obvious tautologies; a statement such as *A woman is a woman* is never interpreted as a tautology but as something like *A woman must be expected to behave as male chauvinist pigs expect women to behave.*

Mr Isard pointed out that in addition to presuppositions there are also 'expectations' that determine the normalcy of a discourse. E.g., I would react differently if my question *'How did you come to Cambridge?'* were answered by him (a) *'By plane'*, (b) *'By hover-craft'*, (c) *'By space-ship'*. That is certainly correct and must be considered in a theory of discourse. The problem is of an even more direct sort. I said that to use or accept a definite description, the interlocutors must presuppose unique existence of a certain natural phenomenon. This too requires modification. A definite description may be used and will be accepted even if there is only a certain 'expectation' that there is (exactly) one phenomenon of a certain kind, cf. *'Where do your parents live?'*, asked by a person who does not know whether his interlocutor's parents are still alive. Even if there is no prior 'expectation', we may accept a definite description on the authority of the user (and may 'learn' in that fashion that there is (exactly) one phenomenon of the kind), e.g. when we read in the newspaper *The Vice Foreign Minister of Swaziland will visit the US*...Even if there is no specific 'expectation' it must still be 'plausible' that there should be (exactly) one phenomenon for the definite description to refer to. I do not know how 'expectability' and 'plausibility', in addition to 'presuppositionality', will eventually be represented formally in a theory of discourse, but I agree that they will have to be represented.

Preference semantics

YORICK WILKS

Abstract

Preference semantics (PS) is a set of formal procedures for representing the meaning structure of natural language, with a view to embodying that structure within a system that can be said to understand, rather than within what I would call the 'derivational paradigm', of transformational grammar (TG) and generative semantics (GS), which seeks to determine the well-formedness, or otherwise, of sentences. I argue that the distinction is not a trivial one, at least not if one genuinely wants to develop a model of human competence. For rejecting utterances is just what humans do not do. They try to understand them.

I outline a system of preference semantics that does this: in operation it has access to the senses of words coded as lexical decomposition trees, formed from a finite inventory of semantic primitives. For each phrase or clause of a complex sentence, the system builds up a network of such trees with the aid of structured items called templates and, at the next level, it structures those networks with higher level items called paraplates. At each stage the system directs itself towards the correct network by always opting for the most 'semantically dense' one it can construct. I suggest that this opting for the 'greatest semantic density' can be seen as an interpretation of Joos' (1972) 'Semantic axiom number one'.

I argue that the analysis of quite simple examples requires the use of inductive rules of inference which cannot, theoretically cannot, be accommodated within the derivational paradigm. I contrast this derivational paradigm of language processing with the artificial intelligence (AI) paradigm, and suggest that even if, as appears to be the case, GS is as it were shifting from one paradigm to the other, there are certain pitfalls remaining in the way of any easy assimilation of deductive processes within a language processor. I argue that some of the principles underlying the PS approach will be needed for any adequate treatment of inference in natural language.

Introduction

In this paper I want to oppose a method of semantic analysis to the contemporary paradigm. By that I mean the transformational grammar (TG)-generative semantics (GS) one, rather than recent developments in modal logic and set theory. It seems to me that attacking the claims of the latter about natural language may be fun, but it is not a pressing matter in the way that criticizing GS is. For GS has gone so far in the right direction, towards a system for understanding natural language adequately, that perhaps with one more tiny tap the whole carapace of the 'derivational paradigm' might burst.

What I intend by that phrase is the picture of language imported into linguistics from proof theory by Chomsky. Both TG and GS claim to devote themselves to the production of bodies of rules that would perform repeated derivations, and so pass from some initial symbol to an ultimate surface string, that is to say a well-formed sentence. The field of all possible derivations with such a body of rules is taken to define the class of well-formed sentences of the language in question: those that can be produced by derivation in that way are 'well formed', those that cannot are not. This description is not, in its essentials, in dispute.

I have argued elsewhere (1971) that there are good abstract reasons for thinking that this sorting cannot, even in principle, be done: at least not if the task is taken to be one of sorting the meaningful sentences of a language from the meaningless ones. The reason is simply that, given any disputed utterance, we could not know formally of it that it was not meaningful, because speakers have the ability to embed odd-looking utterances in stories so as to make them meaningful in the context of use. However, even if this gigantic sorting task could be done, it has no connection whatever with Lakoff's recently expressed (1973) desideratum for GS, as opposed to TG, that it should take 'into account the fact that language is used by human beings to communicate in a social context'. And no generative linguist to my knowledge, whether of the TG or GS persuasion, has ever unambiguously rejected Chomsky's original sorting-by-derivation as the central task of linguistic theory. In this paper I want to argue that there are at least two sorts of example, quite simple examples, that cannot be analysed adequately within the derivational paradigm. To do so, I describe a non-standard system of semantic analysis that can deal with such examples. I describe the system in a rough and ready way, with nothing like an adequate justification, or motivation as the fashionable word is, of its primitive elements and assumptions. Linguists who dislike non-standard systems, and are prone to consider them 'unmotivated' per se should skip immediately to the discussion section so as not to miss the substantive point of this paper.

The preference semantics (PS) system I shall describe is at present functioning as part of an analysis and generation system for natural language programmed on a computer (see Wilks (1973a,b): one with no independent syntax base, everything being handled through the strong semantic representation described. This, I argue, provides an additional argument for its adequacy in handling natural language, over and above the mere labelling of examples. I assume, too, that such a system cannot be dismissed as 'mere performance': partly because, as I shall show, it explicates real competencies of human understanders inadequately treated in TG/GS systems; and in part because the intellectual weight of the 'competence-performance' distinction is insufficient to dismiss systems that merely differ from the conventional TG/GS paradigm.

An outline of preference semantics

A fragmented text is to be represented by an interlingual structure consisting of TEMPLATES bound together by PARAPLATES and Common-Sense (CS) INFERENCES. These three items consist of FORMULAE (and predicates and functions ranging over them and over sub-formulae), which in turn consist of ELEMENTS.

ELEMENTS are sixty primitive semantic units used to express the semantic entities, states, qualities and actions about which humans speak and write. The elements fall into five classes, which can be illustrated as follows (elements in upper case):

(a) *entities*: MAN (human being), STUFF (substances), THING (physical object), PART (parts of things), FOLK (human groups), ACT (acts), STATE (states of existence), BEAST (animals), etc.; (b) *actions*: FORCE (compels), CAUSE (causes to happen), FLOW (moving as liquids do), PICK (choosing), BE (exists), etc.; (c) *type indicators*: KIND (being a quality), HOW (being a type of action), etc.; (d) *sorts*: CONT (being a container), GOOD (being morally acceptable), THRU (being an aperture), etc.; (e) *cases*: TO (direction), SOUR (source), GOAL (goal or end), LOCA (location), SUBJ (actor or agent), OBJE (patient of action), IN (containment), POSS (possessed by), etc.

FORMULAE are constructed from elements and right and left brackets. They express the senses of English words; one formula to each sense. The formulae are binarily bracketed lists of whatever depth is necessary to express the word sense. They are written and interpreted with, in each pair at whatever level it comes, a dependence of left side on corresponding right. Formulae can be thought of, and written out, as binary trees of semantic primitives, and in that form they are not unlike the lexical decomposition trees of Lakoff and McCawley.

Consider the action *drink* and its relation to the formula (or binary tree):

((*ANI SUBJ)(((FLOW STUFF)OBJE)(*ANI IN)(((THIS(*ANI (THRU PART)))TO)(MOVE CAUSE)))))

*ANI here is simply the name of a class of elements, those expressing animate entities namely, MAN, BEAST and FOLK (human groups). In order to keep a small usable list of semantic elements, and to avoid arbitrary extensions of the list, many notions are coded by conventional sub-formulae: so, for example, (FLOW STUFF) is used to indicate liquids, and (THRU PART) is used to indicate apertures.

Let us now decompose the formula for *drink*. It is to be read as an action, preferably done by animate things (*ANI SUBJ) to liquids ((FLOW STUFF)OBJE), of causing the liquid to move into the animate thing(*ANI IN) and via (TO indicating the direction case) a particular aperture of the animate thing; the mouth of course. It is hard to indicate a notion as specific as *mouth* with such general concepts. But it would be simply irresponsible, I think, to suggest adding MOUTH as a semantic primitive, as do semantic systems that simply add an awkward lexeme as a new 'primitive'. Lastly, the THIS indicates that the part is a specific part of the subject.

The notion of preference is the important one here: SUBJ case displays the preferred agents of actions, and OBJE case the preferred objects, or patients. We cannot enter such preferences as stipulations, as many linguistic systems do, such as that of Katz and Postal (1964) with 'selection restrictions', where, if such a restriction is violated, the result is 'no reading'. For we can be said to drink in the atmosphere, and cars are said to drink gasoline. It is proper to prefer the normal, but it would be absurd, in an intelligent understanding system, not to accept the abnormal if it is described. Not only everyday metaphor, but the description of the simplest fictions, require it.

Just as elements are to be explained by seeing how they function within formulae, so formulae, one level higher, are to be explained by describing how they function within TEMPLATES, the third kind of semantic item in the system. The notion of a template is intended to correspond to an intuitive one of message: one not reducible merely to unstructured associations of word senses.

A template consists of a network of formulae grounded on a basic actor-action-object triple of formulae. This basic formula triple is located during initial analysis in frames of formulae, one formula for each fragment word in each frame, by means of a device called a bare template. A bare template is simply a triple of elements which are the heads of three formulae in actor-action-object form.

For example: *Small men sometimes father big sons*, when represented by a string of formulae, will give the two sequences of heads:

KIND MAN HOW MAN KIND MAN

and

KIND MAN HOW CAUSE KIND MAN

(CAUSE is the head of the verbal sense of *father*; *to father* is analysed as *to cause to have life*.)

The first sequence has no underlying template; however, in the second we find MAN CAUSE MAN which is a legitimate bare template. Thus we have disambiguated *father*, at the same time as picking up a sequence of three formulae which is the core of the template for the sentence. It must be emphasized here that the template is the sequence of formulae, and not to be confused with the triple of elements (heads) used to locate it.

It is a hypothesis of this work that we can build up a finite but useful inventory of bare templates adequate for the analysis of ordinary language: a list of the messages that people want to convey at some fairly high level of generality (for template matching is not in any sense phrase-matching at the surface level). The bare templates are an attempt to explicate a notion of a non-atomistic linguistic pattern: to be located whole in texts in the way that human beings appear to when they read or listen.

Let me avoid all further questions of analysis in order to illustrate the central processes of expansion and preference by considering the sentence:

[1] The big policeman interrogated the crook

Let us take the following formulae for the four main word senses:

(1) *policeman*:
((FOLK   SOUR)(((((NOTGOOD   MAN)OBJE)PICK)(SUBJ MAN)))

i.e., a person who selects bad persons out of the body of people(FOLK). The case marker SUBJ is the dependent in the last element pair, indicating that the normal 'top first' order for subject-entities in formulae has been violated, and necessarily so if the head is also to be the last element in linear order.

(2) *big*: ((*PHYSOB POSS)(MUCH KIND))

i.e., a property preferably possessed by physical objects (substances are not big)

(3) *interrogates*: ((MAN SUBJ)((MAN OBJE)(TELL FORCE)))

i.e. forcing to tell something, done preferably by humans, to humans.

(4a) *crook*: ((((NOTGOOD ACT)OBJE)DO)((SUBJ MAN))

i.e. a man who does bad acts. And we have to remember here that we are ignoring other senses of *crook* at the moment, such as the shepherd's

(4b) crook:
((((((THIS BEAST)OBJE)FORCE)(SUBJ MAN))POSS)(LINE THING))

i.e., a long straight object possessed by a man who controls a particular kind of animal.

The analysis algorithm will have seen the sentence as a frame of formulae, one for each of its words, and will look only at the heads of the formulae. Given that MAN FORCE MAN is in the inventory of bare templates, then one scan of a frame of formulae (containing formula (4a) for *crook*), will have picked up the sequence of formulae labelled above (1), (3), (4a), in that order. Again when a frame containing formula (4b), the shepherd's sense of *crook*, is scanned, the sequence of formulae (1) (3), (4b) will also be selected as a possible initial structure for the sentence, since MAN FORCE THING is also a proper bare template sequence.

We now have two possible template representations for the sentence after the initial match; both a triple of formulae in actor-action-object form. Next, the templates are expanded, if possible. This process consists of extending the simple networks we have so far: both by attaching other formulae into the network, and strengthening the bonds between those already in the template, if that is possible. Qualifier formulae can be attached where appropriate, and so the formula (2) – for *big* – is tied to that for *policeman* in both templates. But now comes a crucial difference between the two representations, one which will resolve the sense of *crook*.

The expansion algorithm looks into the formulae expressing preferences and sees if any of the preferences are satisfied: as we saw formula (2) for *big* prefers to qualify physical objects. A policeman is such an object and that additional dependency is marked in both templates: similarly for the preference of *interrogate* for human actors, in both representations. The difference comes with preferred objects: only the formula (4a) for human crooks can satisfy that preference, the formula (4b), for shepherds' crooks, cannot. Hence the former template network is denser by one dependency, and is preferred over the latter in all subsequent processing: its connectivity (using numbers for the corresponding formulas, ignoring the *the*s, and using one arrow for each dependency established) is:

$$2 \to \to 1 \to \to 3 \leftarrow \leftarrow 4a$$

and so that becomes the template for this sentence. The other possible template was connected as follows:

$$2 \to \to 1 \to \to 3 \leftarrow 4b$$

and it is now discarded.

Thus, the sub-formulae that express preferences express both the meaning of the corresponding word sense, and can also be interpreted as implicit procedures for the construction of correct templates. This preference for the greatest semantic density works well, and can be seen as an expression of what Joos (1972) calls 'semantic axiom number one', that the right meaning is the last meaning, or what Scriven (1972)[1] has called 'the trick, in meaning analysis, of creating redundancies in the input'. This uniform principle works over both the areas that are conventionally distinguished in linguistics as syntax and semantics. There is no such distinction in this system, since all manipulations are of formulae and templates, constructed out of elements of a single type.

As a simple example of linguistic syntax, done by preference simply to illustrate the general principle, let us take the sentence:

[2] John gave Mary the book

onto which the matching routine will have matched two templates, with heads as follows, since it has no reason so far to prefer one to the other:

```
John   gave   Mary the       book
MAN-GIVE - - - - - - - - - - - - - THING
MAN-GIVE-MAN
```

The expansion routine now seeks for dependencies between formulae, in addition to those between the three formulae constituting the template itself. In the case of the first, a GIVE action can be expanded by any substantive formula to its immediate right which is not already part of the template, (which is to say that indirect object formulae can depend on the

---

[1] It has been pointed out to me that Quillian's work (1968) does contain a preferential metric, and Dr J. Hurford (private communication) has told me that he has been forced to some preference principle in studying derivations of number structures from a linguistic base.

corresponding action formula). Again *book* is qualified by an article, which fact is not noticed by the second template. So then, by expanding the first template we have established in the following dependencies at the surface level, where the dependency arrows '→' correspond to relations established between formulas for the words they link.

John→gave←book←the
↑
Mary

For the present purpose, we are omitting any indication by arrow of the preference of *give* for a human agent, because it occurs equally in both expansions. Now, if we try to expand the second template by the same method, we find we cannot, because the formula for *Mary* cannot be made dependent on the one for *give*, since in that template *Mary* has already been seen, wrongly of course, as a direct object of giving, and it cannot be an indirect object as well. So then, the template with heads MAN GIVE MAN cannot be expanded to yield any dependency arcs connecting formulae to the template; whereas the template with heads MAN GIVE THING yields two dependency arcs on expansion, and so corresponds to the preferred representation. This method can yield virtually all the results of a conventional grammar, while using only relations between semantic elements.

The limitation of the illustrative examples, so far, has been that they are the usual short example sentences, whereas what we actually have here is a general system for application to paragraph length texts. I will now sketch in, for two sorts of case, how the system deals with non-sentential text fragments with a general template format.

In the actual implementation of the system, as an analysis system, an input text is initially fragmented, and templates are matched with each fragment of the text. The input routine partitions paragraphs at the occurrence of any of an extensive list of KEY words. The list contains almost all punctuation marks, subjunctions, conjunctions and prepositions. In difficult cases, described in detail in (Wilks (1972a)), fragmentations are made even though a key word is not present, as at the stroke in *John knows | Mary loves him*, while in other cases a fragmentation is not made in the presence of a key word, such as *that* in *John loves that woman*.

Let us consider the sentence *John is | in the house*, fragmented into two parts at the point marked by the stroke. It should be clear that the three part template, of standard agent-act-action form, cannot be matched onto the fragment *John is*. In such a case, a degenerate template with heads MAN

BE DTHIS is matched onto the two items of this sentence; the last item DTHIS being a dummy object, indicated by the D.

With the second fragment *in the house* a dummy subject DTHIS fills out the form to give a degenerate template with heads DTHIS PBE POINT. The PBE is the same as the head of the formula for *in*, since formulae for prepositions are assimilated to those for actions and have the head PDO or PBE. The fact that they originate in a preposition is indicated by the P, so distinguishing them from straightforward action formulae with heads DO and BE. POINT is the head of the formula for *house*, so this bare template triple for the fragment only tells us that *something is at a point in space*. At a later stage, after the preliminary assignment of template structures to individual fragments, TIE routines attach the structures for separated fragments back together. In that process the dummies are tied back to their antecedents. So, in *John is in the house*, the DTHIS in the MAN BE DTHIS template for the first fragment of the sentence, ties to the whole template for the second fragment, expressing where John is.

It is very important to note that a preference is between alternatives: if the only structure derivable does NOT satisfy a declared preference, then it is accepted anyway. Only in that way can we deal naturally with metaphor.

So, in examples like:

[3] I heard an earthquake / singing / in the shower

(with fragmentation as indicated by slashes), as contrasted (given that the fragmentation programme is sensitive to *ing* suffixes) with:

[4] I heard / an earthquake sing / in the shower

we shall expect, in the first case, to derive the correct representation because of the preference of notions like singing for animate agents. This is done by a simple extension of the density techniques discussed to relations between structures for different fragments (the TIE routines), in this case, by considering alternative connectivities for dummy parts of templates.

Thus, there will be a dummy subject and object template for /singing/, namely DTHIS CAUSE DTHIS, based on the formula

singing: ((*ANI SUBJ)((SIGN OBJE)(((MAN SUBJ)SENSE) CAUSE)))))

which is to say, an act by an animate agent of causing a human to experience some sign (i.e., the song)

Now the overall density will be greater when the agent DTHIS, in the template for *singing*, is tied to a formula for *I* in a preceding template, than when it is tied to one for *earthquake*, since only the former satisfies the preference for an animate agent, and so the correct interpretation of the whole utterance is made.

But, and here we come to the point of this example, in the second sentence, with *sing*, no such exercise of preference is possible, and the system must accept an interpretation in which the earthquake sings, since only that can be meant.

Other kinds of preference are of objects for certain preferred functions: thus it is expressed in the formula for *book* that its preferred function is to be read. Also, adjective qualifiers express preferred kinds of entity to qualify. Thus *big* has a formula expressing a preference for qualifying objects, and so in the expansion of a representation for *The big glass is green* we would get a denser, and so preferred, structure for the object, rather than for the substance, glass.

In order to give a rough outline of the system, I have centred upon the stages of analysis within the individual fragment. After the application of the routines described so far, TIE routines are applied again to the expanded templates in a wider context: the same techniques of expansion, dependency and preference are applied between full templates for different fragments of a sentence or paragraph. At that stage, (1) case ties are applied (using the same cases as occur within formulae at a lower level); (2) the equivalence of active and passive forms is established; (3) dummies are attached to 'what they stand for' as I indicated with the 'earthquake example'; and, importantly, (4) anaphoric ties are settled.

The TIE routines apply PARAPLATES to the template codings, using the same density techniques one level further up, as it were. Paraplates are objects with the form of two connected templates, and each paraplate in stack defines one case application of an English preposition. Consider the following three schematic paraplates for *in*, where the predicates and functions of which each paraplate consists may fall in any of five positions, for the preposition itself always comes in the place of the action of the second template:

FIRST TEMPLATE			SECOND TEMPLATE		
AGENT	ACTION	OBJECT	AGENT	ACTION	OBJECT
	(PRMARK *DO)	(2OBCAS INST GOAL)		(IN *DIRE)	(FN₁(CONT THING))
	(PRMARK *DO)			(IN *DIRE)	(FN₁(CONT THING))
	(PRMARK *DO)	(2OBHEAD NIL)		(IN LOCA)	

*DIRE is a direction case marker (covering two subcases: TO, mentioned above, and FROM), 2OBCAS and 2OBHEAD are simply predicates that look at both the object(third) formulae of the template in hand, and of the preceding template, i.e., at two objects. 2OBHEAD is true iff the two have the same head, and 2OBCAS is true iff they contain the same GOAL or INSTrument subformula. The predicates like PRMARK are satisfied iff the representation of the fragment's mark (the text item on which the fragment depends under the corresponding interpretation: *put* in this case) is an action whose head is in the class of elements *DO, a wide class covering the majority of actions including *putting*. The lower case words simply explain which sense of *in* is the one appropriate to the paraplate in which it occurs. When the system is functioning as a translator these generation items will in this case be different French prepositions, to be generated when the corresponding paraplate 'fits'. The general result after a paraplate has fitted is that two templates have been linked by a correct case tie.

Now consider the sentence,

[4] I put the key / in the lock

fragmented at the stroke as shown. Let us consider that two templates have been set up for the second fragment: one for *lock* as a fastener, and one for raising lock on a canal. Both formulae may be expected to refer to the containment case. We apply the first paraplate and find that it fits only for the template with the correct (fastener) sense of *lock*, since only there will 2OBCAS be satisfied, i.e., where the formulas for *lock* and *key* both have a subformula under GOAL indicating that their purpose is to close something. The second paraplate will fit with the template for the canal sense of *lock*, but the first is a more extensive fit (indicated by the order of the paraplates, since the higher up the paraplate list, the more non-trivial template functions a paraplate contains) and is preferred. This preference has simultaneously selected both the right template for the second fragment and the correct paraplate linking the two templates for further generation tasks.

If we now take the sentence,

[5] He put the number / in the table

with two different templates for the second fragment (corresponding to the list and flat object senses of *table* respectively) we shall find that the intuitively correct template (the list sense) fails both the first paraplate and the second, but fits the third, thus giving us the *make part of* sense of *in*, and the right (list) sense of *table*, since formulae for *number* and (list) *table* have the same head SIGN, though the formula for (flat, wooden) *table* does not. Conversely, in the case of

[6] He put the list / in the table

fitting the correct template with the second paraplate will yield the *into* sense of *in* (case DIREction) and the physical object sense of *table*; and this will be the preferred reading, since the fit (of the incorrect template) with the third paraplate yields the *make part of a list* reading in this case. Here we see the fitting of paraplates, and choosing the densest preferential fit, which is always selecting the highest paraplate on the list that fits, thus determining both word sense ambiguity and the case ambiguity of prepositions at once. Paraplate fitting makes use of the deeper nested parts (essentially the case relations other than SUBJ and OBJE) of the formulae than does the template matching.

The TIE routines also deal with simple cases of anaphora on a simple preference basis. In cases such as

[7] I bought the wine, / sat on a rock / and drank it

it is easy to see that the last word should be tied by TIE to *wine* and not *rock*. This matter is settled by density after considering alternative ties for *it*, and seeing which yields the denser representation overall. It will be *wine* in this case since *drink* prefers a liquid object.

In more complex cases of anaphora, that require access to more information than is contained in formulae, templates or paraplates, the system brings down what I referred to earlier as common-sense (CS) inference rules. Cases that require them will be ones like the sentence:

[8] The soldiers fired at the women and I saw several of them fall

Simple semantic density considerations in TIE are inadequate here because both soldiers and women can fall equally easily, yet making the choice correctly is vital for a task like translation because the two alternatives lead to differently gendered pronouns in French. In such cases the PS system applies a CS rule, whose form, using variables and subformulae, would be $X(((\text{NOTPLEASE}(\text{LIFE STATE}), \text{OBJE})\text{SENSE}) \rightarrow X(\text{NOTUP MOVE})$ For rough expository purposes such a rule is probably better expressed as '$X[\text{hurt}] \rightarrow X[\text{fall}]$', where the words in square brackets correspond informally to the subformulae in the rule. The rules are applied to 'extractions' from the situations to form chains, and a rule only ultimately applies if it can function in the shortest, most-preferred, chain.

The way the CS inferences work is roughly as follows: they are called in at present only when TIE is unable to resolve outstanding anaphoras, as in the present example. A process of extraction is then done and it is to these extractions, and the relevant templates, that the CS rules subsequently apply. The extractions are quasi-inferences from the deep case structure of formulas. So, for example, if we were extracting from the template for *John drank the water*, unpicking the formula for *water* given earlier would extract that some liquid was now inside an animate thing (from the containment case), and that it went in through an aperture of the animate thing (from the directional case). Moreover, since the extractions are partially confirmed, as it were, by the information about actor and object in the surrounding template, we can, by simple tying of variables, extract new quasi-templates equivalent to, in ordinary language, *the water is in John*, etc. These are (when in coded form) the extractions to which the CS rules apply as it endeavours to build up a chain of extractions and inferences. The preferred chain will, unsurprisingly, be the shortest.

So then, in the 'women and soldiers' example we extract a coded form, by variable tying in the templates, equivalent to [women][hurt], since we can tell from the formula for *fired at* that it is intended to hurt the object of the action. We are seeking for partial confirmation of the assertion 'X? [fall]', and such a chain is completed by the rule given, though not by a rule equivalent to, say, 'X[hurt]$\rightarrow X$[die]', since there is nothing in the sentence as given to partially confirm that rule in a chain, and cause it to fit here. Since we are in fact dealing with subformulae in the statement of the rules, rather than words, 'fitting' means an 'adequate match of subformulae'.

It is conceivable that there would be an, implausible, chain of rules and extractions giving the other result, namely that the soldiers fall: [soldiers] [fire];X[fire]$\rightarrow X$[firedat]$\rightarrow X$[hurt], etc. But such a chain would be longer than the one already constructed and would not be preferred.

The most important aspect of this procedure is that it gives a rationale for selecting a preferred interpretation, rather than simply rejecting one in favour of another, as other systems do (see discussion below). It can never be right to reject another interpretation irrevocably in cases of this sort, since it may turn out later to be correct, as if the 'women' sentence above had been followed by *And after ten minutes hardly a soldier was left standing*. After inputting that sentence the relevant preferences in the example might be expected to change. Nonetheless, the present approach is not in any way probabilistic. In the case of someone who utters the 'soldiers and women' example sentence what he is to be taken as meaning is that the women fell. It is of no importance in that decision if it later turns out that he intended to say that the soldiers fell. What was meant by that sentence is a clear, and not merely a likelihood matter.

It must be emphasized that, in the course of this application, the CS rules are not being interpreted at any point as rules of inference making truth claims about the physical world. It is for that reason that I am not contradicting myself in this paper by describing the CS approach while arguing against deductive and TP approaches. The clearest way to mark the difference is to see that there is no inconsistency involved in retaining the rule expressed informally as 'X[fall] → X [hurt]' while, at the same time, retaining a description of some situation in which something animate fell but was not hurt in the least. There is a clear difference here from any kind of deductive system which, by definition, could not retain such an inconsistent pair of assertions.

Such rules are intended to cover not only 'world knowledge' examples like the last example, but also such cases as:

[9] In order to construct an object, it usually takes a series of drawings to describe it

where, to fix the second *it* as *object* and not *series* (though both yield equivalent semantic densities on expansion) we need a CS inference rule in the same format that can be informally expressed as 'an instrument of an action is not also an object of it'. The point of such rules is that they do not apply at a lexical level like simple facts (and so become an unmanageable totality), but to higher level items like semantic formulae and cases. Moreover, their 'fitting' in any particular case is always a 'fitting better than' other applicable rules, and so is a further extension of the uniform principle of inference by density.

Discussion

Two points about the general procedures I have described are of some topical theoretical importance. Firstly, the notion of preferring a semantic network with the greatest possible semantic density is a natural way of dealing not only with normal semantic disambiguation, like the 'policeman' example [1] above, but with metaphor. For example, if we know from the lexical tree for *drink* that, as an action, it prefers human actors, then, in any given context in which a human actor is available, it will be preferred to any non-human actor, since its presence creates a dependency link and increases the semantic density of that context. So, in

[10] The crook drank a glass of water

it would correctly opt for the human and discard the shepherd's staff sense of *crook*. Yet in the case of

[11] My car drinks gasoline

it would accept the automobile sense, since no animate actor is available to be preferred. This all seems obvious and natural, but is in fact very hard to accommodate within the derivational paradigm of TG and GS, where there must either be a stipulational rule requiring, say, animate actors for drinking (in which case [10] is rejected, although perfectly correct), or there is a rule which permits both [10] and [11] to be derived, in which case it is hard to see how a structure involving a shepherd's staff is to be excluded (as it properly should be). PS cannot formally be accommodated within the conventional derivational paradigm because it is equivalent to running another derivation with a different set of rules (after dropping a stipulation about actors for *drink* in this case). Yet it makes no real sense in the conventional paradigm to talk of re-running a derivation after an unsatisfactory result.

A second lacuna in the derivational paradigm is the lack of a natural way of dealing with what one might call knowledge of the real world, of the sort required for the analysis of [8] above. Lakoff (1971) seems to think that such cases are to be dealt with, within the derivational paradigm, by calling such assumptions as are required 'presuppositions' and using a conventional first-order deductive apparatus on them. The question I want to discuss briefly is whether such apparatus can be fitted into the derivational paradigm.

The new development in linguistic theory that GS brought, it will be remembered, can be expressed in Lakoff's (1972) claim that 'the rules relating logical form to surface form are exactly the rules of grammar'. In order to make my most general point below, let me digress briefly upon the last quotation, and summarize the results of detailed argument established elsewhere (Wilks (1972b)). The difficulty in discussing the quoted claim hinges upon what exactly 'relate' in that sentence is to be taken to mean.

With GS, as with all such theses, there are two ways of looking at them: one is to take the words as meaning what they appear to mean; the other is to assume that they mean something quite different. The first approach gives us what I shall call the *translation* view or the *consequence* view depending on how we take the word 'relate' in that last quotation. The second approach would give what I could call the *renaming* view. By that I mean that when Lakoff speaks of logical form he doesn't mean that in any standard sense, but as some linguistic structure, either familiar or of his own devising. In either case, on the renaming view, GS would not really be *about* logic at all, and disputes about it would be wholly an internal matter for linguistics. When Chomsky (1971) and Katz (1971) write of GS as 'notational variant' of Chomsky's work they are taking the renaming view.

The consequence view is the most obvious possibility, namely that the 'relates' is by inference, valid or otherwise, and that the well-formedness of sentences is settled by whether or not they can be inferred from logical forms. Much of the evidence for the assumption that this is Lakoff's view is circumstantial, but it is reinforced by his introduction of rules of inference with 'It is clear that there is more to representing meanings than simply providing logical forms of sentences' Lakoff (1972:606). That quotation seems to rule out the translation view: that logical forms are the meaning, or 'backbone', of sentences and can be related to them by mere rules of translation. The translation view also becomes less plausible when one remembers how much of Lakoff's discussion of these matters is about inference: if GS were really about translation into logical form (which may be equivalent to the 'transformations preserve meaning' view (see Partee (1971)), then inference would have no place at all in a discussion of natural logic. So then, the consequence view must be Lakoff's view if he has a firm view. Three clear and simple considerations tell against it:

First, There is just no clear notion available of inference going from logical forms to sentences. Rules that cross the logical form-sentence boundary are rules of translation.

Second, There is the problem of 'reverse direction': how could one, even in principle, analyse sentences with reverse inference rules to produce logical forms. Reversing inference rules is to produce falsehood, as in *if this is not coloured then it is not red*. What possible interpretation could we attach to such a procedure in the context of GS? It is true that the relation of a sentence to its presuppositions has the required 'inferential direction', but no one has ever seriously suggested that the premisses required for the solution of examples like sentence [8] will in general be presuppositions, in any sense of that over-worked word. In the case of [8], it is clear that the information required for its solution is *not* presuppositional.

And third, Any 'consequence interpretation' of GS will find itself committed to the view that logical falsehoods are ill-formed in some sense, and so should not be generated by a proper linguistic system. This will lead to difficulties with apparently well-formed sentences that might well be held to express implicit logical falsehoods, such as:

[12] I have just proved arithmetic complete

An immediate result at this point in the argument is that, given the consequence interpretation of GS, a GS system could never be used as an analysis system, and so could surely never function so as to take account of 'social context' in the way Lakoff would like. At the very least it requires some more explanation as to how that can be done with a system that is, in principle, non-analytic.

My principal critical point is that the inductive inferences that analysis of examples like [8] requires cannot be incorporated into the derivational paradigm on the consequence interpretation. The use of inductive premisses is not like the use of entailments, where if something is true then something else must be. If inductive premisses or inferential rules are inserted into a derivational system then that system simply must make mistakes sometimes. And so it must mis-analyse or, within the generative task, it must mis-sort sentences. It only makes sense to use such inferences within a system that is capable, in principle, of finding out it has gone wrong and trying again. Such systems have been developed within what may be called the 'artificial intelligence' AI approach to language processing. They cannot be TG or GS systems, where the derivation simply runs and that is that.

The weaker way out of this dilemma for GS would be to save the derivational paradigm and give up a consequence interpretation. The latter could be achieved either by accepting the 'renaming view', which would be most unpalatable I suspect, or by accepting a weaker interpretation of the inference rules like that adopted by PS. That is, so to interpret the rules of inference as to remain wholly within what Carnap called the 'formal mode'. As I described them, CS rules equivalent to *hurt things tend to fall* are fitted on by preference, but are never interpreted as making truth claims about the future course of the physical world. They are merely used to make claims about what a sentence asserts, not about the course of events, or about what the speaker meant. So, the successful application of the quoted CS rule to [8] allows us to infer that the speaker asserted that the women fell. However, if the speaker follows [8] immediately with

[13] And after ten minutes hardly a soldier was left standing as the gas drifted toward them across the marshes

then we may say that the speaker has merely contradicted himself in some weak sense. And, on this hypothetical approach, one might decline to analyse adequately utterances with self-contradictions. And, if point (3) above is correct, then GS must already decline their analysis, since they are 'ill-formed', so this extra proviso should cause no problems. The advantage of this form of interpretation of rules would be that it keeps linguistics self-contained and out of the morass of probability and inductive logic.

However, reconsideration of examples like [10] and [11] shows that the elaborate compromise just described is not possible and that one must adopt the stronger approach, or, to change the metaphor, see that the door has been open behind one all the time, and simply give up the derivational paradigm in favour of an 'intelligent' metasystem. This is essential for examples like the *car drinks gasoline* case above, whose analysis requires some process equivalent to running the derivation again with different rules – and hence some metasystem available to administer such a re-running. And PS, is I believe, an economical way of describing such a system.

There should be nothing very revolutionary in suggesting that the derivational paradigm be quietly abandoned. Its acceptance has for some time been inconsistent with the real everyday practice of generative linguists, which is to do informal analyses of difficult and interesting example sentences (see Wilks and Schank (1973) for a detailed development of this point), and hardly ever to derive or generate a sentence. In a recent paper Fillmore (1972) too seems to have been questioning, from a very different starting point, the most general description of their activities that modern linguists have inherited without question.

If the stronger approach is to give up the derivational paradigm and adopt the AI one (where I am using that term very loosely to cover any formal approach to language processing that admits of wholly extra-derivational procedures), then the question arises as to whether the deductive procedures that Lakoff now (1971) envisages as part of linguistics can and should be retained. There would clearly no longer be the barriers to the use of deductive processes that existed within the derivational paradigm. Would there be others?

I think there are several very general difficulties about the use of a deductive system for assigning structure to natural language, and some of these have emerged already within the AI paradigm, and are worthy of attention by generative linguists. One difficulty concerns the theoretical problem of specifying firm procedures that would allow any particular deductive solution to be carried through. Here I refer to the enormous problems of search and strategy within domains of theorems. These are very large problems that cannot be discussed here. A smaller but persistent one can be illustrated again with regard to sentences [8] and [12].

In the AI paradigm, unlike the derivational one, a system analysing [8] would have the opportunity to reconsider its solution (that the women fell) on encountering [13] in some social context. What one might call the 'standard AI approach' (for example, Winograd (1972)) explains its moves at this point roughly as follows: if we analyse [8] with the aid of the inductive generalization, and later information shows us that the inference was false (i.e. we encounter some form of contradiction), we will simply retrace our steps to some earlier success point in the procedure and try again with the new information.

The persistent trouble with this sort of answer (and there is no better one) is that there is no general test of logical consistency available, even in principle, and it is too much to hope that a text would correct our misinferences immediately, by making the interposed sentence between [8] and [13] *But it was not the women who fell.*

Paradoxically, it is this sort of deductive approach that Lakoff seems to be embracing (1971) without seeing that it requires not only the wider AI paradigm but consistency heuristics as well. It may be worth pointing out that, even if this strong deductive AI approach were to have adequate consistency heuristics, it would still be inadequate as a natural language analyser. For example, one of its assumptions is that speakers always use correct logic in their utterances. But consider the following silly children's story:

[14] I have a nice dog and a slimy snake. My dog has white furry ears. All animals have ears but my snake has no ears, so it is an animal too. I call it Horace.

Since the story contains a logical error, any deductive analyser for solving anaphora problems must conclude that it is the dog that is called Horace, since only that conclusion is consistent with what it already knows. Whereas any reader can see that Horace is a snake.

My hope is that PS can at some point be extended, still within the 'formal mode' and not making deductive claims, so as to cover in natural language whatever the human competencies about consistency may turn out to be, and my hunch is that they will require shallow chains of commonsense reasonings, drawn from a wide data base, rather than the narrow longer chains of the deductive sciences proper. But even if further research should show this particular approach to be inadequate, the need would still exist for some theory of linguistic inference, one not simply obtained second-hand from logicians, for that will never do. The derivational paradigm has shielded linguists from the pressure to explore this important area, but as the paradigm falls gradually away, the need will become clearer and more acute.

REFERENCES

Chomsky, N. (1971). 'Deep structure, surface structure and semantic interpretation'. D. O. Steinberg and L. A. Jacobvits, eds., *Semantics*. Cambridge.

Fillmore, C. (1972) 'On generativity'. In S. Peters, ed., *Goals of Linguistic Theory*. Englewood Cliffs, N.J.

Joos, M. (1972). 'Semantic axiom number one', *Language*, **48,** 257-65.

Katz, J. (1971). 'Generative semantics is interpretive semantics', *Linguistic Inquiry*, **2**:3, 313-31.

Katz, J. & Postal, P. (1964). *An Integrated Theory of Linguistic Descriptions*. Cambridge, Mass.

Lakoff, G. (1971). 'The role of deduction in grammar'. In C. Fillmore and D. T. Langendoen, eds., *Studies in Linguistic Semantics*. New York.

—— (1972). 'Linguistics and natural logic'. In D. Davidson and G. Harman, eds., *Semantics of Natural Language*. New York.

—— (1973). Letter. In *New York Review of Books*, **22,** No. 1, 340.

Partee, B. (1971). 'On the requirement that transformations preserve meaning'. In C. Fillmore and D. Langendoen, eds., *Studies in Linguistic Semantics*. New York.

Quillian, R. (1968). 'Semantic memory'. In M. L. Minsky, ed., *Semantic Information Processing*. Cambridge, Mass.

Scriven, M. (1972). 'The concept of comprehension'. In J. B. Carroll and R. O. Freedle, eds., *Language Comprehension and the Acquisition of Knowledge*. Washington D.C.

Wilks, Y. (1971). 'Decidability and natural logic', *Mind*, **80,** 497-520.

—— (1972a). *Grammar, Meaning and the Machine Analysis of Language*. London.

—— (1972b). 'Lakoff on natural logic'. Stanford A.I. Project Memo No. 161.

—— (1973a). 'An artificial intelligence approach to machine translation'. In R. Schank and K. Colby, eds., *Computer Models of Thought and Language*. San Francisco.

—— (1973b). 'Understanding without proofs', *Proc. Third Internat. Conf. on Artificial Intelligence*. Stanford.

Wilks, Y. and Schank, R. (1973). 'The goals of linguistic theory revisited', *Lingua*, **34,** 301-26.

Winograd, T. (1972). *Understanding Natural Language*. Edinburgh.

VI SEMANTICS AND SURFACE SYNTAX

Arguments for assigning tense meanings after certain syntactic transformations apply

JOSEPH EMONDS

In this paper I will consider a topic previously treated by T. R. Hofmann (1969). Hofmann proposes a solution in his article to the problem posed by the ambiguity of the English surface verbal form 'have + past participle' (i.e. 'have – V – en') in those dependent clauses whose verbs cannot exhibit either a present or simple past tense morpheme. Such clauses are the so-called 'non-finite' clauses: participles, gerunds, and infinitives of various types. I will examine and expand on Hofmann's solution, try to show its inadequacies, and then propose what I hope is a more promising alternative. In my proposal, the semantic tense values of clauses[1] are assigned according to the distribution of tense markers in trees, subsequent to the application of certain syntactic transformations.

I have been greatly aided by the discussion of tense in chapters XXIII and XXIV of O. Jespersen (1964), to which I will be referring throughout the paper.

At the outset I want to emphasize that in my analysis, as in Hofmann's, *syntactic* tense markers occur not only in surface structure *but also*, with different and more regular distribution, in syntactic deep structures. That is, the deep structure existence of these syntactic tense markers is justified by the fact that we can more easily characterize their distribution in deep structure; yet, I will claim that these markers contribute to meaning only by virtue of their position in trees subsequent to the application of many transformational rules.

I.

Hofmann shows that the distribution of the surface verbal form, *have* + V + *en* (where *en* represents the past participle morpheme in English), with respect to time adverbs, is different in clauses which contain present or simple past tense forms (finite clauses) than in clauses without these forms (non-finite clauses).

---

[1] I will speak of the perfect construction (*have* – V – *en*) as a tense throughout the article.

In finite clauses, certain time adverbs are compatible with the present perfect tenses (*have* + *s*/Ø + V + *en*) but not with the simple past tense, while others are compatible with the simple past tense but not with the present perfect tense. (*s*/Ø represents the present tense morpheme, which is phonetically an *s* in the third person singular and otherwise null.) The following examples demonstrate this correlation:

(1) He *arrived last Tuesday*
I am lonely because they *flew* to Chicago *yesterday*
The men who *were* working here *last year* are now unemployed
He *drank* a litre of vodka *three days ago*
The police believe that the letter *was* destroyed *at midnight* (non-repetitive sense)

*He *has arrived last Tuesday*.
*I am lonely because they *have flown* to Chicago *yesterday*
*The men who *have been* working here *last year* are now unemployed
*He *has drunk* a litre of vodka *three days ago*
*The police believe that the letter *has been* destroyed *at midnight* (non-repetitive sense)

(2) **As of this moment*, he *didn't* arrive
*I am lonely because they *now wrote* me about their good times
*Those who *were* studying *since six a.m.* are tired
*Unless he *drank* a litre of vodka *by tomorrow*, he will lose the fortune
*The police believe that the letter *was* destroyed *by now*

As of this moment, he *hasn't arrived*
I am lonely because they *have now written* me about their good times
Those who *have been* studying *since six a.m.* are tired
Unless he *has drunk* a litre of vodka *by tomorrow*, he will lose the fortune
The police believe that the letter *has been* destroyed *by now*

This difference in distribution no doubt reflects the fact that the *meanings* of the simple past tense and the present perfect tense are (i) distinct, and (ii) incompatible with the meanings of the two classes of time adverbs concerned. How these incompatibilities are to be formally represented is not the concern of this paper; with Hofmann, I simply take them in unclear cases as tests for when verbs have 'past' and 'perfect' meanings.

Hofmann claims that past time adverbs, such as those italicized in (1) above, can occur in just those clauses which contain *ed*. Although he is not completely explicit on this point, he clearly means that this co-occurrence restriction is defined on deep structures. Similarly, he claims that perfect tense adverbs, such as those italicized in (2), can occur in those deep structure clauses which contain *have – en* (PERF), (Hofmann (1969:32–3)). However, as Hofmann points out, the surface form *have – V – en* occurs in surface structure with past time adverbs in a variety of constructions:

(3) *Infinitives which result from 'subject raising'*

He is (was) believed to have destroyed the letter at midnight

Compare:

It is believed that he destroyed the letter at midnight.
*It is believed that he has destroyed the letter at midnight.

John appears to have been in Africa last year
It appears that John was in Africa last year
*It appears that John has been in Africa last year

We consider the law to have been improperly enforced last year
We consider that the law was improperly enforced last year
*We consider that the law has been improperly enforced last year

Participles which result from 'relative clause reduction' or other sources

Anyone having worked here yesterday is free to go
Anyone who worked here yesterday is free to go
*Anyone who has worked here yesterday is free to go

Having been overworked yesterday, I would like an easy job today
Since I was overworked yesterday, I would like an easy job today
*Since I have been overworked yesterday, I would like an easy job today

Our spaceship, having been in orbit twice last year, is now in need of repairs
Our spaceship, which was in orbit twice last year, is now in need of repairs
*Our spaceship, which has been in orbit twice last year, is now in need of repairs

Gerunds

I regret having seen that movie a month ago
I regret that I saw that movie a month ago
*I regret that I have seen that movie a month ago
They wouldn't approve of John's not having graduated last year
It is my having acted so foolishly yesterday that has ruined us

Clauses containing the modal auxiliaries

John must have drunk a litre of vodka yesterday
They should have done that three years ago
You ought to have attended last year
The letter may have been destroyed at midnight
She needn't have worked so hard last Tuesday
?They can't have left a week ago

Infinitives with for-phrase subjects in surface structure

They would hate it for us to have used the car last week
Cadillacs are too expensive for them to have bought one last year
For the plane to have been on time yesterday would have been quite
a surprise

A particularly interesting type of clause in which *have* – V – *en* appears with past time adverbs is what we can loosely term 'counterfactual clauses' (Jespersen's 'preterits of imagination'). In such clauses, the past tense morpheme *ed* appears to express the presupposition of the falseness of the clause it appears in, rather than the semantic past that occurs with past time adverbs and not present or perfect time adverbs. Such counterfactual clauses are permitted after the conjunctions *if* and *as if*, and the imperative *suppose*, and are required after the verb *wish*.

(4) If John *wanted* us *now*, he would send a letter
I wish that John *knew* French *by now*
If you *were* there *tomorrow*, they would be satisfied
He wishes that you *wouldn't* come *tomorrow*

Further confirmation that the underlined verb forms in (4) do not have the past time meaning is given by the fact that past time adverbs are not permitted in the same clause:

(5) *If you were here three days ago, I would be happier
    *He wishes that you came yesterday
    *If only anyone knew French last year, we could save some money
    *He wishes that you wouldn't do that yesterday

Counterfactual clauses resemble non-finite clauses in that the past meaning is expressed by *have – V – en*; this is shown by the possibility of co-occurrence with past time adverbs:

(6) If John had wanted us yesterday, he would have sent a letter
    He wishes that you had come yesterday
    If only anyone had known French last year, we could have saved some money
    He wishes that you wouldn't have come three days ago

Before discussing further the use of *have – V – en* to express the semantic past, it should be emphasized that *have – V – en* also expresses the perfect meaning (i.e., co-occurs with perfect tense adverbs) in all the constructions just discussed:

(7) *Infinitives which result from subject raising*

He is believed to have destroyed the letter by now
John seems to have been in Africa since the outbreak of the war
We consider the election to have been decided since six a.m.

Participles

Anyone having worked here since six a.m. is free to go
Having been overworked since I was a child, I would now like an easy job
Our spaceship, having been in orbit now since Tuesday, is in need of repairs

Gerunds

I don't regret not having seen that movie as of this moment
They wouldn't approve of John's not having graduated by now
It is my having acted so foolishly since I arrived that has ruined us

Clauses containing modal auxiliaries

John must have drunk a litre of vodka by now
They should have been studying since six a.m.
You ought to have attended at least once by now
That letter may have been destroyed by now
They can't have seen a girl since they left for the war

Infinitives with for-phrase subjects in surface structure

They would hate it for us to have used up all the gas by now
Cadillacs are too expensive for them to have owned since the war
For the plane to have now finally arrived is a great relief

Counterfactual clauses

If John had wanted us since his arrival, he would have sent a letter
He wishes that Mary had arrived by now
If only anyone had learned French since their arrival, the group
could have saved money
He wishes that John had learned French by now

Since Hofmann assumes that the clauses with past time adverbs in (3) cannot contain PERF (*have – en*) in deep structure, there must be a transformation which inserts PERF into such clauses (Hofmann (1969:34)). For purposes of this discussion, we can change Hofmann's formulation of this rule slightly, and introduce it as follows: (PAST is the feature corresponding to the morpheme *ed*)

PERF-insertion: $\text{PAST} - (\text{PERF}) \Rightarrow \emptyset - \text{PERF} \ / \ X\_\_\_Y$

How is the context $X\_\_\_Y$ of PERF-insertion to be specified exactly? Basically, it will have to include specification of the various kinds of clauses listed in (3), and a specification of the counterfactual context. One such context can be given as $[_S\_\_\_X_S]$; this is the position of PAST in the infinitives formed by subject raising and in participles formed by relative clause reduction or other rules. A second context is $[_S W - \text{MODAL}\_\_\_ X_S]$.[1] A third context for gerunds is $[_S NP - \text{POSS}\_\_\_X_S]$, and a fourth for infinitives with *for*-phrase subjects is $[_S for - NP\_\_\_X_S]$. A final context

[1] The modals *will* and *can* (in some of its uses) are exceptions in that their semantic pasts are expressed by the morpheme *would* and *could*.

for PERF-insertion is a *deep structure* PAST formative in counterfactual complements to *wish, suppose, if*, etc.[1] It is not necessary for our purposes to collapse these contexts formally in the most precise way possible; the main point is that considerable complexity is involved in the context of Hofmann's PERF-insertion rule.

In all the above contexts except for counterfactual clauses, a rule for deleting the present tense morpheme $s/\emptyset$ is also needed. For in all types of infinitives, participles, and gerunds, there is no third person singular verb ending *s*, and the verb *to be* in these constructions does not exhibit the present finite forms *am, is, are*, but rather the form *be* (plus *ing* or *en*). Furthermore, the present tense morpheme $s/\emptyset$ never appears after modals. Examples:

(8) *John is believed to has destroyed the letter at midnight
　　*Anyone hits by unemployment should protest
　　*For the plane to has been on time yesterday would have been quite
　　a surprise
　　*John musts have drunk a litre of vodka yesterday

Thus, there is another rule in the grammar which shares many and perhaps all of the contexts of PERF-insertion; as formulated here, it may or may not have to include the counterfactual clause context:

$$\text{TENSE-deletion:} \begin{bmatrix} \text{TENSE} \\ -\text{PAST} \end{bmatrix} \Rightarrow \emptyset \ / \ \text{X}\underline{\quad}\text{Y}$$

We can now establish an order between PERF-insertion and TENSE-deletion, and generalize TENSE-deletion at the same time. There are many instances when the semantic past in a non-finite clause is expressed by a present rather than a perfect infinitival or participial form. According to Jespersen (1964:247), the present infinitive in surface structure 'refers not only to present time, but generally to the same time as indicated by the main verb'.

(9) John was rumoured to be hunting *last month*
　　Mary appeared to be well *three days before her death*
　　The crowd demonstrating here *yesterday* contained lots of women
　　Most of us, not being at work *last month*, couldn't afford movies
　　They are talking about buying clothes *in the twenties*
　　John's being arrested *last spring* woke his friends up to reality

---

[1] Jespersen also mentions the 'preterit of imagination' (counterfactual) that may occur after the idioms 'It's about time that...', 'it's high time that...'

The boss didn't like it for us to be late *last year*
The other team was too tall for us to beat *last year*

It is difficult to find sentences of this type which have independent[1] past time adverbs in both the main clause and the non-finite subordinate clause, but in many of the above examples the adverb clearly occurs in the non-finite clause. (The middle four examples are of this type.) Further, the paraphrases of certain of the above examples which most probably derive from the same deep structure sources as these latter contain past tenses in the dependent clauses:

(10) It was rumoured that John was in Africa last month
It appeared that Mary was well three days before her death
The crowd which was demonstrating here yesterday contained lots of women
Most of us, since we weren't at work last month, couldn't afford movies
That John was arrested last spring woke his friends up to reality
The boss didn't like it if we were late last year

Following Hofmann, the presence of the (italicized) past time adverbs in the non-finite clauses of (9) means that they must be derived from deep structure sentences which contain *ed*. Since TENSE-deletion already applies in the types of non-finite clauses under discussion, the most natural solution is to allow TENSE-deletion to apply when TENSE is either +PAST or −PAST, and to restrict PERF-insertion in some fashion so that it does not apply to $\begin{bmatrix} \text{TENSE} \\ +\text{PAST} \end{bmatrix}$ when the latter expresses time 'simultaneous' to the main clause. For purposes of exposition, let us say that TENSE exhibits an additional optional feature ±SIMUL. There is then a definition of the following sort governing the distribution of this feature:

SIMULTANEITY CONDITION: Time adverbs in a clause whose TENSE is +SIMUL must be interpretable as simultaneous with the time of the verb in the next higher clause.

We can reformulate PERF-insertion to be sensitive to the feature SIMUL:

PERF-insertion: $\begin{bmatrix} \text{TENSE} \\ +\text{PAST} \\ -\text{SIMUL} \end{bmatrix}$ (PERF) $\Rightarrow \emptyset - \text{PERF} / X\underline{\quad}Y$

[1] By this I mean two past time adverbs which could not just as well appear together in one of the clauses.

This rule will leave unchanged the deep structure *ed* in the dependent clauses of (9). In order to delete it, we order a generalized TENSE-deletion rule after PERF-insertion:

TENSE-deletion: TENSE $\Rightarrow \emptyset$ / X___Y

In both of these rules, the context X——Y refers to the environments for gerunds, infinitives, participles, clauses with modals, and counterfactuals discussed earlier. We can make the contexts for the two rules exactly the same by including the counterfactual context in the TENSE-deletion rule, *provided* the rule inserting $\begin{bmatrix} \text{TENSE} \\ \text{PAST} \end{bmatrix}$ (that is, *ed*) into counterfactuals *follows* TENSE-deletion. The grammar including these three ordered rules, PERF-insertion, TENSE-deletion, and the 'counterfactual rule', I will refer to below as grammar A.

2.

In this section, I would like to make some criticisms of the grammar of English ('grammar A') which accounts for the difference in permissible contexts for *have* – V – *en* in non-finite and finite clauses by using Hofmann's PERF-insertion rule.

The first criticism is that grammar A contains two rules, PERF-insertion and TENSE-deletion, which have different effects but operate in the same or nearly the same context, written here for convenience as X___Y. We have seen that X___Y is in fact quite complicated. In order to capture the obvious generalization, there would have to be a notational convention defined in the theory of grammar which would allow writing syntactic transformations of the following sort:

STRUCTURAL INDEX₁ $\Rightarrow$ STRUCTURAL CHANGE₁ ⌐X___Y
STRUCTURAL INDEX₂ $\Rightarrow$ STRUCTURAL CHANGE₂⌐

Although I certainly cannot rule out the possibility that such a convention is needed in the theory of grammar, I am not aware of any convincing syntactic arguments in favour of it. Since there are other criticisms to be made against grammar A, and since the solution proposed in section 4 obviates the need for this convention in this case, I see no reason to introduce an ad hoc formal mechanism for capturing the generalization that PERF-insertion and TENSE-deletion operate in the same (complicated) environment. Rather, the fact that such a generalization cannot be

captured without an ad hoc formal mechanism seems a defect of grammar A.

The second criticism is that the syntactic element PERF is introduced
into the same surface structure position by two entirely distinct processes.
To be precise, let us assume (11) as the phrase structure rule for expanding S.

(11) S → COMP – NP – (MODAL) – TENSE – VP
                                    (PAST)

(COMP = the 'complementizers' *that, than, as, whether, for*, and, in certain uses, *if*.) With (11) in the grammar, the base must introduce PERF as
the first verbal (i.e. TENSE-bearing) element in the VP. In a purely for-
tuitous manner, the PERF-insertion rule has the same effect. According to
this organization of the grammar, English would be no more complicated if
PERF-insertion transformed a deep structure PAST into an auxiliary
different from PERF (*have-ing, let-en*, etc.) or even into a non-verbal
element in the VP, or if PERF-insertion introduced PERF into some
other position (before an NP, etc.). In other words, grammar A does not
capture the fact that the semantic past, in clauses where the normal element
with this meaning (TENSE) is deleted, is expressed by an element which is
generated by the base anyway for expressing a different (but related)
semantic concept, not in some random fashion by some substitute morpheme.

The third criticism is analogous to the second; grammar A introduces
the same syntactic element $\begin{bmatrix} \text{TENSE} \\ +\text{PAST} \end{bmatrix}$ into the same structural position
by two entirely distinct and unrelated formal processes. Rule (11) in the
base generates *ed* under S, and the rule inserting *ed* into counterfactuals
does the same thing accidentally. It should be recalled that this latter
transformation must follow TENSE-deletion, if we maximize regularity in
Hofmann's solution by making PERF-insertion and TENSE-deletion subject to exactly the same contexts. Thus, the generation of *ed* in the base and
the transformational insertion of *ed* would be separated by at least two
transformational rules.

To see more concretely how the grammar of section one does not express
a certain simplicity in the grammar of English, suppose that the counterfactual rule inserted not +PAST with TENSE, but some other feature,
say SUBJUNCTIVE, so that there were a different set of verbal forms for
counterfactual clauses. According to grammar A, such a version of English
would be no more complicated than what we have today. (It is true that

were is sometimes substituted for *was* in counterfactuals, but *were* is clearly a past form, and further, as Jespersen (1964:256) notes, this '*were* is chiefly a literary survival, which does not belong to natural spoken English except in such fixed phrases as *if I were you* and *as it were*'.

Of course, there are languages, more complicated than English in this particular respect, which do have special forms for counterfactuals; however, even in such languages, the special forms such as the subjunctive often have more than one semantic function, indicating that the organization of the grammar suggested in section one may be incorrect for those languages also.

A fourth criticism of grammar A is that it implies that all non-finite clauses in English (at least all those that can contain time adverbs, which includes almost all such clauses) must derive from a deep structure source sentence which dominates TENSE. The possibility that some non-finite clauses do not contain a TENSE in their deep structure is excluded. In section 4 I will argue on independent grounds that gerunds do not co-occur with a TENSE element in deep structure, and that hence the possibility of various classes of time adverbs should not be stated in terms of the deep structure presence or absence of *s/∅*, *ed*, *have – en*, etc.

3.

Is there any way to preserve Hofmann's assumption that various classes of time adverbs depend on the deep structure presence of elements like PAST and PERF in the same clause, and to avoid the criticisms of section 2 at the same time?

There is an alternative to grammar A that accomplishes this in part, but only at the cost of introducing new disadvantages. Suppose we attribute the surface structure 'ambiguity' of PERF (i.e., the ability to co-occur with both past time and perfect time adverbs) in non-finite clauses to a systematic deep structure ambiguity of the PERF element, by replacing (11) with (12).

(11) a. $S \rightarrow COMP - NP - (MODAL) - TENSE - VP$
      $ (PAST)$

   b. $VP \rightarrow (PERF) - \ldots$

(12) a. $S \rightarrow COMP - NP - (MODAL) - TENSE - VP$

   b. $VP \rightarrow \begin{pmatrix} PERF \\ (PAST) \end{pmatrix} - \ldots$

That is, we make PAST an optional deep structure feature on PERF rather than on TENSE, and TENSE, like other categories in the grammar, is assumed to be −PAST (and −N, −V, −PLURAL, etc.) unless marked otherwise by some transformation. TENSE in this way is a sort of 'finiteness' marker which, unless the feature PAST is added to it, is morphologically realized as $s/\emptyset$.

With this approach (call it 'grammar B' for reference), we can continue to suppose that past time adverbs occur in deep structure when PAST occurs in the same clause, and that perfect time adverbs occur only when $\begin{bmatrix} \text{PERF} \\ \text{-PAST} \end{bmatrix}$ is in the same clause.

In grammar B, the TENSE-deletion rule and the rule adding +PAST to TENSE (i.e., *ed*) in counterfactual clauses still operate (in that order). But of course there is no PERF-insertion rule. Instead, the following transformation applies *after* the rule adding +PAST to counterfactuals.

$$\text{PAST-insertion:} \begin{bmatrix} \text{TENSE} \\ -\text{PAST} \end{bmatrix} - \begin{bmatrix} \text{PERF} \\ +\text{PAST} \end{bmatrix} \Rightarrow \begin{bmatrix} \text{TENSE} \\ +\text{PAST} \end{bmatrix} - \emptyset$$

This rule says that a deep structure PAST is represented by *ed* and not by *have − en* only if (i) TENSE is present in a clause, and (ii) it has not already been changed to +PAST by some other rule. PAST-insertion has no need of a context restriction, and so removes the first criticism of section 2. Also, the syntactic element PERF is generated in all its occurrences by a single syntactic process (rule (12b)). Finally, the base rules (12) allow us to assign some non-finite clauses with past-time adverbs a deep structure VP source which does not contain TENSE; and I will argue in section 4 that such deep structures must be included in the grammar of English.

On the other hand, there are a number of objections to grammar B. First, it is still true that $\begin{bmatrix} \text{TENSE} \\ +\text{PAST} \end{bmatrix}$ is inserted into the same structural position by two unrelated rules; the counterfactual rule and the PAST-insertion rule characteristic of grammar B.

Secondly, if we retain Hofmann's assumption that past time adverbs can occur only in deep structure clauses that contain PAST, then the deep structures of the dependent clauses of (9) must contain the element $\begin{bmatrix} \text{PERF} \\ +\text{PAST} \end{bmatrix}$ according to grammar B. But since these dependent clauses do not exhibit *have − V − en*, grammar B must include an ad hoc deletion rule of the following sort:

PERF-deletion: $\begin{bmatrix} \text{PERF} \\ +\text{PAST} \\ +\text{SIMUL} \end{bmatrix} \Rightarrow \emptyset$

A third problem with grammar B is the past perfect tense. In grammar B the deep structure representation of this tense cannot be TENSE – $\begin{bmatrix} \text{PERF} \\ +\text{PAST} \end{bmatrix}$, as this is the deep structure of the simple past tense. On the other hand, we cannot reformulate the PAST-insertion rule so that PERF is optionally 'left behind', because the past perfect is not an optional, synonymous variant of the past tense, as the examples of (13) show.

(13) John had left when Mary arrived ≠ John left when Mary arrived
We had been working since five o'clock ≠ *We were working since five o'clock
?John had been more trustworthy after getting his new post ≠ John was more trustworthy after getting his new post

The only remotely natural solution to this problem would be to allow sequences of PERF in deep structure and to then impose an ad hoc surface structure constraint that not more than one PERF per clause appear in surface structure.[1] But a solution of this type is of no interest if something more insightful can be found.

In the first three sections of this paper I have studied two different ways that a grammar of English might be written consistent with the assumption that the syntactic feature PAST in deep structure is what permits past time adverbs to appear in a clause. In section 1, I followed Hofmann's proposal that the PAST morpheme of finite clauses (*ed*) is the untransformed deep structure PAST element, and in section 3 I assumed that the PAST morphemes of non-finite clauses (*have – en*) is the deep structure past element. Both of these solutions have been seen to have serious defects.

[1] In a few marginal cases one hears what are probably 'errors', in which two auxiliary *haves* occur in the same clause:

?John must have already've left when Mary arrived
? If John had already've left when Mary arrived, there wouldn't have been trouble

Even in these marginal cases, *have* cannot appear uncontracted and other adverbs cannot be freely substituted for *already*:

* John must have previously've left when Mary arrived
* If John had completely've finished when Mary arrived, there wouldn't have been trouble

Further, if such examples were *bona fide* examples of two successive perfect auxiliaries, the surface structure would be *have – have – en – V – en* (i.e., *have had left*, for example). But instead, what occurs marginally is *have 've left*.

In section 4, I propose a grammar of tense for English in which the occurrence of time adverbs depends on the surface structure distribution of TENSE elements, rather than on deep structure distribution.

4.

One possible explanation for the different co-occurrence relations between the perfect form *have* – V – *en* and time adverbs in finite and non-finite clauses is that the perfect morphemes may simply have a different meaning when they follow *s*/∅ (in which case past time adverbs cannot co-occur) and when they occur elsewhere (after *ed* or in a TENSE-less clause). In the latter case, *have* – *en* could be assigned a more general meaning like 'anterior to the time of the next highest verb',[1] which it then contributes to the meaning of the verb it modifies.

According to this view, which of its meanings *have* – *en* contributes to a clause is determined (or 'inserted' or 'interpreted') *after* all the rules producing non-finite clauses of various types apply (subject raising, relative clause reduction, etc.).

It seems to me that this view is quite possibly correct, yet it does deny more or less without proof Hofmann's implicit assumption that *have* – *en* is ambiguous in non-finite clauses. In this last section I will take a slightly more conservative point of view, maintaining with Hofmann that *have* – *en* is ambiguous in non-finite clauses (because it can co-occur with both past time and perfect time adverbs), and still show that the meanings of *have* – *en*, and of TENSE for that matter, should be determined or 'inserted' or 'interpreted' *after* the rules which produce non-finite clauses apply.

One criticism of the grammars based on Hofmann's assumptions of sections 1–3 was that each of the two syntactic elements PAST and PERF were introduced into the same structural positions (and into no other positions) by two distinct grammatical processes.

An obvious way to remedy this is to say that only one rule assigns each of *ed* and *have* – *en* into trees (namely, their lexical entries), and that each of these elements is semantically ambiguous lexically. Let us assume (11) as the phrase structure rule expanding S. Then, representing semantic features by italicized capitals, let us assume that the grammar of English contains the following 'lexical entries' (i.e. ordered triples of syntactic, semantic, and phonological features):

---

[1] In some cases, the next lowest verb is involved:

(i) The boy who Mary shot had insulted her the day before.
(ii) John had left before Mary arrived

$$(14)^1 \begin{bmatrix} V \\ AUX \end{bmatrix} - AFFIX, \begin{Bmatrix} PERF \\ PAST \end{Bmatrix}, \textit{have} - en$$

$$TENSE, \begin{Bmatrix} PAST \\ COUNTERFACTUAL \end{Bmatrix}, ed$$

$$TENSE, -PAST \qquad\qquad , s/\emptyset$$

Under what organization of the grammar do these 'lexical entries' make sense? If the lexical assignment of semantic content were made at the deep structure level, then a clause could seemingly be assigned (optionally) both $-PAST$ and $+PAST$ meanings (from $s/\emptyset - have - en$), or the meaning $+PAST$ 'twice' (from $ed - have - en$). This would have to be prevented by a convention in grammatical theory of the following sort:

TENSE Convention: Each clause (containing a verb) can be assigned at most one semantic tense value.

But still the feature *PAST* in the lexical entry for *have* $-en$ is useless if the lexical information of (14) is added to trees at the deep structure level, for the TENSE convention ensures it will never be used.

However, we can continue to impose the TENSE convention and to use the lexical entries of (14), if the information in these lexical entries is inserted in the tree *after* the rules producing non-finite clauses including TENSE-deletion apply.

Before seeing what the advantages of this approach are, let us examine just the mechanics of assigning TENSE meanings in this way. Consider the following representative sampling of examples examined earlier in this paper.

(15) a. *He has arrived last Tuesday
    b. He arrived last Tuesday
    c. As of this moment, he hasn't arrived
    d. He is believed to have destroyed the letter at midnight
    e. He is believed to have destroyed the letter by now
    f. He is believed to have destroyed the letter
    g. If John wanted us now, he would send a letter
    h.*He wishes that you came yesterday
    i. If John had wanted us yesterday, he would have sent a letter
    j. He wishes that Mary had arrived by now

---

[1] I leave open the possibility that there may be a somewhat redundant *syntactic* feature $\pm$ PAST associated with TENSE, which might be needed for the number agreement rule. Such redundancy between syntactic and semantic features seems to be the rule rather than the exception in language. Cf. French gender, English plurals, German gender, etc., where apparently related yet distinct syntactic and semantic features operate in the grammar.

(Non-finite clauses which contain neither TENSE nor *have – en* will be considered below.)

In (a), the morpheme *s/Ø* assigns −*PAST* to the clause; by the *TENSE* convention, *have – en* must be assigned the *PERF* meaning. This in turn is incompatible with a past time adverb. In (b), *ed* assigns *PAST* to the clause, which is compatible with a past time adverb. In (c), *s/Ø* again assigns −*PAST* to the clause, implying that *have – en* must have the PERF meaning, which is compatible with the perfect tense adverb. In (f), *have – en* can be assigned either the *PERF* or *PAST* meanings, and this means that either a past time or a perfect adverb may be added, as in (d) and (e). In (g), the *would* of the main clause makes obligatory a counterfactual reading of the conjunction *if*, which in turn means *ed* is not interpreted as *PAST*. We will see below that such clauses eventually receive an automatic −*PAST* interpretation, making possible an adverb like *now*. Similarly in (h), the verb *wish* requires a counterfactual complement, meaning that the *ed* does not assign *PAST* to the clause; this in turn makes a past time adverb impossible. In (i), *if* again is obligatorily counterfactual because of the *would* in the main clause, so *ed* has the counterfactual meaning. At this point, the clause is not assigned a TENSE value, so *have – en* may be assigned either the *PAST* or *PERF* meaning, but only the former is compatible with the past time adverb in the same clause. In (j) the situation is similar, except that the perfect tense adverb forces a *PERF* interpretation on *have – en*.

It should perhaps be emphasized that ambiguity of non-productive syntactic morphemes of the type exemplified in (14) is not at all unusual. For example, the English second person pronoun *you* is ambiguous between the singular and plural (cf. *yourself* vs. *yourselves*); the plural of French determiners (*les, ces, des, mes, vos, ses, leurs*, etc.) and of German articles and adjectives is ambiguous with regard to gender; most modern Indo-European languages have first person plural forms ambiguous between the inclusive and the exclusive use; most of the modal auxiliaries in English have two meanings, as discussed at some length in Hofmann's article; many prepositions are ambiguous between time or space or time and causal meanings, etc. In all these cases, it is a question of ambiguity and not non-specificity, and syntactic evidence from the language in question can be brought forth to show that the distinction operates in the grammar of the language.

It should also be noted that at present there is no way to evaluate by a purely formal criterion a 'lexical solution' to the problems posed by tense elements as embodied in the lexical entries in (14) and the TENSE convention,[1] as compared to a 'transformational solution', as embodied by rules like PERF-insertion and a rule inserting *ed* in counterfactual clauses. We have no *a priori* way to measure the relative contribution of lexical entries (at any level) and transformations to the complexity of the grammar. The two solutions can be fruitfully compared only by noting which generalizations each does or does not capture.

We have already seen that the 'lexical solution', by introducing *ed* and *have – en* into trees in only one way, answers one defect of the 'transformational' solutions of grammars A and B. (Section 2 explained this defect in detail.) Further, the lexical solution avoids accidentally repeating a context in two different rules, as was necessary in grammar A. And there is no problem in representing the past perfect tense in deep structure as in grammar B; it has the natural representation *ed – have – en*, as grammar A.

I continue to assume with Hofmann that the possibility of occurrence for various time adverbs depends on the semantic tense values assigned to a clause; but since in the lexical solution these values are assigned only *after* the rules which create non-finite clauses, the lexical solution makes it possible that certain non-finite clauses of surface structure may also be TENSE-less in deep structure. We saw in section 1 that grammar A was not consistent with this position. Thus, if we can argue on independent grounds that there are TENSE-less (non-finite) clauses in deep structure, this would be evidence favouring the lexical solution (or grammar B) over grammar A.

In chapter 3 of my dissertation (Emonds (1970)), I argue that *that*-clauses and infinitives do not have NP status at any level in the grammar of English. Among the numerous arguments given there to this effect, the most important points out how for each NP position in the base (subject position, object position, object of preposition position, possessive position), a grammar of English of higher explanatory power can be obtained by assuming that such clauses never have NP status.[2] I also argue that

---

[1] The term 'lexical solution' is not to be confused with 'lexicalist hypothesis' in Chomsky (1970).

[2] For example, several arguments are given justifying the following surface structure:

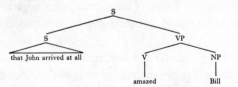

The argument which follows in the text does not in fact depend on this analysis, but only on the non-controversial fact that gerunds are NPs.

gerunds, by contrast, *are* NPs, and should be generated in NP positions in the base by either rule (16) or (17):

(16) NP → S
(17) NP → NP – VP

For convenience, let us repeat the S expansion rule I am using in the 'lexical solution', rule (11):

(11) S → COMP – NP – (MODAL) – TENSE – VP

Richard Kayne has pointed out to me that, given the conclusions of my dissertation, it is definitely preferable to generate gerunds by (17) and not (16). For gerunds never exhibit modals, present or past tense affixes, or the complementizers of finite clauses. All these elements are generated under S but not under VP, according to rule (11), and so they would be automatically and correctly excluded from gerunds by adopting rule (17). It is important to see this is not a trivial point, for there are many instances when gerunds have no *that*-clause (or infinitive) paraphrase:

(18) I would accord *defeating imperialism* a high priority
Bill argued against *the chairman's being allowed to speak*
The importance of *your being here* was overestimated

If rule (16) could generate Ss freely in the positions of the italicized gerunds in (18), sentences with modal auxiliaries would be generated and would have to be marked as ungrammatical deep structures by some special ad hoc device. Since a grammar which generates gerunds with (17) accomplishes the same task by using the least powerful generative device at all useful in grammar, a phrase structure rule, it is hard to see how anything but a notational variant of this solution could be acceptable.

Furthermore, by adopting (17) rather than (16), we can assign English subject pronouns to just those NPs immediately dominated by S (before the application of certain purely stylistic rules), and possessive forms to just those NPs immediately dominated by NP. In all other contexts, English pronouns have objective form. These principles together with rule (17) explain why the subjects of gerunds are in the possessive and not the subjective case.

The only way that grammar A could incorporate most of the advantages of rule (17) would be if it generated gerunds with a sort of stopgap rule of the form NP → NP – TENSE – VP. The appearance of TENSE in this rule is entirely ad hoc, since TENSE generated in this way would always be deleted in grammar A by either PERF-insertion or TENSE-deletion. Furthermore, TENSE would then appear on the right-hand side of two phrase structure rules in grammar A. This would go against a constraint on phrase structure rules observed in practice if not often discussed explicitly: non-phrasal nodes (N, V, A, PREP, MODAL, DET, DEG,[1] COMP, CONJ, PLURAL, EMPH, etc.) do not seem to occur on the right-hand side of more than one phrase structure rule in a given grammar.

Inasmuch as (17) is justified, then, as the deep structure source for gerunds, we can conclude that a lexical solution (or grammar B) is superior to grammar A.

As a final point, it will be recalled that in grammars A and B, the italicized dependent clauses of (9), repeated here for convenience, must contain a PAST element in deep structure.

(9) John was rumoured *to be hunting last month*
   Mary appeared *to be well three days before her death*
   The crowd *demonstrating here yesterday* contained lots of women
   Most of us, *not being at work last month*, couldn't afford movies
   They are talking about *buying clothes in the twenties*.
   John's being arrested last spring woke his friends up to reality
   The boss didn't like it *for us to be late last year*
   The other team was too tall *for us to beat last year*

I suggested in section 1 that this PAST element be assigned a feature +SIMUL to distinguish it from the underlying PASTs which are morphologically realized as *have – en* in non-finite clauses. Grammar A can then describe this distinction fairly easily, as we saw, by making PERF-insertion sensitive to $\begin{bmatrix} \text{PAST} \\ -\text{SIMUL} \end{bmatrix}$, so that TENSE-deletion applies to $\begin{bmatrix} \text{PAST} \\ +\text{SIMUL} \end{bmatrix}$. On the other hand, in grammar B an entirely ad hoc deletion of $\begin{bmatrix} \text{PERF} \\ \text{PAST} \\ +\text{SIMUL} \end{bmatrix}$ must be added to the grammar in order to account for the non-finite clauses of (9).

In the lexical solution, the lexical entries of (14) do not assign any semantic tense value to surface structure clauses not containing *have – V – en*. But such non-finite (and counterfactual) clauses cannot contain any kind of time adverb, without restriction:

[1] DEG = the 'degree' words which modify adjectives (*very, too, as,* etc.).

(19) *John is believed to be in Africa last year
  *John was considered at the meeting to be too harsh in his previous
    decisions

Rather, the present infinitives, participles, and gerunds in (9) obligatorily
express a *tense-simultaneity* with the verb in the next highest clause.[1] As
Jespersen (1964:247) states, 'the present infinitive...refers not only to the
present time, but generally to the same time as indicated by the main verb,
thus:

$$
\text{[Jespersen's examples]} \left\{ \begin{array}{l} \text{It does him good} \\ \text{It did him good} \\ \text{It has done him good} \\ \text{It had done him good} \\ \text{It will do him good} \\ \text{It will have done him good} \end{array} \right\} \begin{array}{l} \text{to take} \\ \text{long walks.} \end{array}
$$

In seeking to describe this phenomenon in the lexical solution, it seems
more appropriate to discard the feature SIMUL and to add an interpretive
principle of the following sort:

TENSE-assignment condition: Clauses which are not assigned tense
values by the lexical entries receive obligatorily the same TENSE
specification as the verb in the next highest clause.

There are some exceptions to this condition, but they would probably be
exceptional in any description of this data. (See above p. 364, n. 1.)
  The TENSE-assignment condition has wider applicability than the way
the feature SIMUL was used in non-finite clauses in grammars A and B. In
those grammars, SIMUL appears in rules so as to permit past time adverbs
with some present infinitives and participles and to exclude them with
others, as in (20):

(20) Walking even a little bit last year did him good
  *Walking even a little bit last year does him good

But in both grammars A and B there would have to be other rules for non-
finite clauses utilizing the feature SIMUL. For example, a rule deleting
will when it carries the feature +SIMUL would be necessary to explain the
examples of (21). (I am assuming that future time adverbs can occur only in

---

[1] An exception is *They were talking about buying clothes in the twenties.* Any description
of this type of data would probably have to treat a gerund of this type differently from
other non-finite clauses of (9).

clauses marked as semantically future; in grammars A and B such clauses would no doubt contain underlying *will*.)

(21)   Walking even a little bit next year will do him good
       Walking even a little bit now is doing him good
       *Walking even a little bit next year is doing him good

       Not owning a house next year will save us on taxes
       *Not owning a house next year is saving us on taxes

       You will later regret not seeing that movie next week
       *He regrets not seeing that movie next week

Such a *will*-deletion rule in non-finite clauses (sensitive to +SIMUL) is not necessary in the lexical solution, given the TENSE-assignment condition.

Similarly, it seems that a deletion of PERF would be necessary even in grammar A (which otherwise has no PERF-deletion rule) to account for the optional lack of *have – en* in the italicized clauses of (22):

(22)   *Telling lies since she was seven* has had an effect on her
       The experience of *being poor since my childhood* has taught me much
       **Telling lies since she was seven* harmed her reputation
       *The experience of *being poor since my childhood* made me pessimistic

Again, such a rule would be obviated in the lexical solution by the more general TENSE-assignment condition.

Thus, a final advantage of the lexical solution proposed in this section over the 'transformational solutions' of grammars A and B is that a general statement can be made on how to interpret so-called 'present' (but in reality TENSE-less) infinitives, participles, and gerunds.

In conclusion, I have proposed in this section that the semantic tense values of clauses be assigned by the lexical entries (14) and the TENSE-assignment condition after the application of certain syntactic transformations (subject raising, relative clause reduction, TENSE-deletion, etc.). I hope I have also shown that only a solution of this type to the problem of the ambiguity of *have – en* raised by Hofmann allows us to capture the necessary generalizations in this domain of linguistic inquiry.[1]

---

[1] Lack of time has prevented me from revising this article to take into account an alternative hypothesis which seems quite plausible, as I now view this topic. As a result, this article takes on more the aspect of a working paper, choosing between certain hypotheses but not taking into consideration others that merit careful attention.
The alternative is this: PERF and PAST may be a single syntactic element PAST′ that

REFERENCES

Chomsky, N. (1970). 'Remarks on nominalization'. R. Jacobs and P. Rosenbaum, eds., *Readings in English Transformational Grammar*. Waltham, Mass.: Ginn and Co.

Emonds, J. (1970). 'Root and structure-preserving transformations'. Reproduced by the Indiana University Linguistics Club, Bloomington, Indiana.

Hofmann, T. R. (1969). 'La transformation de remplacement du constituent "Passé" et ses rapports avec le système modal de l'anglais', *Langages*, **14**, ed. N. Ruwet.

Jespersen, O. (1964). *Essentials of English Grammar*. University of Alabama: University of Alabama Press.

McCawley, J. (1971). 'Tense and time reference in English'. In C. Fillmore and T. Langendoen, eds., *Studies in Linguistic Semantics*. New York: Holt, Rinehart and Winston.

can be generated in two different positions in the base: as a feature co-occurring with TENSE, as in (11) (hence immediately dominated by S), and as a first (optional) element of the VP. This view requires generating non-phrasal nodes which are not lexical categories by more than one rule in the base, which relaxes a restriction in the text; however, other nodes such as NEG and WH may be so generated, meaning that the relaxation in the direction indicated could be correct.

Given this dual source for PAST', non-finite clauses in which *have – en* has a semantic past reading could be derived by deleting only TENSE and not PAST' from the feature bundle TENSE, PAST' and by associating the phonological shape *have – en* with any PAST' which does not co-occur with TENSE. (It might be intuitively more plausible to consider TENSE as simply the 'assertion' marker, and terminologically more accurate to simply replace it with the symbol ASSERTION, which can occur with PAST or simply alone – the latter case being the 'present tense', which is known in many cases to act more like a tenseless form semantically.)

With rules to accomplish these derivations, I think one could still maintain that tense and aspect meanings are assigned to morphemes in deep structure, thereby contradicting the main point of the text. That is, perfect meanings would result from a sequence of TENSE – PAST', but a perfect *form* could also be derived from a deep structure TENSE that does not precede PAST' but rather co-occurs with it, and is then later deleted, leaving only PAST'.

Although I may be misreading the article, I think this is what McCawley is proposing in McCawley (1971), once terminological differences and independent questions such as whether tense and auxiliary elements are verbs, whether verb phrases are sentences, and whether each auxiliary has a verb phrase sister constituent are eliminated.

Given an alternative that preserves deep structure as the locus of semantic interpretation of tense and aspect morphemes, I think it is still an independent question if the TENSE-assignment condition (the determination of the semantic tense of surface clauses which exhibit no tense morphemes) applies at the surface level, but clearly this question should also be re-examined.

Towards a formal treatment of the phenomenon of aspect

CATHERINE FUCHS AND JACQUES ROUAULT

Introduction

The objective towards which we are working is the development of a French Recognition Grammar (FRG) capable of being automatized. Apart from the purely formal aspects (development of the model, logico-mathematical definition of the operators, writing the rules), such an enterprise must necessarily have its basis in a linguistic theory;[1] in this work the essential linguistic concepts are borrowed from A. Culioli (see Culioli (1971) and Culioli, Fuchs, and Pecheux (1970)). The aim of this paper is not to expound or justify the theory, but rather to show how, from this theoretical starting point, the linguistic phenomenon of aspect can be treated within the framework of an FRG.[2]

We shall note very briefly that the chief characteristic of the theory we adopt is that it takes into account the whole dimension of 'utterance'. Our basic assumption is that syntactic structures (to which may be added an interpretation of the lexical units by means of semantic features) cannot on their own satisfactorily account for a certain number of phenomena such as the different roles of determiners, the choice of the passive as opposed to the active, the use of auxiliaries, tenses, 'presenters', etc. Even less can this level of explanation account for the ties of affinity or the rules of exclusion which exist among these different phenomena. Worse still: certain phenomena which seem at first sight to belong to the realm of syntax (e.g. complex sentences, relative clauses) can be treated solely in terms of structural concepts (e.g. 'embedding') only if one takes certain theoretical decisions which are likely to conceal more problems than they elucidate.

Assuming that a 'flexible' syntactic analysis has been carried out in the first levels of the FRG describing the syntactic functions of the different

[1] It is of importance that this theory has been developed from studies made of numerous languages; if this were not the case, our French grammar would be severely limited by the superficial characteristics of this one language.

[2] 'Grammar' should be understood here to have a meaning different from 'syntagmatic grammar'; our aim is to discover operations situated at a sufficiently deep level to escape the specific restrictions of French.

word-groups, we shall in this paper work at a deep level, taking an abstract object, the *lexis*, and considering a series of utterance operations bearing on this object. These operations correspond to the adoption of the lexis by a language user; in a production model, their effect is to associate with each term of the lexis a number of marks (determinations) which enable the lexis to be transformed into a statement. Conversely, the task of the FRG is to distinguish these marks and identify them as signs of the corresponding operations. In this paper we have attempted to develop a formalism which would enable us to describe *aspect*.

The lexis

As we indicated in the introduction, one of the aims of a French Recognition Grammar is the representation of an entry text in terms of abstract concepts (lexes) that exist at a deep level of analysis, and the elucidation of the relationships between lexes. The aim of this section is to define the theoretical framework within which we are working.

The lexis

The lexis diagram. This diagram is made up of three positions and three relations between these positions. The three positions have a meaning of their own, independent of the meaning of the elements which we will later place on them:

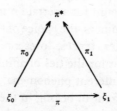

π^* designates a predicative position. Elements which appear in this position 'relate' the elements assigned to the other two positions. ζ_0 and ζ_1 are respectively the point of departure and the point of arrival of the relation.

These three positions are interrelated by π_0, π_1 and π acting in the directions shown on the diagram. π_0, π_1 and π summarize a certain number of extra-linguistic considerations connected with the production of the speech analysed. These considerations form parts of fields of study that at present remain largely unexplored (psycholinguistics, sociolinguistics, ethnolinguistics, . . .).

The lexis. A lexis is obtained by filling the lexis diagram, using constants or variables. In order to avoid going into the problems raised by the nature of constants, we will note simply that constants may be: either *lexical units* (terminal vocabulary) representing 'notions'; or *lexes,* in which case we have embedding of lexes; or *meta-terms.* For example:

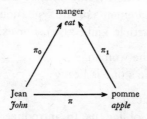

The fact that we can use a given lexical unit as an example in position π^* or position ξ is not attributable to a specific property in that unit which remains immutably associated with it. If such were the case, our work would amount to no more than a sort of coding. In reality, we speak not of three isolated units but of a triple of units ('primitive relation') with which are associated a certain number of speech properties which condition the functioning of the units in question in a particular text.

The nature of the positions in the lexis diagram. We wish to stress the following point: *the lexis exists at a pre-assertive level, that is to say quite independently of its being used by a speaker.*

The only effect of constructing a lexis from three 'notions' is that the notions lose their neutrality with regard to function; thus the notation chosen, which opposes position π^* to the other two positions, takes into consideration the fact that the lexis will be used to form a statement. For a statement to take place there must be, besides the adoption of the lexis by a speaker, an element that is called 'organizing', 'relational' or 'predicative' in various terminologies; it is this element that we assign to position π^*.

But we will be careful not to identify the element assigned to position ξ_0 with the subject, the element assigned to position π^* with the verb, or the element in position ξ_1 with the direct object, even if we use a 'deep' interpretation of these terms that does not involve the active/passive transformation. We will in fact see that the direct object cannot always be placed in position ξ_1: this is the case with verbs like *aider (to help).*

Similarly, to think that the element assigned to position π^* can be embodied in the surface structure only by a verb would be to deny the lexis theory a large part of its originality; in fact we know that in French it can also be embodied at the surface by an adjective, an adverb, a pre-position, etc.

Moreover, the fact that predicative and verb do not necessarily coincide should enable us to explain so-called 'non-verbal' constructions in certain African languages for example. In Bambara, which has a verbal category, we can observe, existing side by side with verbal statements, non-verbal (nominal or adjectival) statements of the type (noun + predicative particle) or (noun + predicative particle + adjective). For example:

(1) a. musò *dò* : it's the woman
    b. fàrà *kà* giri : the stone is heavy

(The particles are in italics.)

These considerations oblige us to introduce a special terminology, clarified by the following definitions:

Definition 1: a '*relater*' is a notion assigned to position π^* of the lexis diagram in such a way that it forms a lexis together with two other assigned notions.

Definition 2:
  (i) an *argument* is a notion assigned to a ξ position in the lexis diagram;
  (ii) the argument assigned to position ξ_0 is the *source* of the lexis relater, and the argument assigned to position ξ_1 is its *target*.

The problem of the number of positions in the lexis diagram. The fact that we have fixed this number at three may cause the reader some difficulty. The 'defence and illustration' of the three-position diagram has been presented from the linguistic point of view in Culioli et al. (1970:19ff).

From a representational point of view, the use of a three-position diagram calls for justification in the following four cases: first, the so-called 'intransitive' verbs, e.g. *L'oiseau vole* (*The bird flies*). To all appearances the position ξ_1 is not filled; if the sentence is compared with *l'oiseau s'envole* (*the bird flies away* – a reflexive verb conveys this meaning in French), one is led to wonder why the number of 'actants' is not the same in the two sentences. We find a similar phenomenon in: *Pierre enfonce des clous avec un marteau* (*Peter drives in nails with a hammer*) and *le marteau enfonce les clous* (*the hammer drives in the nails*). In both cases the disappearance of an 'actant' is connected with the disappearance of the agent, but in the sentence *l'oiseau s'envole* the fact that the elements assigned to ξ_0 and ξ_1 are identical makes the phenomenon much less obvious.

The comparison of French with other languages shows, moreover, that use of the reflexive pronoun varies widely. Thus in Occitan (Journot (1967)) we find reflexive pronouns in expressions where French does not use them:

(2) a. Occ: Quora l'enfant aurà acabat de *se* plorar, *se* dormirà
  b. Fr: Quand l'enfant aura fini de pleurer, il dormira
     When the child has stopped crying, he will sleep
(3) a. Occ: Lo rossinhòu *se* cantèt tota la nuèch
  b. Fr: Le rossignol chanta toute la nuit
     The nightingale sang all night

We also find constructions without a reflexive pronoun in cases where French does use one:

(4) a. Occ: Lo relòtage descroquèt
  b. Fr: L'horlòge *se* déclencha
     The clock started
(5) a. Occ: La carreta reversèt
  b. Fr: La charrette *se* renversa
     The cart tipped over

For all these reasons, we will consider that in such a case the position ξ_1 is filled by a 'pseudo-notion' X' which refers back to the element assigned to position ξ_0. This gives us the following lexis:

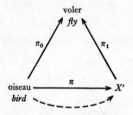

Second, transitive verbs used 'intransitively', e.g. *Pierre mange* (*Peter eats, Peter is eating*). This sentence means either *Peter is eating something at the present moment* (situation), or *Peter is in the habit of eating things, all sorts of things* (property). Here the object is not properly speaking absent but merely indeterminate; we will thus put on position ξ_1 an element represented by Δ which indicates that the object is present at a deep level, though not stated. When a speaker takes up the lexis to use it, one of the operations carried out will be the distinction between situation and property. In function of this distinction the element Δ will become Δ_i in the case of situation, and Δ_a in the case of property. The symbol Δ_i thus refers us to an object capable of being defined in function of the situation, whereas Δ_a refers us to an undefinable object. The lexis which gives rise to the statement *Pierre mange* is therefore the following:

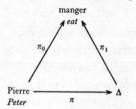

Third, verbs with more than two 'actants', e.g. *Pierre donne un livre au professeur* (*Peter gives a book to the teacher*). The lexis framework is inadequate here; we consider that such a statement results from a general lexis, which we define as follows:

Definition 3. *A general lexis is:*

(i) *either a lexis,*

(ii) *or what is obtained by filling at least one position of the lexis diagram with a general lexis.*

In other words, to obtain a lexis the three positions of the lexis diagram must be filled by 'notions'. When at least one of the places is filled by a lexis (simple or general), we no longer have a simple lexis but, rather, a general one. Only the general lexis, then, has a recursive definition.

In these conditions the above example can be represented by writing first the simple lexis λ: and then by embedding this lexis λ within another lexis. At this point two separate solutions can be envisaged.

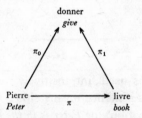

The first consists in assigning λ to position π^* of the lexis diagram to produce the following general lexis:

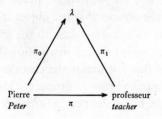

The second solution, which we will adopt for the remainder of this paper, consists in assigning the simple lexis λ to position ξ_0 of the diagram, position π^* being filled by the notion *benef* which refers at surface level to the preposition *à (to)*, for example. In this way we will obtain the general lexis:

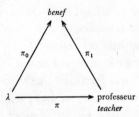

And fourth, adjectives not derived from verbs, and attributive sentences. For example:

(6) Pierre est bon (Peter is good)

This predication of a property about Peter does not necessitate a treatment any different from that of *the dog is a biter*, an expression rendered in Russian as *the dog bites itself*. In other words, we are obliged to fill position ξ_1 with a variable referring back to the notion assigned to position ξ_0, and thus to use the reference symbol (X').

Moreover, in an attributive sentence like (6) it is impossible to tell whether *Pierre* is first or second 'actant'. The distinction ξ_0/ξ_1 seems to have no meaning here; hence the necessity for filling position ξ_1 as shown below.

We therefore obtain the simple lexis:

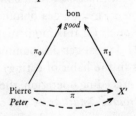

As a second example, consider:

(7) Pierre est professeur (Peter is a teacher)

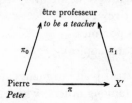

Note that examples (6) and (7) are different in nature, since the ξ_0 apex is filled in the first case by a predicative lexical unit and in the second by a non-predicative lexical unit.

The complexity of a 'relater'. In order to express at the lexis level the concept of verb valency (syntactic level of the statement, see Tesnière (1959)), we are led to speak of the complexity of a relater; this is so as to link our system to traditional linguistic concepts.

Corresponding to verbs of valency *1* and *2*, and to adjectives, we have relaters of complexity *1* (or *2* for verbs like *aider* (*to help*)); corresponding to verbs of valency *n* (where *n > 2*) we have relaters of complexity *n − 1*.

The degree of complexity of a relater is equal to the number of embedded lexes necessary to account for it.

The semantic level of a French Recognition Grammar

This comes within the domain of 'formal semantics' as defined by Culioli. This branch of semantics should be regarded as linked to syntax, and it is only the need for establishing successive stages in the model that obliges us to consider the syntactic and semantic levels as separate. For more details on the relationships between syntax and semantics, see Culioli et al. (1970).

Here we consider the semantic level in the following way. It depends essentially on the recognition and interpretation of *predication operations*, by which we understand:

(a) The *situation/property distinction* which contrasts (8) with (9):
(8) Jean (en ce moment) mange des pommes
   (John is eating apples (at this moment))
(9) Jean a l'habitude de manger des pommes
   (John eats (= is in the habit of eating) apples)
(b) Connected with the preceding operation, the *operations of 'determination' bearing on the 'source' and 'target'*; in other words the problem of articles, which are accounted for by the operations of extraction, 'sign-posting' and 'course'.
(c) *'Thematization'*, which may be neutral, weak or strong, as in (10), (11), and (12) respectively:
(10) Jean mange des pommes
   (John eats/is eating apples)

(11) Il y a (entre autres) Jean qui mange des pommes
   (There is John (among others) who eats/is eating apples)

(12) C'est Jean (et lui seul) qui mange des pommes
(It's John (and only John) who eats/is eating apples)

(d) *Voice*, which is the distinction between active and passive, but which should not be considered as a simple reversal of the direction of a relation.

(e) *Aspect*, which we will have to define, given the existing confusion.

(f) *Modalities*, grouped by A. Culioli into four sub-groups:

M1: affirmative, negative, 'injunctive', interrogative and negative-interrogative.

M2: certain, probable, necessary, etc.

M3: expressing judgement ('it is sad that...', 'fortunately', etc.)

M4: pragmatic, i.e. everything which has to do with relations between subjects.

The present paper concerns aspect only. Another part of our work treats voice and thematization.

Aspect

Introduction

The problem of auxiliaries. In order not to lengthen the text unnecessarily, we will write as ⟨*Jean, manger, pomme*⟩ (⟨*John, eat, apple*⟩) the lexis:

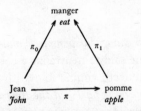

In recognition, this lexis may be derived from statements such as:

(13) a. Jean *est* en train de manger la pomme
(John *is* eating the apple)

b. Une pomme a *été* mangée par Jean
(An apple has *been* eaten by John)

c. C'*est* Jean qui mange la pomme
(It *is* John who eats/is eating the apple)

etc.

As a first approximation, we can say that the auxiliary *être* (*to be*) can indicate either *an aspectual value* (13a) such as an action in progress, not completed; or *voice* (13b) such as passive; or *thematization* (13c), namely, drawing attention to John.

In this section we discuss the following surface forms: *être* (*to be*), *avoir* (*to have*), and the absence of auxiliary, in the cases in which, in French, these are indications of aspect.

Aspect. We need now to define the values which we take to be included under the heading of aspect. The study of languages which possess specific morphological markers of aspect shows that such markers correspond to a variety of values. The number and nature of these values vary from one language to the next, a fact which therefore precludes the possibility of attributing a single interpretable value to the surface sign of 'aspect'. On the other hand, every aspect value is interpretable at the linguistic level; it is possible also to investigate the form it takes in a given language. The reader will find in Fuchs (1971) a list of the principal aspect values. Among these we find, naturally, the pair 'incomplete process'/ 'complete process', which is the value we will study here.

Inventory of surface forms

To study the role of auxiliaries in expressing aspect we begin with the paradigm of the conjugation of the indicative in French. We limit ourselves deliberately to indicative forms in order not to have to treat problems of modality at the same time.

Simple present. E.g. *Jean mange la pomme* (*John eats/is eating the apple*). The simple present can be said to neutralize a certain number of values of time and aspect. It is, indeed, compatible with all the following forms. **present time:** *au moment où je parle* (*at the time of speaking*); **repetition:** *toutes les fois que* (*every time that*); **a-temporal:** *de tout temps* (*timelessly*); **incomplete process:** *être en train de* (*to be in the act of*); **point-of-time process considered in its totality:** *voilà que* (*and suddenly*) (E.g. *Voilà qu'il me serre la main* (*and suddenly he shook my hand*)).

Present formed with 'être en train de' (*to be in the act of*). E.g. *Jean est en train de manger la pomme* (*John is eating the apple*). It is the sign of the 'incomplete' aspect value in present time.

Simple perfect. E.g. *Jean mangeait la pomme* (*John ate/was eating the apple*). It expresses a process which is either single or repeated, is situated in past time, and has 'incomplete' aspect value.

Imperfect formed with 'en train de'. E.g. *Jean était en train de manger la pomme* (*John was eating the apple*). This has the aspect value 'incomplete', situated in past time.

Past indefinite or perfect tense. E.g. *Jean a mangé la pomme* (*John has eaten/ ate the apple*). This can either indicate 'complete' aspect at the present time, as in *at present, it's done* or 'global' aspect – a process considered in its entirety – in the past time, as in *three days ago*.

Pluperfect. E.g. *Jean avait mangé la pomme* (*John had eaten the apple*). This is compatible with the same types of context as the perfect. It therefore can take two values: a 'complete' aspect in past time, or a 'global'aspect specifying two points of reference in the past.

Simple past. This expresses past time and seems to indicate no particular aspect value: the process is presented as happening at a point in time, with no attention given to its beginning or end.

Simple future. This also presents an action at a point in time. In addition, future time involves modal values (purpose, etc.).

Future formed with 'être en train de'. This indicates 'incomplete' aspect in the future.

Future perfect. This indicates 'complete' aspect in the future.

Basis of the formalization

The inventory we have just given shows that three aspect values suffice to account for the paradigm of the indicative in French. These three values are: 'incomplete', 'complete', and 'global'.

To explain the first two of these aspect values, Culioli introduces two operators: the first, O, gives rise to an 'open aspect', presenting the process as it takes place. The F operator ($F = fermé$ (*closed*)) proposed by Culioli produces a 'closed aspect' in the sense that the end of the process has been reached. These two values of aspect are not symmetrical: the 'open' value is primary and the 'closed' value derived (Culioli (1971)).

The formalism we propose here is not very far removed from the one we have just discussed: it is based on three principles and uses four basic operators.

Principles. (a) The formalism must not be simply a rewriting of the surface. If we think we are writing a formalism by merely encoding certain surface signs, we are failing to see that we are explaining nothing, and that we are imposing an arbitrary semantic interpretation.

(b) The formalism must, on the contrary, be situated at a sufficiently abstract level for it to lend itself to a purely formal study, consisting in a search for what can be considered axiomatic and for the rules of deduction controlling the symbols introduced.

(c) Finally, as emphasized by Culioli, such a formalism must be able to be interpreted in natural languages. It is therefore essential that simple rules link the formalism to the speech surface.

The rest of this paper shows the simple way in which we have substantiated the interpretation of the formalism. We note that the axiomatic study of the operators introduced here is far from being finished.

Fundamental operators. (a) We take first *a primitive operator, ε,*[1] *and the form derived from it by duality, ϑ.*[2] The reader should under no circumstances be led by the discussion in this section to think that ε is a rewriting of *être* (*to be*) and ϑ a rewriting of *avoir* (*to have*). Even though this equivalence exists in many cases connected with aspect, it is possible to show that these two operators are often expressed at the surface by a zero term. We will obtain a more accurate idea of their semantic value if we say that ε expresses a coincidence or symmetry (whether of argument or of spatio-temporal determination), while ϑ expresses dissymmetry of argument or spatio-temporal non-coincidence.

(b) We also introduce two operators ρ_0 and ρ_1: at the surface level the first is represented by the present participle, the second by the past participle. We therefore have recognition rules of the type:

R_1: r-ant→ ρ_0 (r) e.g. mangeant→ ρ_0 (*manger*)
     (r-ing)   (eating)   (*eat*)
R_2: r-é→ ρ_1 (r) e.g. mangé→ ρ_1 (*manger*)
     (r-ed   (eaten)   (*eat*)
     r-en...)

Transition from the surface to the formal representation

Note on methodology. We have laid down as a principle that formalization must not consist in simply rewriting the surface: the formalism must, we

---

[1] The reader will take care not to confuse the symbol ε used here with the primitive term in the ontology of Lesniewski (1930).

[2] The idea of introducing 'ε' and its dual is due to Culioli.

stress, be situated at a reasonable level of abstraction – a level necessarily more abstract than the surface to be analysed.

It is, however, possible to start from the speech continuum and arrive at a formal representation: one of the aims of this section is to show how a reasonable handling of surface forms enables us to reach a general formalism. In fact the problem comes down to the choice of surface forms to be used; this choice should eliminate ambiguities, so that it is not possible, for example, to begin with:

(14) Jean mange la pomme (John eats/is eating the apple)

We therefore start from 'post-surface' forms in which each of the aspect values has been interpreted with the help of auxiliaries. To any reader who might accuse us of 'cheating', we would reply that this 'adjustment' is in no way arbitrary or difficult to check. We are simply acting to remove an ambiguity. This removal of ambiguity comes within the scope of a detailed contextual analysis which we cannot present in detail here. Even if it is true that by making this adjustment we jump a step in the development of the FRG, we feel that we are not falsifying data in any important way.

In the case of example (14) the post-surface form is:

(15) Jean est mangeant la pomme (John is eating the apple)

which corresponds to present time and 'incomplete' aspect.

Explanation of the method, using example (14). We therefore start from the post-surface (15). The aspects part of the sentence – which is all that interests us for the moment – is translated as *est mangeant*, or (see R_1) as:

$\varepsilon \rho_0$ *(manger)*

In fact the term $\varepsilon \rho_0$ modifies the whole lexis of which *manger* is the relater:

$\varepsilon \rho_0$ ⟨*Jean, manger, pomme*⟩

By addition of the information that the process is situated in present time – which we write τ_0 – we obtain:

τ_0: $\varepsilon \rho_0$ ⟨*Jean, manger, pomme*⟩

This linear 'framework' gives us some idea of the formalism to use, but it is inadequate to give a functional definition of the syntax of the formal language. To work towards such a definition, we rewrite the above expression as a graph:

(G. 1)

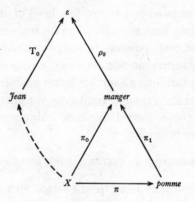

This representation consists first of all of a lexis:

⟨X, *manger*, *pomme*⟩

in which position ξ_0 is filled by the variable X. Since ε signifies, among other things, an identity of argument, this variable X is identified with *Jean* through the term ε at the apex of the graph (G.1). This is indicated by the dotted arrow.

This graph can in turn be written in the following linear form:

τ_0 [*Jean* $\varepsilon\rho_0$ ⟨X, *manger*, *pomme*⟩]

which is the form we shall use here.

The present state of our work does not yet enable us to say what the exact syntax of this formal language is. If the examples cited in this section allow us to have some idea of what it may be, we must nevertheless not forget that the operators introduced here – especially ε – are also used to formalize other concepts. Under these circumstances it is obvious that the axiomatic study of these operators is only beginning.

Study of other cases. We shall consider the following surface forms:

(16) Jean mangeait la pomme
(17) Jean a mangé la pomme
(18) Jean avait mangé la pomme
(19) Jean mangera la pomme
(20) Jean aura mangé la pomme

They generate the following post-surface forms:

(16′) Jean était mangeant la pomme (John was eating the apple)

(17′) Jean est ayant mangé la pomme (John is having eaten…)
(17″) Jean a été mangeant la pomme (John has been eating…)
(18′) Jean était ayant mangé la pomme (John was having eaten…)
(18″) Jean avait été mangeant la pomme (John had been eating…)
(19′) Jean sera mangeant la pomme (John will be eating…)
(20′) Jean sera ayant mangé la pomme (John will be having eaten…)

By writing past time as τ_- and future time as τ_+, we obtain the following graphs:

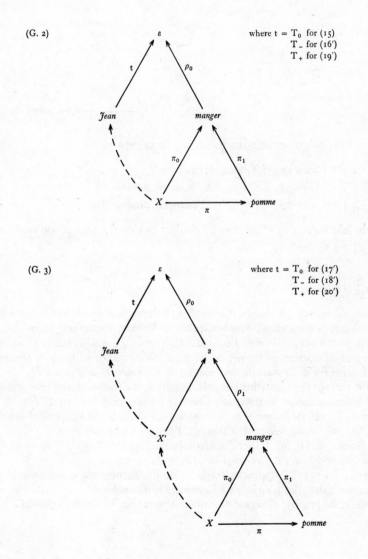

(G. 4)   where t = T_0 for (17″)
                                                 T_- for (18″)

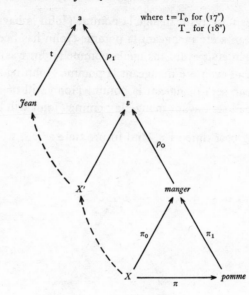

These graphs determine the following linear forms:

(G.2′) t [*Jean* $\varepsilon\rho_0$ $\langle X,$ *manger, pomme* $\rangle$]
(G.3′) t [*Jean* $\varepsilon\rho_0$ $(X'$ $_3\rho_1$ $\langle X,$ *manger, pomme* $\rangle)$]
(G.4′) t [*Jean* $\varepsilon\rho_1$ $(X'$ $\varepsilon\rho_0$ $\langle X,$ *manger, pomme* $\rangle)$]

These last formulae show up the duality between ε and ρ_0 on one hand, $_3$ and ρ_1 on the other.

REFERENCES

Culioli, A. (1971). 'A propos d'opérations intervenant dans le traitement formel des langues naturelles', *Mathématiques et Sciences Humaines*, **34**, 7–15.

Culioli, A., Fuchs, C. and Pecheux, M. (1970). 'Considérations théoriques à propos du traitement formel du langage'. *Documents du Centre de Linguistique Quantitative de la Faculté des Sciences de l'Université de Paris VII.*

Fuchs, C. (1971). 'Contribution préliminaire à la construction d'une grammaire de reconnaissance du français'. *Thèse de l'Université de Paris VII.*

Journot, J. (1967). *Eléments de grammatica occitana.* Montpellier: Publication de la Section Pédagogique de l'Institut d'Etudes Occitanes.

Lesniewski, S. (1930). 'Über die Grundlagen der Ontologie', *C.R. de la Société des Sciences et des Lettres de Varsovie*, **23**, 111–32.

Rouault, J. (1971). 'Approche formelle de problèmes liés à la sémantique des langues naturelles'. *Thèse de l'Université de Grenoble I.*

Tesnière, L. (1959). *Eléments de syntaxe structurale.* Paris: Klincksieck.

On the relations between syntax and semantics

MAURICE GROSS

One of the main objectives of traditional grammarians was to relate form and meaning. This programme ran into many difficulties and was abandoned by structural linguists who found it much more fruitful to concentrate on the voluntarily limited study of the combinatorial properties of words.

Transformational linguists also exclude meaning from the grammar rules they build. However, the definition of a transformational rule (unlike the definition of a distributional rule) explicitly involves meaning, since transformationally related sentences must have identical meanings.[1]

There are important differences in the ways we just referred to the term 'meaning'. Traditional grammars classify forms into families, and attribute to these families absolute categories of meanings.[2] For example, the notion of phrase is a notion of form, so is the notion of *when*-phrase (i.e. adverbial phrase whose left-most word is *when*). Often, the semantic notion /time/ is associated with these forms (i.e. adverbs of time).

The modern formalized version of this activity is usually stated in the general framework of formal logic. On the one hand, the syntactic rules of some formal system[3] define a set of well-formed formulae (here sentence forms), on the other hand, a semantic model provides interpretation for each formula. As in mathematical logic, the question of setting up a dividing line between the syntactic theory and its model constantly arises.[4] In both

---

[1] The definition of distributional rules involves meaning implicitly. Meaning is then part of the global notion of acceptability. Transformationally related sentences may have systematic differences of meaning. For example, one may consider that the declarative sentence *John gave a book to this girl* and the corresponding cleft ones *It is John that gave a book to this girl, It is a book that John gave to this girl, It is to this girl that John gave a book* are transformationally related. Between the source sentence and each of the cleft ones, we observe the same difference: /emphasis/, /contrast/, or the like.

[2] The names of these categories will be written between strokes.

[3] This attitude is by no means the only possible one. As Chomsky has pointed out, performing syntactic descriptions in the framework of the formal systems of mathematical logic implies a particular hypothesis that may turn out to be empirically inadequate. In fact Z. S. Harris (1951:372–3) who first proposed it, has moved towards using algebraic systems, which, owing to their more abstract character, eliminate the possibility of raising certain questions which may not make any linguistic sense (e.g. zeroing of morphemes, directionality of a transformation).

[4] The problems raised by generative semantics relate closely to this question.

the traditional and the formal approach, absolute notions of meaning are needed to interpret the sentences.

Generative grammars provide numerous examples of this approach, and many empirical data, old or discovered within this framework, have been described from just a syntactic point of view. However, despite all kinds of efforts, the study of the semantics of natural languages remains an entirely open field. Many proposals of models of interpretation have been made, but none of the most basic questions has been answered yet. All examples are quite limited with respect to the range of semantic units that come immediately to mind and that seem relevant to semantic descriptions. In fact, they all seem to suffer from the same defect: the lack of empirical basis, and often, a not very careful study of the notions involved raises serious criticisms that may put in question the whole validity of this approach.

For example, most (if not all) traditional grammars associate the notion /time/ to *when*-phrases. But in sentences like *When John makes a mistake, he is unhappy* which are synonymous with *If John makes a mistake, he is unhappy* it is by no means clear why one should attach the concept of /time/ to the phrase, rather than any of the notions /implication/, /condition/, /concomitance/. This type of criticism is fairly general, and applies to all such associations of meaning and form.

Similarly, the semantic notions /true/ and /false/, so widely discussed and formalized in the context of the relations between logic and linguistics, do not seem to have an indisputable empirical basis. For example, it is widely assumed that the sentence

(1) I know that Max has arrived

'presupposes'[1] that the proposition: *Max has arrived* is /true/, while in the sentence

(2) I believe that Max has arrived

the same proposition can be either /true/ or /false/. This difference in 'presupposition' has been attributed to the main verb (i.e. *to know* vs. *to believe*). However, it is by no means clear that the difference that we just observed really holds. In a discourse like *Max's hat and boots are in the entrance, so I know that he has arrived* the subject *I* may have been mistaken by certain

---

[1] The terms 'to presuppose', 'presupposition', although not defined, appear to be used in a technical sense. They are simply to be interpreted as 'to mean partially', 'a part or component of meaning', respectively. For an evaluation of this notion see Kuroda (1973).

clues, and it could be the case that the proposition *Max has arrived* is /false/.

The standard view, namely the first observations we made on (1) and (2), may be correct, but presumably under quite complex linguistic conditions that have not been determined so far. Unless such conditions are clearly stated, the notions /true/ and /false/ may just be as inadequate as the notion /time/ was.

Thus, the absolute notions of meaning that are needed for interpretation, and that have been proposed so far (e.g. notions of time, space, and truth) all appear to be empirically inadequate. Moreover, it is far from obvious to imagine how one should proceed to determine some of them, and how they could be motivated on any empirical and theoretical ground.

The way the semantic notions currently discussed have been arrived at is quite clear. Grammarians and philosophers have performed observations on syntactic classes of sentences or of phrases. Their reading triggered intuitions in the mind of the investigators, and the intuitions were given names that were supposed to reproduce corresponding intuitions appearing in the mind of other students of the same forms. These names are of two main kinds, either words taken from the vocabulary of the language under study, or else they are abstractions whose meaning is technical and defined elsewhere (e.g. logical implication). These two naming activities correspond to two different theoretical attitudes, both easy to criticize: on the one hand one does not see why elementary semantic units should have an observable counterpart (i.e. words) in a natural language, on the other, one does not see why the semantic units should be the ones that constitute the basis of a technical language (e.g. logic) built for reasons that do not have much to do with the study of natural languages. Again, we are faced with the basic empirical problem of semantics: what is a semantic fact?

We already mentioned that there are in generative transformational grammars manipulations of meaning that are of a different kind from the one we just criticized. There, pairs of sentences[1] that are candidates for being related by a transformation are judged to be synonymous or not. Thus, meaning is only involved in comparisons, and *differences* in meaning are detected in this manner. In the physical sciences, it is well-known that *absolute* evaluations of a variable (e.g. temperature) lead always to rather crude results, when compared to *differential* evaluations of the same variable. The situation appears to be the same in linguistics with respect to meaning. Attributing absolute terms to forms is quite problematic, and anyway, has proved to be rather unsuccessful, while comparing the

[1] The status of these pairs should be that of minimal pairs in phonology.

meanings of similar forms may bring to light subtle differences that may be hard to detect directly. This situation has allowed transformational grammarians to handle certain aspects of meaning. But the question of providing interpretations for sentences in terms of units of meaning is not solved. These elements of meaning which have been extracted by differential tests still have to be given names that will make explicit the interpretation of sentences. Such units may have a good empirical adequacy, but the problems we mentioned about naming still remain, and it is hard to see any solution for them.

While attempting to construct a syntactic classification for a large set of simple sentence types (Gross (1975)) we encountered various correlations between forms and meanings which suggested that an empirical study of absolute notions of meaning, while more difficult and less precise than the study of differential units, might not be out of reach. In fact, the main criticisms that have been made about the use of absolute notions are essentially based on the fact that it is always very easy to find counter-examples to any statement involving absolute notions. One of the causes of this situation is that no systematic study of any syntactic phenomenon has ever been made for a natural language. All studies are quite fragmentary, and they only affect a small part of the lexicon, so that it is quite obvious that in no respect is it possible to base a statement on data that reasonably cover a natural language; whence the ease with which one can find counter-examples to statements that are always much too general in comparison with the few examples from which they are extracted. In certain areas of syntax, the study we made avoids this difficulty to a large extent, so that finding counter-examples to our statements will not be as easy as it usually is.

We took as a test case the distribution of about 150 syntactic properties over a lexicon of about 6000 French verbs. The properties we chose turned out to be such that they were relevant to about half of the verbs. This study deals essentially with French complementizers, namely with verbs accepting in at least one of their syntactic positions (i.e. subject or object(s)) at least one of the forms:

que P (*that S*, in English)
si P ou non (*whether S or not*, or *if S or not*)
VΩ (infinitive *VP*)

The 3000 corresponding verbs have been classified mainly according to their pattern of complement(s), which resulted in the definition of 19 classes each containing between 20 and 300 verbs.

Each class has been represented by a matrix. On each row there is a verb, and each column corresponds to a syntactic property. When a verb (i.e. its construction as defined by the class) has a given property, a plus sign is placed at the intersection of the corresponding row and column; a minus sign is placed in the opposite case.

Our syntactic properties are of two types: distributional properties and transformational ones. Some of the distributional properties are clearly semantic and their operational value is rather low. For example, the distinction /human/ vs. /non-human/ has so far turned out to be of little interest, since there are numerous verbs for which there is no sharp distinction (or no distinction at all) between these two terms. Thus /human/ nouns can sometimes be interpreted as /non-human/ subjects, like *brother* in the sentence *My brother functions well.* The reverse is quite frequent too, for example with nouns used as /containers/ of /human/, e.g. *street* in *She amused the whole street.* Again the distinction /human/ vs. /non-human/ does not seem to be relevant to the interpretation of the complement of *to look for.*

Other distributional properties lead to much sharper distinctions. Thus, the distribution of a phrase with a sentential modifier like *the fact that John did it* classified our verbs in a sharply reproducible way, presumably because the occurrence of this phrase is much less dependent on the meaning of its head noun (e.g. we have *I know the facts,* but **I know the fact that John did it*).

The transformational properties that were studied are the ones that are currently found in the literature. In most cases, these properties have been deduced from a small number of examples. The study of a large number of cases led us to revise most of them, introducing new conditions on them, and sometimes revising significantly their formulation. In fact, transformations are only indirectly represented in our tables. Each syntactic property is a structure that a verb may enter into or not. For example, the structure

(A) NP V NP

is such a property, and the corresponding structure

(P) NP est Vpp par NP

with interchanged NPs is another property. It is the pair [(A), (P)] that defines the passive transformation. This definition of the tables allowed us to represent non-transformational relations between different constructions of what ought to be considered as containing the same verb. For example, we observed the existence of pairs like

(3) a. Que Max soit venu a irrité Luc
    (That Max came irritated Luke)

and

    b. Luc s'est irrité auprès de Guy de ce que Max soit venu
    (Luke told Guy that he was irritated that Max came)

Sentences (a) and (b) differ in meaning, but they share several syntactic features: the distributional and semantic nature of the subject in (a) is the same as the one of the *de*-complement in (b), the direct object of (a) is also identical to the subject of (b). Sentence (b) has three arguments,[1] where (a) has only two, and the extra complement *auprès de Guy* which cannot occur in (a)

(4) *Que Max soit venu a irrité Luc après de Guy

adds to the verb the meaning of /saying/. Thus, there does not seem to be any possibility of relating (a) and (b) by transformational means. We could consider that there exist two verbs: *irriter* and *s'irriter*, this position could perhaps be justified by the fact that there are constructions identical in form and similiar in meaning to (b), and involving verbs that do not have the (a) construction:

(5) Luc a protesté auprès de Guy de ce que Max soit venu
    *Que Max soit venu a protesté Luc
(6) Luc s'est plaint auprès de Guy de ce que Max soit venu
    *Que Max soit venu a plaint Luc

Also, there are verbs that have the (a) but not the (b) construction:

(7) Que Max soit venu a ennuyé Luc
    *Luc s'est ennuyé auprès de Guy de ce que Max soit venu

However, through a systematic study of the lexicon, we observed that among the 500 verbs that we described by means of the property

(8) Que S V NP

about 40 also had the construction

(9) NP se V auprès de NP de ce que S

and this correspondence seems to be quite productive, namely it can be extended to other verbs used in (8) in a figurative meaning. On the other

---

[1] We call arguments (of the verb) the subject and the complement(s).

hand, verbs like *protester* that only have the (9) construction are not numerous, we observed fewer than 40 such examples, most of them obtained by a rather difficult extension of some other use of the verb. A typical case would be *soupirer* (*to sigh*) in the sentence

(10) Luc soupire auprès de Léa de ce qu'elle ne vienne plus chez lui

which, although easily understandable, could be rejected by many native speakers as unacceptable.

Thus the solution of two lexical entries does not seem to be justifiable, mainly since it does not capture the relation between (8) and (9). We choose to indicate the relation since our system of representation allows it in a natural way: in our matrix (8) and (9) will be independent properties, and individual verbs like *irriter* will have both.

Another typical example of a non-transformational relation involves pairs of constructions like:

(11) Paul a hurlé à Jean qu'il viendrait
     (Paul shouted to Jean that he would come)
(12) Paul a poussé un hurlement
     (Paul gave a shout)

The constructions (11) and (12) are related morphologically: *hurlement* is a nominal derived from the verb *hurler*; but there is a syntactic and semantic correspondence too, in both sentences: *Paul* is the subject. However, it seems hard to derive (11) from (12) since we observe that the constructions do not have the same complements:

(13) a. *Paul a poussé un hurlement à Jean
     b. *Paul a poussé un hurlement qu'il viendrait
     c. *Paul a poussé un hurlement à Jean qu'il viendrait

similarly, (12) cannot be derived from (11), i.e. from the substructure *Paul hurle* of (11), since *hurlement* can have determiners and modifiers that are not found with *hurler*; for example the source of *un grand nombre* in the sentence

(14) Paul a poussé un grand nombre de hurlements stridents

would be hard to justify.

There is however another observation that indicates the existence of a relation between (11) and (12). We have listed about 150 verbs of /saying/ that have the construction of *dire* (*to say*); among them, 40 have the associated construction (12). In (12), the nominalizing suffixes are highly restricted: *-ment* in 38 cases, and zero in 2 cases. Moreover the pairing is practically nonexistent outside of the class of the verbs of /saying/. We consider this situation as strongly supporting the existence of the indicated relationship. We thus treat certain nominalizations as processes that relate two elementary sentences (which is quite different from the solution in Lees (1960)). The relation is not transformational in Chomsky's sense (Chomsky (1967)), but is considered as such by Harris (1964) who considers the verb *pousser* as an operator acting on a sentence.

Many such cases have led us to make more precise our notion of syntactic property and its relation to transformations. All properties appearing in the columns of our matrices are structures that a verb of a given row enters into or not. Thus, as mentioned, a transformation is a pair of columns. Such pairs are most of the time ordered in generative grammar. But we prefer to consider them as defining a relation,[1] that is, as nonordered. The effect of the relation is to produce a classification of sentence types; between the classes further relations can be defined (Harris (1968)).

The choice of the syntactic properties is primarily determined by the operational quality of the tests that are used. Thus, the property for a verb *V* to enter into a passive form or not when it enters into the construction *NP V NP* provides sharp distinctions among verbs in a large number of cases. As a result of our choice of properties, we have a reasonable guarantee that the classes that we have defined are purely syntactic, taking into account the fact that all traditional attempts, like for example the attempt to relate the existence of passive forms to semantic properties of verbs have always failed.

In a number of cases, it came as a surprise that all the verbs of some of these syntactic classes triggered a common semantic intuition.

For example, we have defined a syntactic class by means of the following properties:

1. the verbs have a direct object, roughly speaking they enter into a structure (P_1): *NP V NP* (*Luc apprècie Max*) without entering into a larger structure like *NP V NP à NP* or *NP V NP de NP* where *à NP* and *de NP* are indirect objects;

2. the *NP* direct object can be the sentential complement *que S* where the main verb of *S* is in the subjunctive, i.e. the verbs enter into the structure (P_2): *NP V que S* (*Luc apprécie que Max soit venu*);

3. the verbs enter into the structure (P_3): *NP V NP de VP* (*Luc apprécie Max d'être venu*) related to the structure (P_2) by the raising (?)

---

[1] 'Relation' is to be taken in its technical sense.

relation *que S→NP de VP*; in (P₃) no nominal *NP* can be substituted for *VP* (i.e. *NP V NP de NP).

These properties, when conjoined, isolate in the French lexicon a set of 60 verbs which all trigger the semantic intuition of /ethical judgement/. This situation should be surprising since in the general case the classes that can be defined by similar syntactic properties are semantically heterogeneous.

In our study, 4 classes out of 19 turned out to be semantically homogeneous; the 3 others are the following:

We defined the class of verbs *V* entering into the construction *NP V VP*, where *NP* is the subject of the infinitive *VP*, and where *VP* can be replaced by the interrogative pronoun *où*. All the members of this class are in some sense verbs of movement from one place to another. E.g.

(15) Guy (descend/court) voir Max

and:

(16) Question: Où Guy (descend/court)-il?
     Answer: Voir Max

while for example, with the same structure:

(17) Guy (aime/doit) voir Max

we do not find the dialogue:

(18) Question: Où Guy (aime/doit)-il?
     Answer: *Voir Max

The class we have described contains about 120 such verbs of movement.

A second class, related to the preceding one, is defined by the construction *NP V NP VP*, where the second *NP* is the subject of the infinitive *VP*, and where this *VP* can be replaced by the interrogative pronoun *où*. Most of these verbs[1] can be interpreted as /causative of movement/. We have

(19) Pierre envoie Guy voir Max
(20) Question: Où Pierre envoie-t-il Guy?
     Answer: Voir Max

---

[1] *Accompagner* in *Luc accompagne Guy voir Eve* is in the class, but is paraphrasable by *Luc va avec Guy voir Eve*, hence it is not /causative/.

and this construction of *envoyer* is synonymous with the causative construction

(21) Pierre fait aller Guy voir Max

where *aller* belongs to the preceding class.
A final class that we have defined corresponds to the construction

(22) Que S V NP

where the NP has a /human/ head noun, and where the subject of V is semantically unrestricted, namely its head noun may belong to any semantic class. In particular we have

(23) Que Guy soit arrivé (amuse/ennuie) Max.

All these verbs are verbs of /sentiment/: the unrestricted subject triggers a feeling in the /human/ direct object.[1] It may be added that this semantic description can also be applied to the class of verbs of /ethical judgement/ already mentioned, but with reversed syntactic relations: the unrestricted direct object triggers a feeling in the /human/ subject.[2]

These examples are by no means accidents, and there are other cases of subclasses of verbs (with respect to our classification) such that a syntactic definition leads to a set of verbs which are all semantically related. For example we can define a class by the structural property:

(24) NP V que S à NP

all of its verbs must have a sentential direct object, and an indirect object with the preposition *à*. This class is quite heterogeneous, but a subclass of these verbs defined by the following properties is homogeneous:

1. the verbs have a sentential direct object *que S* in an indicative form that undergoes equi-*NP* deletion, when the subject of *S* is co-referential with the subject of V:

(25) a. Je dit à Max que je me suis évanoui

⇒

b. Je dit à Max m'être évanoui

---

[1] There are semantically analogous verbs which are syntactically different. For example *plaire* (*to please*) has an unrestricted subject too, but an indirect /human/ object with the preposition *à*.

[2] In certain associated constructions the order of the arguments is similar, though reversed here. We have for example: *Luc hait Eve/Luc a de la haine pour Eve* but *Eve dégoute Luc/Luc a du dégout pour Eve*.

2. the verbs also have a sentential direct object in subjunctive form that undergoes equi-NP deletion when the subject of S is co-referential with the indirect object of V:

(26) a. Je dit à Max qu'il s'en aille

⇒

    b. Je dit à Max de s'en aller

The verbs that are defined by these properties are all verbs of /saying/, and, as mentioned, there are about 150 of them.

Although the semantic notions appearing in each class are 'absolute' notions, they are perceived in a remarkably consistent way by all native speakers. This remark is the basis of what we call semantic homogeneity. But these classes are remarkably homogeneous too from a purely syntactic point of view. The notion of syntactic homogeneity that we are attempting to define is based on observations made on our classification.

As we have already observed, our material can be viewed as a binary matrix of 3000 by 150. Each description of a verb (i.e. each row) has been transferred to a punched card, so that computer programs (Bely and Vasseux (1973)) can easily extract from the general matrix various types of subclasses. For example, we have constructed the set of classes which is such that each class contains only verbs that have exactly the same syntactic properties. For 3000 verbs, we obtain 2000 classes, and when we studied the classes containing more than one verb, we noticed that it was easy to find new syntactic properties that divided these classes into further subclasses containing only one verb. Thus, we can assert that in French there are no two verbs that have exactly the same syntactic properties. Examination of the columns leads to a similar observation: there are no two syntactic properties that have the same distribution over the lexicon. As a consequence all relations between sentences, whether transformational or not, have exceptions. This picture of the syntactic structures of a natural language indicates that a large number of irregularities are present. How to deal with them is not clear,[1] but it is fairly obvious that the irregularities are by no means randomly distributed. In order to separate 3000 verbs in 2000 classes, 12 properties are sufficient, but we had to use more than 150 of them to obtain this result. This indicates that a large

---

[1] In Gross (1975) we suggested an approach to this problem which arises under nearly the same conditions in phonology (Lightner (1972)). Other similar studies have been performed with similar results: Boons et al. (1975) have studied 4000 verbs without sentential arguments, Giry (1972), 1500 nominal constructions of the type *faire N* (e.g. *faire des compliments, faire la vaisselle*), and Picabia (1970), 1200 adjectives with sentential subject and/or sentential complement.

amount of redundancy is present in our matrix, and in particular that the contents of certain rows on the one hand, and of certain columns on the other, are related. Such relations appear to be more numerous for the semantically natural classes than for the other cases. Examples of these numerical differences are given in Table I where it is quite apparent that the semantic classes that we have defined have a high proportion of constant columns, i.e. of columns containing either +signs or −signs.

TABLE I

	No. of constant columns	Total no. of columns
Vs of /ethical judgement/	17	30
Vs of /movement/	15	28
Vs /causative of movement/	20	28
Vs of /sentiment/	4	19
Vs in $NP\ V\ que\ P\ à\ N$	2	45
Vs in $NP\ V\ que\ P$	0	36

The ratios of the number of constant columns to the total number of columns are respectively 0.5, 0.5, 0.7, and 0.25 for the semantic classes, but −0.05 and 0 for the syntactic classes. Such differences seem to be significant. The fact that the ratio is relatively low for the Vs of /sentiment/ is due to the large number of Vs in this class (i.e. 540), and to the presence of morphological rather than syntactic properties. It is important to remember that the semantic notions that we have deduced are not *characterized* by the syntactic properties we have been using. There are verbs which semantically are covered by our definitions, but that do not appear in our syntactic classes. For example: the verbs of /ethical judgement/ can also be tagged verbs of /sentiment/, and these two types do not have the same syntactic properties. Secondly, the verb *marcher* (*to walk*) is not in the syntactically defined class of verbs of /movement/, although semantically it does not seem very different from *courir* (*to run*). And thirdly, in the construction already mentioned

(3) b. Luc s'est irrité auprès de Guy de ce que Max soit venu

s'irriter is semantically a verb of /saying/. However, its syntactic structure: $NP\ V\ auprès\ de\ NP\ de\ ce\ que\ P$ is rather different from the one of *dire* (*to say*) (indirect sentential complement, and a different preposition for the receiver of the message).

At any rate, our examples appear to be clear cases of relations between absolute semantic notion and syntactic properties. However, the way the relationship should be described is by no means obvious. Our observations could be stated in the following general way:

Let $S_1, S_2, \ldots, S_i, \ldots$ be absolute semantic notions. Let $P_1, P_2, \ldots, P_j, \ldots$ be syntactic properties. The rules that relate meaning and shapes are of the form

(R) $\Sigma \rightarrow \Pi$

where Σ and Π are boolean combinations of the S_is and the P_js respectively.

A few remarks about such rules can already be made that may turn out to be quite general. In our examples, Σ was reduced to one S_i (e.g. /sentiment/) or to two (/causative/ of /movement/), that is, Σ was composed of a small number of very intuitive notions. On the other hand Π was made of a rather large number of syntactic properties (i.e. the columns that were constant in a class), and these properties are by no means intuitive: it is very hard (if at all possible for the moment) to imagine a process by which they could be learned by a child or an adult. If the rules (R) had further specific properties, they might be considered as the basis of an empirically adequate theory of learning.[1]

However, even the few examples that we have presented force us to look at the rules (R) from several different points of view, without there being, for the moment, any empirical way of deciding how to formulate them in a precise way.

Thus, each of the semantic classes that we defined seems to contain one verb which, in some sense, is semantically minimal: for the verbs of /ethical judgement/ *aimer* (*to like*) would be this element; for the verbs of /movement/ we would consider *aller* (*to go*) to be minimal; and for the verbs of /saying/ we would take *dire* (*to say* or *to tell*).

In all these cases, the other verbs of the class (or a large majority of them) would be interpreted with the meaning of the minimal element, together with some extra notions that would account for the difference of meaning. But there are many ways of expressing this situation.

Let us consider the verbs of /saying/. In French, practically any verb that can be interpreted as corresponding to an emission of sound or of

---

[1] Element S_i like /sentiment/ may have to be considered as combinations of simpler S's; the same often happens with syntactic properties. Thus the difference in size of the two members of a rule R may not be essential; what is crucial for a theory of learning is to explain how the very complex non-conscious properties P_j are acquired. We propose that the child starts from the conscious and intuitive, hence cultural S_i's, and that a universal process associates these with the syntactic properties.

light can be used syntactically and semantically as a verb of /saying/.[1] We
have for example sentences like

(27) Luc (bégaie/ronronne) à Guy (de venir/qu'il est ici)
     (Luc stammers/purrs) to Guy (to come/that he is here))

Such sentences can be paraphrased by:

(28) Luc dit à Guy (de venir/qu'il est ici) en (bégayant/ronronnant)

Moreover, the construction (28) appears to be acceptable only with *dire*
(the minimal verb) as main verb:[2]

(29) *Luc bégaie à Guy (qu'il est ici/de venir) en ronronnant
(30) *Luc ronronne à Guy (qu'il est ici/de venir) en bégayant

One might describe these restrictions by means of a standard transformational solution: thus the syntactic properties that have been observed for
the verbs of /saying/ would only be attributed to the verb *dire*. All other
verbs of /saying/, namely all verbs that indicate an emission of sound or of
light, would be considered as intransitive verbs. Independently, it can be
observed that *dire* is the only verb which has obligatory complements (at
least in declarative sentences), i.e. which cannot be considered as intransitive. Then a transformation would relate (27) and (28) by deleting the
minimal element *dire* and by inserting the intransitive verb in the former
position of *dire*. Morphological adjustments then take place. Such a solution accounts for the meaning and the syntactic properties of the set of
described structures. Moreover it is morphologically simpler than an
analysis along the lines of generative semantics (Joshi (1972), McCawley
(1968), Postal (1970), Ross (1971)), aside from the grammatical elements
(*en*, *-ant*), the only zeroed element is the root of *dire* which is recoverable
since in our sense the minimal verb is lexically unique.

The same type of solution could be used for the verbs of /movement/:[3]
all the verbs except (minimal) *aller* can be considered as intransitive and
the same transformation as above could be used, which results in:

(31) Max va voir Guy en courant
     ⇒
(32) Max court voir Guy

---

[1] Also constructions that describe certain gestures can be used as verbs of /saying/: *Luc
fait signe de la tête à Guy (qu'il est ici/de venir)* (to nod).

[2] Constructions of the type (28) might be acceptable with other verbs than *dire*, provided that some kind of semantic inclusion holds between the two verbs of /saying/.

[3] Notice that sentences like *Max (monte/descend) voir Guy en courant* are acceptable.
This observation is to be related to the remark of n. 2, above.

The verbs of /ethical judgement/ cannot, however, receive a similar treatment. We do not observe the same relations between the minimal verb *aimer* and the others. Most of them cannot be used intransitively, and if they could, they would not yield the paraphrase observed before:

(33) *Max aime Guy en adorant
(34) *Max aime Guy en haïssant
⇒
(35) Max hait Guy

Rather, these verbs seem to be compounded of *aimer* and some adverbial adjunction. This hypothesis is supported by the fact that practically all of them cannot be used with certain adverbs, like, for example, the comparative *mieux* (*better*):

(36) *Max adorerait mieux venir
(37) *Max haïrait mieux venir

while with *aimer*, we do have

(38) Max aimerait mieux venir

Also, under the same conditions, negations are difficult to accept at least without contrastive effect:

(39) ?*Max n'adore pas venir
(40) ?*Max ne hait pas venir

while *Max n'aime pas venir* is acceptable.

Thus, the verbs of this class could perhaps be viewed as composed of *aimer* and some /intensity/ adverbial and/or a negation. Such an analysis resembles the analyses proposed within the framework of generative semantics. However, we are not concerned with the theoretical problems raised in this context. We only want to point out that the first type of solution that we have proposed is not quite general, and that processes which involve factorization of words may have to be used also in order to describe the structure of the lexicon.

Thus, we seem to be advocating here an empirical approach to semantics that is largely based on syntax, but the separation between syntax and semantics has never been very sharp. It is clear that distributional and transformational grammars are all based on combinatorial processes acting on morphemes, while the rest of the study of language is called semantics.[1]

---

[1] It seems even more difficult to separate pragmatics from semantics.

This dichotomy, essentially based on various formal properties, seems very hard to justify, and linguists have noticed that many problems arise within such a framework, which, to a certain extent, do not seem to be significant. As a consequence, we have shifted our main interest to the empirical data, considering that the study of natural languages should comply with the rules which all experimental sciences obey. One of our main concerns is the reproducibility of data. Most (if not all) of the data in syntax originates from experiments that consist in building strings and checking whether they are acceptable or not. Such experiments turn out to be reproducible in a large number of cases. Other experiments are possible that use other types of intuitions than the intuition of acceptability. As already mentioned, most of the experiments that use (absolute) semantic intuitions have turned out to be non-reproducible, and this has led structural linguists to abandon them completely. But some of these experiments might be reproducible, and that is what our examples are meant to suggest.[1] Thus, it seems to us that a dichotomy should be made, but one based on the criterion of reproducibility: experiments that are reproducible whether syntactic or semantic, yield facts that constitute the subject matter of linguistics, while the rest of the intuitions should be dealt with in philosophy.

REFERENCES

Bely, N. and Vasseux, Ph. (1973). *Le système de gestion de la grammaire du L.A.D.L.* Paris: L.A.D.L.

Boons, J. P., Guillet, A. and Leclère, C. (1975). *La structure des phrases simples en français* (Constructions sans complétives). 3 volumes. Paris: L.A.D.L.

Chomsky, N. (1967). 'Remarks on nominalization'. In R. Jacobs and P. Rosenbaum, eds., *Readings in English Transformational Grammar*. Waltham, Mass.: Blaisdell.

Chomsky, N. and Miller, G. A. (1963). 'Introduction to the formal analysis of natural languages.' In *Handbook of Mathematical Psychology*, **2**, 269–322. New York: Wiley.

Culioli, A. (1971). 'A propos d'opérations intervenant dans le traitement formel des langues naturelles', *Mathématiques et Sciences Humaines*, **34**, 7–15.

Giry, J. (1972). 'Analyse syntaxique des constructions du verbe "faire"'. Thèse. Paris: L.A.D.L.

Gross, M. (1975). *Méthodes en syntaxe*. Paris: Hermann.

Harris, Z. S. (1951). *Methods in Structural Linguistics*. Chicago: Chicago University Press.

---

[1] Culioli (1971) has proposed an interesting set of concepts of meaning that appear to be reproducible.

—— (1964). 'The elementary transformations'. In *Papers in Structural and Transformational Linguistics* (1970), pp. 482–532. Dordrecht: Reidel.

—— (1968). *Mathematical Structures of Language*. New York: Wiley.

Joshi, A. K. (1972). 'Factorization of verbs: an analysis of verbs of seeing.' Mimeographed.

Kuroda, S. Y. (1973). 'Geach and Katz on presupposition'. Mimeographed.

Lees, R. B. (1960). *The Grammar of English Nominalizations*. La Haye: Mouton.

Lightner, T. M. (1972). *Problems in the Theory of Phonology*. Edmonton: Linguistics Research, Inc.

McCawley, J. (1968). 'Lexical insertion in a transformational grammar without deep structure'. In *Papers from the Fourth Regional Meeting of the Chicago Linguistic Society*. Chicago: Chicago Linguistic Society.

Picabia, L. (1970). 'Etudes transformationelles de constructions adjectivales en français'. Thèse. Paris: L.A.D.L.

Postal, P. (1970). 'On the surface verb "remind" ', *Linguistic Inquiry*, **1**, 37–120.

Ross, J. R. (1971). 'Act.' In R. Jacobs and P. Rosenbaum, eds., *Readings in English Transformational Grammar*. Waltham, Mass.: Blaisdell.

Logical expressive power and syntactic variation in natural language

EDWARD L. KEENAN

I will argue here[1] that the task of formally defining logical structures (LS) for natural languages (NL) has a linguistic interest beyond the immediate one inherent in representing logical notions like *entailment, presupposition, true answer to,* etc. The reason is that LS can be used as a basis for describing, and in some cases explaining, certain kinds of syntactic variation across NL. Below we consider three types of comparison between LS and the surface structures (SS) which can be used to express them in different NL.

In the first comparison we will demonstrate that NL differ significantly in their capacity to form restrictive relative clauses. We explain this variation in terms of the *Principle of Conservation of Logical Structure* (Keenan (1972b)).

In the second comparison we show that NL differ in their capacity to stipulate the co-reference of NP positions, but we provide no explanation for this variation.

And in the third comparison we show that the expression of indirect questions (indQ) varies in restricted ways across NL and propose a *Principle of Logical Variants* which explains this on the basis of the LS we propose for indQ.

1. Type 1 comparison

Here we compare LS with the SS which can be used to express them in various NL. Obviously if a LS can be naturally expressed in some NL but

---

[1] Many of the generalizations made in this paper concerning cross language variation required data from a large variety of languages. I should here like to express my thanks to the following linguists and students of language for their help in obtaining the data from the indicated languages: R. Beynon – Welsh; M. Butar-Butar – Batak; B. Comrie – Persian, Turkish, Polish, and Russian; R. P. G. de Rijk – Basque; K. Ebert – Fering (N. Frisian) and especially for making available her field notes on Kera; G. Gembries – Old and Middle English; J. Hawkins – German; R. Hull – Korean; A. Janhunen – Finnish; J. Payne – Welsh; A. Salmond – Maori; P. Sgall – colloquial Czech; A. Sinha – Hindi; H. van Riemsdijk – Zurich German; and B. Vattuone – Genoese.

not others then the former are logically more expressive *in that respect* than the latter.

For example the LS expressed by the relative clauses (RC) in (1)–(3) below are not naturally expressible in English, but they are in the NL indicated:

(1) *Arabic*

alrajul   allathi *hua* wa ibnahu thahabu ille New York
the man that   *he* and son-his went   to New York
*'the man that he and his son went to New York'

(2) *Welsh*

het   y   gwn   y   dyn a'   *i* gadewodd ar y   ford
the hat that I-know the man who *it* left   on the table
*'the hat that I know the man who left (it) on the table'

(3) *Zurich German*

də baəb wo də hanz z kryγt   glæwbt daz d   maria
the boy that the Hans rumour believes that the Mary
ən aakfalə heb
him attacked has
*'the boy that Hans believed the rumour that Mary attacked (him)'

Nor are these possibilities merely isolated facts about Arabic, Welsh, and Zurich German. As indicated by our glosses, these NL differ from English in that they characteristically present a personal pronoun in the NP position relativized. (We henceforth refer to such NL as +PRO, and NL like English which do not present such pronouns as −PRO.) To verify that the greater expressive power of the +PRO languages was in fact due to the presence of the pronoun in the RC we tested RC formation in a variety of 'difficult' environments in several +PRO languages and compared the results with the corresponding environments in −PRO NL. The results are summarized in Table I.[1]

---

[1] Concerning the less well known NL in Table I we note the following: Aoba-1 is one of 12 'melanesian' languages (whose names our informant did not know) spoken on the island of Aoba, the New Hebrides. We arbitrarily designated our informant's language as Aoba-1. It is spoken in the village of Nagea, Longana District.

Batak (Toba dialect) is a Malayo-Polynesian language spoken in Sumatra. The Czech entry refers to colloquial Czech, not literary Czech which uses relative pronouns rather than a constant *rel*-marker with personal pronouns retained in the positions relativized. Gilbertese is a 'micronesian' language spoken in the Gilbert Islands. Kera is a 'Chadic' language spoken in the south of Chad near Fianga. Urhobo is a Kwa language spoken in the delta region of Nigeria; and Malagasy is a Malayo-Polynesian language spoken throughout Madagascar.

TABLE I

Relativization is possible into:

	co-NP	VP-S	NP-S	IndQ	RC	Conj	Oblique	Poss-NP
+PRO								
Aoba-1	yes	yes	yes	yes	no?	yes	yes	yes
Arabic	yes	yes	no	yes	yes	yes	yes	yes
Batak	yes	yes	no	no	no	yes	yes	yes
Czech	no	yes	no	yes	yes	yes	yes	yes
Genoese	yes	yes	yes	yes	yes	yes	yes	yes
Gilbertese	no	yes	no	yes?	no	yes	yes	yes
Hebrew	yes	yes	yes	yes	yes	yes	yes	yes
Kera	**	yes	no	yes	yes	**	yes	yes
Persian	yes	yes	yes	yes	yes	yes	yes	yes
Urhobo	yes	yes	**	no	no	**	yes	yes
Welsh	no	no	yes	yes	yes	yes?	yes	yes
Zurich German	no?	yes	yes	yes	no	yes	yes	yes
−PRO								
English	no	yes	no	yes?	no	yes	yes	yes
Russian	no	no	no	no	no	yes	yes	yes
Finnish	no	no	no	no	no	yes	yes	yes
Hindi	no	no	no	no	no	yes	yes	yes
Malagasy	no	yes	no	no	no	no	no	no
Tagalog	no	no	no	no	no	no	no	no

KEY. *Rows*: the entries are largely self explanatory, save ** which means that the context specified by the column heading does not arise in a natural way.

Columns: co-NP: a single member of coordinate NP, as in 'the man and *the woman* live in Chicago'; *VP-S*: sentence complements of verbs, as in 'John thinks that Mary kissed *the man*'; *NP-S*: sentence complements of N, as in 'John believes the rumour that Mary kissed *the man*'; *indQ*: indirect question, as in 'John knew which man kissed *the woman*'; *RC*: relative clauses, as in 'I saw the man who kissed *the woman*'; *Conj*: both sides of an overt coordinate conjunction in different grammatical cases, as in '*The man* entered the room and Mary kissed *the man*'; *Oblique*: an object of a pre- or post-position, as in 'John hid the money under *the bed*'; *Poss-NP*: a genitive, as in '*The woman*'s cow died'.

Clearly the +PRO languages generally permit the formation of RC in a greater variety of environments than do the −PRO languages. Why? We feel that it is because the +PRO languages present in surface more of the logical structure of the RC than do the −PRO languages and that in general the logically more perspicuous expression can be used in otherwise more difficult positions (where an NP position is 'difficult' if there are many NL that do not permit it to be relativized at all).

To see this, consider that, logically speaking, a RC determines ($\approx$ refers to) an individual (or set of individuals) by first specifying a larger set – that referred to by the head NP – and then restricting that set to those member(s) of which a particular logical sentence – hereafter *the restricting sentence* – is true. Thus for an individual to be correctly referred to by (4),

(4) the girl that John gave the book to

the individual must, in the first place, be a girl, and in the second place, be such that the sentence *John gave the book to her* is true of her. But now compare (4a), the SS of (4), with that of (4b), its natural rendition in Hebrew, a +PRO language.[1]

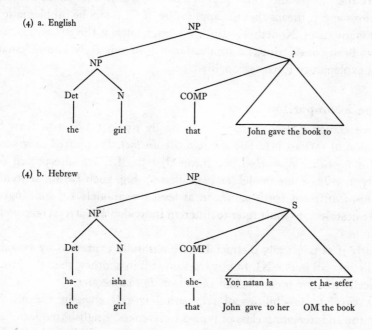

(4) a. English

(4) b. Hebrew

Clearly in Hebrew the restricting sentence of LS is fully presented in surface, since the presence of the pronoun *la* means that the subordinate clause in (4b) has the full SS of a sentence. But in (4a) the subordinate clause in English lacks an NP in an essential argument position of the main verb *give* and consequently is not a SS sentence. Clearly then the +PRO languages present more of the LS of RC in surface than do the −PRO languages.

[1] We are ignoring here the logical properties of the definite determiner since, for purposes of our examples, they do not distinguish the Hebrew and the English RC.

It seems natural to attempt to generalize this point to the following explanatory principle:

Conservation of Logical Structure (CLS)
Let x be a logical structure and let x_i and x_j be distinct surface structures (from possibly distinct NL) which express x. Then if x_i presents more of x than does x_j the syntactic transformations which generate x_i apply in a greater range of cases (or at least in more 'difficult' cases) than those which generate x_j.

Admittedly our inability to measure how much logical structure has been presented by some SS in a particular case, and our inability to measure the 'range' and 'difficulty' of cases to which a sequence of transformations apply, means that the application of CLS will be problematic in a great many cases. Nonetheless, in a few cases, such as the RC comparison we have been considering, its application will be relatively unproblematic and its explanatory force reasonably clear.

2. Type 2 comparison

Here we compare two or more semantically distinct LS with their SS expression in various NL. (By *semantically distinct*, as opposed to *semantically* (or *logically*) *equivalent*, we mean that the LS are interpreted differently in at least one model (state of affairs). E.g. such LS for sentences must have different truth values in at least one model; LS for singular definite descriptions must refer to different individuals in at least one model, and so on.)

Clearly if semantically distinct LS are naturally expressed by syntactically distinct SS in one NL but by the same SS in another, then the former is logically more expressive than the latter, *in that respect*.

The varying possibilities of stipulating co-reference in various NL determine an interesting class of type-2 differences. English (modern), and many NL, stipulate co-reference by contrasting marked and unmarked forms of pronouns as in (5).

(5) a. John hit himself
     b. John hit him

Clearly the marked pronoun in (5a) forces us to understand that the person hit was the same as the one doing the hitting, whereas this is not the case in (5b). Thus the situations in which (5a) is true need not coincide with those in which (5b) is true, and consequently the LS of (5a) is distinct from that of (5b).

Note that the stipulation of co-reference above need not be expressed in surface by pronoun marking. In a few NL at least, a contrast between a pronominal form and a deletion is used in such cases. (Where helpful in the examples below we use matching subscripts to mark NPs whose co-reference is being stipulated; otherwise different subscripts will be used.):

(6) *Japanese*
Taro$_i$ -wa $\emptyset_j$ /zibun$_i$-o tataita
Taro$_i$ him$_j$/himself$_i$ struck

(7) *Arosi* (Solomon Islands)
a. E urao$_i$ na rubuia $\emptyset_j$
   the woman$_i$ hit   her$_j$
b. E urao$_i$ si a rubuia haria$_i$
   the woman$_i$ hit   self$_i$

In light of these examples one might feel that universally NL could stipulate co-reference between subjects and objects of verbs. But this is not the case. In (8)–(12) the NL cited characteristically do not stipulate co-reference between subjects and objects, and are thus logically less expressive than e.g. Modern English

(8) *Middle English*[1] (Chaucer, *The Knight's Tale*)
a. He leyde hym, bare the visage, on the beere (v. 2877)
   (*He* = Theseus, *hym* = Arcite, as is clear from context.)
b. At Thebes, in his contree, as I sayde,
   Upon a nyght in sleep as he hym leyde (v. 1384)
   (*he* = Arcite, *hym* = Arcite.)

(9) *Fering* (A north Frisian dialect)
John hee ham   ferreet
John has him/himself betrayed

(10) *Maori* (New Zealand)
ka patu ia ki a   'ia
hit   he OM person him/himself
                (mkr)
'he hit him/himself'
Gilbertese
E tara*ia*   Teerau
he-hit him/himself Teerau

---

[1] My especial thanks go to Genevieve Gembries, Universität Stuttgart, who worked through many Old and Middle English texts and found several 'minimal pairs' of the sort cited in (8).

(12) *Tahitian* (Tryon (1970))

'Ua ha'apohe 'oia 'iana
was-kill   he him/himself
'He killed him/himself'

Furthermore, as the 'distance' between NPs increases it becomes more difficult to stipulate co-reference. An interesting pair in this regard are subjects of verbs like *think* and the subjects of their sentence complements. English for example does not generally stipulate co-reference in these positions. Thus the pronoun in (13),

(13) John thinks that he is clever

does not change in form according as it is stipulated to refer to John or not, even though we might conceivably expect something like (14):

(14) *John thinks that he-self is clever

Some languages however, e.g. Japanese and Korean, can stipulate co-reference in these positions by contrasting reflexive and non-reflexive pronouns:

(15) *Korean*

$$\text{John}_i\text{-eun}\begin{Bmatrix}\text{keu}_j\text{-ka}\\\text{keu-chacin}_i\text{-i}\end{Bmatrix}\text{yeonglihatago sankaghabnita}$$

$$\text{John}_i\text{ top}\begin{Bmatrix}\text{he}_j\text{ subj}\\\text{he}_i\text{ self subj}\end{Bmatrix}\text{clever}\qquad\text{thinks}$$

'John$_i$ thinks that he$_j$/he$_i$ is clever'

A few other languages use an emphatic form of the pronoun (e.g. *òn* vs. *ó* in Yoruba, *to* vs. *wi* in Kera) to stipulate co-reference in such positions, leaving the unemphatic form to be interpreted as not being co-referential with the matrix subject:

(16) *Yoruba*

Ojo ro   pe (òn /ó) mu sasa
Ojo$_i$ thinks that (he$_i$/he$_j$) is clever

(17) *Kera*

Golsala dig   minti (to /wi) bi cuuru
Golsala thinks that   (he$_i$/he$_j$) is intelligent

Furthermore, use of the pronoun/deletion contrast appears a more frequent way to mark co-reference in these cases than for subjects and objects of the same verb. (Note that in the examples below we only consider pairs of sentences differing solely by the presence or absence of the pronoun: in particular the *that*-complementizer is retained in the cases without pronouns.)

(18) *Finnish*[1]

John$_i$ luuli että (Ø$_i$ /hän$_j$) oli sairas

John$_i$ thought that (he$_i$/he$_j$) was sick

(19) *Malagasy*

Nihevitra Rabe$_i$ fa notadiavin- dRasoa (Ø$_i$ /izy$_j$)

thought Rabe$_i$ that looked for by Rasoa (he$_i$/he$_j$)

'Rabe$_i$ thought that (he$_i$/he$_j$) was being looked for by Rasoa'

(20) *Polish*

Jan$_i$ powiedział, ze (Ø$_i$ /on$_j$) przyjdzie

John$_i$ said that (he$_i$/he$_j$) would come

NL then are logically different in that they vary with regard to the NP positions that are naturally stipulated as being co-referential. But for the moment we can offer no general explanation for this variation.

3. Type 3 comparison

Here we compare the SS expression of LS which are distinct but semantically equivalent (that is, they are always interpreted in the same way in a given model). Clearly distinguishing the SS expressions of such LS does *not* increase the logical expressive power of a NL. Consequently we might expect that (other things being equal) NL would vary according as they more naturally expressed the one or the other in surface. The *Principle of Logical Variants* below makes this intuition more precise. To state it we shall first make explicit a notational convention tacitly used earlier. Namely, for any natural language L_i and any logical structure x, x_i will denote any surface structure in L_i which expresses x. Secondly, we define:

Definition 1: Logical structures x and y are *logical variants in a logical context F* just in case Fx and Fy are logically equivalent. That is, just in case putting either x or y in the context F yields logically equivalent results.

We can now propose the following explanatory principle:

Principle of Logical Variants (PLV)

If x and y are logical variants in a context F then languages vary naturally according as they express x_i or y_i in the context F_i.

[1] Finnish can also stipulate co-reference in these positions by deleting the *että*-complementizer and using a non-finite verb in the subordinate clause.

Clearly the more interesting applications of PLV would be in the cases where the variants x and y are themselves semantically distinct but have their differences neutralized in the context F. For then logically expressive NL would have different SS for x and y and this difference would signal a difference in meaning; hence such NL would not in general be indifferent as to which surface structure x_i or y_i was used in an arbitrary context. But PLV precisely specifies one context where we do expect indifference – namely, those in which, for independent logical reasons, the meaning differences between the SS is neutralized.

Here we shall claim that the LS of singular definite RC (21a) and that of wh-questions (21b) are logical variants in the contexts determined by indirect question frames, e.g. 'John knows——', 'John remembers——', etc., as they appear in (21c).

(21) a. the student that left early
      b. Which student left early?
      c. John knows which student left early

Clearly (21a) and (21b) are not logically equivalent so their LS must be distinct. Now if we can establish that their LS are variants then PLV will predict that NL will vary according as the object clauses of indQ have the form of a RC or of a wh-question (Q).

Let us note first that this prediction appears to be correct to a large extent. Thus in many NL – e.g. Finnish, Tagalog, Korean – the form of a simple Q does not change when it is embedded in indQ contexts:

(22) *Finnish*
      a. Millä veitsellä   John tappoi   kanan?
          Which knife-with did John kill (the) chicken?
      b. Mary ei tiennyt millä veitsellä   John tappoi kanan
          Mary not know which knife-with John killed chicken
          'Mary didn't know with which knife John killed the chicken'

And, as is well known, in many other NL (English, French, and to a lesser extent, German), the form of a simple Q changes only slightly when embedded in indQ frames.

What is perhaps less well known is that there are also many NL in which the object clauses in indQ are identical with (or in a few cases merely very similar to) singular definite relative clauses. E.g.

(23) *Yoruba*
      a. *Relative Clause*
          Ọkunrin (na) ti   obinrin na lu

man   (the) that woman the hit
'the man that the woman hit'
b. *Wh-question*
Ọkunrin wo- ni obinrin na lu?
man   which foc woman the hit
'Which man did the woman hit?'
c. *Indirect question*
Tale mọ   ọkunrin ti   obinrin na lu
Tale knows man   that woman the hit
'Tale knows which man the woman hit'

Note that in (23c), if the interrogative form *woni* is used instead of the relative form *ti* the result is clearly ungrammatical:

(23) d. *Tale mọ ọkunrin woni obinrin na lu

Other NL in which such object clauses are like RC are: Shona, Malagasy, Urhobo, Roviana (Solomon Islands), Sa (New Hebrides), and Kera (Chad). In fact in English we often get both RC and Q structures in indQ. Thus the (a) and (b) sentences below are paraphrases (at least on one reading).

(24) a. John knows the route the plane will take
b. John knows which route the plane will take
(25) a. John knows the year that Mary was born in
b. John knows which year Mary was born in
(26) a. John knew in advance the horse that would win
b. John knew in advance which horse would win

Clearly then if we can show that the LS of Q and of singular definite RC are variants in indQ frames then PLV will explain the variation we have observed in those positions. Below we present informally the main lines of such a demonstration. The analysis of direct questions is based on that in Keenan and Hull (1973a).

First, within the formal logic we provide distinct LS for such RC and Q. The former have, roughly, the form: (the, NP_x, S) which can be read as *the NP which is such that S* (where S is a logical sentence (formula) having a free occurrence of the variable x). Semantically, such structures are interpreted as the unique member of the universe of discourse which is in the set of things that the noun phrase NP_x is interpreted as and of which the sentence S is *true*. Logical questions on the other hand have the form ($which$, NP_x, S) which can be read as *Which NP is such that S?* Semantically they are interpreted as operators which combine with answer phrases (= definite NPs) to form a logical sentence. That is, question-answer pairs are treated as propositions, things that determine truth values in a model. And in particular, restricting ourselves for purposes of exposition to singular questions, a definite NP will be a *true* answer to $(which, NP_x, S)$ just in case it is interpreted as the unique NP_x of which S is true. A true answer to such a question then will always refer to (be interpreted as) the same object that (the, NP_x, S) refers to.

Second, we add to the logic a class of transitive predicates K, K_1, $K_2, \ldots (= know, remember,$ etc.) which form intransitive predicates from either NPs of the form (the, NP_x, S) or from questions. Thus within the logic we have two formally distinct types of sentence, represented roughly as in (27) and (28) below. Now, to show that the LS of RC and Q are variants in indQ frames, we must specify the truth and falsehood conditions for (27) and (28) in a way which both accounts correctly for their consequences, presuppositions, etc., and which shows that they are logically equivalent – that is, that (27) and (28) have, in effect, the same truth and falsehood conditions.

(27)

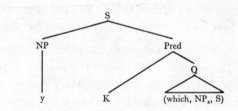

'y knows (remembers, etc.) which NP is such that S'

(28)

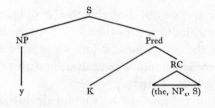

'y knows (remembers, etc.) the NP which is such that S'

We shall informally suggest such a definition But notice first why it is plausible that the definitions should be such as to determine the logical equivalence of (27) and (28). (28) says in effect that John can identify the referent of *the NP which is such that S*. And (27) says that John knows an answer to the question *which NP is such that S?* But to know an answer to such a question is precisely to be able to identify its true answer set, and this is just the referent of *the NP which is such that S*.

Consider now LS having the form (27). A formal statement of their semantics is given in Hull (this volume). The intuition he formalized is this: to say, e.g. that *John knows which student Mary invited* is to say that John knows an informative answer to the question *Which student did Mary invite?* (An answer is informative in a model if it is true but not necessarily so, i.e. there are other models in which it is a false answer.) Such an answer is given by a noun phrase NP' which *identifies* the student that Mary invited. That is, the LS of NP' *is the student that Mary invited* is both true and informative. So to say that John knows which student Mary invited is to say that, for some such NP', *John knows that NP' is the student Mary invited*. More generally then:

Definition 2: $(y, K, (which, NP_x, S))$ is true in a model $\mathcal{M}$ iff there is an NP' such that:

(i) NP' is a true informative answer to $(which, NP_x, S)$ in $\mathcal{M}$ and

(ii) $(y, K \text{ that } (NP' = (the, NP_x, S))$ is true in $\mathcal{M}$

(We are assuming here the formal semantics of factives, e.g. *know that*, etc., given in Keenan (1972a).)

Concerning (28), the intuition that we want to formalize in sentences like *John knows the route the plane will take* is that John can identify the referent of the RC *the route the plane will take*. (Note that it is not the personal sense of *know*, as in *to know John* that we are trying to capture. Rather it is the more sophisticated use, as in *to know who John is*. In several NL of course this ambiguity does not arise since these meanings are expressed by different verbs, e.g. *connaître* vs. *savoir* in French, *kennen* vs. *wissen* in German, etc.) Now to be able to identify the referent of a RC is, linguistically, to be able to refer to it (using of course some noun phrase NP') in an alternative, that is, informative, way. There must then be some such noun phrase NP' equal in reference to the RC and such that John knows that the equality holds. Somewhat more generally then,

Definition 3: $(y, K, (the, NP_x, S))$ is true in a model $\mathcal{M}$ iff there is an NP' such that:

(i) $(NP' = (the, NP_x, S))$ is true and informative in $\mathcal{M}$ and

(ii) $(y, K \text{ that } (NP' = (the, NP_x, S))$ is true in $\mathcal{M}$

Clearly condition (ii) here is identical to the corresponding condition in Definition 2. And condition (i) here is equivalent to condition (i) in Definition 2 since it says in effect that NP' informatively identifies the true answer set of the question $(which, NP_x, S)$. Consequently the truth conditions of LS of the form (27) and (28) are the same. Similarly we could develop the falsehood conditions of (27) and (28) in a natural way which would show them to be the same. Thus (27) and (28) would be shown to be logically equivalent, and so the LS of relative clauses and wh-questions would be logical variants in contexts determined by indirect questions.[1]

4. A transformational solution to type 3 problems?

The type of variation we have explained in terms of (PLV) might appear to some to be more naturally represented within a transformational framework. That type of solution (hereafter the *T-solution*) would be roughly as follows: posit a single LS for indirect questions and then transformationally derive either RC or Q in these contexts depending on the NL. This solution would appear simpler than ours in that it needs only one type of LS for indQ where we have two. But our solution is to be preferred over the T-solution for two quite general reasons:

First, the T-solution offers no *explanation* as to why it is natural to get both RC and Q structures in indQ. Why for example do we not get focused (= cleft, in English) sentences in these positions? They are syntactically similar in many ways to RC and Q, as argued in Schachter (1973) and Keenan and Hull (1973b). Furthermore, why are we indifferent to the difference between RC and Q only in indQ? Why not generally? PLV provides an explanation for this (assuming that something like our LS for RC and Q are correct). Note that even if transformations deriving RC and Q from the same source in indQ contexts could be independently motivated we would still want an explanation as to why NL permit the existence of transformations which derive SS which are both syntactically and, generally, semantically distinct, from the same source in certain contexts.

And second, the T-solution creates a great many syntactic problems not created by our approach:

In the first place, it is clear that RC and Q will each have to have their own syntactic source in general (since they are syntactically distinct structures having in general a different distribution). So the common source for RC and Q in indQ will have to be different from at least one of these independently needed underlying structures, which means that surface RC or Q (or possibly both) will be derived from two distinct sources. This is inelegant and counter-intuitive (since there is in general no reason to think that either RC or Q have two distinct syntactic structures).

---

[1] The logical properties of indirect questions are not well known, and any proposal for representing their LS at this point will not be definitive.

And in the second place, the more syntactically distinct two types of SS are the less natural it is to derive them from the same source. Now although RC and Q are syntactically similar in many respects they are never systematically identical and the differences run deeper than the surface distribution of determiners (e.g. *the* vs. *which*). Thus quite generally, in any given NL the NP positions that can be relativized are not exactly the same as those that can be questioned. Some of the differences are language specific, and some are rather more general.

In the former category we might cite the following facts from German and English. In German many speakers find it difficult or impossible to relativize into sentence complements of verbs like *glauben* (= *think*) but it is often possible to question these positions:

(29) *German*
    a. Du glaubst, daß Fritz das Mädchen liebt
       You think   that Fritz the girl   loves
       'You think that Fritz loves the girl'
    b. Wen glaubst du, daß Fritz liebt?
       'Who do you think that Fritz loves?'
    c. *Das Mädchen, das du glaubst daß Fritz liebt
       'the girl that you think that Fritz loves'

On the other hand, in English we can 'simultaneously' relativize into NPs occurring across coordinate conjunctions in different grammatical cases, but the corresponding question is ill-formed:

(30) a. the man who came early and who(m) Mary attacked
     b. *Who came early and Ø/who Mary attacked?

(Note that the question *Who came early and who did Mary attack?*, while well-formed, does not simultaneously question two NP positions. That is, it does not request the identification of one individual with two properties; rather it requests two identifications of individuals, each of which has one property.)

Finally, concerning the more language general differences in the formation of RC and Q, we feel that in general RC formation is a more esoteric process than Q formation. It is likely that all NL allow the major and near-major NP positions of main verbs to be questioned. (Even in very elementary grammars of languages we usually find a list of question words like *who?*, *what?*, *when?*, *where?*, *whose?*, etc.) On the other hand, many NL have only very restricted RC forming means. (See Keenan and Comrie

(1972) for a detailed justification of this claim.) For example many Malayo-Polynesian languages can only relativize on subject NPs.

A particularly nice differentiating position in this respect is genitives (e.g. '*the woman*'s cow died'). This position is often difficult to relativize, and in several languages – e.g. Tagalog, Basque, Malagasy, Fering – it is not naturally relativizable at all. Yet genitives can usually be questioned:

(31) *Basque*[1]

  a. Apaiz-aren   liburuak irakurri ditut
     priest-the-of books   read   have-them-I
     'I have read the priest's books'

  b. Noren liburuak irakurri dituzu?
     who-of books   read   have-them-you
     'Whose books have you read?'

  c. *liburuak irakurri ditudan   apaiza
     books   read   have-them-I-rel priest-the
     'the priest whose books I have read'

Similarly in Fering we have an interrogative *whose* (= *Hokkers?*) and we do as well in Tagalog (*Kaninong?*).

In conclusion, I have attempted to represent three types of syntactic variation across languages in terms of the logical structures needed to represent the consequences, presuppositions, etc. of NL structures. In two of these cases we were able to propose explanatory principles, that of *Conservation of Logical Structure* and the *Principle of Logical Variants*, which enabled us to explain the observed variation.

REFERENCES

Hull, R. (1973). 'A semantics for superficial and embedded questions in natural language'. This volume.

Keenan, E. (1972a). 'On semantically based grammar', *Linguistic Inquiry*, **3**, No. 4, 413–61.

—— (1972b). 'The logical status of deep structures'. To appear in the *Proceedings of the 11th International Congress of Linguists*. Bologna, Italy.

Keenan, E. and Comrie, B. (1972). 'Noun phrase accessibility and universal grammar'. Paper read at the winter meetings of the Linguistic Society of America.

---

[1] The examples here are due to R. P. G. de Rijk and represent the indigenous way of forming RC (e.g. head noun to the right of the subordinate clause, as is normal for SOV languages). Some dialects, under the influence of Romance, can in addition form RC with the head noun to the left of the subordinate clause, and this type does admit of relativization on genitives.

Keenan, E. and Hull, R. (1973a). 'The logical presuppositions of questions and answers'. In J. Petöfi and D. Franck, eds., *Präsuppositionen in der Linguistik und der Philosophie* (1973). Frankfurt: Athenäum.

—— (1973b). 'The logical syntax of direct and indirect questions'. To appear in *Parasession of the Ninth Regional Meeting of the Chicago Linguistic Society*. Chicago: Chicago Linguistic Society.

Schachter, P. (1973). 'Focus and relativization', *Language*, **49**, No. 1, 19–46.

Tyron, D. (1970). *Conversational Tahitian*. Canberra: Australian National University Press.

Clausematiness

JOHN R. ROSS

1.

In the past decade or so, it has been traditional, within the broad framework of transformational grammar, to account for the difference in grammaticality between (1a) and (1b) by making reference to the theoretical notion of *clausemate*.

(1) a. Frederick$_i$ knows himself$_i$
    b. *Frederick$_i$ knows that we are fond of himself$_i$

Since the reflexive pronoun and its antecedent are *clausemates* in (1a),[1] but not in (1b), as this kind of account goes, only the former string is possible' for English reflexivization is subject to a clausemate condition.

My purpose in this paper is not to improve on this traditional analysis of reflexivization, which seems clearly correct in its essential points, but rather to argue that the term *clausemate* itself must be changed from the binary, on-off, predicate it has always been taken to be (that is, two nodes were either clausemates or not – there was no middle ground), and replaced by a quantifiable predicate of *clausematiness*, which allows the formulation of such statements as (2).

(2) In tree R, A and B are more clausematey than are A and C

This quantifiable predicate forms one axis of a *squish*, the type of model of interaction between two linguistic parameters that I have diagrammed schematically in (3).[2]

---

[1] This term, as far as I know, was first used in Postal (1971). For the purposes of this paper, it makes no difference whether the term *clausemate* is used, or some functional equivalent like 'elements of the same simplex sentence', 'mutually command', 'dominated by all and only the same occurrences of S', etc. In various treatments of reflexivization and related problems, all of these and probably more can be attested in the literature. I have adopted Postal's term here purely on the ground that it is morphologically easier to find a degreeable adjective based on it than is the case with some of the others. Nothing rests on this decision, however.

[2] It is unfortunate, but English does not seem to have any pair of terms which would match the snappiness of the German *X-Haftigkeit* [= having property X to some degree] and *X-Süchtigkeit* [= addicted to X to some degree], so I will have to make do with the two terms I have used in (3).

422

(3)

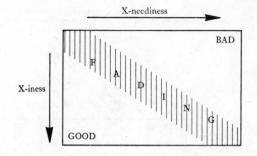

The 'GOOD' and 'BAD' of (3) refer to grammaticality judgements and rule valences (that is, specifications as to whether rules are obligatory, or optional, or do not apply, under various conditions), where grammaticality is linked with obligatoriness, as will become clear from the actual squish of clausematiness which is shown in (4).

The use of the ' $\cong$ ' sign at the bottom of (4) is to establish a rough correspondence between rule valences and degrees of grammaticality. As a working hypothesis, I will assume the correctness of the correspondences in what follows.

To claim that two parameters interact to form a squish is to claim that the values of grammaticality/valence in the cells of each row will decrease monotonically from higher levels of grammaticality/valence to lower ones, if the rows are read from left to right, and also that the values in the cells of each column will decrease monotonically, reading from bottom to top.

When a cell's value interrupts the monotonic decline of a row, it is *horizontally ill-behaved*. Such cells are indicated by the placing of two vertical bars at the sides of the offending cell, as has been done in the fifth cell of the third row of (4). The corresponding type of *vertical ill-behaviour* is marked with parallel horizontal lines, as in the first cell of row 3.

Thus, since I know of no mitigating factors which could be appealed to to account for the various ill-behaved cells of (4), it is not possible at present to maintain the claim that there exists a squish of clausematiness, in the precise sense in which I intend 'squish' to be taken. Rather, (4) must be referred to as a *squishoid* – something which approximates the type of ideal squish that is suggested by (3).

Below, in section 2, I will present the various facts on which (4) is based. If my assessment of these facts is correct, it will be necessary to modify linguistic theory in the way I have suggested – to replace the discrete metalinguistic predicate 'clausemate' with a non-discrete, 'squishy', term like 'clausematey (to some degree)'.

(4) *The clausematiness squish(oid)*

Clausemate-neediness →

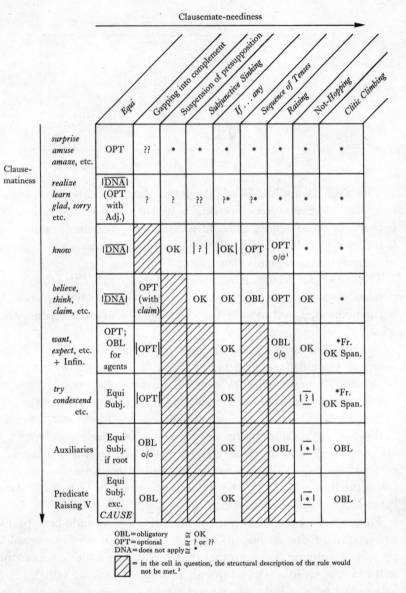

Clausematiness		Equi	Gapping into complement	Suspension of presupposition	Subjunctive Sinking	If...any	Sequence of Tenses	Raising	Not-Hopping	Clitic Climbing
	surprise amuse amaze, etc.	OPT	??	*	*	*	*	*	*	*
	realize learn glad, sorry etc.	|DNA| (OPT with Adj.)	?	?	??	?*	?*	*	*	*
	know	|DNA|	▨	OK	| ? |	|OK|	OPT	OPT o/o¹	*	*
	believe, think, claim, etc.	|DNA|	OPT (with *claim*)	▨	OK	OK	OBL	OPT	OK	*
	want, expect, etc. + Infin.	OPT; OBL for agents	|OPT|	▨	▨	OK	▨	OBL o/o	OK	*Fr. OK Span.
	try condescend etc.	Equi Subj.	|OPT|	▨	▨	OK	▨	▨	|?|	*Fr. OK Span.
	Auxiliaries	Equi Subj. if root	OBL o/o	▨	▨	OK	▨	OBL	|*|	OBL
	Predicate Raising V	Equi Subj. exc. *CAUSE*	OBL	▨	▨	OK	▨	▨	|*|	OBL

OBL = obligatory ≅ OK
OPT = optional ≅ ? or ??
DNA = does not apply ≅ *

▨ = in the cell in question, the structural description of the rule would not be met.²

¹ The 'o/o' sign means 'varies according to dialect'. For example, the o/o in the seventh box of row 3 of (4) means that not all speakers find sentences like (i), in which *Raising* has applied to *know*, grammatical.

(i) I know Selford to dote on pizza

² For example, the shading of the four cells at the bottom of column 6 of (4) is necessitated by the fact that tense is only marked in finite clauses (by definition). Thus we cannot see whether the rule of Sequence of *Tense* applies to the complements of such verbs as *try* or not. Shaded cells are therefore irrelevant for the investigation of the question of whether or not there is a squish in the area under study.

The first line of defence for the linguistic theorist who has abandoned the claim that all metalinguistic predicates can be considered to be discrete, but who does not wish to go 'further away' from this claim than is absolutely necessary, would be, I would imagine, the claim that while most predicates should continue to be regarded as discrete, a few, such as 'clausematey' must be allowed to vary in the way suggested in (3) – to participate in squishes. The notion 'well-behaved matrix' would seem to be rather easily characterizable in a formal way, and thus could be taken to be a minimal departure from a discrete theory.

This is in fact the position that I would like to maintain myself, were it not for the ill-behaved cells in (4) and in other squishoids I have studied.[1] Unless future research should reveal such ill-behaviour to be accountable for on the basis of presently unperceived factors, linguistic theory will be stuck with the task of characterizing the set of possible squishoids. My decision to view such actual arrays of data as (4) as manifestations of underlying true squishes should be seen as a hope that the future will not be so black as it now looks.

2.

2.1. *Equi*

This rule, which is described in detail in Postal (1970), has the effect of deleting the subject of a non-finite complement under identity with some NP in the matrix clause. Thus (5a) may become (5b), under the application of this rule.

(5) a. o/o I was surprised for me to be repulsive to Og.[2]

Equi

b. I was surprised—to be repulsive to Og.

[1] Cf. Ross (1973b, c).

[2] As indicated by the 'o/o' prefix on (5a), speakers' judgements differ with respect to the grammaticality of row 1 sentences in which *Equi* has not applied. While I have not made an extensive study of this phenomenon, my impression is that at least three parameters affect the grammaticality of un-*Equi*-ed sentences like (5a).

A. Person. Most speakers find third-person sentences without *Equi* inferior to first-person sentences (5a) or second-person ones (i). Thus (ii) is worse than (5a) or (i).

  (i) Were you surprised for you to be repulsive to Og?
  (ii) Zoth$_i$ was surprised for him$_i$ to be repulsive to Og

B. Agentivity. For many speakers, the retention of a co-referential agentive subject produces less grammatical strings than result if a non-agentive subject is retained. Thus (5a), which contains a non-agentive subject, is superior to (iii), whose subject is agentive.

  (iii) I was surprised for me to kick Worthington Preppeogh III

This rule is basically optional (*pace* n. 1 below) for the subset of the class of emotive factive[1] predicates which are like *surprise*, a sample of whose members appears in (6).[2]

(6) *surprise, amuse, amaze, shock, appal, disgust, terrify, fascinate, horrify, interest, repel, bewilder, puzzle, bother, bore, devastate,* etc.

Though there are many individual differences separating the members of this group,[3] it is my impression that they behave fairly homogeneously with regard to the syntactic phenomena I will be treating, and it is this class whose behaviour is summarized in the top row of (4).

The next row is based on the behaviour of the smaller class of factives, some emotive, some not, that are listed in (7).

(7) a. *realize, learn, discover, find out*
    b. *glad, sorry, happy, sad*

Actually, the situation with respect to this parameter in *Equi* situations is quite obscure to me, for (iv), which is the *Equi*-ed version of (iii), still sounds equally strange to me.

(iv) I was surprised—to kick Worthington Preppeogh IV.

It cannot be claimed that no non-finite complements denoting volitional activities are permissible with the emotive factives of the first row of (4), for if no *Equi* is possible, the sentences are unimpaired. Cf. (v).

(v) I was surprised for Bob to kick Worthington Preppeogh III

These remarks on agentivity are obviously part of the general problem discussed below in connection with the factors influencing the valency of *Equi* with verbs like *want* and *expect*. I will thus say no more here.

C. Contrast. For some speakers, a contrastively stressed retained co-referential subject, even an agentive one, is superior to a non-contrastively stressed one. Thus (vi) and (vii) are superior to (iii), for these speakers.

(vi) I was surprised for *me* to kick Worthington Preppeogh III, and not *yóu*
(vii) I was surprised for *me* to kick Worthington Preppeogh in as many places as *Lou the Toe Gróza* did

The various possible interactions of such parameters as these on non-*Equi*-ed sentences like (5a) would seem likely to bear much further scrutiny.

[1] Cf. Kiparsky and Kiparsky (1970) for discussion of these terms.
[2] By citing these predicates in their verbal forms, I do not mean to suggest that the verbs are basic. In fact, I would hold, with Lakoff (1970), that *surprised* underlies *surprise* and *surprising*; that (i) gives rise to either (ii) or (iii), through the application of the rule Lakoff refers to as *Flip*.

(i) I was surprised that you ordered prawns
(ii) That you ordered prawns was surprising to me
(iii) That you ordered prawns surprised me

[3] Thus while we would expect to find *repelled,* *repelling, *repel,* paralleling the forms of *surprise* that show up in (i)–(iii) of n. 2 above, in fact we find, for the second of these, *repellent,* instead of an *ing*-form. I will disregard many such differences below.

I have made no exhaustive search, so I do not know whether there are other predicates that should be included in (7), but this partial list will suffice for the purposes of this paper.

The verbs of (7a) do not undergo *Equi*, as is shown by the ungrammaticality of (8).[1]

> (8) a. *Bill realized to have defended himself well
> b. *Ann found out to be holding her breath

The adjectives, however, do: cf. (9).

> (9) a. We are happy to be able to bilk you
> b. We are sorry to have to rat on you
> c. We are glad to be out of your reach

The verb *know*, which constitutes a row of (4) by itself, does not undergo *Equi*, as is shown by *(10).

---

[1] To be sure, the verb *learn* does show up in sentences in which *Equi* has applied, such as (i).

(i) Bill learned to talk loud

However, such sentences as this have a 'how to' interpretation that is not shared by *Equi*-ed clauses that appear as complements of verbs of the class of (6). And the complements of *learn* must express volitional activities, as is suggested by the contrast in (ii)

(ii) Bill learned to talk loud $\left\{ \begin{array}{l} \text{on purpose} \\ \text{*accidentally} \end{array} \right\}$

Also, the infinitival complements of *learn* typically exclude aspect (cf. *(iii) and *(iv)),

(iii) *Benny learned to have been polite.
(iv) *Shorts learned to be arriving that late

and cannot appear with subjects (cf. *(vi)).

(vi) *I learned for you to apply early

All of these properties are approximately the reverse of the behaviour of the *surprise*-class, as is suggested by the grammaticalities of (vii)–(xi).

(vii) * Bill was surprised to talk too loud
(viii) Bill was surprised to talk too loud $\left\{ \begin{array}{l} \text{?*on purpose} \\ \text{?accidentally} \end{array} \right\}$
(ix) ? Benny was surprised to have been polite
(x) Shorts was surprised to be arriving that late
(xi) I was surprised for you to apply early

Finally, *learn to* is a volitional activity, while *be surprised*, etc. (and *learn that*) are not (cf. (xii)–(xiv)).

(xii) Learn to tie your toes!
(xiii) ?* Be surprised to be swarthy! (only OK as a stage direction)
(xiv) * Learn that he didn't leave!

It thus would seem that the active *learn to* is only an apparent counter-example to the claim that the factive verbs of (7a) do not undergo *Equi*.

(10) *I knew to have been servile.[1]

The 'verbs of thinking' of row 4 of (4), a sample of which are shown in (11),

(11) *think, believe, claim, suppose, imagine, guess,* etc.

also prohibit *Equi*, in general, (cf. (12)), with the exception of *claim*, which is the only verb in English in this class to allow the kind of *Equi* that is possible with the *surprise*-class and the adjectives of (7b). Cf. (13).

$$
(12) \quad \text{*Fred} \left\{ \begin{array}{l} \text{thought[2]} \\ \text{believed} \\ \text{supposed} \\ \text{imagined} \\ \text{guessed} \end{array} \right\} \text{to have fooled us}
$$

(13) Fred claimed to have fooled us

---

[1] Again, as was the case with *learn*, there is a use of *know* which allows *Equi* to apply with complements that express activities – cf. (i).

$$
(i) \quad \text{Brain knew to} \left\{ \begin{array}{l} \text{play dumb} \\ \text{*have a way about him} \end{array} \right\}
$$

This *Equi*-able *know* has mysterious restrictions governing its appearance. Thus it will only appear with certain auxiliaries (cf. (ii)),

$$
(ii) \quad \text{Brain} \left\{ \begin{array}{l} \left\{ \begin{array}{l} \left\{ \begin{array}{l} \text{will} \\ \text{?might} \\ \text{?*may} \\ \text{*must} \\ \text{*can} \end{array} \right\} \text{know} \\ \text{*has known} \\ \left\{ \begin{array}{l} \text{must} \\ \text{may} \\ \text{will} \\ \text{could} \end{array} \right\} \text{(not) have known} \end{array} \right\} \text{to play dumb}
$$

and it may be related to the equally weird restrictions governing the distribution of a peculiar construction that involves *teach* – cf. (iii).

$$
(iii) \quad \left\{ \begin{array}{l} \text{That} \\ \text{It} \\ \text{The flood} \\ \text{Your leaving} \\ \text{*That you left} \\ \text{*Sam} \end{array} \right\} \left\{ \begin{array}{l} \text{will} \\ \text{may} \\ \text{*must} \\ \text{could} \\ \text{*can} \end{array} \right\} \text{(*not) teach Joe to talk back}
$$

where the complement should not be taken to mean 'how to talk back', but rather 'that he[1] should not talk back'.

At any rate, the fact that there is a use of *know* which permits the application of *Equi* should not distract us from concluding from the ungrammaticality of such sentences as *(10), which would parallel grammatical sentences like (5b), that *know* does not permit *Equi*.

[2] Once more, there is a construction involving *think to* that allows *Equi*. Cf. (i)

(i) Did you think to turn out the lights?

The application of *Equi* to the complement of *claim* should be considered to be optional, since although (14) is bad for most speakers,

(14) *Fred claimed for Ann to have been perjuring herself

if *Ann*, the subject of the complement, is raised to become the object of *claim*, the resulting structure, while ungrammatical in itself (cf. *(15)),

(15) *Fred claimed Ann to have been perjuring herself.

is so merely because it violates the output condition described in Postal (1974). This condition prohibits certain verbs which undergo *Raising* into object position from appearing in surface structures in the V position of verb phrases of the structure shown in (16),

(16) V NP$_R$ S

where the NP$_R$ was raised out of the subject of S.

If the raised NP$_R$ is subsequently removed from its post-V position by some rule, the resultant structure is somewhat improved. Thus compare *(15) with the ameliorated sentences in (17).

(17) a. ?It was Ann that Fred claimed to have been perjuring herself
　　 b. ?Ann Fred claimed to have been perjuring herself .

I must point out in passing that it is something of a mystery as to why only *claim*, of all the English verbs of thinking in (11), should be able to undergo *Equi*, since the translations of most of the verbs in (11) in other languages seem routinely to undergo this rule. Cf. the German and French sentences in (18) and (19).

(18) Karl meinte/glaubte, uns reingenommen zu haben
　　　　　opined/believed us　in taken　　　　to have
　　 'Karl believed that he had taken us in'

(19) Charles croyait　nous avoir　décus
　　　　　　believed us　to have deceived.
　　 'Charles believed that he had deceived us'

Its meaning is roughly 'remember to', and it is a weak negative polarity item (cf. Baker (1970) for an explanation of this term), as the examples in (ii)–(iv) show.

(ii) Mary may $\left\{ \begin{matrix} \text{not} \\ ?* \underline{\quad} \end{matrix} \right\}$ think to turn out the lights

(iii) I $\left\{ \begin{matrix} \text{doubt} \\ ?? \text{ know} \end{matrix} \right\}$ that Mary will think to turn out the lights

(iv) $\left\{ \begin{matrix} \text{If} \\ ?? \text{ Since} \end{matrix} \right\}$ Mary thought to turn out the lights,
　　 our power bill will be low

I will not be concerned with this use of *think* in this paper.

The situation that obtains with respect to *Equi* for the predicates listed in (20), whose behaviour is described in the fifth row of (4),

(20) *want, expect, plan, hope, intend, desire, like, hate, prefer,* etc.

is the following: while *Equi* must apply if the subject of the complement is an agent (cf. *(21b)),

(21) a.   I want to pick up this cabinet later
   b.   *I want (for) myself to pick up this cabinet later[1]

for many speakers, this deletion is only optional if the subject to be deleted has any other semantic function. Cf. the various grammaticalities in (22).

(22) a.   I want (myself) to be renominated unanimously
   b.   We expect (? ourselves) to be leading by noon
   c.   They$_i$ hope (for them *(selves)$_i$)[2] to be insanely popular
   d.   You might not like it for you (*rself) to spend a life as a galley slave[3]

One fact of interest is that even in the few contexts, such as pseudo-clefts, where *want* can show up with a tenseless *that*-clause (cf. the contrast between (23a) and (23b),

(23) a.   *I want that Bob be tickled
   b.   What I want is that Bob be tickled

this *that*-clause exhibits behaviour paralleling the contrast between (21) and (22). That is, (24a), whose *that*-clause is subjected by a non-agentive NP, is possible, but (24b), whose subject is an agent, is not.

(24) a.   What I want is that I be renominated unanimously
   b.   *What I want is that I pick up this cabinet later

This fact strongly suggests the correctness of the suggestion in Kiparsky and Kiparsky (1970) that *Equi* can operate 'into' *that*-clauses, converting them to non-finite clauses as a part of its operation. For if *Equi* could not

---

[1] To be sure, such sentences as (21b) can be used in [+ Couch] contexts in which the speaker wishes to suggest that he has several personalities, not all of which are under his control. In such cases, however, it is not clear that the condition of co-referentiality that restricts *Equi* is in fact met. Thus while the split personality speaker might use (21b) to describe the conflict of wills within him, I doubt that he could use (21a) in this same sense.

[2] The notation 'A(*B)C' means 'AC is grammatical, but ABC is not'. In other words, AC cannot have B added to it.

The notation 'A *(B)C' means just the reverse: 'ABC is grammatical, but AC is not.' In other words, in this case, B cannot be subtracted from ABC. And 'A ?*(?B)C' and the like would be short for '?*AC/?ABC'.

[3] I have no idea how to explain the contrast in reflexivizability between (22c) and (22d).

look into *that*-clauses, the ungrammaticality of *(24b) could not be treated as arising from the same violation that ungrammaticalizes (21b): the failure to *Equi* a co-referential agent in the class of predicates in (2).

When we move to the sixth row of (4), which summarizes the behaviour of such predicates as those in (25),

(25) a. *try, condescend, attempt, seek, deign, manage, struggle, begin, stop, keep, continue*, etc.; *bribe, cajole, motivate, have*, etc.
   b. *able, capable, wary, kind, sweet*, etc.

the obligatoriness of *Equi* increases, in a sense. For not only are such sentences as those in (26), where *Equi* could have applied and did not, atrocious,

(26) a. *Fred$_i$ condescended for himself$_i$ to emerge as a candidate
   b. *Lovejoy$_i$ struggled for himself$_i$ to understand the riddle of creation
   c. *Toadley$_i$ is able for himself$_i$ to appear almost human

but also such sentences as those in (27), where *Equi* cannot even be considered, because of the lack of co-referentiality, must be rejected.

(27) a. *Fred condescended for me to emerge as a candidate
   b. *Lovejoy struggled for Horace to understand the riddle of creation
   c. *Toadley is able for Andromedans to appear almost human

This fact, first noted in Perlmutter (1971), had led to the adoption of the term *equi-subject* for predicates such as those in (25). All equi-subject predicates must have, in remote structure, a complement whose subject is co-referential with some controlling NP in the clause of the predicate in question, and all such predicates must also undergo *Equi* in every derivation in which they appear.

It is important to note, in connection with the discussion of examples (21)–(24) and the discussion above (p. 452, n. 2) about the valency of *Equi* when applying to the class of predicates like *surprise*, that all equi-subject predicates require their complements to denote a volitional act, whose subject NP is the agent of the act.[1]

---

[1] This is true only of the transitive variants of *begin, continue, stop*, etc. Cf. Perlmutter (1970a) for details.

To continue to the seventh row of (4), what I mean by the term *auxiliary verb* is such predicates, in English, as those in (28).

(28) *can, may, must, need, ought* (to), *shall, will be, have* (in certain uses)

There is evidence, which I will not recapitulate here (cf. Ross (1969, 1972a) for details), which suggests that these elements should be taken to be complement-taking predicates, most occurring, like *begin*, both in transitive, equi-subject constructions, as suggested in (29),

(29)

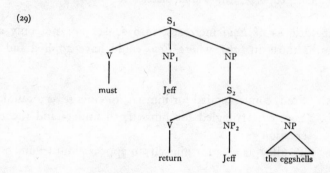

and in intransitive constructions, like (30), to which *Raising* will apply obligatorily, making NP_2 a right sister of V_1.

(30)

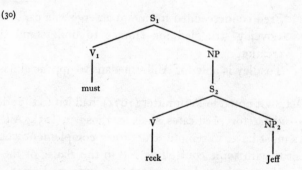

When *Equi* has deleted NP_2 in (29), and when *Jeff* has been placed into subject position by McCawley's rule of *Subject Formation*,[1] (29) and (30) will appear as (31) and (32), respectively.

(31) Jeff must return the eggshells
(32) Jeff must reek

---

[1] I have here adopted McCawley's VSO analysis of English (cf. McCawley (1970) for details), but none of the conclusions I draw about the non-binary nature of the predicate of clausemateness rests on this assumption.

Both of these are of the surface form shown in (33).

(33) NP – auxiliary verb-V-X

Note in particular that no NP can intervene between the auxiliary verb and the verb of its complement, as would be the case if there were an auxiliary in English which was like *want* in being able to occur with complements whose subjects were not necessarily deleted. It seems that this is one of the properties that any predicate that grammarians are willing to call an auxiliary must have: up to differences in order, auxiliaries must conform to (33).

Thus it would seem that we must impose upon all auxiliaries the condition that they be equi-subject predicates if transitive, and that they obligatorily undergo *Raising* if intransitive. Both halves of this disjunctive requirement must be met, if I am correct in my belief that all auxiliaries must 'hit' the target suggested in (33).[1]

Passing on to the eighth row of (4), we find essentially the same situation as with auxiliaries, though with *Predicate Raising*, additional unclarities arise because of the complexity of the arguments motivating the postulation of this process, a complexity that has led to the rejection of the rule in some quarters. For the purposes of this paper, I will assume the existence of such a process,[2] and make some inconclusive remarks about the classes of predicates which can be fused together by its operation.

[1] Of course, the fact that this requirement must be stated in this disjunctive fashion makes the two-*begin* hypothesis advocated in Perlmutter (1970a) and Ross (1972a) appear highly suspect. This is not the place to attempt to improve on this hypothesis, however, for whatever defects this analysis has, it is hard for me to imagine a way of analysing *prove*, *threaten* and *sure* as anything but predicates with two places (or more) in (i) – (v) below,

   (i)   I proved to Leon that Dick was tricky
   (ii) That Mel was there proved to Leon that he had known
   (iii) The medium threatened that he would sue
   (iv) The brass threatened Jeff with disbarment
   (v) We are not sure $\left\{ \begin{array}{l} \text{of his loyalty} \\ \text{(as to/?of) whether we want an igloo} \end{array} \right\}$

and yet such sentences as (vi)–(viii) seem to indicate strongly that they must also appear in such intransitive remote structures as (30).

   (vi) There proved (*to Leon) to have been some tampering
   (vii) This tack threatens to be taken incessantly
   (viii) Careful track is sure to be kept of all my movements

Thus the two-predicate analysis looks inescapable for some predicates, and some other way out of the problem posed by the disjunctive specification mentioned at the beginning of this footnote must be sought.

[2] In Ross (1972b), I argue that even theories in which there is no syntactic transformation of *Predicate Raising* must contain a cognate and functionally equivalent condition on possible lexical items.

To give an example of the way the rule operates, consider the conversion of (34a) into (34b).

(34) a.

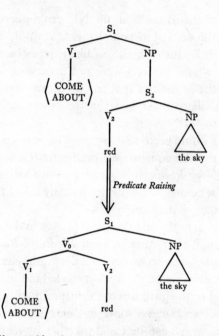

Morphological rules will specify that the realization of the inchoative pro-verb, V_1 of (34b), in construction with *red*, is the suffix *-en*, which will ultimately yield from (34a) the surface string (35).

(35) the sky redden

In other contexts, V_1 shows up as a prefix (*enlarge*) or as ϕ (*thin*). I will not be concerned with such morphological problems below, however.

One obvious fact about the operation of *Predicate Raising* is that it will only operate to fuse together verbs one or both of which are 'colourless', in a sense which is fairly clear intuitively, but which has long resisted theoretical explication. What I mean by 'colourless' will emerge from a comparison of the fused verbs in column (36a) with their composite parts in column (36b)

(36) a.   i. dead   b.   i. NOT – alive
         ii. die   ii. COME ABOUT – dead
         iii. kill   iii. CAUSE – die
         iv. bring   iv. CAUSE – come
         v. look for   v. TRY – FIND

vi. liken vi. SAY – like
vii. ridicule vii. SAY – ridiculous
viii. remind viii. strike – like ($\cong$ THINK-like)[1]
ix. visible ix. ABLE – be seen

It is the capitalized predicates in (36b) that are semantically colourless, in the sense that I intend. And with the exception of NOT, which has a syntax all its own, and of the predicates CAUSE and SAY, all of these other colourless predicates share with auxiliaries the disjunctive requirement of obligatorily undergoing *Raising* or of being equi-subject predicates.

There is no evidence which would show the need for postulating an intransitive alloform of CAUSE, and it can never meet the structural description of *Equi*, for such structures as (37) must be ruled out semantically, unless it can be argued that the V_1 of this structure surfaces as the *do* that is the subject of discussion in Ross (1972b).[2]

[1] For an extensive discussion of a predicate-raising analysis of some uses of *remind*, and of the difference between *strike* and *think*, cf. Postal (1970a).

[2] This possibility is an attractive one, for otherwise it will be necessary to allow predicates to specify that the subjects of their complements *not* be identical to some matrix NP. But since CAUSE would be the only such predicate, as far as I know, postulating a feature like [-Equi Subject] would seem to be counter-indicated. Note that such verbs as *scream*, *yell*, etc. in (i)–(ii), despite seeming to require a feature like [-Equi Subject],

(i) Jeff$_i$ screamed for $\left\{\begin{array}{l} \text{me} \\ \text{her} \\ * \text{ him(self)}_i \end{array}\right\}$ to leave

(ii) We yelled for $\left\{\begin{array}{l} \text{you} \\ \text{him} \\ * \text{ us} \\ * \text{ ourselves} \end{array}\right\}$ to shut up

in fact can be analysed as being normal equi-subject predicates, where the obligatory identity obtains between the complement subject and the indirect object of the matrix, as suggested in (iii),

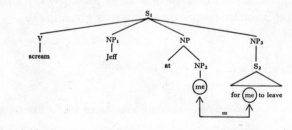

(iii)

with the additional wrinkle that *scream, yell*, etc require non-co-reference of the NPs in the position of NP$_1$ and NP$_2$. Cf. *(iv, v).

(iv) Jeff$_i$ screamed at $\left\{\begin{array}{l} \text{me} \\ \text{her} \\ *\text{him(self)}_i \end{array}\right\}$ for NP to VX

(37)

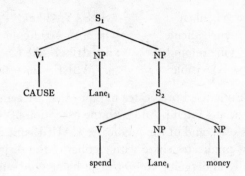

In any event, CAUSE, among the verbs that induce *Predicate Raising*, is a clear counter-example to the claim of the first cell of the eighth row of (4) to the effect that all such predicates are equi-subject, for the rough underlying structures suggested by (38) will all be transformed into their corresponding members in (39) by the operation of *Predicate Raising*.

(38) a. Bill CAUSE [Fred see the turtle]
  b. Bill CAUSE [Fred know of our visa problems]
  c. Bill CAUSE [the horse gallop]
(39) a. Bill show Fred the turtle
  b. Bill inform Fred of our visa problem
  c. Bill gallop the horse

While I have not made an extensive search through lexicon for types of predicates that trigger *Predicate Raising*, and while the capitalized predicates of (36b) do not exhaust the list of such predicates, the only other predicate that I know of beside CAUSE that is not like auxiliaries in having the disjunctive condition OBL *Raising*/equi-subject imposed upon it is the predicate SAY. A list of some of the many verbs in whose decomposition this colourless predicate enters is given in (40).

(v)   We yelled at $\left\{\begin{array}{l} \text{you} \\ \text{him} \\ \text{*us} \\ \text{*ourselves} \end{array}\right\}$ for NP to VX

Such non-co-reference requirements within clauses are familiar from such examples as those in (vi)

(vi) * Fred$_i$ is near himself$_i$
(vii) * The marbles$_i$ are on themselves$_i$

Thus CAUSE would be the only case where a feature like [-Equi Subject] would be used.

(40) a.   i. acquit   b.   i. SAY (or FIND) – innocent
         ii. convict   ii. SAY (or FIND) – guilty
        iii. praise/brag   iii. SAY – good
        iv. criticize   iv. SAY – bad
        v. liken   v. SAY – like
        vi. ridicule   vi. SAY – ridiculous
        vii. pooh pooh   vii. SAY – pooh pooh
        viii. apologize   viii. SAY – sorry
        ix. accuse/confess   ix. SAY – responsible

I have no idea why CAUSE and SAY should be exempt from the OBL *Raising*/equi-subject condition, or why it should be that no more exempt predicates exist, as far as I know.

To sum up the evidence presented so far that there is a squish of clausematiness, the rule of *Equi* proceeds from being optional with the verbs of row 1 of (4), to being obligatory with agent subjects in row 5, to being governed by the equi-subject condition from rows 6 to 8. However, the fact that rows 2 through 4 do not allow *Equi* to apply, as well as the behaviour of CAUSE and SAY weakens seriously the force of this progression. Thus evidence from *Equi* for a squish of clausematiness is at best inconclusive.

2.2. *Gapping*

Turning now to *Gapping*, the rule that converts (41a) to (41b),[1]

Gapping

(41) a. He wore pants, and I wore a toga
     b. He wore pants, and I   a toga

we note that it minimally deletes an identical verb, but may also delete other identical constituents, as we see from the variety of possible gappings shown in (42) – (44) below.

(42) a. He wore pants at work, and I wore pants at home

Gapping

     b. He wore pants at work, and I   at home

---

[1] Cf. Ross (1970) for some discussion of this rule.

(43) a. He wore pants at home on Sundays, and I wore pants at home
          on Mondays

                         Gapping

    b. He wore pants at home on Sundays, and I   on Mondays

(44) a. He wore pants at home on Sundays to flimflam the neighbours,
          and I wore pants at home on Sundays to enrage our goat

                         Gapping

    b. ?He wore pants at home on Sundays to flimflam the neighbours,
          and I to enrage our goat

It seems, then, that contrary to Ross (1970), not only identical verbs can
be gapped, but also an indefinite number of other identical constituents.
Nor need the gapped constituents be contiguous, as the following example
shows.

(45) a. He wore pants at home on Sundays, and I wore a toga at home
          on Mondays

                         Gapping

    b. He wore pants at home on Sundays, and
          I   a toga   on Mondays

The gapping of other constituents than the verb, however, is only
possible when the verb has been gapped.[1] Thus in (42b), the direct object
pants is gappable, but only because the verb *wore* is also gapped. In a structure like that of (46a), which has non-identical, hence ungappable verbs,
the object, *pants*, cannot be deleted.

(46) a. He bought pants, and I wore pants

                    Gapping

    b. *He bought pants, and I wore

I thus suggest, as a way of describing these facts, the analysis sketched in
(47).

(47) *Gapping*
    a. (OPTIONAL) Delete identical verbs

---

[1] Devising a formal procedure for ascertaining this is left as an exercise for the interested reader.

b. (OBLIGATORY) If step (a) has applied, delete any other identical constituents

The reason for making (47b) obligatory can be seen from the fact that the sentences of (48)–(51), which parallel the *b*-versions of the sentences in (42)–(45), except that (47b) has not been applied, are ungrammatical, in varying degrees.

(48) He wore pants at work, and I $\left\{ \begin{array}{c} \text{*pants} \\ \text{**them} \end{array} \right\}$ at home

(49) He wore pants at home on Sundays, and

$$I \left\{ \begin{array}{l} ** \left\{ \begin{array}{c} \text{them} \\ \text{pants} \end{array} \right\} \text{(there)} \\[2ex] * \underline{\quad\quad} \left\{ \begin{array}{c} \text{at home} \\ \text{there} \end{array} \right\} \\[2ex] \left\{ \begin{array}{c} \text{**them} \\ \text{?*pants} \end{array} \right\} \quad \text{at home} \end{array} \right\} \text{on Mondays}$$

(50) He wore pants at home on Sundays to flimflam the neighbours,

$$\text{and I} \left\{ \begin{array}{l} ** \left\{ \begin{array}{c} \text{them} \\ \text{pants} \end{array} \right\} \left\{ \begin{array}{c} \text{there} \\ \text{at home} \end{array} \right\} \left\{ \begin{array}{c} \text{then} \\ \text{on Sundays} \end{array} \right\} \\[3ex] ** \left\{ \begin{array}{c} \text{there} \\ \text{at home} \end{array} \right\} \left\{ \begin{array}{c} \text{then} \\ \text{on Sundays} \end{array} \right\} \\[1ex] \text{etc.} \end{array} \right\} \text{to enrage}$$

our goat

(51) He wore pants at home on Sundays, and

$$I \quad\quad \text{a toga} \left\{ \begin{array}{c} \text{??there} \\ \text{?*at home} \end{array} \right\} \text{on Mondays}$$

If we accept the two-step account of *Gapping* given in (47), then what are we to say of the fact that *to wear* need not be gapped in (52), even though the main verb, *want*, has been gapped?

(52) a. He wants to wear pants, and I want to wear a toga

Gapping

b. He wants to wear pants, and
I   to wear a toga
c. He wants to wear pants, and
I   a toga

It seems to me that the probable source of the difference between *pants*, *at home*, and *on Sundays*, on the one hand, and *to wear* on the other, is that the latter is not a clausemate of the gapped verb *want*, while the former three constituents are all clausemates of the gapped verb *wore*. Thus it would appear that (47b) should be made obligatory only for identical clausemates, and otherwise optional.

However, the central claim of the present paper is that there are degrees of clausematiness. We might thus expect to find the degree of obligatoriness with which (47b) applies varying with the height of the gapped predicate in terms of (4). And roughly, this is the situation that obtains.

Consider first row 1. Note first that (53a) can only be gapped to (53b), not to (53c).

(53) a. He was surprised that he had been sent to Paris, and I was
surprised that I had been sent to Rome

Gapping

b. He was surprised that he had been sent to Paris and
I   that I had been sent to Rome
c. *He was surprised that he had been sent to Paris, and
I   to Rome[1]

The reason here is simple – *Gapping* cannot 'go down into' *that*-clauses. Let us therefore perform *Equi* on both clauses of (53a), which yields (54).

(54) He was surprised to have been sent to Paris, and
I   was surprised to have been sent to Rome

---

[1] Of course, (53c) is not out on all readings, for this string can mean what (i) means.

(i) The fact that he had been sent to Paris and I (had been sent) to Rome surprised him

(53c) is only starred because it cannot have arisen from (53a) via *Gapping*.

To this sentence, *Gapping* has a hope of applying. If only the highest predicate, *be surprised*, is gapped, (55a) results. But if not only this predicate, but also the identical complement, *to have been sent*, is gapped, the result is (55b).

(55) a. ??He was surprised to have been sent to Paris, and
    I   to have been sent to Rome
   b. ??He was surprised to have been sent to Paris, and
    I   to Rome

In my speech, at least, *Gapping* is far less possible for emotive factive predicates, or 'into' (in an I hope obvious sense of this term) their subjectless non-finite complements, than is the case with such predicates as *want*. For the predicates of row 2 of (4) which allow *Equi* to apply, i.e. such adjectives as those cited in (7b), I find the situation slightly improved, but not yet perfect. Cf. the sentences in (56).

(56) a. He was glad to have been sent to Paris, and
    I   was glad to have been sent to Rome

Gapping

   b. ?He was glad to have been sent to Paris, and
    I   to have been sent to Rome
   c. ?He was glad to have been sent to Paris, and
    I   to Rome

Since *know*, as pointed out above, does not allow *Equi*, we cannot check to see whether *Gapping* can go into its complement, for as the ungrammaticality of (53c) suggests, no *that*-clauses can be 'pierced' by *Gapping*. It is for this reason that the third box from the top of column 2 of (4) is shaded.

Since most of the predicates of row 4 do not allow *Equi*, we cannot check to see how they behave under *Gapping*, except for *claim*, which does allow *Equi*. And as (57) shows, *Gapping* can optionally go into the complement of this verb.

(57) a. He claimed to have been sent to Paris, and
    I   claimed to have been sent to Rome

Gapping

   b. He claimed to have been sent to Paris, and
    I   to have been sent to Rome

c. He claimed to have been sent to Paris, and
   I   to Rome

As the fact that both (57b) and (57c) are grammatical suggests, the verbs of row 5 of (4) allow *Gapping* optionally to pierce their complements, and the same is true for the predicates of row (6), as is shown by the fact that both (58b) and (58c) are grammatical.

(58) a. He deigned to wear pants, and
        she deigned to wear a toga

Gapping

b. He deigned to wear pants, and
   she   to wear a toga
c. He deigned to wear pants, and
   she   a toga

When we reach auxiliaries, however, the situation is different. Roughly speaking, the facts are described by the generalization in (59).

(59) No auxiliary verb can gap unless its complement can (and does) gap with it

The need for adding this further condition to the formulation of *Gapping* given in (47) can be seen from the sentences in (60).

(60) a. He was squeezing a tennis ball, and she was greasing a shoe

Gapping

b. ??He was squeezing a tennis ball, and
    she   greasing a shoe
c. He was squeezing a tennis ball, and
    she was squeezing a shoe

Gapping

d. *He was squeezing a tennis ball, and
    she   squeezing a shoe
e. He was squeezing a tennis ball, and
    she   a shoe

As the dubiousness of (60b) shows, the progressive auxiliary does not like to gap alone. For me, however, (60b) still contains traces of English. But in (60d), I find total ungrammaticality, because not only has the *be* been gapped alone (which would reduce the grammaticality of the output to '??' at best), but also the 'clean-up' part of (47), (47b), has not applied to remove the highly clausematey constituent *squeezing*. Of course, when (47b) has applied, (60d) becomes the fully grammatical (60e).

It would have been nice if the fairly complex condition stated in (59) were adequate to describe the behaviour of all the auxiliaries, but for my speech at least, this is, alas, not so. The auxiliaries seem to be subject to (59) in varying degrees, with these degrees roughly corresponding to the linear ordering in Chomsky's classic formula, (61).

(61)   [Tns(Modal)(Perfect)(Progressive)(Passive)]
       Aux   ∧   ∧   ∧ Aux
              have en   *be ing*   *be en*

For me, it seems to be the case that the further an auxiliary element is to the right in (61) – that is, the closer it comes to the verb – the less it is subject to (59). Thus the passive *be* is less constrained than the progressive *be*, as can be seen from the fact that the sentences of (62) are better than the corresponding sentences in (60).

(62) a.   He was driven to Aix, and
          she was taken to Ghent

                    Gapping

     b.   ?He was driven to Aix, and
          she   taken to Ghent
     c.   He was driven to Aix, and
          she was driven to Ghent

                    Gapping

     d.   ??He was driven to Aix, and
          she   driven to Ghent
     e.   He was driven to Aix, and
          she   to Ghent

And the perfect *have* seems to produce systematically worse violations of (59) than does the progressive *be*, as can be seen by comparing (60) with (63).

(63) a.   He has taken the Star   of Pittsburgh, and
        she has stolen the Moon of Altoona

Gapping

b. ?*He has taken the Star   of Pittsburgh, and
      she   stolen the Moon of Altoona
c.   He has taken the Star   of Pittsburgh, and
      she has taken the Moon of Altoona.

Gapping

d. *He has taken the Star   of Pittsburgh, and
      she   taken the Moon of Altoona
e.   He has taken the Star   of Pittsburgh, and
      she   the Moon of Altoona

However, modals seem not to produce worse violations than *have*, as a comparison of (63) and (64) shows.

(64) a.   He may stay inside, and
        she may go   to the beach

Gapping

b. ?*He may stay inside, and
      she   go to the beach
c.   He may stay inside, and
      she may stay outside

Gapping

d. ??He may stay inside, and
      she   stay outside
e.   He may stay inside, and
      she   outside

Indeed, it seems to me that (64d) is significantly better than (63d) or (60d), a fact for which I have no explanation. Basically, however, the generalization stated in (59), appropriately squishified to reflect the fact of the increasing verbiness of the elements of the right of (61), provides as good a first approximation to the behaviour of auxiliaries under *Gapping* as

I will attempt to formulate in this paper. And for the purpose of establishing the correctness of the claim that *Gapping* provides evidence for a squish of clausematiness, the important fact to note in the above discussion is the fact that while gapping the verbs of rows 4, 5, and 6 of (4) is possible without it being necessary to gap their complements (cf. the grammaticality of (57b), (52b), and (58b), respectively), this is not possible with the auxiliaries. The various levels of ungrammaticality manifested by (62d), (60d), (63d) and (64d) show that their complements are clausematey enough to make the clean-up part of (47), namely (47b), obligatory, if the verbal deletion part of (47), namely (47a), has applied.

And of course this is even more true of the predicate-raising verbs of row 8 of (4). For observe what would result if the abstract verb CAUSE, represented by *-en* in (65a), could delete. (65b) is 'splendidly ungrammatical', to use a felicity coined by Larry Horn.

(65) a. He deepened the groove, and
   I   widened   the bolt

Gapping

b. ***He deepened the groove, and
   I   wide   the bolt

To recapitulate, I began this subsection with an investigation of the operation of *Gapping*, and came to the conclusion that this process was best formulated in two steps. In the first, an identical verb is optionally deleted. Then in the second step, all other identical constituents of the clause whose verb has bitten the dust are also purged, sometimes optionally, sometimes obligatorily, with the valency of this second 'clean-up' deletion being a function of the clausematiness of the deleted verb and the constituents to be cleaned up. The force of this case for the primary topic of this paper should be clear: without a quantifiable predicate of clausematiness, no unified treatment of the behaviour of all of the verb classes of (4) could be given.

2.3. *Suspension of presupposition*

Since the publication of Kiparsky and Kiparsky (1970), an impressive number of papers have appeared which have focused on the crucial presuppositional property of factivity.[1] There are hosts of thorny problems

---

[1] Some important recent works include Horn (1972) and Karttunen (1971).

and hotly debated issues in this area, all of which I will ignore, for the purposes of this paper. What *will* concern me is the circumstances under which such propositions as the one expressed in (66),

(66) The sun had touched Peoria, Illinois briefly on May 22, 1913, by noon

which I take to be generally held to be false by students of recent Illinoisian history, can appear in the complements of such factive predicates as appear in (7) and (8) above without any feeling of presupposition failure. As (67) shows, this is not possible under most circumstances, for people who believe (66) to be false.

(67) a. *Elmer $\left\{ \begin{array}{l} \text{was (not)} \left\{ \begin{array}{l} \text{shocked} \\ \text{glad} \end{array} \right\} \\ \text{(never)} \left\{ \begin{array}{l} \text{realized} \\ \text{knew} \end{array} \right\} \end{array} \right\}$ that (66)

   b. *Was Elmer $\left\{ \begin{array}{l} \text{surprised} \\ \text{glad} \end{array} \right\}$ that (66)?

That is, even under negation and questioning, the complement of a factive predicate continues to be presupposed, as has often been remarked. Hence the anomaly of the sentences of (67).[1]

However, there are some contexts in which some types of sentences like those in (67a) can appear without causing presupposition failure. One case in point is counter-factual *if*-clauses. Thus compare the anomalous sentences of (67a) with the progressively less anomalous sentences in (68).

(68) a. *If Elmer were shocked that (66), he would tell us about it

   b. ?If Elmer $\left\{ \begin{array}{l} \text{realized} \\ \text{were glad} \end{array} \right\}$ that (66), he would tell us about it

   c. If Elmer knew that (66), he would tell us about it

Since only the predicates in the three top rows of (4) can be factive, there is no way to check the predicates of the bottom five rows to see whether they can suspend their presuppositions of factivity. I have therefore shaded the bottom five cells of column 3. Thus the only relevant sentences are like those in (68).

What these sentences indicate is that complements whose elements are of

---

[1] No theoretical significance should be attached to my use of '*' to designate both ill-formedness and presupposition failure. The point at issue remains unaffected by this question of terminology.

an exceedingly low clausematiness with the elements of the next sentence up are sentences that can be strongly presupposed. It is almost as if there were a stronger wall separating the two clauses in predicates high up in (4) than exists between the clauses of predicates lower down in (4). The height of this wall also determines the degree to which *Equi* and *Gapping* will be able to penetrate the complement clause, as we have seen.

There is an interesting parallel between *Gapping* and presupposition suspension, with respect to the difference between *that*-clauses and subjectless infinitival complements. As I pointed out above, while *Gapping* cannot pierce *that*-clauses (i.e., (53a) cannot be realized as (53c)), it has a better chance of piercing the *Equi*-ed infinitival remnants of these *that*-clauses (thus when *Gapping* pierces the complement of (54), the not totally useless (55c) results).

And similarly, though both of the sentences in (69) presuppose the truth of their complements,

(69) a. He was surprised that he had been sent to Paris
     b. He was surprised   to have been sent to Paris

to my ear, this presupposition is easier to suspend for the latter sentence than for the former.

(70) a. If he were surprised that he had been sent to Paris, he would tell us about it
     b. If he were surprised to have been sent to Paris, he would tell us about it

That is, it is easier to use (70b) without believing in the truth of (71)

(71) He had been sent to Paris

than it is to use (70a).

My conclusion from these two cases, which show that both the piercing of complements by *Gapping* and the suspension of presuppositions of factivity are easier for infinitives than for *that*-clauses, is that the predicate *clausematey* does not depend merely upon the semantactic class of the matrix predicates we have been focusing on, but also on the superficial form of the complement.

2.4. Subjunctive Sinking

The next process I will discuss has to do with the appearance in certain contexts of verb forms that look, except for first and third person singular *were*, like past tense forms of verbs. Some examples of these forms and the contexts they appear in are shown in (72).

(72) a. If he were here, he'd parboil you
     b. I wish that he knew it
     c. It is as if he were a talking fungus

What is of relevance for (4) is the fact that it is sometimes possible for whatever process it is that produces these subjunctive forms to introduce them into the complement of a predicate, as long as the predicate itself has been made subjunctive. Thus compare the sentences in (73).

(73) If he (ever) thought that I $\left\{ \begin{array}{l} \text{was} \\ \text{were} \end{array} \right\}$ sick, he'd write to me

The form that interests me here is not the subjunctive verb *thought*, but rather the *were* in its complement. Let us say that the process of subjunctivization proceeds down into the tree from the top, first producing *thought*, and then 'sinking' into the complement to produce *were*.

This process of *Subjunctive Sinking* is slightly recursive for me, for I can get (74):

(74) If I thought he were$_1$ able to prove that
     I $\left\{ \begin{array}{l} \text{was} \\ \text{?were}_2 \end{array} \right\}$ sick, I'd stop malingering

However, as the two variants of (73) show, this sinking is not obligatory, and if *were*$_1$ does not appear, but rather the non-subjunctive past tense form *was*, then *were*$_2$ cannot occur. Cf. (75).

(75) *If I thought he was able to prove that I were sick, I'd stop malingering

While I have found that not all speakers will allow subjunctives to sink, as in (73) and (74), I have found no speaker for whom (75) is better than (74).

There are a number of other semantactic constraints on the operation of this rule, some of which can be seen from the constellation of grammaticalities in (76) – (78),

(76) If I believed (*the claim) that he were sick, I'd write to you

(77) If I thought $\left\{\begin{array}{l}\text{that he were sick and (that) she were well}\\ \text{that he were sick and ?(that) she was well}\\ \text{*that he was sick and (that) she were well}\\ \text{that he was sick and (that) she was sick}\end{array}\right\}$

I'd write to you

(78) a. If that he $\left\{\begin{array}{l}\text{was}\\ \text{*were}\end{array}\right\}$ sick were known, I'd write to you

b. If it were known that he $\left\{\begin{array}{l}\text{was}\\ \text{were}\end{array}\right\}$ sick, I'd write to you

and these are extremely interesting, but I will not digress to investigate them here. What I will show is that subjunctives can only sink into the clauses of subjunctivized matrix predicates which are fairly clausematey with elements of their complements.

To see this, consider the sentences in (79)–(82), which correspond to the top four rows of (4).

(79)   If I were surprised that he $\left\{\begin{array}{l}\text{was}\\ \text{*were}\end{array}\right\}$ sick,

I'd write to you

(80) a. If I discovered that he $\left\{\begin{array}{l}\text{was}\\ \text{??were}\end{array}\right\}$ sick, I'd write to you

b. If I were glad that he $\left\{\begin{array}{l}\text{was}\\ \text{??were}\end{array}\right\}$ sick, I'd write to you

(81)   If I knew that he $\left\{\begin{array}{l}\text{was}\\ \text{?were}\end{array}\right\}$ sick, I'd write to you

(82)   If I claimed that he $\left\{\begin{array}{l}\text{was}\\ \text{were}\end{array}\right\}$ sick, I'd have

to prove it

The remaining boxes of column 4 of (4) are shaded, because they cannot be checked to see whether *Subjunctive Sinking* can penetrate them, for they are not tensed, and English only manifests an indicative-subjunctive contrast in tensed clauses. Thus they are irrelevant for the purposes of establishing my claim.

While not all speakers will agree on the absolute values of grammaticality that I have assigned in (79)–(82) – in particular, many will balk at applying *Subjunctive Sinking* at all – I have encountered none who would order them differently than I have above. Thus this process would seem to provide clear support for postulating a squish.

2.5. If ... any

A similar phenomenon concerns the distribution of negative polarity items[1] like *any* in *if*-clauses. As is well known, *any* cannot just appear anywhere: cf. *(83).

(83) *You had any money.

However, such clauses as (83) can be coaxed into appearing if they are under the spell of *negative triggers* like the italicized phrases of (84).

(84) a. *If* you had any money, it's gone now
    b. I *doubt* that you had any money
    c. They *never* told me that you had any money

All of these triggers allow the appearance of *any*s indefinitely far away: cf. (85).

(85) a. *If* he thinks that everybody feels that I said that you had any money, he's wrong
    b. I *doubt* that he would admit that Fred believed that you had any money
    c. They *never* told me that people had wanted you to have any money

Some of these triggers are stronger than others: they allow the *any* to be 'further away', in a sense that I will not define, than do the weaker triggers. One of the weakest triggers is *if*, and the sentences in (86)–(93) show that clausematiness interacts with whatever process is involved in blessing some *any*s and dooming others.

(86) *If he is surprised that you had any money, your horoscope was right.[2]

---

[1] For some discussion of the incredibly tangled world in which such items live, cf. Baker (1970) and Horn (1972).

[2] There is, unfortunately, a red herring in (86) which I can see no way to avoid. The problem is that the emotive factive predicates are themselves negative triggers, as can be seen from (i).

(i) It is $\left\{\begin{array}{l} \text{*likely} \\ \text{*true} \\ \text{surprising} \\ \text{horrifying} \\ \text{shocking} \\ \text{amazing} \end{array}\right\}$ that you had any money

Thus the first clause of (86), minus the *if*, is pretty good, and is improved a lot by the

(87) ?*If he discovers that you had any money, your horoscope was right

(88) If I knew that you had any money, I'd ask you for a contribution

(89) If he thinks that you had any money, he'll never stop pestering you

(90) If he wants you to have any money, he'll give you some stock

(91) If he tried to find you any money, he'd be arrested

(92) If you have had any money, you are hiding it well

(93) If he shortens any poles, I'll fix his wagon

In these sentences, we can see that *if* is a strong enough trigger to pierce all but the least clausematey of the complements. Thus clearly there is an interaction between trigger strength and clausematiness – an extremely complex interaction about which much more would have to be said, in a fuller treatment of this phenomenon. But for now, I will let the matter rest with the preliminary account I have given.

2.6. Sequence of Tenses

This phenomenon, which has been insightfully and stimulatingly studied in Costa (1972), is manifested in the awkwardness of (94c).

(94) a. It seems to me that it may rain
     b. It seems to me that it might rain
     c. *It seemed to me that it may rain
     d. It seemed to me that it might rain

Speaking *very* roughly (cf. Costa (1972) for a much more satisfactory formulation), we can say that the rule of *Sequence of Tense* (*SOT*) copies a matrix verb's past tense onto the tense of its complement, thus neutralizing such tense contrasts as can appear in the complements of present-tense verbs.

It is, of course, highly misleading to characterize the subtle difference in meaning between (94a) and (94b) as a 'tense contrast', which term could be more aptly used to speak of the difference between (95a) and (95b).

(95) a. It seems to me that he can play tennis today
     b. It seems to me that he could play tennis yesterday

addition of the polarity item *at all*, which functions as a kind of secondary trigger. Cf. (ii).

(ii) He is surprised that you had any money ?(at all)

Thus (86) can occur, but not under the relevant reading, in which *any* is triggered by *if*, and not by the predicate *surprised*.

It would be more accurate to say that what *SOT* must do is exclude, under certain circumstances, *that*-clauses whose tensed auxiliary contains one of the words in (96a), while allowing the words in (96b).

(96) a. *am/are/is; have/has; can, may, will, shall;* V(s)
   b. *was/were; had; could, might, would, should;* Ved[1]

As far as I know, there is no semantic cohesion to either class – the members of (96a) merely share the syntactic property of being forbidden to occur in certain past-tense complements.

The interaction of *SOT* with clausematiness can be seen in sentences (97)–(100).

(97) I was surprised that it $\left\{ \begin{array}{c} \text{??may} \\ \text{*might} \end{array} \right\}$ rain

(98) I was glad that it $\left\{ \begin{array}{c} \text{?may} \\ \text{?*might} \end{array} \right\}$ rain

(99) I knew that it $\left\{ \begin{array}{c} \text{may} \\ \text{might} \end{array} \right\}$ rain

(100) I thought that it $\left\{ \begin{array}{c} \text{*may} \\ \text{might} \end{array} \right\}$ rain

Another fact, pointed out in Costa (1972), which suggests a scalar arrangement for the verbs in (97)–(100), concerns the behaviour of the deictic time adverb *now*. In isolation, *now* is awkward in simple past sentences:

(101) ??There was now a hope of victory

However, sentences like (101) are progressively more acceptable as the complements of predicates like those in (97)–(100), when these occur in the past tense. Cf. (102)–(105).

(102) ??I was surprised that there was now a hope of victory
(103) ?I was glad that there was now a hope of victory
(104) I knew that there was now a hope of victory
(105) I thought that there was now a hope of victory

---

[1] It is of interest that the modal *must*, for reasons of its own, is neither in list (96a) nor in list (96b). That is to say, such sentences as (i) are out, whether *must* is read as *has to* or as *had to*.

(i) * It seemed to me that you must sweep the

floor $\left\{ \begin{array}{c} \text{yesterday} \\ \text{today} \end{array} \right\}$

The facts, for my speech, seem to be as follows: with past-tense verbs from the class of (11), past-tense clauses containing *now* can often appear as complements. This is never possible for the predicates of class (6), while the predicates of class (7) lie somewhere between these extremes. It is, to return to the wall metaphor, as if the wall between matrix and complement for (6)-type predicates is too high for a matrix past tense to 'get over', to ease the awkwardness occasioned by such time clashes as those which make clauses like (101) awkward.

However, things appear to be a good deal more complex in this area than I have indicated, and I am not sure that clausematiness plays more than a minor role in *SOT* restrictions. That is, while it does seem to be correct to claim that *SOT* is obligatory for predicates like those in (11), and that it never applies for predicates like those in (6), what calls the shots for such intermediate cases as *know* and the predicates in (7) is related to factivity, as Costa shows. In particular, in her footnote 4, having observed that the semi-factive verb *discover* is non-factive when it is negated and its complement contains *any*, she cites the following contrasting cases:

(106) Bill didn't discover that there $\left\{\begin{array}{l}\text{were} \\ \text{?*are}\end{array}\right\}$ any people on Mars

(107) Bill didn't discover that there $\left\{\begin{array}{l}\text{were} \\ \text{are}\end{array}\right\}$ some people on Mars

Her hypothesis is that *SOT* is obligatory in non-factive complements, and blocked in factive ones, a hypothesis that is strikingly confirmed by the parallels between the presence of *any* and the application of *SOT* which appear in (106)–(107). If future research should provide further corroboration for this hypothesis, it would have the effect of relegating column 6 of (4) to the status of a function of column 3, thus thinning the matrix somewhat. I will leave the matter open, for the present, and close this rather inconclusive discussion with one last observation.

The modal *may*, used epistemically, can be synonymous with one reading of the predicate *possible*. Thus (108a) and (108b) are synonymous.

(108) a. It is possible that Jim has already achieved sobriety
     b. Jim may have already attained sobriety

Presumably, to assert either of these sentences is to make a factual assertion – to state that a certain state of affairs is possible. Interestingly, however, predicates of types (102)–(105) differ among themselves with respect to whether such clauses can appear as their complements, as examples (109)–(112) show.

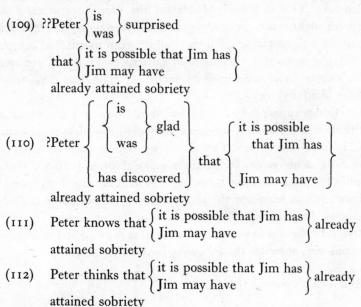

(109) ??Peter $\left\{\begin{matrix} \text{is} \\ \text{was} \end{matrix}\right\}$ surprised

that $\left\{\begin{matrix} \text{it is possible that Jim has} \\ \text{Jim may have} \end{matrix}\right\}$ already attained sobriety

(110) ?Peter $\left\{\begin{matrix} \left\{\begin{matrix} \text{is} \\ \text{was} \end{matrix}\right\} \text{glad} \\ \text{has discovered} \end{matrix}\right\}$ that $\left\{\begin{matrix} \text{it is possible} \\ \text{that Jim has} \\ \text{Jim may have} \end{matrix}\right\}$ already attained sobriety

(111) Peter knows that $\left\{\begin{matrix} \text{it is possible that Jim has} \\ \text{Jim may have} \end{matrix}\right\}$ already attained sobriety

(112) Peter thinks that $\left\{\begin{matrix} \text{it is possible that Jim has} \\ \text{Jim may have} \end{matrix}\right\}$ already attained sobriety

This seems not to be a restriction on expressions involving logical possibility, but rather on a broader class of epistemic expressions: propositions involving logical necessity, such as the synonymous pair in (113),

(113) a. It is certain that Jim has already attained sobriety
      b. Jim must have already attained sobriety

seem, to my ear, to produce sentences as unacceptable as (109)–(110), when combined with predicates of type (6) or (7). Cf. (113) and (114).

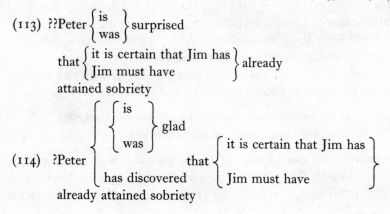

(113) ??Peter $\left\{\begin{matrix} \text{is} \\ \text{was} \end{matrix}\right\}$ surprised

that $\left\{\begin{matrix} \text{it is certain that Jim has} \\ \text{Jim must have} \end{matrix}\right\}$ already attained sobriety

(114) ?Peter $\left\{\begin{matrix} \left\{\begin{matrix} \text{is} \\ \text{was} \end{matrix}\right\} \text{glad} \\ \text{has discovered} \end{matrix}\right\}$ that $\left\{\begin{matrix} \text{it is certain that Jim has} \\ \text{Jim must have} \end{matrix}\right\}$ already attained sobriety

It would be highly desirable if these facts could be reduced to some possibly parallel cases involving disjunction. Thus note that both (115a) and (115b) can be used to make a factual claim.

(115) a. Either Rickie did it, or Johnny is lying
      b. Either Bobby or Johnny has fibbed under oath

However, embedding such disjunctions as the complements of predicates of the types (6) and (7) produces weak sentences. Cf. (116) and (117).

(116) ??Peter $\begin{Bmatrix} \text{is} \\ \text{was} \end{Bmatrix}$ surprised

  that $\begin{cases} \text{either Richie did it or Johnny is lying} \\ \text{either Bobby or Johnny has fibbed under oath} \end{cases}$

(117) ?Peter $\begin{Bmatrix} \begin{Bmatrix} \text{is} \\ \text{was} \end{Bmatrix} \text{glad} \\ \text{has discovered} \end{Bmatrix}$

  that $\begin{cases} \text{either Ritchie did it or Johnny is lying} \\ \text{either Bobby or Johnny has fibbed under oath} \end{cases}$

What all of these cases seem to suggest is that some facts are more equal than others, and that some predicates, those near the top of (4), can only be used fully acceptably if their complements express what we might call 'hard facts', or 'super facts'. The parallels between possibility and disjunction would be an immediate consequence of the possible worlds analysis of possibility advanced in Horn (1972), but the fact that certainty-expressions, such as those in (113), do not constitute super facts would not be automatically accounted for, if I have understood the possible worlds account correctly.

At any rate, I believe that some such distinction between kinds of facts can be used to account for the awkwardness of the examples in (97) and (98) in which *SOT* has not applied. And I must relegate the further exploration of the connections between Costa's hypothesis about factivity and *SOT*, on the one hand, and 'hard' and 'soft' facts, if such a distinction should prove to be a useful one, on the other, to a future paper. For the purposes of this present work, all that can be safely said is that there may be some connection between *SOT* and clausematiness, but that this connection may turn out to be reducible to a function of factivity.

2.7. Raising

The rule of *Raising*, whose operation is described with great care in Postal (1974), converts such sentences as those in (118) into the corresponding sentences of (119).

(118) a. It is likely that Fritz will win.
      b. I expect that Fritz will win
(119) a. Fritz is likely to win
      b. I expect Fritz to win

Raising can never apply to (6)-type predicates, as (120) suggests.

(120) a. *I was surprised that there was no soup
      b. *I was surprised there to be no soup

It might be objected that the fact that (120a) cannot raise to (120b) is not all that interesting, for *surprised* is, after all, an adjective,[1] and no adjectives can undergo *B-Raising*, Postal's term for the raising of a complement subject to derived object position, as in the conversion of (118b) to (119b). Thus the fact that such transitive adjectives as *afraid, sure, aware*, etc., cannot raise (cf. *(122)) could explain the badness of *(120b).

(121)   I was $\left\{ \begin{array}{l} \text{afraid} \\ \text{sure} \\ \text{aware} \\ \text{etc.} \end{array} \right\}$ that there was no soup

(122) *I was $\left\{ \begin{array}{l} \text{afraid} \\ \text{sure} \\ \text{aware} \\ \text{etc.} \end{array} \right\}$ there to be no soup.

However, since adjectives can undergo *A-Raising*, the raising of the embedded subject into derived subject position, as the grammaticality of (119a) shows, we must place an additional constraint upon *Raising* in order to prevent the conversion of such sentences as those in (123) into their corresponding clauses in (124).

---

[1] As can be seen from the fact that it can be modified by *very* and can follow *seem*, both of which are adjectival litmi.

(i)   Dorothy was very surprised at Jeff
(ii) You seem surprised that your cucumbers are not oblate

$$(123) \quad \text{It is} \begin{cases} \text{surprising} \\ \text{disgusting} \\ \text{appalling} \\ \text{interesting} \\ \text{etc.} \end{cases} \text{that there is no soup}$$

$$(124) \quad \text{*There is} \begin{cases} \text{surprising} \\ \text{disgusting} \\ \text{appalling} \\ \text{interesting} \\ \text{etc.} \end{cases} \text{to be no soup}$$

Similarly, the above-mentioned regularity about adjectives could be appealed to to explain the impossibility of such sentences as those in *(125), which contain type (7b) predicates that have undergone *Raising*,

$$(125) \quad \text{*Mel was} \begin{cases} \text{glad} \\ \text{sorry} \\ \text{happy} \\ \text{sad} \end{cases} \text{there to be no soup}$$

but verbs like those in (7a) do not undergo *Raising* either, with the weak exception of *discover* (cf. (126)),

$$(126) \quad \text{a.} \quad \text{*Mel} \begin{cases} \text{realized} \\ \text{learned} \end{cases} \text{there to be no soup}$$

$$\text{b.} \quad \text{*Mel found} \begin{cases} \text{there out} \\ \text{out there} \end{cases} \text{to be no soup}$$

c. ?Mel discovered there to be no soup

so the rule must be additionally constrained in some way.

The verb *know* does undergo *Raising* – cf. (127) –

(127) Mel knew there to be no soup

as do the predicates in (11), by and large. Cf. (128).

$$(128) \quad \text{Mel} \begin{cases} \text{*thought} \\ \text{believed} \\ \text{*claimed} \\ \text{supposed} \\ \text{imagined} \\ \text{??guessed} \end{cases} \text{there to be no soup}$$

As was noted above, *claim* must be lexically marked in such a way as to prohibit such structures as (16) from surfacing, and the same is true of *think*. If *think* is passivized, as in (129),

(129) There was thought (??by Ted) to be no soup

things are improved, though for some reason, the badness of (130a) cannot be repaired by yanking out the object of *thought* – cf. (130b).

(130) a. *Mel thought Twiggy to have defended herself well
      b. ?*It was Twiggy that Mel thought to have defended herself well

To my ear, this avenue of repair is slightly more viable with *claim* than with *think*, but I am not at all confident of this judgement.

Curiouser and curiouser, while passivization will improve the *thought*-version of (128) – cf. (129) – the passive of the *claimed*-version retains most of its ungrammaticality. Cf. (131).

(131) ??There was claimed (by Mel) to be no soup

Needless to say, I have no explanation for these differences.

One other way to improve clauses which result when *Raising* applies to *think* is to delete certain kinds of *be* – thus *(132a) can become (132b).

(132) a. *Mel thought Ted to be $\left\{ \begin{array}{l} \text{incompetent} \\ \text{a fool} \end{array} \right\}$

      b. Mel thought Ted $\left\{ \begin{array}{l} \text{incompetent} \\ \text{a fool} \end{array} \right\}$

Thus the various ungrammaticalities in (128) should not obscure the basic generalization that governs this class of verbs: *Raising* is optional.

With respect to verbs of the class (20), *Raising* can apply to most of them, and for some of them, it is even obligatory. Cf. (133).

(133) a. I want (*for) there to be no soup
      b. I expect (for) there to be no soup
      c. I plan ??(for) there to be no soup
      d. I hope *(for) there to be no soup
      e. I intend (for) there to be no soup
      f. I desire ?(for) there to be no soup
      g. I like (*for) there to be no soup
      h. I hate ??(for) there to be no soup
      i. I prefer (for) there to be no soup

In these sentences, the presence of *for* means that *Raising* has not been applied. The judgements in such cases vary wildly from speaker to speaker – I have been able to detect no regularity with respect to which of the verbs in (20) raise and which do not. The only firm claim that I can make is that I know of no one who allows (133d) without *for*, presumably a reflection of the fact that *hope* takes a *for*-phrase object (*hope for action* vs. *want* (**for*) *action*). And, though *plan* can show up with *for*, it can also do without (*plan* (*for*) *a party*), so the undeletability of *for* in (133d) seems safely traceable to the impossibility of **hope a party*.

The salient fact about (133) is that for many speakers, there are some verbs in the class of (20) for which *Raising* is obligatory [for me, this is so for *want* and *like*], whereas I know of no one for whom any predicate in one of the rows above row 5 of (4) requires *Raising* to apply. That is, *Raising* cannot be lexically governed in such a way as to be made obligatory until row 5.[1]

With respect to row 6 of (4), cell 7 describes the behaviour of predicates like those in (25). Since such predicates as *try, condescend, deign, manage*, etc., and *bribe, cajole, motivate*, etc., in (25a) must be analysed as being equi-subject predicates, to account for such facts as the non-synonymy of (134a) and (134b),

(134) a. Mr McX condescended to sit next to Hoppy
b. Hoppy condescended to be sat next to by Mr McX

as well as the impossibility of *(135) (cf. Postal (1974) for details),

(135) *There condescended to be a grope-in

we see that only such predicates as *begin, stop, continue*, etc., can even meet the SD of *Raising*. And since no verbs in this class form sentences like *(136),

$$(136) \ *It \begin{Bmatrix} began \\ stopped \\ continued \\ etc. \end{Bmatrix} \begin{Bmatrix} for\ there\ to\ be\ riots \\ there\ being\ riots \end{Bmatrix}$$

it is clear that *all* members of this class obligatorily undergo *Raising*. The same is true for all non-equi-subject auxiliaries: as a class, all must undergo *Raising*.

---

[1] For some discussion of the crucial theoretical property of *governability*, cf. Lakoff (1970).

And proceeding to the lowest row of (4), we cannot form a decision as to whether the derivation of all such sentences as (137) must involve *Raising*,

(137) Dearly likened me to a cockroach

or whether all syntactically necessary information can be produced by merely applying *Predicate Raising*. At present, too little is known about the details of the way *Predicate Raising* applies for it to be possible to come to a clear decision in this case – hence I have shaded in the lowest cell of column 7 of (4).

Summing up, then, the interaction of clausematiness and *Raising*, we see that for predicates that have a high wall between their complements and themselves, no *Raising* is possible. As we proceed down (4), with the wall getting lower, *Raising* becomes optional, then obligatory for particular lexical items in a class, and finally, for rows 6 and 7, obligatory for these classes, not merely for particular items, but for *all* items. Thus as clausematiness increases, the valence of *Raising* proceeds monotonically towards obligatory application.

2.8. Clitic Climbing

In this section, I will give an extremely broadbrush characterization of another immensely complex area: the behaviour of clitic pronouns. These are words like those cited in (138).

(138) *French Clitics*
  me (1st sing.)
  te (2nd sing.)   le (masc.)   lui (sing.)
  se (refl.)   +la (fem.) +   +y+en+V
  nous (1st pl.) les (pl.)   leur (pl.)
  vous (2nd pl.)

$$\text{DO or IO} + \begin{bmatrix} \text{3rd pers.} \\ \text{DO} \end{bmatrix} + \begin{bmatrix} \text{3rd pers.} \\ \text{IO} \end{bmatrix} + \text{Place} + \text{Part}$$

Often, these words must appear in fixed orders relative to the verb (usually, as in French), or to some structurally defined position within their clause,[1] and generally, they are heavily constrained as to their order among themselves by a variety of output conditions.[2] In French, any sequence of clitics must conform to the order chart given in (138).

---

[1] Thus in Serbo-Croatian, all clitics must occur in a fixed order in the second position of a clause.

[2] An important and extensive discussion of such a case appears in Perlmutter (1971).

Since the NPs that clitics fill the function of typically occur in other positions in remote structure than those that they occupy in surface structure, it is generally held that they are transformationally moved from their remote location to their surface location by some such rule as (139).

(139) *French clitic placement*

$$X - V - Y - \text{clitic} - Z \quad \text{OBL}$$

1	2	3	4	5	$\Rightarrow$
1	4+2	3	0	5	

This rule will operate, correctly, to convert the structure underlying (140a) into that underlying (140b),

(140) a. Nous – avions – deux copies – de ça – hier

   we   had   two   copies   of that   yesterday

      X   V   Y   clitic   Z

   b. Nous en avions deux copies hier.

where the clitic *en* means 'of it'.

However, unless somehow constrained, this rule could also convert (141a) into (141c), instead of into (141b).

(141) a. Je crois   que nous avions deux copies de ça

        I   believe that we   had   two   copies of that

   b. Je crois que nous en avions deux copies

   c. *J'en crois que nous avions deux copies

In this case, a general principle, (142), provides an account for the unacceptability of (141b).

(142) In no language can a clitic be moved out of a clause with a subject

The phrase 'clause with a subject' is meant to cover whatever would correspond to *that*-clauses (*that he bring/brings it*), as well as any construction that would correspond to English *for NP to VX*-constructions (*for him to bring it*) or English *Acc/Poss-Ing*-constructions (*him/his bringing it*). I know of no language that would allow a rule cognate to (139) to chop any clitic, say one corresponding to *it*, out of such constructions.

Note that if (142) is a roughly correct formulation, it will have two nontrivial consequences. Consider the case of Italian, which has a rule deleting unstressed subject pronouns. Thus (143a) would, unless *io* 'I' and *tu* 'you' were stressed, become (143b).

(143) a. Io so   che tu sai   questo
         I know that you know this
         ⇓ *Pronoun Deletion* ⇓
      b. φ Credo che ·   φ sai questo
         'I know that you know this'

If *questo* in (143) is replaced by *lo* 'it', which is a clitic pronoun, and which must therefore be cliticized by the Italian rule that is cognate to (139), as in (144),

(144)   So   che lo sai
         I know that it you know

         'I know that you know it'

we find that *lo* still remains within the embedded clause. That is, neither in Italian nor in any other language known to me is the position of clitics affected by the operation of the rule of *Pronoun Deletion*. All clauses whose subjects are deleted by this rule behave like clauses with subjects for the purposes of the generalization stated in (142).

This suggests two things: first, it provides evidence for the existence of a rule like *Pronoun Deletion*, for otherwise subjectless clauses like *che lo sai* in (144) will not be parallel to clauses like *che Pietro lo sa* 'that Peter knows it', clauses whose nonpronominal subject shows up in surface structure. Second, it is likely that *Pronoun Deletion* must universally be ordered extremely late.

As to the question of whether clitic positioning is affected by other rules which delete, or otherwise remove, subjects, no universal answer can be given: languages differ with respect to which of these rules affect clitics, and especially with respect to which of the lexical items that undergo these rules affect the operation of the rules of clitic positioning.

An example will make this point clearer. In Italian, there is a rule of *Equi*, cognate with the English rule, which deletes complement subjects under identity with a controller NP. Thus (145a) becomes (145b),

(145) a. Pietro$_i$ volera che lui$_i$ fosse   famoso
         Peter$_i$ wanted that he$_i$ be(subj) famous
         ⇓ *Equi* (OBL)
      b. Pietro$_i$ voleva   φ essere famoso
         Peter   wanted   to be (inf.) famous

where the deletion of the subject de-finitizes the verb, as in many languages, resulting in the conversion of the subjunctive *fosse* to the infinitive *essere*.

If the resulting infinitive phrase contains a clitic, as is the case with (146a) a rule cognate with, but stronger than, (139), can optionally position this clitic to the left of the matrix verb, as in (146b).

(146) a. Pietro voleva leggere lo
        Peter wanted to read it
    b. Pietro lo voleva leggere

If this option is not taken, the clitic *lo* must be cliticized to the complement verb, which results in a fusion of the infinitive and clitic into a single word, with concomitant loss of the final vowel [e] which would otherwise show up at the end of the infinitive. In this case, the result is (147).

(147) Pietro voleva leggerlo

Let us refer to sentences like (146b), in which a clitic from a complement has been attached to a matrix verb, as *clitic-climbed clauses*. What emerges from a point-by-point comparison of three Romance languages – French vs. Italian, and Spanish – is that they differ with respect to the number of predicates which allow the formation of clitic-climbed clauses. In French virtually no predicates do – the only exceptions being the auxiliary verbs *avoir* 'to have' and *être* 'to be' and a few predicate-raising verbs like *faire* 'to make', *voir* 'to see', etc.[1]

Thus (148a), which corresponds in French to (146a), cannot undergo *Clitic Climbing* to produce *(148b).

(148)a. Pierre voulait lire   le
         Peter wanted to read it
    b. *Pierre le voulait lire

Rather, rule (139) must treat *lire le* as a clause, attaching *le* to the complement verb *lire*, as in (149), which corresponds to (147), except that while Italian clitics are suffixed to infinitives, French clitics are prefixed to them.

(149) Pierre voulait le lire
     'Peter wanted to read it'

However, for the verb *faire*, clitics must climb. Thus in (150a), which parallels (148a) in being a case of a matrix verb with an infinitival comple-

---

[1] For a detailed analysis of *faire*-type constructions cf. Kayne (1969).

ment,[1] we find that (150b), a clitic-climbed clause, is grammatical, while (151), which parallels (147) and (149), is ungrammatical.

(150) a. Pierre faisait   lire   le par Michel
       Peter   was making to read it by Michael
    b. Pierre le faisait lire par Michel
       'Peter was making Michael read it'

(151)   *Pierre faisait le lire par Michel

Similarly, though one might analyse the past-tense forms which are made up of a form of *avoir* and the past participle as another case of verb + complement, we find nothing but clitic-climbed clauses – thus (152a) must become (152b), not (153).

(152) a. Pierre a   lu   le
       Peter   has read(p.p.) it
    b. Pierre l'a [=le + a] lu
       Peter read it

(153)   *Pierre a le lu

Thus in French, we find that clitics must climb past the causative verb *faire* and the auxiliaries *avoir* and *etre*, but cannot climb past any other verbs.

In Italian, the class of clitic-climbed clauses is far greater. Thus it appears that all speakers allow clitic-climbed variants like (146b) for the following verbs:[2]

(154) *volere* want   *osare (di)* dare (obs.)
      potere be able   *sapere*   know how to
      dovere have to   *solere (di)* be accustomed (obs.)
      usare (di) used to   *continuare a* continue
      ardire (di) desire (obs.)   *cominciare a* begin
                                      andare a   be on the way to

      stare per be about to
      stare V + ndo (progressive)
      cercare di try
      rifiutare di refuse

---

[1] For my present purpose, I will disregard the fact that the embedded agentive subject of *lire*, namely *Michel*, shows up in a *par*-phrase in (150b). Cf. Kayne (1969) for a discussion of the processes which produce this phrase, and Comrie (1973) for a penetrating discussion of some universal aspects of cognate conversions, in a wide variety of languages.
[2] I am grateful to Donna Jo Napoli for providing me with this data.

In addition, most speakers consulted by Napoli allowed clitics to climb with *provare a* 'try', but there was considerably less agreement among speakers as to whether climbing was possible with verbs from the following list:

preferire (di)	prefer
desiderare (di)	desire
odiare (di)	hate
amare (di)	love
degnare (di)	deign
dubitare (di)	hesitate
detestare (di)	detest
giurare di	swear
godere di	enjoy
tentare di	try
smettere di	stop

There do seem to be some verbs which no speakers will allow to undergo *Clitic Climbing*. According to Napoli's data, *dimenticare di* 'forget to' is such a verb. Thus no one allows (156a) to climb to (156b) – only the unclimbed (157) is possible.

(156) a.　Pietro dimenticava　di leggere lo
　　　　　Peter　was forgetting of to read it
　　　b. *Pietro lo dimenticava di leggere
(157)　　　Pietro dimenticava di leggerlo
　　　　　'Peter was forgetting to read it'

It thus appears necessary to mark each verb in Italian lexically as to whether or not it will permit clitics in its complement to climb out and attach to it. No structural differences between the verbs of (154) and (155) have been discovered, and semantic explanations seem unlikely to turn up, given the semantic closeness of *cercare*, *provare*, and *tentare*. The classes of predicates that can appear in clitic-climbed clauses are highly variable from speaker to speaker, so no solution other than lexical marking seems to be available, in this case.

However, as in French, all speakers require clitics to climb in causative constructions with *fare* 'to make'. Thus (158a) must climb to (158b)–(159) is ungrammatical.

(158) a.　Pietro faceva mangiare lo a　Giacomo
　　　　　Peter　made　to eat　　it to Jack

b.   Pietro lo faceva mangiare a Giacomo
'Peter was making Jack eat it'
(159)   *Pietro faceva mangiarlo a Giacomo

Finally, Italian parallels French in requiring clitics to climb past auxiliary verbs like *avere* 'to have' and *essere* 'to be'. To exemplify this with the
first of these, note that in (160a), as in the structurally parallel (152a), the
clitic *lo* must climb to precede *ha* 'has', as in (160b). If the clitic does not
climb, the result, *(161), is ungrammatical.

(160) a.   Pietro ha letto   lo
Peter has read(p.p.) it
b.   Pietro lo ha letto.
'Peter read it'

(161)   *Pietro ha $\left\{ \begin{array}{l} \text{lettolo} \\ \text{lo letto} \end{array} \right\}$

Turning now to Spanish, we find a situation in which *Clitic Climbing* is
essentially the same as in Italian. As in French and Italian, clitics must
climb in sentences whose main verb is the causative *hacer*, 'to make'. Thus
lo in (162a) must climb to precede *hizo* in (162b). The unclimbed version
(163), is ungrammatical

(162) a.   Pedro hizo leer   lo a Juan
'Peter made to read it to John'
b.   Pedro se lo hizo leer a Juan[1]
'Peter made John read it'
(163)   *Pedro hizo leerselo a Juan

Also, clitics must climb past the auxiliary verbs *haber* – 'to have' and *ser*
'to be': (164a) must be realized as (164b), not as (165).

(164) a.   Pedro ha leido   lo
Peter has read(p.p.) it
b.   Pedro lo ha leido
'Peter read it'
(165)   *Pedro ha leido lo

However, apart from the cases of causatives and auxiliaries, clitics never
have to climb. They *can* climb, however, from the complements of many,

[1] The *se* of (162b) is a third-person dative clitic copy of *a Juan*. This copying, which need
not concern us here, is required in sentences contaning indirect objects.

but not all, verbs. As in Italian, there is variation from speaker to speaker, and the dominant impression is that semantic 'colourlessness', in the sense used above in connection with (36), is a prerequisite for *Clitic Climbing*. For example, though *andar a* can have the meaning of immediate future ('be going to'), which is relatively colourless, or 'be on the way to', which is more colourful, when in a clause without climb clitics, only the former reading survives in a clitic-climbed clause. An example of this is provided by the contrast between (166a) and (166b).

(166) a. Voi a ver la
      I go to see her

      'I am going to/will see her'
      'I am on the way to see her'

   b. La voi a ver
      Her I go to see

      'I am going to/will see her'

In addition, there is a regularly definable class of verb + infinitive constructions which never allow *Clitic Climbing*. These are discussed in Hankamer (1972): they are cases in which the infinitive is paraphrasable by a tensed clause, cases that parallel those in (13), (18) and (19). An example appears in (167): when (167a) is converted, by optional *Equi*, to (167b), the lower clitics cannot climb to precede the upper verb *dicen* 'they say': they stay before the auxiliary *haber*. Compare *(167c) with (167d).

(167) a. Los generales dicen que (ellos) han visto lo
        the generals say that (they) have seen him.

Equi (OPT)

    b. Los generales dicen haber visto lo
    c. *Los generales lo dicen haber visto
    d. Los generales dicen haberlo visto
       The generals say that they saw him

Hankamer argues that a transderivational account is necessary: clitics climb only where no *que*-clause paraphrase is available. If I am right in my claim that verbs like *say* and other predicates of the classes of rows 1 to 4 of (4) universally erect greater clause-boundaries between themselves and their complements than do rows 5 to 8, then an alternative formulation in terms of some criterial value of a variable feature of clausematiness could be proposed. As of now, I see no way to distinguish between these quite different-sounding analyses, so I will leave the matter open.

The discussion of this section has focused on one single process involving the interaction of clitics and clausematiness, namely *Clitic Climbing*. I would like to point out in passing that there are other processes in Romance languages which suggest a connection with clausematiness. I will describe two.

The first concerns the choice of auxiliary verb in forming compound past tenses. Most verbs use a form of the verb *have* and a past participle to express past tense, but some verbs, typically verbs of motion, form this type of past with a form of the verb *be*. Thus note the contrasts in (168) for French, and in (169) for Italian.

(168) a. Paul a   mangé
         Paul has eaten

         'Paul ate'

      b. Paul est allé
         Paul is gone

         'Paul went'

(169) a. Guglielmo ha mangiato
         William   has eaten

         'William ate'

      b. Guglielmo è andato
         William   is gone
         'William went'

In Italian, however, the choice *have* vs. *be* is not confined to an auxiliary in construction with a past participle of the class of (169b), but rather, can influence the choice of the auxiliary of certain matrix verbs, when the matrix verbs appear as past participles. An example of this kind of 'upward' influence, which is a clear violation of the putatively universal Influencer Constraint proposed in Ross (1973a) appears in (170).

(170) a. Guglielmo ha potuto   mangiare
         William   has been able to eat

         'William could eat'

      b. Guglielmo è potuto   andare
         William   is been able to go

         'William could go'

The class of predicates that allows this type of selection varies from from speaker to speaker: Donna Jo Napoli informs me that for her, only the verbs in (171) allow this upward influence.

(171) *continuare a* to continue
cominciare a to begin
potere to be able
dovere to have to

Though some speakers include *volere* in this class, Napoli does not. The phenomenon thus would seem to require lexical marking to account for it.

The second phenomenon concerns a rule of French which optionally moves the quantifier *tous* 'all', when this quantifier has been floated rightwards off of a clitic, as in (172),

(172) Marie a voulu les voir tous
Marie has wanted them to see all
'Marie wanted to see them all'

to follow the auxiliary *avoir*, as has happened in (173).

(173) Marie a tous voulu les voir

Disregarding details of the operation of this rule, let us note merely that it will only apply to move *tous* to the left of a very small set of verbs – compare (173) with (174).

$$
(174) \quad \text{Marie a tous} \left\{ \begin{array}{l} \text{pu} \\ \text{?essayé de} \\ \text{*condescendu de} \end{array} \right\} \text{les voir}
$$

$$
\text{'Marie} \left\{ \begin{array}{l} \text{was able to} \\ \text{tried to} \\ \text{condescended to} \end{array} \right\} \text{see them all'}
$$

For many speakers, the rule cannot apply at all, and for some, only for the verb *vouloir* 'to want'.

What makes these two processes of interest for the concerns of this paper is the light that they shed on the problem of proposing a universal function of clausematiness, one based on the semantic colourlessness of the matrix verb, in the sense of 'colourless' that was discussed above in connection with (36).

Since some speakers allow (173) but none of the sentences in (174), we might conclude that the inequality stated in (175) obtains,

(175) ABLE > WANT

where the ' > ' means 'has more semantic colour than'. If we then were to make clausematiness a function of colour, such that highly colourful predicates erected higher 'walls' between themselves and their complements than did relatively less colourful predicates, we would predict that no two clausematiness-sensitive processes in any language could differ among themselves in that one would apply with ABLE and not with WANT, while the other did the reverse.

Regrettably, this extremely strong claim is impossible to maintain, as a comparison of (173)–(174) with (171) shows. For Napoli's dialect, we must conclude that WANT (*volere*) > ABLE (*potere*), with respect to the upward selection of the perfect auxiliary.

Further, as I pointed out above, the fact that *cercare di* (for all speakers), *provare a* (for most), and *tentare di* (only for some) allow *Clitic Climbing*, while all have roughly the meaning of 'try', suggests that no semantically-based, universal, total ordering of all predicates with respect to a variable property of clausematiness will prove possible.

Nonetheless, it may yet be possible to establish a universal sequence of sets of predicates, such as that shown in (176).

(176)

$$\left\{ \begin{array}{l} \text{WANT} \\ \text{ABLE} \\ \text{FUTURE} \\ \text{NECESSARY} \\ \text{PROGRESSIVE} \\ \cdot \\ \cdot \\ \cdot \end{array} \right\}_A < \left\{ \begin{array}{l} \text{BEGIN} \\ \text{STOP} \\ \text{TRY} \\ \text{MANAGE} \\ \cdot \\ \cdot \\ \cdot \end{array} \right\}_B < \left\{ \begin{array}{l} \text{CONDESCEND} \\ \text{AVOID} \\ \text{HASTEN} \\ \cdot \\ \cdot \\ \cdot \end{array} \right\}_C \cdots$$

Speakers could differ among each other with respect to which of the elements of a set was set off from its complement by greater clause boundaries, but all would agree that any predicate from set A would have lower boundaries than any from B or C, and that any from B would have lower boundaries than any from C.[1]

In a way, the extremely rough classes of predicates that characterize the vertical dimension of (4) constitute a first attempt to establish such an ordered sequence of unordered classes.

To sum up the interaction of *Clitic Climbing* and clausematiness, I have

---

[1] Hindle and Sag set up precisely such a sequence of environment classes in their extremely important paper on *anymore*. Cf. Hindle and Sag (1974).

proposed that universally, no clitic can climb out of a clause with a subject (cf. (142)). The other side of this coin is the generalization stated in (177):

(177) No language can prohibit a clitic from climbing out of the complement of an auxiliary verb

In other words, I suggest that the notions of *clausematey* and *auxiliary* are interdependent, and that certain syntactic phenomena, such as the positioning of clitics, the obligatoriness of *Gapping*, etc., are universally defined as being functions of clausematiness.

3.

To conclude, I have presented evidence in section 2 which argues for a squish of clausematiness. The facts concerning the eight processes discussed suggest that in the course of derivations, the 'walls' that separate matrix verb and complement, walls which prevent the operation of these eight processes, can sometimes be lowered. One operation which lowers these walls (alternatively, which increases clausematiness) is the optional *Equi* which applies to emotive factives – cf. the contrast between (53c) and (55b) on the one hand, and the contrast between (70a) and (70b) on the other.

Put in a different way, as we proceed from the top of (4) to the bottom, we notice an increasing dependence of complement on matrix. Thus for the higher rows, *Equi* is never obligatory – the complement can appear as a tensed clause in surface structure, while this is not possible for the lower rows, which require that the complement subject not appear next to its verb, either by virtue of having been raised or deleted. And the gapping of the predicates of the higher rows does not require the gapping of their complements, as is the case for the lower rows. And the tense of the complements of the higher rows is independent of the tense of their matrix, a situation which also ceases to obtain when the lower rows are reached. And the process of *Clitic Climbing*, which is restricted to the innermost of clauses, applies obligatorily for rows 7 and 8 of (4), and (hopefully) implicationally thereafter: if a language allows clitics to climb out of the complements of predicates like those in row 5, which are not equi-subject predicates, then presumably it will allow clitics to climb out of the complements of predicates which are equi-subject, like those of row 6, though the reverse may not always obtain.

At present, however, the data on which this squish are based are too limited for me to do more than speculate about the degree to which they are universal. Also, it should be seen as part of a work in progress (cf. Ross (in preparation)), in which I argue that the variables contained in some chopping rules are stronger than those contained in others. The present work has considered only one rule which chops over a variable – *Clitic Climbing*. But in Ross (in preparation), I argue for such inequalities as those in (178),

(178) *Pseudo-Cleft Formation > Question Formation > Adverb Preposing*

where ' > ' means 'stronger than'.

That is, (178) predicts that whenever adverbs can be preposed, constituents can be questioned, and that whenever they can be questioned, they can be pseudo-clefted, but that the reverse predictions do not hold. In connection with an implicational sequence of restrictiveness of environment, such as that shown in (179),

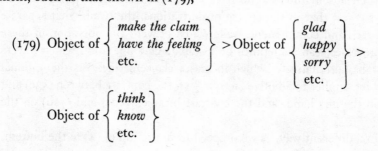

Where ' > ' means 'more restrictive than', (178) will generate the small squish shown in (180).

(180)

		Strength of variables →		
		Adv. Pre-posing	*QF*	*Pseudo-Cleft Formation*
Restric-tiveness of environ-ment ↓	Obj. of *make the claim*	*	*	OK
	Obj. of *glad, sorry*	*	OK	OK
	Obj. of *know think*	OK	OK	OK
		(181)	(182)	(183)

The judgements on the basis of which (180) is justified can be found in (181)–(183).

(181) a.   I made the claim that you would pay up tomorrow

$$\Downarrow \quad \textit{Adverb Preposing}$$

b.   *Tomorrow I made the claim that you would pay up
c.   I am glad that you will pay up tomorrow

$$\Downarrow \quad \textit{Adverb Preposing}$$

d.   *Tomorrow I am glad that you will pay up
e.   I think that you will pay up tomorrow

$$\Downarrow \quad \textit{Adverb Preposing}$$

f.   Tomorrow I think that you will pay up

(182) a.   ?*Who did you make the claim that you had invited?
b.   Who are you glad that you have invited?
c.   Who do you think that you have invited?

(183) a.   What I made the claim that we had rewired is the grandfather clock
b.   What I am glad that we have rewired is the grandfather clock
c.   What I think that we have rewired is the grandfather clock

It is the purpose of Ross (in preparation) to argue that when all other chopping rules are 'blended into' the implicational series in (178), an extended series of environments like those of (179) can be found whose interaction with the full set of chopping rules will be a squishoid which contains (180) as a subpart.

And clearly, the matrix in (4) must combine with this full squishoid of variable strength to produce a fuller characterization of the notion 'syntactic variable'.

At present, I must concede that while the evidence that I have discussed seems to indicate fairly strongly the need for distinguishing the top 5 rows of (4) from each other, and the bottom two rows from each other, I have not been able to build a persuasive case for distinguishing rows 5 and 6, which is precisely the area of greatest inter-speaker variation, with respect to areas like cliticization.

What the import is of attempting to set up such a squish as (4) is the following: clearly though much lexical marking is necessary in the middle ranges, the at present still imprecise notion of colourlessness seems to be

474   JOHN R. ROSS

involved in various quite different-seeming processes in many languages. These processes cannot be studied in isolation from each other – the colourlessness of *have* and *be* that makes it obligatory for clitics to climb past them is the same as the relative colourlessness of the verbs of thinking, when compared to the relative colourfulness of the emotive factives.

Until much more cross-linguistic evidence has been assembled, it will be premature to attempt, in even as preliminary a fashion as that of Ross (1973c), to find numerical values for a variable feature [α Clausematey], $0 \le \alpha \le 1$, though this will eventually prove feasible, hopefully.

But in the meantime, until the numbers come, it is my hope that this paper will alert other researchers to the possibility that semantactic processes of highly diverse kinds – deletions, like *Gapping*; rules of influence, like *SOT*; ascensions, like *Raising*; and chopping rules, like *Clitic Placement* – may all be dancing to the same drum: the height of the wall between superordinate and subordinate clauses.

Acknowledgements

The research on which this paper was based was supported in part by a grant from the National Institute of Mental Health (Grant Number 5 PO1 MH13390-08), whose help I am very grateful for.

In addition I would like to thank several friends who have given me {a hand/ hands(?)} in avoiding whichever of the reefs in the treacherous waters, of cliticization in Romance that this paper has *not* foundered on: for French, Suz Fischer, for Spanish, Yvonne Bordelois and Jim Harris, and for Italian, Donna Jo Napoli.

I would also like to express my collective thanks for chortles received, to various Slavists among an audience of the Chicago Linguistic Society, before which I first read, in the fall of 1972, a version of this paper containing some home-made Serbo-Croatian examples. The Slavists, by their well-timed guffaws, cleared this version of at least *those* inadequacies.

As for all the others...

REFERENCES

Baker, Carl Leroy. (1970). 'Double negatives', *Linguistic Inquiry*, **1**:2, 169–86.
Comrie, Bernard (1973). 'Causatives and universal grammar'. Unpublished multilith, King's College Research Centre, University of Cambridge.
Costa, Rachel (1972). 'Sequence of tenses in that-clauses', *Chicago Linguistic Society*, **8**, 41–51.
Hankamer, Jorge (1972). 'Analogical rules in syntax', *CLS*, **8**, 111–23.
Hindle, Donald, and Sag, Ivan (1974). 'Some more on *anymore*'. To appear in Roger Shuy, ed., *Proceedings of the NWAV II Conference*. Washington, D.C.: Georgetown University Press.

Horn, Laurence Robert (1972). *On the Semantic Properties of Logical Operators in English*. Unpublished doctoral dissertation, University of California.

Karttunen, Lauri (1971). 'Some observations on factivity', *Papers in Linguistics*, 4:1, 55-69.

Kayne, Richard (1969). *The Transformational Cycle in French Syntax*. Unpublished doctoral dissertation, Massachusetts Institute of Technology.

Kiparsky, Paul, and Kiparsky, Carol (1970). 'Fact'. In Manfred Bierwisch and Karl-Erich Heidolph, eds., *Progress in Linguistics*, pp. 143-73. The Hague, Holland: Mouton.

Lakoff, George (1970). *Irregularity in Syntax*. New York: Holt, Rinehart, and Winston.

McCawley, James D. (1970). 'English as a VSO language', *Language*, 46, 286-99.

Peranteau, Paul, Levi, Judith N. and Phares, Gloria C. (eds.) (1972). *Papers from the Eighth Regional Meeting of the Chicago Linguistic Society*. Chicago: Chicago Linguistic Society. [= *CLS* 8].

Perlmutter, David M. (1970a). 'The two verbs *begin*.' In Roderick A. Jacobs and Peter S. Rosenbaum, eds., *Readings in English Transformational Grammar*, pp. 107-19. Waltham, Massachusetts: Ginn and Company.

—— (1970b). 'Surface structure constraints in syntax', *Linguistic Inquiry*, 1:2, 187-255.

—— (1971). *Deep and Surface Structure Constraints in Syntax*. New York: Holt, Rinehart, and Winston.

Postal, Paul M. (1970a). 'On the surface verb *remind*', *Linguistic Inquiry*, 1:1, 37-120.

—— (1970b). 'On coreferential complement subject deletion', *Linguistic Inquiry*, 1:4, 439-500.

—— (1971). *Crossover Phenomena: A Study in the Grammar of Coreference*. New York: Holt, Rinehart, and Winston.

—— (1974). *On Raising*. Cambridge, Massachusetts: MIT Press.

Ross, John Robert (1969). 'Auxiliaries as main verbs.' In William Todd, ed., *Studies in Philosophical Linguistics – Series One*, pp. 77-102. Evanston, Illinois: Great Expectations.

—— (1970). 'Gapping and the order of constituents.' In Manfred Bierwisch and Karl-Erich Heidolph, eds., *Progress in Linguistics*, pp. 249-59. The Hague, Holland: Mouton.

—— (1972a). 'Doubl-ing', *Linguistic Inquiry*, 3:1, 61-86.

—— (1972b). 'Act'. In Donald Davidson and Gilbert Harman, eds., *Semantics of Natural Languages*, pp. 70-126. Dordrecht: D. Reidel.

—— (1973a). 'Slifting'. In Maurice Gross, Morris Halle, and Marcel-Paul Schützenberger, eds., *The Formal Analysis of Natural Languages*, pp. 133-69. The Hague, Holland: Mouton.

—— (1973b). 'A fake NP squish.' In C. J. N. Bailey and Roger Shuy, eds., *New Ways of Analyzing Variation in English*, pp. 97-140. Washington, D.C.: Georgetown University Press.

—— (1973c). 'Nouniness'. In Osamu Fujimura, ed., *Three Dimensions of Linguistic Theory*, pp. 137-257. Tokyo, Japan: The TEC Company.

—— 'Variable strength.' (In preparation).